MARYLAND MARRIAGES, 1778-1800

Compiled by
Robert Barnes

GENEALOGICAL PUBLISHING Co., Inc.

Copyright © 1978
Genealogical Publishing Co., Inc.
1001 N. Calvert St., Baltimore, MD 21202
All Rights Reserved
First printing, 1978
Second printing, 1979
Third printing, 1993
First printing in paperback, 2005
Library of Congress Catalogue Card Number 77-88843
International Standard Book Number 0-8063-0791-9
Made in the United States of America

CONTENTS

FOREWORD

This book is a compilation of all marriages recorded from 1778 to 1800 in church records which are on deposit at the Maryland Historical Society in Baltimore and at the Hall of Records in Annapolis. Also included are a number of extant marriage license returns filed annually by ministers, showing which marriages they had performed by virtue of a license issued by the county clerks. In addition, this work includes the marriage licenses on file at certain county courts, especially Harford, Dorchester, and Allegany Counties. In some cases the marriage licenses for a particular county had already been published, and in a few cases the marriage licenses were not readily accessible to the compiler, so these have not been included. Following the List of Sources is a bibliography of published marriage records which the researcher may wish to consult.

In this book, as in the first volume of *Maryland Marriages*, covering the years 1634-1777 and published in 1975 by the Genealogical Publishing Co., Inc., the marriages are arranged alphabetically by the groom's last name. Following his name are the date of marriage and the name of the bride. Additional pertinent information found in the record, such as the names of parents of either party or references to previous marital state or place of origin, is included. In the last column there is a code designation for the source of each marriage, followed by a dash and then the page number on which that marriage is found in the record source. The list of sources used, with their code designations and location, immediately precedes the list of marriages. A surname index of brides is given at the end of the book.

Some records came to the author's attention after preparation of the camera-ready transcript had begun, and these are grouped as Addenda. Finally, marriages for the period 1634 to 1777 which were not listed in the first volume of *Maryland Marriages* are included here in the Appendix.

As in the first volume every attempt has been made to spell the name exactly as it appeared in the register, so spelling variants should be checked. From time to time the same marriage was recorded in two different sources with a difference in spelling of names or perhaps a difference in dates. In all such cases the discrepancies have been noted. The user of the book will have to make his own judgement as to which of the variants is correct. Where two dates are given it is possible that the earlier date is the date the marriage license was issued and the later date that on which the ceremony was actually performed.

The author especially wishes to thank the following persons: the staffs of the Hall of Records and the Maryland Historical Society; Mr. J. Harlan Livezey for making available a copy of the original marriage license book of Harford County; Mr. John Dern for marriages from the marriage register of Pastor John Casper Stoever; Mrs. Mary K. Meyer and Mrs. Edwin Carothers for invaluable assistance; and finally Dr. Neal Brooks of Essex Community College and the author's wife and son for help with the index.

LIST OF SOURCES

In the following list the initials DAR refer to records at the
Daughters of the American Revolution Library in Washington; MHS
to records at the Maryland Historical Society in Baltimore, and
HR to records at the Hall of Records in Annapolis.

ALLEGANY COUNTY

1 AL - Allegany County Marriage Licenses, 1791-1796, published in
the National Genealogical Society Quarterly, XX, 52-53.

2 AL - Marriage Register of Rev. William Shaw of the Methodist
Episcopal Church, 1792-1800, published in DAR Magazine,
Aug.-Sept. 1965, pp. 700-701.

3 AL - Allegany County Marriage Licenses, 1797-1800, compiled
by Margaret D. Cupler and Helen S. Hinkle, in "Early
Allegany County Records, 1737-1825," typescript, MHS.

ANNE ARUNDEL COUNTY

1 AA - All Hallows Parish; copy made in 1888 by Lucy H. Harrison,
at MHS.

2 AA - St. Margarets Parish; copy made in 1890 by L. H. Harrison,
at MHS.

3 AA - St. James Parish; copy made in 1891, by L. H. Harrison, at
MHS.

4 AA - Marriage License Returns made by various ministers, found
in Scharf Papers, MS. 1999, at MHS. Ministers who filed
returns were: Rev. James Magill (filed 8 Nov. 1777, 5 Nov.
1778, 8 Nov. 1779); Rev. Walter Magowan (filed 17 Nov.
1778, 11 Dec. 1779); Rev. David Lowe (filed 6 Nov. 1778);
Rev. Nelson Reed (filed 17 Nov. 1787, 1 Sept. 1788; 19
Nov. 1790;); Rev. Jonathan Forrest (filed 14 Nov. 1787, 21
Oct. 1788, 31 Oct. 1789, 18 Jan. 1791); Rev. Ignatius Pigman (filed 12 Jan. 1787); Rev. James Riggin (filed 14 Sept.
1788); Rev. Thomas John Claggett (filed 6 June 1789); Rev.
John Hagerty (filed 17 Oct. 1789); Rev. Ezekiel Cooper
(filed 6 Nov. 1790; marriages were undated and dates were
taken from Brumbaugh, Md. Records); unsigned list beginning
with Rezin Spurrier in Jan. 1790 to Charles Brown in Octo-
ber 1790, dates taken from Brumbaugh; Rev. Lemuel Green
(filed 29 Nov. 1790, some dates taken from Brumbaugh, 10

May 1791, 15 Sept. 1796, 4 Nov. 1797, 2 Nov. 1798); Rev.
John Chalmers (filed 30 Dec. 1791, 20 Nov. 1792); Rev. John
Bowen (filed Oct. 1792); Rev. Charles Dorsey (filed 26 Nov.
1792, 1 Nov. 1793, 1 Dec. 1798); Rev. Richard Parrott (7
Dec. 1792); Rev. Jacob Linton (31 Oct. 1792); Silvester
Hutchinson (31 Oct. 1792); Rev. John Long (12 Dec. 1792);
Rev. John Bloodgood (20 July 1793, 17 Oct. 1793); Rev. Jo-
seph Wyatt (10 Nov. 1795, some marriages were in Baltimore
Co., 14 Nov. 1798, 14 Nov. 1799, 14 Nov. 1800); Rev. Ben-
ton Riggen (filed 19 Feb. 1795, some marriages were in Bal-
timore and Harford Counties, 2 Oct. 1798); Rev. Greenbury
Ridgely (29 Oct. 1795, 9 Jan. 1797, 7 Nov. 1797, 2 Jan.
1799, 27 Dec. 1799, 10 Feb. 1801, 30 Dec. 1801); Rev. Rez-
in Cash (13 Oct. 1796); Rev. John Deborah (24 Nov. 1795);
Rev. Nathaniel Burton Mills (31 Aug. 1796);Rev. Charles
Stewart of Charles (4 May 1798, 19 July 1799); Rev. James
E. Higgins (13 May 1799); Rev. George Roberts (25 April
1800).
Where dates of marriages were not included in the mini-
ster's returns, dates in parentheses were taken from Anne
Arundel County Marriage Licenses published in Brumbaugh.

5 AA - St. Annes Parish; copy made in 1889 by L. H. Harrison; 2
vols. at MHS.

BALTIMORE COUNTY

1 BA - St. James Parish; copy made by L. H. Harrison, at MHS.

2 BA - St. Johns Parish; register 1768-1852 at HR.

3 BA - St. Pauls Parish; copy made by L. H. Harrison at MHS.

4 BA - St. Thomas Parish; copy made by L. H. Harrison, at MHS.

5 BA - First Presbyterian Church, Baltimore; copy of register made
in 1906, at MHS.

6 BA - Marriage Register of Rev. Lewis Richards, pastor of First
Baptist Church, Baltimore, 1784-1818, MS. 690 at MHS.

7 BA - New Jerusalem (Swedenborgian) Church, Baltimore; copy of
register at MHS.

8 BA - First Methodist Episcopal Church, Baltimore, copy of register at MHS.

9 BA - Otterbein German Evangelical Reformed Church, Baltimore,
copy of register, 1798-1850, made in 1903 at MHS. This
transcription was compared to another one made by Holdcraft
also at MHS.

10 BA - First German Reformed Church, Baltimore, copy of register
at MHS. Marriages start on p. 178 with date of 1783;
marriages beginning in 1788 were published in Bulletin
of Maryland Genealogical Society, XVI (May 1975), pp. 65
ff.

11 BA - Marriage License Returns made by various ministers, found
in Scharf Papers, MS. 1999, at MHS.
-1, Returns of Rev. Thomas Chase of St. Pauls Parish,
filed 19 Nov. 1778.
-2, Returns of Rev. George Worsley, late Rector of St.
Johns Parish, now rector of Port Tobacco Parish,

filed 22 May 1781.
-3, Returns of Rev. William West, Rector of St. Pauls
Parish, filed 22 Nov. 1779 (included only those marriages not already taken from St. Pauls Parish Register).
-4, Returns of Rev. William West, filed 19 Nov. 1780.
-5, Returns of Rev. William West, filed 27 Nov. 1782.
-6, Returns of Rev. William West, filed 6 Nov. 1783.
-7, Returns of Rev. William West, filed 30 Nov. 1734.
-8, Returns of Rev. William West, filed 30 Nov. 1785.
-9, Returns of Rev. William West, filed 16 Nov. 1786.
-10, Returns of Rev. William West, filed 20 Nov. 1787.
-11, Returns of Rev. William West, filed 29 Nov. 1738.
-12, Returns of Rev. William West, filed 15 Nov. 1789.
-13, Returns of Rev. William West, filed 21 Nov. 1790.
In all cases of Rev. West's returns, only those marriages not already recorded in the parish register
were included.

12 BA - Marriage Register of Rev. John Allen, Rector of St. Johns
Parish, 1796-1815, at HR.

13 BA - Marriage Register of Rev. John Coleman, Rector of St.
Johns Parish, 1779-1809, No. 13867 at HR.

14 BA - Marriage License Returns of Rev. Patrick Allison, pastor
of First Presbyterian Church, Baltimore, in Scharf Papers,
MS. 1699, MHS.   Only marriages not already found in the
church register were included.
-1, Return filed 1 Nov. 1779.   -2, Return filed 1 Nov.
1780.   -3, Return filed 1 Nov. 1781.   -4, Return filed
1 Nov. 1782.   -5, filed 1 Nov. 1783.   -6, filed 1 Nov.
1784, -7, filed Nov. 1785.   -8, filed 1 Nov. 1736.   -9,
filed 1 Nov. 1787. -10, filed 1 Nov. 1788.   -11, filed
1 Nov. 1789.   -12, filed 1 Nov. 1790.   -13, filed 21 Nov.
1791.   -14, filed 13 Nov. 1792.   -15, filed 9 Nov. 1793.
-16, filed 15 Nov. 1794.   -17, filed 17 Nov. 1795.   -18,
filed 1 Nov. 1796.   -19, filed Nov. 1797.   -20, filed
Nov. 1798.   -21, filed Nov. 1799.   -22, filed Nov. 1800.

15 BA - Marriage License Returns of Rev. John Turner, Baptist
Minister, Scharf Papers, MS. 1999, at MHS.
-1, filed 31 Jan. 1789. Dates in parentheses are supplied
from "Baltimore County Marriage Licenses, 1777-1799,"
typescript at MHS.
-2, filed 28 Nov. 1789. Dates in parenthese are supplied
as above.
-3, filed 30 Nov. 1790. Dates in parentheses supplied
as above.
-4, filed 30 Nov. 1791. Dates in parentheses supplied
as above.

16 BA - Marriage License Returns of Rev. Richard Whatcoat, of the
Methodist Episcopal Church, Scharf Papers, MS. 1999, at
MHS.
-1, filed 9 Sept. 1786.   -2, filed 26 Nov. 1787 (by Nov.
1787 Rev. Whatcoat was in Hampshire Co., Va.).   -3,
filed Nov. 1785. -4, filed 2 Nov. 1793.

17 BA - Marriage License Returns of Rev. John Davis, Scharf Papers, MS. 1999, at MHS.
-1, filed 28 Nov. 1777.

18 BA - Marriage Licenses Returns of Rev. John Hagerty, Scharf
Papers, MS. 1999, at MHS.

-1, filed 4 Nov. 1788. -2, filed 16 Nov. 1790. -3, filed 26 Nov. 1791. -4, filed 16 Nov. 1792. -5, filed 4 Nov. 1793. -6, filed 29 Nov. 1794.

19 BA - Marriage License Returns of Rev. Lewis Richards, Scharf Papers, MS. 1999, at MHS. Only marriages not included in his marriage register were abstracted. Most of his returns were merely duplicates of his register. The returns which contained new marriages were: -3, filed 28 Nov. 1788; -4, filed 26 Nov. 1789; -7, filed 30 Nov. 1792; -8, filed 29 Nov. 1793; -9, filed 29 Nov. 1794; -11, filed 22 Nov. 1796; -12, filed 29 Nov. 1797; -13, filed Nov. 1798; -14, filed Nov. 1799.

20 BA - Marriage License Returns of Ezekiel Cooper, Scharf Papers, MS. 1999, at MHS. -1, filed 25 Nov. 1789. Dates in parentheses are from "Baltimore Co. Marr. Lic., 1777-1799," at MHS.

21 BA - Marriage License Returns of Thomas Foster, Scharf Papers, MS. 1999, at MHS. -1, filed 10 Nov. 1789.

22 BA - Marriage License Returns of Rev. Benton Riggin, Scharf Papers, MS. 1999, at MHS. -1, filed 2 Nov. 1789. -2, filed 28 Oct. 1793.

23 BA - Marriage License Returns of Rev. Nelson Reed, Scharf Papers, MS. 1999, at MHS. -1, filed 2 Nov. 1789. -2, filed 10 Nov. 1791. -3, filed 19 Nov. 1792.

24 BA - Marriage License Returns of Rev. William Gill, Scharf Papers, MS. 1999, at MHS. -1, filed 23 Nov. 1786.

25 BA - Marriage License Returns of Rev. William Ringgold,Scharf Papers, MS. 1999, at MHS. -1, filed 24 Nov. 1785.

26 BA - Marriage License Returns of Henry Wills, Scharf Papers, MS. 1999, at MHS. -1, filed 5 Oct. 1790.

27 BA - Marriage License Returns of John Cole, Scharf Papers, as above. -1, filed 19 Nov. 1790.

28 BA - Marriage License Returns of Emory Pryor, Scharf Papers, as above. -1, filed 8 Nov. 1791, but all marriages took place in Dorchester Co., except the Crisfield-Wilson marriage which was in Kent Co. -2, filed 20 Nov. 1792.

29 BA - Marriage License Returns of Rev. Daniel Kurtz, Scharf Papers, as above. -1, contains marriages performed 1786-1790. -2, filed 1 Nov. 1791. -3, filed 1 Nov. 1792.

30 BA - Marriage License Returns of Rev.Philip Bruce, Scharf Papers, as above. -1, filed 7 May 1791.

31 BA - Marriage License Returns of Rev. John Robinson, Scharf

Papers, as above.
-1, filed 8 Oct. 1791.

32 BA - Marriage License Returns of Rev. Robert Green of Methodist Episcopal Church, Scharf Papers, as above.
-1, filed 14 Nov. 1792.

33 BA _ Marriage License Returns of Rev. George Hagerthy, Scharf Papers, as above.
-1, filed 15 Nov. 1791.

34 BA - Marriage License Returns of Rev. Sylvester Hutchinson, Scharf Papers, as above.
-1, filed 18 Nov. 1791.

35 BA - Marriage License Returns of Rev. Joseph J. G. Bend, Rector of St. Pauls Parish, Scharf Papers, as above. Only those marriages not already found in the parish register were included.
-1, filed 27 Nov. 1793. -2, filed 24 Nov. 1794. -3, filed 23 Nov. 1795. -4, filed 24 Nov. 1796. -5, filed 25 Nov. 1797. -6, filed 27 Nov. 1798.

36 BA - Marriage License Returns of Rev. John Fitch Oliver, Rector of St. Thomas Parish, Scharf Papers, as above.
-1, filed 26 Dec. 1794.

37 BA - Marriage License Returns of George Cannon, Scharf Papers, as above.
-1, filed 28 Oct. 1794.

38 BA - Marriage License Returns of Morris Howe, Scharf Papers, as above.
-1, filed 15 Oct. 1794. Some marriages were performed in Somerset Co.

39 BA - Marriage License Returns of John Chalmers, Scharf Papers, at MHS.
-1, filed 27 Oct. 1794 in Baltimore Co., but most were performed in Kent and Queen Annes Co.

40 BA - Marriage Licenses of Bishop (later Archbishop) John Carroll of the Roman Catholic Church, Scharf Papers, as above.
-1, filed 20 Oct. 1795. -2, filed 1796. -3, filed Nov. 1797.

41 BA - Marriage License Returns of Augustin Smith, Scharf Papers, as above.
-1, filed 28 Nov. 1795.

42 BA - Marriage License Returns of Anthony Garnier, Scharf Papers, as above.
-1, filed 28 Nov. 1795.

43 BA - Marriage License Returns of Joshua Jones, Scharf Papers, as above.
-1, filed 6 Nov. 1795.

44 BA - Marriage License Returns of Francis Beeston, Scharf Papers, at MHS.
-1, filed 1 Nov. 1795. -2, filed 1 Nov. 1797.

45 BA - Marriage License Returns of Absolom Butler, Scharf Papers, as above.

-1, filed 14 Aug. 1797. -2, filed 8 Sept. 1798. -3, filed 6 Aug. 1799.

46 BA - Marriage License Returns of various ministers for the year 1796, Scharf Papers, as above. Only five marriages were found in this return.

47 BA - Marriage License Returns of Rev. John Ireland, Scharf Papers, as above. `
-1, filed 3 Nov. 1797; list began 22 Dec. 1795.

48 BA - Marriage License Returns of Rev. George Roberts, Scharf Papers, as above.
-1, filed Oct. 1800. -2, filed Dec. 1800.

49 BA - Marriage License Returns of Nicholas Snethen, Scharf Papers, as above.
-1, list for 1800.

50 BA - Zion Lutheran Church, Baltimore, copy of register at MHS. On p. 387 are marriages for 1786, divided between "auser der gemenda," and 'im der gemenda." Some may have taken place in 1787. Only marriages not already found in the marriage license returns of Rev. Daniel Kurtz were abstracted.

51 BA - Marriage Licenses issued by William Gibson, Clerk of Baltimore County, between 15 Dec. 1784 and 24 Nov. 1787. The minister who performed the ceremony is in parentheses. Copied from Liesenring, "Maryland Marriages, 1777-1804," at MHS.

CALVERT COUNTY

1 CA - Marriage License Returns of various ministers, found in Scharf Papers, MS. 1999, at MHS.
-1, return of Rev. Francis Lauder, filed 3 Nov. 1778.
-2, return of Rev. Lauder, filed 24 Nov. 1779.
-3, return of Rev. Lauder, filed 28 Nov. 1780.
-4, return of Rev. William Phebus, filed 22 Sept. 1788.
-5, return of Rev. Thomas John Claggett, Rector of All Saints Parish, Calvert Co.; copied by Christopher Johnston, in his transcript of the register of Christ Church Parish, at MHS.

2 CA - Christ Chuch Parish, copy of register made by Christopher Johnston, at MHS.

CAROLINE COUNTY

1 CR - St. Johns Parish, transcript of register made by George B. Wilson and published in Bulletin of the Maryland Genealogical Society, XVI (1975), 73-79.

CARROLL COUNTY

1 CL - St. Luke's (Winter's) Lutheran Church, copy of register made by Pastor Frederick S. Weiser, at MHS.

LIST OF SOURCES

2 CL - Zion Evangelical Lutheran Church, Manchester, Parish Register, 1784-1853, transcript by Pastor F. S. Weiser, at MHS.

CECIL COUNTY

1 CE - St. Stephens Parish Register; copy made by L. H. Harrison in 1892, at MHS.

2 CE - St. Mary Ann's Parish Register; copy made by L. H. Harrison in 1891, at MHS.

CHARLES COUNTY

1 CH - Trinity Parish Register; copy at MHS.

2 CH - Marriages in Charles County, Maryland, "1779-1781," published in DAR Magazine, LXI, 233 ff.; actually covers period 1778-1801. No statement is made as to where these marriages were taken from, but they were probably abstracted from the marriage license returns of various ministers.

3 CH - Records of the Congregation of Upper and Lower Zachiah, Mattawoman, and St. Marys (Bryantown), 1793-1861; copy made by Mrs. Frank P. (Louise) Scrivener, at MHS. The marriage records make note of various dispensations made due to consanguinity between the parties.

4 CH - Marriage License Returns of Rev. John McPherson, Scharf Papers, MS. 1999, at MHS. -1, filed 24 Nov. 1778. -2, filed 20 Nov. 1779. -3, filed 21 Nov. 1780.

5 CH - Marriage License Returns of Rev. Henry Fendall, Scharf Papers, as above. -1, filed March 1778.

6 CH - Marriage License Returns of Rev. Benjamin Roles, Scharf Papers, as above. -1, filed 13 Nov. 1779.

7 CH - Marriage License Returns of Rev. John Bolton, Scharf Papers, as above. -1, filed 13 Nov. 1779.

DORCHESTER COUNTY

1 DO - Dorchester Parish, typed transcript of a copy "transcribed from the original, May 1851," at MHS.

2 DO - Dorchester County Marriage Licenses, photocopy of transcript made in 1929 by Dr. Elias Jones, at MHS.

LIST OF SOURCES

FREDERICK COUNTY

1 FR - Zion Lutheran Church, Middletown, transcript made by Charles T. Zahn in 1934, at MHS.

2 FR - First German Evangelical Reformed Church, Frederick, copy made in 1903, at MHS.

3 FR - Frederick County Marriage License Returns, 1791-1801, Scharf Papers, MS. 1999, at MHS.

4 FR - Frederick County Marriage Licenses, 1778-1800, copied from the originals at the court house, and published in the DAR Magazine, Vol. 85.

5 FR - Moravian Church Register, 1759-1871, translated by Henry J. Young, 1942, at MHS.

6 FR - St. Peter's Lutheran Church, Woodsboro, transcript edited and arranged by Dr. Coral Gordon, 1962, at MHS.

7 FR - Ministerial Records of Pastor Johann Casper Stoever, transcribed and graciously made available to the author by Mr. John Dern of Redwood City, Cal., from HSP Am. 725, Ms. at the Historical Society of Pennsylvania in Philadelphia. Parties are described as of "Monakeseus" (or Monocacy), except for Margaretha Neffin of "Cruz Creek," who married Joh. Georg Schacteler.

HARFORD COUNTY

1 HA - St. Georges Parish Register, copy made by L. H. Harrison, at MHS.

2 HA - Marriage Register of Rev. John Allen for St. Georges Parish, 1795-1816, at HR.

3 HA - Marriage Licenses at Harford County Court House, Bel Air, transcribed by the author. Marriages in the first part of the register may have actually taken place a year earlier than that indicated in the copy of the marriage license book available to the public. Marriages listed as occurring starting in March 1791 probably have the correct date.

4 HA - Original Lists of Marriage Licenses, photocopy made available to the author by Mr. J. Harlan Livezey, Esq., of Aberdeen.

5 HA - Marriage License Returns filed by Rev. William West by licenses issued by John Lee Gibson, Clerk of Harford Co. Court, in Scharf Papers, MS. 1999, at MHS; filed with Baltimore Co. Marriage License Returns.

LIST OF SOURCES

HOWARD COUNTY

1 HO - Christ Church, Queen Caroline Parish, copy of register made in 1892/3 by L. H. Harrison, at MHS.

KENT COUNTY

1 KE - St. Pauls Parish, copy of register, at MHS.

2 KE - Shrewsbury Parish, copy of register made in 1898 by L. H. Harrison, at MHS.

3 KE - Marriage License Returns of Rev. Christopher Spry, filed 7 November 1792, Scharf Papers, MS. 1999, at MHS.

4 KE - Kent County Marriage Licenses, 1796-1798, published in B ulletin of Maryland Original Research Society, I, 65-73. Items marked with an asterisk after the page number have dates that are open to question.

MONTGOMERY COUNTY

1 MO - Marriage License Returns of Rev. John Carroll, Scharf Papers, MS. 1999, at MHS.
-1, filed 20 Nov. 1778.   -2, filed Nov. 1777.

2 MO - Marriage License Returns of Rev. Joseph Threlkeld, Scharf Papers, as above.
-1, filed 16 Nov. 1778.

3 MO - Marriage License Returns of Rev. Clement Brooke, Scharf Papers, as above.
-1, filed 7 Nov. 1778.

4 MO - Marriage License Returns of Rev. Alexander Williamson, Scharf Papers, as above.
-1, filed 2 Nov. 1778.

5 MO - Prince Georges Parish, copy of register made by L. H. Harrison in 1890, at MHS.

6 MO - Marriage License Returns of Rev. Slingsby Linthicum, Scharf Papers, as above.
-1, filed 31 Oct. 1798.

7 MO - Marriages Recorded in Diary of Hezekiah Wilson, published in National Genealogical Society Quarterly, VI, 27-31.

8 MO - Trinity Church, Georgetown, D. C., Marriages, 1795-1805, from Vol. 175, Archives of Georgetown University, transcribed by the Genealogical Records Committee of the District of Columbia, D.A.R., Vol. 47 of their records, at the DAR Library.

LIST OF SOURCES

PRINCE GEORGES COUNTY

1 PG - Prince Georges Parish Register, 1711-1798, indexed by Mrs. Irvin C. Brown, typescript at MHS.

2 PG - Marriage License Returns of various ministers, Scharf Papers, MS. 1999, at MHS.
  -1, returns of Rev. Thomas Digges, filed 26 Nov. 1778, 30 Nov. 1779, and 6 Dec. 1780.
  -2, returns of Rev. Walter Hanson Harrison, filed 25 Nov. 1777, 27 Nov. 1778, and Nov. 1779.
  -3, returns of Rev. Edward Gantt, filed 11 Nov. 1778, 4 Nov. 1779, 20 Nov. 1780, and 22 Nov. 1782.
  -4, returns of Rev. William Duke, filed 19 Nov. 1789, and and 20 Nov. 1790.
  -5, returns of Rev. Osborn Sprigg, filed 1 Dec. 1781.
  -6, returns of Rev. James Hunt, filed 12 Feb. 1778.
  -7, returns of Rev. Thomas John Claggett, filed 20 Nov. 1780.

3 PG - St. Johns Piscataway Parish, copy of register made in 1884 by L. H. Harrison, at MHS.

4 PG - Christ Church, Washington Parish, marriages copied by Livingston Manor Chapter, D. C. D. A. R., in Vol. 69 of Genealogical Records of District of Columbia, D.A.R., at DAR Library.

QUEEN ANNES COUNTY

1 QA - St. Lukes Parish, copy of register made in 1904/5, at MHS.

SAINT MARYS COUNTY

1 SM - Marriages performed by Rev. James Walton, S. J., at Newtown, published in Maryland Historical Magazine, LI (June 1956), 135-137.

2 SM - Marriages performed by Rev. Ignatius Baker Brooke, at Newtown, published in Maryland Historical Magazine, LI (June 1956), 138.

3 SM - St. Andrews Parish, copy of register made in 1907 by L. H. Harrison, at MHS.

4 SM - William and Mary Parish, photostat of original register, at MHS.

SOMERSET COUNTY

1 SO - Coventry Parish, copy of register made in 1899/1900 by L. H. Harrison, at MHS.

LIST OF SOURCES

2 SO - Somerset County Marriage Licenses, typescript at MHS.

3 SO - Somerset Parish, copy of register made by C. H. B. Turner and typed by Esther R. George, 1942, at MHS.

TALBOT COUNTY

1 TA - St. Peters Parish, copy of register made by L. H. Harrison in 1895, at MHS.

WASHINGTON COUNTY

1 WA - Marriage License Returns of various ministers, Scharf Papers, MS. 1999, at MHS.

2 WA - Marriage Register of Pastor Jacob Goering, c.1791-1792, transcribed by Pastor Frederick S. Weiser, typescript at MHS.

3 WA - St. Johns Evangelical Lutheran Church, Hagerstown, Vol. I of marriages, burials, and miscellaneous transcribed by Mrs. Warren D. (Louise L.) Miller, typescript at DAR Library.

WICOMICO COUNTY

1 WI - Stepney Parish, original register at HR.

WORCESTER COUNTY

1 WO - Worcester County Marriage Licenses, 1795-1800, typescript at MHS.

2 WO - St. Martins Parish, typescript copy of register, 1722-1340, at MHS.

SOCIETY OF FRIENDS

1 SF - Gunpowder Monthly Meeting, abstracts of records compiled by Bliss Forbush, at MHS.

2 SF - Nicholite Marriage Records compiled by Kenneth L. Carroll, 'in "More About the Nicholites," in Maryland Historical Magazine , XLVI (1951), 288-289.

3 SF - Pipe Creek Monthly Meeting, abstracts of records compiled by Mrs. Bliss A. Forbush, at MHS.

4 SF - Third Haven Monthly Meeting, copy of marriage records made in 1903, at MHS.

LIST OF SOURCES

5 SF - Clifts Monthly Meeting, records published serially in the
Bulletin of the Maryland Genealogical Society, beginning
XIII (Aug. 1972), p. 22.

6 SF - West River Meeting, records published serially in the
Bulletin of the Maryland Genealogical Society, beginning
XIV (May 1973).

7 SF - Cecil Monthly Meeting, photocopies of original records at
MHS. Marriages 1778-1800 found in Vol. I, pp. 108-122,
and Vol. III, pp. 489-510.

8 SF - Baltimore Monthly Meeting, microfilm of original records
at HR.

9 SF - Deer Creek Monthly Meeting, microfilm of original marriage
register, 1761-1822, at HR.

10 SF - Nottingham Monthly Meeting, Register of Births and Deaths,
which contains a few marriages; microfilm of original
records at HR.

11 SF - Nottingham Monthly Meeting, Register of Marriages, 1730-
1889; microfilm of original records at HR.

PUBLISHED SOURCES

Anne Arundel County: Marriage licenses for 1777-1820 published
in Gaius M. Brumbaugh, Maryland Records, Colonial, Revolutionary,
County and Church, from Original Sources, 2 vols. (1915-1918).
Repr. Baltimore: Genealogical Pub. Co., 1967.

Baltimore City and County: Marriage Licenses, 1777-1799, typescript at MHS.

Caroline County: Marriage Licenses, 1774-1815 pub. in Pennsylvania Magazine of History and Biography, XXVIII, 209 ff., repr.
by Genealogical Pub. Co., 1975. Marriage Licenses for 1774-
1781 were published in National Genealogical Society Quarterly,
XXIII (No. 2), p. 33. Marriage Licenses, 1774-1825, were
published by Raymond B. Clark, Jr., and Sara Seth Clark, St.
Michaels, Md., 1969.

Cecil County: Marriage Licenses, 1777-1840, pub. by Genealogical
Pub. Co., 1974. Marriage Licenses 1777-   , pub. by Raymond B.
Clark, Jr., in The Maryland and Delaware Genealogist, beginning
Vol. X.

Charles County: marriages performed by various ministers published in Brumbaugh, Maryland Records.

Dorchester County: Marriage Licenses, 1780-1855, published by
Katherine W. Palmer, Cambridge, Md., 1960. Marriage Licenses,
1790-1802, published in Publications of the Pennsylvania Genealogical Society, VIII (March 1923), 252-260.

Frederick County: Marriage Licenses, 1778-1781, published in J.
Thomas Scharf, History of Western Maryland, 2 vols. (1882).
Repr. Baltimore: Genealogical Pub. Co., 1968. Marriages per-

formed by various ministers in Brumbaugh, Maryland Records, II,
497 ff. Records of Marriages and Burials in the Monacacy Church
in Frederick County, Maryland, and in the Evangelical Lutheran
Congregation in the City of Frederick, Maryland, 1743-1811, by
Frederick S. Weiser.   Washington, National Genealogical Society, 1972.

Harford County: marriages performed by Rev. George Worsley, pub.
in Brumbaugh, Maryland Records, II, 494-495. Marriage Licenses,
1779-1838, pub. in Publications of the Genealogical Society of
Pennsylvania, VIII (March 1922),pp. 151-163 (must be used with
care).

Kent County: Marriage Licenses, 1799-1850, published by Raymond
B. Clark, Jr., and Sara Seth Clark, St. Michaels, Md., 1972.

Montgomery County: marriages performed by various ministers, pub.
in Brumbaugh, Maryland Records, II, 513 ff. Marriage Licenses,
1798-1800 pub. in Scharf, History of Western Maryland, I, 662-
664. Marriages of Rock Creek Parish, 1796-1801, pub. in Thomas,
Chronicles of Colonial Maryland, pp. 225-229.

Prince Georges County: Marriage Licenses, 1777-1801, pub. in Brumbaugh, Maryland Records, I, 93 ff. Marriages from the Register
of Rev. Thomas Read, Prince Georges Parish, 1796-1808, pub. in
Brumbaugh, Maryland Records, II, 557 ff. Marriage Licenses
1777-1824 published in New England Historic Genealogical Register, beginning Vol. LXXIII. Marriage Licenses, 1777-1886, by
Helen W. Brown, pub. by Genealogical Pub. Co., 1973.

Queen Annes County: Origins and History of St. Peter's Church,
Queenstown, Maryland, 1637-1976, by Rev. Edward B. Curley,
c. 1976, contains baptisms and marriages. Marriage Licenses,
1787-1788, pub. in Maryland and Delaware Genealogist, XIV, pp.
45-46.

St. Marys County: Marriage Licenses, 1794- , pub. in Maryland
and Delaware Genealogist, beginning Vol. X. Marriage Licenses
1794-1864, pub. in Brumbaugh, Maryland Records, I, 313 ff.
Marriages performed by various ministers pub. in Brumbaugh, II,
535 ff. The Jesuit Missions of St. Marys County, Maryland, by
Edwin F. Beitzell, © 1960, contains marriage records from
several Roman Catholic parishes.

Talbot County: Marriage Licenses, 1794-1824, pub. by Raymond B.
Clark, Jr., and Sara Seth Clark, Washington, 1965. The History of
St. Joseph's Mission, Cordova, Maryland, 1765-1965, by Loleta
Callahan et al., Cordova, Md., 1965, contains marriage records,
1760-1802.

Washington County: marriages performed by various ministers,
pub. in Brumbaugh, Maryland Records, II, 522 ff.

```
(?), (?), c. 30 Jan. 1794, Lithy Chilston          7 BA-1
(?), (?), Aug. 1795, Nancy Brittingham             1 WO
(?), (?), 30 Sept. 1795, Elizabeth Smith           3 HA-24
(?), Abraham, 16 Aug. 1786, by Rev. Pigman; Ann Roughton  4 AA
(?), David, (date not given), (wife's name not given)  5 BA-6
(?), John, slave to Mrs. Hoxton; 2 March 1793, Mary Beady,
     mulatto                                       3 CH-161
(?), Lambert, 31 July 1796, Daphne (?), both belonging to
     the Baltimore Company                         3 BA-327
(?), Loudon, 10 July 1796, Becky (?), slaves of Christopher
     Hughes                                        3 BA-327
(?), Richard, 1 Jan. 1794, Judith (?), negroes    50 BA-394
(?), Richard, 11 Dec. 1794, Sylvia (?), blacks    50 BA-396
(?), Sampson, 1794, Daphne (?), blacks            50 BA-394
(?), Titus, negro, 30 July 1796, Hannah Armstrong  1 WO
Aakins, William, 26 Sept. 1794, Keziah Hurley      2 DO
Abbitt, David, 4 Sept. 1784, Ann Bond              3 HA-9
Abbott, John, 12 July 1798, Anne Little            3 BA-360
Abbott, William, 11 Jan. 1798, Priscilla Forman    4 KE-65
Abel, Aaron, 29 June 1785, Elizabeth Phillips      2 DO
Abel, Philip, 13 May 1799, Priscilla Freeman       3 BA-371
Abell, Arthur, 12 Jan. 1784, Henrietta Raily       3 SM-61
Abell, Clarke, 3 June 1779, Catherine Hutchins,    3 SM-57
Abell, Edward, 7 Nov. 1778, Statia Taylor          3 SM-57
Abell, John, 4 June 1780, Elizabeth Abell          3 SM-58
Abell, John, 23 Oct. 1790, Sarah Thomas            4 FR
Abercrombie, John, 17 Nov. 1791, Eleanor Hendrickson  6 BA
Abercromby, Robert, 5 Aug. 1787, Martha Smallwood  3 PG-253
Abey, Peter, 25 July, 1778, Elizabeth Heffner      4 FR
Able, John, 5 (Jan.? or June?) 1780, Magdaline Decloe  4 FR
Abraham, John, 12 Nov. 1785, Monica Reynolds      11 BA-9
Abraham, Thomas, (date not given), Sarah Nunen     3 BA-229
Ackerman, George, 31 Aug. 1790, M. Bose           29 BA-1
Ackerman, Philip, 3 June 1794, Cath. Fisher       29 BA-5
Ackman, Charles, 11 May 1796, Sarah Walker         2 DO
Acres, Thomas, 13 Jan. 1798, Elizabeth Berry       3 BA-354
Acton, Henry, 22 Dec. 1796, Mary Ann Pagett        3 PG-442
Adair, Philip, 25 Feb. 1798, Elizabeth Tudor       7 BA-4
Adams, Abraham, 15 Dec. 1792, by Rev. Dorsey; Rebeckah
     Shipley; see also 4 FR                        4 AA
Adams, Abraham, 14 April 1798, Mary Albaugh        4 FR
Adams. Alexander, 14 April 1795, Elizabeth White, widow;
     maiden name given as McLure; 3 BA-301        35 BA-1
```

```
Adams, Andrew, 25 Jan. 1797, Mary Taylor          2 SO-1
  3 SO gives the date as 26 Jan. 1797
Adams, Isaac, 7 July 1796, Hetty Taylor          29 BA-7
Adams, Isaac M., 19 Sept. 1797, Leah Wood         2 SO-1
Adams, James, 24 Nov. 1789, Elizabeth Welch       3 PG-256
Adams, James, 15 April 1793, Lyda Meredith        4 FR
Adams, John, 13 Sept. 1781, Mary Jones            2 DO
Adams, John, 23 March 1788, Susanah Brown         3 PG-254
Adams, John, 19 Jan. 1798, by Rev. Wyatt, Henrietta Phillips
                                                  4 AA
Adams, John, 22 Jan. 1799, Eleanor Collyer        5 MO-115
Adams, John Whittingham, 17 May 1797, Sally Disharoon;
  2 SO-1 gives date as 16 May 1797                3 SO
Adams, Joseph, 19 Jan. 1791, Biddy Curran         4 FR
Adams, Joshua, 13 Sept. 1781, Henrietta Fitzchew  2 DO
Adams, Joshua, c.1792, by Rev. Chalmers; Ann Kelly 4 AA
Adams, Levin, 14 Aug. 1781, Elce Lee              2 DO
Adams, Levin, 10 Dec. 1785, Elizabeth Wrotten     2 DO
Adams, Moses, son of Eusebius and Rachel (dec.); 3rd day,
  4 mo., 1788, Olive Thatcher, dau. of Richard and Abigail
  Thatcher of Kennet Twp., Chester Co., Penna.    4 SF-188
Adams, Nathan, 28 July 1797, Charity Howard       2 SO-1
Adams, Philip, 12 Feb. 1799, Esther Prior         2 SO-1
Adams, Samuel, 28 Dec. 1777, Sarah Nelson         2 CH-233
Adams, Samuel, 26 May 1789, Agnes Thompson       10 BA-192
Adams, Stephen, 20 Nov. 1778, Henrietta Low       1 SM-137
Adams, Stoughton, 29 May 1799, Mary Sanders      29 BA-10
Adams, Thomas, 4 Sept. 1794, Susanna Adams        2 AL-700
Adams, Thomas, 16 Oct. 1798, Mary Rounds          2 SO-1
Adams, William, 5 Nov. 1778, Mary Grey            2 PG-2
Adams, William, 12 Feb. 1783, Eleanor Wagner      3 HA-7
Adams, William, 26 March 1796, Hannah Hallan      3 BA-321
Adams, William, 24 July 1798, Patty Stewart       3 BA-361
Adams, William, 4 Dec. 1798, Rebecca Hall         2 SO-1
Addison, Christ'n, 2 June 1799, Hannah Corwell   50 BA-405
Addison, George Mitchel, 27 April 1800, by Rev. Ridgely;
  Elizabeth Scott                                 4 AA
Addison, John, 11 Oct. 1792, Sarah Leitch         1 BA-4
Addison, Robert, 14 Aug. 1779, Remela Darlon      4 FR
Ader, John, 27 Nov. 1783, Sarah Anst              4 FR
Aderton, Joseph, 1 Aug. 1799, Ann Latimer         2 CH-233
Adkins, David, 19 Feb. 1798, Mary Waller          1 WO
Adkins, William, 20 July 1793, Elizabeth King     4 FR
Adkison, Francis, 20 May 1780, Eliza Phillips    11 BA-4
Adlington, Joseph, 1 Dec. 1799, Hannah Gilberthorpe 3 BA-381
Adlum, Joseph, 7 Nov. 1798, Ann McPhail           3 HA-27
  2 HA-351 gives the date as 8 Nov. 1798.
Adlum, Thomas, 23 March 1799, Sarah McCasky       3 HA-28
  2 HA-351 gives the date as 7 April 1799.
Adrion, Christian, 5 June 1799, Hannah Cornwell  29 BA-10
Ady, James, 12 July 1789 Mary Rickets            23 BA-1
Ady, Joshua, 6 Nov. 1792, Mary Ford               1 BA-4
Aggis, William, 28 July 1780, Ann Anderson        3 BA-180
Ainsworthy, John, 16 Jan. 1780, Mary Ainsworthy   3 SM-58
Airs, Littleton, 29 Jan. 1799, Sally Hitch        2 SO-1
Airy, Richard, 21 July 1800, Catherine Coghlan    2 DO
Aisquith, John, 3 June 1779, Mary Chesley         3 SM
Aiter, Abraham, 17 April 1781, Elizabeth Reigh    4 FR
Aiter, David, 12 April 1797, Elizabeth Stoner     4 FR
Akers, Henry, 1 Dec. 1793, Sarah Tully            2 DO
Akers, William, 27 April 1785, Nancy Daugherty    2 DO
Albach, Martin, 27 June 1786, Cath. Bohmer        2 FR-1105
Albaugh, Abraham, 18 June 1791, Margaret Adams    4 FR
Albaugh, David, 16 March 1782, Mary Harter        4 FR
Albaugh, George, 20 June 1798, Catherine Springer 4 FR
```

```
Albaugh, John, 26 Jan. 1793, Mary Smith              4 FR
Albaugh, Samuel, 9 June 1793, Hannah Whiteneck       4 FR
Albers, Barend, 4 Sept. 1800, Christ. Cath. Anderson 50 BA-408
  See also 29 BA-11.
Albers, Lueden, 6 Jan. 1798, Eva Diffendoerfer       10 BA-198
Albright, Andrew, 11 July 179-(?), Elizabeth Cobenheifer
                                                      5 BA-1
Albright, George, 28 May 1800, Ann Scriver           29 BA-11
Albright, Henry, 8 Jan. 1781, Anna Margaret Swawin    4 FR
Albriton, Charles, 4 Jan. 1781, Catherine Burridge    2 CH-233
Alburger, Samuel, 23 May 1798, Rebecca Garrettson     6 BA
Alby, William, 22 Jan. 1778, Keziah Riston            2 PG-3
Alcock, Joseph, 27 May 1794, Sarah Rook              18 BA-6
Alcock, Samuel, 19 Jan. 1793, Rhoda Evans             2 DO
Alder, Robert, 26 July 1790, Mary Nice               15 BA-3
Alderkin, Zedekiah, 15 Dec. 1800, Eunice Hitchborn    7 BA-4
Aldridge, Abraham, 3 Dec. 1795, Mary Haley            3 BA-313
Aldridge, John, 14 Nov. 1783, Mary Lakin              4 FR
Aldridge, John, 1 May 1792, Margaret Limes            5 BA-1
Aldridge, Thomas, 4 Feb. 1791, Mary Blackburn         4 FR
Aldridge, Thos., 23 Aug. 1798, Cath. Meyers          29 BA-9
Ale, Daniel, 12 Oct. 1778, Modelane Keller            4 FR
Alexander, (?), 21 Sept. 1780, Ann Reenor, blacks    11 BA-4
Alexander, Ashton, 26 Dec. 1799, Catherine Hanson Thomas 4 FR
Alexander, John, 30 June 1785, Sarah Cole             2 DO
Alexander, John, 25 Oct. 1795, Elizabeth Bagfort      3 BA-311
Alexander, Robert, 27 June 1790, Rebecca Hayes        1 BA-2
Alexander, Robert, 4 Sept. 1800, Jane Clendenning     3 HA-30
Alexander, William, 3 May 1795, Rachel Thornton       6 BA
Alexander, William, 14 May 1799, Polly Harwood Stockett,
  dau. of Thomas Noble Stockett and his wife Mary     1 AA-162
Alfort, John, 19 Aug. 1780, Margaret Ashman           4 FR
Alhausen, Just., 20 Nov. 1800, Ann Roberts           50 BA-408
Alin, Chlaeh (sic), 28 Oct. 1780, Henly Linkins       2 CH-233
Alison, George, 3 Dec. 1798, Christina Zimmerman      2 FR-1105
All, Benjamin, 12 Nov. 1778, Sarah Pitts             11 BA-1
All, Edward, 15 Jan. 1784, Mary Sutton               11 BA-7
All, John, 15 July 1798, Comfort Young                6 MO
Allan, Henry H., 18 Aug. 1798, Elizabeth Bother       2 DO
Allcock, Samuel, 29 April 1790, Rhody Sheehy          2 DO
Allcock, William, 20 Aug. 1791, Bridget Pearson       6 BA
Allein, Richard, 23 Jan. 1780, Phebe Dixon            1 CA-3
Allein, William, 1 Dec. 1778, Elizabeth Cowen         1 CA-2
Allen, Bartholomew, 7 Jan. 1778, Sarah Thomas        11 BA-1
Allen, Bartholomew, 20 Jan. 1782, Frances Ramsey      2 CH-233
Allen, George, 6 Jan. 1782, Sarah Lowe                2 PG-3
Allen, Henry Hill, 23 May 1795, Eliza Byus            2 DO
Allen, Isaac, 23 Dec. 1800, Mary Herring              3 HA-30
  2 HA-352 gives date as 24 Dec. 1800.
Allen, James, 9 Jan. 1781, Sarah Williams             2 CH-233
Allen, James, 5 Sept. 1792, Mary Sanks               18 BA-4
Allen, Jesse, 16 Oct. 1796, Catherine Cox             6 BA
Allen, John, 14 May 1778, Sarah Merekin              11 BA-1
Allen, John, 30 Oct. 1781, Virlinda Lanham            2 PG-5
Allen, John, 7 April 1785, Elizabeth Lee              6 BA
Allen, John, 12 Oct. 1786, Ann Piles                  3 PG-251
Allen, John, 1 Feb. 1789, Catherine Elizabeth Hawkins 3 BA-221
Allen, John, 23 March 1790, Christiana Penny          3 BA-228
Allen, John, 30 Nov. 1796, Lucretia Brumbly           1 WO
Allen, John, 9 April 1799, Elizabeth McCurdy          2 SO-1
Allen, Lucas, 9 April 1797, Catherine Emmert          3 BA-343
Allen, Philip, 8 June 1778, Jane Grimes               4 FR
Allen, Reuben, 3 Jan. 1796, Anne Wingat               3 BA-317
Allen, Richard, 19 Feb. 1778, Catherine Proctor      11 BA-1
Allen, Thomas, 18 Dec. 1800, Elizabeth Egnew          5 BA-1
```

Allen, Will'm, 7 March 1791, Sarah Dean   3 BA-229
Allen, William, 12 April 1798, Hannah Bond   3 HA-27
  See also 12 BA-370.
Allen, William, 3 Dec. 1800, Mary Sollers   6 BA
Allender, John, 20 July 1789, Hanna Jervis   20 BA-1
Allender, John Day, 13 Aug. 1790, Martha Barnaby 18 BA-2
Allender, Joseph, 30 Jan. 1800, Mary Biays   5 BA-1
Allender, Nicholas, 26 June 1797, Sarah Bradford 3 HA-26
  2 HA-349 gives the date as 29 June 1797.
Allender, William, 19 Nov. 1788, Ann Sollars   6 BA
Allens, James, 6 Jan. 1782, Sarah Williams   3 HA-5
Allibone, Benjamin, 14th day, 2 mo., 1787, Phebe Stedman 6 SF
Allingham, Stephen, 19 April 1781, Jemima Richards 2 PG-5
Allison, Elisha, 19 June 1796, Ann Shepperd   3 BA-323
Allison, George, 15 June 1797, Christina Zimmerman 4 FR
Allison, Henry, 25 May 1779, Margaret Dillian   3 SM-57
Allison, Jno. B., 20 April 1797, Eliz. Higgins   5 MO-114
Allison, Patrick, 15 March 1787, by Rev. Isaac S. Keith; Mary
  Buchanan   5 BA-1
Allison, Robert, 9 July 1780, Sarah Turner   3 HA-2
Allisson, Henry, 22 June 1796, Elizab. Linton   2 FR-1105
Allmon, David, 3 July 1790, Eliza Traverse   18 BA-2
Allsip, Richards, 28 Sept. 1780, Keziah (House?) 1 CA-3
Allwell, William, 15 April 1790, Sarah Kedie   11 BA-13
Allwine, Jno., 9 June 1796, Cath. Weynemeyer   29 BA-6
Ally, Shadrack, 1782, Elizabeth Gates   2 CH-233
Alricks, Hermanus, 1 Jan. 1791, Jane Liggat   4 FR
Alricks, West, 21 Feb. 1794, Ann Peyton   4 FR
Alter, Adam, 8 March 1798, Eliz. Ernst   29 BA-9
Alter, Christian, 28 Dec. 1797, Nancy Wooding   6 BA
Alter, David, 20 Oct. 1796, Barb. Mohr   50 BA-400
Alter, Frederick, 21 Oct. 1790, P. Moore   29 BA-1
Alter, Jno., 19 Dec. 1795, Susannah Giles   29 BA-7
Alter, Jno., 4 April 1800, Mary Simon   29 BA-11
Altvater, Henry, 11 Dec. 1794, Hannah Garretson 50 BA-396
Alwait, Hugh, 11 Dec. 1800, Rebecka Densey   48 BA-2
Alward, Azel, 16 Oct. 1800, Sally McCammon   3 BA-393
Alwart, Hugh, 11 Dec. 1800, Rebecka Densy   8 BA-2
Alwell, Samuel, 22 Dec. 1778, Mary Maccoy   2 PG-3
Alwill, William, 8 June 1780, Sarah Philips   11 BA-4
Ambrose, John, 1 Aug. 1794, Catherine Lynn   4 FR
Ambrosins, Christopher, 9 Oct. 1787, Cath. Getzendanner 2 FR-110!
Amerson, Charles, 8 April 1797, Philipena Crampton 4 FR
Amelung, Frederick M., 3 May 1797, Louise Sophia Furnival
  4 FR
Amie, J. B. J. A., 27 June 1797, H. F. Joullain Dupuy 44 BA-2
Ammitt, Wm., 11 June 1793, Rebecca Roles   18 BA-5
Amos, Luke, 26 Nov. 1794, Sarah Gallion   3 HA-23
  7 BA-1 gives the date as 27 Nov. 1794.
Amos, Mordica, 18 Jan. 1789, Pacience Spiers   23 BA-1
  The marriage took place in Washington Co.
Amos, William, 19 Nov. 1779, Mary Sinclair   3 HA-1
Amos, Zachariah, 23 Jan. 1792, Susannah Mutchmer 3 HA-21
Amoss, Benjamin, 5 Nov. 1800, Margaret Conn   3 HA-30
Amoss, James, son of William and Hannah, 4th day, 11 mo.,
  1790, Hannah Lee, dau. of David and Rebecca   1 SF
Amoss, James, 23 Feb. 1798, Jane Bell   3 HA-27
Amoss, James, of J., 4 Dec. 1799, Mary Amoss   3 HA-28
Amoss, Robert, 2 Jan. 1792, Elizabeth Amoss   3 HA-21
Amoss, William, 6 June 1799, Ruth Sutton   3 HA-28
Ancrum, Jacob, 20 March 1779, Elizabeth Clark   4 FR
Anderson, Abraham, 26 Aug. 1798, Jane Camoren   6 BA
Anderson, Daniel, 29 Feb. 1785, Rachel Wearin   3 HA-9
Anderson, Edward, 14 Dec. 1797, by Rev. Ridgely; Susanna
  Danielson   4 AA

Anderson, Geo., 25 March 1781, Martha Presbury   11 BA-2
Anderson, Henry, 12 July 1792, Sarah Alexander   2 DO
Anderson, Henry, 23 Oct. 1799, Eliza Crawford   5 BA-1
Anderson, Jabez, 2 Jan. 1796, Elizabeth Gocoghegan   3 BA-317
Anderson, James, 15 Feb. 1781, Catherine McComas   2 CH-233
Anderson, James, 4 April 1781, Sarah Hill   3 HA-3
Anderson, James, 12 Feb. 1782, Cassandra McComas   3 HA-6
Anderson, James M., Jr., 16 Feb. 1797, Elizabeth B. Hands
   4 KE-65
Anderson, John, 12 June 1779, Catherine Loney   4 FR
Anderson, John, 26 May 1783, Susanna Brown   3 BA-185
Anderson, John, 25 Dec. 1787, Jean Gibbs   3 PG-253
Anderson, John, 10 April (1797?), Elizabeth Ship   4 FR
Anderson, Joseph, 22 Jan. 1797, by Rev. Green; Sarah Coulter
   4 AA
Anderson, Levin, 13 Aug. 1792, Mary Phillips   2 DO
Anderson, Robert, 25 Nov. 1789, Sarah Cole   15 BA-2
Anderson, Robert, 15 March 1796, Mary Brashears   2 FR-1105
Anderson, Robert, 11 Jan. 1798, Elizabeth Hicks   45 BA-2
Anderson, Stephen, 22 Oct. 1798, Nancy Cahoon   1 WO
Anderson, Thomas, 1 Sept. 1788, Sarah Brinsfield   2 DO
Anderson, William, 16 June 1778, Sarah Wayman   2 PG-2
Anderson, William, 22 June 1778, Mary Sullivan   11 BA-1
Anderson, William, 26 Sept. 1778, Cavey Brashears   4 FR
Anderson, William, of Kent Co., Del., 31 Aug. 1791, Ann
   Causey of Caroline Co.   2 SF
Anderson, William, 1 Feb. 1793, Mary McDonald   5 BA-1
Anderson, William, 12 May 1796, Anna Thomas   4 FR
Anderson, William, 11 April 1799, Mary Roe   3 BA-370
Anderwig, Lancelot, 21 Dec. 1797, Sarah Turner   3 PG-443
Andrew, James, 13 May 1798, Mary Bell   2 DO
Andrew, Maddox, 1 March 1792, Premela (sic) Kell   28 BA-2
Andrew, Robert, 5 Jan. 1795, Eleanor Toby   3 BA-299
Andrew, Russell Rea, 12 April 1796, Mary Orem   2 DO
Andrew, William, 26 Feb. 1781, Catherine Blackburn   3 HA-3
Andrew, William Holland, 13 Feb. 1794, Mary Galloway   6 BA
Andrews, Abraham, 17 March 1780, Mary Hanson   3 HA-1
Andrews, Edw'd Burns, 25 March 1796, Eleanor Davies   6 BA
Andrews, Isaac, 3 Feb. 1790, Mary Woodland   2 DO
Andrews, Levin, 16 May 1785, Sarah Starling   2 DO
Andrews, Levin, 9 April 1793, Charlotte Barnes   2 DO
Andrews, Medford, 25 Jan. 1794, Sarah Parker   2 DO
Andrews, Nathaniel, 18 March 1797, Caroline Andrews   2 DO
Andrews, Randolph, 2 Oct. 1799, Sarah (Barnet?)   29 BA-10
Andrews, Stanaway, 31 Jan. 1786, Mary Moore   2 DO
Andrews, Stephen, 31 Jan. 1788, Nancy Staplefort   2 DO
Andrewson, Dickeson, 6 May 1779, Ann Belcher   11 BA-3
Andros, Thomas, 21 Jan. 1800, Delilah Fisher   2 FR-1105
Angell, James, 25 Dec. 1788, Mary Barney   5 BA-1
Angell, William Christopher, 26 Nov. 1791, Nancy Traverse
   2 DO
Ankrom, Aaron, 30 April 1783, Mary Marley   4 FR
Annis, Thomas, 2 Sept. 1797, Mary Dunn   3 HA-26
   2 HA-350 gives the date as 7 Sept. 1797.
Annis, William, 3 Sept. 1793, Margaret Thompson   3 BA-275
Ansell, Sam'l, 12 Jan. 1786, Priscilla Graves   4 FR
Ansley, Wm., 5 Aug. 1800, Polly Carsey   2 SO-1
Anspach, Henry Nicholas, 19 Feb. 1799, Elizabeth Furnival
   3 BA-368
Antes, Adam, 8 Jan. 1793, Christina Schmit   2 FR-1105
Anthony, Nathan, 2 Nov. 1798, Hester Clark   4 KE-65
Apollo, Lewis Benjamin, 4 Jan. 1794, Polly Starchberger 4 FR
Apollo, Lewis Benj'm, 13 Feb. 1796, Catherine Slicker 4 FR
Apolo , Benj., 19 June 1800, Mary Usher   2 FR-1105
Appel, Christ'n, 1789, Rosina Sohnin, widow   50 BA-388

```
Appel, Wm., 1791, C. Bohlson                           50 BA-391
Apple, Christian, 3 Jan. 1792, Margaret Herns           3 BA-255
Apple, Christian, 30 Sept. 1795, Sarah Wilson           6 BA
Apple, Christian, 11 Sept. 1798, Anne Fowler            3 BA-363
Appleby, Charles, 26 July 1793, by Rev. G. Ridgely; Ruth
    Wood                                                4 AA
Appleby, John, 26 Sept. 1796, Elenor Fair Jacob         3 BA-329
Appleby, William, 7 Aug. 1796, by Rev. Ridgely; Ruth
    Shadows                                             4 AA
Appleby, William, 17 April 1800, by Rev. Ridgely; Rebecca
    Barry                                               4 AA
Applegarth, James, 31 Jan. 1799, Amelia Beckwith        2 DO
Applegarth, Philemon, 10 Aug. 1793, Nancy Howell        2 DO
Applegarth, Robert, 6 April 1787, Sally Thomas          2 DO
Applegarth, William, 24 Sept. 1791, Nancy Busick        2 DO
Appold, Andrew, 25 Feb. 1800, Nelly Decker             29 BA-11
Appold, Lewis Benjamin, 9 June 1800, Mary Usher         4 FR
Archebald, Samuel, 28 March 1778, Catherine Cook        4 FR
Archer, Hugh, 15 Sept. 1780, Mary Virginia (?)          3 AA-416
Archer, John, 21 Nov. 1797, Elizabeth Kittleman         6 BA
Archey, Edward, 23 Nov. 1797, Eliz. Allison             5 MO-114
Archman, Henry, 30 Dec. 1784, Sarah Hanly              11 BA-8
Arel, George, 19 Jan. 1785, Sarah Dremen                3 HA-10
Armer, Samuel, 2 Oct. 1788, Susanna Swan                3 BA-218
Armiger, John, 6 Feb. 1781, Williaminah Whitington      3 AA-417
Armiger, Leonard, 4 Sept. 1794, Rebecca Brown           3 AA-424
Armiger, Samuel, 13 Oct. 1788, by Rev. Foreest; Elizabeth
    Scott                                               4 AA
Armiger, William, 1 Jan. 1784, Jane Whittington         3 AA-420
Armitage, Jno., 5 July 1785, Sarah Linton              11 BA-8
Armitage, John, 7 Sept. 1788, Jane Wright               6 BA
Armitage, John, 28 July 1795, Elenor Jones              3 BA-307
Armitage, John, 3 March 1799, Sarah Gwinn               3 HA-28
Armitage, Roger, 7 March 1799, Peggy Hays               6 BA
Armitage, Wm., 28 March 1784, Eliza Bonfield           11 BA-7
Armond, Andrew, 29 June 1794, by Rev. Ridgely; Rebecca
    Reynolds                                            4 AA
Armor, Wm., 1 July 1784, Rachel Puntney                11 BA-7
Armstead, Isaac, 15 April 1795, Barbara Turner          6 BA
Armstrong, Ephraim, 5 June 1797, Susan Cowarden         4 KE-65
Armstrong, Ford, 27 Sept. 1794, Susanna Murphy          7 BA-1
Armstrong, James, 25 Aug. 1778, Margaret Risdale       11 BA-1
Armstrong, James, 2 Nov. 1779, Susanna Wells           11 BA-3
Armstrong, James, 30 Oct. 1800, Elizabeth Douglas       3 BA-394
Armstrong, John, 18 Nov. 1790, Patience Lorton          5 BA-1
Armstrong, John, 14 Aug. 1791, Elizabeth Edwards        3 HA-21
Armstrong, John, 31 July 1798, Ann Colby                4 KE-65
Armstrong, Joseph, 19 Dec. 1799, Jane Alexander         4 FR
Armstrong, Joshua, 12 July 1795, Nancy White            6 BA
Armstrong, Robert, 7 April 1796, Elizabeth Cresap       1 AL-53
Armstrong, Solomon, 6 Dec. 1792, Margaret Griffin       3 BA-259
Armstrong, William, 21 Feb. 1796, Esther Dungen         5 BA-1
Armsstrong, William, 21 Dec. 1797, Ann Athey            3 PG-443
Armsworthy, Bennett, 11 Feb. 1800, Susanna Cissell      4 SM-184
Armsworthy, Daniel, 21 Dec. 1800, Elizabeth Newton      4 SM-184
Armwood, 11 July 1800, Gertrude Harper                  1 WO
Arnal (?), Peter, 10 Dec. 1795, Elizabeth Gregory       6 BA
Arnest, Caleb, 6 Jan. 1784, Ann Helm                   11 BA-7
Arnett, Ezekiel, 26 Dec. 1797, Mahala Evans             2 DO
Arnett, Henry, 22 Dec. 1792, Nancy Vain                 2 DO
Arnett, Levi, 9 June 1785, Rebecca Pickering            2 DO
Arnett, Thomas, 5 Sept. 1787, Tamsey Knott              2 DO
Arnett, William, 24 May 1781, Sarah Reed                2 DO
Arnett, William, 23 June 1794, Molly Mereday            2 DO
Arnold, Anthony, 22 Aug. 1782, Frances Leatherman       4 FR
```

```
Arnold, David, 1 March 1793, Eleanor Pearrie          4 FR
Arnold, Harris, 30 Sept. 1795, Elizabeth Downen       2 DO
Arnold, John, 20 May 1798, Ann Holbrook               6 BA
Arnold, Joshua, 4 Aug. 1796, Mary Wood                6 BA
Arnold, Peter, 21 Feb. 1793, Elizabeth Kettleman      6 BA
Arnold, Peter, 24 Dec. 1797, Sarah Holbrook           6 BA
Arnold, Peter, 21 March 1799, Peggy Cord              6 BA
Arnold, Peter, 23 March 1799, Nancy Perry             4 FR
Arnold, Samuel, 12 Sept. 1800, Mary Ann Jolly         2 AL-701
Arnold, William, 4 Sept. 1786, Elizabeth Allen        3 PG-251
Arnot, Joseph, 18 Oct. 1793, Ann Conelly             50 BA-393
Arvin, William, 27 Sept. 1789, Elizabeth Hardcastle   1 BA-2
Asbridge, William, 12 June 1798, Catherine Tregoe     2 DO
Asburn, John, 20 Nov. 1792, Nancy Gray                6 BA
    19 BA-7 gives the groom's name as John Ashbaw.
Ashburner, John, 25 July 1800, Anna Gibson            3 BA-388
Asher, Abraham, 9 Jan. 1800, Mary Thompson            6 BA
Asher, Anthony, 15 May 1794, Mary Adams              29 BA-5
Asher, John, 25 April 1799, Chloe Freer               6 BA
Ashford, John, 28 Jan. 1779, Anne Elgin               2 PG-2
Ashley, Benjamin, 29 July 1793, Catherine Bibby      19 BA-8
Ashley, John, 24 Dec. 1798, Sarah Blackiston          4 KE-65
Ashley, Thomas, 2 Feb. 1784, Rebecca Grace            3 HA-8
Ashly, Greenberry, 5 Oct. 1797, by Rev. Ridgely; Mary
    Marsh                                             4 AA
Ashman, Henry, 5 June 1784, Elizabeth Moyer           4 FR
Ashman, Thomas, 2 July 1796, Margaret Leathorn        3 BA-327
Ashman, William, 27 Dec. 1792, Rebecca Boyce         16 BA-4
Ashmead, John, 14 July 1800, Catherine Jordan         3 HA-29
Ashton, Henry Alex., 25 May 1778, Mary Dent           4 CH-1
Ashton, John, 3 May 1800, Susannah Fulton             3 HA-29
Ashwell, Barnett, 16 Jan. 1793, Sarah Forrest        18 BA-5
Askew, Jno., 22 Dec. 1800, Eliz. Jones               29 BA-12
Askew, Jonathan, 14 Dec. 1793, Mary Porter            3 BA-279
Askew, Joshua, 23 Sept. 1784, Eliza Williamson       11 BA-7
Askew, William, 10 Dec. 1784, Sarah Calwell           1 BA-7
Askey, Michael, 4 Jan. 1782, Susanna Burket           3 AA-418
Asque, John, 4 Oct. 1779, Sarah Woolverton            4 FR
Asquith, David, 2 Oct. 1791, Frances Nichols          1 BA-3
Ater, Abraham, 21 Feb. 1785, Catherine Reighe         4 FR
Ater, Abraham, 30 March 1799, Charity Ephlen          4 FR
Athay, Zephniah, 13 Nov. 1790, Lucy Duckett           3 PG-257
Athein, Horatio, 12 June 1791, Mary Schann            2 FR-1105
    4 FR gives the bride's name as Mary Showne.
Atherton, William, 10 April 1792, Temperance Bower   29 BA-3
Athey, Hanson, 9 April 1798, Mary Long                3 PG-443
Athey, Joseph, 27 Jan. 1798, Mariah Wheeling          4 FR
Atkinson, Angeloe, 30 Nov. 1795, Sarah Hudson         1 WO
Atkinson, Isaac, 6 Feb. 1800, Nelly Inloes            6 BA
Atkinson, Milby, 13 Aug. 1800, Polly Trayhearn        1 WO
Atley, Joseph, 10 Sept. 1791, Ann Smith               3 PG-258
Atmore, William, 19 March 1800, Lilian Morrow         3 BA-384
Atwell, Benjamin, 16 Jan. 1781, Sarah Kidd            3 AA-417
Atwell, John, 4 Sept. 1797, Anne Lewis                4 FR
Atwell, Thomas, 25 May 1800, Elinor Worthin           7 MO-29
Atwell, William, 29 Jan. 1799, Elizabeth Rawlings     1 AA-163
Aubert, Martin, 9 March 1789, Catherine Feterley      4 FR
Augenbaugh, John, 10 June 1800, Susanna Little        3 BA-387
Auld, Capt., 30 Oct. 1800, Betsy Mauldin              7 BA-4
Auld, Hugh, 25 July 1793, Zipporah Wilson            18 BA-5
Auld, John, 20 Dec. 1790, Sarah Carroll               2 DO
Auman, Andrew, 29 March 1785, Barb. Lutter            2 FR-1105
Aushutz, Jacob, 19 Aug. 1792, Sybillina Foltz        50 BA-392
Austen, William, 5 Sept. 1800, Milly Clark            2 SO-1
Austin, Hezekiah, 15 Dec. 1796, Eliz. Odle            5 MO-113
```

```
Austin, Isaac, 17 Dec. 1797, Mary G. Malcomb          3 SO
Austin, Isaac R., 16 Dec. 1797, Martha G. Halcomb     2 SO-1
Austin, John, 15 Feb. 1799, Cassandra Odle            5 MO-115
Austin, Lawrence, 29 July 1788, Rebecca Perrigo       18 BA-1
Avalon, Philip, 10 Oct. 1799, Elizabeth Conner        4 FR
Avery, Robert, 25 May 1794, Mary McBride              3 BA-287
Avis, David, 21 Sept. 1779, Ann Ferguson              3 AA-415
Avis, John, 23 Nov. 1780, Sarah Aisquith              1 CA-3
Ayers, Samuel, 21 Jan. 1794, Margaret Gaines          2 AL-700
Aylon, Richard, 14 March 1793, Jane Avenpold          4 FR
Aylworth, John, 8 Nov. 1788, Elizabeth Wilson         6 BA


B...hitt (?), Joshua, c.1792 in Washington Co., by Rev.
   Chalmers; Eliz. Nelson                             4 AA
Babbs, James, Feb. 1778, Delila Porter                11 BA-1
Babcock, Clark, 23 Feb. 1796, Margaret Flinn          3 BA-317
Babelitz, Pet., 28 Jan. 1783, Elis. Merkysin          2 CL-82
Babes (?), John, 17 Oct. 1780, Ann McCubbin,          11 BA-4
Babs, Thomas, 14 Feb. 1799, by Rev. Ridgely; Rachel Pum-
   phrey                                              4 AA
Bachelor, William, 16th day, 8 mo., 1788, Elizabeth Jones
   2 SF-289
Bachley, John, 14 Oct. 1783, Mary Ristar              10 BA-178
Bacon, Lemuel, 17 Dec. 1783, Mary Stocker             11 BA-7
Baden, Benja., 30 Jan. 1793, Eliza Whitington         22 BA-2
Bader, Dominic, 3 Jan. 1800, Marie Rabbon             10 BA-200
Baehr, George, 30 Jan. 1791, Elizab. Koblentz         2 FR-1108
Baer, George, 29 Jan. 1786, Mary Adams                2 FR-1107
Baer, George, Jr., 13 April 1788, Cath. Hauer         2 FR-1108
Baer, John, 25 Dec. 1788, Mary Thomas                 2 FR-1108
Bagens, John, 7 June 1783, Catherine Whitenack        4 FR
Bager, Geo. Samuel, 7 April 1789, Cath. Bossert       2 FR-1108
Bagford, William, 16 Nov. 1796, Ann Creigh            45 BA-1
Baggarly, Hezekiah, 23 Dec. 1797, Charlotte Orme      6 MO
Baggarly, James, 20 Oct. 1798, Elizabeth Smith        6 MO
Bagley, William, 7 Jan. 1790, Susanna Husbands        1 BA-2
Bail, Robert P., 10 Oct. 1796, Mary Ann Davies        5 BA-2
Bailey, Daniel, 27 March 1782, Catherine Carson       3 HA-6
Bailey, Evan, 28 March 1798, Mary Ervin               6 BA
Bailey, James, 1791, Christina Weiderman              50 BA-390
Bailey, James, 27 Nov. 1800, Polly Felter             3 AL-7
Bailey, John, 28 Sept. 1794, Rebecca Bell             4 BA-76
   36 BA-1 gives the date as 24 Sept. 1794.
Bailey, Jones, 19 Dec. 1781, Salinah Renshaw          3 HA-5
Bailey, Levin, 27 Jan. 1795, Margaret Lowder          3 BA-299
Bailey, William, 2 Sept. 1784, Mary Rachob            4 FR
Bailey, William, 18 June 1796, Phebe Ferrin           4 FR
Bailiss, Elias, 29 Jan. 1782, Rachel Barcellay        3 HA-6
Baillie, Alex., 27 April 1797, Mary Doyle             2 AL-700
Baillie, Andrew, 1 Oct. 1779, Mary Leftrich           2 CH-233
Bailly, Samuel, 19 Nov. 1795, Mary Ann Dorsey         35 BA-1
Baily, Adam, 1790, Susanna Lutz                       50 BA-389
Baily, Amos, 10 Feb. 1796, Anne Reams                 3 BA-317
Baily, Joseph, 21 Sept. 1790, Susanna Hedges          2 FR-1108
Bain, Daniel, 7 Feb. 1793, Elizabeth Spedden          2 DO
Bain, William, 6 Aug. 1783, Mary Howland              11 BA-6
Bainbridge, Absalom, 12 April 1790, Elizabeth Beatty  4 FR
Bainbridge, Edmond, 26 Sept. 1781, Catziah Bainbridge 4 FR
Bair, Henry, 6 Nov. 1779, Eliz'th Shellman            4 FR
Bakeoven, Peter, 25 April 1798, Catharine Hulk        6 BA
Baker, Adam, 17 Sept. 1794, Juliana Layman            4 FR
Baker, Allen, 17 Oct. 1797, Susanna Pennington        45 BA-2
Baker, Archibald, 10 July 1799, Anna Wait             1 WO
Baker, Basil, 25 Nov. 1790, Ann Linch                 4 FR
```

```
Baker, Charles, 12 Sept. 1781, Elizabeth Tuder          3 HA-5
Baker, Charles, 25 Oct. 1800, Mary Crebs                3 BA-394
Baker, Christian, 25 Aug. 1783, Mary Creichebaum        4 FR
Baker, Elam, 27 Aug. 1782, Keturah Baker                11 BA-5
Baker, Ephraim, 31 March 1796, Sacey Reimy              3 BA-321
     35 BA-4 gives the bride's name as Tacy Reimey.
Baker, Frederick, 29 March 1789, Catherine Baker        4 FR
Baker, Frederick, 14 June 1797, Susanna Buzzard         4 FR
Baker, Henry, 1 May 1786, Eliz. Geringer                2 FR-1107
Baker, Henry, 15 Sept. 1797, Priscilla Coke             4 FR
Baker, Howard, 6 April 1782, Ann Philips                2 CH-233
Baker, Isaac, 23 Nov. 1780, Ann Stewart                 2 CH-233
     3 HA-5 gives the date as 22 Nov. 1781.
Baker, Jennis Helming, 29 May 1797, Susanna Johanna Gerardina
     Van Noemes                                         5 Ba-3
Baker, John, 13 Aug. 1780, Delia Presbury               3 HA-2
Baker, John, 23 Jan. 1783, Mary Doyel                   11 BA-6
Baker, John, 29 June 1794, Mary Dungan                  6 BA
Baker, John, 8 Feb. 1798, Elizabeth Standiford          6 BA
Baker, John, 1 Feb. 1799, Polly Harder                  4 FR
Baker, Jonathan, 12 Dec. 1800, Polly Hickman            1 WO
Baker, Larkin, 7 Dec. 1799, Margaret Mark               4 FR
Baker, Manning, 13 Sept. 1796, Rebecca Clair            3 BA-329
Baker, Morris, 20 Aug. 1782, Jane Haithorn              3 HA-7
Baker, Morris, 14 Aug. 1798, by Rev. Dorsey; Rachel Gladman
     4 AA
Baker, Nathan, 24 March 1791, Belinda Bosley            1 BA-3
Baker, Nathaniel, 30 April 1778, Anne Grover            1 CA-1
Baker, Nathaniel, 7 May 1782, Sarah Daniels             3 HA-6
Baker, Peter, 21 June 1789, Elizabeth Foy               4 FR
Baker, Philip, 12 Feb. 1799, Margaret Stoker            4 FR
Baker, Riley, 19 June 1797, Priscilla Carmichael        2 SO
Baker, Samuel, 3 Aug. 1797, Elizabeth Paca              3 PG-443
Baker, Thomas, 12 June 1784, Mary Taylor                11 BA-7
Baker, William, 1 Jan. 1782, Jane Davis                 3 SM-59
Balden, John, 3 May 1798, Elizabeth Jones               3 BA-358
Baldry, William, 25 June 1789, Mary Green               3 BA-221
Baldwin, Abraham, 27 May 1798, Sarah Jenny              6 BA
Bale, John, 1 Oct. 1796, Honor Murry                    4 FR
Ball, Dan'l, 31 March 1779, Catherine Boyer             4 FR
Ball, Gerret, 11 Jan. 1787, Eliz. Cecil                 2 FR-1107
Ball, James, 20 Feb. 1779, Rachel Hinton                4 FR
Ball, Jos., 21 Dec. 1797, Ally Phelps                   2 FR-1109
Ball, Samuel, 29 June 1794, Eliz. Veal                  29 BA-5
Ball, Samuel, 18 May 1799, Judith Magacy                3 BA-371
Ball, Thomas, 14 May 1797, Calista Corner               1 TA-311
Ball, William, 21 Oct. 1790, Elis. Dukehart             29 BA-1
Ball, William, 12 Feb. 1797, Anna Pamela Green          3 BA-342
Ball, William, 5 Dec. 1797, Eliz. Arnold                2 FR-1109
Ballard, Daniel, 6 July 1797, Dorothy Waters            2 SO
Ballard, Michael, 11 Aug. 1787, Elizabeth Page          3 BA-228
Ballard, Robert, 13 July 1780, Rebecca Plowman          11 BA-4
Ballinger, William, son of William and Cassandra, 20th day,
     7 mo. 1797, Lydia Smith, dau. of John and Elizabeth of
     Harford Co.                                        3 SF
Balsell, Christian, 9 Sept. 1786, Catherine Yantz       4 FR
Balser, John, 7 May 1782, Elizabeth Lydey               4 FR
Balszel, Jacob, 11 Jan. 1787, Charlotte Christ          2 FR-1107
     4 FR gives the bride's name as Charity Christ.
Balt, Christian, 3 Aug. 1799, Cath. Zahn                50 BA-406
Baltimore, William, 8 Oct. 1800, Ann Cook               2 DO
Baltzell, Daniel, 24 Nov. 1799, Sus. Gittinger          2 FR-1109
Balzell, Charles, 10 June 1794, Elizab. Fulton          2 FR-1109
Balzell, Jacob, 10 May 1796, Anna Campbell              2 FR-1109
Bamfler, Johann, 26 Jan. 1800, Catherine Maakbein       10 BA-200
```

```
Bandel, Geo., 31 Dec. 1800, Eliz. Boss          29 BA-12
Bane, Patterson, 20 Aug. 1800, Rebecca Luckie    3 HA-30
Banester, Joseph, 29 March 1797, Elizabeth Thomas 4 KE-65
Banis, John, 4 Dec. 1800, Martha Mitchel        50 BA-408
Bankard, Abraham, 18 July 1789, Modolena Erb     4 FR
Banks, Andrew, 5 Feb. 1795, Catherine Bowen      6 BA
Banks, David, 10 Jan. 1782, Eliza Miller        11 BA-5
Banks, David, 7 Oct. 1787, Katherine Grant       6 BA
Banks, Henry, 19 Nov. 1799, Polly Messick        2 SO
Banks, Wm., 11 Sept. 1788, Sus'a Connaway       11 BA-11
Bankson, James, 6 Nov. 1783, Sarah Hull         11 BA-6
Bankson, Jno., 5 May 1787, Mary Mickle          11 BA-10
Banneday, Jno., 26 April 1787, Mary Harrien     11 BA-10
Banninger (or Barringer), Francis, 24 Sept. 1778, Ann Hobson
     2 MO-1
Bannister, Benjamin, 24 Dec. 1778, Grace Holland 1 CA-2
Bantom, Gabriel, 18 Dec. 1792, Juanity Lee       2 DO
Bantz, Henry, 9 Aug. 1788, Cath. Schmidt         2 FR-1108
Bantz, Johannes, 1 Feb. 1795, Catharina Kunz    10 BA-196
Barbarin, Louis, 16 Dec. 1794, Maria Corbet      3 BA-296
Barbarin, Louis, 23 Sept. 1797, Elizabeth Moore  3 BA-350
Barber, Elijah, 7 Dec. 1787, Nancy Todd          2 FR-1108
Barber, James, 19 May 1782, Sarah Rogers         3 BA-184
Barber, John, 12 Sept. 1795, Elizabeth Rider     4 BA-77
Barber, John, 10 Aug. 1799, Margaret Richards    3 BA-375
Barbine, Charles, 26 Jan. 1786, Mary Harthmann  10 BA-186
Barclay, Henry, 23 Nov. 1788, Frances Nicholson  3 PG-255
Barclay, James, 16 June 1800, Mary Griffith      2 DO
Barclay, William, 18 Dec. 1794, Mary Evans       3 PG-440
Bard, James, 10 May 1778, Martha Griffis        11 BA-1
Bare, George, 29 Jan. 1791, Elizabeth Cublentz   4 FR
Bare, John, 13 May 1797, Elizabeth Brown         4 FR
Barefoot, William, 29 Sept. 1786, Eleanor Morgun 24 BA-1
Barentz, Heinr., 16 March 1794, Caroline Linck  50 BA-394
Barford, Richard, 17 Feb. 1794, Lydia Sparrow    6 BA
Bargelt, John, 2 June 1795, Bashie Night        10 BA-196
Bargesar, Daniel, 8 April 1797, Sarah Gates      4 FR
Barker, John, 10 Jan. 1784, Margaret Atwell      3 AA-418
Barker, John, 29 Jan. 1793, Elizab. Mugg         2 FR-1108
Barker, Samuel, 25 Jan. 1797, Ann Mocabee        4 FR
Barker, William, 27 March 1783, Rachel Franklin  3 AA-419
Barker, William, 19 Feb. 1785, Suzanna Griffith  4 FR
Barkley, George D., 1788, Sophia Warwick        50 BA
Barklie, Thomas, 1 Nov. 1798, Jane McCormick     5 BA-3
Barkman, David, 26 Sept. 1799, Margaret Griffis  6 BA
Barkman, Peter, 28 May 1779, Ulianna Crandler    4 FR
Barkshire, Henry, 15 Feb. 1779, Cresilla Burton  4 FR
Barkus, Daniel, 24 Oct. 1793, Cassandra Elliott  2 AL-700
Barkus, Moses, 15 Dec. 1796, Nancy Thompson      2 AL-700
Barlow, Zachariah, 17 Dec. 1779, Eleanor Hickman 4 FR
Barnaby, Elias, 8 June 1788, Rachel Riffett      3 BA-217
Barnard, James, 1 July 1800, Esther Humbertson   2 AL-701
Barnard, Michael, 9 Dec. 1797, Caty Strong       4 FR
Barnard, Notley. See Barnet, Notley.
Barnee, Thos., 21 Aug. 1785, Barb. Neuschwangar  2 FR-1107
Barnes, Adam, 5 Aug. 1784, Ruth Shipley          3 BA-188
Barnes, Amos, 12 May 1783, Rebecca Wood          3 HA-7
Barnes, Basil, 23 Jan. 1791, Mary Lanham         3 PG-258
Barnes, Caleb, 12 Oct. 1780, Margaret Walker     4 FR
Barnes, David, 27 Aug. 1787, Elizabeth Hall      4 FR
Barnes, Dawson, 29 Sept. 1794, Mary Poole        4 FR
Barnes, Elijah, 17 Aug. 1784, Cath. Shipley     11 BA-7
Barnes, Foard, 30 Nov. 1792, Ann Gilmor          3 HA-22
Barnes, George, 6 June 1797, Catherine Sigler    2 AL-700
Barnes, Henry, 4 Feb. 1790, Ann Lanham           3 PG-256
```

```
Barnes, Henry, (Aug. or Sept.) 1798, Abigail Barnes      2 AL-701
Barnes, James, 22 March 1781, Sarah Fort                 3 HA-3
Barnes, James, 27 May 1783, Sarah Jarris                 4 FR
Barnes, James, 24 Dec. 1795, Nancy Harrison              4 FR
Barnes, John, 7 Jan. 1786, Caroline McNamara             2 DO
Barnes, John, 15 July 1786, Debitha Taylor               4 FR
Barnes, Jno., 6 April 1789, Ruth Barnes                 11 BA-12
Barnes, Leonard, 11 Oct. 1790, Nancy Price               2 FR-1108
Barnes, Levin, 26 April 1795, Mary Sholl                29 BA-6
Barnes, Levin, 4 July 1795, Milly Coulbourne             2 DO
Barnes, Mace, 26 March 1785, Mary Keene                  2 DO
Barnes, Michael, 1 Oct. 1788, Elizabeth Kemp             4 FR
Barnes, Moses, 25 April 1789, Mary Lake                  2 DO
Barnes, Rezin, 7 Sept. 1792, by Rev. Dorsey; Essenah
   Barnes                                                4 AA
Barnes, Richard, 17 Dec. 1783, Sarah Kidd                3 HA-8
Barnes, Robson, 8 Sept. 1792, Elizabeth Barns            2 DO
Barnes, Thomas, 3 Jan. 1795, Ann King                    4 FR
Barnes, Thomas, 15 Oct. 1796, Elizabeth Lake             2 DO
Barnes, Vachel, 15 May 1788, Charity McDougal            4 FR
Barnes, William, 12 Sept. 1791, Deborah Onion            4 FR
Barnes, William Parker, 9 June 1799, Mary Osborne        3 BA-372
Barnes, Zadock, 28 Jan. 1794, Elizabeth Paulson          4 FR
Barnet, Charles, 26 March 1795, Ann Burton               7 BA-2
Barnet, George, 2 July 1795, Rebecca Smith              29 BA-6
Barnet, James, 2 July 1796, Polly Fitzgerald             3 BA-327
Barnet, Luke, 25 April 1796, Catherine Pinkley           4 FR
Barnet, Michael, before 12 Feb. 1778, Dolly Adams        2 PG-6
Barnet (Barnard), Notley, 2 Oct. 1800, Elsey Ragan       2 AL-701
Barnet, Peter, 4 Jan. 1790, M. Owings                   29 BA-1
Barnet, Phillip, 18 June 1795, Sarah Gilbert             7 BA-2
Barnet, Robert, 30 May 1786, Nancy Stallings             2 FR-1107
Barnet, Robert, 18 March 1796, Margaret Kemp             4 FR
Barnett, Archibald, 22 June 1782, Elizabeth Lucas        4 FR
Barnett, Charles, 24 March 1795, Ann Burton              3 HA-24
Barnett, Jacob, 12 Feb. 1788, Catherine Hissey           3 BA-216
Barnett, Robert, 29 May 1786, Nancy Stallings            4 FR
Barnett, Thomas, 20 Sept. 1784, Nancy Griffith           2 DO
Barnett, Thomas, 18 Jan. 1800, Rebecca Manning           2 DO
Barnett, William, 23 Nov. 1780, Sarah Piggman            4 FR
Barney, John, 4 Dec. 1786, Mary Wallace                  6 BA
Barney, Joseph, 4 Aug. 1789, Elizabeth Jones             4 AA
Barney, Samuel, 30 July 1799, Eve Bryer                 29 BA-10
Barney, William, 2 May 1799, Rebecca Ridgely             3 BA-371
Barnhart, Peter, 9 Sept. 1795, Elizabeth Hains           4 FR
Barns, Eleven, 4 Sept. 1783, Hannah Slack               11 BA-6
Barns, Ephraim, 19 Aug. 1794, Eleanor Barnes             4 FR
Barns, Jesse, 18 Dec. 1795, Elizabeth Morris             2 DO
Barns, Thomas, 5 March 1793, Sarah Wingate               2 DO
Barnsley, Joseph, 14 June 1792, Elizabeth Hall           3 BA-256
Barnthisell, Christopher, 5 Oct. 1794, Catherine Grove   4 FR
Barr, Hugh, 26 Nov. 1783, Priscilla James                4 FR
Barrack, Frederick, 19 Sept. 1797, Mary Simon            4 FR
Barran, William, 28 June 1799, Sarah Brownley            6 BA
Barrance, Richard, 25 July 1798, Ann Rawson              6 BA
Barret, Edward, 2 Oct. 1786, by Rev. Turner; Catherine
   Kitten                                               51 BA-30
Barret, John, 3 Oct. 1796, Mary Hagerty                  3 BA-329
Barrett, James, 4 March 1800, Catherine Layfield         1 WO
Barrett, John, 31 Aug. 1788, Margery Braithwaite         3 BA-211
Barrett, John, 17 Oct. 1799, Catherine Ruke              3 BA-379
Barrett, Joseph Loudon, 26 Sept. 1789, Elizabeth Williams
   3 PG-255
Barrett, Nehemiah, 18 Dec. 1793, Winey Cummings          1 AL-52
Barrett, William, 23 Feb. 1783, Margaret Malley          3 SM-61
```

```
Barrey, John, 30 Aug. 1792, by Rev. Bowen; Mary Watkins  4 AA
Barrick, Christian, 15 Feb. 1793, Catherine Hoover        4 FR
Barrick, George, 11 May 1783, Nancy Waters                4 FR
Barrick, Henry, 9 Sept. 1780, Margaret Keller             4 FR
Barrick, William, 22 May 1778, Catherine Heartsock        4 FR
Barrick, William, 29 Sept. 1792, Mary Scholes             4 FR
Barrington, Joseph, 1 April 1797, Martha Fisher           4 FR
Barron, William, 8 June 1786, Elizabeth Hooper Hicks      2 DO
Barrs, John, 5 Feb. 1784, Sarah Stevens                   3 AA-420
Barrs, Leonard, 14 Nov. 1779, Mary Griffin                1 CA-2
Barry, Jacob, 1 June 1788, by Rev. Forrest, Mary Disney   4 AA
Barry, John, 6 March 1790, Elis. Dieffenderfer            29 BA-1
Barry, Laban, 10 Oct. 1778, Anne Walls                    11 BA-1
Barry, Lavalin, 14 March 1795, Jamimah Stansbury          6 BA
Barry, Michael, 26 May 1798, Elizabeth Ward               6 BA
Barry, Standish, 11 Oct. 1788, Nancy Thompson             3 BA-218
Barry, William, 21 June 1778, Mary Ann Smith              2 PG-3
Bart, Jacob, 30 Aug. 1796, Mary Schmit                    2 FR-1109
Bartels (or Bortels), (?), 18 April 1797, Cath. Lau       29 BA-8
Bartholow, (?), 1790, (?) Kennerly                        50 BA-389
Bartholomew, Thos., 1790, An. Ben                         50 BA-389
Bartholow, Thomas, 29 Aug. 1798, Ann Nelson               4 FR
Barthy, William, 19 Nov. 1780, Ann Smoot                  2 CH-233
Bartlett, Richard, son of Joseph, 6th day, 12 mo., 1780,
    Rebecca Edmondson, dau. of Wm.                        4 SF-166
Barton, Asael, 27 Dec. 1791, Susanna Millikin             1 BA-4
Barton, Edward, 2 Dec. 1786, Ann Harris                   2 SF
Barton, James, 6th day, 4 mo., 1782, Mary Ann Jenkins     2 SF-288
Barton, James, 4 Jan. 1798, Rachel Smith                  7 BA-3
Barton, John, 7 June 1792, Judith Adams                   3 PG-437
Barton, Joshua, 18 April 1783, Mary Amos                  3 HA-7
Barton, Thomas, 24 June 1785, Mary Pearce                 11 BA-8
Barton, Thos., 8 Nov. 1798, Nancy Stiner                  29 BA-10
Barton, William, 29 March 1798, Ann Biddle                1 TA-309
    See also 6 BA.
Bary (or Barry), Philip, 2 July 1795, by Rev. Ridgely; Sarah
    Disney                                                4 AA
Basford, Benjamin, 10 Jan. 1782, Elizabeth Sheckels       3 AA-418
Basford, Benjamin, 4 May 1788, Ann Wittington             4 AA
    Marriage performed by Rev. Riggin.
Bash, And'w, 21 Nov. 1780, Barbara Hanes                  4 FR
Bashears, Belt, Feb. 1790, Milly Duvall                   4 AA
Basil, James, 16 Oct. 1790, Rebecca Read                  4 AA
Basil, John, 31 Jan. 1781, Ruth Nichols                   2 PG-5
Basset, Richard, 16 Feb. 1797, Priscilla Boyer            4 KE-65
Basset, Nehemiah, 22 Dec. 1793, Winnie Cummings           2 AL-700
Bassett, Thomas, 23 Jan. 1783, Mary Harris                2 DO
Bast, Jacob, 11 Oct. 1796, Cath. Heckedarn                2 FR-1109
Bastford, Henry, 16 Dec. 1794, by Rev. Ridgely; Mary Watkins
    4 AA
Bastian, Anthony, 10 Aug. 1779, Catherine Fogle           4 FR
Baston, Isaac, 7 July 1783, Elizabeth Boneville           2 DO
Bateman, Benjamin, 6 Aug. 1796, Anne Hutton               6 BA
Bateman, John, 13 Sept. 1786, Ann Oakley                  2 CH-233
Bateman, John, 14 Sept. 1797, Martha Galloway             6 BA
Bateman, Levin, 28 Oct. 1788, Ann Simpson                 2 CH-233
Bateman, Richard, 22 Dec. 1782, Mary Ann Hatton           2 CH-233
Bateman, Richard, 23 Dec. 1800, Margaret Wakefield        2 CH-233
Bateman, Tezreel, 18 Nov. 1782, Sarah Simks               2 CH-233
Bates, Rowland, 23 May 1778, Margaret Wooten              11 BA-1
Batson, George, 12 Dec. 1795, Susanna Calbfleish          4 FR
Batson, John, 16 Jan. 1791, Rachel Kirth                  3 BA-234
Battenfeld, Jacob, 18 Sept. 1798, Eliz. Emmerich          2 FR-1109
Batter, William, 26 Dec. 1781, Eliza Myers                11 BA-5
Batterson, John, 23 April 1783, Martha Meeks              3 HA-7
```

Battis, Azor, 20 Sept. 1800, Fanny Stranger; free negroes
   3 BA-392
Bauer, Christ'n, 1788, Marg. Iar   50 BA-388
Bauer, Conrad, 14 Nov. 1797, Eliz. Schmidt   2 FR-1109
Bauer, Johannes, 2 Dec. 1784, Christina Beider   10 BA-184
Bauer, Martin, 2 Nov. 1787, (?) Becker   29 BA-1
Bauer, Wilhelm, 11 July 1784, Ida Reely   10 BA-182
Baulderson, John, 24 April 1793, Milky Baker   18 BA-5
Bauman, Daniel, 15 Nov. 1791, Cath. Let   2 FR-1108
Bausman, Lorentz, 27 Oct. 1789, Cathrina Riz   10 BA-194
Baxley, George, 5 Sept. 1793, Mary Merryman   18 BA-5
Baxley, John, 16 July 1793, Mary Stevenson   18 BA-5
Baxley, Thomas, 10 July 1796, Elizabeth Coale   6 BA
Baxter, Barnet, 18 Sept. 1783, Ruth Haile   11 BA-6
Baxter, Jacob, 5 Feb. 1782, Johanna Vance   11 BA-5
Baxter, James, 21 June 1792, Ann Bower   19 BA-7
   6 BA gives the groom's name as Dexter.
Baxter, Jas., 18 Oct. 1798, Sarah Bradburn   50 BA-404
Baxter, Nicholas, 2 Feb. 1792, Sarah Perigo   6 BA
Baxter, Nicholas, 26 Nov. 1797, Mary Pierce   6 BA
Bay, Hugh, 1 March 1785, Sarah Turner   3 HA-10
Bayard, John Hodge, 15 April 1784, Rebecca Edelen   4 FR
Bayard, John Morris, 8 Oct. 1788, Margaret Carrick   4 FR
Bayer, Abraham, 20 June 1786, Eva Beringer   2 FR-1107
Bayer, David, 8 Nov. 1785, Sarah Krumm   2 FR-1107
Bayer, John, 28 Dec. 1796, Mary Borkhardt   2 FR-1109
Bayer, Ludwig, 23 Jan. 1785, Polly Hildebrand   10 BA-184
Bayer, Mich'l, 4 Jan. 1785, Catherine Delaplank   4 FR
Bayer, Peter, 22 May 1787, Anna Mary Mossetter   2 FR-1108
Bayless, Augustin, 5 Jan. 1785, Pamelia Brown   3 HA-9
Bayley, Philip, 6 Jan. 1778, Mary Morgan   11 BA-1
Bayley, Sam'l, 11 Nov. 1779, Mary Campbell   4 FR
Baylis, Augustin, 4 Dec. 1785, Eliz. Brown   11 BA-9
Bayly, Hezekiah, 5 March 1778, Jane Evans   2 MO-1
Bayly, Josiah, 26 April 1796, Leah Lockerman   2 DO
Bayly, Stephen, 18 Dec. 1799, Priscilla Waller   2 SO
Bayly, Thomas, 27 March 1796, Sarah Nevitt Muir   2 DO
Bayly, Thomas, 17 Nov. 1800, Betsey Cooper   2 SO
Bayman, Thos., 15 Nov. 1779, Mary Smith   4 FR
Baynard, James, son of Nathan and Sarah, 17 April 1787,
   Rebekah Mason, dau. of William Winchester Mason   1 CR-73
Baynum, Wm., 30 Nov. 1795, Betsey Carey   1 WO
Bayzand, William, 19 Feb. 1794, Susanna Aisquith Moore 3 BA-281
Beach, Ebenezer, 27 Nov. 1794, Eleanor Smoot   29 BA-6
Beach, John, 13 Jan. 1789, Catherine Wolf   5 BA-2
Beach, Joseph, 31 Dec. 1799, by Rev. Ridgely; Mary Beach
   4 AA
Beach, Tho., 8 Oct. 1782, Mary Hendrickson   11 BA-5
Beachamp, Charles, 14 July 1794, Sarah Gadd   2 DO
Beachem, John, 25 Dec. 1783, Elizabeth Sticker   3 BA-186
Beachwood, Josa., 18 Nov. 1796, Wealthy Paine   1 WO
Beagor, Richard, 2 June 1795, Elizabeth Fullhart   10 BA-196
Beal, Francis, 12 April 1778, Penelope Ford   2 CH-233
Beal, John, 26 Sept. 1797, Milla Biscoe   4 KE-65
Beal, Josias, 14 Dec. 1780, Mary Hellen   3 SM-58
Beal, Zephaniah, 22 March 1800, by Rev. Ridgely; Lotty Ray
   4 AA
Beale, Benjamin, 5 May 1778, Ann Bardle   4 FR
Beale, Davault, 11 Nov. 1791, Mary Hildebrand   4 FR
Beale, Thomas Keibard, 8 Sept 1799, Isabella Clarke   3 BA-377
Beall, Andrew, 21 Nov. 1782, Mary Beall   2 PG-3
Beall, Asa, 6 Feb 1794, Elizabeth Beall   1 AL-52
Beall, Bennett, 8 Jan. 1789, Ann Morriss   3 PG-255
Beall, Christopher, 11 Jan. 1780, Ann Brooke   2 PG-1
Beall, Colmore, 3 April 1786, Mary Shekells   4 FR

```
Beall, Colmore, 2 Nov. 1791, Jean Offutt              4 FR
Beall, Daniel, 17 April 1790, Catherine Bingan        4 FR
Beall, David, 24 Aug. 1791, Mary Davis                1 AL-52
Beall, Elijah, 29 June 1797, by Rev. Green; Ann Long  4 AA
Beall, Elisha, 17 Oct. 1783, Jane Perry               4 FR
Beall, George, 19 Oct. 1790, Margaret Hamilton        4 FR
Beall, Isaiah, of Thomas, 5 Dec. 1795, Ann Pullen     1 AL-53
Beall, James, 10 May 1787, Ann Mitchell               3 PG-252
Beall, John, 5 April 1795, Ann Fowler                 3 PG-441
Beall, John B., 26 Nov. 1796, Eleanor Beatty          4 FR
Beall, John Fendall, 10 April 1787, Margaret Beall Hanson
   3 PG-252
Beall, Jonathan, 8 May 1794, Elizabeth Williams       3 PG-440
Beall, Joseph, 13 Jan. 1785, Henrietta Biggs          4 FR
Beall, Nathaniel, 5 Feb. 1788, Ann Head               4 FR
Beall, Ninian, 7 March 1780, Ann Maria Stricker       4 FR
Beall, Ninian, 25 July 1790, Christina Stoll          2 FR-1108
Beall, Peter, 9 Oct. 1779, Margaret Weddle            4 FR
Beall, Richard, 30 Dec. 1794, Casander Hillery        3 PG-440
Beall, Robert, 11 Aug. 1787, Ann Aldridge             4 FR
Beall, Robert B., 6 Jan. 1791, Elizabeth Berry        3 PG-258
Beall, Theodore, 5 June 1790, Susanna Eve Greenfield  4 FR
Beall, Thomas Brooke, 12 April 1799, Harriet West     4 FR
Beall, Upton, 29 Dec. 1796, Matilda Price             4 FR
Beall, Walter, 1 May 1794, Jean Waring                3 PG-440
Beall, William, 8 March 1796, Isabella Ramsy          2 FR-1109
Beall, William, 15 March 1796, Mary Winroad           2 FR-1109
Beall, William, 19 Dec. 1798, Elizabeth Walker        4 FR
Beame, George, 24 Jan. 1782, Sarah McAllister         11 BA-5
Beamer, Adam, 12 Feb. 1785, Mary Albaugh              4 FR
Beamer, Matthias, 4 Sept. 1786, Christena Boyer       4 FR
Beamer, Phillip, 20 Oct. 1796, Rachel Barton          7 BA-3
Bean, Benjamin, 9 Dec. 1779, Rebecca Evans            2 PG-3
Bean, Edmond, 23 May 1797, Elizabeth Wood             2 HA-349
Bean, George, 23 Dec. 1790, Armintta Jones            3 PG-257
Bean, Jacob, 20 Sept. 1786, Mary Myers                4 FR
Bean, John, 26 June 1781, Anne Heming                 3 SM-59
Bean, Richard, 14 Sept. 1797, Prudence Kelly          5 MO-114
Beane, George, 14 Oct. 1778, Anne Dillion             3 SM-57
Beane, William, 23 Sept. 1797, Elizabeth Garaner      4 FR
Beanes, Colmore, 20 April 1778, Milicent Tyler        2 PG-3
Beanes, Francis, 14 Aug. 1789, Martha Haff            4 FR
Beanes, John Hancock, 19 Feb. 1786, Henrietta Dyer    3 PG-251
Beans, John H., 24 May 1795, Herriot Clagett          3 PG-441
Bear, Richard, 25 Dec. 1779, Ann Burns                11 BA-4
Beard, Alexander, 23 July 1790, Mary Bride            11 BA-13
Beard, John, 4 Aug. 1781, Mary Cheshire               2 DO
Beard, Jonathan, 28 March 1791, by Rev. Green; Rebecca
   Stockett                                           4 AA
Beard, Joseph, 12 Oct. 1799, Eliz'th Leakin           8 BA-1
Beard, William, 23 Dec. 1791, Patty Roberts           4 FR
Beard, Zebulon, 5 June 1798, Polly Wingate            2 DO
Beare, William, 1 June 1782, Elizabeth Rudecill       4 FR
Bearing, James, 22 Aug. 1779, Patience Hipsley        5 BA-2
Beasman, George, 18 Nov. 1790, Sally Glover           6 BA
Beaston, Peregrine, 24 Aug. 1786, Naomi Alexander     2 DO
Beatherds, Isaac, 26 Dec. 1797, Sally Richards        1 WO
Beatle, Henry, 20 Feb. 1794, Rachel Welsh             18 BA-6
Beatty, Archibald, 18 April 1784, Frances Fancit      3 HA-8
Beatty, Elijah, 7 July 1785, Susanna Hagan            4 FR
Beatty, (Fair?), 16 May 1785, Isabella Fisher         3 HA-10
Beatty, John, 22 Dec. 1799, Ann Beall                 2 AL-701
Beatty, Thos., 26 May 1779, Jane Waters               4 FR
Beatty, Thomas Johnson, 5 Nov. 1795, Achsah Chamier Holliday
   4 BA-77
```

```
Beauchamp, Daniel, 18 Feb. 1797, Anne Moore              2 SO
Beauchamp, Jesse, 14 Aug. 1799, Lydia Baker             2 SO
Beauchamp, Joseph, 2 Dec. 1796, Betsey More             2 SO
Beauchamp, Thomas, 13 Feb. 1798, Anne Lockwood          2 SO
Beauchamp, William, 16 Feb. 1798, Minty Adams           2 SO
Beauford, William, 13 Sept. 1780, Sarah Gardner        11 BA-4
Beaupre, Louis Nau, 14 Oct. 1795, Victoire Bardon      44 BA-1
Beaven, John, 8 Dec. 1796, Verlinda Gibbons             3 PG-442
Beavens, James, 27 March 1799, Peggy Kellaem            1 WO
Beavens, John, 14 Jan. 1800, Polly Rounds               1 WO
Beavens, Joseph, 30 Sept. 1798, Elizabeth Thompson      3 BA-363
Beavens, Mills, 31 Dec. 1798, Barshaba Richards         1 WO
Becht, Jacob, 29 May 1800, Mary Schenk                  2 FR-1109
Bechtel, George, 18 March 1794, Esther Eller            2 FR-1109
Beck, Anthony, 14 May 1795, Ann Barnes                  4 FR
Beck, George, 8 April 1797, Ann Jefferies               4 KE-65
Beck, Godfrey, 22 Sept. 1800, Eliz. Haas               29 BA-11
Beck, James, 3 April 1797, Ann Copper                   4 KE-65
Beck, Jeremiah, 23 Dec. 1797, Mary Night                4 FR
Beck, John, 22 Nov. 1778, Sarah Hamilton                2 PG-3
Beck, John, 12 Sept. 1781, Mary Johnson                 3 HA-5
Beck, John, 6 Dec. 1794, Ann Miller                    44 BA-1
Beck, Matthew, 2 Dec. 1779, Sarah Roberts               3 HA-1
Beck, Rezin, 18 Jan. 1798, Dorcas Turner                6 MO
Beck, Samuel D., 28 Aug. 1793, by Rev. G. Ridgely, Martha
    Webb                                                4 AA
Beck, William, 4 Jan. 1797, Elizabeth Howard            4 KE-65
Beckebach, Geo., 24 Dec. 1792, Mary Magd. Baulus        2 FR-1108
Beckebach, Michael, 26 Aug. 1798, Mary Barthelma        2 FR-1109
Beckenbaugh, George, 21 Oct. 1791, Elizabeth Simmerman  4 FR
Beckenbaugh, George Peter, 15 Dec. 1785, Susanna Keffauver
    4 FR
Becker, Conrad, 25 May 1795, Mary Jost                  2 FR-1109
Becker, Henry, Jr., 5 Sept. 1786, Catherine Miller      4 FR
Beckett, Humphrey, 31 Oct. 1777, Lydia Sunderland       1 CA-5
Beckett, John, 3 Oct. 1778, Mary Walker                 2 PG-2
Beckett, Marshew, 25 Dec. 1790, Ann Higgins             3 PG-257
Beckett, Wm. Levin, c.1792, by Rev. Chalmers; Mary (Clarke?)
    4 AA
Beckibaugh, George, 22 Dec. 1792, Mary Powlas           4 FR
Beckley, John, 12 Nov. 1797, Ann Cambell               45 BA-2
Beckwith, Benedict, 30 Jan. 1800, Eliz. White           5 MO-116
Beckwith, David, 23 Sept. 1786, Catherine Jutsice       4 FR
Beckwith, Henry, 20 Sept. 1784, Sarah Mitchell          2 DO
Beckwith, Henry, 16 Oct. 1789, Mary Taylor              2 DO
Beckwith, Nehemiah, 11 Nov. 1785, Kneely Mitchell       2 DO
Beckwith, Samuel, 20 Aug. 1793, Susanna Durbin          1 AL-52
Beckwith, Thomas, 14 Nov. 1789, Sarah Wheeler           2 DO
Beckwith, William, 28 March 1788, Martha Elder          4 FR
Beckwith, William, 23 Feb. 1790, Rachel Jacobs          6 BA
Beckworth, William, 24 Sept. 1778, Priscilla Jenkins    2 PG-2
Bednum, Jno., 16 Aug. 1794, Eliz. Smith                29 BA-5
Beeler, George, 15 April 1794, Elizab. Molledor         2 FR-1109
    4 FR gives the bride's name as Mullidore.
Beeman, James, 16 Aug. 1795, Amelia Johnson             3 BA-307
Beeman, Moses, 30 Aug. 1795, Sarah Layport              2 AL-700
Been, Daniel, 5 Feb. 1795, Ann Pope                     3 PG-440
Beene, Samuel, 21 Dec. 1794. Elizabeth (?)              3 PG-440
Beever, William, 4 June 1778, Susannah Temple           4 FR
Behler, Andrew, 28 July 1791, Mary Hodge               29 BA-2
Behn, John H., 18 Sept. 1798, Violet Bryden             5 BA-3
Beigler, Henry, 18 May 1786, Barbara Flukein            4 FR
Beinbrech, Conrad, 10 Nov. 1791, Magdalena Thomas       2 WA-16
Beishan, John Lanesort, 7 March 1796, Frances Chaddick  6 BA
Bela, John Baptiste, 25 Sept. 1796, Winy Brady          3 BA-329
```

```
Bell, Alexander, free black, 8 Jan. 1792, Eleanor Pine,
   slave of Wm. Paterson                          3 BA-255
Bell, Booz, 20 Nov. 1799, Mager Twyford           2 DO
Bell, Edward, 4 Aug. 1799, Nancy Kennedy          6 BA
Bell, Jacob, 3 Sept. 1799, Mollie Mills           2 SO
Bell, John, 10 Jan. 1797, Polly Marshall          2 SO
Bell, John, 18 Aug. 1800, Grace Luckie            3 HA-29
Bell, Lloyd, 1 May 1785, Eliza Jones             11 BA-8
Bell, Peter, 1 Jan. 1789, Magdalen Schmit         2 FR-1108
Bell, Richard, 26 Feb. 1797, Ann Bell             7 MO
Bell, Russel, 7 Aug. 1794, Maria Stauvern        29 BA-5
Bell, Thomas, 10 Jan. 1799, Euphania McCotter     2 DO
Bell, William, 1 Feb. 1797, Polly Pitts           1 WO
Bellinger, Jean Phillipes Etienne, 1 April 1794, Polly
   Gardner                                        6 BA
Bellowsob, William, 8 March 1800, Lucretia Fowler 8 BA-1
Belmare, Francis, 12 Oct. 1794, by Rev. Ridgely; Elizabeth
   Anderson                                       4 AA
Belt, Benjamin, Jr., 7 Feb. 1782, Mary Wells      2 PG-3
Belt, Carlton, 26 Feb. 1799, Elizabeth Jones      7 MO-29
Belt, James, 3 Jan. 1798, Eleanor Moore           3 BA-354
Belt, Jeremiah, 5 March 1778, Priscilla Gant      2 PG-2
Belt, Jeremiah, 9 Nov. 1796, Ann West             4 FR
Belt, John, 5 April 1791, Sarah Hyfield           4 FR
Belt, Joseph, 8 Oct. 1793, Ellin Randall          5 BA-2
Belt, Lloyd, 16 Dec. 1790, El. Causlet Mit. Thomas 2 FR-1108
   4 FR gives the bride's name as Eliz'th Causlet Met-
   calfe Thomas.
Belt, Middleton, 27 Aug. 1782, Ann Belt           2 PG-3
Belt, Mordecai, 25 April 1799, Priscilla Parish  45 BA-3
Belt, Stephen, 17 July 1781, Monica Jones         2 PG-5
Belton, Francis, 18 Oct. 1789, Mary Barney       11 BA-12
Belton, William, 11 Sept. 1790, Marg't Smith     11 BA-13
Beltz, Peter, 14 Nov. 1787, Magdalen Moll         2 FR-1107
Bence, Jacob, 27 Feb. 1790, Barbara Kemp          4 FR
Bendall, Bennett, 25 Dec. 1799, Mary Thomas       2 DO
Bendall, Matthew, 11 June 1791, Nancy Auld        2 DO
Bender, Jacob, 14 Dec. 1794, Catharina Stein     10 BA-196
Bender, John, 1788, Elis. Hoss                   50 BA-388
Benfield, Richard, 8 April 1792, Ann Smith        3 BA-257
Bengel, Conrad, 1 Feb. 1795, Marie Holmes    /   10 BA-196
Bennet, Edward, 10 June 1780, Mary Ward           3 BA-181
Bennet, Geo., 21 Jan. 1782, Mary Philips         11 BA-5
Bennet, James, 2 March 1794, Ann Roberts          3 AA-424
Bennett, Benjamin, 24 Nov. 1780, Rebecca James    4 FR
Bennett, Caleb, 8 Nov. 1785, Cath. Willson       11 BA-8
Bennett, Daniel, 11 April 1788, Sarah Johnson     4 FR
Bennett, Frederick, 27 March 1794, Amelia Keene   2 DO
Bennett, Isaac, 11 Jan. 1800, Susannah Miller    29 BA-11
Bennett, Jesse, 20 Dec. 1779, Priscilla Knight    4 FR
Bennett, John, 29 April 1786, Mary Plummer        4 FR
Bennett, Jno., 16 Nov. 1794, Sally Jackson       29 BA-6
Bennett, John, 29 Dec. 1795, Cassandra Benton     4 FR
Bennett, John, 2 April 1800, Nancy Cook           2 DO
Bennett, Joseph, 11 June 1798, Elizabeth Lindon   5 BA-3
Bennett, Patrick, 3 Nov. 1780, Mary Squires      11 BA-2
   See also 2 CH-233.
Bennett, Peter, 10 Oct. 1799, Sarah G. Selby      3 BA-379
Bennett, Philip, 4 June 1795, Sarah Gilbert       3 HA-24
Bennett, Richard, 20 Feb. 1798, Sally Tully       2 SO
Bennett, Stephen, 1 Dec. 1791, Catherine O'Neall  6 BA
Bennett, Thos., 10 June 1780, Marg't Ashbow      11 BA-4
Bennett, Thomas, 30 Oct. 1798, Comfort King       3 BA-365
Bennett, Thomas, 19 May 1800, Lilly Soward        2 DO
Bennett, William, c.1792 in Frederick Co. by Rev. Chalmers;
   Mary Scholes                                   4 AA
```

```
Bennett, William, 9 Dec. 1799, Mary Jones          2 DO
Bennett, Wm. Purnell, 28 March 1800, Dolly Johnson 1 WO
Bennington, William, 12 Jan. 1780, Isabella Wilson 3 HA-1
Bennitt, Jeffries, 18 Dec. 1792, Eleanor Benton    4 FR
Bennitt, Nathan, 14 March 1795, Deborah Holland    4 FR
Benser, Johann Henry, 17 March 1799, Maria Elizabeth Klin-
    der (or Klinekeim)                             9 BA-142
Benson, Benjamin, 6 Oct. 1792, Allender Sullivan  18 BA-4
Benson, James, son of Benjamin and Hannah, 30th day, 4 mo.,
    1794, Elizabeth Price, dau. of Mordecai and Rachel 1 SF
Benson, John, 5 July 1800, Sophia Cropper          1 WO
Benson, Joseph, 25 Feb. 1796, Lovey Mills          2 DO
Benson, Lawton, 20 Dec. 1794, by Rev. Benton Riggin;
    Elizabeth Burk                                 4 AA
Benson, William, 26 Oct. 1797, Rachel Hensey       5 MO-114
Benston, Ephraim, 11 March 1800, Sucky Roberts     2 SO
Bentley, Abner, 6 April 1782, Ruth Wood            4 FR
Bentley, Absolom, 4 April 1795, Ruth Bentley       4 FR
Bentley, Caleb, of Loudon Co., Va., son of Joseph and Mary
    of Chester Co., Penna.; 20th day, 4 mo., 1791, Sarah
    Brooke, dau. of Roger and Mary                 6 SF
Bentley, Solomon, 15 March 1781, Rebecka Wood      4 FR
Bently, Levy, 4 May 1790, Sarah Harlan             2 FR-1108
Bently, John, 2 Oct. 1790, Ann Thompson            3 BA-228
Bentum, Chas., 26 Oct. 1799, Eliz. Kohl           29 BA-10
Bentz, George, 6 April 1788, Elizab. Gomber        2 FR-1108
    4 FR gives the bride's name as Gumbare.
Bentz, Jacob, 20 Jan. 1799, Cath. Steckel          2 FR-1109
    4 FR gives the bride's name as Stickle.
Bentzen, Peter, 5 July 1795, Rebecca Andrews      29 BA-6
Berding, Derrick, 16 Jan. 1800, Hannah Hanson     29 BA-11
Berg, Peter, 8 Aug. 1786, Cath. Berg               2 FR-1107
Berghman, Christopher, 10 Aug. 1784, Maria Pantz   4 FR
Berien, Walter, 12 Jan. 1790, Charity Simpson      2 CH-233
Berkly, Thos., 19 Jan. 1790, Priscilla Bean        3 PG-256
Berkman, Peter, 3 June 1779, Catharine Litchard    4 FR
Berminham, Wm., 26 July 1795, Elizabeth Trumbo    29 BA-6
Bernard, Barneby, 14 June 1797, Mary R. Dickerson  1 WO
Bernard, Thomas, 14 Oct. 1783, Eleanor Reardon    11 BA-6
Bernheissel, Matthias, 10 Oct. 1791, Christina Weinbrenner
    2 WA-16
Berntheisel, Christoph, 5 Oct. 1794, Cath. Grof    2 FR-1109
Berrage, Edward, 9 Feb. 1784, Mary Lyne           11 BA-7
Berridge, William, son of William and Grace (born 21 Aug.
    1776); 4 Oct. 1798, Sally Peterkin             1 TA-308
Berry, Andrew, 18 March 1797, Mary Gilberthorpe    3 BA-342
Berry, Basil, 15 Jan. 1780, Eleanor McCauly       11 BA-4
Berry, George, 6 March 1778, Margaret Limbrich     2 MO-1
Berry, George, 26 Aug. 1790, Eleanor Carback       6 BA
Berry, John, 2 March 1783, Elizabeth Willett       2 CH-233
Berry, Ryon, 12 June 1783, Ann Owen                2 CH-233
Berry, William, 19 Dec. 1797, Mary Cole            3 PG-443
Berry, William, 27 July 1800, Kezia Ebling         2 AL-701
Berryer, Abraham, 8 June 1797, Margaret Hughes     4 FR
Bertrand, John Peter, 17 Feb. 1795, Amanda Victoire Sophia
    Vatinel                                       44 BA-1
Beshang, John, 13 May 1784, Elizabeth Rogers       3 HA-8
Besse, Clodius, 15 April 1784, Margaret Mealy      3 BA-187
Best, James, 1 June 1800, Elizabeth Adams          3 BA-386
Bestpitch, John, 5 June 1788, Rhody Booze          2 DO
Bestpitch, Jonathan, 9 June 1783, Ibby Waters      2 DO
Bestpitch, Jonathan, 2 July 1794, Margaret Lane    2 DO
Bestpitch, Peter, 11 Aug. 1800, Aidy Hurley        2 DO
Bethune, Louis, 11 April 1784, Ann Smithers       11 BA-7
Betton, Thomas S., 30 June 1798, Ann Catherine Rapp 6 BA
```

```
Betts, Solomon, 24 Nov. 1796, Araminta Alexander      3 BA-333
Betz, Conrad, 11 April 1786, M. Streher              29 BA-1
Bevan, Richard, 25 Dec. 1795, Ann Guffey              6 BA
Bevans, James, 10 Jan. 1793, Mary Rusk               6 BA
Bevans, Joseph, Nov. 1787, Ann Griff..(?)           11 BA-10
Bevans, Joshua, 1793, Lindy League                  50 BA-393
Bevard, Charles, 1 Feb. 1798, Amelia Chance          3 HA-27
Bevard, James, 4 Feb. 1798, Amelia Chance            2 HA-350
Bevard, John, 20 Nov. 1787, Esther Smith             4 FR
Beverbach, Jacob, 25 Sept. 1796, Cath. Horn         10 BA-198
Beveridge, John, 16 July 1780, Ann Cobbart           1 CA-3
Beveridge, Wm., 12 June 1784, Ann Adams             11 BA-7
Bevins, Jno., 6 July 1794, Rachel Burk              50 BA-395
Bevins, Joshua, 10 Nov. 1785, Eleanor Wilson        11 BA-8
Beyer, David, 5 Nov. 1785, Sarah Crum                4 FR
Bias, James, 10 June 1784, Sarah Jackson            11 BA-7
Biays, James, 12 May 1796, Sarah Trimble             5 BA-2
Biays, Joseph, 26 March 1797, Elizabeth May          5 BA-3
Bibby, John, 14 Jan. 1784, Cathe. Stoller           11 BA-7
Bibby, Matthew, 3 April 1797, Rebecca Mann           2 DO
Biddeson, Jeremiah, 15 Nov. 1785, Elizabeth Bond     6 BA
Biddle, John, 6 Jan. 1794, by Rev. G. Ridgely; Elenor
  Davis                                              4 AA
Biech, William, 29 June 1797, Elizabeth Price        3 BA-346
Bier, John, 28 Oct. 1784, Uliana Snider              4 FR
Bier, Philip, Jr., 10 Nov. 1798, May Miller          4 FR
Bigges, Gilbert, 7 May 1791, Sarah Rice              5 BA-2
Biggon, Heugh, 25 Nov. 1778, Sarah Hewey             4 FR
Biggs, Fred'k, 17 Oct. 1795, Mary Wilson             4 FR
Biggs, Jacob, 25 June 1785, Eve Moon                 4 FR
Biggs, Jacob, 23 Dec. 1794, Christena Borghman       4 FR
Biggs, John, 16 Dec. 1779, Susanna King              2 PG-3
Biggs, John, 20 Nov. 1782, Prescilla Willson         4 FR
Bigham, Thomas, 20 March 1799, Margaret McNair       4 FR
Bignal, Joseph, 19 Feb. 1780, Eleanor Smith         11 BA-4
Billingslea, James, 14 Sept. 1797, Elizabeth Matthews 2 HA-350
Billingsley, Clement, 21 Nov. 1786, Eleanor Warren   2 CH-233
Billingsley, James, 11 Sept. 1797, Elizabeth Matthews 3 HA-26
Billingsley, John, 28 Oct. 1782, Charity Ford        2 CH-233
Billingsley, Walter, 26 Jan. 1783, Clemency Preston  3 HA-7
Binns, Simon, 4 Jan. 1790, Sarah Wildman             4 FR
Binns, Thomas, 24 Jan. 1795, Amelia Durham           7 BA-1
  3 HA-24 gives the groom's name as Thomas Nelson Binns.
Bins, Simon, Jan. 1790, Sarah Wildman                2 FR-1108
Birckhead, James, 2 Feb. 1797, Elizabeth Sullivan    2 DO
Birckhead, Thomas, 7 Dec. 1797, Elizabeth Waters     1 BA-8
Bird, Charles, 11 (Jan.?) 1798, Margaret Barton      5 MO-114
Bird, John, 6 Sept. 1788, by Rev. Claggett; Elizabeth
  Swain                                              4 AA
Bird, Littleon, 13 Jan. 1800, Sally Tyler            2 SO
Bird, Samuel, 30 March 1795, Sarah Dyson             4 FR
Bird, Thomas, 16 Dec. 1780, Jemima Wheeler           2 PG-5
Bird, Thomas, 20 Dec. 1797, Anna Flemming            1 WO
Bird, Thomas, 19 March 1799, Sarah Records           2 SO
Birk, John, 20 April 1798, Denny Wright              2 SO
Birkhead, Christopher, 24 May 1787, Ann Wright      11 BA-10
Birkhead, Francis, 9 April 1780, Margaret Simmons    3 AA-416
Birkhead, Nehemiah, 8 Feb. 1781, Sarah Ward          3 AA-417
Birkhead, Seaborn, 22 Jan. 1778, Ann Harrison        3 AA-414
Birkhead, William, 21 Oct. 1797, Sally Weatherly     2 SO
Birkholtz, David, 10 July 1799, Adelheid Roseman    29 BA-10
Biscoe, Thomas, 27 Nov. 1782, Margaret Bennet        3 SM-60
Bisho, Nicholas, 12 Dec. 1794, Nancy Turine          5 BA-2
Bishop, Benjamin Freder'k, 15 July 1800, Ann Echel  29 BA-11
  50 BA-407 gives the date as 4 July 1800.
```

```
Bishop, John, 17 Sept. 1789, Hannah Cooper          2 FR-1108
Bishop, John, 26 Oct. 1797, Susannah Johnson        6 BA
Bishop, Nath., 6 May 1798, Nancy Freshwater         1 WO
Bishop, Samuel, 18 Oct. 1796, Mary Smith            1 WO
Bishop, William, 3 June 1794, Patience Hilton       6 BA
Bishop, William, 1 June 1797, Caty Speer            6 BA
Bissett, Thomas, 10 April 1800, Hannah Todd         6 BA
Bitch, Samuel, 30 March 1794, Sarah Milson         10 BA-196
Bittel, Jacob, 24 June 1791, Rachel Todd            2 FR-1108
Bitters, John, 22 Sept. 1796, Elizabeth Donovan     3 BA-329
Bittle, John, 21 July 1797, Elizabeth Mullinieux    4 FR
Bitzer, Anthony, 29 May 1794, Eunice Ball           2 AL-700
Bivens, John, 9 Sept. 1784, Mary Wilson            11 BA-7
Bixler, Jacob, 29 Nov. 1795, Barb. Grebel           2 FR-1109
Black, Christopher, 20 Dec. 1787, Elizabeth Barlow  3 BA-216
Black, Daniel, 31 Aug. 1797, Mary Bobo              2 AL-700
Black, George, 23 Nov. 1780, Grace Brown            3 HA-3
Black, Henry, 30 Oct. 1798, Rachel Buckley          6 BA
Black, Henry, 29 Nov. 1799, Susanna Whitmore        4 FR
Black, James, 6 June 1795, Mary Carroll             3 BA-305
Black, James, 11 Dec. 1798, Margaret Wilson         4 KE-65
Black, Robert, 20 Jan. 1800, Elizabeth Barnes       6 BA
Black, Samuel, 3 Oct. 1782, Jane Johnson            3 HA-7
Black, William, 1 Jan. 1793, Bathsheba Barlow       6 BA
Blackburn, John, 5 Feb. 1787, Elizabeth Magruder    3 PG-252
Blackburn, Thomas, 29 Oct. 1796, Jane Squire        4 FR
Blackburn, Wm., 11 Feb. 1779, Ann Carr              4 FR
Blackiston, Daniel, 3 Nov. 1796, Elizabeth Smith    4 KE-65
Blades, Handy, 19 March 1799, Comfort Blades        1 WO
Blades, James, 9 June 1798, Sarah Melvin            1 WO
Blades, Samuel, 26 Aug. 1796, Tabitha Jones         1 WO
Blair, Robert, 30 Oct. 1800, Nancy Richardson       1 WO
Blake, Ebenezer, 15 Nov. 1798, Ruth Headington      6 BA
Blake, Thomas, Jr., 27 April 1779, Mary Smith       3 AA-415
Blakeney, John, 4 Nov. 1796, Lydia Regan            6 BA
Blancher, Peter, 4 April 1781, Mary Ross            3 HA-3
Blaney, Jones, 7 Dec. 1800, Mary Streett            3 HA-30
Bleany, Nath'l, 31 July 1785, Eliza Tate           11 BA-8
Blickenstaffer, David, 7 Jan. 1793, Uliana Shurtz   4 FR
Blickenstaffer, Yost, 31 Aug. 1799, Margaret Fuller 4 FR
Blizard, John, 18 Jan. 1799, Leah Burbage           1 WO
Block, Andrew, 12 April 1790, El. Mitchel          29 BA-1
Blocker, George, 30 April 1797, Rosanna Essing      2 AL-700
Bloom, John, 3 Oct. 1798, Elizabeth Engel           4 FR
Blot, Francis, 25 May 1797, Patty Meyer             3 BA-345
Blot, Johann, 22 April 1800, Rosina Caas           10 BA-200
Bloxam, Southy, 8 Oct. 1789, Leah Marien            2 DO
Bloxom, John, 30 Oct. 1784, Fanny Lewis             2 DO
Bloyd, John, 11 Jan. 1796, Mary Willis              2 DO
Blugher, George, 28 March 1797, Rosanna Essing      3 AL-4
Blunt, Edward, 27 Aug. 1778, by Rev. Magowan; Elizabeth Trott
     4 AA
Blunt, Walter or Washer, 29 Jan. 1778, Sarah Jackson 4 MO-1
Boardman, James, c.1792, by Rev. Hutchinson; Ruth Shepherd
     4 AA
Boarman?, Robert, 1 Feb. 1796, Mary Wheeler         3 HA-24
Bobbs (or Botts), Jacob, 21 Feb. 1782, Jane Smith   3 HA-6
Bobo, Henry, 15 Aug. 1799, Sarah Black              2 AL-701
Bockemiller, John. Aug., 28 Feb. 1799, Eliz. Bossett 50 BA-405
Bocklop, Charles, 7 Aug. 1785, Cath. Lang           2 FR-1107
Bocklop, Charles, 22 May 1787, Christina Pahl, widow 2 FR-1108
Bocky, George, 22 April 1787, Christina Haas        2 FR-1108
Bod (or Buch), Johannes, 29 Aug. 1799, Sophia Vincek (or
     Vincent, or Winkick)                           9 BA-143
Boden, Samuel, 7 Oct. 1800, Sus. Mahn               2 FR-1109
```

```
Bodley, Chas., 29 May 1799, Mary Rusk              29 BA-10
Bodley, Robert, 8 Feb. 1800, Margaret Webb          2 DO
Bodley, Thomas, 29 July 1787, Mary Rutter           6 BA
Boehmer, Hy., 2 Aug. 1785, Ann. M. Albach           2 FR-1107
Bogen, Anth'y Fred'k, 7 Dec. 1784, Mary Koontz      4 FR
Boget, Michael, 28 Feb. 1793, Elizabeth Wilson      6 BA
Boggs, James, 27 Aug. 1794, Margaret Stickle        4 FR
Bohmer, Fred'k, 5 Aug. 1794, Sus. Lenhard          29 BA-5
Boid, William, 10 May 1797, Martha Lin              4 KE-65
Bolgiano, Francis, 25 May 1799, Betsey Weller      29 BA-10
Boller, Philip William, son of Henry and Maria Elizabeth,
  9 April 1794 (at Bethlehem), Catherine Lanius     5 FR-7
Bolton, Francis, 16 April 1781, Marg't Howser       3 BA-181
Bolton, Richard, 21 Jan. 1778, Mary Gormon         11 BA-1
Bombarger, Wm., 11 May 1786, Christina Matts       11 BA-9
Bonar, James, 2 March 1779, Mary Stewart            5 HA
Bonar, James, 1 April 1785, Agnes Baker             3 HA-9
Bonar, William, 30 May 1781, Elizabeth Grifeth      3 HA-4
Bond, Barnet, 27 Dec. 1785, Sarah Harryman         11 BA-9
Bond, Barnet, 14 Jan. 1790, Ruth Hughes             6 BA
Bond, Christopher, 13 Dec. 1787, by Rev. Turner; Sarah
  Pindell                                          51 BA-30
Bond, Edward, 5 Feb. 1778, Catherine Pindell       11 BA-1
Bond, Henry, 5 March 1778, Elizabeth Gorsuch       11 BA-1
Bond, James, 11 July 1799, Julia McCurd             5 BA-3
Bond, James, 17 April 1800, Henry Sword             4 SM-184
Bond, John, 6 Sept. 1791, Catherine Devin           3 HA-21
Bond, John, son of Samuel, 18 Jan. 1794, Cynthia Richardson
  3 HA-23
Bond, John P., 16 Nov. 1797, Polly Davis           45 BA-2
Bond, Mordecai, 4 Oct. 1796, Hannah Hughes          1 BA-7
Bond, Nicodemus, 29 Aug. 1789, Mary Stevenson      15 BA-2
Bond, Peter, 20 March 1794, Elizabeth Morris       18 BA-6
Bond, Thos., 24 July 1783, Sarah Jordan            11 BA-6
Bond, Thomas, 22 Dec. 1791, Ann Talbott             1 BA-4
Bond, Thomas, 22 Oct. 1795, Mary Hall               3 PG-441
Bond, Thomas, 9 Aug. 1797, Elizabeth Harryman       6 BA
Bond, William, 3 Nov. 1796, Susannah Cromwell       6 BA
Bond, William Stodard, 14 June 1792, Mary Hayward   2 DO
Bond, Zacheus, 19 Jan. 1797, Cassandra Lee Morgan   1 BA-7
  See also 3 HA-26.
Bone, John, 9 Dec. 1796, Sarah Piles                3 AL-4
Boner, James, 1 March 1780, Mary Stewart            3 HA-1
Boney, Thomas, 31 Oct. 1780, Sarah Fleet            1 CA-3
Bonfield, John, 23 Dec. 1783, Cassandra Stansbury  11 BA-7
Bonham, Malachi, 24 Sept. 1789, Mary Williamson     4 FR
Bonn, Joseph, 31 Oct. 1795, Ann Hall               29 BA-6
Bonn, Philip, 22 Nov. 1796, Madlen. Helmling       29 BA-8
Bonnady, Jas., 7 May 1780, Lurana Hines            11 BA-4
Bonnawell, Edward, 10 Jan. 1799, Patty Barn         1 WO
Bonner, Matthias, 27 Dec. 1779, Ann Maria Nicholson 11 BA-4
Bonnifant, Benjamin, 11 Feb. 1798, Anne Brown       6 MO
Bonion, Joseph, 1 April 1799, Fanny Harris          6 BA
Bonnet, Joseph, 15 Nov. 1796, Marian Ferrand        6 BA
Bonsell, Jesse, 2 June 1795, Mary Stapleton         5 BA-2
Bontz, John, 9 Sept. 1797, Elizabeth Birely         4 FR
Booger, Jacob, 21 Aug. 1790, Elizabeth Crist        4 FR
Boogher, Frederick, 16 Oct. 1791, Christina Margareta Hultz
  4 FR
Bookey, Mathias, 22 April 1780, Christena Grush     4 FR
Boon, John, 10 Nov. 1792, by Rev. G. Ridgely; Sarah
  Griffith                                          4 AA
Boon, John Cockey Robert Burley, 16 June 1791, Elisabeth
  Hale; see also 3 BA-253                           18 BA-3
Boon, Robert, 10 Aug. 1797, by Rev. G. Ridgely; Nancy
  Hancock                                           4 AA
```

```
Boone, Alexius, 8 Jan. 1779, Mary Smith           2 CH-233
Boone, John, son of Capt. Jno. and Elizabeth, 22 Nov. 1792,
    Sarah Griffith, dau. of Charles               2 AA-115
Boos, Nicholas, 26 Dec. 1786, Anna Maria Remer   10 BA-188
Booth, Basil, 9 March 1780, Eliz. Henry           1 SM-137
Booth, Michael, 24 Sept. 1797, Susannah Fitzgerald 6 BA
Booth, William, 14 July 1792, Jane Kayl           3 BA-256
Booze, James, 30 Dec. 1799, Jane Meredith         2 DO
    1 DO-40 gives the date as 9 Jan. 1800.
Booze, John, 21 April 1790, Mary Sanders          2 DO
Booze, Joseph, 1 April 1788, Grace Daugherty      2 DO
Booze, Zebulon, 16 April 1799, Dozilla Shenton    2 DO
Boquet, James, 17 Jan. 1779, Elizabeth Saxe       1 CA-2
Borckhardt, Joseph, 1 Sept. 1789, Mary Hansey     2 FR-1108
Bordley, John, 2 Aug. 1798, Catherine Starck      3 BA-361
Bordley, Thomas, 15 Nov. 1798, Sarah Gould        4 KE-65
Bordley, William Clayton, 10 July 1798, Margaret Keener
    3 BA-360
Borein, John, 11 Aug. 1786, by Rev. Turner; Sarah Slyder
    51 BA-30
Boring, Joshua, 23 Jan. 1797, Jane Camack         4 FR
Borkhardt, George, 14 Sept. 1795, Hannah Hedge    2 FR-1109
Born, Jacob, son of Daniel, 1 Sept. 1789, Anna Margaret
    Weller, dau. of John and Maria Barbara        5 FR-8
Boroff, Valentine, 24 March 1794, Margaret Cose   4 FR
Bosham, Levin, 24 Jan. 1799, Ann Whayland         3 SO
Boshan, Daniel, 2 Sept. 1793, Alice McGaw         3 HA-23
Boshell, Joseph, 12 Aug. 1797, Betsy Keene        2 DO
Boshockney, Thomas, 16 Sept. 1784, Biddy McDonald 11 BA-7
Bosler, John, 27 March 1796, Mary Flanagan       35 BA-4
Bosley, Bazil, 2 May 1793, Rebecca Chamberlin     1 BA-5
Bosley, Elijah, 7 May 1789, Hannah Wilmot         1 BA-2
Bosley, George?, 13 May 1798, Kitty Hogan        29 BA-9
Bosley, Isaac, 17 Feb. 1793, Elizabeth Hutchins   1 BA-5
Bosley, James, 6 Nov. 1799, Hannah Hughes         1 BA-9
Bosley, Joshua, 4 Nov. 1779, Ann Gott             3 AA-415
Bosly, William, 7 Feb. 1782, Eliza Anderson      11 BA-5
Boss, Hays, 9 May 1797, Eleanor Perrigo          47 BA-1
Bossert, David, 21 Feb. 1786, Catherine Schuck    2 FR-1107
Bost, Peter, 17 Feb. 1785, Catherine Illspach    10 BA-184
Boston, Isaac, 7 July 1783, Elizabeth Boneville   2 DO
Boston, Levin, 21 Jan. 1781, Gatrude Benston      1 SO-199
Boston, Richard, 14 Feb. 1799, Keziah Peaks       3 BA-368
Boswell, Elijah, 11 April 1782, Ann Carrington    2 CH-233
Boswell, Elkanah, 3 Jan. 1790, Ann Morland        3 PG-256
Boswell, Horatio, 18 Jan. 1798, Sarah Dement      3 PG-443
Boswell, Joseph, 19 Dec. 1793, Elizabeth Jones    4 BA-75
    36 BA-1 gives the date as 14 Dec. 1793
Boswell, Philip, 19 Nov. 1791, Charlote Pacser    3 PG-258
Boswell, Walter, 14 Oct. 1779, Eleanor Smallwood  2 CH-233
Bosy, Charles, 28 Jan. 1783, Mary Bear           11 BA-6
Boteler, Alexander, 9 Jan. 1792, Elizabeth Philpott 4 FR
Boteler, Arthur, 12 Sept. 1797, Eliz. Sweringer   2 FR-1109
    4 FR gives the bride's name as Swearingen.
Boteler, Henry, 24 Aug. 1793, Mary Eastburn       4 FR
Botham, John, 5 Jan. 1798, Polly Layfield         1 WO
Botham, Levin,, 22 Jan. 1799, Anne Whayland       2 SO
Botner, John, 7 April 1796, Eliza Sherwood        3 BA-321
Botten?, Rob't, 11 Nov. 1784, Ann Ross           11 BA-8
Bottenberg, Mich'l, 8 May 1800, Mary Jendes       2 FR-1109
Bottenfield, Jacob, 18 Sept. 1798, Elizabeth Emeris 4 FR
Bouchier, Arthur, 1790, Fanny McElleltor?        50 BA-389
Bouis, Jno., 4 Dec. 1800, Martha Mitchell        29 BA-12
Boulding, Jehu, 16 May 1795, Mary Askew           7 BA-2
Bounds, John, 2 Dec. 1800, Nancy Nutter           1 WO
```

```
Bounds, Jones, 16 May 1778, Elizabeth Richardson     1 WI-116
Bounds, William, 8 Sept. 1798, Peggy Wailes          3 SO
   2 SO gives the froom's name as William Bounds, Jr.
Bourmaster, John W., 18 Sept. 1779, Mary Eve Dowlan  4 FR
Bourne, Sylvanus, 17 Oct. 1797, Rebecca Mercer Haslett 5 BA-3
Bousom, John, 27 Nov. 1778, Elizabeth Wedden         4 FR
Boute, John, 2 July 1796, Louise Gersois             3 BA-327
Bowan, John, 13 Oct. 1785, Sarah Anderson            3 HA-10
Bowden, Thomas, 9 Dec. 1780, Eleanor Mahany          4 FR
Bowden, William, 6 June 1778, Elizabeth Ryley        4 FR
Bowe, William, 3 Nov. 1778, Mary Mason               2 PG-2
Bowen, Charles, 16 April 1779, Martha Gray           1 CA-2
Bowen, Edward, 29 Nov. 1792, Rebecca Stansbury       6 BA
Bowen, Elisha, 10 Dec. 1784, Catherine Spence        3 HA-9
Bowen, James, 1 Jan. 1783, Margaret Robison          3 BA-184
Bowen, John, 5 Nov. 1778, Sarah Tucker               1 CA-2
Bowen, John, 16 Dec. 1779, Sus'a Piercy              11 BA-4
Bowen, John, 18 Nov. 1790, Dinah Battee              6 BA
Bowen, John, 23 Jan. 1798, Polly Caudry              1 WO
Bowen, Jonathan, 22 May 1790, by Rev. Reed; Elizabeth Bowen
   4 AA
Bowen, Josias, 24 Nov. 1791, Sarah Stansbury         6 BA
Bowen, Josias, 18 May 1797, Prudence Stansbury       6 BA
Bowen, Sabret, 4 Jan. 1792, Elizabeth Umphreys       6 BA
Bowen, Solomon, 20 June 1786, Jemima Merryman        24 BA-1
Bowen, William, 21 July 1789, Elizabeth Hetherington 15 BA-2
Bowen, William Jones, 20 June 1793, Marg't Murphy    3 BA-269
Bowens, Thomas, 15 Dec. 1793, Louisa Barnes          2 FR-1108
Bower, Martin, 17 June 1780, Barbara Handshew        4 FR
Bower, Philip, 17 Nov. 1780, Sarah Perry             4 FR
Bowering, John, 7 Oct. 1799, Margaret Martin         5 BA-3
Bowers, George, 29 Oct. 1799, Catherine Ryane        6 BA
Bowers, John, 3 Nov. 1793, Hannah Bronnell           1 BA-5
Bowers, John, 3 Nov. 1793, Hannah Broadwell          3 HA-23
Bowhanan, John, 22 July 1783, Easter Smith           1 SO-198
Bowie, Peter, 20 Sept. 1798, Mary Clements           4 FR.
Bowie, Thomas, 26 Jan. 1794, Margaret Belt           2 PG-439
Bowie, William, 19 Dec. 1788, Ann Card               4 FR
Bowie, William Sprigg, 23 Dec. 1781, Elizabeth Sprigg 2 PG-3
Bowlas, Jacob, 18 Feb. 1792, Marg'r Beckibaugh       4 FR
Bowler, Peter, 3 Jan. 1785, Susan Cowan              3 HA-9
Bowler, Peter, 17 July 1788, Rachel Coen             1 BA-1
Bowles, Jno., 17 Feb. 1784, Mary Strabble            11 BA-7
Bowles, John, 21 Aug. 1797, Eve Beckenbaugh          4 FR
Bowlin, John, 10 Feb. 1796, Ally Hobbs               3 BA-317
Bowling, Samuel, 20 Feb. 1787, Mary Ann Plumer       2 FR-1107
   4 FR gives the bride's name as Plummer.
Bowlis, Henry, 26 April 1798, Elizabeth Routzawn     4 FR
Bowman, George, 18 Feb. 1796, Sarah Howse            5 MO-113
Bowman, Henry, 19 June 1800, Sarah Weaver            6 BA
Bowman?, Robert, 1 Feb. 1796, Mary Wheeler           3 HA-24
Bowman, Samuel, son of Samuel and Ann (dec.), 6th day, 7
   mo., 1791, Sarah Tyler, dau. of John (dec.) and
   Elizabeth                                         4 SF-201
Bowness, William, 9 March 1788, Esther Adams         2 DO
Bowser, Isaac, 2 June 1796, Violet Legget            29 BA-7
Bowsinger, Henry, 5 Oct. 1784, Barbara Shrader       4 FR
Bowyer, Wm., 19 June 1780, Ann Forrester             11 BA-4
Boyce, Augustus, 15 Jan. 1793, Sabina Hall           3 HA-22
Boyce, Hugh, 11 Oct. 1797, Eleanor Mooney            3 BA-351
Boyce, Roger, 3 Dec. 1797, Hannah Day                2 HA-350
Boyd, Adam, 13 Sept. 1796, Violet Boyd               3 BA-329
Boyd, Abraham, 26 Jan. 1800, by Rev. Ridgely; Elizabeth
   Iglehart                                          4 AA
Boyd, Andrew, 26 June 1783, Mary McCay               4 FR
```

```
Boyd, Andrew, 1786, Hetty Everson                 50 BA-387
Boyd, Andrew, 18 Aug. 1787, H. Everson            29 BA-1
Boyd, Benjamin, 21 Dec. 1794, by Rev. Ridgely; Rebecca
    Duvall                                         4 AA
Boyd, Edward, 10 Aug. 1800, Mary Hoffman           2 FR-1109
Boyd, Francis, 24 April 1778, Ruth Teves          11 BA-1
Boyd, John, 2 Jan. 1796, by Rev. Cash; Frances Harrison 4 AA
Boyd, John, 9 Jan. 1797, Avarilla Mitchell         3 HA-25
Boyd, John, 24 Jan. 1797, Arabella Mitchell       47 BA-1
Boyd, John, 31 Oct. 1799, Hannah Smith             2 FR-1109
Boyd, Joseph, 26 Jan. 1800, by Rev. Ridgely; Elizabeth
    Last?                                          4 AA
Boyd, Robert, 10 June 1797, Mary Echart            3 AL-4
Boyd, William, 6 May 1800, Sarah Keatly            3 BA-386
Boye, Anthony, 27 Aug. 1794, Sarah Brown           3 BA-291
Boyer, Abraham, 20 June 1786, Eve Bearinger        4 FR
Boyer, Adam, 4 July 1799, Charlotte Mantz          4 FR
Boyer, David, 9 Dec. 1800, Ann Kincaid             7 BA-4
Boyer, Hugh, 12 Oct. 1797, Eleanor Mooney         47 BA-1
Boyer, Jacob, 25 July 1779, Catherine Link         4 FR
Boyer, John, 27 Aug. 1785, Agnes Boyes            11 BA-8
Boyer, John, 21 Dec. 1796, Mary Burckhart          4 FR
Boyer, Joseph, 1 Nov. 1779, Mary Stoll             4 FR
Boyer, Nicholas, 27 Nov. 1794, Margaret Ireland   18 BA-6
Boylan, Thomas, 19 Feb. 1789, Mary Good            4 FR
Boyle, Anthony, 2 April 1782, Jane Partridge       2 DO
Boyle, Daniel, 23 April 1796, Susanna Carrice      4 FR
Boyle, Jno., 1 Oct. 1789, Marg't Boyle            11 BA-12
Boyle, John, 22 Jan. 1797, Ann Talbott             4 FR
Boyle, Thos., 6 Oct. 1794, Mary Gross             29 BA-5
Boyle, William, 9 Dec. 1792, Mary Evans            5 BA-3
Boyles, Anthony, 12 Oct. 1787, Dorothy Keene       2 DO
Boyles, Henry, 20 Aug. 1794, Rebecca Barons        1 AL-53
    2 AL-700 gives the date as 21 Aug. 1794, and the
    bride's name as Rebecker Barkus.
Boyrley, Frederick, 31 May 1783, Eliz'th Motter    4 FR
Boyrley, George, 18 March 1779, Eliz'th Inch       4 FR
Boysene, Thomas, 1 Aug. 1799, Elizabeth Robinson   6 BA
Bozman, Thomas, 11 Feb. 1800, Rachel Scott         2 SO
Bradburn, Alexander, 26 Feb. 1795, Sarah Taylor    6 BA
Bradburn, William, 22 Dec. 1778, Eliz. Edelen      1 SM-137
Bradfield, Jas., 24 Jan. 1782, Ruth Wheeler       11 BA-5
Bradford, Annamia, 18 April 1796, Nancy Richards   1 WO
Bradford, Avery, 8 Jan. 1799, Sophia Riggin        2 SO
Bradford, George, 20 April 1785, Margaret Talbott  3 HA-9
Bradford, William, 5 Aug. 1786, Sarah Snider       3 BA-211
Bradhurst, Benjamin, 14 March 1790, Delila Young   6 BA
Bradley, Dan'l, 29 July 1782, Ann Lester           4 FR
Bradley, Edward, 17 March 1785, Clara Rutledge     3 HA-9
Bradley, Nathan, 25 June 1788, Elizabeth Lankford  2 DO
Bradley, Patrick, 8 July 1794, Rachel James        4 FR
Bradley, Purnell, 9 Jan. 1792, Ann Hackett         2 DO
Bradley, Robert, 17 April 1787, by Rev. Allison; Ruth
    Howard                                        51 BA-30
Bradley, Wm., 18 Nov. 1779, Jane Fulliston         4 FR
Bradshaw, John, 3 Jan. 1793, Sarah Hubbard         2 DO
Bradshaw, Samuel, 12 Oct. 1797, Rebecca Hubbard    2 DO
Bradshaw, William, 23 May 1795, Catherine Mathews  4 BA-77
Brady, Jno., 9 April 1791, Eliz. Long             29 BA-2
Brady, Thomas Gerard, 11 May 1782, Susanna Brown   2 CH-233
Braithwaite, William, 18 May 1786, Kitty Brookover 4 FR
Bramble, David, 4 Aug. 1788, Rhoda Sears           2 DO
Bramble, Edmondson, 8 Feb. 1790, Brace Booze       2 DO
Bramble, Edmondson, 13 Jan. 1796, Keziah Bramble   2 DO
Bramble, Elias, 23 Dec. 1791, Keziah Shorter       2 DO
```

Bramble, Gabriel, 3 July 1788, Sarah Stanford   2 DO
Bramble, William, 15 Feb. 1784, Mary Dean   2 DO
Branch, John, 29 Feb. 1788, Rebecca Strawble   3 BA-217
Brand, George, 15 Dec. 1785, Pleasance Norwood   11 BA-9
Brandenberger, Sam'l, 8 May 1780, Madelaine Hargerhymer 4 FR
Brandenbergh, Fred'k, 22 Feb. 1782, Eliz'th Sibert   4 FR
Brandenbergh, Henry, 10 July 1793, Elizabeth Gorner   4 FR
Brandenburg, William, 15 June 1795, Christena Martin   4 FR
Brandenburger, Jacob, 13 Feb. 1787, Eliz. Rein   2 FR-1107
Brandenburger, John, 13 April 1794, Phoebe Garner   2 FR-1109
Brandenburger, Math., 16 Dec. 1787, Barb. Keller   2 FR-1108
Brandt. Christian, 7 Feb. 1786, Rosina Walter   2 FR-1107
   4 FR gives the bride's name as Rosanna.
Braner, George Heinr., 18 Jan. 1795, An. Marg. Waters 50 BA-396
Brannan, Thomas, 27 Dec. 1799, Jane Ford   3 HA-1
Brannen, Thomas, 16 May 1778, Mary Sheppard   3 BA-174
   11 BA-1 gives the bride's name as Shepherd.
Brannian, John, 23 June 1791, Sarah George   1 BA-3
   3 HA-21 gives the date as 21 June 1791.
Brannock, George, 17 Jan. 1789, Sidney Woodland   2 DO
Brannock, John, 27 Nov. 1792, Keziah Thomas   2 DO
Brannock, Moses, 17 Nov. 1791, Rebecca Parker   2 DO
Brannock, Thomas, 13 March 1797, Elizabeth Ginnan   2 DO
Brannon, William, 23 Dec. 1780, Sarah Smith   3 HA-3
Branson, William, 2 Jan. 1791, Margret Smith   3 BA-234
Brashear, Ely, 14 May 1799, Julia Magruder   4 FR
Brashears, Belt, 28 April 1792, Ann Cook   4 FR
Brashears, John Pottinger, 24 Dec. 1778, Ann Pumphrey 2 PG-3
Brashears, Jonathan, 14 June 1781, Mary Brown   2 PG-5
Brashears, Joseph, 7 Jan. 1781, Mary Cross   2 PG-5
Brashears, Selburn, 15 Feb. 1795, Eleanor Proctor   3 AA-424
Brashers, Levi, 5 Jan. 1793, Frances Lambeth   22 BA-2
Brass, Philip, 15 Nov. 1789, Henrietta Moore   4 AA
   Rev. Reed performed the ceremony.
Brathelow, Michael, 18 Aug. 1792, Ann Nelson   4 FR
Bratten, John, 4 Dec. 1795, Piercey Grey   1 WO
Bratten, John S., 31 Jan. 1798, Polly Quinton   1 WO
Brauer, G. Henry, 18 Jan. 1795, A. Marg. Wolens   29 BA-6
Braughan, John, 2 May 1794, Rebecca Thompson   2 DO
Braughan, Thomas, 28 July 1797, Sarah Wheatley   2 DO
Braun, Michael, 26 March 1786, Rosina Jantz   2 FR-1107
Braund, Joseph, 23 May 1780, Emily Maddox   2 CH-233
Brave, Jacob, 13 Sept. 1799, Rebecca Nixon   4 FR
Brawner, Thomas, Jr., 16 Feb. 1798, Elizabeth Need   4 FR
Bray, Jas., 7 Dec. 1796, Marg. Maloney   29 BA-8
Brayfield, John Baptist, 15 April 1787, Uliana Whitmore 4 FR
Brayfield, Sam'l, 14 April 1796, Jane Pancoast   2 FR-1109
Brayn, Joseph, 17 Oct. 1778, Martha Matthews   4 FR
Brayson, Wm., 1791, Magd. Hauston   .   50 BA-391
Brazier, Robert, 10 Dec. 1797, Sarah Davis   12 BA-370
Breedin, Joseph, 21 Jan. 1779, Susanna Stallions   1 CA-2
Breedin, Robert Hammett, 29 Sept. 1782, Anne Nuthall   3 SM-60
Breerwood, Job, 22 Jan. 1793, Leah Mace   2 DO
Breerwood, John, 2 Aug. 1781, Ann Wheeler   2 DO
Breerwood, Jonathan, 25 June 1781, Sophia Reed   2 DO
Breerwood, Jonathan, 14 Dec. 1784, Sarah Sanders   2 DO
Breerwood, Joshua, 27 Oct. 1792, Hagar Barnes   2 DO
Breerwood, Joshua, 18 Dec. 1795, Seney Mace   2 DO
Breerwood, Levin, 21 Dec. 1798, Margaret Bestpitch   2 DO
Breisz, Adam, 23 Dec. 1800, Mary Stoll   2 FR-1109
Breisz, John, 23 Feb. 1796, Eliz. Lafever   2 FR-1109
Brelefelt, Henry, 26 Nov. 1790, Margaret Hanke   29 BA-12
Brenan, John, 3 Nov. 1799, Elizabeth Blake   3 BA-380
Brengle, Christian, 18 Oct. 1788, Elizabeth Devilbiss 4 FR
Brengel, Lohrentz, 22 June 1788, Cath. Sheffy   2 FR-1108
   4 FR gives the groom's name as Lawrence.

Brenshelt, Conrad, 5 Nov. 1799, Cath. Reis   29 BA-11
Brent, William Chandler, 24 May 1786, Eleanor Neale   2 CH-234
Brentsinger, John Christian, 1 April 1798, Marie Dorothy
    Schotten, widow, formerly Meyer   9 BA-142
Brerton, Parker, 6 July 1796, Ann Christopher   3 SO
Breses, Aquila, 5 April 1795, Ann Robinson   3 PG-441
Brest, Clement, 20 Nov. 1796, Patsy Collins   29 BA-8
Brevitt, Joseph, 29 Nov. 1798, Cassandra Woodland   12 BA-370
Brewer, James, 31 Aug. 1797, Margaret Young   2 HA-350
Brewer, John, 26 April 1788, by Rev. Reed; Mary Williams
    4 AA
Brewer, Nich's, 16 Feb. 1787, Juliet Salt   11 BA-10
Brewer, Zachariah, 26 Jan. 1778, Dorothy Cecil   1 SM-137
Brewitt, John, 14 May 1784, Mary Swop   10 BA-180
Breyley, Simon, 22 Aug. 1779, by Rev. Mitchell; Ann Boyle
    1 WA
Brian, Dan'l, 16 Oct. 1786, Deborah Magruder   11 BA-9
Brian, Isaac, 10 Dec. 1796, Juliana Schock   29 BA-8
Brian, John, 7 Oct. 1788, Mary Dreeves   3 BA-211
Brian, Michael, 25 Nov. 1797, Mary Miller   3 BA-352
Brian, Richard, 30 Nov. 1799, Elizabeth Potter   3 BA-381
Briant, Samuel, 19 Dec. 1799, by Rev. Ridgely; Nackey Wood
    4 AA
Brice, James, son of John and Sarah, of Annapolis, 24 May
    1781, Juliana Jenings, dau. of Thomas and Juliana 5 AA-280
Brice, Jno., 24 Sept. 1782, Mary Ann Robinson   11 BA-5
Bricher, John, 10 Feb. 1799, Nancy Boyer   4 FR
Bridenhart, John, 15 April 1795, Mary Lowdermilk   1 AL-53
Briff, William, 12 Oct. 1793, Catherine Jones   2 DO
Briggs, Isaac, of Georgetown, printer, son of Samuel and
    Mary of Philadelphia; 27th day, 8 mo., 1794, Hannah
    Brooke   6 SF
Briggs, James, 5 Dec. 1797, Temperance Ensor   5 BA-3
Briggs, Robert, 25 Dec. 1788, Priscilla Jefferson   2 FR-1108
Bright, Edward, 24 Feb. 1793, (?) Vanskike   2 AL-700
Bright, James, 14 Jan. 1784, Sarah West   2 DO
Bright, James, 25 May 1800, Mary Ann Tidings   1 AA-162
Bright, Richard, 16 June 1792, Elizabeth Tregoe   2 DO
Brightman, John, 16 Aug. 1799, Polly Pittay   3 BA-376
Brightwell, John, 4 Jan. 1785, Mary Dobson   2 FR-1107
    4 FR gives the bride's name as Marg. Dobson.
Brightwell, Richard, 6 Dec. 1787, Betty Howard   2 FR-1108
Brightwell, William, 20 Aug. 1785, Mary Waddle   4 FR
Brill, Frederick, 16 Dec. 1784, Elizabeth Reisen   10 BA-184
Brin, John, 25 April 1779, Elizabeth Harding   3 SM-57
Brin, Nicholas, 5 Dec. 1797, Anna Maria Margaret Tilghman
    4 KE-65
Brinsfield, Elijah, 13 Sept. 1781, Sarah McAllister   2 DO
Brinsfield, Thomas, 16 Oct. 1783, Nancy Hutchinson   2 DO
Brintsfield, John, 13 Dec. 1780, Elethe Hutchinson   2 DO
Brion, Hanson, 22 Feb. 1797, Nancy Holland   1 WO
Briscoe, John, 14 Feb. 1784, Eleanor Magruder   4 FR
Briscoe, John, 1 July 1795, Jane Delashmutt   4 FR
Briscoe, Ralph, 8 March 1792, Sarah Delashmutt   2 FR-1108
Briscoe, Richard Sothorn, 29 Nov. 1796, Theadocia Stone
    McPherson   3 PG-442
Briscup, Jonathan, 29 Dec. 1798, Elizabeth Vansant   4 KE-65
Brish, Henry, 11 March 1797, Harriette Murray   4 FR
    45 BA-1 gives the date as 14 March 1797, and the
    bride's name as Henrietta Murray.
Brishe, David, 13 Sept. 1788, Barbara Pentz   4 FR
Brittingham, Isaac, 29 Sept. 1796, Betsey Townsend   1 WO
Brittingham, Joseph, 28 Nov. 1796, Catharina Borkes 10 BA-196
Brittingham, Wm., 30 July 1796, Polly Goottee   1 WO
Broadhag, Charles F., 24 June 1793, Elizabeth Alexander 1 AL-52

```
Broadhead, William, 25 Oct. 1797, Sally Weatherby        3 SO
Broadway, Joseph, 28 June 1798, Easter Knotts            4 KE-65
Brock, Thomas, 15 Feb. 1787, Mary Perrigo                6 BA
Brodess, Jonathan, 21 March 1791, Rosanna Saunders       2 DO
Brodess, Joseph, 19 March 1800, Mary Pattison            2 DO
Brodess, Thomas, 19 June 1781, Anne Higgins              2 DO
Brodess, Thomas, 23 Feb. 1785, Elizabeth Bestpitch       2 DO
Brodess, Thomas, 22 June 1790, Dorothy McGraw            2 DO
Brodess, William, 20 Jan. 1792, Margaret Slaughter       2 DO
Brodis, Jonathan, 7 March 1783, Ann Aaron                2 DO
Brohawn, John, 13 Sept. 1783, Mary Edmondson             2 DO
Brohawn, Patrick, 6 July 1783, Rebecca Jones             2 DO
Broke, Ferdinand, 2 April 1799, Hannah Cornwall          5 BA-3
Bromwell, John, 18 May 1798, Frances Willis              4 KE-65
Brook, Matthew, 28 Dec. 1784, Ann Fearson                2 CH-234
Brook, Samuel, 4 Aug. 1783, Clara Oyrich                 2 DO
Brooke, Bazil, 24 Nov. 1797, Mary Patrick                6 BA
Brooke, Gerrard, son of Basil, 22nd day, 4 mo., 1789,
     Margaret Thomas, dau. of Richard                    6 SF
Brooke, James, son of Basil, 21st day, 6 mo., 1797,
     Hester Boone, dau. of Isaac and Hannah              6 SF
Brooke, Richard, 29 Dec. 1795, Cassandra Prigg           2 HA-349
Brookover, Thomas, 9 March 1786, Mary Thomas             2 FR-1107
Brooks, Charles, 5 Sept. 1797, Priscilla Phillips        2 DO
Brooks, Edward, 20 Dec. 1795, Cassandra Prigg            3 HA-24
Brooks, James, 9 Dec. 1781, Martha Gardiner             11 BA-5
Brooks, James, 8 Dec. 1800, Judah Seward                 2 DO
Brooks, Samuel, 23 Aug. 1797, Margaret Covington         4 KE-65
Brooks, Thomas, 16 July 1798, Sarah Blake                3 HA-27
     2 HA-350 gives the date as 17 July 1798.
Brooner, Elias, 13 May 1780, Mary Ann Zimmerman          4 FR
Brooner, John, 9 Oct. 1779, Susanna Delauter             4 FR
Brother, Henry, 5 Jan. 1793, Elizabeth Brengle           4 FR
Brother, Valentine, 8 Jan. 1795, Margaret Shell          4 FR
Brothers, Francis, 28 Nov. 1786, by Rev. Turner; Frances
     Chapman                                            51 BA-30
Brotherson, Ch's Moore, 19 July 1790, Jane Stansbury    11 BA-13
Brotherton, Thos., 15 Oct. 1783, Blanche Pickett        11 BA-6
Broughton, Josiah, 1 May 1798, Esther Scott              2 SO
Brow, John, 10 Nov. 1793, Catherine Perkins              3 BA-279
Brow, John, 15 Nov. 1796, Mary Kelly                     3 BA-333
Brown, Abraham, 27 Sept. 1795, Elizabeth White           6 BA
Brown, Alexander, 24 March 1795, Anne Jones              5 BA-2
Brown, Anderton, 11 Aug. 1786, Sarah Dawson              2 DO
Brown, Andrew, 1 Jan. 1778, Barsheba Richardson          1 SO-196
Brown, Aquila A., 30 Dec. 1794, Sarah Cresap             1 AL-53
Brown, Arthur A., 31 Dec. 1794, Sarah Cresap             2 AL-700
Brown, Charles, Oct. 1790, Micha Owings                  4 AA
Brown, Clement, 16 Sept. 1795, Mary Brown                2 DO
Brown, David, 7 Nov. 1791, Jemima Elder                  6 BA
Brown, Dennys, 20 Nov. 1798, by Rev. Dorsey; Rebeccah
     Porter                                              4 AA
Brown, Edward, 15 March 1785, Sarah Richards            11 BA-8
Brown, Edward, 13 April 1797, Elizabeth K---(?)         45 BA-1
Brown, Elihu, son of Isaac and Lydia (Slater) Brown, 29th
     day, 5 mo., 1782, Margaret Brown, dau. of Joseph and
     Hannah (Wilson) Brown                               1 SF
Brown, Emanuel, 18 March 1798, Betsy Game                2 SO
Brown, Emanuel, 20 May 1800, Nancy Wooden                2 SO
Brown, Frederick, 19 Feb. 1788, Sarah Willson            3 BA-217
Brown, Frederick, 23 July 1796, Catherine Engle          4 FR
Brown, George, 11 Jan. 1781, Rebecca Denny               2 CH-234
Brown, George, 6 Jan. 1782, Margaret Dennis              3 HA-5
Brown, George, 22 Nov. 1792, Frances Cussens             3 HA-22
Brown, George, 9 Jan. 1797, Isabella Corke               4 KE-65
```

```
Brown, Henry, 25 March 1783, Acha Sollers              11 BA-6
Brown, Henry, 4 June 1793, Ann Stevenson                4 FR
Brown, Henry, 22 June 1797, Catherine Wise              4 FR
Brown, James, 5 Dec. 1780, Henna Hitchcock              2 CH-234
   3 HA-5 gives the date as 2 Dec. 1781.
Brown, James, 19 Dec. 1782, Elizabeth Stansbury        11 BA-6
Brown, James, 20 May 1792, Elizabeth Hackett            1 QA-65
Brown, James, 30 Oct. 1800, Sarah Condon                6 BA
Brown, James, 22 Dec. 1800, Priscilla Dudle             2 DO
Brown, Jesse, son of David and Susanna, 5th day, 5 mo., 1791,
   Dorothy Matthews, dau. of George and Dorothy (Miller)
   Matthews                                             1 SF
Brown, John, 7 May 1778, Elizabeth Davies               5 BA-1
Brown, John, 1 Oct. 1778, Alice Noding                  2 MO-1
Brown, John, 2 Oct. 1783, Hannah Black; mulattoes      11 BA-6
Brown, John, 11 June 1784, Ketura Henry                 2 DO
Brown, John, 14 Aug. 1791, Rebecca Short                5 BA-2
Brown, John, 16 June 1796, Mary Wilkerson               6 BA
Brown, John, 15 Nov. 1796, Mary Kelly                  35 BA-4
Brown, John, 10 Dec. 1796, Betsy Ann Cunningham         6 BA
Brown, John, 18 Oct. 1798, Elisabeth Morris             3 BA-364
Brown, John, 29 July 1799, Mary Read                    6 BA
Brown, John, 14 Dec. 1797, Sarah Gassaway               6 BA
Brown, Joseph, 10 July 1783, Henrietta Clarke           3 AA-417
Brown, Joseph, 28 Aug. 1787, Sarah Stouder              4 FR
Brown, Joseph, 12 July 1791, Dolly Griffith             2 DO
   28 BA-1 gives the date as 13 July 1791.
Brown, Joshua, 23 Oct. 1791, Mary McMacken              6 BA
Brown, Joshua, 6 June 1799, Nancy Algier               45 BA-3
Brown, Josiah, 16 Aug. 1790, Jehosheba Kirk             5 BA-2
Brown, Leonard, 19 April 1799, Fanny Foster            29 BA-10
Brown, Levi, 23 Dec. 1797, Elizabeth Handley            2 DO
Brown, Mathew, 17 Jan. 1799, Eliz. Frick               29 BA-10
Brown, Michael, 25 March 1786, Rosanna Yantz            4 FR
Brown, Moses, 30 April 1797, Mary Snowden              44 BA-2
Brown, Nicholas, 17 Jan. 1799, Polly Stocksdale        45 BA-3
Brown, Peregrine, 28 July 1781, (?) Proctor             3 HA-4
Brown, Richard, Sr., 17 July 1794, Ann Wood             3 AA-424
Brown, Robert, 30 April 1795, Elizabeth Modock          3 PG-441
Brown, Samuel, 21 Aug. 1791, Deborah Inman              4 FR
Brown, Solomon, 5 April 1781, Susannah Porters          3 HA-3
Brown, Thomas, 11 May 1778, Lydia Ann Chambers          4 FR
Brown, Thomas, 10 Nov. 1778, Mary Love                  2 PG-3
Brown, Thomas, 31 July 1785, Mary Betz                 10 BA-184
Brown, Thomas, 11 Oct. 1785, Mary Elliott               5 BA-2
Brown, Thomas, 28 April 1790, Elizabeth Smith           3 BA-228
Brown, Thomas, 30 Sept. 1790, Ann McGregory             6 BA
Brown, Thomas, 4 March 1793, Margaret Watts            18 BA-5
Brown, Thomas, 29 July 1793, Hannah Murrey              1 BA-5
Brown, Thomas, 17 Feb. 1794, Eleanor Gordon             3 HA-23
   7 BA-1 gives the date as 19 Feb. 1794.
Brown, Thomas, 31 Oct. 1794, Jane Camel                 3 BA-293
Brown, Thomas, 17 Sept. 1795, Rebecca Elliott           7 BA-2
Brown, Thomas, 4 March 1797, Mary Colgan               44 BA-2
Brown, White, 6 Oct. 1786, Ann Withgott                 2 DO
Brown, White, 15 Dec. 1792, Sarah Thomas                2 DO
Brown, William, 26 April 1778, Dorcas Woodward          1 CA-1
Brown, William, 12 Dec. 1782, Mary Hammond              3 AA-419
Brown, William, 20 June 1783, Elizabeth Thompson        3 HA-8
Brown, William, 12 Jan. 1784, Leah Dickerson            1 SO-196
Brown, Wm., 15 Nov. 1789, Ann Parsons                  11 BA-12
Brown, William, 27 Jan. 1791, by Rev. Green; Nackey Wilson
   4 AA
Brown, William, 20 June 1795, Mary Mattox               6 BA
Brown, William, 30 July 1795, Lovey Woodland            2 DO
```

```
Brown, William, 18 Jan. 1796, Amelia Bestpitch        2 DO
Brown, William, 23 Jan. 1797, Leah Wilson             1 WO
Brown, William, 29 April 1800, by Rev. Ridgely; Elizabeth
  Shipley                                             4 AA
Browner, Daniel, 27 July 1800, Elizabeth Hoffman      6 BA
Browning, Edward, 22 April 1791, Priscilla Soper      4 FR
Browning, Elias, 12 March 1788, Susannah Cullom       4 FR
Browning, Jeremiah, before 12 Feb. 1778, Lucy Mitchel 2 PG-6
Browning, Joseph, 30 May 1796, Mary Haff              4 FR
Browning, Lewis, 28 Dec. 1793, Margaret Philips       4 FR
Browning, Sam'l, 10 Feb. 1792, Nancy Hobbs            4 FR
Browning, Zadock, 26 Dec. 1793, Mary Browning         2 FR-1109
Bru---(?), Andrew H., 1 Nov. 1800, Maria E. Solomon   6 BA
Bruce, John, 19 Jan. 1800, Mary Cullison              4 SM-184
Bruff, Charistopher, 3rd day, 1 mo., 1788, Mary Berry, dau.
  of James                                            4 SF-183
Bruff, Robert, 22nd day, 3 mo., 1798, Ruth Neall, dau. of
  Solomon and Ruth                                    4 SF-214
Bruff, Samuel, 11 Aug. 1800, Matilda Marshall         2 DO
Bruhst, Wilhelm, 17 April 1788, Catherine Nuordenius  10 BA-190
Brumagin, John, 17 April 1795, Mary Thompson          2 DO
Brumbly, Jabez, 25 Oct. 1796, Martha Tarr             1 WO
Brummel, Joseph, 21 Dec. 1797, Elizabeth Fawble       45 BA-2
Bruner, Peter, 4 Oct. 1782, Margaret Gunn             4 FR
Brunner, Jacob, 29 Aug. 1784, Margaret Kline          4 FR
Brunner, Jacob, 13 Aug. 1786, Magd. Schneider         2 FR-1107
Brunner, Peter, 26 April 1789, Cath. Sim              2 FR-1108
  4 FR gives the groom's name as Peter Brunner of Peter,
  and the bride's name as Catherine Sinn.
Brunner, Peter, Aug. 1796, Elizabeth Haber, widow of Schmidt
  5 FR-10
Brunt, Thomas, 12 Aug. 1796, by Rev. Cash; Verlinder Smith
  4 AA
Bryan, Benjamin, 16 Dec. 1781, Frances Massey         2 CH-234
Bryan, Charles, 1 April 1793, Penelope Sherwood       2 DO
Bryan, Dan'l, 2 Sept. 1785, Frances Shields         , 11 BA-8
Bryan, James, 29 Aug. 1793, Amey Hall                 4 FR
Bryan, James John, 2 Aug. 1792, Isabella Jones        2 DO
Bryan, John, 16 Jan. 1780, Eliz'th Carhill            4 FR
Bryan, Lewis, before 30 Nov. 1779, Margaret Church    2 PG-1
Bryan, Luke, 6 Jan. 1780, Eleanor Harryman            11 BA-4
Bryan, Nicholas, 19 Sept. 1793, Deborah Gorsuch       6 BA
Bryan, Richard, 23 Feb. 1795, Sarah Timbrell          3 BA-299
Bryan, Richard, 3 Oct. 1796, Mary Steele              3 PG-442
Bryan, Thomas, 25 July 1793, Massy Plummer            2 FR-1108
Bryan, Thomas, 5 Sept. 1799, Kitty Hunt               3 BA-377
Bryerly, Robert, 30 Dec. 1783, Sarah Moore            3 HA-8
Bryley, Simon, 21 Aug. 1779, Ann Boyle                4 FR
Bryner, John, 18 Jan. 1798, Araminta Turner           4 KE-65
Bryon, Peter, 28 Jan. 1794, Eleanor Broughton         29 BA-5
Brysen, James, 22 Nov. 1795, Elizabeth Stevenson      3 BA-313
Bryson, John, 25 March 1786, Catherine Green          6 BA
Bryson, Nathan Gregg, 20 Oct. 1799, Susanna Prentiss  5 BA-3
Bucey, Henry, 26 Sept. 1778, Ann Trueman              4 FR
Bucey, Henry, 11 Aug. 1792, Ann Maccattee             4 FR
Buchanan, James, 26 Nov. 1787, Susanna Young          5 BA-2
Buchanan, James A., 1 Jan. 1793, Elisabeth Calhoun    5 BA-2
Buchanan, Moses, 15 Oct. 1780, Eleanor (?)            3 SM-58
Buchanan, Wm., 27 Aug. 1782, Cath. Myers              11 BA-5
  3 BA-185 gives the date as 27 Aug. 1783.
Buchanan, Wm., 10 Nov. 1799, Hepzibah Perine          6 BA
Bucher, Barthol., 18 Sept. 1785, Sus. Walter          2 FR-1107
Buck, Christopher, 9 Oct. 1790, Kezia Gorsuch         11 BA-13
Buck, John, 19 Nov. 1793, Catherine Merryman          1 BA-6
Buck, John, 14 March 1799, Agness Hickson             6 BA
```

```
Buck, Jno., 12 Nov. 1800, Cath. Sanford            29 BA-12
Buck, Joshua, 11 June 1778, Sarah Crook            11 BA-1
Buck, William, 9 Sept. 1800, Ellen Bosley           6 BA
Buckey, George, 21 April 1787, Christena Haas        4 FR
Buckey, Peter, 13 April 1794, Christena Martena      4 FR
Buckey, Peter, 16 May 1796, Mary Salmon              4 FR
Buckey, Valentine, 29 Jan. 1793, Charlotte Ramsbergh 4 FR
Buckias, John, Jr., 9 April 1796, Elizabeth Wey      4 FR
Buckingham, George, 1 March 1788, Hester Tener      18 BA-1
Buckingham, Thomas, 3 May 1793, Mary Stophel         3 BA-266
Buckingham, William, 5 Sept. 1778, Margaret Gladman 11 BA-1
Bucklers, Henry, 17 Nov. 1797, Rachel Gilberthorpe   3 BA-352
Buckley, Thomas, 25 July 1796, Rachel Garrison       3 BA-327
Bucky, George, 8 Oct. 1796, Susanna Kreiger          2 FR-1109
Bucky, Valentine, 9 Nov. 1790, Eliz. Stricker        2 FR-1108
Bucky, Valent., 29 Jan. 1793, Charl. Remsperger      2 FR-1108
Budd, John, 18 June 1781, Rebecca Tolley             2 DO
Budd, John, 24 Nov. 1794, Barbara Brooke             2 DO
Budulph, Zebulon, 16 Oct. 1797, Abigail Murray       4 KE-65
Buell, William H., 3 Oct. 1798, Eleanor Hughes       6 BA
Buger, Jno., 1793, Eleanor Stewart                  50 BA-393
Buldge, Henry, 10 March 1797, Elizabeth Price        5 BA-2
Bulger, Henry, 28 March 1793, Mary Kittleman         3 BA-265
Bulger, Martin, 13 June 1779, Mary Logue            11 BA-3
Bull, Isaac, 1 March 1780, Sarah Love                3 HA-1
Bull, Jacob, 17 June 1781, Esther Bull               3 HA-4
Bull, John, 8 Dec. 1793, Delia Standiford            3 HA-8
Bull, Stephen, 24 Aug. 1793, Hannah Sulph            3 BA-271
Bull, William, 26 Aug. 1781, Avarilla Hanson         3 HA-4
Bull, William, 2 June 1785, Mary Bussey              3 HA-9
Bullen, John, son of Charles and Elizabeth (born 11 April
   1767), 9 March 1794, Mary Harrison, dau. of William
   and Sarah (born 24 Dec. 1773)                     1 TA-309
Bullen, Simon, 27 Aug. 1791, Jane Willson           18 BA-3
   See also 3 BA-235.
Bullett, Thomas James, 21 Dec. 1789, Mary Harrison   2 DO
Bumbery, John, 30 April 1784, Mary Baltrop           2 CH-234
Bumbury, Simmons, 24 Sept. 1795, Nancy Bride        42 BA-1
Bumrides, James, 24 Nov. 1785, Margaret Slater       5 BA-2
Bunker, Job, 29 July 1795, Mary Anderson             6 BA
Bunker, Moses, 8 May 1798, Margaret Franciscus       5 BA-3
Buntz, Jacob, 8 Sept. 1793, Rachel Coleman          18 BA-5
   1 KE-250 states that the bride was a dau. of Charles
   Coleman.
Burbage, Edward, 3 July 1795, Mary Smack             1 WO
Burby, James, 10 Sept. 1800, Susanah Elward          8 BA-2
Burch, Edward, before 30 Nov. 1779, Ann Spink        2 PG-1
Burch, Henry, 27 June 1791, Susanna Suit             3 PG-258
Burch, John, 7 Nov. 1797, Fanny Miller               3 BA-352
Burch, Joseph, 7 Dec. 1788, Eleanor Taylor           2 PG-4
Burch, Thomas, 27 July 1780, Susanna Talburt         2 PG-7
Burch, Thomas, 7 Sept. 1794, Verlinda Hardevy        3 PG-440
Burch, Zachariah, 27 Dec. 1786, Mildred Robey        3 PG-252
Burckhart, George, 12 Sept. 1795, Hannah Hedge       4 FR
Burckhart, Joseph, 5 Oct. 1793, Margaret Stephanus   4 FR
Burckhartt, John, 20 June 1789, Catherine Markle     4 FR
Burckhartt, Nathaniel, 15 April 1786, Margaret Simmons 4 FR
Burckitt, George, Jr., 9 June 1785, Ann Hobbs        4 FR
Burden, John, 7 June 1781, Clina Squires            11 BA-1
Burditt, William, 8 May 1777, Rachel Moberly         4 AA
   Rev. Magill performed the ceremony.
Burges, William, 5 Nov. 1790, Caran Nicholls         4 FR
Burgess, Benjamin, 5 Nov. 1780, Agnes Battie         3 AA-416
Burgess, Edward, 25 June 1781, Margaret Thomson      2 PG-5
Burgess, John, 21 Oct. 1779, Eleanor Magruder        2 PG-2
```

```
Burgess, Jno., 29 June 1785, Eleanor Welsh            11 BA-8
Burgess, John, 19 June 1800, Elizabeth Merchant        3 BA-387
Burgess, John M., 27 Feb. 1794, Elizabeth Coolidge     3 PG-439
Burgess, Joseph, 31 Dec. 1779, Sarah Gray        ·     2 PG-1
Burgess, Richard, 8 March 1778, Mary Gassaway          4 AA
     The ceremony was performed by Rev. Magill.
Burgess, Richard, Jr., 17 Sept. 1782, Mary Coolidge    2 PG-3
Burgess, William, 1790, by Rev. Forrest; Caran Nichols 4 AA
Burgess, William, 30 Oct. 1800, by Rev. Ridgely; Susanna
     Coale                                             4 AA
Burgher, Adam, 17 May 1793, Susanna Smith              4 FR
Burgoine, Jacob, 1 May 1796, Ann Gardner               5 BA-2
Burk, David, 2 March 1788, Elizabeth Murphy           10 BA-190
Burk, Greenbury, 17 Aug. 1796, Rhoda Davis            35 BA-4
Burk, John, 10 Nov. 1785, Eleanor Redden Gash         11 BA-8
Burk, Joseph, 29 July 1787, Mary Hamilton             11 BA-10
Burk, Michael, 15 Aug. 1778, Mary Woods               11 BA-1
Burk, Richard, 12 Jan. 1792, Hannah Dunn              18 BA-4
Burk, Samuel, 14 Aug. 1800, Polly Hynes               48 BA-1
     See also 8 BA-2.
Burk, Thomas, 26 June 1795, Rebecca North              5 BA-3
Burk, Thomas, 4 Oct. 1798, Sarah Hines                 5 BA-3
Burk, Thomas, 20 July 1799, Mary Leary                 3 BA-374
Burk, William, 24 Jan. 1797, Amelia Willis             4 KE-65
Burke, John, 22 Aug. 1793, Eliza Barns                18 BA-5
Burke, John, 28 Dec. 1796, Susannah Templeton          3 HA-25
     2 HA-349 gives the date as 25 May 1797.
Burke, Theobald, 20 March 1783, Eliza Flaherty        11 BA-6
Burkhart, Daniel, 7 Dec. 1791, Elizabeth Burkhart      2 WA-17
Burkhart, Nathaniel, 16 April 1786, Margaret Simmons   2 FR-1107
Burkitt, Christopher, 21 Oct. 1780, Eliz'th Hobbs      4 FR
Burkitt, Joshua, 17 May 1792, Elizabeth Nellson        4 FR
Burkitt, John, 24 Jan. 1796, Sarah Knabs              10 BA-198
Burland, John, 11 Nov. 1792, Mary Neil                 3 BA-257
     3 BA-258 gives the date as 10 Nov. 1792.
Burmingham, Wm., 9 June 1789, Eliza Herring           11 BA-12
Burn, Dennis, 18 Oct. 1793, Sarah Cord                 3 BA-275
Burn, Edward, 14 April 1800, Sarah Bramble             2 DO
Burn, Henry, 29 June 1799, Polly Hogans                2 DO
Burn, Heugh, 24 July 1779, Sarah Temple                4 FR
Burn, James, 27 Sept. 1787, Hannah McCasky            11 BA-10
Burn, John, 29 May 1792, Mary Ann Dorsey McDonald      3 BA-256
Burn, John, 9 Nov. 1798, Sarah Wiggins                 4 KE-65
Burn, Thomas, 12 May 1792, Mary Vickers                2 DO
Burn, Thomas, 5 Aug. 1796, Barthulah Ross              2 DO
Burnee, Thomas, 19 Aug. 1785, Barbara Nicewarmer       4 FR
Burneham, Christopher, 4 Dec. 1779, Sarah McClure     11 BA-4
Burneston, Isaac, 17 Jan. 1792, Anna Rutter           18 BA-4
Burneston, Jos., 5 Aug. 1787, Julianna Grof            2 FR-1108
     4 FR gives the parties' names as Joseph Burniston,
     Jr., and Juliana Grove.
Burneston, Tho., 7 Nov. 1780, Ellen Elkins            11 BA-4
Burnet (Peter?), 1790, (Mary?) Owings                 50 BA-389
Burnet, John, 28 Nov. 1788, Hannah Spencer             1 BA-1
Burnet, Stephen, 12 March 1783, Anastatia Jones        3 SM-61
Burnham, Jno., 4 May 1784, Rebecca Davis              11 BA-7
Burnham, John, Jr., 17 Sept. 1787, by Rev. Turner; Agnes
     Morrison                                         51 BA-30
Burnham, Jos., 10 Feb. 1800, Marg. Austin             29 BA-11
Burnor, Alexander Peter, 3 Feb. 1794, Margaret Lushrow 3 BA-281
Burns, Adam, 5 April 1795, Mary Bull (or Baill)        6 BA
Burns, Andrew, 28 Dec. 1788, Mary Bussey               1 BA-1
Burns, Michael, 1 Oct. 1788, Eliz. Kemp                2 FR-1108
Burns, Sam'l, 10 May 1799, Cath. Hoit                 29 BA-10
     50 BA-405 gives the date as 14 May 1799.
```

Burrell, Allen, 20 March 1789, Susannah Wood   3 PG-255
Burrell, George, 22 July 1780, Elizabeth Lince   4 FR
Burrell, Thos., 5 Feb. 1789, Mary Adams   11 BA-12
Burrell, Thomas, 24 May 1791, Lindy Grimes   6 BA
Burridge, Thomas, 18 Jan. 1782, Joanna Chapman   2 CH-234
Burris, Jonathan, 30 June 1799, Eliz. Kimes   2 AL-701
Burris, Thomas, 28 June 1794, Ann Lanham   4 FR
Burroughs, Thomas, 15 Dec. 1785, Jane Moorehead   11 BA-9
Bursey?, Edward, 9 Jan. 1785, Ann Burgess   11 BA-8
Burtes, John, 5 Sept. 1795, Ellin Price   5 BA-2
Burtles, William, 28 June 1789, Sarah Wathen   2 CH-234
Burton, Francis, 15 Aug. 1780, Elizabeth Abbot   2 PG-7
Burton, Henry, 1 May 1779, Catherine Hill   4 FR
Burton, Jacob, 5 June 1790, Mary Swearingen   4 FR
Burton, John, 6 Dec. 1798, Mary Sodden   6 BA
Burton, Joseph, 10 Dec. 1798, Rebecca Ritter   3 BA-366
Burton, Thomas, 1 March 1778, Mary Harriman   11 BA-1
Burton, Thomas, 25 March 1786, Leah Welsh   11 BA-9
Burton, William, 5 April 1798, Mary Fowler   6 BA
Busby, James, 10 Sept. 1800, Susanna Edward   48 BA-1
Busey, Henry, 7 June 1795, Sarah Powell   3 AA-424
Busey, Thomas, 5 April 1797, Elizabeth Beall   4 FR
Bush, Edward, 21 May 1792, Achsah Leatherbury   29 BA-2
Bush, George, 11 Oct. 1791, Eliz. Grall   2 FR-1108
Bush, Greenbury, 17 Aug. 1796, Rhoda Davis   3 BA-327
Bush, John, 10 Dec. 1782, Anna Elizabeth Stauffer   5 FR-10
Bush, John George, 13 April 1798, Justine Charlotte Boden-
    sick   4 FR
Bushears, John Walker, 14 Sept. 1794, Easther Soper   3 PG-440
Bushell, Leonard, 25 May 1800, by Rev. Wyatt; Nancy Baker
    4 AA
Busick, Ayers, 27 April 1790, Mary Keene   2 DO
Busick, James, 10 March 1781, Ann Wood   2 DO
Busick, John, 4 Dec. 1790, Nancy Foreman   2 DO
Busick, Joshua, 25 Dec. 1793, Betsy Elliott   2 DO
Busick, Nathan, 2 March 1785, Naomi North   2 DO
Busick, Seney, 6 Feb. 1788, Anne Keene   2 DO
Buskirk, John, 30 June 1793, Jane Workman   2 AL-700
Bussard, Joseph, 14 Sept. 1778, Mary Sheffer   4 FR
Bussey, Thos. D., 4 Feb. 1796, Mary Bennett   29 BA-7
But, Johann George, 22 Dec. 1799, Catherine Kaiserin   10 BA-198
Butcher, Barth'w, 21 Sept. 1795, Eliz'th Plumb   44 BA-1
Butcher, John, 26 Oct. 1778, Susanna Hinselagh   11 BA-1
Buth, Thomas, 18 Oct. 1797, Ann Brown   4 KE-65
Butler, David, 18 April 1799, Susan Maria Johns   3 BA-370
Butler, Elisha, 18 Feb. 1783, Eliza Martin   11 BA-6
Butler, James, 2 Dec. 1779, Rebecca Welsh   3 AA-415
Butler, John, (5 April 1790), Rebecca Simpson   15 BA-3
Butler, John, 1 Feb. 1793, Elizabeth Proctor   3 CH-161
    "disp. for consang. in 3rd degree."
Butler, Joseph, 1 Aug. 1778, Mary Ogle   4 FR
Butler, Peter, 13 April 1786, Anne Silver   4 FR
Butler, Richard, 20 May 1786, Amelia Fischer   4 FR
Butler, Richard, 29 Dec. 1792, Sarah Botts   1 BA-5
Butler, Richard, 30 Dec. 1792, Sarah Butler   3 HA-22
Butler, Sam'l, 9 Dec. 1796, Frederica Brownson   29 BA-8
Butler, Thomas, 29 Dec. 1795, Jane Gittings   2 FR-1109
Butler, Tobias, 13 Jan. 1792, Elizabeth Smith   4 FR
Butler, Tobias, Jr., 14 July 1794, Catherine Crist   4 FR
Butler, William, 10 Oct. 1788, Delilah Gittings   4 FR
Butler, William, 24 Feb. 1789, Delilah Browning   2 FR-1108
Butt, Hieronymus, 1790, (?) Corran   50 BA-389
Butt, Humphrey, 23 July 1795, by Rev. Ridgely; Alla
    Donialson   4 AA
Butt, Zadoc, 10 Nov. 1787, Margret Grantt   3 PG-253

```
Butter, Samuel, 10 March 1800, Nancy Anderson        1 WO
Button, Eli, 6 Feb. 1792, Rebecca Wroten             2 DO
Button, Reine Guillaume, 15 Jan. 1795, Jane Matthews 3 BA-299
Button, Robert, 22 Jan. 1800, Mary Durding           8 BA-1
Button, Roger, 4 Nov. 1788, Ally Sebree              1 CA-3
Button, William, 2 Jan. 1797, Ibby Adams             2 DO
Buxton, Jno., 12 Jan. 1796, Eleanor Macoy            5 MO-113
Buxton, John, 13 Nov. 1798, Mercy Soper              4 FR
Buxton, Thomas, 24 Nov. 1796, Fanny Mocbee           5 MO-113
Buzzard, Jno., 12 Jan. 1795, Nancy Hufford           4 FR
Byal, Wm., 8 Aug. 1782, Eliza Stafford               11 BA-5
Byfield, Abraham, 7 April 1793, Patience Corbin      6 BA
Byfield, Robert, 16 Feb. 1779, Mary Falconer         4 FR
Byford, Henry, 2 May 1790, Mary McClure              1 BA-2
Byrne, Bartholomew C., 7 April 1798, Maria Hamilton  6 BA
Byrne, William, 2 Jan. 1787, Mary Hildebrand         4 FR
Byshop, John, 18 Oct. 1798, Mary Speer               6 BA
Byus, Joseph, 4 Jan. 1792, Jinney Hughes             2 DO
Byus, William, 30 May 1783, Sarah Linthicum          2 DO


Cable, Geo., 23 Oct. 1783, Belinda Hicks             11 BA-6
Cables, Jacob, 21 March 1799, Catherine Mike         6 BA
Cabrera, John, 9 Nov. 1794, Jane Mitchell            44 BA-1
Cabril, William, 29 Feb. 1781, Mary Rigdon           3 HA-3
Cadennan, Francis, 22 Oct. 1797, Biddy Bryan         3 BA-351
Cadle, Griffith, 8 Dec. 1785, Agnes Tevis            11 BA-9
Cahay, Nathaniel, 12 May 1799, Lydia Garner          4 SM-184
Cahil, William, 29 Nov. 1783, Eliza Russell          11 BA-7
Cahill, William, 11 Aug. 1798, Mary Farlan           7 BA-4
Cahoa, John, 17 May 1778, Joanna Bennett             11 BA-1
Cain, John, 8 Jan. 1797, Mary Geber                  2 FR-1117
Caine, Henry, 16 Aug. 1796, Sarah Grimes             4 BA-78
Calder, Nathaniel, 30 Dec. 1790, Cassandra Chew      4 FR
Calder, Robert, 1 Aug. 1798, Jerushe Miers           4 KE-66
Caldwell, John, 9 Dec. 1796, Elizabeth Cole          4 KE-66
Caleb, Henry, 11 Feb. 1784, Sarah Galoush            11 BA-7
Calef, Jno., 18 Nov. 1784, Achsah Knight             11 BA-8
Calfus, Lewis, 30 June 1789, Eve Weller              10 BA-194
Calhoon, James, 29 Dec. 1778, Catherine McAter       4 FR
Calhoon, Thomas, 9 Sept. 1795, Nancy Taylor          1 WO
Calhoun, Alexander, 27 March 1794, Sarah Clemments   5 BA-4
Callahan, Joseph, 17 Oct. 1800, Nancy Henderson      1 WO
Callahan, Samuel, 6 July 1788, by Rev. Reed; Nancy Carr  4 AA
Callahan, William, 11 Sept. 1797, Susanna Downs      6 BA
Callahane, John, 24 Feb. 1778, Susannah Sherwood     2 PG-2
Calmes, George, 23 Jan. 1783, Mary Price             4 FR
Calpfleish, John, 6 Oct. 1781, Catherine Foutz       4 FR
Calvert, James, 6 Oct. 1792, Elizabeth Shadders      6 BA
Calwell, John, 11 Feb. 1796, Mary Purle              5 BA-4
Calwell, Thomas, 14 Feb. 1793, Sally Gallion         3 HA-22
Calwell, William, 20 Nov. 1800, Eleanor Gundall      3 HA-30
Cambel, James, 15 Sept. 1785, Linny Hyatt            2 FR-1117
Camden, Charles, 17 Dec. 1793, Elizabeth Camden      4 FR
Camden, Henry, 7 July 1793, Mary Sprigg              4 FR
Camel, John, 1 April 1788, Eliz. Harbin              2 FR-1117
Campbell, Arch'd, 1 June 1786, Eliza Hindman         11 BA-9
Campbell, Archibel, 29 Jan. 1792, Sarah M'Donald     2 FR-1117
Campbell, Arthur, 30 Dec. 1788, Ann Lovejoy          2 PG-4
Campbell, Bennett, 23 Dec. 1799, Catherine Devilbiss 4 FR
Campbell, Eneas, 24 Dec. 1793, Henrietta Chaney      4 FR
Campbell, Jacob, 5 Sept. 1794, Barbara Beckinbaugh   4 FR
Campbell, James, 2 Nov. 1779, Clare Sehorn           4 FR
Campbell, James, 9 Sept. 1785, Linney Hyatt          4 FR
Campbell, James, 6 Jan. 1790, Frances Moody          5 BA-4
```

```
Campbell, James, 30 March 1794, Sarah Sewel            2 FR-1117
Campbell, John, 16 March 1784, Mary Carter             4 FR
Campbell, John, 18 May 1788, Marion Maxwell            3 BA-217
Campbell, John, 3 March 1796, Polly Craton             5 MO-113
Campbell, John, Jr., 9 April 1796, Ann Cummings        4 FR
Campbell, John, 12 June 1796, Sarah Howard             6 BA
Campbell, John, 17 Sept. 1796, Biddy O'Donnell         3 BA-329
Campbell, John, 23 Dec. 1796, Elizabeth Hobbs          4 FR
Campbell, Jno., 30 Dec. 1798, Priscilla Oden           5 MO-115
Campbell, John, 8 Nov. 1800, Betsy Rowan               2 SO
   3 SO gives the date as 9 Nov. 1800.
Campbell, Johnston, 1 Nov. 1785, Henrietta Bryerly     3 HA-10
Campbell, Joseph Murray, 30 Jan. 1798, Grace Hewet     6 BA
Campbell, Mathias, 9 May 1778, Teney Voagh             4 FR
Campbell, Matthew, 19 Dec. 1795, Susanna Stull         4 FR
Campbell, Peter, 4 Feb. 1799, Altha Wilkins            3 BA-368
Campbell, Robert, 1 Jan. 1792, Catharine Smith         6 BA
Campbell, Thomas, 8 April 1800, Leah Dorman            2 SO
Campbell, Thomas J., 30 March 1797, Sarah Sinclair     6 BA
Campble, John, 10 May 1791, Anne Winegarden            2 FR-1117
Canby, Jno., 2 Dec. 1795, Hannah Brune                50 BA-398
Candle, James, 6 March 1780, Ann Richards              4 FR
Cane, Thomas, Sr., of Kent, Del., 12 June 1790, Frances
   Smith of Caroline Co.                               2 SF
Cann, Francis, 11 Oct. 1797, Mary Gale                 4 KE-66
Cann, James, 10 Jan. 1798, Mary Redding                4 KE-66
Cann, John, 1 June 1795, Margaret Helmes               3 BA-305
Canne, Antoine, 4 Nov. 1800, Elisa Crosgrove           3 BA-394
Canner, John, 5 Aug. 1778, Hannah Mammes              11 BA-1
Cannon, James, 29 Aug. 1799, Mary Johnson              2 DO
Cannon, Jesse, 23 Feb. 1787, Fanny Brown               2 DO
Cannon, John, 23 Oct. 1790, Elizabeth Linganfelter     4 FR
Cannon, Luke, 11 Dec. 1783, Betsy Rumbley              2 DO
Cannon, Sailes, 17 Dec. 1789, Mary Hopkins Macmahan    1 TA-299
Cannon, Thomas, 2 Jan. 1798, Charlotte Talbot          2 SO
Cannon, William, 24 June 1798, Sarah Sterling          1 DO-40
Canol (or Carroll), Patrick, 1 Jan. 1795, Elizabeth Hays
   3 PG-440
Canowls, Ch's, Aug. 1784, by Rev. Higinbotham, Ruth Stans-
   bury                                               11 BA-7
Cantle, Barnett, 15 April 1794, Catharine McLaughlin   5 BA-4
Cantwell, James, 20 Dec. 1796, Frances Lacey           2 SO-11
Cantwell, Joseph, 7 Dec. 1791, Mary Sewers             2 DO
Capito, George, 10 Sept. 1796, Gertraut Reckman       50 BA-400
Capoot, Jeremiah, 6 Aug. 1794, Mary Taylor             5 BA-4
Capp, Stephen, 10 Nov. 1793, Nancy Fowler              6 BA
Cappedon, Christian, 8 Oct. 1792, Eliz. Wyant         29 BA-3
Carawan, Frederick, 16 Sept. 1794, Levinia Booze       2 DO
Carbury, Henry, 8 Dec. 1792, Cevilla (Sybilla) Schnertzer
   4 FR
Carey, Dennis, 6 May 1798, Judy Moore                  3 BA-358
Carey, Hugh, 1790, Phebey McChilton                    5 BA-389
Carey, James, 20 July 1779, Mary Hodge                 4 FR
Carey, James, of Balto. Town, son of Jno. Carey of Balto.
   Co., 6th day, 9 mo., 1786, Martha Ellicott, dau. of
   John of Balto. Co.                                  6 SF
Carey, James, 17 July 1795, Charlotte Carlisle         4 FR
Carey, Jeremiah, 30 June 1797, Margaret Kellie        29 BA-8
Carey, John, 15 Dec. 1785, Ann Knight                 11 BA-9
Carl, David, 12 Feb. 1792, Barbara Grof                2 FR-1117
Carlile, Samuel, 22 July 1782, Ann Taylor              3 HA-6
Carlisle, James, 1788, Nancy Murray                   50 BA-388
Carlyle, John, 18 Feb. 1790, Elizabeth Lane            5 BA-4
Carmack, William, 16 Aug. 1791, Sarah Richards         4 FR
Carmady, Darby, 14 Aug. 1791, Susanna Gordon          18 BA-3
```

Carman, Andrew, 27 Aug. 1782, Mary Davis   3 HA-7
Carman, Wm., 17 Oct. 1799, Ann Cunningham   6 BA
Carmichael, (Jas. or John?), 23 Feb. 1797, Eliz. Landers
    29 BA-8
Carmine, Daniel, 28 Jan. 1791, Magga Tunis   2 DO
Carnaghan, James, 26 Oct. 1797, Catherine Miller   6 BA
Carnan, Charles Ridgely, 17 Oct. 1782, Priscilla Dorsey
    11 BA-5
Carnan, Morris, 12 Jan. 1792, Cordelia Greenfield   18 BA-4
Carney, John, 13 Nov. 1793, Elizabeth Crist   4 FR
Carney, John, 13 April 1797, Esther Hudd   3 BA-343
Carney, Mich'l, 30 Jan. 1781, Margaret English   4 FR
Carney, Thos., 16 May 1795, Sarah Baxley   29 BA-6
Carns, Thos., 12 Aug. 1794, Marg. Heelstrunk   29 BA-5
Carpenter, Allen, 9 May 1795, Anne Skuse   3 BA-305
Carpenter, Isaac, 4 Jan. 1794, Lydia Reed   29 BA-5
Carpenter, Jacob, 3 July 1800, Polly Horn   3 BA-387
Carpenter, John, 28 Jan. 1779, Frances Perry   2 PG-2
    See also 2 CH-234.
Carpenter, John, 24 Dec. 1793, Helen Gwinn   3 BA-279
Carper, Philip, 1 Oct. 1797, Catherine Drill   4 FR
Carr, Aquila, 21 April 1786, by Rev. Turner; Susannah Bond
    51 BA-29
Carr, Benjamin, 10 Feb. 1795, Ann Trott   3 AA-424
Carr, Felix, 4 June 1795, Catherine Figgance   3 BA-305
Carr, James, son of Aquila and Susanna (Parrish) Carr; 15th
    day, 8 mo., 1787, Elizabeth Price, dau. of Samuel and
    Ann (Moore) Price   1 SF
Carr, John, Feb. 1779, Rachel Purnell   3 AA-415
Carr, John, 15 July 1780, Margaret Bryerly   3 HA-2
Carr, John, 3 July 1781, Elizabeth Pindell   3 AA-417
Carr, John, 7 Dec. 1788, Mary Keller   2 FR-1117
Carr, John, 15 Aug. 1797, Eleanor Herron   3 BA-348
Carr, Joshua, 29 Dec. 1800, Sarah Withgott   2 DO
Carr, Samuel, 12 Jan. 1783, Jane Russel   3 AA-419
Carr, Samuel, 28 April 1795, Eleanor B. Carr   3 PG-441
Carr, Thomas, 29 Jan. 1793, Cath. Gashauer   2 FR-1117
Carr, William, son of Aquilla and Susanna (Parrish) Carr;
    3rd day, 8 mo., 1791, Sarah Herbert, dau. of William
    and Ann   1 SF
Carreck, Marrien, 22 Jan. 1795, by Rev. Ridgely; Margaret
    Webb   4 AA
Carrell, Samuel, 20 Oct. 1788, Elizabeth Williams   18 BA-1
Carrens, Thomas, 16 May 1780, Ruth Baldwin   4 FR
Carrick, George, 12 Dec. 1796, Carey Baker   3 BA-333
Carrick, Marreen, 1 Oct. 1782, Elizabeth Jones   2 PG-3
Carrico, James, widower, 5 April 1796, Marianna Carrico
    "disp. for consang. in 2nd to 3rd degree"   3 CH-162
Carrico, Wilfred, 9 Jan. 1798, Eleanor Moore   3 CH-162
Carrill, W., 29 Jan. 1779, Elizabeth Fee   4 FR
Carrington, Samuel, 8 Jan. 1782, Milly McDonald   2 CH-234
Carrol, Charles John, 26 May 1795, Jennet Brown   3 AA-424
Carrol, James, 18 Dec. 1787, Sophia Gough, dau. of Harry
    Dorsey Gough   2 BA-11
Carrol, John, 9 May 1779, Elizabeth Hamilton   2 CH-234
Carrold, James, 7 April 1792, Susanna Galwith   3 PG-436
Carroll, Benjamin, 25 Dec. 1792, Mills Proctor   1 BA-5
Carroll, Caleb, 18 Feb. 1789, Elizabeth Corkin   2 DO
Carroll, Charles, 14 Oct. 1789, Susanna Lord   2 DO
Carroll, Charles, 3 Feb. 1795, by Rev. Ridgely; Elizabeth
    Warfield   4 AA
Carroll, Daniel, 10 Jan. 1779, Ann Maccubbin   5 MO-115
Carroll, Daniel, 30 Sept. 1800, Betsy Greenwood   2 DO
Carroll, James, formerly James Maccubbin of Annapolis, 20
    Dec. 1787, Sophia Gough, dau. of Harry D. Gough   3 BA-221

```
Carroll, John, 16 June 1780, Isabella Cowen          3 HA-2
Carroll, John, 5 Feb. 1790, Mary Willis              2 DO
Carroll, John, 30 Nov. 1800, by Rev. Ridgely; Mary Duvall
    4 AA
Carroll, Joshua, (18?) July 1800, by Rev. Wyatt; Sarah
    Goodwin?                                         4 AA
Carroll, Levi, 21 Nov. 1796, Rebecca Corkrin         2 DO
Carroll, Levin, 14 Oct. 1797, Mary Goslee            2 DO
Carroll, Patrick, 30 Oct. 1792, Rachal Corkran       2 DO
Carroll, William, 14 Nov. 1783, May Tuchstone        3 HA-8
Carron, William, 13 Feb. 1786, Anne Aldridge         5 BA-4
Carson, Henry, 14 Nov. 1798, Louise Strider          9 BA-142
Carson, John, 31 Dec. 1789, Hannah Haas              2 FR-1117
Carson, Joseph, 28 Jan. 1800, Eliz. Clay            29 BA-11
Cartee, Daniel, 30 Nov. 1783, Susanna Griffee        5 BA-3
Carter, Arthur, 27 June 1793, Bathan Beall           4 FR
Carter, Charles Stowards, 4 June 1798, Sarah Berry   3 BA-359
Carter, George, 23 Dec. 1782, Gizzel Brawner         2 CH-234
Carter, Henry, 7 Feb. 1779, Elizabeth Hogan          3 SM-57
Carter, Henry, (19 Feb. 1791), Eleanor Arthurton    15 BA-4
Carter, James, 17 Jan. 1786, Ann Ennalls Hooper      2 DO
Carter, Jeremiah, 7 Oct. 1788, Mary Ann Roberts      2 DO
Carter, Jethro, 13 Oct. 1796, Hetty Matthews         3 SO
Carter, John, 6 Sept. 1783, Mary Hambleton           4 FR
Carter, John, 4 June 1784, Mary Bowyer               3 HA-8
Carter, John, 4 March 1790, Ann Thomas               2 FR-1117
Carter, John, 15 Nov. 1791, Elizabeth Clarridge      2 DO
Carter, John, 10 Jan. 1796, Jane Guffey?             6 BA
Carter, John, 6 Nov. 1779, Mary Ford                 3 BA-380
Carter, Joseph, 25 June 1780, Bathia Sindol         11 BA-4
Carter, Joshua, 28 June 1796, Cath. Springer         2 FR-1117
Carter, Richard, 18 Dec. 1790, Mary Beall            4 FR
Carter, Thomas, 6 March 1780, Mary Roach             4 FR
Carter, Thos., 25 Jan. 1797, Christina Nicholl      29 BA-8
Cartey, Thomas, 1 March 1780, Margaret Nicholls      4 FR
Cartwright, Abraham, 21 Jan. 1783, Mary Hart         2 BA-11
    11 BA-6 gives the groom's name as Abram.
Cartwright, Abraham, 3 April 1800, Elizabeth Stevenson 6 BA
Carty, Francis, 1 Oct. 1792, Magdalen Juel           1 BA-4
Carty, John, 18 Dec. 1796, Elizabeth Fellers         3 BA-333
Carver, William, 10 Aug. 1779, Eliza Condon         11 BA-3
Carvill, Thomas, 31 July 1798, Mary Ringgold         4 KE-66
Cary, William, 2 June 1793, Maria Barbara Fritchie   4 FR
Case, Robert, 14 March 1789, by Rev. Hagerty; Rachel Basil
    4 AA
Case, Robert, c.1799, by Rev. Steuart; Eleanor Yieldhall
    4 AA
Casey, John, 11 Aug. 1778, Philoclea Edgworth (or Dogworth)
    1 MO-1
Cash, Dawson, 7 Oct. 1798, Jemima Beens              5 MO-115
Cash, John, 8 Feb. 1782, Chloe Callico               2 CH-234
Cash, John, c.1792 in Washington Co., by Rev. Chalmers;
    Elizabeth Roberts                                4 AA
Cash, Jonathan, 4 April 1796, Sarah Fitzgerald       4 FR
Cash, Wm., 26 March 1779, Casse Nicholls             4 FR
Cashman, Timothy, 21 Oct. 1795, Maria Bell           3 BA-311
Cashman, Wm., 4 Feb. 1796, Sarah Brown              29 BA-7
Caslick, Edward, 17 Dec. 1785, Lucretia Ward         2 DO
Caslow, Samuel, 16 July 1798, Catharine Marr         3 BA-360
Cassat, Peter, 4 Jan. 1798, Susan Stansbury          3 BA-354
Cassell, Abraham, 23 April 1782, Catherine Linganfelter
    4 FR
Cassell, Dan'l, 8 May 1785, Mary Ollix               4 FR
Cassidy, Patrick, 9 July 1778, Hannah Read          11 BA-1
Casson, Joseph, 16 Jan. 1798, Sarah Cosden           4 KE-66
```

```
Castill, Francis, 8 March 1795, Marg. Halter            50 BA-396
Castillo, John, 23 Aug. 1798, Anne Jones                 3 BA-348
Castle, Thomas, 21 May 1797, Eliz. Messerle              2 FR-1117
Caswell, Josiah, 17 March 1796, Nancy Scott              5 BA-4
Caswell, Thomas, 18 April 1795, Jane Leary               3 BA-301
Caterow, Charles, 4 March 1797, Catherine Christ         4 FR
Cathell, John, 9 Dec. 1796, Priscilla Ward               1 WO
Catholick, Edward, 13 Feb. 1782, Mary Vinson             2 DO
Catlin, Thomas, 27 Dec. 1798, Milly Beauchamp            2 SO
Cato, Edward, 30 Jan. 1796, Sinah Marton                 3 BA-317
Caton, Nicholas, 22 March 1780, Mary Hackett             3 HA-1
Catrup, James, 2 Feb. 1797, Polly Swan                   1 TA-313
Catrup, Lemmon John, 16 Nov. 1800, Eliz'th Hopkins       1 TA-314
Caudry, Wm., 8 Nov. 1797, Sally Bowen                    1 WO
Caufman, Henry, 7 April 1798, Elizabeth Hardman          4 FR
Caulfield, Robert, 10 Dec. 1778, Phebe Hayes             5 BA-3
Caulk, James, 17 Dec. 1800, Priscilla Sewell             2 DO
Caulk, Tho. Ward, 26 May 1785, Hannah Leas              11 BA-8
Causey, Henry, 20 Aug. 1785, Mary Wallace                2 DO
Causey, John, 8 July 1798, Betty Cannon                  1 DO-40
Cavey, John, 15 Dec. 1785, Ann Knight                   11 BA-9
Cavey, Thomas, 17 Oct. 1789, by Rev. Hagerty; Elizabeth
     Donaldson                                           4 AA
Cavill, John, 29 March 1798, Anne Perry                  3 BA-357
Cawood, John, 1 Jan. 1786, Elizabeth Warde               3 PG-251
Cawood, Smallwood, 18 June 1787, Elizabeth Smallwood     3 PG-253
Cawood, Stephen, 20 Oct. 1786, Catherine Hepsabah Emerson
     3 PG-251
Cawood, Stephen, 14 June 1792, Elizabeth Ann Fendall     3 PG-437
Cawood, William, 6 June 1782, Martha Beale               2 CH-234
Cealin, George, 16 Jan. 1800, Elisabeth Garner           3 BA-382
Cecil, Benjamin, 29 Jan. 1798, Ann Fisher                4 FR
Cecil, Henry, 12 Jan. 1789, Sarah Hinton                 2 FR-1117
Cecil, John, 24 Feb. 1798, Mary Linton                   4 FR
Cecill, George, 16 Dec. 1797, Elizabeth Linton           4 FR
Celman, Wm., 18 July 1780, Mary Frazier                 11 BA-4
Chadbourne, Joseph, 17 Nov. 1779, Ann Gates              4 FR
Chader, James, 19 Nov. 1795, Sarah Jourdan               3 BA-313
Chaires, John, 23 July 1798, Mary Findley                4 KE-66
Chairs, John, 1 March 1797, Mary Start                   4 KE-66
Chairs, Thomas, 12 Aug. 1797, Mary Start                 4 KE-66
Chamberlain, Robins, 30 Jan. 1794, Mary Crookshanks      3 BA-281
Chamberlain, Samuel, 22 June 1798, Ann Jenkins           3 HA-27
Chambers, Daniel, 17 Nov. 1791, Martha Childs           34 BA-1
Chambers, John, 21 July 1799, Eleanor Busk               6 BA
Chambers, Mathew, 20 Nov. 1800, Cath. Mummy             29 BA-12
Chambers, Wm., 30 July 1783, Judith Harvey              11 BA-6
Chambers, Wm., 4 Feb. 1787, Susanna Porter              11 BA-10
Chambers, William, 14 Dec. 1794, Rebecca Evans           3 BA-296
Chambers, William, 6 Dec. 1796, Ann Thrift               7 BA-3
Chambers, William, 6 Nov. 1799, Elizabeth Doyle          3 HA-28
     2 HA-351 gives the date as 7 Nov. 1799.
Chamblin, William, 28 Oct. 1797, Nancy Chamblin          4 FR
Champlin, Hugh, 23 March 1789, by Rev. Hagerty; Elizabeth
     Hinder                                              4 AA
Chance, Daniel, 18 Aug. 1798, Sarah Gray                 4 KE-66
Chance, Rich., 3 April 1786, Barthulah Green             2 DO
Chance, William, 9 Nov. 1796, Amelia Fountain            4 KE-66
Chancey, George, Jr., 14 Nov. 1796, Frances Rebecca Dorsey
     3 HA-25
Chancy, Thomas, 21 April 1795, Susanna Stockwell         1 AL-53
Chandler, James, 3 Jan. 1800, Nancy West                 5 BA-4
Chandler, John, 5 Sept. 1782, Catherine Posey            2 CH-234
Chandler, John, 10 Nov. 1782, Eleaner Goring             2 CH-234
Chandler, Joseph, (26 April 1788), Eleanor Cables       15 BA-1
```

Chandler, Nathan, 9 April 1782, Cicely Davis   4 FR
Chandless, John Hurle, 1 Sept. 1793, Sarah Anderson   3 BA-275
Chaney, Abel, 17 March 1785, Ruth Johnson   11 BA-8
Chaney, Benjamin, 22 March 1791, Elizabeth Brown   3 HA-21
Chaney, Charles, 17 Oct. 1799, Sarah Dunham   3 BA-379
Chaney, Ezekiel, 6 Sept. 1794, Mary Balzel   1 AL-53
  2 AL-700 gives the date as 7 Sept. 1794, and the bride's
  name as Mary Belzeb.
Chaney, Jonn, 27 Feb. 1781, Elizabeth Garretson   2 CH-234
Chaney, Thomas, 4 Oct. 1792, by Rev. Bowen; Jemima Goodman
  4 AA
Chaney, Thomas, 6 Dec. 1798, by Rev. Ridgely; Mary Williams
  4 AA
Changeur, Leon, 30 June 1795, Josephine Gripiera Montalebor
  44 BA-1
Chany, William, 15 Sept. 1796, by Rev. Cash; Susannah Stalins
  4 AA
Chapman, Christopher, 21 Dec. 1798, Eliz. Rous   29 BA-10
Chapman, James, 20 Feb. 1798, Rachel Merryman   45 BA-2
Chapman, James, 1 June 1800, Eleanor Isher   6 BA
Chapman, John, 12 Nov. 1778, Elizabeth Kelly   11 BA-1
Chapman, John, 1 June 1780, Sarah Jonke   2 CH-234
Chapman, Thomas, before 12 Dec. 1792, by Rev. John Long;
  Clare Taylor   4 AA
Chappell, Erasmus, 23 June 1791, Sally Beard   2 DO
  28 BA-1 gives the date as 27 June 1791.
Chappell, Sam'l, 5 Aug. 1792, Sarah Tice   6 BA
Chappell, Thomas, 11 Jan. 1781, Eleanor Harvey   3 AA-417
Chariot, Pier, 6 Sept. 1794, Guidai Richards   19 BA-9
  6 BA gives the groom's name as Peter Per Chariot.
Charles, (?), 17 Dec. 1782, Mary (?); free negroes   11 BA-6
Charles, Henry, 17 Jan. 1793, Mary Wright   2 SF
Charles, Isaac, 2nd day, 1 mo., 1779, Sophia Rauly   2 SF-288
Charles, Isaac, 2 Oct. 1798, Elizabeth Windows (sic) 2 DO
Charles, Isaac, 31 July 1800, Elizabeth Bell   2 DO
Charles, John, son of Solomon, 4th day, 11 mo., 1789,
  Elizabeth Stapleford, dau. of Raymond Stapleford   4 SF-196
Charles, Solomon, 28 Oct. 1794, Mary Furbas   2 DO
Charles, Williss, 14 Jan. 1786, Sarah Wright   2 SF
Charlton, John W., 25 Sept. 1790, Elizabeth Beatty   4 FR
Chartress, John, 23 Dec. 1799, Betsey Lucas   3 BA-381
Chase, Thorndick, 10 Feb. 1785, Mary Jacobs   11 BA-8
Chauncey, George, 17 Nov. 1796, Rebecca Frances Dorsey
  12 BA-370
Cheiny, Charles, 2 Nov. 1777, by Magill; Lucretia Gardiner
  4 AA
Cheney, Charles, 3 Feb. 1780, Elizabeth Waters   2 PG-3
Cheney, Francis Tubman, 15 May 1780, Elizabeth Costin 3 SO
Cheney, John, 19 Dec. 1780, Elizabeth Fennell   2 PG-5
Cheney, Rezin, 6 Jan. 1799, by Rev. Ridgely; Rebeckah
  Harvey   4 AA
Cheney, Thomas, 18 July 1779, by Rev. Magowan; Elizabeth
  Sunderland   4 AA
Cheney, William, c.1799, by Rev. Steuart; Ann Steuart 4 AA
Chenoweth, Richard, (8 Feb. 1790), Sarah Belt   15 BA-3
Chenowith, Arthur, (25 Nov. 1791), Elizabeth Baxter 15 BA-4
Chenowith, Thomas, 10 Aug. 1777, Anne Carroll   17 BA-1
Chesholm, Thomas, 25 Jan. 1796, Comfort Rigdon   3 HA-24
Chesley, John, 5 Jan. 1779, Mary Ashcum Parran   1 CA-2
Chesolm, Thomas, 28 Jan. 1796, Sarah Rigdon   2 HA-349
Chesran, David, 24 Dec. 1797, Mary Hanel   5 BA-4
Chessy, Henry, 3 Oct. 1779, Unis Bramble   2 DO
Chessy, John, 31 Oct. 1799, Sarah Anderson   2 DO
Cheston, Daniel, 2 Nov. 1796, Catherine Holland   6 BA
Cheverlin, Jesse, 12 Feb. 1780, Catherine Guither   3 SM-58

Cheves, Daniel, 3 Oct. 1795, Mary Carnes   3 BA-311
Chew, John, 25 July 1780, Margaret Kent   3 AA-416
Chew, Richard, 2 May 1780, Frances Holland   3 AA-416
Chew, Rev. Thomas John, 14 Nov. 1793, Margaret Crab Johns
  3 PG-438
Chew, Thomas Sheredine, 25 Feb. 1790, Elizabeth Morgan   1 BA-2
Chew, William, 9 June 1787, Rebecca Holton   6 BA
Chicard, Baptista, 8 Nov. 1794, Rachel Eyres   3 BA-296
Chilcoal, Benjamin, 1 July 1783, Comfort McClain   4 FR
Chilcoat, Joshua, 21 Oct. 1789, Rebecca Arnold   10 BA-194
Chilcoat, Richard, 13 Dec. 1786, by Rev. Turner; Elizabeth
  Cole   51 BA-30
Chilcott, Elijah (7 Feb. 1789), Elizabeth Ensor   15 BA-2
Child, Benjamin, 18 Sept. 1781, Mary Roberts   3 AA-417
Childerson, William, 22 May 1783, Rebecca Hopkin   2 DO
Childs, Benjamin, 4 Oct. 1792, Elizabeth Evans   23 BA-3
Childs, Edward, 8 Oct. 1792, Minty (?); blacks   2 FR-1117
Childs, Henry, 7 Feb. 1793, Sarah Smith   22 BA-2
Childs, James, 29 Dec. 1799, Polly Newcomer   3 BA-381
Childs, John, 7 May 1778, by Rev. Magowan; Ann Owings   4 AA
Childs, John, 6 Feb. 1798, Sarah Wheeler   45 BA-2
Childs, William, 18 Dec. 1781, Mary Willett   2 PG-3
Chillison, William, 12 March 1785, Sarah Woolford   2 DO
Chilman, John, 2 July 1796, Elizabeth Moore   6 BA
Chilson, Walter, 16 June 1799, Hannah Martin   12 BA-370
Chilton, James, 25 June 1778, Cath'r Burns   2 MO-1
China, Nathan, 29 Nov. 1787, Sarah Mansfield   6 BA
China, Zephania, 23 Jan. 1783, Ruth Lewis   11 BA-6
Chinn, John Yates, of Va., 8 Dec. 1796, Sarah Fairfax
  Carter   3 BA-333
Chinworth, Thomas, 1 Jan. 1788, Rachel Norris   1 BA-1
Chiseldine, Seneca, 4 Nov. 1779, Elizabeth Biscoe   3 SM-57
Chiseley, John, 30 Oct. 1784, Elisabeth Flanagan   5 BA-3
Chissel, John, 14 Feb. 1779, Ann Sindal   6 BA
Chiswell (sic), Benj., 4 April 1787, by Rev. West; Barbara
  Wagers   51 BA-30
Chizum, Josiah, 30 Oct. 1792, Mary Webster   2 DO
Chord, Henry, 24 July 1791, Eleanor Randall   6 BA
Chrisman, John, 17 June 1796, Peggy Stonesifer   1 AL-53
Christ, Peter, 16 April 1797, Margaret Mang   2 FR-1117
Christian, Anthony, 16 June 1798, Elisabeth Welsh   3 BA-359
Christian, Jno., 26 April 1795, Cath. Jordan   29 BA-6
Christie, Gabriel, 18 Nov. 1779, Priscilla Hall, dau. of
  Capt. John Hall of Cranbury; see also 3 HA-3   1 HA-392
Christie, James, 27 Dec. 1785, Rebecca Birmingham   11 BA-9
Christophel, Jno., 31 March 1800, Marg. Crowel   29 BA-11
Christopher, Ebben, 4 Nov. 1798, Polly Sturgis   1 WO
Christopher, Eli, 3 May 1796, Lotte Driskele   1 WO
Christopher, Elijah, 4 March, 1800, Sarah Bratten   1 WO
Christopher, George, 20 Dec. 1799, Major Willing   1 WO
Christopher, Henry, 24 Dec. 1792, Rosanna Johnson   2 DO
Christopher, Jno., 31 March 1800, Margaret Crowel   50 BA-407
Christopher, Joseph, 11 Jan. 1790, Sarah Woollen   2 DO
Christopher, Thomas, 18 May 1797, Nancy Tuvey   47 BA-1
Chun, Lancelot, 4 Nov. 1792, Martha Ridgely   2 FR-1117
Chunn, Charles Courts, 11 Dec. 1788, Sarah Cooksey 1 CH-208
Church, Roswell, 3 Sept. 1793, Ruth Murray   6 BA
Church, Samuel, 27 July 1793, Hannah Pitcher   5 BA-4
Churchman, Enoch, 1 Feb. 1792, Martha Norris   3 HA-21
  1 BA-4 gives the date as 2 Feb. 1792.
Churchman, John Frederick, 25 Feb. 1787, Mary Tucker   4 FR
Cicly, Henry, 4 March 1794, Hester Workman   2 AL-700
Cile, Peter, 18 Sept. 1780, Eliz'th King   4 FR
Cissell, Joshua, 29 Dec. 1787, Mary Readen   3 PG-254
Cissill, William, 5 Dec. 1793, Margret Cole   3 PG-438

```
Clabaugh, Charles, 17 Aug. 1779, Eliz'th Hill        4 FR
Clackner, Adam, 23 Dec. 1798, Rebecca Gill          29 BA-10
Clagett, Henry, 23 Nov. 1798, Julia Hawkins          4 FR
Claggett, Joseph W., 29 Aug. 1782, Eleanor Digges    2 PG-3
Claiborne, George Wythe, 20 Dec. 1794, Mary King Hellen
   3 BA-296
Clancey, John, 19 July 1785, Elizabeth Yuslice       4 FR
Clancey, Roger, 26 June 1795, Lydia Bale             4 FR
Clansey, Patrick, 18 July 1795, Hanna Hogan          3 BA-307
Clapham, Col. Josias, 30 Aug. 1783, Dorcas Johnson   4 FR
Clapham, Sam'l, 26 Sept. 1797, Elizabeth Johnson     4 FR
Clapp, Stephen, 10 Nov. 1793, Nancy Fowler          19 BA-8
Clarage, Cloudsberry, 21 Nov. 1797, Sarah Bryson     6 BA
Clarck, Raphael, 8 Aug. 1797, Martha Peterson        3 BA-348
Clare, Benjamin, 23 May 1799, Charlotte Bevins       3 BA-371
Clarey, James, 16 July 1791, Sarah Thorp            33 BA-1
Clarey, John, 3 Nov. 1781, Sarah Walker              4 FR
Claridge, Young, 14 Aug. 1781, Elizabeth Barns       2 DO
Clark, Abraham, 5 Jan. 1780, Elizabeth Evans         2 PG-3
Clark, Benjamin, 5 Feb. 1793, by Rev. G. Ridgely; Elizabeth
   Gambol                                            4 AA
Clark, Charles, 6 May 1793, Mary Mills               2 DO
Clark, Daniel, 20 June 1798, Mary Stevens            2 DO
Clark, Elisha, 25 Nov. 1790, Elizabeth Porter        6 BA
Clark, George, 10 Aug. 1785, Lydia Garrett           3 HA-9
Clark, Hugh, 23 April 1798, Rebecca Morse            4 KE-66
Clark, Ignatius, 6 July 1780, Ann Hilton             2 CH-234
Clark, James, 23 Dec. 1784, Barbara Rock            11 BA-8
Clark, James, 18 May 1797, Mary Ann Birmingham       6 BA
Clark, John, 5 May 1793, Mary Whaley                 3 BA-266
Clark, John, 15 Nov. 1794, Cassandra Anderson        1 BA-6
Clark, John, 8 Aug. 1795, Abiel Shepherd             1 AL-53
Clark, John, 23 Feb. 1796, Charlotte Bobbin          3 BA-317
Clark, John, 16 May 1796, Mary Greenwood             2 DO
Clark, John, 13 March 1797, Ann Elston               6 BA
Clark, Joseph, 21 Jan. 1796, Hannah Howard           7 BA-3
Clark, Oliver, 3 Sept. 1795, Sophia North            5 BA-4
Clark, Peter, 1 March 1778, Frances Lewin            3 AA-414
Clark, Peter, 4 July 1781, Elizabeth Wadley          3 BA-181
Clark, Richard, 4 Sept. 1798, Nancy Bell             1 WO
Clark, Thomas, 23 Dec. 1781, Ann Hall                2 PG-3
Clark, Thomas, 21 Sept. 1784, Susanna Mansfield      4 FR
Clark, Wm., 19 April 1778, Mary Hopewell             1 SM-137
Clark, William, 23 April 1778, by Rev. Magill; Dina White
   4 AA
Clark, William, 8 Oct. 1780, Levina Warfield         2 PG-3
Clark, William, 6 Jan. 1798, Rachael Grimes          7 BA-4
Clark, William, 24 May 1798, by Rev. Ridgely; Elizabeth
   Clark                                             4 AA
Clark, William, 19 Dec. 1800, Mary Webb              1 WO
Clark, William P., 31 July 1800, by Rev. Ridgely; Juliet
   Gaither                                           4 AA
Clarke, Abraham, 20 Dec. 1792, by Rev. G. Ridgely; Mima
   Jones                                             4 AA
Clarke, George, 4 Nov. 1800, Jane Abell              4 SM-184
Clarke, Henry, 25 Dec. 1777, Elizabeth Beckett       2 PG-2
Clarke, Ignatius, 24 Dec. 1799, Jane Theobald        4 SM-184
Clarke, John, 29 April 1783, Hannah Maydwell         3 BA-191
Clarke, John, 13 Aug. 1797, Priscilla Dodd          47 BA-1
Clarke, John, 16 Jan. 1798, Margaret Bomberger       6 BA
Clarke, John, 19 Dec. 1800, Anne Hosgood             3 BA-396
Clarke, Patrick, 27 Aug. 1798, Margaret Reading      3 BA-362
Clarke, Richard, 26 Oct. 1778, Margaret Berry       11 BA-1
Clarke, Samuel, 9 March 1785, Mary Lucas            11 BA-8
Clarke, Seth, 3 Nov. 1795, Cassandra Browning        4 FR
```

```
Clarke, Thomas, 14 Sept. 1798, Priscilla Bevins        3 BA-363
Clarke, William, 18 Oct. 1781, Monica Woodward         3 SM-59
Clarke, William, 24 Dec. 1789, Dorcas Fitz            11 BA-13
Clarke, Wm., 4 Feb. 1799, Cath. Shrade                29 BA-10
Clarridge, James, 16 Feb. 1792, Sally Mills            2 DO
Clary, Ashford Dowden, Dec. 1789, Elizab. Smith        2 FR-1117
Clary, Ashford Dowden, 18 July 1795, Sarah Neighbours  4 FR
Clary, Daniel, 2 Jan. 1789, Rachel Penn                4 FR
Clary, Zachariah, 20 May 1793, Delilah Penn            4 FR
Clash, Perry, 27 Dec. 1796, Lucretia Wheatley          1 TA-313
Claus, Stephen, 26 May 1793, Gosina Holland           10 BA-196
Clay, Adam, 10 Jan. 1793, Elizabeth Hardinger          4 FR
Clay, John, 21 Aug. 1790, Nancy Jones                  4 FR
Clay, Samuel, 19 March 1793, Rachel Grimes             4 FR
Claypoole, Septimus, 8 June 1797, Elizabeth Polk      47 BA-1
Clayton, Joseph, 18 Aug. 1796, Sarah Wells             3 BA-327
Claywell, Wm., 2 Sept. 1796, Rachel Johnson            1 WO
Cleave, Joseph, 17 Sept. 1798, Mary Paul               4 KE-66
Clefford, Michael, 18 March 1781, Pheby Eatan          4 FR
Clements, Basil, 5 Dec. 1794, Cloe Green               4 FR
Clements, Edward, 27 Nov. 1782, Eliza Morris          11 BA-6
Clements, Edward, 4 March 1796, Charlotte Wade         3 BA-321
Clements, James, 3 Sept. 1794, Mary Landraken         35 BA-2
Clements, Walter, 28 Aug. 1782, Nancy Garrett          2 CH-234
Clements, William, 24 July 1797, Winifred Hardey       4 FR
Clements, William H., 18 July 1789, Eleanor Jenkins    4 FR
Clements, Zach., 28 Feb. 1790, Ann Clements            3 PG-257
Clemments, Madngo, 4 June 1797, Elizabeth Marlow       3 PG-438
Clemmons, William, 17 Dec. 1781, Mary James            3 HA-5
Clendenen, John, 27 May 1793, Elizabeth Glasgow        3 HA-22
Clenerd, Francis, 21 Sept. 1785, Sarah Weltzhamer      4 FR
Clerkson, Thomas, 20 July 1785, Elizabeth Tompanks    10 BA-184
Cleyburn, William Dandridge, 21 June 1778, Ann Dandridge
   2 CH-234
Clifford, Dennis, 30 Sept. 1799, Eleanor Johnson       3 BA-378
Clifton, Thomas, 18 July 1795, Lydia Hopkins     .     5 BA-4
Cline, David, 28 July 1799, Catharine Shakes           3 BA-374
Cline, Henry, 19 July 1778, Mary Jumper                4 FR
Clingling, William, 8 March 1784, Jane Gilmore         3 HA-8
Clingman, John, 17 Dec. 1797, Ann Wise                 5 BA-4
Clinton, Thomas, 6 June 1794, Catherine Michael        4 FR
Cloninger, Philip, 28 Nov. 1797, Modelina Hennickhouser
   4 FR
Clooney, James, 3 Sept. 1794, Mary Landraken           3 BA-293
Clopper, Peter, 11 Sept. 1794, Mary Golding            5 BA-4
Clopper, Peter, 1 Dec. 1799, Rachel Wells              5 BA-4
Close, Christian, 26 Dec. 1786, Cath'e Grant          11 BA-10
Close, David, 1 Nov. 1797, Mary Bentley               47 BA-1
   3 BA-352 gives the date as 1 Nov. 1798.
Close, George, 21 Feb. 1782, Elizabeth Fowl            3 HA-6
Cloud, Isaac, slave; 20 March 1799, Rachel Johnson, free
   black                                               3 BA-369
Cloudsbury, Kirby, 24 July 1796, Sarah Hopkins         1 TA-322
Cloudsley, Thomas, 18 Nov. 1800, Jane Summers, alias
   Cooper                                              3 BA-395
Club, Leven, 3 Sept. 1786, Rhoda Short                 3 PG-251
Club, Matthew, 21 Nov. 1793, Drucilla White            3 PG-438
Clubb, William, 3 Jan. 1797, Ann Notley                3 PG-442
Clyma, Peter, 5 May 1778, Eleanor Pile                 4 MO-1
Coal, Christopher A., 1 April 1798, Sarah Claton        5 MO-115
Coal, George, 9 Oct. 1794, Sarah Biddison              3 BA-293
Coale, Charles Caple, 24 March 1793, Sarah Rhoades     3 BA-265
Coale, Dennis, 2 Dec. 1788, Ann Dawson                 4 FR
Coale, Isaac, 21 Nov. 1797, Sarah Ridgely              2 FR-1117
Coale, James, 11 March 1788, Mary Carter               2 FR-1117
```

```
Coale, John, 23 May 1779, Elizabeth Stevens           5 BA-3
Coale, John, 4 June 1797, Rachel Young                6 BA
Coale, Joseph, (24 Dec. 1788), Sofia Osborne         15 BA-2
Coale, Thomas of William, 7 Oct. 1781, Sarah Ridgely  1 HO-220
Coale, Thomas, 16 Feb. 1797, by Rev. Ridgely; Rachel Gardner
    4 AA
Coale, Thomas, 27 Dec. 1798, Elizabeth Dorsey         6 BA
Coale, William, 24 April 1794, Elizabeth Bowen        6 BA
Coaleman, James, 27 Dec. 1781, Alisannah Pendergast   3 HA-5
Coard, Arthur, 28 July 1784, Bathias Swann            3 HA-8
Coard, Asbury, 4 March 1784, Sarah Daws               3 HA-8
Coates, Francis, 25 Dec. 1794, Charlotte Linton       3 BA-296
Coats, James, 9 March 1793, Rachel Jackson            6 BA
Coats, John, (born 11 July 1751), 22 June 1779, Susannah
    Murray                                            1 TA-313
Cobb, John, 19 Jan. 1782, Hannah Ealey                3 HA-6
Coblentz, Adam, 12 Feb. 1788, Elizabeth Kahlmannin    1 FR-59
Cochran, George, 21 Dec. 1780, Eleanor Shaw           2 CH-234
Cochron, Heugh, 29 Oct. 1779, Eliz'th Hobston         4 FR
Cock, Sam'l, 15 Dec. 1783, Mary Ogle                  4 FR
Cockey, Caleb, 8 Jan. 1789, Sally Rutter              6 BA
Cockey, John, 18 Aug. 1785, Mary Cole                11 BA-8
Cockey, Joshua, 28 April 1793, Polly Jones            6 BA
Cockey, Joshua F., 21 Dec. 1797, Elizabeth Fowble    45 BA-2
Cockey, Thomas, 11 March 1788, Ruth Brown             6 BA
Cockey, Thomas, of Edward, 26 Sept. 1795, Elizabeth Owings
    6 BA
Cockey, Thomas Dye, 10 Jan. 1788, Elizabeth Cockey    6 BA
Cockey, Thomas Dye, 26 March 1793, Ann Risteau        6 BA
Cockrall, Thomas, 3 March 1798, Sarah Wiley           6 BA
Cockran, George, 24 Dec. 1780, Eleanor Shaw          11 BA-2
Cockran, Wm., 11 May 1783, Ann McGill                11 BA-6
Cocky, Joshua, 23 Feb. 1782, Henrietta Cromwell      11 BA-5
Coe, James, 1 Feb. 1798, Sarah Hart                   6 BA
Coe, Jesse, 8 Nov. 1784, Abrillea Norris              4 FR
Coe, Wm., 13 Jan. 1791, Hannah Barber                 6 BA
Coffee, John Dowden, 21 Dec. 1785, Darcus Roberts     4 FR
Coffey, Charles, 7 Jan. 1794, Mary Colsten            2 DO
Coffin, Lemuel, 28 March 1780, Catherine Creable      4 FR
Coffin, William, 18 Nov. 1795, Elizabeth Vinson       2 DO
Coghlan, William, 10 Nov. 1794, Catherine Kirk       40 BA-1
Cohe, William, 29 Sept. 1797, Rebecca Richardson      4 KE-66
Cohee, John, 6 Dec. 1797, Susanna Wilson              4 KE-66
Cohen, Isaac, 9 Aug. 1797, Peggy Moore                3 BA-348
Cohoon, Nathan, 6 Feb. 1780, Betty Adams              1 SO-205
Cohoun, Moses, 28 April 1784, Eleanor Stewart         5 BA-3
Cohrman, Georg, 21 May 1795, Magd. Walzen            50 BA-397
Coil, George, 7 July 1792, Elizabeth King             4 FR
Coil, Samuel, 17 April 1778, Catherine Brady         11 BA-1
Colbert, Simon, 12 Dec. 1778, Eleanor Reed            4 FR
Colbert, William, 6 Dec. 1796, Bridgett Howard        2 SO-11
Colby, William, 15 April 1799, Rebecca Brown          4 FR
Cole, Abraham, 14 Dec. 1790, Cecil Gist               6 BA
Cole, Benjamin, 29 Jan. 1799, Margaret Sullivan       6 BA
Cole, Elijah, 19 Feb. 1792, Patsey Phillips           6 BA
Cole, Elijah, 26 March 1800, Rachel Trapnall          6 BA
Cole, Ezekiel, 5 Aug. 1793, Sarah Courtney            3 HA-22
Cole, George, 12 May 1778, Priscilla Hocker           4 AA
Cole, Giles, c.1791, Sarah Osborne                   15 BA-4
Cole, Godfrey, 23 May 1789, Eliz. Keener             29 BA-1
Cole, James, 31 March 1797, Catherine Hollis          3 HA-26
    2 HA-349 gives the date as 4 April 1797.
Cole, James, 16 April 1798, Anne Christopher          3 BA-357
Cole, John, 27 Dec. 1782, Marg't Cunningham          11 BA-6
Cole, John, 8? Nov. 1785, Eleanor Maratta            11 BA-8
```

```
Cole, John, 30 April 1796, Priscilla Drew              3 HA-25
   7 BA-3 gives the date as 1 May 1796.
Cole, John, 4 Feb. 1797, Mary McDonough                5 BA-4
Cole, Joshua (13 Oct. 1789), Ann Lee                  15 BA-2
Cole, Nathan, 18 March 1790, Darcus Tudor              6 BA
Cole, Philemon, 27 Nov. 1800, Elizabeth Rutter         6 BA
Cole, Richard, 7 Sept. 1786, Catherine McSherry        4 FR
Cole, Robert, 1 Jan. 1800, Ann Fenwick                 4 SM-184
Cole, Samuel, 15 Nov. 1786, by Rev. Turner; Sarah Haile
   51 BA-30
Cole, Skipwith, 22 Jan. 1797, Elizabeth Gilbert        2 HA-349.
Cole, Stephen, 30 Nov. 1792, Rachel Gorsuch           32 BA-1
Cole, Thomas, 18 May 1782, Jane Hart                  11 BA-5
Cole, Thomas, 18 Dec. 1798, Martha Tracey              6 BA
Cole, Thomas, 13 Nov. 1799, Elisabeth Smith            3 BA-380
Cole, Thomas, 17 April 1800, Elizabeth Welsh           6 BA
Cole, Vincent, 24 July 1777, Anne Orum                17 BA-1
Cole, William, 30 March 1793, Cathorine Laughlin      22 BA-2
Cole, William, 4 Feb. 1795, Sarah Hamilton             7 BA-2
Cole, William H., 27 Aug. 1799, Elizabeth Magors       4 FR
Colebourn, Elijah, 15 Jan. 1799, Hetty Austin          1 WO
Coleby, Charles, 14 May 1792, Rachel Bird             18 BA-4
Coleman, Charles, 15 March 1791, Lydia Forwood         1 BA-3
Coleman, John, 16 Sept. 1783, Mary Rainier            11 BA-6
Coleman, John, 5 Dec. 1787, Leah Springfield           3 BA-213
Coleman, John, 24 May 1794, Margaret Savage            1 AL-53
   2 AL-700 gives the date as 26 May 1794, and the bride's
   name as Mary Savage.
Coleman, John, 29 Jan. 1799, Fanny Horsefoot           3 BA-367
Coleman, John, 10 Oct. 1799, Elizabeth Wheeler         8 BA-1
Coleman, Joseph, 27 Feb. 1792, Rebeckah Justice        4 FR
Coleman, Joseph, 30 Jan. 1793, Mary McMechan           3 BA-258
Coleman, Nich's, 9 Nov. 1786, Sarah Bond              11 BA-9
Coleman, Samuel, 31 Oct. 1799, Charlotte Bobbet        6 BA
Coleman, William, 31 July 1784, Anne Labesius          5 BA-3
Coleman, William, 12 June 1793, Sinah Allen            3 BA-269
Coleshine, Earnest, 10 Oct. 1786, Eliz'th Showe        4 FR
Colliberger, John, 16 Nov. 1791, Susanna Dutrow        4 FR
Collick, Levin William, 25 Dec. 1800, Amy Black        1 WO
Collier, John, 8 Oct. 1778, Esther Hardy              11 BA-1
Collier, Layfield, 22 Aug. 1797, Sally White           1 WO
Collier, Levin, 12 Feb. 1799, Betsy Porter             2 SO
Collier, Robert, 24 April 1797, Catty Ritchie          2 SO-11
Collings, James, 27 Nov. 1794, Sarah Moonshot          3 BA-296
Collings, John, 23 Nov. 1799, Susanna Hagan            6 BA
Collings, Richard, 8 May 1797, Fanny Brown             5 BA-4
Collins, Alexander, 24 Dec. 1799, Polly Isham          2 SO
Collins, Belitha, 7 Jan. 1800, Comfort Irons           1 WO
Collins, Edward, 29 Feb. 1796, Cassy Collins           3 HA-25
   7 BA-3 gives the date as 1 March 1796 and the bride's
   name as Cassandra.
Collins, Ephraim, 4 Oct. 1781, Charity Combess         3 HA-5
Collins, George, 26 Dec. 1790, Sarah Bailey            1 BA-3
Collins, Henry, 29 Oct. 1785, Mary Irons               3 HA-10
Collins, Hodijah, 12 Aug. 1791, Mary Gromett           4 FR
Collins, Humohrey, 15 Feb. 1785, Sarah Bell            2 FR-1117
Collins, Isaac, 3 Jan. 1798, Tabitha Stevenson         1 WO
Collins, Jacob, 25 June 1781, Hannah Mearty            3 HA-4
Collins, James, 20 Feb. 1780, Christian Turner Davis   2 PG-7
Collins, James, 24 April 1780, Eliza Davis            11 BA-4
Collins, James, 8 Feb. 1797, Polly White               1 WO
Collins, James, 30 Aug. 1798, Mary Donellan            3 BA-362
Collins, James, 26 Feb. 1799, Martha Davis             1 WO
Collins, James W., 24 April 1800, Sarah Daugherty      6 BA
Collins, John, 10 May 1778, Elizabeth Scroggen         4 CH-1
```

```
Collins, Jno., 24 Jan. 1790, Amelia Church              11 BA-13
Collins, John, 15 July 1800, Betsey Davis                1 WO
Collins, Joseph, 10 May 1791, Comfort Jones              6 BA
Collins, Joshua, 13 Jan. 1793, Mary Rubey                2 FR-1117
Collins, Matthew, 27 Nov. 1785, Sus. Bowlass             2 FR-1117
Collins, Maynard, 8 Jan. 1779, Sarah Jones               5 HA
Collins, Patrick, 5 Feb. 1780, Eliz'th Pepper            4 FR
Collins, Robert, 27 April 1797, Sarah Ritchie            3 SO
Collins, Thomas, 23 Feb. 1796, Betty Malcomb             3 SO
Collins, Timothy, 21 April 1778, Elizabeth McFee        11 BA-1
Collins, Walton, 18 July 1797, Martha Townsend           1 WO
Collins, William, son of Thomas and Rebecca, 10 Oct. 1782,
    Emme Kibble                                          1 WI-117
Collins, William, 28 Dec. 1784, Judith Waters           11 BA-8
Collins, William, 6 Jan. 1798, Sarah Summers             4 KE-66
Collison, Benjamin, 14 April 1787, Mary Young            2 DO
Collison, James, 3 June 1799, Elizabeth McCollister      2 DO
Collison, Jeremiah, 14 Dec. 1786, Ann Howland           11 BA-10
Colly, Wm., 15 April 1799, Rebecca Brann                 2 FR-1117
Colsten, Gladstone, 1 Nov. 1791, Mary Voss               2 DO
Colsten, Thomas, Jr., 10 Jan. 1791, Margaret Mace        2 DO
Colston, Edmund, 5 Jan. 1786, Mary Shehawn               2 DO
Colston, Jesse, 21 July 1800, Nancy Colston              2 DO
Colston, Thomas, 23 April 1781, Elizabeth Colston        2 DO
Colston, Thomas, Jr., 17 July 1784, Britania Wallace     2 DO
Combs, Cuddie, 26 Feb. 1793, Abigail Tremble             2 AL-700
Comegys, Cornelius, 15 Oct. 1798, Mary Gould             4 KE-66
Commeger, William, 10 July 1796, Martha Clarke           7 BA-3
Commer, Peter, 28 Aug. 1800, Mary Longston               2 AL-701
Compston, John, 29 June 1778, Sarah Knotts               4 FR
Compton, Alexander, 4 Oct. 1782, Mary Joy                2 CH-234
Compton, John, 20 Aug. 1795, Elizabeth Jacobs            4 FR
Compton, John, Jr., 12 Oct. 1795, Rebecca Clarke         1 AL-53
Compton, Joseph, 27 Oct. 1798, Ann Paine                 4 FR
Comyn, Patrick, 7 June 1785, by Rev. Turner; Nancy Deaver
    51 BA-29
Conaway,George, 1 June 1800, by Rev. Wyatt, Elizabeth Roboson
    4 AA
Conaway, Greenbury, 12 April 1796, by Rev. Ridgely; Sarah
    Cadle                                                4 AA
Cocnklin, Jno., 20 Dec. 1785, Mary Merritt              11 BA-9
Condon, David, 16 Oct. 1797, Catherine Gotsailech        4 FR
Condon, James, 24 Dec. 1788, Elizabeth Adams             2 DO
Condon, Richard, 6 Jan. 1787, Arey Franklin              4 FR
Condon, William, 20 Oct. 1786, Ruth Welsch               4 FR
Condon, Wm., 13 Oct. 1787, Sarah Penn                    4 FR
Condon, Zachariah, 8 Dec. 1789, Rachel Elliott           4 FR
Condon, Zachariah, 17 Dec. 1799, Eleanor Todd            4 FR
Condrum, William, 8 May 1781, Elinor Stuard              3 HA-4
Conly, John, 19 Aug. 1781, Honor Kemp                    3 BA-182
Conn, James, 2 Jan. 1786, Agness Sparks                  5 BA-4
Conn, William, 9 Feb. 1799, Catherine Boteler            4 FR
Conna, Peter, 27 Aug. 1800, Polly Longshore              3 AL-6
Connally, Andrew, 22 July 1796, Rhoda Gray               2 DO
Connally, Christopher, 18 May 1790, Mary Nicolls         2 DO
Connard, John, 13 Oct. 1784, Susannah West               3 HA-9
Connell, James, 27 March 1800, Betsy Cromwell            3 BA-384
Connelly, John, 7 Oct. 1783, Mary Conner                11 BA-6
Connely, Rob't, 18 May 1780, Eleanor Heartley           11 BA-4
Conner, Benjamin, 1 April 1797, Grace Coulbourn          2 SO-11
Conner, Edward, 13 Dec. 1783, Rachel Forbes              3 BA-189
Conner, Elijah, 24 March 1797, Nancy Otten               2 SO-11
Conner, James, 25 Sept. 1778, Eliz'th Sipes              4 FR
Conner, John, 18 Dec. 1783, Sarah Lankford               1 SO-205
Conner, John, 12 July 1788, Mary Stewart                 2 DO
```

Conner, Lawrence, 7 Aug. 1790, Elizabeth Appleby   4 FR
Conner, Patrick, 5 Nov. 1796, Polly Larman or Larmaur   1 AL-53
Conner, Wm., 14 or 16 Oct. 1788, by Rev. Claggett, Eleanor
     Wevil   4 AA
Connerly, Thomas, 12 Oct. 1793, Levina Simmons   2 DO
Connolly, Lawrence, 12 Nov. 1799, Barbara Cook   3 BA-380
Connon, Wm., 1 Jan. 1790, Ann Murphy   11 BA-13
Connor, James, 24 May 1795, Elizabeth Graham   3 BA-305
Connor, Thos., 1791, Sarah Bankson   50 BA-391
Connoway, America, 17 Dec. 1793, Mary Saddler   6 BA
Connoway, Charles, 9 May 1784, Catherine Gardner   3 BA-187
Connoway, George, c.1798, by Rev. Riggin, Elizabeth
     Pettibone   4 AA
Connoway, Michael, before 12 Dec. 1792, by Rev. John Long;
     Belinda Jean   4 AA
Connoway, Rich'd, (12 May 1789) Barbara Barnett   15 BA-2
Connoway, William, 12 April 1795, Hanna Stewart   3 BA-301
Conor, William, 7 Feb. 1796, Elizabeth Harris   3 PG-442
Conradt, Henry, 17 April 1787, Mary Leth   2 FR-1117
     4 FR gives the bride's name as Mary Late.
Conrod, John, 30 May 1784, Sarah Enloes   11 BA-7
Conroy, Barnaby, 17 July 1781, Jane Spicer   3 BA-182
Conroy, Edward, 19 May 1795, Jemima Angus   4 FR
Constable, John, 9 Dec. 1780, Ann Fuller   2 PG-5
Constable, John, 8 Oct. 1795, Elizabeth Galaway   6 BA
Constable, Sam'l, 27 March 1785, Rebecca Dobston   2 FR-1117
Constable, Wm., 1790, Priscilla Cooke   50 BA-390
Constant, Richard, 25 March 1790, Elizabeth Coward   6 BA
Constantine, Edward, (20 Aug. 1788), Catherine Dimmitt
     15 BA-1
Contee, Benjamin, 30 March 1788, Sarah Rt. Lee   2 CH-234
Contwell, Thomas, 27 Aug. 1795, Sally Smith   5 BA-4
Conway, James, 24 Nov. 1792, Amelia Elizabeth Atkinson   5 BA-4
Conway, John, 8 Jan. 1797, Sarah Steele   3 BA-341
Conway, Samuel, 19 May 1792, Sarah Henry   3 BA-256
Conway, William, 25 Aug. 1792, Sarah Atkinson   3 BA-256
Coogle, Adam, 10 Aug. 1787, Catherine Nave   4 FR
Coogle, John, 26 Oct. 1797, Ann Green   6 BA
Cook, Aaron, 6 Aug. 1794, Nancy Wood   2 DO
Cook, Bartholomew, 13 Nov. 1794, Mary Pickering   2 DO
Cook, David, 24 Oct. 1799, Ellen Brady   6 BA
Cook, Elijah, 12 May 1778, Jean (McKeen?)   4 MO-1
Cook, Emanuel, 23 Feb. 1797, Ann Gosnell   45 BA-1
Cook, Greenbury, 20 Nov. 1788, Ann Baseman   3 BA-218
Cook, Henry, 1 June 1779, Mary Lambert   4 FR
Cook, Henry, 4 April 1784, Elizabeth Ratclift   2 DO
Cook, Henry, 28 Jan. 1799, Margaret Bennett   2 DO
Cook, Hodson, 17 April 1790, Elizabeth LeCompte   2 DO
Cook, Hodson, 10 Sept. 1798, Rebecca Hayward   2 DO
Cook, Jas., 2 Dec. 1793, Margaret Nappt?   29 BA-5
Cook, Jeremiah, son of Stephen and Hannah, 22nd day, 2 mo.,
     1786, Rachel Farquhar, dau. of Allen and Sarah   3 SF
Cook, Jesse, 18 Nov. 1795, Lotty Abbott   2 DO
Cook, John, 10 April 1779, Susannah Wilson   4 FR
Cook, John, 18 July 1782, Eleanor Connolly   3 HA-5
Cook, John, 11 July 1795, Catherine Mixendorff   4 FR
Cook, Moses, 23 Jan. 1799, Elizabeth Hayward   2 DO
Cook, Samuel, 16 May 1792, Sarah Dawson   2 DO
Cook, Samuel, 4 Oct. 1798, Henrietta Attix   4 KE-66
Cook, Stanley, 1 Dec. 1781, Salina Vickers   2 DO
Cook, Thomas, 23 June 1778, Mary Simpson   11 BA-1
Cook, Thomas, 17 Dec. 1782, Mary Soward   2 DO
Cooke, Richard, 23 Nov. 1800, Elizabeth Van Wycke   3 BA-395
Cooke, Samuel, 26 June 1792, Charlotte Holland   6 BA
Cookerly, John, Jr., 9 Sept. 1796, Alice Fleming   4 FR

```
Cooksey, Hezekiah, 13 July 1780, Eliza Grey              2 CH-234
Cookus, Michael, 10 May 1784, Elizabeth Kile            4 FR
Cooley, John, 8 Dec. 1780, Sarah Gilbert                3 HA-3
Cooley, William, 7 July 1785, Elizabeth Bay             3 HA-9
Coomes, Aden, 2 Oct. 1794, Pamilia Williams             2 FR-1117
Coomes, Baalis, 3 June 1799, Sarah Richardson           4 FR
Cooms, Richard, 1782, Clare Green                       2 CH-234
Coonce, John, 5 Aug. 1780, Catherine Roar               4 FR
Coonce, Nicholas, 14 May 1796, Rebecca Danford          1 AL-53
Cooper, Adam, 12 Oct. 1786, Rebecca Hammilton           2 FR-1117
Cooper, Arch'b'd, 8 Nov. 1779, Mary Ramsay              4 FR
Cooper, Calvin, 20 Feb. 1800, Margaret Palmer           3 BA-383
Cooper, George, 16 June 1777, Ann Southern              3 BA-173
Cooper, George, 14 Aug. 1787, Elizabeth Sweitner        6 BA
Cooper, James, 7 Dec. 1786, Naomy Ramsey                4 FR
Cooper, James, 1 March 1793, Leah Brannock              2 DO
Cooper, John, 24 March 1794, Susanna Beach              3 BA-285
Cooper, John, 30 April 1797, Elisabeth McLane           3 BA-344
Cooper, Joseph, 27 Nov. 1799, Mary Clarke               6 BA
Cooper, Philip, 13 Feb. 1797, Sarah Green               3 HA-25
Cooper, Robert, 29 Aug. 1791, Cath. Harlin              2 FR-1117
Cooper, Robert Clark, 14 Dec. 1793, Rebecca Griffen     6 BA
Cooper, Samuel, 13 July 1788, Martha Roberts            3 BA-205
Cooper, Thomas, 6 Oct. 1778, Catherine Gill            11 BA-1
Cooper, Thomas, 7 July 1781, Margaret Summers           3 BA-185
Cooper, Wm., 17 Dec. 1779, Mary Harrison                4 FR
Cooper, William, 27 April 1797, Patience Jackson        2 SO-11
Cooperider, Elias, 8 March 1780, Susanna Iseminger      4 FR
Cope, David, 30 July 1788, Nancy Willis                 2 DO
Cope, John, 26 March 1783, Mary Cooper                  2 DO
Cope, William, 14 Jan. 1782, Leah Knott                 2 DO
Cope, William, 26 Sept. 1786, Keziah Addison            2 DO
Cope, William, 22 June 1793, Milcah Hammond             2 DO
Copeland, James, 30 Dec. 1789, Rebeckah Chrisholm       4 FR
Copeland, John, 28 Aug. 1794, Margaret Cowan            3 HA-23
Copenhaver, John, 19 June 1790, Barbara Miller          4 FR
Copens, Heinrich, 25 March 1788, Margaretha Milderman  10 BA-190
Corban, Joseph, 29 April 1783, Mary Corban             11 BA-6
  "not first but second cousins."
Corbin, Elijah, 16 Feb. 1785, by Rev. Davis; Sarah Kelly
  51 BA-29
Corbin, Joseph, 17 June 1790, Eleanor Grover            6 BA
Corbin, Nathan, 11 Oct. 1785, Susanna Anderson         11 BA-8
Corbin, Nathan, 7 April 1800, Sophia Enloes             3 HA-29
Corbin, Peter S., 25 June 1800, Molly Stockly           1 WO
Corbin, Thomas, 11 May 1790, Nancy Turner               1 BA-2
Corbin, Thomas, 5 May 1795, Eleanor Sinwall             6 BA
Corbin, William, 30 Sept. 1781, Salley Politte          1 SO-204
Corbus, Conrad, 9 Jan. 1794, Fanney Potter              2 AL-700
Corby, John, 19 Sept. 1799, Jane Gordon                 3 BA-377
Corckhill, Thomas, 27 Nov. 1800, Anne Cole              3 BA-395
Cord, Abraham, 22 Oct. 1798, Mary Ford                  6 BA
Cord, Amos, 22 Jan. 1798, Elizabeth Swaine              3 HA-27
  2 HA-350 gives the date as 23 Jan. 1798.
Cord, Aquila, before 2 Nov. 1789, Milcah Browning      22 BA-1
Cord, Jno., 29 Nov. 1794, Marg. Wilson                 29 BA-6
Cord, John, 13 Feb. 1797, Rebecca Wilson                3 HA-25
Cordery, Nathan, 24 July 1798, Dorcas Ayers             2 AL-701
Cordery, Noble, 23 Nov. 1794, Elizabeth Cordery         2 AL-700
Cordingly, William Welch, 28 Feb. 1796, Ann Moore       5 MO-113
Cordray, Covington, 20 Dec. 1797, Ann Winwright         3 SO
Corkran, Edward, 21 Dec. 1792, Sabana Rowen             2 DO
Corkran, James, 18 Dec. 1788, Telitha Carroll           2 DO
Corkran, Peter, 18 Jan. 1790, Elizabeth Bell            2 DO
Corkran, Timothy, 10 Oct. 1780, Mary A. Hubbard         2 DO
```

```
Corm, Daniel, 12 July 1787, Elizabeth Pontany        6 BA
Cornall, John, 11 March 1786, Jennet O'Neall         4 FR
Cornelius, Daniel, 18 May 1797, Sarah Tharp          4 KE-66
Cornelius, Joseph, 25 April 1787, Jemima Mason       6 BA
Cornell, William, 30 Dec. 1789, Hannah Griffith      6 BA
Cornish, Levin, 28 Sept. 1793, Milly Govare          3 BA-275
Cornmiller, Jacob, 4 Oct. 1792, Jane Robinson        6 BA
Corse, Israel, son of David, dec.; 21st day, 5 mo., 1795,
     Lydia Troth, dau. of William                    4 SF-207
Corse, Thomas, 25 May 1792, Elizabeth Gray           2 DO
Corsey, Henry D., 26 July 1800, Mary Oliver          6 BA
Coryton, Josiah, 25 Oct. 1795, Catherine Lynn        3 PG-441
Cosden, Jeremiah, 5 June 1794, Elenor Buchanan       3 BA-287
Cosley, Thomas, 20 Sept. 1780, Jane Timmons          3 HA-2
Cossen, Nicholas, 11 Aug. 1794, Rebeckah Wilson      4 FR
Cost, George, 29 Dec. 1798, Mary Harshman            4 FR
Cost, Jacob, 2 Dec. 1799, Mary Magdalene Cross       4 FR
Coston, Isaac, 19 April 1797, Sarah Adams            2 SO-11
Cothel, James, 21 May 1795, Charity Harryman         6 BA
Cotherill, Thomas, 23 Oct. 1796, Margaret Hughes     6 BA
Coton?, Charles Warren, 4 Aug. 1792, Henrietta Mowbray  2 DO
Cotreal, William, 20 June 1785, Margarett Berry      2 DO
Cottingham, Daniel, 10 March 1796, Polly Tilghman    1 WO
Cottingham, Ephraim, 15 April 1790, Jemima Bird      1 SO-205
Cottingham, Isaac, 29 Jan. 1799, Susanna Lambden     1 WO
Cottingham, James, 18 Dec. 1798, Grace Cottingham    1 WO
Cottingham, John, 15 April 1787, Prissilla Fleming   1 SO-204
Cottingham, Thomas, 23 June 1796, Rhoda Townsend     1 WO
Cottman, Lazarus, 7 Jan. 1797, Betsey Bishop         1 WO
     3 SO gives the date as 11 Jan. 1797.
Cotty, Edward, 12 May 1781, Mary Yoakley             3 HA-4
Couch, Chas., 1791, Franc. Bowlen                   50 BA-391
Couenhoun, William, 29 Aug. 1785, by Rev. Turner; Eleanor
     Pindell                                        51 BA-29
Coughran, Jno., 25 May 1786, Mary Dunnavin          11 BA-9
Couhns, Jacob, 15 July 1800, Polly Salway            3 BA-388
Coulbourn, William, 2 March 1799, Betsy Coulbourn    2 SO
Couling, James, 5 April 1778, Elizabeth Sollers     11 BA-1
Coulter, Alexander, 29 March 1792, Hetty McCaskey    5 BA-4
Coulter, Alex'r, 26 Jan. 1797, Jane McCoone         29 BA-8
Coulter, Alexander, 1 Nov. 1799, Rebecca Jennings    4 FR
Coulter, John, 3 Feb. 1788, Mary McCaskey            5 BA-4
Coulter, John, 3 Nov. 1796, Margaret McIlroy         5 BA-4
Coulter, John, c.1798, by Rev. Riggin; Elizabeth McCubbin
     4 AA
Council, Henry, 15 July 1793, Sarah Tubman           2 DO
Councilman, George, 12 June 1798, Sarah Fitch        6 BA
Councilman, John, 6 Aug. 1778, Mary Turnpaugh        5 BA-3
Counsellor, Conrad, 27 April 1799, Eliz. Bryand     29 BA-10
Countz, Henry, 4 Aug. 1778, Ann Bowman               2 MO-1
Courtenay, Henry, 10 Jan. 1799, Isabella Purviance   5 BA-4
Courtenay, James, 18 Nov. 1794, Mary Mitcheson       5 BA-4
Courtenay, Rob't, 30 Sept. 1790, Eliza Burland      11 BA-13
Courtney, Hollis, 18 March 1791, Eleanor Everest     3 HA-21
Cousins, George, 11 Sept. 1794, Elizabeth White      7 BA-1
     3 HA-23 gives the date as 10 Sept. 1794.
Cousins, John, 5 Feb. 1799, Elizabeth Jackson        3 HA-28
Covel, Jonathan, 1790, by Rev. Forrest; Ann Forrest  4 AA
Coventon, Levin, 18 May 1795, Mary Green             3 BA-305
Cover, Jacob, 31 May 1785, Elizabeth Rudecill        4 FR
Covington, (?), 19 Dec. 1797, Ann Winwright          2 SO-11
Covington, Jesse, 26 April 1796, Nancy Gates         3 SO
Covington, Philip, 26 Feb. 1778, Prissey Nicholson   1 WI-121
Covington, Wm., 6 June 1799, Sally Tingle            1 WO
Cowall, Thomas, 12 Nov. 1786, Elizabeth Davidson     3 BA-227
```

Cowan, Alexander, 29 June 1795, Rhoda Hubbert   3 BA-305
Cowan, Benjamin, 6 Feb. 1783, Martha Knight   3 HA-7
Cowan, .Thomas, 19 Feb. 1785, Mary Richardson   3 HA-10
Cowan, William, 17 Nov. 1787, Catherine Stewart   3 BA-203
Coward, Slaytor, 7 Dec. 1795, Betsy Pritchett   2 DO
Cowarden, James, 20 April 1798, Ann Grant   4 KE-66
Coware, Lewis, 2 Jan. 1783, Milly Banks; free negroes 11 BA-6
Cowen, Alexander, 23 May 1799, Mary Elizabeth   6 BA
Cowen, Leonard, 15 May 1791, Mary Fowler   1 BA-3
Cowley, John, 16 Jan. 1800, Sarah Young   7 MO-29
Cowman, Joseph, son of Jno. and Sarah; 23rd day, 2 mo.,
    1786, Mary Snowden, dau. of Sam'l and Elizabeth   6 SF
Cowman, Thomas, 15 Nov. 1798, Henrietta Harwood   1 AA-163
Cox, Abraham, 8 Dec. 1778, by Rev. Mitchell; Elizabeth Clark
    1 WA-
Cox, Charles, 7 Dec. 1794, Ann King   3 PG-440
Cox, Charles, 28 May 1797, Ann McZinny   1 TA-314
Cox, Daniel, 11 Feb. 1782, Sarah Noel   2 DO
Cox, Elisha, 14 Aug. 1787, Milly Frasier   4 FR
Cox, George, 29 May 1797, Biddy Lewis   3 BA-345
    See also 29 BA-8.
Cox, Isaac, son of Isaac, 2nd day, 8 mo., 1786, Lydia Parratt,
    dau. of Aaron   4 SF-180
Cox, James, 8 Dec. 1796, Catherine Fulford   3 BA-333
Cox, John, 2 Sept. 1778, Margaret Howard   2 CH-234
Cox, John, 2 Sept. 1782, Ann Shermentine   3 SM-60
Cox, Jno. M., 18 Dec. 1798, Eleanor Gray   5 MO-115
Cox, Jonathan, 4 April 1792, Susanna Bailie   1 AL-52
Cox, Joseph, 26 June 1798, Elizabeth Shields   3 HA-27
    See also 12 BA-370.
Cox, Josias, 26 March 1799, Polly Milbourn   2 SO
Cox, Matthew, (24 Sept. 1789), Rebecca McMackin   20 BA-1
Cox, Robert, 15 Sept. 1791, Jennet Johnston   6 BA
Cox, Sam'l, 10 Nov. 1785, Elizabeth Hopkins   5 BA-3
Cox, William, 12 Feb. 1782, Selina Lindsey   2 CH-234
Cox, William, 20 Sept. 1783, Catherine Lintz   4 FR
Cox, William, 23 Nov. 1791, Dorcas Edwards   18 BA-3
    See also 3 BA-254.
Cox, William, 26 May 1796, Charlotte Taylor   3 PG-442
Cox, William, 22 Feb. 1798, Rebecca Tipton   45 BA-2
Cox, Wm., 23 Dec. 1798, Liley Kelly   5 MO-115
Cox, William, 15 Oct. 1799, Mary Chambers   3 BA-379
Cox, Young, 29 April 1781, Anna Margaret Freeland   3 AA-417
Coxe, James, 7 Sept. 1780, Sophia Kennedy   5 BA-3
Coy, John, 28 March 1793, Martha Gallion   3 HA-22
Cozens, John, 7 Feb. 1799, Elizabeth Jackson   2 HA-351
Crabb, Ralph, 3 May 1787, Mary Thomas   4 FR
Crabb, Thomas, 4 Jan. 1795, Mary Adlum   4 FR
Craber, Bostian, 4 July 1795, Allear Hutchison   4 FR
Crabs, Jeremiah, 4 Oct. 1798, Mary Crabs   4 FR
Crabster, John, 19 Nov. 1783, Susanna Little   4 FR
Crabston, John, 9 June 1796, Sarah Culver   7 BA-3
Cracroft, Luke, 23 Dec. 1797, Alice Hall   3 BA-353
Cradal, Anton, 1 March 1789, Anna Maria Magener   10 BA-192
Crafford, Jas. B., 14 March 1799, Ann Allison   5 MO-115
Craford, Alexander, 14 Jan. 1796, Sara Ryan   3 BA-317
Craft, Jacob, 17 March 1798, Averilla Taylor   29 BA-9
Craft, Jonathan, 26 Dec. 1780, Lillia Palmer   2 DO
Craft, Nathan, 15 Feb. 1791, Leah Saunders   2 DO
Craft, Thomas, 22 March 1798, Betsy Messeck   2 DO
Craft, William, 6 Dec. 1799, Ann Bestpitch   2 DO
Crage, John, 18 June 1792, Elizabeth Ennalls   2 DO
Craig, Colin, 24 April 1794, Sarah Hill   3 BA-285
Craig, Thomas, 12 May 1800, Mary Woolford   2 DO
Craig, William, 2 June 1800, Alice Saunders   2 DO

```
Cross, Jacob, Sept. 1790, Rachel Murphy               4 AA
Cross, John, 16 Jan. 1798, Mary Williams             45 BA-2
Cross, Lewis, 18 June 1796, Mary Buckias              4 FR
Cross, Nicodemus, 9 Jan. 1794, Barbara Gladman        6 BA
Cross, Robert, 12 June 1794, Charlotte Lewis          3 BA-287
Cross, Robert, 3 March 1795, Catherine Hildebrand     5 BA-4
Cross, Thomas, 22 Oct. 1780, Elizabeth Virmilion      2 PG-3
Crossby, James, 5 Sept. 1785, Deborah Runnel          2 FR-1117
Crossmug, John, 6 May 1793, Elizabeth Riley           4 FR
Croswell, Hanse, 17 Nov. 1798, Mary Montgomery        2 SO
Crouch, James, 28 Aug. 1798, Catherine Jones          4 KE-66
Crouch, Thomas, 27 Dec. 1790, Elizabeth McGowan       1 BA-3
Crouder, Laty, 27 Aug. 1778, Lovess Woolf            11 BA-1
Crouse, John, 20 May 1780, Catherine Umsatt           4 FR
Croutz, Joseph, 13 Dec. 1799, Mary Jeffries           6 BA
Crow, James, 11 June 1789, Rachel Tevis               6 BA
Crow, Peter, 21 March 1799, Sophie Trimble            2 AL-701
Crow, William, 28 Feb. 1785, Sarah McCoy             11 BA-8
Crow, William, 19 Sept. 1793, Mary Humberson          2 AL-700
Crowder, Joseph, 5 Aug. 1798, Judith Classey          3 BA-361
Crowell, John, 15 Sept. 1792, Susan Dagar             4 FR
Crowl, Michael, 7 April 1780, Mary Hosplehawn         4 FR
Crown, Conrad, 2 Aug. 1796, Catherine Shroyer         4 FR
Croxall, James, 11 March 1788, Eleanor Gittings       3 BA-217
Croxall, John, 26 Nov. 1791, Isabella Hanna          28 BA-1
Crum, Abraham, 6 March 1797, Susanna Ringer           4 FR
Crum, Ephraim, 11 Jan. 1796, Hannah Creager           4 FR
Crum, Evan, 19 Aug. 1795, Sarah Hertzog               2 FR-1117
Crum, Isaac, 28 Nov. 1791, Susanna Plummer            4 FR
Crum, John, 5 March 1785, Mary Crum                   4 FR
Crum, John, 5 Feb. 1793, Rebecca Crum                 2 FR-1117
Crum, Wm., 7 Dec. 1792, Amelia Wise                   4 FR
Crum, William, 29 Dec. 1793, Elizabeth Levy           2 FR-1117
   "at the poor house."
Crumston, Joshua, 19 Nov. 1798, Eve Grable            4 FR
Crumwell, Wm., 22 Jan. 1799, Sarah Groff              2 FR-1117
Crus, Christopher, 28 July 1799, Margaret Bedlenburg  9 BA-143
Crusey, Robert, 25 June 1781, Jane Wells              4 FR
Cryer, John, 30 April 1784, Elizabeth Lee             2 DO
Cufford?, John, 3 Nov. 1782, Mary Sangsture           3 HA-7
Culbertson, Samuel, 19 Aug. 1782, Eleanor McKean      4 FR
Culbertson, William, 19 April 1778, Harriet Robinson 11 BA-1
Cullee, Jesse, 20 July 1800, Rachael Ricketts         3 BA-388
Cullember, Nathaniel, 8 Nov. 1778, Cassandra Bourn    1 CA-2
Cullen, Jacob, 15 Nov. 1797, Grace Riggin             2 SO
Cullen, William, 16 Jan. 1798, Hetty Maddux           2 SO
Cullen, William, 1 Oct. 1799, Ibby Douglas            2 SO
Culler, Jacob, 23 Dec. 1795, Mary Storm               4 FR
Cullidan, George, 7 Feb. 1797, Cath. File            29 BA-8
Cullin, Travers, 16 May 1797, Eleanor Hall           29 BA-8
Cullison, Jesse Stansbury, 31 Aug. 1784, Sus'a Picket 11 BA-7
Culliston, Jeremiah, 23 Sept. 1780, Margaret Chisholm 4 FR
Culliun, John, 30 Aug. 1792, Mary Shehawn             2 DO
Cullom, William, 12 Oct. 1790, Elizabeth Northcraft   4 FR
Culp, Henry, 6 Nov. 1790, Catherine Adlum             4 FR
Culp, Michael, 13 April 1790, Maria Sophia Grosh      4 FR
Culver, Henry, 9 Jan. 1798, Mary Patterson            5 MO-114
Culver, Levi, 1 June 1797, Elizabeth Stallings        2 HA-349
Cumberledge, Geo., 31 March 1789, Rachel Barber       2 FR-1117
Cummiger, William, 15 July 1796, Martha Clarke        3 HA-25
Cummin, Mark, 7 Aug. 1800, Mary McDole                2 HA-352
Cumming, Herman, 7 Sept. 1779, by Rev. Mitchell; Mary James
   1 WA
Cumming, James, 25 Aug. 1778, Casiah Coale            4 FR
Cummins, Andrew, 18 Nov. 1789, Nancy Phillips         2 DO
```

```
Cummins, John, 6 Sept. 1791, Margaret Lee              2 DO
Cummins, Joseph, 10 Jan. 1792, Henry (sic) Lee         2 DO
Cunningham, Andrew, 11 Oct. 1798, Elizabeth Black      6 BA
Cunningham, Daniel, 16 Oct. 1797, Ann Amoss            3 HA-26
  1 BA-8 gives the date as 19 Oct. 1797.
Cunningham, George, 30 Sept. 1800, Ann Gilbert         3 HA-30
Cunningham, Henry, 25 May 1796, Frances Sprucebanks    3 HA-25
  7 BA-3 gives the date as 26 May 1796.
Cunningham, John, 30 Jan. 1787, Margaret Mather        5 BA-4
Cunningham, Jno., 27 Jan. 1793, Mary Emery            50 BA-393
Cunningham, John, 10 Dec. 1794, Catherine Leary        3 BA-296
Cunningham, John, 25 Dec. 1795, Mary Puely             3 BA-313
Cunningham, Jno., 11 March 1798, Rachel Britt         50 BA-403
Cunningham, Michael, 26 Dec. 1782, Leah Rowles        11 BA-6
Cunningham, Peter, 10 Dec. 1780, Elizabeth Bird        4 FR
Cunnyngham, Robert, 23 May 1783, Elizabeth Adams       3 BA-190
Curran, William, 16 July 1792, Elizabeth Buckingham    3 BA-256
Curry, Charles, 18 Jan. 1793, Provey Flood             4 FR
Curry, George, 19 Oct. 1781, Eleanor Sturgeon          3 HA-5
Curry, James, 4 Dec. 1781, Kezia Kidd                  3 HA-5
Curry, James, 4 Jan. 1800, Nancy Thompson              2 HA-351
Curry, Jno., 12 Aug. 1786, Mary Sneak                 11 BA-9
Curry, Robert, 22 April 1797, Jane Bird                4 KE-66
Curry, William, 3 Aug. 1781, Ann Smith                 3 HA-4
Curry, William, 9 Nov. 1800, Sarah Dean                2 FR-1117
Curson, Richard, Jr., 13 March 1794, Elizabeth Moale   3 BA-285
Curtain, Jas., 5 July 1798, Ann Hay                   29 BA-9
Curtin, Dennis, 11 March 1787, Ann Freeman             3 PG-252
Curtin, Thomas, 23 Feb. 1797, Jane Graves              6 BA
Curtis, Benjamin, 1 July 1790, Deborah Perrigo         6 BA
Curtis, Edmund, 27 Feb. 1796, Elizabeth Kirby          3 BA-317
Curtis, Eleazer, 8 Sept. 1788, Bridget Harnes          3 BA-218
Curtis, Henry, 31 Aug. 1778, Hannah Fulston            4 FR
Curtis, Jacob, 13 Feb. 1800, Elizabeth Deagan          5 BA-4
Curtis, Jno., 5 Jan. 1784, Peggy Edwills              11 BA-7
  See also 3 BA-228.
Curtis, John W., 12 Oct. 1797, Peggy Hayward           2 SO-11
Curtis (or Cordray), Thomas, 30 Nov. 1797, Peggy Bloodsworth
  2 SO-11; see also 3 SO.
Curts, Nicholas, 31 March 1798, Margaret Burkhart      4 FR
Cushion, Robert, 25 June 1789, Susa Shipley           11 BA-12
Cushion, Thomas, 30 May 1795, Catharine Smith          3 BA-305
Cutler, Edward, 12 April 1779, Mary Asbill             4 FR
Cutshall, George, 3 April 1784, Hannah Hammond         4 FR


Dabler, William, 25 Dec. 1800, Elizab. Jones           2 FR-1123
Dads, Emanuel, 1 Jan. 1799, Mary Pierce                4 AA
  The ceremony was performed by Rev. Ridgely.
Daer, Jacob, 15 April 1798, Maria Scherer             10 BA-198
Daffin, Robert, 16 Jan. 1781, Eliza Simmonds           3 SM-59
Daft, John, Nov. 1779, Anna Spalden                    1 SM-137
Daignan, Michael, 1 Jan. 1789, Elizabeth Durney        2 DO
Dail, James, 20 Dec. 1786, Leah Jones                  2 DO
Dail, Moses, 9 Sept. 1795, Mary Jones                  2 DO
Dail, William, 29 Sept. 1785, Anne Barnes              2 DO
Daily, Michael, 12 Aug. 1797, Mary Barnes              4 KE-67
Daiskit, Samuel, 21 Jan. 1794, Mary Skinner            3 PG-439
Dakly, John Scroggan, 15 June 1778, Mary Ann Mahoney   2 CH-234
Dale, Jacob, 29 March 1800, Charlotte Truitt           1 WO
Dale, John Peter, 17 Dec. 1793, Catherine Lemon        4 FR
Dale, William, 26 Feb. 1800, Sarah Godfrey             1 WO
Daley, Daniel, 27 Dec. 1798, Elizabeth Killen          3 BA-366
Daley, John, 31 Jan. 1798, Ally Keefe                  3 BA-354
Daliquet, John Bapt., 22 Sept. 1795, Eliz'th McSherry 44 BA-1
```

```
Dall, James, 21 Jan. 1790, Charlotte Lane           11 BA-13
Dall, James, 20 Nov. 1794, Sarah Brooke Holliday     1 BA-6
Dallam, Francis, 22 April 1781, Martha Smith         3 HA-4
Dallam, John, 13 May 1781, Mary Willson              3 HA-4
Dallam, Josiah William, 24 Jan. 1800, Henrietta Mary Jones
    8 BA-1
Dallam, Richard, 30 Dec. 1792, Margaret Carlile      3 HA-22
Dallam, Richard, 28 March 1799, Priscilla Paca       2 HA-351
    3 HA-28 gives the date as 25 March 1799.
Dallas, Walter R., 14 March 1786, Catherine Crook    6 BA
Dally, Ebenezer, 30 May 1794, Mary Philips           2 FR-1122
Dalrymple, John, 31 Oct. 1782, Martha Marr           3 AA-419
Dalrymple, John, 25 March 1787, Mary Waters         11 BA-10
Dament, Daniel, 4 March 1799, Hannah Deckensheets    4 FR
Dancer, William, 16 Sept. 1798, Susannah Brien       6 BA
Dancy, John, 27 Nov. 1786, Rebecca Hardy             3 PG-251
Danecobe, Jac. Bernard, 21 March 1797, Sally Evans   6 BA
Danecker, Carl, 26 Dec. 1796, Elizab. Keppenhuster  50 BA-400
Daniel, Elias M., 20 Nov. 1800, Margaret Goldin      5 MO-116
Danield, James, 25 July 1799, Dorcas McChoow         8 BA-1
Daniels, Anthony, 17 March 1793, Anna Maria Murray   5 BA-5
Danielson, Moses, 25 May 1800, by Rev. Ridgely; Sarah Penn
    4 AA
Danielson, Thomas, 15 Oct. 1799, by Rev. Ridgely; Elizabeth
    Chaney                                           4 AA
Dannenberg, Frederick William, 16 April 1795, Dorothea
    Koenig                                          40 BA-1
Danner, Jacob, 21 Dec. 1784, Christina Brand        10 BA-184
Danner, Zacharias, 8 Oct. 1799, Marg. Zayer          2 FR-1123
Dannilly, Michael, 27 Jan. 1783, Cath'e Sadler      11 BA-6
Darbey, Caleb, 24 May 1792, Sarah Gartrill           4 FR
Darby, Jno., 19 Jan. 1799, Harriet Milbourne         7 BA-4
Dare, Nathaniel, 22 Jan. 1778, Jean Gray             1 CA-1
Darley, Michael, 17 Sept. 1788, Caroline Miller      3 BA-218
    See also 3 BA-229.
Darling, John, 16 Aug. 1800, Ann Dunlavey            6 BA
Darnall, Gerard, 1 Feb. 1781, Sarah Hurley           2 PG-5
Darnell, Henry, 3 Sept. 1788, Mary Leek              4 FR
Darnell, Philip, 3 Nov. 1788, Lucy Perrill           4 FR
Darr, John, 28 Nov. 1795, Catherine Stoner           4 FR
Dasheel, Benjamin, 25 Dec. 1777, Ann Yoe             1 CA-5
Dashiel, Col. George, 5 Oct. 1799, Sally Dennis Lane 1 WO
Dashiell, Arthur, Sr., 13 Nov. 1798, Betsy Phillips  2 SO
Dashiell, Benjamin, 24 March 1798, Elizabeth Robertson 2 SO
Dashiell, Daniel, 4 Sept. 1796, Polly Dashiell       3 BA-329
Dashiell, George, 1 Sept. 1798, Sarah Wilson         2 SO
    3 SO gives the date as 26 Sept. 1798.
Dashiell, George, 18 Feb. 1796, Molly Jones          3 SO
Dashiell, Henry, 23 Feb. 1797, Jane Cottingham       3 SO
    2 SO gives the date as 21 Feb. 1797.
Dashiell, Henry, 24 Jan. 1799, Mary Leeke            3 BA-367
Dashiell, Ichabod, 25 Nov. 1800, Priscilla Dashiell  2 SO
Dashiell, John, 5 April 1796, Polly Handy            3 SO
Dashiell, Joseph, Jr., 25 Aug. 1779, Jeane Evans     1 WI-111
Dashiell, Mitchell, of Mitchell, 29 Feb. 1779, Mary Hust
    1 WI-115
Dashiell, Robert, 14 June 1789, Rebecca Stewart, dau. of
    William                                          1 WI-133
Dashiell, Thomas, Jr., 22 Jan. 1798, Elizabeth Wailes 2 SO
Dashiell, Thomas, 28 Oct. 1800, Anne Porter          2 SO
Dashings, Joseph, 14 July 1795, Eliza Mannings       4 BA-77
Daster, Jno. B., 8 Sept. 1798, Cath. Burgoyne       29 BA-9
Daub, Jacob, 4 March 1794, Eliz. Merckle             2 FR-1122
Daughaday, Abraham, 1 Aug. 1794, Susannah Wheeler    6 BA
Daughaday, John, 21 Sept. 1794, Mary Hales           6 BA
```

Daughaday, John, 22 Oct. 1795, Rachel Leakins   6 BA
Daughaday, Johnsey, 6 Dec. 1798, Susannah Owings   6 BA
Daughaday, Joseph, 12 June 1790, Sarah Taylor   6 BA
Daugherty, Dickason, 1 Sept. 1785, Esther Lord   1 SO-207
Daugherty, George, 5 Nov. 1795, Catherine Gerhart 4 FR
Daugherty, John, 1 April 1800, Ann Chauncey   3 HA-29
Daugherty, Samuel, 17 Jan. 1782, Hannah Ealey   3 HA-5
Daugherty, William, (27 April 1790), Ruth Towson 15 BA-3
Daughy, Patrick, 5 Nov. 1800, Eliz. Dixon?   29 BA-12
Davage, Henry, 4 Nov. 1794, Sarah Crow   4 FR
Davenport, Jonathan, son of Joseph and Elizabeth, 4th day,
  3 mo., 1790, Margaret Dukehart, dau. of Valerius and
  Margaret   1 SF
Davenport, Nicholas, 8 Sept. 1791, Rachell Demmitt 6 BA
Davenport, Sims, 8 Feb. 1781, Eliza Harris   3 AA-417
Davey, John, 28 June 1796, Ruth Dorsey   4 FR
David, John, 15 July 1780, Sarah Finley   3 HA-2
Davidson, Andrew, 18 July 1779, Anne Stokes   5 BA-4
Davidson, Andrew, 19 Nov. 1795, Mary Somerville 5 BA-5
Davidson, David, 17 Nov. 1796, Dorcus Harris   4 FR
Davidson, James, before 12 Dec. 1792, by Rev. John Long;
  Mary Stewart   4 AA
Davidson, Jas. or Jos., 16 Oct. 1799, Eliz. Betson 29 BA-10
Davidson, Job, 17 May 1778, Elizabeth Miller   11 BA-1
Davidson, John, 11 Jan. 1788, by Rev. Reed; Ann McCauley
  4 AA
Davidson, Jno., 29 Sept. 1798, Lydia Lowman   29 BA-9
Davidson, Luke, 7 April 1788, Barthula Turnbull 2 DO
Davidson, Robert, 20 May 1795, Mary Dance   5 BA-5
Davidson, Samuel, 25 Nov. 1787, Jane Dunbar   6 BA
Davidson, William, 29 May 1798, Hidey Cornelius 5 BA-5
Davies, Joseph, 31 Oct. 1780, Sarah Miller   1 CA-3
Davies, Josiah, 21 Dec. 1780, Margaret Hallock   5 BA-5
Davis, Abijah, 4 Jan. 1796, Catherine Pointer   1 WO
Davis, Ambrose, 25 Aug. 1785, Elizabeth Grover 3 BA-190
Davis, Ambrose, 20 May 1800, Bewly White   2 FR-1123
Davis, Amos, 22 Oct. 1797, Mary Carson   6 BA
Davis, Aquilla, 15 July 1800, Mary Stainton   2 DO
Davis, Archibald, 15 April 1790, Jane Carback   6 BA
Davis, Barnabas, 23 June 1786, Elizabeth Hobbs   4 FR
Davis, Barney, 28 Aug. 1796, Mary Mitchell   3 BA-327
Davis, Benjamin, son of Benjamin, 1 Oct. 1787, Mary Wood,
  dau. of Peter and Elizabeth   1 CH-207
Davis, Benjamin, 30 Oct. 1792, Catherine Weaver 4 FR
Davis, Benjamin, 3 Jan. 1798, Sarah Matthews   2 SO
Davis, Benj., 24 Feb. 1798, Eliz. Thresher   5 MO-115
Davis, Caleb, 21 Dec. 1800, Nancy Cannon   2 DO
Davis, Charles, 3 Jan. 1799, Laurady Howse   5 MO-115
Davis, Christian, 25 July 1784, Mary Sweeting   11 BA-7
Davis, Daniel, 9 Feb. 1786, Mary Leech   11 BA-9
Davis, Daniel, 16 May 1800, Nelly Bell   2 SO
Davis, Edw'd, 3 May 1785, Cath. Louderman   11 BA-8
Davis, Edward, 27 Dec. 1793, Ann Grunden   3 HA-23
Davis, Elihu, 13 May 1794, Hannah Stansbury   3 BA-287
Davis, Elzey, 27 Feb. 1798, Mary Knight   2 SO
Davis, Ennalls, 18 Dec. 1799, Nancy Willson   2 DO
Davis, Ezekiel, 17 March 1785, Mary Cotteral   11 BA-8
Davis, Francis, 2 May 1790, Sarah Eliot   2 FR-1122
Davis, Francis, free black; 4 Nov. 1796, Milly, slave of
  John Ker   3 BA-333
Davis, Francis William, 9 Nov. 1790, Elizab. Parrish 2 FR-1122
Davis, Frederick, 22 Oct. 1799, Martha Hammond 1 WO
Davis, Gaither, 4 Dec. 1800, Eliz. Birmingham   29 BA-12
Davis, George, 28 Sept. 1781, Ann Grant   3 HA-5
Davis, George, 13 Aug. 1795, Elizabeth Scott   3 HA-24
  See also 2 HA-349/

```
Davis, Gilbert, 13 Jan. 1784, Eliza Ratcliff             11 BA-7
Davis, Handy, 6 July 1797, Rhoda Burbage                  1 WO
Davis, Henry, 5 Oct. 1783, Eliza Robinson                11 BA-6
Davis, Henry, 26 Oct. 1790, Mary Norman Morris            3 PG-257
Davis, Henry, 5 April 1798, Sarah Butler                 45 BA-2
Davis, Henry Ferguson, 22 Jan. 1795, Elizabeth Britt     44 BA-1
Davis, Ichabod, 25 Jan. 1785, Delilah Randal             11 BA-8
Davis, Ignatius, 22 May 1798, Margaret Wootton            5 MO-115
Davis, Jacob, 14 May 1787, Mary McAllister               10 BA-188
Davis, James, 23 July 1779, Elizabeth Brookes             2 PG-2
Davis, James, 25 Sept. 1791, Elizabeth Hudson             6 BA
Davis, James, 21 Feb. 1797, Hannah Jenkins Adkins         1 WO
Davis, James, 17 April 1797, Hannah Birch                 1 WO
Davis, Jarret, 4 April 1795, Elizabeth McDonald           4 FR
Davis, John, 15 July 1780, Rachael Wooden                11 BA-4
Davis, Jno., 20 Jan. 1782, Mary Brown                    11 BA-5
Davis, John, 4 May 1782, Mary Potter                      4 FR
Davis, John, 10 Dec. 1782, Mary Bosly                    11 BA-6
Davis, Jno., 4 or 14 Dec. 1784, Sarah Vaughan            11 BA-8
Davis, John, 19 Dec. 1787, Elizabeth Widmeyer             4 FR
David, John, (20 Feb. 1789), Elinor Dorsey               15 BA-2
Davis, John, 22 Feb. 1790, Sarah Dixon                    2 DO
Davis, John, 25 July 1790, Sophia Brown                   6 BA
Davis, John, 18 June 1795, Mary Burdan                   44 BA-1
Davis, John, 21 Feb. 1797, Sarah Vansant                  4 KE-67
Davis, John, 26 Dec. 1798, Eleanor Beatty                 6 BA
Davis, John, 6 Nov. 1799, Mary Jones                      2 SO
Davis, Jonathan, 7 Dec. 1799, Mary Smith                  4 FR
Davis, Joseph, 6 Aug. 1779, Ann How                       4 FR
Davis, Joseph, Aug. 1784; by Rev. Higginbothom; Eliza
    Anchors                                              11 BA-7
Davis, Joseph, 30 Aug. 1787, Sarah James                 11 BA-10
Davis, Kidwallader, 25 Dec. 1792, Margaret Porter        18 BA-5
Davis, Levi, 30 July 1792, Eleanor Whitmyer               4 FR
Davis, Ludwick, 15 Sept. 1783, Susanna Yates              4 FR
Davis, Luke, 30 May 1784, Anne Shepherd                  11 BA-7
Davis, Marmaduke, 12 April 1795, by Rev. Ridgely; Drusilla
    Forrest                                               4 AA
Davis, Martin A., 5 Aug. 1798, Nancy Baily                1 WO
Davis, Matthias, 21 Dec. 1788, Rachel Maynard             2 FR-1122
Davis, Matthias, 21 June 1797, Betsey Handy               1 WO
Davis, Mordecai, 16 Feb. 1782, Elizabeth Geddard          3 HA-6
Davis, Moses, 18 May 1779, Anne Evans                     3 SM-57
Davis, Moses, 21 July 1782, Cathrine Dunn                 5 BA-5
Davis, Nath'l, 16 Feb. 1785, by Rev. West; Marg't Hutson
    51 BA-29
Davis, Nehemiah, 1 May 1795, Abigail Howard               1 WO
Davis, Noah, 15 May 1797, Elizabeth Adams                 2 SO
Davis, Peter, 13 Dec. 1779, Ann King                     11 BA-4
Davis, Reuben, 13 Nov. 1796, Ellen Taylor                 2 FR-1122
Davis, Rezin, 15 March 1782, Nancy Phillips               4 FR
Davis, Richard, 10 Feb. 1782, Margaret Lansdale           2 PG-3
Davis, Robert, 9 July 1778, Ann Collins                   1 AA-156
Davis, Robert, 1 April 1782, Susanna Ratcliff            11 BA-5
Davis, Samuel, 21 April 1778, Rebecca Bucey               2 MO-1
Davis, Samuel, 8 Oct. 1795, Deborah Renshaw               6 BA
Davis, Samuel, 2 Oct. 1799, Polly Baker                   8 BA-1
Davis, Samuel, 26 Aug. 1800, Ann Davis                    1 AA-162
Davis, Samuel, 2 Sept. 1800, Rachel Walls                 2 FR-1123
Davis, Solomon, 23 July 1798, Sarah Denwood Smith         2 DO
Davis, Solomon, 20 Aug. 1799, Mary Simkins                2 AL-701
Davis, Thomas, 8 Dec. 1782, Marg't Tippett               11 BA-6
Davis, Thos., 2 Aug. 1795, Marg. Young                   29 BA-6
Davis, Thomas, 21 April 1796, Catherine Worthington       5 MO-113
Davis, Thomas, 8 June 1800, Rebecca Beard                 1 AA-161
```

```
Davis, Tilghman, 16 Oct. 1799, Polley Willson           2 DO
Davis, Turner, 21 Dec. 1796, Mary Bowen                 1 WO
Davis, Warrington, 28 Aug. 1798, Polly Smack            1 WO
Davis, Will'm, 13 Jan. 1784, Marg't Burkhead           11 BA-7
Davis, William, 11 Dec. 1794, Mary McMahon              5 BA-5
Davis, William, 30 June 1796, Ruth Owings               5 BA-5
Davis, William, 16 Feb. 1797, Elizabeth Butter         45 BA-1
Davis, William, 4 Sept. 1798, Mary Parker               1 WO
Davis, William Luckett, 15 Feb. 1785, Elizabeth Hungerford
    4 FR
Davis, William S., 11 May 1795, Sarah Stubbs            3 BA-305
Davis, William Worthington, 21 July 1790, Margaret Muse 2 DO
Davis, Zachariah, 5 Jan. 1778, Sarah Wright             2 CH-234
Davis, Zachariah, 11 Nov. 1794, Elizabeth Hyatt         4 FR
Daw, Joseph, 25 March 1786, Sarah Carr                 11 BA-9
Dawes, Mordecai, 15 Feb. 1781, Elizabeth Goddard        2 CH-234
Dawley, John, 21 May 1796, Nancy Abbott                 2 DO
Dawney, Henry, 10 Sept. 1799, Martha Hill               3 HA-28
    12 BA-370 gives the date as 12 Sept. 1799.
Daws, Benjamin, 6 April 1784, Rachel Magniss            3 HA-8
Daws, Edward, 29 Dec. 1793, Ann Grunden                 1 BA-6
Dawson, Benjamin, 21 March 1783, Mary Simmons           4 FR
Dawson, Elisha, 5th day, 11 mo., 1785, Lydia Harris     2 SF-288
    "both of Caroline Co."
Dawson, Jacob, 20 May 1780, Sarah North                11 BA-4
Dawson, James, 6 Feb. 1796, Elizabeth Middle            3 HA-25
Dawson, James, 25 April 1798, by Rev. Wyatt; Elizabeth Norris
    4 AA
Dawson, John, 5th day, 1 mo., 1778, Anne Harriss        2 SF-288
Dawson, John, 24 Dec. 1784, Elizabeth McFarlin          2 DO
Dawson, John, 12 April 1788, Mary Hagan                 4 FR
Dawson, Jno., 6 Aug. 1795, Frances Caulk               29 BA-6
Dawson, John, 2 Feb. 1799, Susanna Harbord              3 BA-367
Dawson, John, 10 Dec. 1800, Nancy Cox                   3 BA-396
Dawson, Joseph, 3 Jan. 1781, Sarah Dawson               2 DO
Dawson, Lenard, 15 Aug. 1797, Mary Wolf                 2 AL-700
Dawson, Nicholas, 27 Aug. 1781, Elizabeth Bayne         4 FR
Dawson, Obadiah, 4 July 1782, Polly Watts               2 DO
Dawson, Philemon, 22 May 1794, Jane Henderson           3 BA-287
Dawson, Richard, 18 Feb. 1784, Ann Dawson               4 FR
Dawson, Severn, 26 Feb. 1798, Kitturah Jones            2 DO
Dawson, William, 22 April 1789, Ann Gilbert             4 FR
Dawson, William, 13 April 1790, Susanna Hurst           2 DO
Dawson, William, 19 March 1795, Ann Robertson           6 BA
Day, Edward, 11 Nov. 1787, Mary Presbury               11 BA-10
Day, Edward, 15 Jan. 1793, Sarah How                    3 PG-438
Day, Edward, 2 May 1799, by Rev. Wyatt; Sarah Lewis     4 AA
Day, James, 27 May 1778, Elizabeth Jonston             11 BA-1
Day, John, 24 Jan. 1784, Mary Ann Wetherell             3 HA-8
Day, John, 29 Feb. 1788, Sarah Allender                 2 BA-11
Day, Joshua, 29 Oct. 1784, Sarah Hanson                 3 HA-10
Day, Luke, 6 Oct. 1789, Mary How                        3 PG-255
Day, Thomas, 27 Aug. 1778, Hannah Dean                 11 BA-1
Day, Thomas, 8 Aug. 1800, Sarah Baker                   3 BA-389
Dayhuff, Henry, 26 Oct. 1788, Sarah Parkinson           6 BA
Days, Henry, 1 Oct. 1796, Ruth Tall                     4 FR
Deacons, Ambrose, 26 Jan. 1780, Ann Chatham             2 CH-234
Deaden, Jacob, 27 July 1800, Eleanor Bone               3 BA-388
Deakin, Michael, 20 Oct. 1779, Rebecca Cooke            2 PG-3
Deakins, James, 8 June 1797, Margaret James             3 AL-4
Deakins, John, 20 June 1797, Mary James                 2 AL-700
Deakins, Stephen, 2 May 1796, Elizabeth Freland         1 AL-53
Deal, John, 2 Feb. 1790, Catherine Burckhardt           4 FR
Deal, Michael, 26 May 1794, Nancy Agnew                 3 BA-287
Deal, Nathaniel, 10 July 1794, Rachel Crosby            3 AA-424
```

```
Deal, Peter, 18 Dec. 1790, Mary Eliot                        4 FR
Deale, Henry, 23 Feb. 1783, Margaret Disney                  3 AA-419
Deale, Henry, 18 Nov. 1794, Mary Eckard                      4 FR
Deale, Richard, 3 May 1781, Febe Lattin                      3 AA-417
Deame, Robert, 7 Nov. 1778, Eliz'th Reynolds                 4 FR
Dean, Barnabas, 15 Dec. 1798, Elizabeth Frishour             4 FR
Dean, Barney, 21 Nov. 1790, Catherine Ratliffe              11 BA-13
Dean, David, 7 April 1795, Nancy Griffith                    2 DO
Dean, George, 18 Nov. 1781, Elizabeth Wheatley               2 DO
Dean, Henry, 21 Sept. 1786, Polly Keene                      2 DO
Dean, Henry, 20 Aug. 1791, Sarah Melvill                     2 DO
     28 BA-1 gives the date as 21 Aug. 1791, and the bride's
     name as Milvin.
Dean, Henry, 18 Dec. 1798, Rebecca Stokes                    2 DO
Dean, John, 22 Aug. 1787, Maria Bihmer                       6 FR-201
Dean, John, 8 Jan. 1791, Mary Ann Abbott                     2 DO
Dean, Joshua, 18 Sept. 1790, Nanny Jones                    11 BA-13
Dean, Laben, 18 Oct. 1784, Franky Griffith                   2 DO
Dean, Levi, 7 Feb. 1788, Mary Whiteley                       2 DO
Dean, Nathaniel, 12 Feb. 1789, Dolly Dean                    2 DO
Dean, Richard, 9 May 1796, Sarah Bootbe                      2 DO
Dean, Robert, 10 Dec. 1791, Margret Young                    3 BA-254
Dean, Thomas, 8 June 1794, by Rev. Ridgely; Peggy Armond
     4 AA
Deane, Hezekiah, 17 March 1778, Rebecca Lowndes              5 BA-4
Dear, John, 13 Aug. 1785, Hannah Mann                        6 BA
Death, Jacob, 8 Jan. 1799, Elizabeth Miller                  3 BA-367
Deaver, Abraham, 25 June 1778, Ann Lakin                     4 FR
Deaver, Francis, 21 Dec. 1786, Betty Wilson                  6 BA
Deaver, Francis, 3 Jan. 1790, Nancy Stansbury                6 BA
Deaver, Hugh, 12 April 1782, Margaret Smith                  3 HA-7
Deaver, Hugh, 18 Feb. 1798, Darby Holbrook                   5 BA-5
Deaver, John, 3 Aug. 1789, by Rev. Hagerty; Honner Wroth
     4 AA
Deaver, Micajah, 3 April 1792, Dianna Ellis                  3 HA-21
Deaver, Misel, 26 Dec. 1799, Sarah Frazier                   4 FR
Deaver, Richard, 7 Oct. 1790, Deborah Pierce                 6 BA
Deaver, William, 27 July 1784, Rachel Chinea                 3 BA-188
Deaver, William, 3 Jan. 1785, Elizabeth Standley             3 HA-10
Deavor, Mr., 9 Nov. 1780, Rebecca Shipley                   11 BA-4
Deavour, John, 12 May 1781, Mary Fowler                      3 HA-4
Deberry, George, 14 Dec. 1797, Caty Upcraft                  4 FR
De Bonne, Anthony, 18 Nov. 1796, Sally Lang                  2 SO
Debrular, George, 12 July 1791, Arminta Nutterville          1 BA-3
     3 HA-21 gives the date as 11 July 1791.
Debruler, Greenbury, 23 May 1799, Rachel Healy               3 HA-28
     See also 12 BA-370.
De Carnap, Caspar, 27 Dec. 1794, Elizabeth Richardson       10 BA-196
Decker, George, 16 Aug. 1792, Susanna Forney                10 BA-194
Decker, Jacob, 9 May 1788, (?) Tornbach                     29 BA-1
De Corsey, Henry, 26 July 1800, Mary Oliver                  6 BA
Deegan, Patrick, 24 Oct. 1799, Polly McComas                12 BA-370
Deems, Fried'k, 1790, H. Skyles                             50 BA-390
Deeran, John, 18 Sept. 1798, Deborah Dormer                  2 HA-350
Deerdarf, Ab'm, 21 Feb. 1781, Cath. Bowersmith               4 FR
De Forrest, Henry, 21 May 1790, Rachel Conklan              18 BA-2
Degenhardt, Christian, 20 Dec. 1784, An. M. Miller           2 FR-1122
Degeon, Joseph, 21 Sept. 1800, Margaret Gorril               2 HA-352
Degin, (?), 13 Aug. 1793, Sarah McEmmery                    50 BA-393
De Haven, Andrew, 11 Nov. 1792, Esther Kempf                 2 FR-1122
De Haven, Peter, 26 June 1787, Mary Cellars                  2 FR-1122
De Hof, Nicholas, 6 March 1787, Sus. Cath. Vogel             2 FR-1122
Dehoof, Philip, 11 Sept. 1789, Elizabeth Ebbert              4 FR
Deiwelbisz, George, 5 April 1790, Sus. Berg                  2 FR-1122
Delehay, James, 3 Aug. 1781, Statia Sewell                   2 DO
```

Digges, Ignatius, 16 Nov. 1800, Charlotte Murphy   3 BA-395
Digner, Charles, 25 Dec. 1798, Polly Clark   2 SO
  3 SO gives the date as 26 Dec. 1798.
Dikes, George, 1 Oct. 1799, Dolly Evans   1 WO
Dill, Thomas, 3 Jan. 1786, Amelia Carter   2 DO
Dill, Zachariah, 29 April 1792, Mary Ann Crisp   3 KE
Dillehunt, John, 2 Jan. 1796, Harriet Newman   3 BA-317
Dilling, Henry, 25 Nov. 1800, Loie Andrew   2 DO
Dillion, Edward, 29 June 1792, Ann Tasker   3 HA-21
Dillireu?, Samuel, 22 May 1799, Elizabeth Watkins   6 BA
Dilman, Jacob, 1788, Margaretha Widman   50 BA-388
Dilworth, John, 24 Oct. 1795, Priscilla Williams   4 FR
Dilworth, Joseph, 16 Nov. 1784, Ann Allen   11 BA-8
Dilworth, William, 16 Sept. 1788, Kesia Greenfield   1 CA-4
Dimmitt, Burch, 14 Jan. 1797, Catherine Legross   3 BA-341
Dimmitt, Henry, 17 Nov. 1796, Elizabeth Bond   45 BA-1
Dimmitt, William, 1 Sept. 1796, Nancy Trapnall   1 BA-7
Dimond, William, 29 July 1800, Elizabeth Stafford   49 BA-1
Dinam, William, 5 Dec. 1797, Sarah Pinix   3 HA-26
Dines, Jeremiah, 7 June 1784, Ann Ward   2 DO
Dines, Jeremiah, 7 Oct. 1795, Rebecca Harding   2 DO
Dinjes, Philip, 1 Dec. 1793, Susanna Norhen   10 BA-196
Dinning, James, 4 June 1799, Nancy Vaughn   45 BA-3
Dinsmore, Thomas, 19 Jan. 1798, Hannah Dodd   5 BA-5
Dirga, Pearl. See Pearl Durkee.
Disneigh, John, 13 Nov. 1800, Margaret Hunt   3 BA-395
Disney, Edward, 3 Dec. 1795, by Rev. Ridgely; Margaret
  Watkins   4 AA
Disney, James, 22 March 1783, Mary Weems   3 AA-419
Disney, Richard, 7 Nov. 1799, by Rev. Ridgely; Sarah
  Disney   4 AA
Disney, Snowden, 2 Oct. 1793, by Rev. G. Ridgely; Rachel Dever
  4 AA
Disney, Solomon, 5 May 1796, Rachel Fitz   6 BA
Disney, William, 11 March 1794, Ruth Spurrier   4 AA
  The ceremony was performed by Rev. G. Ridgely.
Dittarlaw, Butler, 8 Sept. 1796, Elizabeth Webster   3 PG-442
Ditto, Abraham, 23 May 1796, Ann Amoss   3 HA-25
Ditzenback, Adam, 15 April 1788, Elizabeth Houleman   3 BA-219
Ditzenback, Peter, 15 April 1788, Susa. Mercin   11 BA-11
  See also 3 BA-219.
Divatt, Dennis, 2 Jan. 1796, Mary Martin   6 BA
Diver, Jonathan, 7 Jan. 1784, Eliza McKiney   3 AA-420
Divers, John, 8 May 1788, Belinda Eagleston   6 BA
Dives, William, 28 Aug. 1800, Rachel Jacobs   2 DO
Divine, Thomas, 4 Dec. 1800, Jane Suter   3 BA-396
Divos, William, 16 Dec. 1780, Rebecca Kain   3 HA-3
Dixon, Benja., 29 April 1779, Ann McAdow   5 HA
  3 HA-1 gives the date as 27 April 1780.
Dixon, Jacob, 1781, Mary Lancaster   2 CH-235
Dixon, John, 26 Jan. 1800, Margaret Wright   6 BA
Dixon, John Hattin, 9 May 1798, Mary Tobery   4 FR
Dixon, Ralph, (2 Nov. 1791), Rachel Parks   15 BA-4
Dixon, Robert, son of Isaac, 28th day, 2 mo., 1780, Ann
  Berry, dau. of James   4 SF-160
Dixon, Samuel, 10 Jan. 1792, Eleanor Scott   2 CH-235
Dixon, Thos., 1 Sept. 1782, Eliza Frazier   11 BA-5
Dixon, Thomas, 9 Aug. 1787, Susanna Pollite   1 SO-128
Dixon, William, 24 Sept. 1783, Lidia Winnell   3 AA-420
Dixon, William, 20 Aug. 1789, Mary Roe   1 SO-208
Dixon, William, 17 Feb. 1797, Leah Dikes   1 WO
Dize, John, 2 Dec. 1800, Chloe Evans   2 SO
Dizney, William, 12 Jan. 1789, Elizabeth Parks   6 BA
Doake, James, 15 Sept. 1796, Polly Henry   5 BA-5
Dobbins, Thomas, 19 July 1789, Mary Wild   6 BA

```
Dobson, William, 22 Sept. 1778, Mary Ray            4 FR
Dockarty, Samuel, 23 Jan 1781, Han. Caley           2 CH-235
Dod, James, 15 Jan. 1790, Ann Marthes               3 PG-256
Dod, John, 7 June 1782, Ann Bond                    11 BA-5
Dodd, Abraham, 21 March 1797, Elisabeth Smith        3 BA-343
Dodd, John, 17 July 1783, Ann Hagardine, dau. of William
    and Tamsey                                      1 CR-74
Dodd, John, 6 Oct. 1798, Margaret Dinsmore          3 BA-364
Dodds, John, 6 Nov. 1798, Margaret Dinsmore         35 BA-6
Dodds, Philip, 16 April 1798, Susanna Smith          4 FR
Dodds, Samuel, 26 April 1797, Margaret Manahan       4 FR
Dodge, Daniel, 15 Jan. 1799, Ruth Ragan             6 BA
Dodge, Samuel, 10 Oct. 1793, Ann Stansbury          6 BA
Dodge, William, 12 July 1794, Elizabeth Woodland    2 DO
Dodson, Elijah, 1 Sept. 1789, Mary Karr             2 FR-1122
Dodson, Joseph, 8 Dec. 1787, Mary Hambleton         2 DO
Dodson, Joseph, 23 April 1798, Priscilla Barnett    2 DO
Doe, Joseph, 10 Oct. 1778, Mary Jones               11 BA-1
Doerr, Jacob, 4 Feb. 1787, Marg. Wintz              2 FR-1122
Dofler, Geo., 11 June 1798, Cath. Spanseiler        2 FR-1122
Doherty, Cornelius, 13 Nov. 1796, Mary James        45 BA-1
Doland, John, 29 March 1779, by Rev. Mitchell; Elizabeth
    Jones                                           1 WA
Doll, George, son of Jos., 11 March 1799, Cath. Schmit  2 FR-1122
Doll, John, 28 Jan. 1800, Sus. Kortz                2 FR-1123
Dolle, Henry, 24 April 1796, Cath. Gall             29 BA-7
Dolphin, John, 16 June 1778, Elizabeth Hults        11 BA-1
Dolton, Henry, 4 June 1781, Eleanor Russell         2 PG-5
Donahoo, Daniel, 14 June 1780, Mary Treadaway       3 HA-2
Donahoo, Daniel, 18 Jan. 1785, Sarah Wood           3 HA-10
Donaldson, Elijah, 30 Dec. 1781, Mary Ann Chiney    2 PG-3
Donaldson, Renald, 2 Dec. 1800, Eliz. Sellers       29 BA-12
Donaldson, Richard, (21?) April 1798, by Rev. Wyatt;
    Margaret Rhods                                  4 AA
Donaldson, William, 25 Feb. 1796, Priscilla Chamberland
    3 BA-317
Donally, James, 3 April 1798, Mary McKensie         3 BA-357
Donavin, John, 6 Nov. 1780, Frances Gilbert         3 HA-3
Doncaster, James, 28 Feb. 1779, Keziah Wyatt        2 PG-3
Donn, Moses, 20 Dec. 1796, Mary Messick             2 SO
Donnaldson, Bayly, 11 April 1778, Milly Cockarel    2 MO-1
Donnaway, William, 15 July 1800, Sophia Wilkins     1 WO
Donnell, Patrick, 23 Sept. 1794, Margaret Bryce     1 BA-6
Donnellan, Nehemiah, 19 June 1794, Mary Mull        3 BA-287
Donnigan, John, 1 June 1778, Catherine Herbert      11 BA-1
Donoghy, Francis, 30 Oct. 1800, Elisabeth Donnolly  3 BA-394
Donohoe, Teague, 19 May 1797, Elizabeth Handy       1 WO
Donovan, Ephraim, 28 March 1791, Charlotta Taylor   1 BA-3
Donovan, James, 1 Feb. 1795, Mary Mehan             3 BA-299
Donovan, Thomas, 28 May 1781, Rachel Greenard       3 HA-4
Donovan, Thomas, 4 Aug. 1787, by Rev. Davis; Ann Cole  51 BA-30
Donoven, William, 29 April 1789, Esther Trenter     4 FR
Doolan, John, 30 Dec. 1799, Mary Joanna (?)         3 BA-381
Dooley, Edward, 28 Sept. 1782, Mary Smith           3 HA-7
Dooley, John, 23 July 1782, Catharine Poteet        3 HA-7
Dorchester, Wm., 17 Feb. 1781, Mary Trencer         4 FR
Dorman, Cornelius, 26 Oct. 1784, Anne Casement      5 BA-5
Dorman, William B., 10 May 1794, Julian Gorsuch     3 BA-287
Dormon, James, 13 Sept. 1781, Tabitha Willess       1 SO-126
Dorney, Frisby, 16 Oct. 1797, Ann Hozier            4 KE-67
Dorothy, John, 3 Oct. 1798, Mary Dise               2 SO
Dorrity, Francis, 3 March 1798, Priscilla Edds      4 KE-67
Dorrity, Joseph, 20 Dec. 1779, Margaret Carroll     5 BA-4
Dorsey, Amos, 13 May 1784, by Rev. Robison; Polly Dorsey
    11 BA-7
```

```
Dorsey, Basil, 25 March 1782, Tabitha Richardson      4 FR
Dorsey, Basil, 12 Aug. 1792, Harriet Harris           2 FR-1122
Dorsey, Baz'l John, 5 Sept. 1786, Polly Hanes        10 BA-188
Dorsey, Ch's, Aug. 1784, by Rev. Higginbothom; Eliza
    Anchors                                          11 BA-7
Dorsey, Clement, 12 Dec. 1799, Priscilla Hebb         4 SM-184
Dorsey, Daniel, 16 March 1779, by Rev. Magill; Eleanor
    Dorsey                                            4 AA
Dorsey, Dennis, 10 Nov. 1788, Tarisha Elder           6 BA
Dorsey, Edward, 23 Feb. 1786, Susanna Lawrence        6 BA
Dorsey, Edward, 25 March 1786, Eliza Dorsey          11 BA-9
Dorsey, Eli, 26 Nov. 1778, by Rev. Magill; Sara Worthington
    4 AA
Dorsey, Elias, 8 June 1779, Susanna Snowden           5 BA-4
Dorsey, Elias, 17 Feb. 1788, Polly Lawrence          18 BA-1
Dorsey, Ely, (21 Feb. 1778), Ellis Barnes            25 BA-1
Dorsey, Evan, 6 Jan. 1789, Sus. Lawrence              2 FR-1122
Dorsey, Greenbury, 24 Feb. 1784, Sarah Hobbs          4 FR
Dorsey, Henry, son of Edward, 5 Feb. 1795, Elizabeth Smith-
    son; see also 1 BA-7                              3 HA-24
Dorsey, James, 8 Feb. 1787, Rachel Choysman          10 BA-188
Dorsey, James Maxwell, 15 Nov. 1798, Martha McComas  12 BA-370
Dorsey, John, 29 April 1781, Hannah Day               3 HA-24
Dorsey, John, 15 July 1788, Martha Chesum             2 DO
Dorsey, John, 2 Dec. 1792, Jemima Gist                6 BA
Dorsey, John, 26 April 1798, by Rev. Ridgely; Elizabeth
    Stringer                                          4 AA
Dorsey, John, 30 Nov. 1799, Eleanor Cochran           4 FR
Dorsey, John E., 14 Dec. 1799, Margaret Hudson        3 BA-281
Dorsey, John Lawrence, 20 Dec. 1785, Rachel Bonham    4 FR
Dorsey, Johnsa, 9 March 1788, Sarah Hammond           2 FR-1122
Dorsey, Joseph, 27 July 1780, Mille Gillis            5 BA-4
Dorsey, Joshua, 16 Feb. 1789, H. Hammond             29 BA-1
Dorsey, Joshua, 15 Sept. 1795, Janet Kennedy          4 FR
Dorsey, Josias, 31 Dec. 1798, Sophia Dorsey           4 FR
Dorsey, Lloyd, 26 Jan. 1797, Anna Green               5 MO-114
Dorsey, Michael, 27 Sept. 1796, Elizab. Poole         2 FR-1122
    4 FR gives the groom's name as Michael Dorsey of John.
Dorsey, Nicholas Worthington, 14 Dec. 1-79, Rachel Warfield
    2 PG-3
Dorsey, Owen, 15 Oct. 1797, Henrietta Dorsey          7 BA-3
Dorsey, Pat., 28 May 1782, Marg't Hobbs              11 BA-5
Dorsey, Phillip, 13 Dec. 1787, Elizabeth Joyce        3 BA-216
Dorsey, Reason, 9 Aug. 1797, Frances Cromwell         3 HA-26
    2 HA-350 gives the date as 10 Aug. 1797.
Dorsey, Richard, 22 Jan. 1796, Anne Wayman            5 MO-113
Dorsey, Richard, 18 March 1798, Rebecca Willis        1 DO-39
    2 DO gives the date as 16 March 1798.
Dorsey, Samuel, 25 Jan. 1795, Clementia Preston       7 BA-1
Dorsey, Thomas Beal, 3 Feb. 1784, Achsah Dorsey      11 BA-7
Dorsey, Thomas Beale, 28 Nov. 1797, by Rev. Dorsey; Sarah
    Dorsey Merryweather                               4 AA
Dorsey, Vachel, 5 March 1778, Elizabeth Batty        11 BA-1
Dorsey, Vachel, 13 March 1792, Ann Poole              2 FR-1122
Dorsey, Vachel, 5 April 1798, Elizabeth Dorsey        3 BA-357
Dorsey, William, 2 April 1781, Elizabeth Worthington  4 FR
Dorsey, William, Jr., 27 Jan. 1789, Sophia Dorsey     4 FR
Dorsey, William, 21 May 1793, Rachel Hobbs            4 FR
Dotson, John, 7 Jan. 1784, Eliza Stinett              3 AA-420
Dougherty, Hugh, 3 March 1791, Ann Stertz or Stutz   29 BA-2
Dougherty, Jno., 30 Sept. 1784, Marg't McCormick     11 BA-7
Dougherty, John, 11 April 1791, Mary Woolrick         6 BA
Dougherty, John, 3 April 1800, Ann Chauncey           2 HA-352
Dougherty, Joseph, 23 May 1796, Joyce Holmes          3 BA-323
Douglas, Alexander, 1 Dec. 1790, Hannah Heron         2 DO
```

```
Douglas, Benjamin, 27 Oct. 1782, Sarah Marshall          2 CH-235
Douglas, James, 27 April 1780, Mary Addington            3 AA-416
Douglass, George, 23 May 1795, Frances Boucher          29 BA-6
Douglass, Charles, 9 Jan. 1796, Rebeckah Hall            4 FR
Douglass, William, 26 April 1778, Eliza Gentle           2 MO-1
Doulind, John, 21 April 1795, Ann Gilberthorp            6 BA
Dove, Mark, 17 May 1779, Betsy LeCompte                  2 DO
Dowd, Charles, 26 Nov. 1798, Margaret Moore              3 BA-365
Dowdal, James, 28 Jan. 1793, Sarah Hogan                 6 BA
Dowden, Michael, 6 Feb. 1792, Mary Dunn                  4 FR
Dowden, Thomas, 3 Sept. 1778, Annie Campbell             2 MO-1
Dowel, Richard, 21 Dec. 1788, Lydia Davis               23 BA-1
Dowell, Benj'n, 15 April 1788, Barb. Springer            2 FR-1122
Dowell, John, 22 Jan. 1778, Priscilla Sunderland         3 AA-414
Dowell, Richard, 7 April 1795, Margaret Towney           3 AA-424
Dowell, Thomas, 21 Jan. 1784, Sarah Batson               3 AA-420
Dowlan, Charles, 30 May 1778, Anne Brannegan            11 BA-1
Dowland, Luke, 9 Feb. 1799, Hannah Gilberthorpe         29 BA-10
Dowlin, James, 12 Oct. 1792, Mary Neilson                6 BA
Dowling, Edward, Jan. 1794, Mary Gordon                  2 FR-1122
Downes, Rich'd, 15 Aug. 1796, Eliz. Rose                 5 MO-113
Downes, Robert, 29 Sept. 1792, Allafar Witzell           3 BA-257
Downes, Thomas, 10 June 1794, Susannah Marsh             5 BA-5
Downes, Wm., 3 June 1791, Sarah Jones                   29 BA-2
Downes, William, 13 Feb. 1794, Margaret Burns            3 BA-281
Downey, Alexander, 17 Feb. 1795, Mary Tucker             2 FR-1122
Downey, James, 7 Jan. 1790, Priscilla Bond               6 BA
Downey, John, 15 June 1784, Emy Stoxall                  5 BA-5
Downey, John, 11 Nov. 1800, Betsey Owings                5 BA-5
Downey, Robert, 14 Oct. 1800, Rachel Sutherland          4 BA-78
Downey, Wm., 23 Sept. 1796, Dorothy Parks               29 BA-7
Downhour, Jacob, 20 Jan. 1785, Eliza Folk               11 BA-8
Downing, James, 22 Sept. 1784, Acena Waters              4 FR
Downing, Joseph, 23 April 1799, Elizabeth Webster        3 HA-28
Downing, Richard, 16 July 1781, Margaret Webb            3 HA-4
Downing, Samuel, 15 July 1785, Priscilla Webb            3 HA-9
Downs, Benjamin, 2 Oct. 1788, Blanch Hampton             1 BA-1
Downs, Henry, 15 Aug. 1790, Deleah Enlows                1 BA-2
Downs, Henry, 30 Nov. 1793, Sarah Barnes                39 BA-1
Downs, John, 13 Dec. 1789, Elizabeth Underwood           3 PG-256
Downs, Will'm, 27 Dec. 1779, Mary Roland                 2 PG-7
    See also 2 CH-235, which gives groom's name was
    Wilson Downs.
Downy, Robert, 14 Oct. 1800, Rachel Sotherland           1 BA-9
Dowson, Obediah, 29 June 1792, Ann Delehay               2 DO
Dowson, Obediah, 27 Sept. 1796, Thula Brannock           2 DO
Doxey, Jeremiah, 24 March 1799, Mary Higginson           4 SM-184
Doye, John, 18 April 1786, Sarah Graston                10 BA-186
Doyle, Andrew, before 25 Nov. 1789, Elizabeth Fields    20 BA-1
Doyle, Jacob, 20 June 1799, Cath. Duttro                29 BA-10
Doyle, John, 13 Sept. 1786, Sophia Adamson               4 FR
Doyle, Thos., 28 March 1780, Marg't Mahaly              11 BA-4
Doyne, John, 20 Aug. 1794, Mary Meyers                   3 BA-291
Drake, Jno., 1 Aug. 1782, Sarah Crag                    11 BA-5
Drake, William, 17 Oct. 1780, Elizabeth Hinckle          4 FR
Drake, William, 7 June 1800, Catherine Leckler           3 BA-386
Drane, Anthony, 26 Dec. 1778, Anne Smith                 2 PG-2
Draper, Ira, 20 Feb. 1800, Margaret Leary                3 BA-383
Dreaden, Isaac, 15 Sept. 1797, Mary Alexander,           1 WO
Dreaden, Mills, 14 Nov. 1798, Betsy Winder Murry         2 SO
Dreadin, James, 12 April 1800, Dolly Holston             1 WO
Drebert, Andreas, 28 Dec. 1788, Catharina Jeger         10 BA-192
Drebert, Christian, 17 June 1792, Maria Forney          10 BA-194
Dresser, Alfred, 2 Oct. 1796, Rachel Powers              3 BA-329
Drew, Henry, 18 June 1784, Sarah Henderson               3 HA-8
```

```
Drew, Michael, 3 May 1781, Eliz'th Woolf            4 FR
Driscoll, Florence, 27 Aug. 1799, Elizabeth Ashburner  3 BA-376
Driscoll, Florence, 22 Nov. 1800, Eliz. Groce     29 BA-12
Driskele, Elgate, 15 April 1796, Anna Dykes         1 WO
Driver, James, 3 May 1792, by Rev. Dorsey; Lucy Hobbs  4 AA
Drone, Wm., 16 Sept. 1786, Susanna Sheckells        4 FR
Drown, Job, 29 Oct. 1799, Sophia Clark              6 BA
Drowry, Ignatius, 25 March 1793, Mary Goldsborough  4 FR
Drum, Peter, 8 Dec. 1795, Sarah Hansey              2 FR-1122
Druman, James, 19 Nov. 1798, Sarah Starling         2 FR-1122
Drummond, Hugh, 24 Feb. 1784, Elizabeth Cadle       3 BA-186
Drura, William, 4 Feb. 1799, Elizabeth Langford     2 DO
Drury, Jerningham, 14 April 1790, by Rev. Cooper; Sarah Hill
     4 AA
Dryden, Littleton, 15 May 1791, Peggy Levingston    2 SO
Dryden, Milby, 11 Feb. 1800, Mary Patrick           8 BA-2
Dryden, Stephen, 29 Jan. 1796, Catherine Dryden     1 WO
Dryden, William, 1 Aug. 1780, Philipena Kisinger    4 FR
Dubin, John, 17 Feb. 1800, Sarah Clifford           2 AL-701
Dubourg, Mich'l, 6 Jan. 1793, Elizabeth Grainger    3 BA-258
Dubre, Joseph, 20 Nov. 1794, Mary Kiser             3 HA-23
     7 BA-1 gives the date as 22 Nov. 1794.
Ducatel, Edm'd, 28 May 1795, Ann Pineau            44 BA-1
Duchart, (?), 21 Sept. 1784, Elizabeth Dotter      10 BA-182
Duck, Christoph, 28 June 1789, Charlotte Jugel     10 BA-192
Ducker, John, 5 March 1790, Eliza Bissett           4 FR
Duckert, Thomas, 7 Jan. 1796, Mary Clagett          3 PG-442
Dudderer, Samuel, 11 April 1791, Elizabeth Dickensheets  4 FR
Dudley, Joseph, 9 April 1778, Anne Lauter or Laten 11 BA-1
Dudley, Joshua, 9 April 1777, Catherine Stewart     3 BA-174
     The marriage was sworn to on 12 June 1779 by Anne
     Smith, Edward McLure, and Sarah McLure.
Duett, Whittington, 17 May 1799, Lovey Davey        2 SO
Duff, John, 10 Sept. 1780, Mary Hudson             11 BA-4
Duffey, John, 18 Oct. 1796, Hannah Grimes           3 BA-329
Duffield, Richard, 13 Feb. 1787, Mary Macat         6 BA
Dugan, Cumberland, 31 Oct. 1786, Margaret Kelso     5 BA-5
Dugan, Henry, 25 March 1799, Charlotte Pierpoint    3 BA-369
Dugan, James, 7 June 1783, Honor Masterson         11 BA-6
Dugan, Thomas, 28 Aug. 1783, Rebecca Fowler        11 BA-6
Dugar, Peter, 30 Dec. 1793, Elizabeth Tully         3 BA-279
Duhig, Oliver, 15 June 1792, Catherine Headekin    28 BA-2
Duke, William, 28 May 1793, Hester Condon           1 BA-5
Dukes, Christopher, 2 Aug. 1785, Jane Graves       11 BA-8
Dukes, Christopher, 23 March 1797, Jane Dukes       6 BA
Dukes, John, 8 Jan. 1800, Tabitha Allen             1 WO
Dulany, Hany, 6 May 1800, Rhoda Goddard             2 SO
Dulany, Peter, 27 Sept. 1778, Bridget Fitzgerald   11 BA-1
Duley, Barton, 8 March 1778, Martha Baker           4 MO-1
Duley, Thomas, 6 Feb. 1778, Elizabeth Bateman       4 CH-1
Duley, William, 20 June 1798, Elizabeth Kitely      3 HA-27
     12 BA-370 gives the date as 21 June 1798.
Duley, Zachariah, 2 June 1798, Ann Lazenby          6 MO
Dulin, Peregrine, 14 Jan. 1800, Henrietta Vickars   2 DO
Dulst, George, 2 June 1800, Wilhelmina Hinckles    10 BA-200
Dumerte, John, 25 June 1782, Elizabeth Keepots      5 BA-5
Dumes?, George, 24 March 1793, Ruth Coward          6 BA
Dunbar, William, 7 Jan. 1798, Martha Wells          6 BA
Duncan, George, 15 June 1797, Sarah Evans           2 HA-349
Duncan, James, 4 April 1787, Sarah Leach            2 CH-235
Duncan, Josiah, 20 Oct. 1795, Martha M. Dale        1 WO
Duncan, Levi, 26 May 1797, Leah Purnell             1 WO
Duncan, Perry, 13 Aug. 1778, Elizabeth Nooke       11 BA-1
Duncan, William, 4 Sept. 1790, Martha Talbott      26 BA-1
Duncan, William, 27 March 1798, Esther Holland      1 WO
```

```
Dungan, Benjamin, 22 Aug. 1797, Anne Rusk              6 BA
Dungan, Thomas, 28 Sept. 1797, Mary Gray              3 BA-351
Dungan, Wm., 23 Jan. 1791, Elizabeth Brand            6 BA
Dunham, William, 17 Oct. 1799, Polly Chaney           3 BA-379
Dunkin, William, 21 July 1788, Mary Dukin             6 BA
Dunn, Henry, 31 May 1786, by Rev. West; Kesiah Brown 51 BA-30
Dunn, Moses, 22 Dec. 1796, Mary Mezick                3 SO
Dunn, Moses, 7 Aug. 1798, Sukey Jones                 2 SO
Dunn, Richard, 14 Jan. 1795, Sarah Bateman            3 HA-24
Dunn, Richard, 20 May 1798, Mary Larramore            3 SO
  2 SO gives the date as 3 May 1798.
Dunn, Thomas, 24 April 1798, Mary Warthan             4 FR
Dunn, Thomas, 28 Oct. 1800, Mary Warthin              7 MO-29
Dunn, William, 1 Jan. 1794, Sarah Newnam             39 BA-1
Dunning, Dennis, 24 Sept. 1789, Nancy Dutton         11 BA-12
Dunning, John, 4 March 1786, Ruth Mansfield           4 FR
Dunning, John, 21 Nov. 1799, Lydia Wilson             2 HA-351
Dunnington, Hezekiah, 9 Oct. 1780, Ava Magriger       2 CH-235
Dunnock, Levin, 10 Oct. 1793, Sarah Moore             2 DO
  The date is also given as 12 Oct. 1793 in the same
  source.
Dunnock, Levin, 13 Sept. 1796, Elizabeth King         2 DO
Dunstible, James, 15 June 1794, Mary Ann McCande      6 BA
Dunston, Jno., 26 July 1787, Marg't Burk             11 BA-10
Dunston, Thomas, 1 Jan. 1789, Ann Liget               1 BA-1
Dunswell, Sam'l, 8 March 1799, Polly Gutchey         29 BA-10
Dunwick, Isaac, 24 Sept. 1789, Jane Ray               3 BA-234
Dunwoody, Rob't, 20 Sept. 1784, Eleanor Kidd         11 BA-7
Dunwoody, Robert, 28 Feb. 1796, Ann McCann           29 BA-7
Duphorn, Simon, 30 June 1795, Barbara Boose           4 FR
Duppel, Benj'n, 22 March 1796, Eliz. Reitenauer       2 FR-1122
Durbin, Benjamin, 9 May 1793, Liddy Lenger            1 AL-52
Durbin, Cornelius, 29 Jan. 1789, Mary Harrison        4 FR
Durbin, John, 1 July 1791, Margaret Poulson           4 FR
Durbin, John, 12 Feb. 1800, Sarah Clifford            3 AL-6
Durbin, Thomas, 5 Oct. 1780, Clemence Litton          3 HA-2
Durff, Jacob, 21 Nov. 1780, Juliana Grindler          4 FR
Durham, Thomas, 20 Feb. 1791, Rachel Shoudy           1 BA-3
Durham, Zacharias, 11 March 1792, Lucia Husband       1 BA-4
Durkee (Dirga), Pearl, 5 Jan. 1794, Joanna Gailes     3 BA-281
Durkee, Pearl, 16 March 1797, Mary Hankey             3 BA-342
Durm, Davis, 17 April 1797, Alla Ross                 4 KE-67
Dusky, Joshua, 8 Jan. 1798, Dolly Brown               2 DO
Dust, John, 15 Jan. 1785, Elizabeth Pritchett         4 FR
Dutro, George, 23 Dec. 1792, Elizabeth Stansbury      3 BA-259
Dutterar, John, 21 Aug. 1779, Catherine Summers       4 FR
Dutterer, Conrad, 21 Jan. 1799, Susanna Soolser       4 FR
Duttero, Mr., 25 Dec. 1793, Peggy Baker               4 FR
Duttero, John, 27 Aug. 1792, Susanna Worman           4 FR
Duttero, John, 20 Nov. 1795, Mary Nusbaum             4 FR
Dutton, David, 1 Feb. 1792, Leah Healy                3 BA-255
Dutton, John, 24 June 1800, Amelia Cannen             3 HA-29
Dutton, John, 26 June 1800, Amelia Carman             2 HA-352
Dutton, Robert, 22 March 1785, Mary Walsham           3 HA-9
Dutton, Roger, 31 Oct. 1800, Shela Wright             2 SO
Duttro, Conrad, 5 Aug. 1794, Frances Karr             4 FR
Duttro, David, 26 Feb. 1797, Mary Crickbaum           3 AL-4
Duttro, David, 28 Feb. 1797, Mary Barkus              2 AL-700
Duvall, Beal, 21 Aug. 1794, Anne Dean                 3 BA-291
Duvall, Benjamin, 9 Feb. 1799, Sarah Thompson         4 FR
Duvall, Charles, 14 June 1778, Casia Brashears        2 PG-2
Duvall, Claudius, 3 Oct. 1797, Elizabeth Carmack      4 FR
Duvall, Colmore, 5 Feb. 1791, by Rev. Chalmers; Elizabeth
  Peach                                               4 AA
Duvall, Dan'l, 6 May 1784, Sarah Conn                11 BA-7
```

Duvall, Henry, 19 Sept. 1800, by Rev. Wyatt; Elizabeth Boone
  4 AA
Duvall, Isaac, 18 Dec. 1800, by Rev. Ridgely; Charlotte Black-
  ston   4 AA
Duvall, Jeremiah, 2 Feb. 1793, by Rev. Dorsey; Elizabeth
  Warfield   4 AA
Duvall, Job, 28 Nov. 1798, by Rev. Ridgely; Margaret Hands
  4 AA
Duvall, John, 27 Nov. 1798, Rebecca Rawlings   1 AA-163
Duvall, Levi, 23 April 1784, Ann Duvall   4 FR
Duvall, Mareen, 2 Nov. 1780, Mary Duvall   2 PG-3
Duvall, Mareen, 8 July 1789, Rachel Howard   4 FR
Duvall, Mark Brown, 17 Jan. 1793, by Rev. G. Ridgely; Sarah
  Duvall   4 AA
Duvall, Marsh Mareen, 29 Oct. 1792, Rebeckah Wilson   4 FR
Duvall, Marsh Mareen, 2 Dec. 1795, Ann Fowler   4 FR
Duvall, Noah, 10 May 1795, by Rev. Ridgely; Anne Eaglen 4 AA
Duvall, Rob't, 7 April 1787, Eliza Kirsted   11 BA-10
Duvall, Samuel B., 28 Jan. 1796, by Rev. Samuel Hill; Jemima
  Jones   46 BA-1
Duvall, Walter, 22 May 1798, by Rev. Ridgely; Sarah Duvall
  4 AA
Dwyer, William, 9 May 1797, Elizabeth Briscoe   4 KE-67
Dye, Daniel, 2 March 1797, Martha Wells   2 AL-700
Dye, William, 30 Sept. 1795, Rachel Wells   2 AL-700
Dye, William, 23 Oct. 1800, Mary Hammett   3 BA-394
Dyer, Aaron, son of Joseph and Joanna, 29th day, 4 mo.,
  1779, Elizabeth Dawes, dau. of Isaac and Mary   1 SF
Dyers, Isaac, 22 Jan. 1797, Susanna Williams   45 BA-1
Dykes, William, 24 Dec. 1795, Margaret Chaddick   6 BA
Dyrumple, Jesse, 19 Feb. 1784, Ann Duke   3 AA-420
Dysart, James, 18 Oct. 1792, Catherine Ellender   6 BA
Dyson, Bennett, 8 Oct. 1783, Verlinda Chunn   2 CH-235
Dyson, John Baptist, 28 Aug. 1790, Mary O'Nele   4 FR

Eaden, Thomas, 6 May 1797, Matilda Clark   4 KE-67
Eader, Abrah., 22 Feb. 1785, Cath. Reich   2 FR-1126
Eader, Adam, 18 Oct. 1788, Elizabeth Kitterman   4 FR
Eades, Jno., 24 Oct. 1782, Sarah Holton   11 BA-5
Eagan, Jno., 31 Aug. 1783, Mary Clements   11 BA-6
Eagerton, John, 9 Dec. 1798, Fanny Burch   3 BA-366
Eagle, Henry, 10 Dec. 1796, Mary Kendall   4 KE-67
Eagleston, Abraham, 24 Nov. 1792, Jane Austine   6 BA
Eagleston, Abraham, 5 Nov. 1797, Rebecca Hughes   6 BA
Earle, Thomas, 29 Oct. 1791, Rhoda Busick   2 DO
Early, Benjamin, 29 Jan. 1789, Jane Cocley   2 PG-4
Earnest, Geo., 10 Oct. 1793, Rachel Borth   18 BA-5
Earnst, Jacob, 21 June 1785, Mary Smith   4 FR
Easley, Kemble, 25 July 1800, Ann Ratcliffe   2 CH-235
Eason, Harman, 10 Sept. 1782, Sarah Shanks   2 DO
Eastburn, Robinson, 17 May 1790, Sarah Boteler   4 FR
Eastentor, John, 12 Dec. 1799, Mary Bradley   8 BA-1
Easum, James, 3 Nov. 1788, Delilah Parker   1 WO
Easterday, Christian, 5 June 1795, Cath. Geddis   4 FR
Eaton, Edward, 2 Feb. 1782, Dolly Valliant   2 DO
Eaton, John, 13 Jan. 1795, Rachel Pearsons   2 FR-1126
Eaton, William, 19 May 1793, Nancy Bryan   2 FR-1126
Ebdidge, William, 26 Dec. 1799, Anne Davis   3 BA-381
Eberhard, (?), 1790, (?) Block   50 BA-389
Ebert, George Adam, 2 Nov. 1793, Catherine Fout   4 FR
Ebert, John, 30 Oct. 1783, Margaret Ming   4 FR
Ebert, John, 11 Dec. 1788, Elizabeth Odle   19 BA-4
Ebert, Philip, 19 April 1779, Mary Swadner   4 FR
Ebhart, Harthman, 16 Jan. 1789, Elisabeth Bornet   10 BA-192

```
Ebling, Abijah, 4 June 1799, Sarah Morson or Morrison    2 AL-701
Eccard, Bernhard, 16 May 1785, Marg. Parnewill          1 FR-59
Eccles, Samuel, 14 April 1791, Ann Dunwoody             6 BA
Eccleston, John, 13 Aug. 1785, Rebecca Hodson           2 DO
Eccleston, John, 10 April 1794, Mary Sullivan           2 DO
Eccleston, Thomas, 23 Sept. 1800, Polly Beckwith        2 DO
Eccleston, Thomas Firman, 15 April 1782, Milcah Pitt    2 DO
Eckel, Philip, 19 Oct. 1791, Mary Tinges                29 BA-2
Eckman, Jacob, 29 July 1797, Catherine Pitenger         4 FR
Eckman, Michael, 14 Jan. 1800, Mary Jacob               2 FR-1126
Eddire, James, 11 May 1778, Mary Hammond                4 FR
Edelen, Clement, 6 Nov. 1780, Ann Simpson               2 PG-1
Edelen, Oswald, 25 Oct. 1787, Mary Thompson Bond        2 CH-235
Edelin, Edward, 12 Feb. 1782, Eleanor Boarman           2 CH-235
Edelin, Francis, 8 Nov. 1779, Sarah Thompson            2 CH-235
Edelin, George, 14 May 1785, Sarah Edelin               2 CH-235
Eden, Garret, 2 June 1797, Agnes Watson                 6 BA
Eden, Jeremiah, 2 May 1791, Mary Summers                3 HA-21
Eden, Jeremiah, 11 Aug. 1799, Betsy Rogers              29 BA-10
Eden, Robert, 16 March 1781, Minah Coale                5 BA-5
Edes, William, 20 June 1799, Margaret Pannell           6 BA
Edgar, Arnold, 13 Sept. 1798, Hilly Wallace             2 DO
Edgar, Henry, 10 Feb. 1789, Margaret Smith              2 DO
Edgar, William, 17 Dec. 1798, Keziah Foxwell            2 DO
Edgell, Henry, 19 April 1791, Keziah Wrotten            2 DO
Edmondson, James, 15 March 1797, Lydia Clark            1 TA-315
Edmondson, John, 11 Dec. 1794, Sarah Mann               2 DO
Edmondson, Joseph, 11 April 1799, Elizabeth Simmons     2 DO
Edmondson, Pollard, 26 March 1789, Elizabeth Airey      2 DO
Edmondson, Samuel, son of Francis and Rachel (dec.), 14th
     day, 10 mo., 1797, Susanna Kemp, dau. of Benjamin
     (dec.) and Ann                                     4 SF-212
Edmondson, Thomas, 16 July 1798, Sarah Smith            2 DO
Edmondson, William, of Kent Co., Del., son of Francis and
     Rachel (dec.), 17th day, 1 mo., 1795, Ann Kemp, dau. of
     Benjamin (dec.) and Ann                            4 SF-205
Edmondson, William, son of James, 1st day, 5 mo., 1788,
     Sarah Regester, dau. of John                       4 SF-190
Edmonston, Alex'r, 20 June 1791, Cassandra Jones        6 BA
Edmonston, Thomas, 3 Dec. 1793, Ruth Sheckell           2 FR-1126
Edward, negro belonging to David Crafford, 9 April 1798,
     Linny, negro                                       5 MO-115
Edwards, Abraham, 4 Oct. 1786, Ellen Jones              2 FR-1126
Edwards, Cadwalader, 3 Dec. 1786, by Rev. Pigman; Sarah
     Chalmers                                           4 AA
Edwards, David, 3 Aug. 1785, Eliza Kettle               11 BA-8
Edwards, Headen, 9 June 1793, Susannah Beall            4 FR
Edwards, Heathcote, 15 July 1784, Dorcas Towson         11 BA-7
Edwards, Jas., 22 May 1794, Ann McCollom                50 BA-394
Edwards, John, 4 June 1778, Mary Turner                 2 CH-235
Edwards, John, 22 Aug. 1778, Mary Leech                 4 MO-1
Edwards, John, 24 Feb. 1794, Ann Winfield               4 FR
Edwards, Paul, 12 Sept. 1785, Sarah Travolet            10 BA-184
Edwards, Philip, 28 March 1793, Ann Rawlings            3 BA-265
Edwards, Thomas, 10 June 1787, Mary Adams               5 BA-5
Edwards, Thomas, before 4 May 1798, by Rev. Stewart; Rachel
     Beard                                              4 AA
Edwards, Thomas, 13 Sept. 1798, Anne Gordon             5 BA-5
Edwards, Thomas, 6 Dec. 1798, Mary Turner               4 KE-67
Edwards, Wm., 10 Jan. 1782, Martha Dugmore              11 BA-5
Edwards, William, 20 June 1789, by Rev. Hagerty; Ann Chalmers
     4 AA
Edwards, William, 6 Jan. 1799, Sophia Lerouett          3 BA-367
Ehrenberg, Phillip, 11 Feb. 1799, Magdalena German      10 BA-198
Eichenbrode, Daniel, 7 Aug. 1792, Elizabeth Yost        4 FR
```

Eichendorf, Christian, 30 Sept. 1800, Leonore Petre   29 BA-11
    50 BA-408 gives the groom's name as Christ'r.
Eichler, Christ'n, 17 March 1793, Salome Kamer   50 BA-393
Eigenbrod, John, 22 April 1800, Susanna Sanger   5 FR-24
Eiglehart, Edw'd, 15 Dec. 1788, Sophia Herrine   11 BA-12
Eisennagel, Thos., 20 Sept. 1785, Sus. Spanseiler   2 FR-1126
Eislen, Fred'k, 23 March 1795, Sarah Cole   29 BA-6
Elbert, Solomon, 19 May 1797, Charlotte Elliott   2 DO
Elder, Delecah?, 7 Nov. 1798, by Rev. Dorsey; Sarah Lindsey
    4 AA
Elder, Elijah, 28 July 1778, by Rev. Magill; Mary Davidge
    4 AA
Elder, James, 12 June 1779, Eliz'th Burn   4 FR
Elder, James, 7 May 1792, Kitty Hughes   4 FR
Elder, John, 9 Sept. 1794, Margaret Greenwood   6 BA
Elder, Michael, 2 Jan. 1794, Pleasant Petticoat   6 BA
Elfry, William, 20 April 1799, Nancy Grace   29 BA-10
Elgar, Joseph, Jr., son of Joseph and Margaret; 19th day,
    11 mo., 1800, Ann Wright, dau. of Joel and Elizabeth
    (Farquhar) Wright   3 SF
Elgin, William, 18 June 1780, Ann Anderson   2 CH-235
Eli, David, 19 Sept. 1797, Catherine Ditto   4 FR
Elias, George, 15 April 1797, Catherine Linaweaver   4 FR
Elis, Lewis, 1790, (?) Leary   50 BA-390
Elison, Daniel L., 2 Sept. 1795, Ann Logsdon   1 AL-53
Ellenbach, John, 11 Feb. 1790, Marg't Flock   4 FR
Ellenor, William, 19 Feb. 1795, Barbara Berner or Bemer
    1 BA-7
Eller, Jacob, 14 Oct. 1792, Marg. Willjard   2 FR-1126
Elleroe, Jas., 1791, M. Wilson   50 BA-391
Ellicott, David, 28 Sept. 1778, Martha Evans   5 BA-5
Ellicott, Elias, 26th day, 4 mo., 1786, Mary Thomas, dau.
    of Evan   6 SF
Ellicott, George, son of Andrew, 29th day, 12 mo., 1790,
    Elizabeth Brooke, dau. of James   6 SF
Ellicott, John, 8 April 1779, Cassandra Hopkins   5 BA-5
Ellicott, Nathaniel, 5 Sept. 1790, Elizabeth Ellicott   5 BA-5
Ellinder, George, 12 Feb. 1792, Sarah Grimes   1 BA-4
Ellinsworth, Israel, 1 Feb. 1782, Barbara McCabe   1 WI-114
Elliot, John, 4 Oct. 1795, Nancy David   4 FR
Elliot, Samuel, 22 Nov. 1780, Mary Richardson   3 AA-416
Elliot, Thomas, 3 Feb. 1796, Mary Hinton   4 FR
Elliott, Benjamin, 29 Jan. 1791, Rachel Bestpitch   2 DO
Elliott, Benjamin, 16 Jan. 1794, Mary Griffin   2 DO
Elliott, Constantine, 10 Oct. 1798, Phebe Langrell   2 DO
Elliott, Edward, 22 Nov. 1796, Keziah Elliott   2 DO
    1 DO-39 gives the date as 24 Nov. 1796.
Elliott, Eli, son of John and Sarah (Millhouse), 20th day,
    9 mo., 1798, Margaret Hughes, dau. of Jesse and Eliza-
    beth   3 SF
Elliott, Hooper, 16 April 1779, Nancy Taylor   2 DO
Elliott, James, 17 Dec. 1799, Mary Slaughter   3 BA-381
Elliott, Jason, 16 June 1800, Mary Orem   2 DO
Elliott, John, 26 Dec. 1800, Elizabeth Cook   2 DO
Elliott, Joseph, 27 Oct. 1783, Leah Elliott   2 DO
Elliott, Joseph, 15 Feb. 1797, Charlotte Elliott   2 DO
Elliott, Planner?, 4 Sept. 1794, Rhoda Elliott   2 DO
Elliott, Samuel, 12 Nov. 1780, Mary Richardson, dau. of
    Richard and Elizabeth   6 SF
Elliott, Samuel, 6 March 1793, Margaret Hayward Waggoman
    2 DO
Ellis, Chas., 29 Nov. 1800, Rachel Fultz   29 BA-12
Ellis, Eleazer, 7 Oct. 1791, Rebecca Onion   4 FR
Ellis, Elija, 29 Dec. 1779, Susannah Watson   2 PG-7
Ellis, Hezekiah, 6 Sept. 1778, Ann Briggs   2 MO-1

Ellis, Jno., 29 June 1782, Rebecca Barnes   11 BA-5
Ellis, Jno., 22 Oct. 1796, Sarah McCoone   29 BA-7
Ellis, Thomas, 27 May 1784, Hannah Meredith   4 FR
Ellis, Wm., 3 Aug. 1799, Margaret Ansley   6 BA
Ellit, Nich's, 4 April 1799, Mary Stiles   29 BA-10
Ellott, Thomas, 9 Oct. 1781, Susanna Bevard   3 HA-5
Elphinstone, David, 19 April 1791, Lydia Hambleton 3 BA-235
    See also 31 BA-1.
Elson, Henry, 2 Sept. 1790, Rachael Low   11 BA-13
Elston, Thomas, 21 Aug. 1794, Eliza Duncin   18 BA-6
Elvans, William, 13 Sept. 1795, Elisabeth Rogers   5 BA-5
Elwert, Thomas, 11 July 1799, Susanna Matthews   5 BA-5
Elwes, Will'm, 12 May 1795, Ann Frances Bourdon   44 BA-1
Elwood, Thomas, 20 Oct. 1794, Elizabeth Devine   3 BA-293
Ely, David, 14 July 1781, Susanna Myers   4 FR
Ely, George, 11 Dec. 1800, Catherine Davis   3 BA-396
Ely, Jacob, 6 Aug. 1799, Mary Renner   4 FR
Ely, John, 24 Dec. 1792, Jane Meeks   3 HA-22
Elzey, Isaac, slave of George Hall; 28 June 1795, Rachel
    Cornish, free black   3 BA-305
Emberson, John, 9 Dec. 1790, Rebecca Simpson   3 PG-257
Emberson, William, 27 Dec. 1789, Mary Ann Simson   3 PG-256
Emerich, Philip, 13 Jan. 1797, Eliz. Miller   29 BA-8
Emich, Henry, 30 Nov. 1794, Eliza Fauntz   50 BA-396
Emich, Mortius, 13 April 1795, Elizabeth Eirich   10 BA-196
Emmerson, Aquila, 16 Dec. 1792, Susanna Simpson   3 PG-437
Emmerson, John, 20 Jan. 1791, Elizabeth P. Colegate 6 BA
Emmert, Philip, 8 April 1797, Sarah Brown   35 BA-5
Emmitt, William, 30 March 1790, Henrietta Coale   4 FR
Emmitt, Wm., 15 March 1798, Sarah Zimmerman   29 BA-9
Emmory, Adam, 16 Dec. 1779, Sarah Hipps   4 FR
Emory, Bryan, 7 Nov. 1797, Frances Atkinson   4 KE-67
Emory, Thomas, 23 Sept. 1779, Elizabeth Hopewell   3 SM-57
Engel, George, 3 Dec. 1789, Cath. Yung   2 FR-1126
Engel, George, 8 Sept. 1799, Sus. Jung   2 FR-1126
Engel, Peter, 20 Aug. 1799, Mary Renner   ◡   2 FR-1126
England, Jacob, 30 June 1790, Mary Joice   6 BA
England, Joseph, 30 Oct. 1783, Eliza Rowland   11 BA-6
Engle, George, 3 Dec. 1789, Catherine Young   4 FR
Engle, George, 7 Sept. 1798, Susanna Young   4 FR
Engle, Peter, 17 Aug. 1799, Mary Renner   4 FR
Engle, Thomas, 16 Aug. 1794, Margaret Hurst   3 BA-291
Englebrecht, John, 1 Oct. 1785, Margaret Houx   4 FR
Englebright, Jno., 3 May 1785, Marg't Wood   11 BA-8
Englebright, Michael, 27 June 1795, Elizabeth Stull 4 FR
Engler, Peter, 5 Feb. 1790, Susanna Hoffman   4 FR
Enlows, Henry, 27 Feb. 1791, Nancy Simpson   1 BA-3
Ennalls, Bartholomew, 16 Nov. 1799, Nancy Ervin   2 DO
Ennalls, Henry, 1 June 1785, Sarah Goldsborough   2 DO
Ennalls, Joseph, 20 Feb. 1796, Mary Hodson   2 DO
Ennalls, Thomas, 1 July 1794, Elizabeth Richardson 2 DO
Ennalls, William, 16 Jan. 1796, Harriet Byus   2 DO
Ennis, Joshua, 2 May 1785, Sarah Peterkin   11 BA-8
Ennis, Outten, 12 Jan. 1798, Polly Gladden   1 WO
Ennis, Samuel, 8 Nov. 1798, Elizabeth Wright   1 WO
Ennis, Samuel, 17 Nov. 1800, Rachel Marshall   1 WO
Ensey, Dennis, 10 Oct. 1797, Elizab. Crawford   2 FR-1126
Ensloe, Joseph, 26 May 1785, Mary McGacky   11 BA-8
Ensor, Abram, 2 March 1783, Cath'e Dicks   11 BA-6
Ensor, Abraham, Jr., (18 Dec. 1787), Barthia Brooks 15 BA-1
Ensor, James, 23 Jan. 1798, Nancy Dean   6 BA
Ensor, John, 13 May 1779, Urith Gorsuch   5 BA-5
Ensor, John, 21 Dec. 1797, Eleanor Smith   45 BA-2
Ensor, Nathan, 1 Oct. 1787, by Rev. West; Mary Brooks 51 BA-30
Ensor, William, 22 Nov. 1791, Rachel Conales   5 BA-5

Eodman, Edward, 19 Dec. 1799, by Rev. Ridgely; Sarah Douglas
    4 AA
Epach, George, 27 April 1790, S. Daner   29 BA-1
Eperle, Christian, 3 Nov. 1789, Elizabeth Morgelin   6 FR-202
Eppert, Henry, 7 May 1787, Elizabeth Snaider   4 FR
Erb, Peter, 27 March 1798, Barbara Grove   4 FR
Erickson, Bernard, 10 Oct. 1797, Hannah Schliepter   29 BA-8
    50 BA-402 gives the date as 30 Oct. 1797.
Erickson, Bernard, 1 Dec. 1798, Judy Coffin   29 BA-10
Ermine, Joseph, 17 Nov. 1799, Nancy O'Brian   3 BA-380
Erring, William, 3 July 1790, by Rev. Cooper; Rachel Brewer
    4 AA
Erskin, Edward, 29 Nov. 1797, Siney Martin   29 BA-9
Ervin, George, 6 April 1800, Martha Wilson   8 BA-2
Esam, James, 14 April 1784, Frances Watts   11 BA-7
Escridge, Woolford, 29 March 1788, Lilly Tall   2 DO
Essex, Isaac, 26 Nov. 1795, by Rev. Cash; Sarah Laine 4 AA
Essex, John, 2 Jan. 1783, Ann Bowen   3 AA-419
Essex, Samuel, 10 April 1788, by Rev. Riggin; Elizabeth
    Ross   4 AA
Esterday, Jacob, 9 Sept. 1796, Rachael Landers   4 FR
Etherton, Thomas, 22 Sept. 1796, Mary Bryan   3 BA-329
Etsler, Daniel, 30 June 1789, Mary Albaugh   4 FR
Euzibi, John, 24 Oct. 1799, Elizabeth Haden   6 BA
Evans, Annanias, 16 May 1800, Priscilla Adkins   1 WO
Evans, Caleb, 5 March 1787, Eva Wedel   2 FR-1126
    4 FR gives the bride's name as Waddle.
Evans, Charles, 20 Dec. 1789, Ann Lamb   6 BA
Evans, Cornelius, 24 Aug. 1799, Rosanna Smith   3 BA-376
Evans, David, 23 Feb. 1792, Elizabeth Barnes   4 FR
Evans, Edmund, 4 Nov. 1797, Rachel Milbourn   1 WO
Evans, Edward, 10 July 1796, Jane Coale   3 BA-327
Evans, Eleazer, 14 Nov. 1796, Mary Nicholls   4 FR
Evans, Elijah, 21 Jan. 1782, Mary Morris   4 FR
Evans, Evan, 28 Aug. 1790, Mary Noon   6 BA
Evans, Evan, 18 Nov. 1800, Delia Gordon   3 BA-395
Evans, Francis, 23 March 1796, Anne Porter   3 BA-321
Evans, Griffith, 6 July 1788, Sarah Hewit   6 BA
Evans, Griffith, 26 Nov. 1792, Mary Burgess   6 BA
Evans, Hooper, 18 May 1791, Fanny Cheshire   2 DO
Evans, James, 2 Feb. 1786, Sarah Meek   4 FR
Evans, Jeremiah, 5 June 1791, Mary Stevenson   6 BA
Evans, John, 23 June 1778, Letitia Ellicott   5 BA-5
Evans, John, 21 Dec. 1786, Verlinda Willcoxon   3 PG-251
Evans, John, 14 Jan. 1789, Rhoda Cope   2 DO
Evans, John, 26 Oct. 1789, Mary Byass   6 BA
Evans, John, 31 Oct. 1795, Johanna Fitzgerald   1 AL-53
Evans, John, 12 Nov. 1795, Elizabeth Shaffer   3 BA-313
Evans, John, 1 Dec. 1795, Sarah Barnes   4 FR
Evans, John, 1 Jan. 1799, Nancy Webb   3 BA-367
Evans, John, 1 April 1800, Miranda Owens   2 FR-1126
Evans, Joseph, 3 Dec. 1789, Eliza Wilcox Davey   11 BA-13
Evans, Joshua, 27 May 1797, Betsey Nelson   1 WO
Evans, Lewis, 5 April 1787, Rachel Ellicott   6 BA
Evans, Peter, 26 July 1796, Nancy Hudson   1 WO
Evans, Philip, 12 Jan. 1786, Mary Hurley   3 PG-251
Evans, Robert, 18 March 1787, Lucy Jones   3 PG-252
Evans, Robert, 17 July 1794, Eve Smith   4 FR
Evans, Robert, 10 Nov. 1797, Elizabeth Elliott   2 DO
Evans, Solomon, 24 Dec. 1799, Polly Bratcher   2 SO
Evans, Wm., 14 Nov. 1781, Susanna Powel   11 BA-5
Evans, William, 14 Jan. 1784, Alasanna Cassimore   3 HA-8
Evans, William, 7 Sept. 1788, Rebecca Fowler   6 BA
Evans, William, 20 Nov. 1795, Rebecca Atkins   2 DO
Evans, William, 13 June 1797, Polly Walston   2 SO

Everard, Wm., 31 May 1800, Eliza Ann Mills   6 BA
Everett, Benjamin, 1 April 1781, Rachel Mitchell   3 HA-3
Everett, James, 26 Oct. 1783, Mary Barnes   3 HA-8
Everett, James, 9 Feb. 1793, Margaret Walker   3 HA-22
Everett, Jno., 8 March 1793, Eleanor Taylor   50 BA-393
Everett, Joseph, 21 Nov. 1795, Clara Wheeler   3 HA-24
Everhart, Jacob, 6 Sept.? 1790, C. Black   29 BA-1
Everhart, Martin, 4 Jan. 1779, Christina Fulsin   4 FR
Everhart, Martin, April 1781, Mary Eve Mock   4 FR
Everhart, Martin, 27 Oct. 1787, by Rev. Turner; Sarah
    McCallister   51 BA-30
Everist, Benjamin, 12 Feb. 1800, Margaret Barnes   3 HA-29
Everist, Nathan, 23 Feb. 1798, Charity Everist   3 HA-27
Everitt, Philip, 21 March 1797, Patty Brown   4 KE-67
Everitt, William, 29 March 1795, Sarah Cooper   1 BA-7
Everley, Peter, 18 June 1797, Ulianna Wistman   4 FR
Everly, John, 27 May 1783, Elizabeth Isaminger   4 FR
Eversfield, John, 7 June 1778, Barbara Brooke   2 PG-2
Everson, Jacob, 5 May 1793, Sophia Parks   3 BA-267
Everson, James, 16 Dec. 1787, Elizabeth Nothay   3 PG-253
Everson, Nathaniel, 2 Aug. 1795, Elsbeth Nash   3 BA-307
Everson, Nich's, 3 Jan. 1800, Cath. Corlbon   29 BA-11
Everson, Richard, 23 Aug. 1792, Mary Lenhart   29 BA-3
Everton, Daniel, 22 July 1783, Eliza Stringer   11 BA-6
Evett, Andrew, 13 April 1781, Eleanora Porter   3 HA-4
Evitt, Woodward, 17 Jan. 1784, Catherine Hiseler   4 FR
Ewald, John, 19 June 1787, Cathrina Bingel   10 BA-188
Everly, Peter, 18 June 1797, Juliana Wiszman   2 FR-1126
Ewers, Jonathan, 27 Aug. 1797, Ann Gregg   4 FR
Ewin, William, 5 Nov. 1799, Mary England   4 FR
Ewing, George, 20 June 1782, Jane Harris   3 HA-6
Ewing, James, 14 April 1784, Mary Kean   3 HA-8
Ewing, Joseph, 13 April 1793, Mary Gorrell   3 HA-22
Ewing, William, 10 Oct. 1785, Elizabeth Billingsley 3 HA-10
Eyler, Jonas, 24 April 1781, Anna Regina Herbach   5 FR-10

Fackrel?, John, Feb. 1790, Mary Felps   4 AA
Fagg, William, 3 Nov. 1778, Priscilla Jones   2 PG-2
Fah, Abraham, 28 March 1790, Mary A. Steiner   2 FR-1128
Fahly, Geo., 23 Feb. 1791, Mary Wolff   2 FR-1128
Fairall (Terral?), Mathew, 19 Jan. 1797, Helhan Barnes 2 AL-700
Fairbank, James, son of James, 30th day, 6 mo., 1780,
    Elizabeth Troth, dau. of Henry   4 SF-162
Fairbanks, Jno., 25 Jan. 1789, Ann Hairman   11 BA-12
Fairbanks, Wm., 30 Nov. 1799, Amelia Butler   29 BA-11
Fairs, Edward, 18 Nov. 1792, Margaret Matthews   3 BA-257
Falconear, John Barkley, 9 April 1798, Ann Maria Shane 4 FR
Falconer, Elisha, 30 April 1794, Sarah Davis   4 FR
Faling, Henry, 3 Jan. 1786, Elizabeth Delauter   4 FR
Fallen, David, 29 May 1798, Esther Purkins   2 SO
Fallon, James, 22 June 1783, Ann Baker   11 BA-6
Falls, Moor, 10 Dec. 1785, Abigail Biddle   11 BA-9
Falls, Moor, 24 Sept. 1796, Rebecca Wilson   5 BA-6
Fannon, Lawrence, 29 Oct. 1788, Ann Henseller   3 BA-213
Fant, Theobald, 14 April 1796, Catharina Schumack   10 BA-198
Faris, Christian, 33 May 1794, Elizabeth Mantz   4 FR
Faris, John, 26 March 1779, Sarah McDonnah   4 FR
Farland, Joseph, 15 May 1791, Mary Frazier   3 BA-256
Farlow, Jesse, 7 March 1797, Sarah Laws   1 WO
Farmer, John, 27 Jan. 1781, Sarah Smith   3 HA-3
Farmer, John, 12 Sept. 1788, Hester Galbraith   18 BA-1
Farmer, William, 23 Nov. 1789, Mary Penn   4 FR
Farsnworth, Jas., 31 Aug. 1782, Jane Murphey   11 BA-5
Farquhar, Amos, 14 March 1796, Jane Moore   4 FR

Farquhar, James, 23 March 1784, Sarah Moore   4 FR
Farquhar, Robert, 12 May 1789, Esther Dodson   4 FR
Farquhar, William, Jr., son of William and Ann (Miller);
    11th day, 10 mo., 1780, Mary Bailey, dau. of John
    and Mary (Nash) Bailey   3 SF
Farquhar, William, son of Allen and Sarah (Moore), 30th
    day, 9 mo., 1784, Elizabeth Talbott, dau. of John
    and Mary   3 SF
Farquhar, William, son of William and Rachel, 24th day, 4
    mo., 1793, Esther Wright, dau. of Isaac and Eleanor
    (Parvin) Wright   3 SF
Farr, John, 25 Nov. 1778, Mary Watts   2 CH-235
Farr, John Baptist, 23 Nov. 1780, Mary Vermilion   2 PG-1
Farroll, Thomas, 12 May 1778, Hannah Dalton   4 FR
Favely, James, 9 Feb. 1797, by Rev. Ridgely; Elizabeth
    Whittle   4 AA
Farver, Adam, 21 June 1779, Eliz'th Keplar   4 FR
Farver, John, 8 May 1783, Rachel Arnold   4 FR
Fassett, John, 20 June 1800, Anna Bravard   1 WO
Fassett, Thomas, 26 April 1800, Sarah Faasett   1 WO
Faubel, Wilhelm, 26 July 1800, Lena Morsitius   10 BA-200
Fauble, Jacob, 18 April 1795, Susanna Hubbard   4 FR
Faulkner, Samuel, 4 Oct. 1799, Mary Brown   3 BA-379
Faurie, Joseph, 13 April 1795, Frances d'Alban   40 BA-1
Fauxall, Thos., 5 Jan. 1792, Eliza French   18 BA-4
Favery, Thos., 1 April 1794, Naomi Coward   6 BA
Favier, John, 15 Dec. 1796, Mary Thompson   44 BA-2
Faw, Abraham, 27 March 1793, Mary Steiner   4 FR
Feburiere, Nicholas, 17 April 1797, Susan Tucker   5 MO-114
Fee, Michael, 10 April 1796, Rebecca Matthews   6 BA
Feichter, George, 15 Jan. 1785, Catherine Snyder   4 FR
Fell, Elijah, 7 May 1791, Priscilla Galloway   6 BA
Fell, Junius, 16 Sept. 1792, Eleanor Wholebrook   6 BA
Fell, Stephen, 21 Feb. 1780, Ann Edwards   3 HA-1
Fell, Wm., 27 May 1800, Ann Haslip   29 BA-11
Fellers, Edward, 23 May 1797, Jane Higdon   3 BA-345
Fellers, Henry, 10 April 1791, Rachael Miller   3 BA-234
Fellows, Edward, 23 May 1797, Jane Higdon   35 BA-5
Fellows, Richard, 25 Dec. 1783, Mary Barlow   11 BA-7
Felton, John, 23 Nov. 1798, Eleanor McHenry   4 FR
Fenell, Stephen, 16 Dec. 1787, Margaret Perry   4 FR
Fenley, Richard, 25 March 1782, Alice Ward   3 HA-6
Fenley, Thomas, 25 Oct. 1795, Chloe Bayne   3 PG-441
Fennell, John, 5 Sept. 1792, Sarah Phrisby   3 HA-222
Fenny, Nathaniel, 28 Aug. 1785, Sarah Dawson   11 BA-8
Fenton (or Trenton?), Anthonio, 23 Jan.1780, Marg't Burk
    11 BA-4
Fenton, Charles, 2 March 1782, Dolly Danily   3 BA-183
Fenwick, Jacob, 20 Nov. 1778, Catherine Ford   1 SM-137
Fenwick, James, 14 Feb. 1786, Henrietta Mary Lancaster   2 CH-235
Ferguson, Daniel, 11 May 1798, Mary Riley   4 KE-67
Ferguson, James, 15 June 1799, Rebecca Tuds   6 BA
Ferguson, Rob't, 5 Oct. 1784, Eliza Vanhorn   11 BA-7
Ferguson, Wm., 3 Aug. 1797, Eunice Davis   1 WO
Fern, Peter, 2 May 1786, Marg. Bennet   2 FR-1128
Fero, Henry, 2 Nov. 1793, Mary Wigal   4 FR
Ferrel, George, 28 Oct. 1798, Eleanor David   4 FR
Ferrel, Wm., 10 Aug. 1800, Mary Burns   2 FR-1128
Ferrell, Thomas, 6 April 1793, Ruth Galloway   1 BA-6
Ferrill, William, 6 Feb. 1798, Elizabeth Vansant   4 KE-67
Fessler, John, 18 Oct. 1782, Elizabeth Baugh   4 FR
Fessler, John, 13 April 1793, Barbara Bough   4 FR
Fethercoil, Jno., 1 Dec. 1781, Catherine Berkman   4 FR
Fid, Paltus?, 8 Dec. 1783, Mary White   3 HA-8
Fiege, Philip, 15 Oct. 1782, Christena Hummell   4 FR

```
Field, Martin, 2 Sept. 1790, Jane Hogan              3 BA-228
Field, Thos., 11 Feb. 1797, Rebecca Thomas           29 BA-8
Fielder, Nicholas, 16 Jan. 1780, Anne Colloson        3 SM-58
Fields, Abraham, 19 March 1778, Johana Peck           2 MO-1
Fields, Elisha, 15 Feb. 1780, Margaret Naylor         2 PG-7
Fields, Jno., 4 May 1797, Mary Madden                 5 MO-114
Fightmaster, Frederick, (12 May 1791), Sarah Kennedy  31 BA-1
   3 BA-234 gives the date as 15 May 1791.
Filius, John, 31 July 1792, Elizabeth Yates           4 FR
   2 FR-1128 gives the date as 5 Aug. 1792.
Filius, Joseph, 15 April 1798, Eliz. Schlicher        2 FR-1128
Fillers, Richard, 7 July 1787, Elizabeth West
Filson, Samuel, 1 April 1800, Mary Cooper             2 FR-1128
Filuse, Joseph, 10 April 1798, Elizabeth Sleicherlan  4 FR
Fin, William, 24 April 1788, Susannah Quay            11 BA-1
Finders, Philip, 26 Dec. 1797, Sarah Lenhard          10 BA-198
Fink, George, 23 May 1795, Rosina Fleishal            29 BA-6
Finkbohner, John, 5 Aug. 1788, Sus. Brucker           2 FR-1128
Finlay, Hugh, 11 Aug. 1788, Sarah Hughes              6 BA
Finley, Alexander, 27 April 1799, Jane Carruthers     3 BA-370
Finley, Jas. or Jos., 19 Sept. 1798, Cath. Gartz      29 BA-9
Finly, Jno., 1791, Marg. Wilson                       50 BA-391
Finn, Peter, 31 Oct. 1782, Mary Wheeler               11 BA-5
Finn, Wm., 12 Jan. 1793, Eliza Harris                 18 BA-5
Finnagan, Henry Patrick, 17 June 1792, Aransa Demaker  1 BA-4
Finnigan, H. Patrick, 25 April 1792, Areanea Slemaker  3 HA-21
Fips, John, 29 Nov. 1779, Mary Collins                11 BA-4
Firby, Jno., 16 May 1793, Marg. Turner                50 BA-393
Firth, James, 11 Oct. 1791, Nancy Hunter              11 BA-3
Fischer, Adam, 10 April 1797, Elizabeth Rowe          4 FR
Fischer, Jonas, 22 Oct. 1798, Anne Cook               4 FR
Fish, Benjamin, 14 April 1785, Aret Ridgely           2 AA-114
Fish, James, 11 Oct. 1791, Nancy Hunter               3 BA-254
Fish, Joseph, 27 Aug. 1796, Jemima Martin             29 BA-7
Fish, Richard, 23 Dec. 1800, Elizabeth Young          7 MO-29
Fish, Robert, 22 Dec. 1796, Eliz. Jeans               5 MO-113
Fishback, John, 19 Feb. 1799, Cath. Beckley           29 BA-10
Fisher, Basil, 29 Dec. 1787, Sophia Paradise          5 BA-6
Fisher, James, 19 Jan. 1800, Sarah Stewart            6 BA-
Fisher, John, 24 Dec. 1778, by Rev. Magill; Aksia Mosgrove
   4 AA
Fisher, John, 24 Nov. 1787, Eleanor Robertson         2 CH-235
Fisher, John, 24 May 1795, by Rev. Ridgely; Margaret Eaglen
   4 AA
Fisher, John, 10 June 1800, Nancy Appleman            6 BA
Fisher, John Frederick, 29 May 1792, Elizabeth Birshall
   3 BA-258
Fisher, Joseph, 6 Aug. 1794, Elisabeth Cruses         5 BA-6
Fisher, Lewis, 18 March 1784, Mary Childs             3 AA-421
Fisher, Ludwick, 26 April 1797, Elizabeth Crawford    4 FR
Fisher, Martin, 6 Feb. 1783, Rebecca Chaulk           3 AA-419
Fisher, Martin, 20 April 1783, Mary Daily             2 CH-235
Fisher, Martin, 24 May 1798, by Rev. Ridgely; Rody Forrest
   4 AA
Fisher, Mich'l, 7 Aug. 1783, Eliza Lucas              11 BA-6
Fisher, Michael, 12 July 1794, Matilda Watkins        1 AL-53
Fisher, Robert, 20 Dec. 1791, Hannah Baker            28 BA-1
Fisher, Thomas, 14 Nov. 1799, Elizabeth Yates         3 BA-380
Fishpaw, John, 16 Aug. 1798, Ann Haile                6 BA
Fishwick, James, 11 Dec. 1787, Mary Craig             3 BA-216
Fiste, Philip, 27 April 1795, Margaret Simmerman      4 FR
Fister, Henry, 11 Jan. 1799, Drusilla Johnson         4 FR
Fitch, Ai. (sic), 27 May 1800, Ann Mercer             29 BA-11
Fitch, Henry, 1 Feb. 1784, Ann Eagleston              11 BA-7
Fitcher, Ezekiel, 5 Nov. 1784, Hagar Robertson        2 DO
```

```
Fitchew, Ezekiel, 7 Jan. 1789, Elizabeth Jones        2 DO
Fitchew, Levin, 10 Dec. 1788, Ann Tall                2 DO
Fite, George, 8 Oct. 1783, Rosanna Pontany            3 BA-189
   11 BA-6 gives the bride's name as Punteny.
Fite, Jacob, 10 March 1791, Nancy Reinecker          29 BA-2
Fite, Peter, 23 Aug. 1782, Mary Clayer                3 BA-183
Fitzgerald, Edward, 27 Oct. 1796, Mary Donovan        3 BA-329
Fitzgerald, Elijah, 12 April 1799, Sarah Lister       2 SO
Fitzgerald, 29 July 1800, Sarah Walston               2 SO
Fitzgerald, John, 24 Aug. 1780, Ann Green             2 CH-235
Fitzgerald, John, 2 June 1795, Mary Drake             3 BA-305
Fitzgerald, John, Oct. 1800, Mary Phelps              2 FR-1128
Fitzgerald, Richard, 25 July 1781, Judith Sutor       3 HA-4
Fitzgerald, Robert, 19 Feb. 1792, Catherine Cook      3 BA-255
Fitzhugh, Peregrin, 11 Dec. 1781, Elizabeth Chew      3 AA-418
Fitzpatrick, Dennis, 13 July 1791, Susanna Trott      4 FR
Fitzpatrick, Hugh, 13 Aug. 1794, Julia Slater        29 BA-5
Fitzpatrick, James, 25 Aug. 1786, Lucy Yeats         10 BA-186
Fitzpatrick, Michael, 3 June 1780, Catherine Collins  3 HA-2
   5 HA gives the date as 6 June 1778, which is more
   likely to be correct.
Fiveash, Peter, 12 May 1784, Charlotte Parks          3 BA-187
Flannigan, Lackey, 14 June 1779, Jane Barnett         4 FR
Flax, Michael, 11 June 1780, Marg't Brannar          11 BA-4
Fleagle, Charles, 26 Oct. 1778, Catherine Fisher      4 FR
Fleagle, Valentine, 11 Aug. 1779, Christena Censor    4 FR
Fleming, John, 10 March 1784, Rachel Davis            4 FR
Fleming, John, son of David, 31st day, 10 mo., 1787,
   Betsy Charles, dau. of Jacob and Mary              4 SF-182
Flemming, Arthur, 13 April 1782, Deborah Bonham       4 FR
Flemming, Arthur, 8 Feb. 1785, Sarah Davis            4 FR
Flemming, Elijah, 4 Dec. 1786, Cathrina Taylor       10 BA-188
Flemming, John, Jr., 16 April 1780, Nelly Quinton     1 SO-26
Flemming, James, 1 July 1794, Elizabeth Kibble       37 BA-1
Fletcher, Baterton, 4 Dec. 1787, Major Stanton        2 DO
Fletcher, Henry, 10 Feb. 1785, Cath. Warrel          11 BA-8
Fletcher, James, 13 June 1797, Mary Campbell          6 BA
Fletcher, Philip, 18 April 1784, Cath'e Wolfe        11 BA-7
Fletcher, Philip, 5 July 1794, Mary Sullivan          4 FR
Fletcher, Thomas, 24 Feb. 1800, Elizabeth Drank       3 BA-383
Fleury, Paul Aime, 28 Oct. 1794, Clare Young          1 BA-6
Fleury, William, 2 July 1782, Esther Maddox           2 CH-235
Flinn, James, 5 July 1796, Elizabeth Cooney           3 BA-327
Flinn, Jno., 30 Nov. 1793, Judith McMahan            29 BA-5
Flisher, John, 9 June 1778, Ezebella Dugmore         11 BA-1
Flood, Jno., 1791, Eleanora Murphy                   50 BA-391
Florance, Nicholas, 19 Aug. 1783, Pamela Woolen       3 BA-185
Florence, Mons., 11 Nov. 1797, Barbara Brown          3 BA-352
Flout, Christopher, 6 Nov. 1792, Hannah Hughes        4 FR
Flower, Charles, 28 Oct. 1780, Mary Hutchins          3 SM-58
Flower, Samuel, 25 Jan. 1779, Janey Bowlaney          4 FR
Flower, Thomas, 5 April 1779, Mary Murphey            4 FR
Flower, Thomas, 2 Dec. 1781, Eleanor Bond             3 SM-60
Floyd, Caleb, 31 May 1793, Eleanor Lee                6 BA
Floyd, Joseph, 31 Dec. 1782, Mary Daughaday          11 BA-6
Floyd, Joseph, 21 Nov. 1787, by Rev. West; Nancy Wheeler
   51 BA-30
Floyd, Joseph, 9 Dec. 1794, Catherine Logue          44 BA-1
Floyd, Sam'l, 1791, Cath. Gross                      50 BA-391
Floyd, Samuel, 15 June 1793, Fanny Somelin            3 BA-269
Floyd, Thomas, 24 Sept. 1795, Ann Todd               43 BA-1
Fluck, Jacob, 4 May 1790, Eliz. Koblentz              2 FR-1128
Fluck, Mat., 15 Jan. 1787, Cath. Jung                 2 FR-1128
Fluck, Peter, 9 July 1797, Mary Hans                  2 FR-1128
Flucke, John, 17 April 1779, Eve Young                4 FR
```

```
Flucke, Mathias, 11 Jan. 1787, Cathe. Young          4 FR
Flucke, Peter, 7 July 1797, Mary Haines              4 FR
Fluhart, Massey, 7 May 1785, Mary Ridgely            4 FR
Fluhart, Stephen, 22 Nov. 1785, Elizab. Randel       2 FR-1128
Flyde, John, 18 March 1799, Elizabeth Powlass        4 FR
Focke, Anthony, 12 March 1797, Biddy Sullivan        3 BA-342
     See also 47 BA-1.
Fogarty, Edw'd, 30 Oct. 1797, Judith Mekin          44 BA-2
Fogel, Jacob, 17 Jan. 1796, Mary Hall                2 AL-700
Fogle, Adam, 26 Jan. 1785, Eliz'th Scaggs            4 FR
Fogle, Adam, 7 Aug. 1787, Sarah Hammett              4 FR
Fogle, Christian, 12 July 1793, Mary Norwood         4 FR
Foist, John, 7 July 1798, Eleanor Farthing           4 FR
Foley, Joseph, 3 Aug. 1795, Mary Burnet              3 BA-307
Folger, Frederic, 7 March 1782, Isabella Emmitt      5 BA-6
Follin, Henry, 23 Feb. 1799, Polly Miles             2 SO
Folmer, Martin, 29 Aug. 1795, M. F. Christiana Penman  29 BA-6
Fonday, Abraham, 28 Dec. 1785, Marg't Grymes        11 BA-9
Fonnerdan, John, 21 Oct. 1783, Marg't Edwards       11 BA-6
Foocks, Levin, 11 Jan. 1788, Nancy Thomas            2 DO
Fooks, George, 21 March 1783, Sarah Bartlett         4 FR
Fooks, Jonathan, 3 Jan. 1800, Eleanor Roach          1 WO
Forbes, James, 9 Oct. 1783, Eliza Foster            11 BA-6
Forbes, James, 6 Dec. 1788, Ann Smith               11 BA-12
Forbes, Jas., 1791, Francisca Keller                50 BA-390
Forbes, John, 21 April 1782, Elizabeth Marshall      2 CH-235
Forbes, Matt., 14 July 1788, Polly Bevans            3 BA-217
Ford, Alexander, before 25 Nov. 1789, Rachel Barns  20 BA-1
Ford, Archabald, 12 June 1791, Elizabeth Athey       3 PG-258
Ford, Barney, 8 Sept. 1783, Mary Cole               11 BA-6
Ford, Benjamin, 1 Sept. 1782, Mary Apriorson         3 HA-7
Ford, Benjamin, 7 Jan. 1800, Margaret Hopkins        4 SM-184
Ford, Edmund, 7 Sept. 1784, Cathrina Bond           10 BA-182
Ford, Frederick, 4 June 1782, Margaret Benjamin      3 HA-6
Ford, Gilbert, 22 Dec. 1796, Esther Adams            2 SO
Ford, Horatio, 16 March 1787, by Rev. West; Elizabeth Gill
     51 BA-30
Ford, Joh., 27 Oct. 1778, Elizabeth Bevens          11 BA-1
Ford, John, 2 Oct. 1781, Winifred Athey              2 CH-235
Ford, John, 23 Dec. 1794, Drussilla Durbin           7 BA-1
Ford, Jos., 20 Nov. 1778, Henrietta Spinks           1 SM-137
Ford, Joseph, 28 April 1779, Margaret Wood           3 AA-415
Ford, Joseph, 31 Dec. 1781, Mary Wood                3 AA-418
Ford, Joseph, 17 Dec. 1799, Polly Peacock            8 BA-1
Ford, Joshua, 10 June 1786, Sarah Cole              10 BA-186
Ford, Joshua, 22 Dec. 1796, Mary Johnson            45 BA-1
Ford, Lloyd, 20 Feb. 1780, Mary Wood                11 BA-4
Ford, Peter, Oct. 1779, Maria Sewell                 1 SM-137
Ford, Thos., 5 May 1785, Nancy Wood                 11 BA-8
Ford, Thomas Cockey Deye, 20 Dec. 1781, Acha Cockey 11 BA-5
Ford, William, 10 April 1785, Mary Sillen            3 HA-10
Ford, William, 5 Aug. 1787, Lucy James              1 BA-1
Foreman, Dan'l, 13 July 1784, Eliza Brown           11 BA-7
Foreman?, Joseph, before 12 Dec. 1792, by Rev. John Long;
     Ann Robinson                                    4 AA
Foreman, Joseph, 30 June 1796, Eliz'th McKeel        1 TA-316
Foreman, Leon'd, 23 March 1782, Rachael Mattox      11 BA-5
Foresith, Samuel, 3 April 1781, Martha Carsons       3 HA-3
Forester, George Will'm, 29 Aug. 1779, Temprence Redgrave
     2 KE-314
Forgason, Daniel, 14 June 1785, Charity Auston       2 FR-1128
Forker?, Patrick, 17 May 1778, Mary Elligan          2 MO-1
Forman, Bartholomew, 15 Dec. 1796, Juliana Crabbin   4 KE-67
Forman, John, 6 Sept. 1797, Elizabeth Jones          4 KE-67
Forman, Valentine, 14 Oct. 1798, Rebecca Lucas       3 BA-364
```

```
Forman, William Lee, 20 Nov. 1790, Jane Spear          5 BA-6
Formwalt, Jacob, 30 March 1793, Cathe. Garnhart        4 FR
Forney, Jno., 3 May 1797, Sarah Boyce                 29 BA-8
Forney, Nicholas, 8 July 1798, Charlotte Potee         3 BA-360
Forquhar, Rob't, 19 May 1789, Esther Dodson            2 FR-1128
Forrest, Josiah, 25 Dec. 1785, Ann Stone              16 BA-1
Forrest, Vincent, 17 Nov. 1778, Sarah Newshaw         11 BA-1
Forrester, Benja., 20 Jan. 1780, Sarah Oram           11 BA-4
Forrester, George, 5 May 1783, Rachael Oram           11 BA-6
Forrester, George, 9 April 1789, Cassandra Gardiner   10 BA-192
Forster, Moses, 8 May 1778, Mary Cavener               4 FR
Forsyth, Isaac, 22 Dec. 1792, Frances Brown            5 BA-6
Forsythe, Jno., 22 June 1796, Cath. Swyman            29 BA-7
Fort, John, 10 Nov. 1797, Elizabeth Beachem           45 BA-2
Fortney, David, 6 May 1800, Elizab. Lewis              2 FR-1128
Fortt, Joshua, 6 Aug. 1799, Anna Tipton               45 BA-3
Forward, Jacob, 22 May 1781, Martha Warren             2 CH-235
Forward, Samuel, 18 June 1795, Ann Perkins             7 BA-2
Forward, William, 2 Jan. 1779, Hannah Harland          4 FR
Forwood, Jacob, 7 May 1782, Elizabeth Warriner         3 HA-6
Forwood, Jacob, 10 Feb. 1789, Martha Jarritt           1 HA-394
Forwood, Samuel, 28 Oct. 1794, Mary Murray             3 HA-23
Forwood, Samuel, 13 June 1795, Ann Perkins             3 HA-24
Fosset, James, 27 June 1779, Anne Fanin or Farrin      2 PG-3
Fossett, Jno., 2 April 1782, Susanna Ellison          11 BA-5
Foster, Basill, 19 April 1778, by Rev. Magill; Mary Penn
   4 AA
Foster, Benj., 14 Feb. 1798, Catherine Prather         3 AL-5
Foster, George, 29 Sept. 1800, Mary McPhail            2 HA-352
Foster, James, 18 Sept. 1799, Rebecca Shanacy          3 BA-377
Foster, John, 7 Dec. 1782, Eliza Liddle               11 BA-6
Foster, Joseph, 24 Dec. 1782, Sarah Tull              11 BA-6
Foster, Joseph, 2 Dec. 1788, by Rev. Claggett; Elizabeth
   Grover                                              4 AA
Foster, Wm., 2 April 1782, Sarah Walker               11 BA-5
Fotten, James, 14 Oct. 1794, Rebecka Fetters           2 AL-700
Fouble, Jacob, 14 Aug. 1784, Margaret Gibbs            4 FR
Fouble, Jasper, 10 Sept. 1789, Eliza Watson           11 BA-12
Fouble, Peter, 14 Oct. 1792, Elizabeth Painter         6 BA
Fouck, George, 11 Nov. 1786, Elizabeth Kemp            4 FR
Foules?, James, 31 Jan. 1795, Ann Hammond              6 BA
Fountz, Jacob, 1792, Mary Emich                       50 BA-392
Fout, Daniel, 6 Aug. 1796, Barbara Fout                4 FR
Fout, Henry, 29 Oct. 1791, Phoebe Creager              4 FR
Fout, Jacob, 20 June 1795, Cath. Faubel               29 BA-6
Fout, Jacob, 6 Feb. 1797, Margaret Smith               4 FR
Fout, Michael, 23 Nov. 1789, Catherine Hufferd         4 FR
Foutch, Heughey, 7 May 1787, Elizabeth Johnson         4 FR
Foutch, John, 28 May 1787, Catharina Specht            1 FR-59
Foutz, George, 6 March 1798, C. Sapp                   3 AL-5
Fowble, Jacob, 22 May 1796, Margaret Hafligh           6 BA
Fowler, Benjamin, 24 March 1796, Mary Hughes           6 BA
Fowler, Edward, 11 May 1799, Eleanor Roberts           2 SO
Fowler, George, 16 April 1791, Eleanor Hammond         6 BA
Fowler, Isaac, 13 Aug. 1795, Nancy Head                6 BA
Fowler, James, 23 Aug. 1789, Mary Woodfield           23 BA-1
Fowler, James, 20 April 1795, Elizabeth Moore          3 BA-301
Fowler, John, 7 Dec. 1790, Nancy Burgee                4 FR
Fowler, John, 21 Dec. 1791, Ann Johnston               6 BA
Fowler, John, 20 April 1798, Mary Huff                 4 FR
Fowler, Martin?, before 15 Sept. 1796, by Rev. Green; Sarah
   Taylor                                              4 AA
Fowler, Rezin, 21 Dec. 1797, by Rev. Ridgely; Rachel Sewell
   4 AA
Fowler, Richard, 31 Jan. 1779, Ann Summers             2 PG-3
```

```
Fowler, Richard, 6 March 1783, Mary Collins         11 BA-6
Fowler, Robert, 30 Nov. 1796, Sarah Fowler           3. SO
  2 SO gives the date as 29 Nov. 1796.
Fowler, Samuel, 3 June 1794, Rebecca Love            6 BA
Fowler, Samuel, 26 Nov. 1794, Mary Reese            3 BA-296
Fowler, Samuel, 13 April 1796, Ann Cavey Adams      29 BA-7
Fowler, Thomas, 10 Oct. 1793, Sarah Barton          3 BA-275
Fowler, William, 8 Oct. 1785, Catherine Garland      3 HA-10
Fowler, William, 17 March 1792, Rebecca Watkins     18 BA-4
Fowler, William James, 6 Feb. 1780, Elizabeth Craig  3 AA-416
Fowler, Zachariah, 19 Sept. 1782, Elizabeth Jones    3 BA-183
Fox, Adam, 2 Nov. 1798, Ann Gaver                    4 FR
Fox, Anthony, 25 May 1780, Eleanor Collins          11 BA-4
Fox, Anthony, 16 Aug. 1782, Sarah Kemp              11 BA-5
Fox, George, 10 Dec. 1799, by Rev. Roberts; Mary Sambling
  4 AA
Fox, Henry, 19 May 1794, Catherine Frey              4 FR
Fox, Henry, 18 Jan. 1799, Leah Zimmerman             4 FR
Fox, Henry, 28 June 1799, Mary Garver                4 FR
Fox, John, 15 Sept. 1798, Catherine Simon            4 FR
Fox, John Hopkins, 21 Dec. 1794, Elizabeth Simon     4 BA-77
Fox, Peter, 1 Nov. 1799, Mary Oyler                  4 FR
Fox, Uriah, 18 April 1794, Grace Sedwith             4 FR
Fox, William, 15 Aug. 1797, Mary Carroll             3 HA-26
  See also 2 HA-350.
Foxwell, Abraham, 27 Dec. 1785, Priscilla Wallace    2 DO
Foxwell, Abraham, 21 March 1788, Hagar Dean          2 DO
Foxwell, John, 13 Aug. 1781, Sarah Woodland          2 DO
Foxwell, Levi, 21 April 1785, Sarah Fallen           2 DO
Foxwell, Roger, 28 March 1785, Comfort Phillips      2 DO
Foxwell, Roger, 16 Feb. 1786, Betsy Foxwell          2 DO
Foxworth, Robert, 16 Sept. 1790, Mary Cottriel       6 BA
Foye, Henry, 6 Feb. 1787, Mary Piecken               4 FR
Frampton, Hubert, 18 Oct. 1788, Mary Vickars         2 SF
Framtom, William, 3rd day, 11 mo., 1781, Marget Goslin  2 SF-288
Frances, Rennick, 15 May 1782, Ann Roddy             3 BA-183
Francis, Charles, 1791, M. Bonsey; blacks, married by per-
  mission                                           50 BA-390
Francis, John, 8 Nov. 1781, Alice Cramphin           2 PG-5
Francks, Henry Taylor, 14 Sept. 1779, Margaret Buskurk  4 FR
Frandenberger, Heinrich, 27 Nov. 1787, Sarah Bondrey  10 BA-190
Frankfurther, Phill., 28 Sept. 1783, Mar. Elis. Munschin
  2 CL-82
Franklin, Alexander, 1 March 1797, Rachel Riley      1 WO
Franklin, Charles, 26 April 1792, Catherine Counsilman
  18 BA-4
Franklin, Garret, 24 March 1796, Elizabeth Burgin    6 BA
Franklin, John, 8 Dec. 1779, Virlinda Cox            2 CH-235
Franklin, John, 10 April 1783, Mary Hopkins          3 AA-419
Franklin, Rezon, 22 Nov. 1798, Elizabeth Goshedg     4 FR
Franklin, Selby, 7 Jan. 1799, Mary B. Vandome        1 WO
Franklin, Tho., 1 June 1786, Marg't Councilman      11 BA-9
Franklin, Thos., 30 June 1796, Charlotte Kirby       1 WO
Franklin, William, 21 Jan. 1779, Isabella Franklin   3 AA-415
Franklin, Wm., 18 July 1797, Anna Riley              1 WO
Fraser, Andrew, 1 Jan. 1792, Catherine Lanham        3 PG-436
Fraser, Francis, 3 June 1792, Mary Perkins           5 BA-6
Fraser, Wm., 12 June 1781, Verlinda Giddings         4 FR
Frasier, John, 25 Oct. 1789, Mary Lanham             3 PG-255
Frazier, Charles, 4 Aug. 1788, Elizabeth Mitchell    2 DO
Frazier, James, 11 Feb. 1783, Margaret Eccleston Byus  2 DO
Frazier, James, 29 Sept. 1783, Elizabeth Hubbert     2 DO
Frazier, James, 7 Dec. 1794, by Rev. Joseph Wyatt; Ann
  Duckett                                            4 AA
Frazier, John, 24 July 1784, Kitty Barron            2 DO
```

```
Frazier, John, 6 Sept. 1798, Barbara Good           4 FR
Frazier, Levin, 14 Jan. 1781, Elizabeth Eccleston   2 DO
Frazier, Levin, 14 Aug. 1784, Elizabeth Lee         2 DO
Frazier, Peter, 8 Dec. 1795, Rebecca Beayer         4 FR
Frazier, Samuel, 29 Aug. 1798, Mary Massey          4 KE-67
Frazier, Solomon, 29 July 1784, Sarah Hight Le Compte 2 DO
Frazier, Solomon, 22 Feb. 1788, Elizabeth Woolford  2 DO
Frazier, William, 6 Feb. 1780, Sarah Jones          3 AA-416
Fream, Richard, 12 Dec. 1791, Susannah Link         6 BA
Frederick, Michael, 27 Oct. 1798, Cath. Shott       29 BA-9
Free, Martin, 27 Sept. 1792, Cath. Roll             50 BA-392
Free, Nic'l, 2 Feb. 1790, Catherine Nigill          3 PG-256
Freeburger, Jacob, 23 Feb. 1799, Mary Parks         6 BA
Freed, Peter, 1 Nov. 1797, Charity Hennickhouser    4 FR
Freeland, Robert, 25 Feb. 1781, Sarah Isaac         3 AA-417
Freelock, John, 30 Aug. 1798, Sidney Walker         3 BA-362
Freeman, James, 8 April 1787, Ann Webster           3 PG-252
Freeman, Patrick, 2 Sept. 1794, Catherine Farmer    3 BA-293
Freeman, Sam'l, 21 Dec. 1785, by Rev. Turner; Mary Burnham
   51 BA-29
Freeman, Thomas, 6 April 1779, Sarah Mitchell       1 CA-2
Freeman, Thomas, 18 Dec. 1783, Chaney Allnut        3 AA-420
Freeman, Thos., 6 Nov. 1787, by Rev. Reed; Mary Talbott
   4 AA
Freer, John, 27 Nov. 1797, Chloe League             3 BA-352
Freeze, Michael, 18 June 1799, Catherine Grabill    4 FR
French, Benjamin, 11 Nov. 1784, Mary Abercrombie    11 BA-8
French, Daniel, 3 Nov. 1781, Rachel Wilson          5 BA-6
French, Dominick, 1793, Mary Shillingsburgh         50 BA-393
French, Jno., 11 Oct. 1796, Marg. Welsh             29 BA-7
French, Othea, 13 Nov. 1788, Eleanor Waters         6 BA
French, Peter, 14 Aug. 1798, Catherine Stagors      6 BA
French, Samuel, 5 April 1798, Lydia Cook            6 BA
Frey, Andreas, 1788, Marg. McCurdy                  50 BA-388
Frey, Daniel, 19 Nov. 1793, Elizab. Christ          2 FR-1128
Frey, George, 26 Aug. 1783, Mary Bayman             4 FR
Frey, Isaac, 29 Jan. 1776, Mary Stone               4 FR
Frey, Jno., 24 Nov. 1799, Lurecia Lucas             5 MO-116
Friberger, George, 11 April 1795, Sophia Shoup      4 FR
Frieberger, Henry, 8 May 1794, Marg. Miller         29 BA-5
Friedrich, David, 15 Jan. 1797, Hanna Lauterjung    50 BA-401
Friend, Jas., 18 June 1787, Susannah Sparrow        6 BA
Fries, Michael, 18 June 1799, Cath. Grabiel         2 FR-1128
Friesbie, George, 27 March 1794, Cath. Breitenbach  29 BA-5
Frinton, Thomas, 3 April 1781, Margaret Hutchcraft  4 FR
Frior, John, 19 Sept. 1784, Catherine Callahan      3 BA-188
Fritzgerald, Wm., 24 June 1791, Molley Purdam       4 FR
Frizzel, Lloyd L., 30 Jan. 1800, Seeny Turner       2 FR-1128
Frizzle, Jacob, 28 Feb. 1780, Margaret McKinley     4 FR
Froelich, John, 19 Jan. 1792, Salome Rothrock       2 FR-1128
Frollett, Joseph, 10 May 1784, Susannah Stallions   3 AA-421
Fromentin, Eligius, 28 May 1800, Betsy Polk         2 SO
Frost, George, 20 April 1789, Ann Mahar             11 BA-12
Frost, John, 20 April 1787, Sarah Krap or Krass     5 BA-6
Frost, John, 20 April 1787, Sarah Thrap             17 BA-9
Frost, John, 14 Feb. 1790, Elizabeth Dorsey         6 BA
Frost, William, 5 July 1795, Elizabeth Haney        7 BA-2
Froud, James, 16 Jan. 1780, Mary Sage               4 FR
Frushour, Adam, Jr., 24 Sept. 1799, Margaret Wandle 4 FR
Frushour, Jacob, 8 April 1799, Susannah Dick        4 FR
Frutscho, Phillip, 4 Oct. 1787, Maria Steitz        10 BA-188
Fry, Enoch, 16 June 1794, Soloma Holtzapple         4 FR
Fry, Joseph, 25 April 1797, Permelia Angling        4 FR
Fry, Thomas, 30 June 1795, Elizabeth Crandell       3 PG-441
Frydinger, Nicholas, 6 Aug. 1796, Esther Kemp       4 FR
```

Frymiller, Jno., 27 June 1798, Eliz. Walter   29 BA-9
Fuchs, Adam, 5 Dec. 1786, Abigail Sellers   6 FR-201
Fuchs, Balthasar, 15 July 1792, Elizabeth Euler   6 FR-202
Fuchs, Henry, 18 Jan. 1799, Leah Zimmerman   2 FR-1128
Fuchs, John, 23 Jan. 1791, Cath. Fuchs   2 FR-1128
Fuchs, John, 18 Sept. 1798, Cath. Simmon   2 FR-1128
Fuchs, Peter, 16 Sept. 1800, Bridget Ingen Hall   2 FR-1128
Fulford, John, 30 Jan. 1794, Sarah Hughes   6 BA
Fulham, Geo., 2 May 1782, Dorothy King   11 BA-5
Fulk, James, 6 Sept. 1780, Sarah Baker   11 BA-4
Fulks, Jacob, 13 Dec. 1792, Priscilla Perkins   1 BA-5
Fuller, Heinrich, 22 Dec. 1789, Catharina De Hoff   6 FR-202
Fuller, Sam'l, 8 April 1783, Eliza Sheers   11 BA-6
Fuller, Thomas, 6 May 1800, Ann Cockerill   2 AL-701
Fullerton, James, 13 Jan. 1791, Sarah Bradford   1 BA-3
Fullerton, Wm., 25 Oct. 1787, Anne Mackin   11 BA-10
Fullum, Mich'l, 11 May 1779, Mary Ropp   4 FR
Fulton, Alexander, 24 Nov. 1797, Sarah Carmick   4 FR
Fulton, George, 3 June 1794, Margaret Hedges   4 FR
  2 FR-1128 gives the date as 7 June 1794.
Fulton, James, 10 Oct. 1786, Anne Christopher   5 BA-6
Fulton, John, 10 Dec. 1799, Lydia Mitchell   3 HA-28
Fulton, Nathaniel, 10 May 1784, Nancy Browning   4 FR
Fulton, Robert, 11 March 1794, Barb. Balzell   2 FR-1128
Fulton, William, 6 Nov. 1800, Mary Davidson   5 BA-6
Furlong, William, 5 May 1791, Sally Johnson   5 BA-6
Furney, Henry, 12 April 1784, Judey Horne   4 FR
Furrow, Mathias, 31 Aug. 1779, Christena Beaghell   4 FR
Fursel, Edward, 17 July 1782, Mary Carroll   3 HA-7
Fusbury, George, 13 Sept. 1789, Eleanor Geany   3 BA-221
Fye, Joseph, 12 March 1790, Ann McClain   4 FR
Fyen, Friedrich, 22 Feb. 1784, Cathrina Boster   10 BA-180

G-(?)-d, Edward, 9 Oct. 1789, by Rev. Claggett; Henrietta
  Lansbury   4 AA
Gabard, John, 8 March 1778, Margaret Lucas   2 CH-235
Gadd, Levin, 20 Aug. 1791, Mary Woollen   2 DO
Gadd, Thomas, 29 Oct. 1797, Elizabeth Smith   2 DO
Gadd, William, 23 April 1791, Nancy Padan   2 DO
Gafford, William, 7 June 1798, Elizabeth Mott   4 KE-68
Gaghen, John, 6 Jan. 1793, Mary Dunsheath   6 BA
Gaikes, Samuel, 12 July 1795, Elizabeth Flood   3 BA-307
Gains, Brian, 17 April 1800, Ann Houdershel   2 AL-701
Gaiter, Ralph, 30 Nov. 1788, Sarah Rowles   3 BA-219
Gaither, James, 6 Nov. 1798, Patience Hall   7 BA-4
Gaither, Ralph, 23 Nov. 1788, Sarah Rowles   11 BA-1
Gale, Thomas, 6 Feb. 1797, Elizabeth Cooper   4 FR
Gale, Thomas, 7 Sept. 1797, Ann Hodges   4 KE-68
Gall, Johan, 1788, Cath. Schaffer   50 BA-388
Gallaher, Daniel, 30 March 1799, Jane Higginbottom   3 BA-369
Gallaher, Francis, 13 Oct. 1800, Margaret Dolan   3 BA-393
Gallaher, John, 24 Dec. 1798, Alce Anna   6 BA
Gallaway, Thomas, 25 Feb. 1780, Catherine Dallas   2 CH-235
Gallion, Alexander, 14 Jan. 1800, Mary Spencer   3 HA-29
Gallion, Gregory, 16 Oct. 1785, Ann Antley   3 HA-10
Gallion, John, 15 Dec. 1796, Mary Garrettson   7 BA-3
Gallop, Joseph, c.1792, by Rev. Linton; Milcah Dorsey 4 AA
Galloway, Absolom, (31 July 1788), Rebecca Chamberlain
  15 BA-1
Galloway, Absolom, 4 May 1799, Mary Merrett   3 HA-28
Galloway, Aquila, 4 April 1792, Ann Barton   1 BA-4
Galloway, Ezekiel, 14 July 1790, Rachel Craig   6 BA
Galloway, Francis, 23 March 1790, Margaret Shocknesey 5 BA-6
Galloway, James, 5 Sept. 1790, Mary Chine   1 BA-2

Galloway, John, 24 Oct. 1780, Wealthy Mildues   11 BA-4
Galloway, Moses, 6 May 1782, Pamelia Owings   11 BA-5
Galloway, Moses, 7 Aug. 1800, by Rev. Ridgely; Sarah Ship-
  ley   4 AA
Galloway, Robert, 2 Sept. 1799, Judy McKafferty   3 BA-377
Galloway, Salathiel, 9 Nov. 1797, Mary Galloway   6 BA
Galloway, Thomas, 25 Feb. 1781, Catherine Dallas   11 BA-2
Galloway, Thomas, 27 Dec. 1791, Mary Molholm   2 WA-17
Galloway, William, 16 Dec. 1783, Sisley Bryan   11 BA-7
Gallup, Joseph, 28 Sept. 1791, Milcah Dorsey   3 HA-22
Gallup, Thomas, 1 Feb. 1792, Phoebe Smith   3 HA-21
Gambia, Richard, 4 April 1781, Sarah Gardner   2 CH-235
Gamble, Thomas, 29 Oct. 1795, Mary McPillon   3 BA-311
Gamble, Thomas, 18 Sept. 1796, Margaret Collins   5 BA-6
Gambrill, Abraham, 30 Jan. 1786, Lily Bryan   2 DO
Game, George, 6 Dec. 1799, Leah Noble   2 SO
Gander, George, 9 July 1778, Rosanna Dillan   4 FR
Gandy, Abraham, 24 Dec. 1793, Sarah Manihan   2 FR-1131
Ganer?, John, 3 Aug. 1797, Deborah Colbertson   7 BA-3
Gantt, Daniel, 5 Oct. 1797, Lucy Anderson   4 FR
Gantt, Edward, 23 April 1795, Letitia Lovejoy   3 PG-441
Gantt, Dr. Thos., 19 Nov. 1780, Miss Ann Reynolds   2 PG-7
Gardiner, Isaac, 13 Jan. 1778, Rebecca Baker   1 CA-1
Gardiner, Jno., 3 Jan. 1790, Rachael Jones   11 BA-13
Gardiner, John Chunn, 1 Oct. 1799, Esther Cowood   2 CH-235
Gardiner, John Francis, 1794, Cath. Jameson   3 CH-161
  "disp. for consang. from 3rd to 4th degree."
Gardiner, Johnsey, 15 Jan. 1778, Martha Grimes   1 CA-1
Gardiner, Jos., 14 April 1793, Dorothea Edelin   3 CH-161
  "disp. for consang. in the 2nd to 3rd degree"
Gardiner, Obed, 3 June 1791, Deborah Gettier   5 BA-6
Gardiner, Richard, 5 May 1778, Mary Davis   11 BA-1
Gardiner, William, 29 June 1780, Keziah Willin   1 CA-3
Gardner, Abraham, 28 Aug. 1796, by Rev. Ridgely; Catherine
  Litchfield   4 AA
Gardner, Henry, 26 March 1798, Elizabeth Reel   4 FR
Gardner, Hezekiah, 18 Sept. 1783, Mary H. McPherson   2 CH-236
Gardner, Isaac, 20 Jan. 1796, by Rev. Cash; Mary Winnell
  4 AA
Gardner, Isaac, 30 Aug. 1798, Rachel Hudson   6 BA
Gardner, Jno., 13 March 1794, Marg. Hoffman   29 BA-5
Gardner, John, 26 Dec. 1797, Cassandra Dowden   5 MO-114
Gardner, John, 9 Jan. 1798, Ann Sadler   45 BA-2
Gardner, Peter, 6 Nov. 1799, Debby Curtis   6 BA
Gardner, William, 10 May 1795, Ann Hahn   5 BA-6
Gardner, William, 4 Feb. 1798, by Rev. Ridgely; Rachel
  Steward   4 AA
Garland, Edmund, 17 Dec. 1792, Christina Young   50 BA-392
Garland, George, 28 Feb. 1797, Mary Messer   3 BA-342
Garman, Benjamin, 5 Jan. 1797, Rachel Barton   6 BA
Garmann, John, 9 Sept. 1792, Catharina Cassel   10 BA-194
Garner, Luke, 21 May 1798, Hannah Powell   4 FR
Garner, Walter, 4 Nov. 1779, Mary Ann Finisee   2 PG-2
Garner, William, 14 Nov. 1779, Mary Ann Finises   2 CH-236
Garner, William, 1 May 1800, Sarah Allen   6 BA
Garnett, And'w, 19 Oct. 1785, Mary Bevington   4 FR
Garnett, Geo., 18 Feb. 1783, Eliz'th Mosserly   4 FR
Garnous, William, 19 Feb. 1794, Jane Tune   3 BA-281
Garret, Barton, 29 Jan. 1778, Ann Butler Gray   2 CH-236
Garret, John Valentine, 28 July 1778, Mary Kelly   11 BA-1
Garrett, Allen, 18 Jan. 1779, Mary Barton Philpott   4 FR
Garrett, Samuel, 20 Nov. 1779, Rebecca Foreman   11 BA-3
Garrettson, Garrett, 18 Sept. 1785, Susannah Olliver   3 HA-9
Garrettson, Thomas, 25 Oct. 1789, Rachel Roberts   22 BA-1
Garrison, Alexander, 16 Sept. 1785, Mary Greenfield   3 HA-10

```
Garrison, James, 5 Jan. 1781, Martha Osborn          3 HA-3
Garrison, Ruthan, 20 Nov. 1797, Mary Gallion         3 HA-26
  1 BA-8 gives the date as 23 Nov. 1797.
Garrot, Aeneas, 4 May 1799, Eleanor Conner           4 FR
Garrott, John, 30 Dec. 1786, by Rev. Claggett; Mary Waron
  4 AA
Garrott, Thomas, 14 Feb. 1799, Eliz. Fee             5 MO-115
Gartner, Geo., 25 Dec. 1786, Hannah Lee             11 BA-10
Gartrell, Jehocophat, 4 May 1799, Eleanor Conner     4 FR
Garvan, Cornelius, 18 Aug. 1800, Mary Shay          50 BA-407
Garvey, George, 21 Nov. 1793, Jemima Cherry         29 BA-5
Gary, Everrard, May 1800, Ann Cloud                  5 MO-116
Gaslin, Smith, 6 April 1791, Nancy Airey             2 DO
Gassaway, Richard, 12 Oct. 1778, Ann Arnold          4 FR
Gassaway, Samuel, 7 Nov. 1789, Nancy Gassaway        4 FR
Gatchel, Samuel H., 18 Oct. 1796, Anne Gray          6 BA
Gaterel, Stephen, 18 Feb. 1779, by Rev. Magill; Mary Cole
  4 AA
Gates, James, 1 Jan. 1783, Lydia Padgett             2 CH-236
Gattert, Valentine, 2 April 1781, Catherine Foy      4 FR
Gatton, Azariah, 29 Sept. 1782, Hesse Veneble        4 FR
Gatton, Richard, 1 July 1785, Jemima Veatch          4 FR
Gatton, Sylvester G., 29 Sept. 1786, Anna Robey      4 FR
Gatton, Thos., 22 Jan. 1799, Ruth Ray                5 MO-115
Gauline, John Baptist, 22 Nov. 1796, Pauline Justine Leuder
  44 BA-2
Gauntt, Thomas, 7 Nov. 1783, Sarah Potts             4 FR
Gavan, Matthew, 4 Oct. 1795, Anne Fitzgerald        40 BA-1
Gaver, Dan'l, 10 March 1795, Susanna Beckibaugh      4 FR
Gaver, John, 18 Nov. 1783, Margaret Black            4 FR
Gaver, Valentine, 18 May 1779, Eliz'th Smitten       4 FR
Gaw, William, son of James and Prudence, 30th day, 1 mo.,
  1799, Isabel Belt, dau. of Richard and Keturah     1 SF
Gay, Henry, 4 Dec. 1779, Judy Silverin               4 FR
Gearish, Francis, 20 May 1798, Rachel Holbrook       6 BA
Gebhart, Peter, 16 Aug. 1796, Elizabeth Haas         4 FR
  2 FR gives the date as 18 Aug. 1796.
Gebhart, Solomon, 11 Nov. 1793, Catherine Werner     4 FR
Geddes, David, 4 Sept. 1796, Elizabeth Courtney      3 BA-329
Geddis, David, 8 Feb. 1794, Lydia Day               14 BA-16
Geddis, George, 11 Dec. 1777, Isabella Hayes         5 BA-6
Geddis, James, 19 Oct. 1786, Marg't Flax            11 BA-9
Gedon, Daniel, 23 Dec. 1800, Susannah Butler         2 FR-1131
Gedultig, Conrad, 25 May 1778, Catherine Snider      4 FR
Geesey, Henry, 12 Jan. 1799, Rosina Ramack           4 FR
Geisler, George Diedrich, 11 Feb. 1798, Elizabeth Nonne-
  berg or Wonneberg                                 10 BA-198
Geissinger, Frantz, 4 April 1790, Sarah Levi         2 FR-1131
Gelaspy, Charles, 20 Nov. 1779, Elizabeth Dunsheath  3 HA-1
Geltzer, Valentin, 21 Aug. 1785, Anna Lena          10 BA-184
Gennow, Frederic, 26 Dec. 1800, Barb. Lots          29 BA-11
Gent, Thomas, 1 June 1796, Judith Landers            3 BA-323
Gentle, George, 21 April 1778, Verlinda Locker       2 MO-1
Geoghegan, Ambrose, 1 May 1778, Margaret Salmon     11 BA-1
Geoghegan, George, 10 July 1788, Eliz. Winder       29 BA-1
Geoghegan, Moses, 18 Feb. 1784, Rebecca Ferguson     2 DO
George, negro belonging to Henry Jones, 28 March 1796,
  Polly, negro belonging to Charles Jones            5 MO-113
George, Henry, 13 March 1795, Marg. Cole            29 BA-6
George, Joseph, 31 Jan. 1790, Rosannah Howard        6 BA
Georgia, Jno., 18 Dec. 1796, Eliz. Gantz            29 BA-8
Gerecht, Justiss, (date not given), Elizab. Drenter  2 FR-1131
German, Benja., 26 Feb. 1784, Rachael Parlett       11 BA-7
German, John, 7 Feb. 1782, Ann Cole                  2 CH-236
German, John, 24 Dec. 1782, Sarah Barny             11 BA-6
```

German, Moses, 10 Nov. 1791, Susannah Dean 6 BA
German, Thomas, 19 Oct. 1785, Zana Bevan 11 BA-8
Germley, Michael, 22 April 1799, Biddy Fockes 3 BA-370
Gernand, John Adam, 19 May 1789, Anna Catherine Weller, dau.
of Jacob and Anna Margaretha 5 FR
Gerrish, Francis, 4 June 1778, Mary Lyon 11 BA-1
Gerry, James, 10 Oct. 1786, by Rev. Turner; Florah Low
51 BA-30
Gess, Jonathan, 22 Aug. 1791, Rebecca Dowel 2 FR-1131
Gest, John, 13 Nov. 1792, Rebecca Hall 3 HA-22
Getee, Henry, 1 Aug. 1792, Mary Barnover 29 BA-3
Gettert, Valentine, 10 March 1792, Catherine Beaghly 4 FR
Getzendanner, Adam, 14 Oct. 1787, Mary An. Kuhns 2 FR-1131
Getzendanner, Balser, 11 June 1794, Phillipena Stull 4 FR
2 FR-1131 gives the date as 12 June 1794, and the bride's
name as Stoll.
Getzendanner, Christian, 1 April 1786, Cath. Ramsbergh 4 FR
2 FR-1131 gives the date as 2 April 1786, and the
groom's name as Gotzendanner.
Getzendanner, Christian, 15 July 1786, Mary Ann Bare 4 FR
Getzendanner, Geo., 22 April 1780, Eliz'th Darr 4 FR
Getzendanner, Henry, 17 April 1800, Hannah Becker 2 FR-1131
Getzendanner, Jacob, son of Adam, 7 Jan. 1797, Elizabeth
Getzendanner; 2 FR-1131 gives the date as 10 Jan.
1797 4 FR
Getzendanner, John, 5 Sept. 1785, Rebeckah Fout 4 FR
2 FR-1131 gives the date as 6 Sept. 1785, and the
bride's name as Faut.
Getzendanner, John, 30 May 1789, Catherine Tabler 4 FR
2 FR-1131 gives the date as 31 May 1789, and the
bride's name as Dabler.
Geyer, Adam, 23 April 1791, Margaret Doss 4 FR
Geyer, Daniel, 9 May 1791, Mary Brengle 4 FR
2 FR-1131 gives the date as 10 May 1791.
Geyer, Henry, 15 Feb. 1795, Elizab. Ireland 2 FR-1131
Geyer, Jacob, 25 July 1794, Elizabeth Lemaster 4 FR
Geyer, John, 20 March 1785, Elizab. Scheffy 2 FR-1131
Geyser, Henry, 7 Feb. 1795, Elizabeth Ireland 4 FR
Ghant, George, 31 Jan. 1782, Elizabeth (?) 2 CH-236
Ghequiere, Charles, 6 Feb. 1785, Harriet Halley 11 BA-8
Giar, John, 19 March 1785, Elizabeth Sheffey 4 FR
Gibb, Elisha, 10 June 1800, Hesse (Merritt?) 1 WO
Gibberthorp, Thomas, 6 Aug. 1792, Rachel Joy 3 BA-257
Gibbins, James, 8 March 1794, Hannah Bush or Busher 3 BA-285
Gibbons, Alexander, 8 Oct. 1792, Rebecca Keith 3 PG-437
Gibbons, Eli, 12 Jan. 1799, Milly Tilghman 2 SO
Gibbons, Francis, 20 Feb. 1780, Rebecca Eden 3 SM-58
Gibbons, Philip, 4 June 1780, Margaret Sinclair 5 BA-6
Gibbs, Abraham, on or about 6 Nov. 1793, Sarah (?) 7 BA-1
Gibbs, John, 2 Aug. 1796, Susanna McDonald 4 FR
Gibbs, John H., c.24 Sept. 1778, Mary Henrietta Dyer 2 PG-2
Gibhard?, Lewis, 25 Feb. 1797, Eliz. Slaughter 29 BA-8
Gibson, Bennett, 30 Jan. 1800, Comfort Grover? 2 DO
Gibson, Francis, 10 Match 1784, Elizabeth Davis 3 HA-8
Gibson, James, 22 June 1784, Catherine Ettyburn 5 BA-6
Gibson, James, 11 Oct. 1798, Nancy Merriday 3 SO
Gibson, James, 2 April 1799, Sarah Ward 6 BA
Gibson, John, 18 March 1781, Ann Gibson 3 AA-417
Gibson, James, 10 May 1795, Elizabeth Joice 3 BA-305
Gibson, Joseph, 28 Oct. 1783, Susanna Jones 11 BA-6
Gibson, Peter, 18 Oct.? 1792, Susanna Shiles? 4 AA
The ceremony was performed by Rev. Parrott.
Gibson, Thomas, 10 March 1778, Caroline Porter 11 BA-1
Gibson, Thomas, 12 Nov. 1789, Eliza Bond 1 BA-2
Gibson, Thomas, 4 Nov. 1792, Nancy Heughs 4 FR

Giddings, Thomas, 30 April 1793, Lyda Perry   4 FR
Gier, George, 1 May 1784, Mary Thomas   4 FR
Giesbert, Daniel, Aug. 1795, Elizabeth Michael   4 FR
Giese, Frederick, 8 Sept. 1783, Mary Baker   4 FR
Giese, Henry, widower, 20 Jan. 1800, Rosina Glatt, dau. of
     George and Maria Elizabeth   5 FR
Giessler, John, 22 May 1789, Barbara Loschni   10 BA-192
Gifford?, John, 3 Nov. 1782, Mary Sangsture   3 HA-7
Gifford, Robert, 17 March 1793, by Rev. G. Ridgely; Hannah
     Meek   4 AA
Gilbert, Aquila, 9 Jan. 1780, Priscilla Gallion   3 HA-1
Gilbert, Benjamin, 26 Feb. 1789, Eleanor Hudson   6 BA
Gilbert, Henry, 18 Feb. 1797, Sarah Smith   4 KE-68
Gilbert, James, 12 Jan. 1783, Mary Johnson   3 HA-7
Gilbert, Jervis, 19 Nov. 1798, Sophia Cole   2 HA-351
     3 HA-27 gives the date as 27 Nov. 1798.
Gilbert, John, 24 Nov. 1780, Mary Strong   2 KE-314
Gilbert, Michael, 18 Nov. 1783, Elizabeth Presbury   3 HA-8
Gilbert, Michael, 7 Aug. 1785, Ann Clark   3 HA-9
Gilbert, Michael, 30 April 1794, Betsy Stiles   3 HA-23
Gilbert, Parker, 21 Sept. 1797, Martha McComas   1 BA-8
     3 HA-26 gives the date as 19 Sept. 1797.
Gilbert, Parker, Jr., 2 Oct. 1800, Martha Hughes   2 HA-352
     3 HA-30 gives the date as 1 Oct. 1800.
Gilbert, Philip, 9 Feb. 1783, Sarah Ruff   3 HA-7
Gilbert, Thomas, 13 July 1779, Hannah Burton   4 FR
Gilbert, Thomas, 29 Oct. 1790, Ruth Fisher   29 BA-2
Gilbert, William, 2 Dec. 1794, Jane Ever   3 HA-23
Gilberthorp, Francis, 13 Nov. 1796, Eleanor Sutherland 6 BA
     19 BA-11 gives the groom's name as Francis Gilbert
     Thorpe.
Gilberthorp, William, 9 Feb. 1800, Elizabeth Hart   3 BA-382
Gilberthorpe, James, 19 April 1798, Sarah Pratt   3 BA-357
Gilburn, Wm., 13 July 1797, Nancy Churchman   29 BA-8
Gilder, Ruben, 5 Oct. 1790, Mary Ashbury Alkin   26 BA-1
Giles, Andrew, 23 Dec. 1797, Aleathe Willis   4 KE-68
Giles, Geo., 9 May 1785, Mary Hollings   11 BA-8
Giles, Joseph, 28 Aug. 1800, Hannah Reed   6 BA
Giles, Sam'l, 11 Dec. 1790, Dorothea Fields   29 BA-2
Giles, Thomas, 18 Dec. 1798, Betsy Leatherbury   2 SO
     Another entry in the same source gives the date as
     21 Dec. 1798. 3 SO gives the date as 15 Jan. 1799.
Giles, William, 7 April 1796, Nancy Israelow   6 BA
Gill, Benjamin, 3 Dec. 1792, Jemima Murray   6 BA
Gill, Charles, 3 March 1787, by Rev. Davis; Priscilla
     Ford   51 BA-30
Gill, Daniel, 30 Sept. 1787, Nelly McCutchins   6 BA
Gill, John, 13 April 1787, by Rev. Davis; Rachel Gill 51 BA-30
Gill, John Price, 29 Nov. 1792, Providence Kirby   19 BA-7
     6 BA gives the groom's name as John Price.
Gill, Joseph, 23 Dec. 1794, Mary Fenley   3 PG-440
Gill, Joshua, 19 Jan. 1799, Jemima Gorsuch   3 BA-367
Gill, Joshua, 9 June 1799, Nancy Goodfellow   45 BA-3
Gill, Nicholas, 13 May 1794, Elizabeth Gill   3 BA-287
Gill, Nicholas, 10 April 1800, Peggy Armstrong   6 BA
Gill, William, 12 May 1783, Rachel Wooden   11 BA-6
Gill, William, 15 June 1793, Mary Gill   6 BA
Gillam, Jacob, 5 Dec. 1782, Lidia Jackson   3 AA-419
Gillam, Lucas, 24 Dec. 1789, Temperance Corbin   1 BA-2
Gillaspie, David, 8 Sept. 1778, Christe Berry   4 FR
Gilleland, John, 23 April 1798, Mary Hays   4 FR
Gilling, James, 12 July 1778, Elizabeth Mates   11 BA-1
Gillingham, James, son of John, of Bucks Co., Penna., 24th
     day, 5 mo. 1786, Elizabeth Hayward, dau. of Wm.
     of A. A. Co.   6 SF

Gillion, Philip, 3 March 1787, Catherine Rowe   4 FR
Gilliss, Jesse, 29 Aug. 1794, Sebrah Lurton?   38 BA-1
Gilliss, Joseph, 6 May 1800, Esther Dashiell   2 SO
Gillnar, John, 5 Feb. 1799, Rachel Darby or Darley   3 BA-368
Gills, Eckhardt, 13 May 1788, Cath. Sulzer   2 FR-1131
Gilmor, John, 26 March 1799, Ann Price   2 AL-701
Gilmore, John, 11 Jan. 1796, Jane Smith   5 BA-6
Gilpin, Bernard, son of Gideon and Sarah, of Del. Co.,
    Penna., 21st day, 8 mo. 1793, Sarah Thomas, dau. of
    Richard Thomas of Mont. Co.   6 SF
Gilpin, William, 1 Oct. 1779, Sebina Violet   2 PG-3
Gingen, George, 19 April 1778, Jenny Wade   4 MO-1
Gipson, James, 8 Oct. 1798, Nancy Merreday   2 SO
Giraud, Alex'r, 29 Oct. 1797, Mary Ryan   44 BA-2
Giraud, James John, 18 June 1796, Anna Harriet Wheeler 6 BA
Gisberd, Abraham, 4 Dec. 1798, Sarah Jenkins   4 FR
Gisenir, John, 10 Nov. 1795, Mary Good   4 FR
Gisse, Peter, 4 June 1795, Susannah Decter   5 BA-6
Gist, John E., 13 Nov. 1783, Frances Trippe   3 BA-191
Gist, Mordecai, 23 Jan. 1778, Mary Sterett   5 BA-6
Gist, Thomas, 2 Dec. 1781, Martha Scott   3 AA-418
Gist, Thomas, 29 July 1785, by Rev. Turner; Ruth Shelly
    51 BA-29
Gittinger, John, 28 April 1795, Marg. Hauck   2 FR-1131
Gittings, Archibald, 13 March 1799, Elisabeth Bosley   1 BA-9
Gittings, Asa, 16 April 1799, Elizabeth Clarke   4 FR
Gittings, James, 23 April 1793, Harriet Sterett   5 BA-6
Gittings, Richard, 20 Nov. 1788, Mary Sterett   5 BA-6
Gittins, John, 10 Sept. 1788, Mary Clements   3 PG-254
Gittleman, Jno., 12 July 1785, Mary Maydwell   11 BA-8
Gitzadanner, Jacob, 9 June 1784, Elizabeth Moyer   4 FR
Gitzadanner, Thos., 13 Oct. 1787, Mary Ann Koontz   4 FR
Givans, James, 22 March 1797, Betsey Lindsey   1 WO
Givans, Robert, 22 Oct. 1795, Rosanna Butler   1 WO
Givans, Robert, 17 Oct. 1797, Ruth Robertson   1 WO
Given, James, 30 Dec. 1794, Elizabeth Green   1 BA-6
Given, Moses, son of James and Isabella, 31st day, 8 mo.
    1797, Ann French, dau. of Israel and Margaret   3 SF
Glading, James, 22 Feb. 1785, Mary Chridening   3 HA-10
Glanding, William, 23 May 1794, Anne Norman   2 DO
Glanvill, Stephen, 31 May 1798, Sarah Stevenson   6 BA
Glasgow, James, 30 July 1797, Elizabeth Revell   3 SO
Glasgow, William, 10 Feb. 1783, Eleanor Morland   2 CH-236
Glazner, John, 22 Sept. 1791, Mary Sneidiker   1 AL-52
Glede, James, 27 Feb. 1798, Comfort Fields   6 BA
Gleeson, Roger, 18 June 1797, Catherine Doryan   44 BA-2
Glendenning, Adam, 10 Oct. 1799, Milcah Gale   3 BA-379
Glenn, Hanson Wm., 24 May 1795, Cath. Penn   29 BA-6
Glenn, James, 16 May 1799, Mary Weaver   5 BA-7
Gleves, Thomas, 4 June 1798, Elizabeth Doyle   3 BA-359
Glissan, Solomon, 4 Feb. 1797, Elizabeth Stallings   4 FR
Glover, James, 25 Jan. 1796, Amy Soward   2 DO
Glover, Joshua, (19 Oct. 1791), Rachel Dorsey   15 BA-4
Glover, Samuel, 24 Feb. 1778, by Rev. Magill; Elizabeth
    Barns   4 AA
Glover, William D., 25 Sept. 1800, Peggy Hodson   2 DO
Glyn, James, 6 April 1779, Elizabeth Roberts   5 BA-6
Glynn, Thomas, 6 Jan. 1788, Catherine Driskell   3 BA-205
Goaler, Thomas, 26 Nov.1798, Hesther Baxter   6 BA
Goar, Thomas, 29 May (?), Marcy Smith   4 FR
Gochea, Chas., 17 April 1793, Mary Froggett   50 BA-393
Goddard, John, 5 Aug. 1787, Susannah Thorn   3 PG-253
Goddard, Wm., 23 June 1783, Ann Rockhold   11 BA-6
Godfrey, Bennam, 22 April 1778, Mary Bullock   11 BA-1
Godfrey, Levin, 11 May 1796, Ann T. Truitt   1 WO

```
Godfrey, William, 22 Feb. 1781, Elizabeth Love         2 PG-5
Godfrith, William, 7 Aug. 1800, Elizabeth Schunk       3 BA-389
Godin, Francis, 17 Nov. 1796, Margaret Meek            5 BA-7
Godman, William, 22 July 1797, Delilah White           1 BA-8
Godwin, George, 21 Dec. 1798, Hannah Curry             4 KE-68
Godwin, Thomas, 8 July 1797, Leah Young                4 KE-68
Godwin, William, 15 July 1797, Delilah White           3 HA-26
Gody, Matthew, 29 April 1783, Mary Mahony              2 CH-236
Goe, Henry Bateman, 16 Feb. 1792, Susanna Gittings     1 BA-4
Goe, William, 7 Oct. 1790, Cassandra Jones             1 BA-3
Goetz, Adam, 24 Aug. 1794, Rachel Vanderberg          29 BA-5
Golan, Joseph, 29 June 1799, Anna Penn                 3 BA-373
Gold, Pollish, 21 July 1793, Sarah Froggett           50 BA-393
Gold, William, 30 May 1789, Sarah Stainton             2 DO
Goldie, Jacob, 6 March 1794, Nancy Davis               4 FR
Goldsborough, Charles, 3 Sept. 1793, Elizabeth Goldsborough
     2 DO
Goldsborough, Charles, 19 April 1798, Ann Stevens      2 DO
Goldsborough, John, Jr., son of John and Caroline, 25 Jan.
     1797, Anna Maria Chamberlaine, dau. of Samuel and
     Henrietta Maria (born 31 March 1774);              1 TA-311
     See also 1 TA-316.
Goldsbury, James, 9 Jan. 1783, Araminta Roberts        3 SM-60
Golman, Jacob, 22 Dec. 1797, Elizabeth Cost            4 FR
Gomber, Jacob, 19 May 1787, Susanna Beatty             4 FR
     2 FR-1131 gives the date as 20 May 1787.
Gonyard, Joseph, 8 Aug. 1794, Susanna Gaurig?         10 BA-196
Good, John, 30 Nov. 1793, Elizabeth Thomas             4 FR
Good, Samuel, 4 Feb. 1790, Eleanor White               3 BA-227
     See also 11 BA-13.
Goodacre, Wm., 8 Jan. 1781, Catherine Donavan          4 FR
Goodfellow, Wm., 1 Oct. 1799, Nancy Butler             6 BA
Goodman, Jacob, 30 July 1796, Catherine Jones          4 FR
Goodman, James, 18 March 1800, Betsy Farrington        2 SO
Goodman, William, Sr., 27 Oct. 1788, Mary Morris       4 FR
Goodrick, Joseph, 5 Aug. 1782, Eliza Nash              2 CH-236
Goodwin, Cabel, 17 July 1793, Mary McMin               2 AL-700
     1 AL-52 gives the date as 16 July 1793, and the
     groom's name as Caleb Goodwin.
Goodwin, Jacob, 19 March 1778, Anne Masey              2 MO-1
Goodwin, John, 25 Dec. 1791, Elizabeth Blinio          3 BA-254
Goodwin, Moses, 18 Feb. 1798, Elizabeth Geoghegan      6 BA
Goodwin, Richard, 5 Feb. 1800, by Rev. Wyatt; Sarah Row-
     lings                                             4 AA
Gootee, Bidcar, 5 Dec. 1791, Rachel Tyen?              2 DO
Gootee, Gabriel, 2 Jan. 1798, Nancy Griffith           2 DO
Gootee, William, 30 Aug. 1796, Leah Anderson           2 DO
Gordon, Alexander, 16 May 1781, Martha McClenlan       3 HA-4
Gordon, Duncan, 23 Dec. 1797, Eleanor Mitchell         5 BA-7
Gordon, George, 7 July 1796, Elizabeth Ober            6 BA
Gordon, James, 26 March 1778, Mary Barkever           11 BA-1
Gordon, James, 30 July 1783, Mary Riddle               3 HA-8
Gordon, John, 8 Aug. 1778, Jane Skinner               11 BA-1
Gordon, Jno., 26 Aug. 1792, Elis. Ort                 50 BA-392
Gordon, Jno., 18 Feb. 1795, Sophia Meyers             29 BA-6
Gordon, Joseph, 2 Nov. 1797, Mary Baltin               4 FR
Gordon, Michael, 6 July 1794, Frances Savage           5 BA-6
Gordon, Nathan, Nov. 1797, Delia Stevenson             3 HA-26
     2 HA-350 gives the date as 2 Nov. 1797.
Gordon, Philip, 27 Nov. 1795, Silby Williams           3 BA-313
Gordon, Philip, 14 July 1797, Delia White              3 HA-26
Gordon, Will'm, 5 May 1784, Thomasin White            11 BA-7
Gordy, Jacob, 13 April 1787, Nancy Grace               6 BA
Gordy, Wm., 8 Dec. 1797, Betsey Mitchell               1 WO
Gore, Amos, 26 Dec. 1779, Drewe Andrew                11 BA-4
```

```
Gore, John, 30 Aug. 1785, by Rev. Turner; Clarissa Clarke
   51 BA-29
Gore, Richard, 8 Nov. 1794, Allay Sandiland          40 BA-1
Gorman, John, 24 Feb. 1777, Mary Shepherd             3 BA-172
Gorman, Thomas, 15 Feb. 1778, Mary Clay              11 BA-1
Gormly, James, 19 Jan. 1789, Jemima Berkly           10 BA-192
Gormond, Henry, 1 June 1785, Priscilla Harrington     2 DO
Gornwell, Henry, 19 Jan. 1798, Mary J. Hinman         1 WO
Gorrell, John, 25 Aug. 1781, Avarilla Griffith        3 HA-4
Gorrell, William, 29 Nov. 1780, Ann Kelly             3 HA-3
Gorsuch, Benja., 5 June 1783, Mary Holland           11 BA-6
Gorsuch, Charles, 2 Nov. 1786, by Rev. Pigman; Rebeckah
   Ditto                                              4 AA
Gorsuch, Dickinson, 27 March 1794, Mary Talbott       1 BA-6
Gorsuch, John, 18 Oct. 1791, Mary McClung            34 BA-1
Gorsuch, John, 22 Dec. 1795, Sarah Galloway           6 BA
Gorsuch, John, 29 Nov. 1797, Mary Riley               6 BA
Gorsuch, Joshua, 25 June 1795, Anne Smith             3 BA-305
Gorsuch, Norman, (8 Nov. 1790), Kitty Gorsuch        15 BA-3
Gorsuch, Robert, 8 Aug. 1782, Sarah Donovan          11 BA-5
Gorsuch, Stephen, 15 Feb. 1798, by Rev. Green; Tabitha
   Johnson                                            4 AA
Gorsuch, Thomas, 27 Feb. 1778, Ellin Chapman         11 BA-1
Gorsuch, Wm., 6 June 1793, Aberella Vaughan          18 BA-5
Gorthener, Phillip, 16 Feb. 1785, Cathrina Gutelach  10 BA-184
Gorthrop, John, 30 Jan. 1794, Sally Sheredine         7 BA-1
Gorvan, Cornelius, 18 Aug. 1800, Marg. May           29 BA-11
Goslee, Levin, 8 July 1800, Nelly Jones               2 SO
Goslee, Levin, 31 July 1800, Elizabeth Moore          2 SO
Goslee, Thomas, 15 May 1798, Nancy Denwood            2 SO
Goslee, William, 12 Sept. 1797, Sarah Newcomb         2 SO
Gosler, Thomas, 22 May 1798, Nancy Denwood            3 SO
Goslin, Henry, 25 Dec. 1786, Ann Carney               4 FR
Goslin, John, 10 Feb. 1783, Elizabeth Airey           2 DO
Goslin, Levin, 22 Jan. 1794, Rachel Rider            38 BA-1
Goslin, William, 14 Sept. 1780, Eleanor Western       5 BA-6
Gosnel, Peter, 1 Nov. 1798, Emma Hill                 4 FR
Gosnel, Philip, 30 July 1786, Mary Ward              11 BA-9
Gosnell, Greenbury, 6 Dec. 1792, Ruth Pinbarton       6 BA
Gosnell, Hoper, 12 Sept. 1787, Susannah Speur        10 BA-188
Gosnell, Peter, 22 Oct. 1793, Mary Mollohan           2 FR-1131
Gossage, Daniel, son of Charles and Eve (Hopkins), (born
   28 Feb. 1760), 28 Nov. 1783, Elizabeth Hopkins     1 TA-318
Gossage, Samuel, 9 Nov. 1796, Elizabeth Bright        2 DO
Gossick, Thomas, 15 April 1800, Elizabeth Lauder      6 BA
Gott, Edward, 13 Dec. 1791, Mary Bond                18 BA-4
Gott, Ezekiel, 7 Sept. 1783, Mary Childs              3 AA-419
Gott, Richard, 17 Dec. 1795, Ruth Bailey              1 BA-7
Gough, John, 28 Oct. 1800, Martha Lowry               3 BA-394
Gough, Salathiel, 26 April 1778, Eliza Sheredine Gray 1 CA-1
Gough, Thomas, 22 Dec. 1778, Margaret Gray            1 CA-2
Gough, William, before 25 Nov. 1789, in A. A. Co.; Mary
   Ann Abbott                                        20 BA-1
Gould, Benjamin, 21 Jan. 1790, Elizabeth Hawkins      1 QA-65
Gould, John, 13 March 1796, Margaret Wheeler          3 BA-321
Gould, William B., 26 Oct. 1792, Martha Mitchell      3 HA-22
Gouldby, William, 24 Feb. 1783, Sarah Smith           2 DO
Gouthrop, John, 30 Jan. 1794, Sarah Sheridan          3 HA-23
Gouty, John, 6 Feb. 1800, Nelly Truitt                1 WO
Goven, Gerard, 2 April 1793, Sarah Giles              3 BA-265
Gover, Ephraim Gittings, 31 Jan. 1793, Elizabeth Gover 1 BA-5
Gover, Robert, 27 Feb. 1781, Mary Miles               3 AA-417
Gover, Robert, 18 April 1797, Martha Wheeler          2 HA-349
Gover, Robert, 11 Nov. 1800, Cassandra Lee            3 HA-30
Gover, William, son of Robert, dec.; 28th day, 12 mo., 1786,
   Sarah Cowman, dau. of John                         6 SF
```

```
Gowtee, John, 7 Aug. 1796, Polly Disharoon              1 WO
Grabill, Moses, 12 April 1799, Elizabeth Bixler         4 FR
Grace, Adam, 3 Dec. 1798, Barsheba Hinkle               3 AL-5
Grace, Bowyer, 25 April 1798, Mary Brooks               3 HA-27
  2 HA-350 gives the date as 26 April 1798.
Grace, Peter B., 4 April 1792, Priscilla Meyer          3 HA-21
Gradultig, George, 18 April 1795, Catherine Hole        4 FR
Grafflin, Jacob, 20 Oct. 1793, Mary Frymiller           6 BA
  See also 19 BA-8.
Grafft, William, 21 Sept. 1784, Cathrina Wod?          10 BA-182
Grafton, Aquila, 8 Aug. 1780, Margaret Perine           3 HA-2
Grafton, Daniel, 1 March 1782, Elizabeth Everett        3 HA-6
Graham, Hugh, 5 Oct. 1796, Sara Loffins                 1 AL-53
Graham, James, 3 Feb. 1785, Mary Scrivener             11 BA-8
Graham, John, 22 Aug. 1798, Hannah Cooper               4 KE-68
Graham, John, 21 Jan. 1800, Sally Collier               2 SO
Graham, John, 8 March 1800, Elizabeth Brent             3 AL-6
Graham, Rubin, 20 April 1798, Rachel Carter             4 FR
Graham, Samuel, 25 Sept. 1787, Amelia Wall              2 DO
Graham, William, 28 June 1778, Sabra Robinson          11 BA-1
Grahame, John Colin, 12 Jan. 1788, Anne Jennings Johnson
  4 FR
Grainger, James, 6 Oct. 1788, Nelly Thomas              2 DO
Grainger, William, 5 Feb. 1790, Rebecca Medford         2 DO
Grallot, Francis, 24 Oct. 1793, Catharine Fisher        6 BA
Gramer, Adam, 15 Sept. 1792, Appelona Devilbiss         4 FR
Grammer, Fred'k, 6 Sept. 1787, Eliz. Countryman        29 BA-1
Granger, Joseph, 28 Sept. 1782, Sarah Gripe            11 BA-5
Granger, Joseph, 4 Nov. 1787, Barbara Weaver            6 BA
Grant, Alexander, 20 March 1783, Mary Johnson          11 BA-6
Grant, Daniel, 7 Aug. 1794, Isabella Nelson             5 BA-6
Grant, John, 16 March 1778, Eliza Greenfield Tyler      2 CH-236
Grant, John, 31 March 1798, Elizabeth Leaver           10 BA-198
Grant, Richard, 19 Jan. 1798, Mary Connican             4 KE-68
Grant, William, 18 Nov. 1790, Catherine Holland         1 BA-3
Grant, William, 12 Feb. 1795, Caroline Glebe            3 BA-299
Grant, William, 10 June 1799, Susanna Dennis            3 BA-372
Grapevine, Frederick, 29 April 1787, Elizabeth Mathews  6 BA
Grass, Henry, 2 Oct. 1794, Elisabeth Isaacks            5 BA-6
Graves, Benjamin 7 Oct. 1787, Elizabeth Crown           3 PG-253
Graves, Ebenezer, 31 Aug. 1797, Mary Anderson           5 BA-7
Graves, Ezekiel, 11 Oct. 1796, Linny Ireland           19 BA-11
Graves, Jeremiah, 3 Oct. 1780, Rachel Craig             3 SM-58
Graves, Richard, 29 May 1798, Charlotte Dorsey          3 HA-27
  2 HA-350 gives the date as 31 May 1798.
Graves, Thomas, 9 Oct. 1783, Eliz'th Cartnail           4 FR
Gray, Archibald, 14 July 1800, Lurana Hurley            2 DO
Gray, Benjamin, 15 Feb. 1778, Mary Stewart              2 CH-236
Gray, Elijah, 11 Nov. 1787, by Rev. Forrest; Mary Lawton 4 AA
Gray, George Howard, 15 Dec. 1800, Sally Law            1 WO
Gray, Greenbury, 3 Aug. 1789, Susanna Chaney            4 AA
Gray, Dr. James, 6 Jan. 1784, Sarah Brooke              3 AA-420
Gray, Jas., 1791, Cath. Lewel                          50 BA-391
Gray, James, 5 April 1800, Catharine Denton             8 BA-1
Gray, James Woolford, 28 April 1787, Elizabeth Griffin  2 DO
Gray, Jesse, 12 July 1798, Sarah Lawrence               1 WO
Gray, John, 27 Nov. 1783, Elizabeth Turner              3 SM-61
Gray, John, 26 April 1792, Lucy Foster                  3 BA-258
Gray, John, before 12 Dec. 1792, by Rev. John Long; Ann
  Todd                                                  4 AA
Gray, John, 14 Dec. 1799, Minta Freeman                10 BA-198
Gray, Joseph, 3 Sept. 1795, Elizabeth Willson           3 BA-311
Gray, Joshua, 30 April 1789, Rebecca Drane             10 BA-192
Gray, Littleton, 27 Feb. 1799, Peggy Smith              1 WO
Gray, Lynch, 30 June 1790, Catherine McLaughlin        11 BA-13
```

```
Gray, Lynch, 24 Dec. 1796, Hannah Denton              6 BA
Gray, Peter, 20 March 1798, Mary Bradburn             3 BA-356
Gray, Richard, 12 Sept. 1778, Rebecca Wilson          2 PG-2
Gray, Richard, son of Robert, 27 Nov. 1781, Elizabeth
   Brewer, dau. of Nicholas; see also 11 BA-5         2 AA-114
Gray, Richard, 8 Jan. 1784, Eliza Gray                3 AA-420
Gray, Rouse, 9 Jan. 1796, Bridgett Cathell            1 WO
Gray, Samuel, 22 Sept. 1787, Anne Rice                5 BA-6
Gray, Samuel, 26 July 1799, Levy Hudson               1 WO
Gray, Thomas, 3 Nov. 1778, Anne Bowen                 1 CA-1
Gray, Wilson, 26 April 1782, Elizabeth Simms          2 CH-236
Gray, Zacharia, 22 July 1777, Susanna Parker          2 CH-236
Gray, Zachariah, 22 Feb. 1781, Sophia Holmes          3 BA-190
Grayham, George, 10 June 1800, Kezia Rumbley          2 DO
Grayham, John, 31 Aug. 1787, Mary McLawley            1 BA-1
Grayham, William, 15 July 1800, Eliza Forbes          2 DO
Greathouse, David, 21 Jan. 1794, Pensillah Goodwin    4 BA-76
Greaves, Absalom, 16 Jan. 1781, Alathia Smith         3 SM-59
Greb, Conrad, 27 Jan. 1793, Mary Eberhard            50 BA-393
Greb?, Conrad, 23 Sept. 1798, Sophia Block           29 BA-9
Greeher, Robert, 1 Oct. 1798, Mary Warren             4 FR
Green, Abram, 26 Feb. 1782, Eliz'th Cole             11 BA-5
Green, Allevatius Thompson, 4 Feb. 1798, Delila Holbrook
   6 BA
Green, Basil, 17 Jan. 1780, Mary Ann Lanham           2 PG-1
Green, Charles, Sept. 1782, Margaret Taysor           4 FR
Green, Charles, 23 Feb. 1798, Ann Lane               45 BA-2
Green, Elisha, 3 June 1783, Priscilla Chamberlain    11 BA-6
Green, Ezekiel, 24 Jan. 1795, Darcus Denton           6 BA
Green, Henry, (21 June 1788), Elizabeth Boreing      15 BA-1
Green, Henry, 15 Jan. 1794, Elisabeth Walters         5 BA-6
Green, Henry, 5 Sept. 1799, Anne Walker               3 BA-377
Green, Isaiah, 27 April 1799, Mary Hanky              6 BA
Green, James, 27 Oct. 1792, Ann Bender               29 BA-3
Green, Jeremiah, 13 Oct. 1793, Elizabeth McConner     2 AL-700
Green, John, 1 July 1788, Cassandra Smithson          1 BA-1
Green, John, 7 Nov. 1790, Alice McKinstry             6 BA
Green, John, 12 June 1793, Priscilla Ball             2 DO
Green, John, 3 Jan. 1797, Rachel Redding              4 KE-68
Green, John, 8 March 1797, Betsy Townsend             1 WO
Green, Joseph, 26 March 1789, Catherine Stansbury     6 BA
Green, Joshua, 5 Dec. 1798, Sally Webster             2 SO
Green, Josias, 24 Nov. 1796, Mary Monk               10 BA-198
Green, Launcelot, 30 Oct. 1794, Elizabeth Carr        3 AA-424
Green, Leonard, 29 Jan. 1778, Anne Brown              1 MO-1
Green, Luke, 10 Oct. 1796, Peggy Wilson               4 FR
Green, Nathan, 30 Nov. 1799, Mary Buck                6 BA
Green, Robert, 26 Aug. 1791, Barbara Chambers         1 AL-52
Green, Samuel, 8 Feb. 1793, Mary Ann Violetta Clements 4 FR
Green, Sam'l, 25 March 1796, Susanna Wrench           4 FR
Green, Samuel, 23 July 1796, Hannah Nailor            3 BA-327
Green, Thomas, 30 Nov. 1792, Margaret Giles           2 DO
Green, William, 25 Nov. 1792, Achsah Stinchcomb      18 BA-5
Green, William, 25 Dec. 1792, Susannah Besit          6 BA
Green, William, 21 Dec. 1795, Chloe League            3 BA-313
Green, William, 29 Sept. 1796, Elizabeth Atwood       4 FR
Green, Zadock, 17 Sept. 1798, Eleanor Holder          2 SO
   3 SO gives the date as 26 Sept. 1798.
Greene, Russell, 7 Oct. 1788, Peggy Sly               5 BA-6
Greener, Dan'l, 6 April 1786, Marg. Shartel          29 BA-1
Greenfield, Jacob, 26 Sept. 1791, Elizabeth Everest   3 HA-21
   1 HA-396 gives the date as 29 Sept. 1791.
Greenfield, Nathaniel, 17 Feb. 1791, Elizabeth Hatton 23 BA-2
Greenfield, Thomas Truman, 7 April 1782, Priscilla Beckett
   3 AA-418
```

```
Greenfield, William, 1 March 1797, Sarah Whaland          4 KE-68
Greengrass, John, 28 Feb. 1779, Catherine Cain            4 FR
Greenlee, James, 8 April 1800, Mary Redham                3 HA-29
Greenly, James, 13 April 1800, Mary Redman                2 HA-352
Greenly, Thomas, 25 April 1800, Mary Howard               3 HA-29
  2 HA-352 gives the date as 27 April 1800.
Greenwell, John Basil, 21 April 1798, Polly Gray          4 FR
Greenwell, Philbert, 13 April 1790, Eleanor Cushman       4 FR
Greenwell, Stephen, 18 Feb. 1783, Henrietta Wise          3 SM-61
Greenwood, Alexander, 16 Feb. 1798, Hetta Lassell         4 KE-68
Greenwood, Benj'n, 19 Sept. 1795, Ann Briggs              29 BA-6
Greenwood, John, 27 Feb. 1788, Mary Delahay               2 DO
Greenwood, Tho., 3 Sept. 1782, Sophia Peddicoat           11 BA-5
Greenwood, Thomas, 28 Aug. 1796, Kezia Stansbury          3 BA-327
Greer, Wm., 14 Sept. 1800, Sarah Ridley                   7 BA-4
Gregary, James, 16 Dec. 1792, Ann Jones                   3 PG-437
Gregg, Thomas, 5 June 1795, Anne Smith                    4 FR
Gregory, David, 7 June 1789, Elizabeth Williams           6 BA
Gregory, James, 20 Nov. 1790, Jane Wigley                 6 BA
Gregory, James, 7 May 1796, Sarah Bond                    6 BA
Gregory, John, 11 Nov. 1783, Cathe. Dunn                  11 BA-7
Gregory, Jno., 14 Jan. 1790, Eliza Grimes                 11 BA-13
Gregory, Ralph, 21 Nov. 1798, Sarah Chenoweth             29 BA-10
Greiner, Michael, 19 Aug. 1792, Sybilla Jendes            2 FR-113]
Grey, Thomas, 14 Jan. 1786, Sarah Marine                  2 SF
Grice, Richard, 3 Jan. 1798, Charlotte Hollins            3 BA-367
Griffen, Thomas, 29 April 1784, Elizabeth Jones           3 BA-186
Griffin, Amos, 18 March 1784, Nelly Dawson                2 DO
Griffin, Baxter, 8 April 1784, Fanny Le Compte            2 DO
Griffin, Belitha, 23 June 1795, Mary Smith                1 WO
Griffin, Belitha, 19 Aug. 1800, Mary Golt                 1 WO
Griffin, Edward, 29 May 1781, Agnes Sheckells             2 PG-5
Griffin, George, 5 June 1783, Polly Cramphin              11 BA-6
Griffin, John, 27 Sept. 1780, Mary Ann Comrick            3 HA-2
Griffin, John, 24 Dec. 1782, Susannah Sunderland          3 AA-419
Griffin, John, Jr., 27 March 1792, Mary Carback           6 BA
Griffin, Joseph, 24 May 1791, Mary Soward                 2 DO
Griffin, Philip, 17 July 1800, Ann Jones                  4 SM-184
Griffin, Rosse, 21 Sept. 1780, Sarah Ratcliffe            2 CH-236
Griffin, Thomas, 29 Jan. 1784, Elizabeth Jarboe           3 SM-61
Griffin, Thomas, 7 Sept. 1790, Ann Nothy                  2 PG-4
Griffin, Walter, 10 April 1796, Elizabeth Pearson         3 BA-321
Griffin, William, 10 July 1795, Jane Chambers             3 BA-307
Griffin, York, 6 June 1790, Susanna Belt                  5 BA-6
Griffin, Zadock, 17 Feb. 1785, Susannah Hunter            4 FR
Griffith, Abraham, 5 Sept. 1796, Elizabeth Thompson       4 FR
Griffith, Caleb, 2 Nov. 1787, Mary Richardson             4 FR
Griffith, Chrisholm, 22 Aug. 1778, Mary Ann Scott         4 FR
Griffith, Edward, 20 Aug. 1790, Ales Todd                 2 DO
Griffith, Elisha, 27 Aug. 1781, Catherine Wollf           4 FR
Griffith, Ely Ridgely, 22 Dec. 1789, by Rev. Reed; Sarah
  Spurrier                                                4 AA
Griffith, Henry, 16 Sept. 1797, Hessey Steward            4 FR
Griffith, Howard, 5 Feb. 1782, Jemima Jacob               2 PG-3
Griffith, James, 8 Dec. 1796, Mary Ford                   45 BA-1
Griffith, John, 22 March 1778, by Rev. Magill; Elizabeth
  Ridgely                                                 4 AA
Griffith, John, 31 July 1783, Mary Craton                 2 DO
Griffith, John, 4 Oct. 1798, Sarah Jeffers                3 BA-364
Griffith, Joseph, 25 Jan. 1781, Elizabeth Griffith        2 DO
Griffith, Joshua, 1 Nov. 1783, Elizabeth Ridgely          4 FR
Griffith, Joshua, 10 June 1798, by Rev. Ridgely; Elizabeth
  Ridgely                                                 4 AA
Griffith, Lewis, 23 May 1789, Mary Booth                  2 DO
Griffith, Lewis, 14 July 1800, Polly Hughes               2 DO
  1 DO-40 gives the date as 17 July 1800.
```

```
Griffith, Luke, 9 Feb. 1784, Ann Beard              11 BA-7
Griffith, Mark, 24 Sept. 1785, Polly Simmons         2 DO
Griffith, Nathan, 2 Jan. 1786, Sally Simmons         2 DO
Griffith, Nathan, 23 March 1793, Susannah Thomas     6 BA
Griffith, Osborn, 12 Aug. 1790, Cassandra Haile      6 BA
Griffith, Peter, 28 Jan. 1794, Helen Hacket          6 BA
Griffith, Philamond, 7 July 1785, Eleanor Jacob      4 FR
Griffith, Reuben, son of Abraham and Mary, 2nd day, 1 mo.,
    1799, Elizabeth Price, dau. of Benjamin and Temperance
    1 SF
Griffith, Richard, 19 Oct. 1789, Margaret Tice       4 FR
Griffith, Richard, 2 June 1796, Ann Thomas           4 FR
Griffith, Robert, 26 June 1788, Elizabeth Keene      2 DO
Griffith, Samuel, 17 Nov. 1778, Mrs. Martha Presbury 1 HA-391
Griffith, Samuel, 19 Nov. 1779, Martha Presbury      3 HA-1
Griffith, Samuel, 21 Dec. 1791, Elizabeth Garrettson 3 HA-21
Griffith, William, 13 April 1780, Ann Wells         11 BA-4
Griffith, William, 4 Aug. 1784, Anna Atkins          4 FR
Griffith, William, 29 Aug. 1793, Ann Frazier         6 BA
Griffith, Zadock, 17 Feb. 1785, Sar. Hantel          2 FR-1131
Griffy, Benjamin, 26 Aug. 1778, Susanna Modisit      2 CH-236
Grimes, Alexander, 23 April 1795, Eleanor Pearl      1 AL-53
Grimes, Basil, 29 Oct. 1793, Betsy Picket            4 FR
Grimes, Benjamin, 17 Jan. 1789, Sarah Grimes         2 PG-4
Grimes, Frederick, 19 March 1798, Margaret Randall   4 FR
    2 FR-1131 gives the date as 22 March 1798.
Grimes, Jeremiah, 21 March 1793, Susanna Tobert      3 PG-438
Grimes, John, 15 Jan. 1778, Dela Hendon             11 BA-1
Grimes, John, 6 Jan. 1789, Sarah King                3 PG-255
Grimes, John, 22 May 1790, Nancy Garrett            26 BA-1
Grimes, John, (2 Oct. 1790), Mary Morrison          15 BA-3
Grimes, Sebastian, 14 Jan. 1794, Mary Watkins        6 BA
Grimes, Sebaston, 4 April 1797, Jemima Bryan         6 BA
Grimes, William, 20 July 1795, Elizabeth Grimes      4 FR
Grimes, William, 7 April 1798, Mary Clance           4 FR
Grinnum, John, 22 Jan. 1799, Rachel King             2 DO
Groason, Samuel, 6 Sept. 1786, Mary Lockerd         10 BA-188
Groff, Henry, 18 Nov. 1790, Eliza Long              11 BA-13
Gronan, Christian, 17 Nov. 1799, Peggy Kammer       10 BA-198
Groom, James, 30 Nov. 1780, Rebecca Kicketts         4 FR
Groom, William, 5 April 1795, Isabella Miller        6 BA
Groom, Wm., 24 July 1796, Mary Ann Kelly             5 MO-113
Groom, William, 21 Aug. 1800, Rebecca Hopkins        3 BA-390
Groome, James, 22 Feb. 1797, Sarah Perkins           4 KE-68
Groomes, James, 5 Feb. 1799, Sarah King              5 MO-115
Grose, Henry, 22 Feb. 1782, Margaret Derr            4 FR
Groseman, Simon, 11 June 1779, Eliz'th Fogle         4 FR
Groshner, Wm., 31 March 1781, Eliz'th Welsh          4 FR
Groshong, Abraham, 6 June 1794, Elizabeth Waggoner   4 FR
Grosjean, Jno. James, 26 Oct. 1790, Mary Trigle     11 BA-13
Gross, Simon, 25 Jan. 1798, Ann Job                  5 BA-7
Gross, William, 10 Sept. 1783, Margaret Burkhart     4 FR
Groteyon, Christian, 22 Aug. 1793, Modelena Elginger 4 FR
Grove, Henry, 31 July 1798, Judith Kephart           4 FR
Grove, John, 14 April 1798, Anne Carroll             3 BA-357
Grove, Martin, 28 Oct. 1797, Catherine Stemple       4 FR
Grove, Peter, 2 Dec. 1793, Barbara Everly            4 FR
Grove, Peter, 11 Aug. 1798, Katy Unglebower          4 FR
Grover, George, 12 April 1798, Elizabeth Benton      6 BA
Grover, John, 3 March 1795, Jemima Fitzgerald        2 FR-1131
Grover, Jonathan Mason, 17 Nov. 1780, Sarah Musgrove 4 FR
Grover, Thomas, 20 Feb. 1784, Priscilla Denton       3 AA-421
Groverman, Anthony, 31 Oct. 1798, Henrietta W. Delius 29 BA-9
Groves, Ezekiel, 11 Oct. 1796, Lenny Ireland         6 BA
Groves, William, 14 Jan. 1781, Jane Eustors          2 CH-236
```

```
Groves, William, 13 Jan. 1782, Jane Hughstone         3 HA-5
Groves, William, 26 Feb. 1794, Sarah Day              3 HA-23
Groves, William, 1 March 1794, by Rev. Benton Riggen;
    Sarah Day                                         4 AA
Grows, John, 30 Jan. 1780, Christiana Jenkins         2 CH-236
Gruber, David, 22 Nov. 1798, Susy Moore               4 FR
Grumbaugh, Simon, 5 Nov. 1795, Phillipena Devilbiss   4 FR
Grunner, Jno., 7 July 1796, Barb. Baker               29 BA-7
Grymes, Geo., 19 May 1782, Christiana Fowler          11 BA-5
Grymes, Wm., 22 Dec. 1785, Sarah Shipley              11 BA-9
Gue, Joseph, 1 Oct. 1789, Ann Dells                   11 BA-12
Guest, Basil, 18 Dec. 1788, by Rev. Hagerty           4 AA
Guest, Job, 14 March 1786, by Rev. Pigman; Hannah Bullen
    4 AA
Guishard, David, 5 March 1789, Rachael Patterson      11 BA-12
Guiseberts, And'w, 9 Dec. 1784, Urith Ridgely         4 FR
Guishard, Mark, 22 Feb. 1796, Catharine McCabe        5 BA-6
Guist, Richard, 28 Nov. 1782, Dorothy Wood            3 AA-419
Gumbare, John, Jr., 12 Dec. 1799, Esther Mantz        4 FR
Gummert, Christian, 27 Dec. 1779, Margaret Road       4 FR
Gump, John, son of John and Elizabeth Juliana, March 1793,
    Anne Maria Williar                                5 FR
Gump, John, 1 Dec. 1797, Mary McGaghey                4 FR
Gump, John George, son of John and Elizabeth Juliana,
    1 Sept. 1789, Anna Elizabeth Frey, dau. of John Daniel
    and Maria Catherine                               5 FR
Gums, Manuel,16 Oct. 1798, Sarah Krebs                3 BA-364
Gun, Alexander, 14 Feb. 1791. Margery McKay           4 FR
Gunby, Benj., 12 July 1796, Esther Sturgis            1 WO
Gunby, John, 23 Jan. 1798, Amelia Chaille             1 WO
Gunby, Kirk, 11 Sept. 1798, Hannah Duncan             1 WO
Gunby, Stephen, 5 May 1796, Ann Stansbury             6 BA
Gunnet, George, 31 July 1800, Nelly Mitchell          3 BA-388
Gunther, Christian Frederick, son of Peter and Maria, 28
    Sept. 1786, Maria Barbara Frey, dau. of John Daniel
    and Maria Catherine                               5 FR
Gurley, Josiah, 25 July 1800, Polly Wright            2 SO
Guth, Henry, 2 July 1795, Francisca Schleman          29 BA-6
Guthrie, Wm., 1 April 1780, Eleanor Elder             4 FR
Guthrow, John, 20 May 1797, Rebecca Joiner            44 BA-2
Guttery, Joshua, 7 Dec. 1783, Susanna Keener          11 BA-7
Gutthrey, William, 23 March 1797, Mary Bateman        6 BA
Gutting, Azariah, 22 June 1794, Mary Selby            3 PG-440
Guttry, Joshua, 2 Dec. 1792, Elizabeth Keener         3 BA-259
Guy, Joseph, 13 Dec. 1780, Sarah Smith                2 CH-236
Guy, Samuel, 27 July 1795, Catherine Darr             4 FR
Guyer, Dennis, 3 May 1797, Jane Oldfield              6 BA
Guyton, Isaac, 21 Nov. 1789, Margaret Hethorn         1 BA-2
Guyton, John Holt, 30 Oct. 1787, Sarah Watkins        1 BA-1
Guyton, Joshua, 12 Jan. 1782, Sarah Mitchell          3 HA-5
Gwin, John, 20 Sept. 1785, Grele Stull                5 BA-6
Gwinn, John, 22 Dec. 1779, Jean Ludwell Bruce         2 CH-236
Gwynn, Robert, 19 Feb. 1797, Elizabeth Gwynn          1 BA-7
Gwynn, William, 23 March 1788, Eleanor Campbell       1 BA-1


Haack, Nicolaus, 13 Jan. 1799, Sophia Louisa Richberin
    10 BA-198
Haas, Michael, 18 Aug. 1788, Sophia Prishe            4 FR
Haas, Valent, 13 April 1794, Elizab. Dodoro           2 FR-1135
Hablisten, Bartholomew, 20 March 1794, Harriote Machaux
    3 BA-285
Hacket, John Brown, 1 Jan. 1793, Anna Maria Thompson  1 QA-65
Hackett, John, 1 Jan. 1788, Jane Grant                3 BA-216
Hackney, Benj. Rhodes, 14 May 1785, Elizabeth Warrant Philpott
    4 FR; 2 FR-1134 gives date as 15 May 1785.
```

```
Hackney, Jacob, 27 Oct. 1784, Mary Garrett          4 FR
Hackney, Samuel, before 31 Aug. 1796, by Rev. Mills;
   Margaret Bristol                                 4 AA
Hadaway, James, 25 May 1797, Ann Every              4 KE-68
Hadaway, Samuel, 5 Nov. 1793, Nancy Harrington      2 DO
Haddely, Benjamin, 18 April 1786, Susanna Covill    4 FR
Hadder, Warren, 21 Dec. 1796, Polly Johnson         1 WO
Hadley, Robert, 3 Jan. 1797, Jane Turner            4 KE-68
Hadley, Robert, 1 Aug. 1798, Hannah Smith           4 KE-68
Haeg, Andrew, 1 Nov. 1785, Mary Wolf                2 FR-1134
Haep, George, 14 Aug. 1792, Cath. Puderbach         2 FR-1135
Haff, Abraham Jr., 27 May 1796, Frances Dern        4 FR
Haff, William M., 7 Sept. 1797, Peggy Dawson        4 FR
Hagan, Benedict, 16 Feb. 1794, Cloe Montgomery      3 CH-161
   "disp. for consang. in 3rd to 4th degree."
Hagan, Francis, 29 Jan. 1788, Margaret Ramsower     4 FR
Hagan, Henry, 17 June 1780, Susanna Hyatt           4 FR
Hagan, Henry, 9 Jan. 1798, Eliz. Padget             3 CH-162
Hagan, Hugh, 1 Aug. 1797, Dorothy Waggoner          4 FR
Hagan, Raphael, 9 Oct. 1782, Rebecca Deviel         2 CH-236
Hagar, George, 8 Dec. 1781, Magdalena Keefhaver     4 FR
Hagar, Jonathan, 17 Nov. 1783, Mary Orendorff       4 FR
Hagarman, Samuel, 16 April 1796, Rebecca Wooden     6 BA
Hageman, Henry F., 8 Sept. 1792, Rebecca Hillmans   6 BA
Hagen, John, 4 Dec. 1793, Mary Bryan                3 BA-279
Hagerman, John, 28 Oct. 1791, Eleanor Gorman        1 AL-52
Hagerty, Daniel, 14 March 1796, Elizabeth Jones     3 HA-25
   2 HA-349 gives the date as 17 March 1796.
Hagerty, George, 19 Dec. 1778, Elizabeth Kennedy    4 FR
Hagerty, John, 16 May 1780, Sarah Cooper            3 BA-179
Hagerty, Mathew, 23 April 1795, Jenny Barret       40 BA-1
Hagerty, Michael, 28 Aug. 1797, Eleanor Carey       3 BA-349
Hagner, Jacob, 1791, Barb. Emich                   50 BA-391
Hagner, John, 5 Oct. 1792, Rebecca Coward           6 BA
Hagon, Francis, 29 Jan. 1788, Marg. Ramsower        2 FR-1135
Hague, Amos, 13 Feb. 1782, Milley Burrell           4 FR
Hague, Hugh, 26 Dec. 1791, Catherine McCoy         28 BA-2
Hague, John, 1 June 1799, Elizabeth Trencham        3 BA-372
Hagwood, Jno., 4 July 1799, Kitty Thomas           29 BA-10
Hahn, Jacob, 27 April 1783, Marie Hildebrechtin     1 CL-29
Hahn, Jno., 15 Sept. 1794, Cath. Ackerman          29 BA-5
Hahn, Peter, 9 April 1798, Eve Smith               29 BA-9
Haiey, John, 3 March 1799, Hannah Johnson           3 HA-28
Hail, Robert, 15 March 1795, Mary Mitchell          6 BA
Haile, Thomas, 20 March 1798, Sarah Edmondson Neighbours
   3 BA-356
Hailey, John, 13 Aug. 1793, Rosannah Kelly          6 BA
Hain, Caleb, 20 March 1788, Sarah Davis             4 FR
Haine, Charles, 24 April 1798, Dorothy Impson       4 FR
Haines, Daniel, 26 Jan. 1782, Ann Sollers          11 BA-5
Haines, Dan'l, 12 March 1799, Nancy Butler         29 BA-10
Haines, John, 7 April 1798, Mary Lipps              4 FR
Haines, Joseph, son of Nathan and Sophia (Price), 20th day,
   1 mo., 1779, Rachel Cookson, dau. of Samuel and Jane
   3 SF
Haines, Joseph, 2 Aug. 1796, Mary Shroyer           4 FR
Haing, Benjamin, 30 Oct. 1798, Rose Swanwick        5 BA-7
Hains, Nathan, 29 Dec. 1788, Ann Murray             4 FR
Hair, James, 7 Dec. 1785, Mary All                  3 HA-10
Haislip, John, 27 Jan. 1780, Easter Nelson          2 CH-236
Haislip, Richard. 27 March 1781, Mary Babington     3 BA-181
Hale, Christian, 4 Feb. 1790, Juliet Cooper        11 BA-13
Hale, Henry, 11 Sept. 1800, Susan Hall, dau. of Aquila
   Hall                                             2 BA-12
Hales, Hugh, 5 Sept. 1799, Jimimah Sewel            6 BA
```

```
Haley, Peter, 18 Dec. 1794, Elizabeth Larey or Lacey      6 BA
Halfpenny, Wm., 8 Jan. 1792, Elizabeth Garrison           6 BA
Halkerstone, John, 4 Nov. 1779, Elizabeth Hanson          2 CH-236
Hall, Alexander F., 21 Sept. 1799, Eliza Byas             6 BA
Hall, Barrick, 26 June 1797, Mary Burgee                  4 FR
Hall, Ben'd Edward, 2 March 1781, Milcah Garrett          3 HA-3
Hall, Benjamin, 3 Jan. 1788, Rachael Pomfrey              3 BA-204
Hall, Benjamin, 20 April 1799, Elizabeth Leakins          4 FR
Hall, Charles, 7 March 1800, Mary Ann Dunsfore            3 BA-383
Hall, Dixon, 9 May 1793, Rebecca Hodson                   2 DO
Hall, Edward, 20 Oct. 1782, Ann Wells                     3 AA-418
Hall, Elisha, 10 Feb. 1783, Ann Turner                    3 AA-419
Hall, Elisha, 1 July 1788, Mary Todd                      3 BA-217
Hall, Ezekiel, 3 Nov. 1796, Elizabeth Hammond             6 BA
Hall, Francis Magruder, 20 Oct. 1795, Mary Hill          40 BA-1
Hall, George, 12 May 1788, Elizabeth Robinson             6 BA
Hall, George, 9 Feb. 1796, Hesse Bowen                    1 WO
Hall, George, 7 July 1799, Hetty Smith                    8 BA-1
Hall, Henry, 12 April 1781, Mary Wells                    3 AA-417
Hall, Henry, 26 June 1787, Rachel Harwood, dau. of Capt.
     Thomas                                               1 AA-160
Hall, Henry, 13 March 1800, Mary Turner                   2 FR-1136
Hall, Jacob, 20 May 1785, Mary Willmott                   3 HA-9
Hall, James, 4 Nov. 1792, Rebecca McGreggory              6 BA
Hall, James, 27 July 1794, Elizabeth Connolly             1 BA-6
Hall, James, 10 March 1796, Ann Beck                      1 QA-65
Hall, Jesse, son of Jesper, 5 Feb. 1784, Patience Jacob,
     widow of Richard Jacob of Joseph                     2 AA-114
Hall, John, 20 June 1795, Margaret Bolan                  4 FR
Hall, John, 24 June 1799, Polly Shenton                   2 DO
Hall, John, 26 Aug. 1799, Solema Evis                     4 FR
Hall, John, 14 Sept. 1800, Elisabeth Randall              3 BA-391
Hall, Jonathan, 1 Oct. 1786, Ann Miller                  11 BA-9
Hall, Joseph, 2 July 1780, Mary McGill                    3 SM-58
Hall, Joseph, 11 March 1784, Nancy Horner                 4 FR
Hall, Joseph, 17 March 1792, Margaret Burkett             4 FR
Hall, Joseph, 24 April 1796, Sarah Day                    3 BA-321
Hall, Joshua, 20 Dec. 1798, by Rev. Ridgely; Martha Hall
     4 AA
Hall, Josiah Carvil, 14 March 1780, Jane Smith           11 BA-4
Hall, Josias, son of John and Barthia Hall of Cranbury,
     28 June 1787, Martha Garrettson, dau. of George and
     Martha                                               1 HA-395
Hall, Nathaniel, 30 Dec. 1777, Mary Hughes                2 PG-2
Hall, Noah, 24 Jan. 1797, Betsy Layfield                  2 SO
Hall, Phillip, 16 June 1799, Leah Price                   2 SO
Hall, Richard D., 15 Jan. 1799, by Rev. Ridgely; Elizabeth
     Perkins                                              4 AA
Hall, Robert, 26 Feb. 1799, Elizabeth Conner              2 SO
Hall, Thomas, 10 Sept. 1778, Anne Ravelling              11 BA-1
Hall, Thomas, 19 March 1793, Isabella Presbury            3 HA-22
Hall, Thomas, 25 Dec. 1797, Polly Chambers                2 SO
Hall, Vachel, 13 Dec. 1796, Margaret Hall                 4 FR
Hall, William, 22 Jan. 1779, Martha Hall                  3 AA-414
Hall, William, 9 April 1782, Martha Duckett               2 PG-3
Hall, William, 2 Dec. 1783, Salina Ramsey                 3 HA-8
Hall, William, 27 Aug. 1795, Mary Flitcher                3 BA-307
Hall, William, 9 Jan. 1797, Sally Edger                   2 DO
Hall, William J., 26 Jan. 1797, Grace Craig               5 BA-7
Hallard, John, 31 March 1780, Hannah Coy                  3 HA-1
Haller, Michael, 26 Aug. 1798, Cath. Rabourn              2 FR-1136
Halstal, John, 16 Feb. 1779, Lucy Downes                  2 PG-3
Ham, Thomas, 13 June 1795, Ann Brown                      6 BA
Hambleton, Benjamin, 6 Oct. 1798, by Rev. Dorsey; Sarah
     Thomas                                               4 AA
```

```
Hambleton, James, 28 June 1788, Cassandra Bond          6 BA
Hambleton, John, 22 Nov. 1787, Elizab. Philips          2 FR-1135
Hambleton, John, 20 May 1790, Phebe Maxwell             1 BA-2
Hambleton, John, 17 June 1793, Margaret Bond            3 HA-22
  See also 1 BA-5.
Hambleton, John, 26 Jan. 1797, Aley Gafford             1 BA-7
  3 HA-25 gives the date as 24 Jan. 1797.
Hambleton, William, 1 May 1796, Susanna Todd            2 FR-1136
Hamby, James, 13 Jan. 1800, Ann Williams                3 HA-29
  2 HA-351 gives the date as 16 Jan. 1800.
Hamby, William, 13 Aug. 1800, Susanna Cowan             3 HA-29
  2 HA-352 gives the date as 14 Aug. 1800.
Hamersley, Henry, 1 Oct. 1786, Olivia Jerningham        2 CH-236
Hammill, Peter. See Hansell, Peter.
Hamilton, Edward, 20 Nov. 1786, Mary Ann Boarman        2 CH-236
Hamilton, Edward, 18 Dec. 1797, Sarah Cummins           2 DO
Hamilton, George, 18 May 1783, Frances Haley           11 BA-6
Hamilton, George, 14 April 1796, Rachel Williams        3 BA-321
Hamilton, James, 9 July 1796, Kitty Bailey              6 BA
Hamilton, Jo., 1790, Mary Welsh                        50 BA-390
Hamilton, John Alexander, 22 June 1795, Eleanor Philpot
  4 FR
Hamilton, John G., 22 Nov. 1794, Eliz. Smallwood        4 FR
Hamilton, John Hance, 3 March 1790, Elizabeth Carroll   2 DO
Hamilton, Robert, 28 May 1790, Elizabeth Andrew         4 FR
Hamilton, William, 25 May 1799, Maria Selman            3 BA-371
Hammer, Henry, 22 June 1792, Mary Miller                6 BA
Hammer, Peter, 1790, Ann Capost                         3 BA-229
Hammersleigh, Charles, 27 April 1799, Barbara Shreup    4 FR
Hammerston, Richard, 18 Dec. 1777, Margaret Worester?   2 PG-2
Hammet, James, 8 May 1797, Mary Brittain               47 BA-1
Hammet, Thomas, 13 Sept. 1795, Mariah Rosanna Stine     5 BA-7
Hammett, Jesse, 10 July 1799, Jane Young                5 BA-8
Hammond, Abrah'm Geo., 20 Nov. 1788, Mary Garetson      6 BA
Hammond, Benj., 26 July 1796, Janet Cottingham          1 WO
Hammond, Bowden, 25 May 1798, Amelia Jones              1 WO
Hammond, Edward, 17 July 1795, Nancy Truitt             1 WO
Hammond, Edward, 19 May 1796, Nancy Howard              1 WO
Hammond, Edward, 26 July 1799, Molly Baker              1 WO
Hammond, George, 12 June 1779, Elizabeth Wells          5 BA-7
Hammond, Isaac, 13 March 1778, Susanna Bond            11 BA-1
Hammond, James, 23 April 1782, Frances Patterson        3 HA-6
Hammond, John, 27 Nov. 1783, Elizabeth McConnell        3 BA-211
Hammond, John, 5 March 1795, Elizabeth Anderson         3 BA-301
Hammond, Jonathan, 18 June 1799, Patsy Pepper           1 WO
Hammond, Lot, 4 March 1797, Elizabeth Davis             4 FR
  2 FR-1136 gives the date as 9 March 1797.
Hammond, Nathan, 8 June 1793, Priscilla Worthington     4 FR
Hammond, Ormond, 27 Jan. 1780, Eliz'th Iuckett          4 FR
Hammond, Philip, (2 Nov. 1790), Mary Clark             15 BA-3
Hammond, Philip, 2 Oct. 1795, Elizabeth Hammond         4 FR
Hammond, Rezin, 10 Jan. 1793, Nancy Joyce               3 BA-258
Hammond, Tho., 17 April 1783, Eleanor Hopham           11 BA-6
Hammond, Thomas John, 26 Jan. 1797, Rachel Gaither      4 FR
  2 FR-1136 gives the date as 5 Feb. 1797.
Hammond, Wm., 12 Oct. 1780, Mary Pindell               11 BA-4
Hammond, William, 9 May 1782, Elizabeth Lloyd           3 AA-418
Hammond, William, 11 Jan. 1797, Betsy Gibbs             1 WO
Hampton, David, 28 Aug. 1783, M. Easter Gordon          3 HA-8
Hamson, Bryan, 18 Feb. 1793, Lucy Hatton                3 PG-438
Han?, Hein., 1789, Jul.? Dehart                        50 BA-388
Hana, Thomas, 15 June 1786, Mary Hanward                5 BA-7
Hance, Benjamin, 2 April 1780, Sarah Dare               1 CA-3
Hance, Richard, 10 June 1781, Mary Simmons              3 AA-417
Hance, Samuel, Jr., 6 Dec. 1778, Sarah Allnut           1 CA-2
```

Hancock, Francis, c.1799, by Rev. Higgins; Jemima Selby 4 AA
Hancock, Stephen, 19 Feb. 1778, Belinda Ridgely   11 BA-1
Hancock, Wm., 9 Oct. 1787, Eliza Hush   11 BA-10
Handcock, James, 31 Dec. 1800, Rachael Ward   1 WO
Hande, Thomas, 12 Jan. 1780, Catherine Whitmer   4 FR
Handley, Handy, 4 May 1786, Nicey Hooper   2 DO
Handley, James, 22 May 1787, Mary Magruder   3 PG-252
Handley, Planner, 30 Aug. 1798, Leah Windows   2 DO
Hands, Ephraim, 25 May 1793, Sarah Garrettson   18 BA-5
Handshaw, John, 1 March 1779, Eliz'th Knowse   4 FR
Handy, Henry, 28 Jan. 1797, Nancy Campbell   2 SO
Handy, John, son of Thomas, 27 Nov. 1788, Sarah Coulbourn,
    dau. of Isaac   1 SO-208
Handy, Joseph, 21 March 1798, Mary Ann Waters   3 SO
Handy, Richard H., 16 June 1798, Betsy Gordon   2 SO
  3 SO gives the date as 17 June 1798.
Handy, Richard Henry, 18 Dec. 1794, Elizabeth Campbell 2 DO
Handy, Robert J. H., 25 Nov. 1800, Molly Selby   1 WO
Hanes, Henry, 3 March 1789, Ruth Peacock   11 BA-12
Hanna, Hugh, 4 Feb. 1782, Rebecca Varne   3 HA-6
Hanna, James, April 1783, Hannah Bayley   3 HA-7
Hanna, John, 22 March 1796, Ann Rogers   2 HA-349
    See also 3 HA-25.
Hannah, Edward, 8 Nov. 1797, Rebecca McLure   5 BA-7
Hannah, John, 28 May 1778, Elizabeth Greenfield   11 BA-1
Hannah, Robert, 25 Jan. 1780, Mary Thomas   3 HA-1
Hannah, Samuel, 19 Jan. 1790, by Rev. Cooper; Mary Marshall
    4 AA
Hannan, John, 4 Jan. 1795, Marg't Towers   44 BA-1
Hannan, William, 12 March 1787, Rebecca Hawkins   11 BA-10
Hanning, Caleb, 22 June 1780, Susanna Kelly   3 SM-58
Hansell (Hamill?), Peter, 20 March 1798, Margaret Poland
    2 AL-701
Hanshaw, Basil, 21 Jan. 1782, Mary Kilmon   11 BA-5
Hanshugh, Fred'k, 23 Oct. 1784, Mary Whitehair   4 FR
Hanson, Anthony, 12 Sept. 1799, Barbara Shaffer   6 BA
Hanson, Benjamin, 12 Oct. 1780, Martha Garrettson   3 HA-2
Hanson, Christopher, 28 Oct. 1781, Airy Rolls   3 BA-182
Hanson, Hollis, 30 April 1782, Mary Dorsey   3 HA-6
Hanson, Jacob, 2 Sept. 1793, Ann Nowers   3 HA-23
Hanson, Jas., 3 March 1782, Aberilla Beven   11 BA-5
Hanson, James, (25 April 1791), Rachel Shippen   15 BA-4
Hanson, John, 4 Dec. 1782, Avarilla Hollis   3 HA-7
Hanson, Peter, 20 June 1797, Hannah Yepson   29 BA-8
Hanson, Samuel, 10 Aug. 1788, Elizabeth Fendall   3 PG-254
Hanson, Theodore, 30 Sept. 1798, Nancy Clay   3 BA-363
Hanson, Walter, 25 Dec. 1781, Sarah Hatch Maddox   2 CH-236
Hanson, Walter, 20 April 1783, Elizabeth Hanson   2 CH-236
Hanson, William, 4 Nov. 1782, Mary Matthews   3 HA-7
Hanway, Francis, 21 Sept. 1793, Belinda Cane   3 BA-275
Harbaugh, Christian, 6 Nov. 1780, Maria Elizabeth Williar,
    dau. of Peter and Elizabeth Magdalena (Schlim)   5 FR
Harbaugh, George, Jr., 25 Aug. 1793, Amey Hall   4 FR
Harbest, Frederick, 9 March 1793, by Rev. Dorsey; Mary Lucas
    4 AA
Harbin, Joshua, 23 July 1778, Ruth Hoskinson   2 MO-1
Harbin, Roswald Nalley, 5 April 1796, Mary Osburn   3 CH-162
Harbin, Thomas, 6 Dec. 1781, Lucy Roby   2 CH-236
Harbot, John, 16 Dec. 1791, Lucy Sherwood   3 PG-436
Harden, John, 13 May 1780, Mary Sessions   3 HA-2
Harden, Robert, 6 Nov. 1797, Sarah Pritchett   2 DO
Hardesty, Edward, 25 Dec. 1792, by Rev. G. Ridgely; Ruth
    Chaney   4 AA
Hardesty, Elisha, 28 Sept. 1780, Sarah Wells   2 PG-3
Hardesty, John, 26 July 1788, by Rev. Reed; Henrietta Chaney
    4 AA

Hardesty, Thos., 24 Dec. 1778, by Rev. Magowan; Jane Crawford
  4 AA
Hardesty, Thomas, 5 Jan. 1797, by Rev. Ridgely; Ann Chaney
  4 AA
Hardesty, William, 29 Nov. 1781, Williaminah Marr   3 AA-418
Hardey, Anthoney, 4 Oct. 1796, Mary Green   3 PG-442
Hardey, Arnold, 5 April 1782, Barbara Fleming   4 FR
Hardey, Henry, 29 Dec. 1796, Frances West   5 MO-113
Hardey, Noah, 14 Jan. 1794, Mary Stone   3 PG-439
Hardikin, John, 19 May 1800, Peggy Carter   2 DO
Hardin, Richard, 28 May 1790, Rachel Crepell   4 FR
Harding, Christopher, 6 Nov. 1800, Anne Lee   3 BA-395
Harding, Edw'd, 12 May 1778, Ann Butler   2 MO-1
Harding, Elias, 9 Jan. 1786, Cassandra Ford   4 FR
Harding, Elias, 24 Feb. 1799, Eleanor Harding   4 FR
Harding, George, 19 Dec. 1789, Lydia Duffith   2 FR-1135
Harding, George, 24 April 1794, Catherine Berger   4 FR
Harding, Gotfried, Feb. 1793, P. Brown   50 BA-393
Harding, Lewis, 5 Dec. 1795, Ann Jarrett   4 FR
Harding, Nich's, 21 May 1782, Sarah Grover   11 BA-5
Harding, Thomas, 5 June 1799, Polly Marchant   3 BA-369
Harding, Vachel, 14 March 1798, Mary Parker   4 FR
Harding, Zephaniah, 12 April 1786, Sarah Howell   4 FR
Hardt, Peter, 6 Dec. 1795, Charlotte Doll   2 FR-1136
Hardy, Baptist, 19 Feb. 1786, Ester Osborn   3 PG-251
Hardy, George, 10 Feb. 1782, Ellanor Stone   2 PG-3
Hardy, James, 7 Jan. 1783, Maty Caldron   3 BA-184
Hardy, Jesse, 3 Nov. 1789, Sarah Wheat   3 PG-255
Hardy, John, 19 Sept. 1800, Sarah Evans   3 BA-392
Hardy, Joseph, 19 March 1798, Mary Waller   2 SO
Hardy, Richard, 30 May 1790, Rachel Crepel   2 FR-1135
Hardy, Thomas, 15 Feb. 1780, Margaret Wilcoxon   2 PG-3
Hardy, Wm., 8 July 1794, Elizabeth Button   6 BA
Hare, Francis, 25 June 1794, Mary Golway   3 HA-23
  1 BA-6 gives the date as 29 June 1794, and the bride's
  name as Mary Galoway.
Hare, Jno., 5 Dec. 1796, Kitty Drisker   29 BA-8
Hargant, John, 24 Sept. 1796, Sarah McLaughlin?   4 FR
Hargate, Abraham, 1 June 1779, Mary Pentrin   4 FR
Hargity, John, 16 May 1780, Sarah Cooper   11 BA-4
Hargrove, Thomas, 29 Dec. 1798, Margaret Buckley   3 BA-366
Haring, Henry, 29 Jan. 1780, Catherine Peckenpaugh   4 FR
Harker, Richard, 13 April 1797, Jemima Lynch   29 BA-8
Harkins, Daniel, 14 July 1797, Biddy Sweeny   47 BA-1
Harkins, John, 3 Sept. 1799, Peggy Powell   3 BA-377
Harlan, Daniel, 19 Feb. 1788, Eliz. Justice   2 FR-1135
Harlan, James, 13 April 1791, Mary Wood   2 FR-1135
Harlan, Jeremiah, 8 Sept. 1800, Esther Stump   3 HA-30
Harlan, Ruben, 21 Dec. 1788, Cath. Richards   2 FR-1135
Harley, Joshua, 18 June 1789, Elizabeth Whitenacht   4 FR
Harley, Thomas, 22 Nov. 1796, Sarah Larrance   4 KE-68
Harlin, James, 18 April 1791, Mary Wood   4 FR
Harlin, Joshua, 5 Jan. 1792, Sarah Wood   4 FR
  2 FR-1135 gives the date as 8 Jan. 1792.
Harman, James, 7 Nov. 1793, Mary Sorter   18 BA-6
Harmon, Jacob, 30 March 1799, Margaret Zealer   4 FR
Harmon, John, 17 May 1794, Elizabeth Shryock   4 FR
Harmun, Martin, 27 Nov. 1796, by Rev. Ridgely; Elizabeth
  Wood   4 AA
Harnet, James, 8 Sept. 1778, Sarah Summerby   11 BA-1
Harp, Laurence, 1 Sept. 1796, Mary Delany   2 HA-349
Harp, William, 16 Sept. 1792, Sarah Diffey   6 BA
Harper, Daniel, 1 Dec. 1792, Eleanor Bramble   2 DO
Harper, Edward, 15 April 1800, Sarah Ann Boswell   5 MO-116
Harper, James, 18 Jan. 1796, Frances Dean   2 DO

```
Harper, Shadrach, 24 July 1799, Amelia Phillips        2 DO
Harper, Thomas, 15 March 1791, Sevela Jones            2 DO
Harper, William, 24 July 1798, Nelly Polk              2 SO
Harriman, Caleb, 5 Nov. 1778, Anne Hawkins            11 BA-1
Harriman, Joshua, 16 Jan. 1785, Sarah Wiley           11 BA-8
Harriman, Wm., 19 June 1780, Mary Greene              11 BA-4
Harrington, Benjamin G., 19 Dec. 1792, Elizabeth Thomas 2 DO
Harrington, Edward, 11 March 1791, Mary Woollen        2 DO
Harrington, James, 5 Sept. 1789, Mary Hooper           2 DO
Harrington, John, 11 Dec. 1783, Sarah Hubbard          2 DO
Harrington, Nathan, 28 Feb. 1787, Elizabeth Hooper     2 DO
Harrington, Peter, 17 July 1783, Elizabeth Ferguson    2 DO
Harrington, Peter, 5 Dec. 1797, Sally Hooper           2 DO
Harrington, Richard, 9 Jan. 1800, Catherine Inglish    2 DO
Harrington, William, 7 Jan. 1800, Anne Durham          2 SO
Harris, Benjamin, 10 April 1795, Amelia Stone          3 AA-424
Harris, Charles, 15 July 1796, Hannah Noble            1 WO
Harris, David, 14 Sept. 1780, Sarah Crocket            5 BA-7
Harris, David, 23 Jan. 1788, Frances Hatton Moale      5 BA-7
Harris, Edward, 31 Aug. 1790, Marg't Sullivan         11 BA-13
Harris, Elias, 17 May 1796, by Rev. Ridgely; Mary Gary 4 AA
Harris, Elzey, 1 March 1798, Mary Knight               3 SO
Harris, George, Jr., son of George and Beulah, 2nd day
   7 mo. 1789, Susanna Hicks Rogers, widow of John
   Rogers and dau. of James and Mary Hicks             1 SF
Harris, Isaac, 24 Jan. 1797, Marget Taylor             2 SO
   3 SO gives the date as 25 Jan. 1797, and the bride's
   name as Margaret Taylor.
Harris, James, 9 Oct. 1781, Elizabeth Madkin           2 DO
Harris, James, son of William, 20th day, 11 mo., 1784,
   Celia Wright                                        2 SF-288
Harris, James, 13 July 1791, Henny Mitchell            2 DO
Harris, James, 10 July 1794, Susannah Daull            5 BA-7
Harris, James, 28 Jan. 1795, Elenor Moore              3 BA-299
Harris, James, 25 Nov. 1797, Temperance Burk           4 KE-68
Harris, James, 17 July 1798, Mary R. Hobbs             2 SO
Harris, James, 18 July 1798, Mary R. Hobbs             3 SO
Harris, John, 11 Feb. 1781, Carther Davis              1 SO-29
Harris, John, 3 March 1783, Mary Elder                 4 FR
Harris, John, 29 Oct. 1785, Rebecca Geoghegan          2 DO
Harris, John, 7 April 1788, Clara Beckwith             2 DO
Harris, Jno., 24 Feb. 1794, Ann Butler                29 BA-5
Harris, Jno., 29 Nov. 1795, Hannah Curtain            50 BA-398
Harris, Jonathan, 29 May 1800, Amelia Wallce           2 DO
Harris, Josias, 3 Aug. 1779, Elizabeth Davis           4 FR
Harris, Josias, 2 Sept. 1781, Catherine Martin         2 CH-236
Harris, Noah, 24 July 1784, Nancy Marshall             2 DO
Harris, Peter, son of James (dec.) and Mary, 22nd day,
   10 mo., 1800, Anna Needles, dau. of Tristram and
   Anna                                                4 SF
Harris, Richard, 19 Dec. 1779, Margaret Hance          1 CA-3
Harris, Robert, 16 Dec. 1778, Jane Grimes              4 FR
Harris, Samuel, 10 March 1778, Clan Legg               3 AA-414
Harris, Samuel, 24 May 1786, Catherine Koonce          4 FR
Harris, Samuel, 26 Nov. 1792, Susanna Gott             4 FR
Harris, Stephen, 15 Jan. 1799, Sally Owens             2 SO
Harris?, Stophel, 6 Feb. 1778, Barbara Hook           11 BA-1
Harris, Thomas, 11 Sept. 1791, Nancy Waters            6 BA
Harris, Thomas, 8 March 1796, Sarah Mills              1 WO
Harris, Thomas, 18 Jan. 1798, Margaret Crabs           4 FR
Harris, Wm., 27 Jan. 1780, Marg't Crouch              11 BA-4
Harris, William, "the 3rd," 20 May 1781, Betty Wilson  3 AA-417
Harris, William, 11 July 1785, Sarah Vickers           2 DO
Harris, William, 14 Nov. 1793, Mary Constable         18 BA-6
Harris, William, 23 June 1796, Alice Rencher           3 SO
```

Harrison, Abraham, 22 Jan. 1792, Lilly Madkins   3 BA-255
Harrison, Charles, 8 Jan. 1778, Isabella Luton   11 BA-1
Harrison, Charles, 18 Jan. 1789, by Rev.
   beth Sewel   4 AA
Harrison, Daniel, 3 March 1796, Elizabeth Tillingsworth
   3 BA-321
Harrison, Elisha, 10 April 1796, Sarah Beale   3 PG-442
Harrison, Geo., 8 June 1783, Agnes Shipley   11 BA-6
Harrison, Grove, 20 July 1786, Hannah Fuller   2 FR-1134
Harrison, Hall, 17 March 1800, Elisabeth Gault   3 BA-383
Harrison, John, 17 July 1779, Betty Clann   4 FR
Harrison, John, 1 Feb. 1780, Rachel Deale   3 AA-416
Harrison, Jno., 4 April 1785, Cathe. Lucas   11 BA-8
Harrison, Joseph, 25 Oct. 1778, Rachel Perry   2 PG-2
Harrison, Kens., 9 March 1780, Sarah Saffle   4 FR
Harrison, Nathan, 21 June 1787, Mary Badan   4 FR
Harrison, Richard, 23 April 1782, Mary Norris   3 AA-418
Harrison, Richard Everingham, 29 June 1790, Sarah Thompson
   1 QA-65
Harrison, Samuel, 10 June 1778, by Rev. Magowan; Susannah
   Johns   4 AA
Harrison, Samuel, 20 Feb. 1788, Elizabeth Showne   4 FR
   2 FR-1135 gives the date as 21 Feb. 1788, and the
   bride's name as Eliz. Schaun.
Harrison, Saphenia, 29 Oct. 1793, Sarah Biddle   2 FR-1135
Harrison, Thomas, 4 Dec. 1779, Jane White   2 PG-3
Harrison, Thomas, 18 March 1783, Eliza Inloes   11 BA-6
Harrison, Rev. W. H., 16 Nov. 1781, Mary Stoddart   2 CH-236
Harrison, Wm., 4 Nov. 1778, Mary Davis   4 FR
Harrison, William, son of Thomas and Elizabeth, 23rd day,
   11 mo., 1791, Ruth Farquhar, dau. of William and
   Rachel   3 SF
Harriss, Josias, 10 Aug. 1797, Elizabeth Logan   3 PG-443
Harriss, Robert, 7 Feb. 1796, Elizabeth Morland   3 PG-442
Harry, Isaac Renatus, 1793, Anna Colln of Lititz   5 FR-53
Harry, Isaac Renatus, 12 Oct. 1795, Maria Barbara Feiser
   5 FR-53
Harry, Jno., 29 Nov. 1800, Rachel Course   29 BA-12
Harryman, George, (8 Feb. 1788), Rachel Bond   15 BA-1
Harryman, John, 17 Feb. 1785, Mary Eaglestone   3 BA-189
Harryman, Nathaniel, 19 Aug. 1790, Mary Oram   6 BA
Harryman, Nathaniel, 8 Oct. 1796, Catherine Oliver   6 BA
Harryman, Stephen, 25 Oct. 1799, Polly Waller   6 BA
Harson, James, 1 Dec. 1795, Rosey Gess   2 FR-1136
Hart, Adam, 6 Sept. 1794, Elizabeth Myers   4 FR
Hart, Benj'n, 17 April 1779, Elizabeth Danniwolf   4 FR
Hart, Benjamin, 1 Feb. 1797, Priscilla Johnson   2 DO
   1 DO gives the date as 4 Feb. 1797.
Hart, Christ'n, 19 Oct. 1778, Eliz'th Richards   4 FR
Hart, Daniel, 18 Jan. 1778, Sarah Beaucard   11 BA-1
Hart, Edward, 2 July 1792, Betsy Davis   2 DO
Hart, Ellis, 1 Aug. 1789, Ann Howard   4 FR
   2 FR-1135 gives the date as 4 Aug. 1789.
Hart, Henry, 12 Dec. 1780, Mary Cartwright   2 BA-11
Hart, Henry, 7 Aug. 1789, R. Ayers   29 BA-1
Hart, Michael, 11 Feb. 1786, Mary Row   4 FR
Hart, Peter, 5 Dec. 1795, Charlotte Doll   4 FR
Hart, Salathiel, 22 June 1797, Milly Smith   1 DO-39
Hart, Thomas, 14 April 1795, Eleanor Groshe   4 FR
Harth, Mich'l, 12 Feb. 1786, Mary Rau   2 FR-1134
Hartley, Joshua, 12 Feb. 1798, Ann Bayne   3 HA-27
   2 HA-350 gives the date as 13 Feb. 1798.
Hartman, John, 5 June 1786, Catherine Sheets   4 FR
Hartman, Paul, 5 March 1800, Margaret Price   6 BA
Hartung, Godfrey, 4 Aug. 1796, Eliz. Valentine   29 BA-7

```
Harvey, Basil, 15 April 1794, Mary Hale              4 FR
Harvey, David, 10 April 1800, Sarah Taylor           2 DO
Harvey, Henry, 24 April 1791, Sarah McDaniel         3 PG-257
Harvey, Henry, 24 Nov. 1793, Cath. Middleton         3 CH-161
Harvey, James, 11 May 1785, Darcus Brown             4 FR
Harvey, James, 7 Feb. 1790, Anne Farel               5 BA-7
Harvey, John, 5 Nov. 1794, Catherine Frampton        2 SF
Harvey, John, 12 March 1799, Hannah Johnson          2 HA-351
Harvey, John, 22 Sept. 1800, Leah Breerwood          2 DO
Harvey, Jonathan, 3 Jan. 1797, Lucy Armstead         3 BA-341
Harvey, Joseph, 1 Dec. 1796, Mary Thompson           3 BA-333
Harvey, Patrick, 28 April 1783, Mary Smith          11 BA-6
Harvey, Richard, 13 Feb. 1798, by Rev. Ridgely; Susanna
     Hardy                                            4 AA
Harvey, Richard, 8 Feb. 1800, Ann Robinson           6 BA
Harvey, Robert, 25 March 1795, Henny Ward            2 DO
Harvey, Samuel, 7 Dec. 1788, by Rev. Claggett; Ann Giddins
     4 AA
Harvey, Samuel, 10 Dec. 1793, Virlinda Fisher        2 FR-1135
Harvey,Thomas, 31 Dec. 1787, Hannah Thornton         3 BA-204
Harvey, Thomas, April 1794, Elizabeth Ann Simpson    3 PG-439
Harvey, William, 7 June 1788, Eleanor Jackson        3 BA-217
Harvey, William, 24 Aug. 1797, Elizabeth Eton        5 BA-7
Harvey, William, 11 Oct. 1797, Margaret Burns        3 BA-351
     See also 47 BA-1.
Harwood, Henry, 11 Dec. 1794, Jane Buckler           3 BA-296
     35 BA-1 states that on the license the bride is named
     Elizabeth Buckley.
Harwood, Thomas, 29 Oct. 1778, Anne White            2 PG-2
Haseleb, Rezin, 3 Oct. 1786, S. Eakley              29 BA-1
Haser, Jesse, 12 March 1789, Mary McCullestor        6 BA
Hasham, Josiah, 26 March 1800, Mary Knopwood?        3 BA-384
Hashelbach, -(?)-, 3 June 1784, Maria Breidenbarth  10 BA-180
Hashelback, Johann George, 14 July 1796, Barbara Cotieln?
     10 BA-198
Haskins, Henry, 3 Sept. 1795, Sarah Austin           2 DO
Haskins, Henry, 29 Oct. 1799, Sarah Vickars          2 DO
Haskins, Joseph, (born 28 Feb. 1762), 23 Oct. 1788, Sarah
     Barclay (born 1 Aug. 1771), dau. of Rev. John Barclay
     1 TA-318
Haslet, Alexander, 15 Feb. 1798, Elizabeth Highjah   5 BA-7
Haslip, John, 23 Oct. 1800, by Rev. Ridgely; Mary Griffith
     White                                           4 AA
Hastotter, David, 20 Dec. 1798, Polly Kintz         45 BA-3
Hatch, David C., 18 Nov. 1800, Polly Reese           6 BA
Hatcheson, Benjamin, 26 Jan. 1796, Marha -(?)-       1 KE-292
Hatcheson, Richard, 4 Nov. 1792, Elizabeth Hurtt     1 KE-291
     & 292
Hathaway, Jethro, 7 May 1795, Eleanor Buckley        5 BA-7
Hatton, Aquilla, 21 June 1798, Delia Parks           6 BA
Hatton, George, 2 July 1786, Eleanor Dent            3 PG-251
Hatton, John, 20 Oct. 1785, Mary Magnus             11 BA-8
Hatton, John, 15 April 1787, Rachel Hatton           6 BA
Hatton, Thomas, 2 Sept. 1784, Mary Ward             11 BA-7
Hatton, Wm., 14 March 1780, Mary Cartey              4 FR
Hauck, John, 12 March 1797, Eliz. Sinn               2 FR-1136
Hauck, Michael, 7 May 1797, Magd. Engel              2 FR-1136
Haucke, George, 4 May 1794, Mary Caword?            50 BA-394
Haucke, Jacob, 26 Oct. 1794, Mary Schliesman        50 BA-396
Hauer, Nicholas, 13 Oct. 1795, Priscilla Dawson      4 FR
Hauffell, George, 1792, Heinr. Hoffman              50 BA-392
Haughey, Hugh, 12 Aug. 1800, Susan Harwood           2 HA-352
Hauser, Adam, 10 June 1791, Sibylla Yantz            4 FR
     2 FR-1135 gives the date as 12 June 1791.
Hauser, Jno., 5 April 1795, Barb. Roh               29 BA-6
```

Hausler, Philip, 1793, Ann Haines   50 BA-393
Hausser, Jacob, 13 Oct. 1787, Cath. Bader   2 FR-1135
Havely, Michael, 25 Dec. 1791, Elizabeth Wolfin   2 WA-17
Havener, Andrew, 9 Feb. 1789, Susanna Haas   4 FR
Haw, Charles, 17 Dec. 1800, Jane Howard   3 BA-396
Hawk, Stephen, 12 July 1798, Agness Hamilton   5 BA-7
Hawk, Thomas, 8 Oct. 1796, Sara Brown   3 BA-329
Hawkins, George, 8 April 1798, Margaret Barton   7 BA-4
Hawkins, John, 28 April 1795, Eleanor Dorsey   7 BA-2
Hawkins, Joseph, 22 April 1787, Ann Shipley   3 BA-191
   See also 11 BA-10.
Hawkins, Joseph, 17 Nov. 1796, Sarah Downy   35 BA-4
Hawkins, Nicholas, 19 June 1799, Mary Chaulk   6 BA
Hawkins, Ralph, 20 Dec. 1792, Susanna Jacobs   3 BA-259
Hawkins, Robert, 8 May 1794, Mary Missee   18 BA-6
Hawkins, Robert, 20 July 1797, Ann Mitchell   3 HA-26
   See also 2 HA-350.
Hawkins, Samuel, 4 Feb. 1785, Hannah Standiford   3 HA-9
Hawkins, Samuel, 20 Nov. 1787, Catherine Pomphrey   18 BA-1
Hawkins, Smith, 5 Nov. 1782, Eleanor Laidlet   2 CH-236
Hawkins, Wm., 16 Dec. 1779, Frances Cuningham   11 BA-4
Hawling, John Wilispen, 25 Oct. 1785, Jemima Fouch   4 FR
Hawman, Peter, 18 Aug. 1781, Elizabeth Hildebrand   4 FR
Hawn, Lewis, 11 Nov. 1799, Elizabeth Pearce   4 FR
Hawn, Michael, 9 Sept. 1778, Christianna Eichelberger 4 FR
Hawood, Jno., 5 Oct. 1794, Sarah Klein   29 BA-5
Hay, Alex'r, 28 July 1796, Juliet Miller   29 BA-7
Hay, Edmond, 7 April 1797, Sarah Whiteacre   4 FR
Hay, Jacob, c.1786, Elisab. Meier   50 BA-387
Hay, Jacob, 12 July 1794, Elizabeth Schally   10 BA-196
Hay, James, 4 Dec. 1786, Jane Dillan   6 BA
Hay, James, 27 April 1797, Mary Cornical   3 BA-344
Hay, Joh., 1791, Barb. Meyer   50 BA-391
Hay, Robert, 13 March 1791, Anna Magruder   3 PG-257
Hay, Wm., 12 May 1791, Sus. Steitz   29 BA-2
Hay, William, 9 Jan. 1798, Ruth Hawkins   3 PG-443
Hayden, James, 4 Sept. 1791, Anne Robertson   2 CH-236
Haydn, Samuel, 15 Feb. 1795, Elizabeth Mahoney   3 BA-299
Haydon, Clement, 13 Jan. 1786, Fowney Wakefield   2 CH-453
Hayes, Edward, 23 Oct. 1798, Maria O'Brien   3 BA-364
Hayes, George, 16 March 1797, "his second wife (unnamed)"
   7 MO-29
Hayly, Samuel, 29 Oct. 1799, Kitty Anderson   3 BA-380
Hayman, Cornelius Riggin, 17 Dec. 1799, Anne Smith   2 SO
Hayman, Hezekiah, 18 March 1800, Hetty Riggin   2 SO
Hayman, Isaiah, 18 Oct. 1796, Peggy Rencher Pollitt   3 SO
Hayne, Charles, (date not given), Rebecca Forman   4 KE-68
Hays, Aaron, 13 Jan. 1786, Elisabeth Brown   10 BA-186
Hays, Allin, 9 Feb. 1792, Cath. Bossert   2 FR-1135
Hays, Archer, 23 Feb. 1781, Hannah Smith   3 HA-3
Hays, George, 9 March 1797, Elizabeth Ridgely   4 FR
Hays, Joel, 11 March 1783, Sarah Crapper   11 BA-6
Hays, John, 29 Jan. 1796, Susanna Howard   4 FR
Hays, John, 23 Oct. 1780, Rebecca Williams   3 BA-180
Hays, Joseph, 7 Feb. 1791, Deborah Wimmer   4 FR
Hays, Notley, 2 Dec. 1788, Sarah Rawlings   4 FR
Hays, Richard, 11 Feb. 1789, Charlotte Norris   4 FR
Hays, Thomas, 2 Dec. 1786, Ann Wilkey   4 FR
Hays, William, 11 Feb. 1796, Cynthia Thompson   3 HA-25
   7 BA-3 gives the date as 13 Feb. 1796.
Hays, William, 4 Jan. 1800, Anna Goulding   7 BA-4
Haythorn, Samuel, 29 June 1800, Ann Rockhold   3 HA-29
Hayward, Henry, 7 Dec. 1797, Harriot Barney   3 BA-353
Hayward, Jacob, 8 May 1800, Elizabeth Brinsfield   2 DO
Hayward, Richard, 19 Dec. 1791, Margaret Hubbert   2 DO

Hayward, Thomas (born 8 Oct. 1771), son of William and Marga-
     ret, 12 May 1795, Mary Smith (born 10 Nov. 1775)   1 TA-319
Hayward, William, 27 May 1789, Mary McGraw   2 DO
Hayward, William, 2 April 1791, Sarah LeCompte   2 DO
Hayward, William, son of William and Sydney, 9th day, 5 mo.,
     1791, Kezia Coates, dau. of Jonathan and Jane   1 SF
Hayward, William, 4 Jan. 1792, Rebecca LeCompte   2 DO
Hayward, William, 5 Dec. 1792, Mary Tregoe   2 DO
Haywood, Isaac, 12 July 1797, Ann Talbott   4 FR
Haywood, Thomas, 16 Oct. 1781, Mary Shermentine   3 SM-59
Hayworth, Johnathan, 11 Dec. 1787, Rebecca Randall   3 BA-214
Haze, Leonard, 24 Aug. 1782, Eleanor Simmons   4 FR
Hazlewood, Thomas, 5 May 1778, Sarah Coffin   4 FR
Hazzard, George, 3 May 1791, "by Rev. Richards of the Bap-
     tist Congregation;" Eleanor Burgess   3 BA-234
     6 BA gives the date as 9 May 1791.
Head, Biggar, 13 Feb. 1779, (?) Livers   4 FR
Head, Cecilius, 8 Jan. 1779, Elizabeth Butler   4 FR
Head, Ignatius, 2 Jan. 1790, Nancy Perry   4 FR
Head, Richard, 4 May 1784, Ruth Bentley   4 FR
Head, Wm. Edward, 27 Aug. 1778, Mary Walker   4 FR
Healy, Thomas, 2 Feb. 1792, Charlotte Holcraft   6 BA
Heaps, Lawrence, 29 Aug. 1796, Mary DuLaney   3 HA-25
Heard, Jacob, 4 Oct. 1796, Mary Dwyer   2 FR-1136
Hearn, Ant'y, 18 Nov. 1794, Sarah Jenkins   44 BA-1
Hearn, Ebenezer, 21 Feb. 1798, Betsey Roach   1 WO
Hearn, Elijah, 5 Sept. 1787, Cassandra Davis   4 FR
Hearn, Greenbury, 15 June 1797, Sarah Grimes   4 FR
Hearn, Mathias, 16 July 1798, Amelia Shipley   4 FR
Hearn, Spencer, 15 April 1797, Eliza Wilson   2 SO
Heart, Peter, 28 Jan. 1777, Sarah Cook   2 PG-2
Heartsock, William, 4 July 1778, Catherine Fogle   4 FR
Heater, Frederick, 26 Aug. 1779, Mary Ann Shroiner   4 FR
Heath, Samuel, 12 Feb. 1789, Eleanor Joyce   3 BA-221
Heath, Samuel, 29 May 1779, Peggy Turpin   2 SO
Heath, William, Sept. 1778, Mary Allwell   11 BA-1
Heather, Michael, 6 Nov. 1784, Rebecca Geoghegan   2 DO
Heathrington, Thomas, 7 Feb. 1793, Sarah Pollock   3 BA-258
Heaton, Jeremiah, 7 Jan. 1799, Mary Fisher   3 HA-27
Heaton, William, 31 July 1794, Eliza Constable   18 BA-6
Hebb, Richard, 2 Feb. 1788, Ann Thomas   4 FR
     2 FR-1135 gives the date as 4 Feb. 1788.
Hebert, Jno. Baptiste, 29 June 1797, Eliz. Tassey   29 BA-8
Heck, Daniel, 1 July 1783, Elizabeth McLain   4 FR
Heck, Peter, 12 April 1789, Hannah Waschebach   2 FR-1135
Heckenmiller, John Conrad, 1 Sept. 1789, Elizabeth Davis
     4 FR
Heckman, Wilh., 9 march 1796, Eliz. Endese   50 BA-399
Heddinger, Michael, 11 July 1793, Catherine Herman   3 BA-270
Hedericks, Thos., 3 June 1784, Christiana Frits   11 BA-7
Hedge, Caleb, 8 Sept. 1788, Mary Dern   4 FR
Hedge, Moses, 14 Nov. 1799, Catherine Waters   4 FR
Hedge, Nicholas, Dec. 1794, Zeruiah Ritchie   4 FR
Hedges, Andrew, 30 April 1792, Christena Cramer   4 FR
Hedges, Jonas, 17 Aug. 1784, Mary Ann Hedges   4 FR
Hedges, Joseph, 21 July 1797, Catherine Baltzell   4 FR
Hedges, Josiah, 4 Nov. 1778, Ann Barnett   4 FR
Hedges, Peter, 24 Sept. 1787, Elizabeth Boyer   4 FR
     2 FR-1135 gives the date as 25 Sept. 1787, and the
     bride's name as Bayer.
Hedges, Shardrick, 3 Aug. 1782, Mary Dickson   4 FR
Hedges, William, 28 Feb. 1790, Leah Duffield   2 FR-1135
Hedly, Anthony, 7 May 1798, Susanna Lewis   29 BA-9
Hedrick, John, 22 Jan. 1792, Margaret Galf   3 BA-255
Hedricks, James, 2 July 1794, Anne Fish   3 BA-291

Heffner, George, Jr., 1 April 1786, Eve Margaret Yantz   4 FR
Heffner, Gotlip, 6 Dec. 1790, Catherine Shafer   4 FR
Heffner, Michael, 8 Oct. 1779, Margaret Reed   4 FR
Heffner, Michael, 6 Sept. 1794, Elizabeth Shafer   4 FR
Hehs, Joseph. See Hess, Joseph.
Heider, Henry, 25 July 1798, Eliz. Law   29 BA-9
Heighten, Josias, 23 Dec. 1790, Rebecca Cawood   4 FR
Heim, Frederick, 13 April 1788, Cathrina Jul. Bleisen   10 BA-190
Heinecke, Frederick, 20 Nov. 1794, Ann Schroeder   29 BA-6
Heishen, Cornelius, 22 Oct. 1793, Elizabeth Weber   10 BA-196
Heisling, Thomas, 6 Feb. 1798, Peggy Randall   10 BA-198
Hellen, Alexander, 16 May 1799, Susanna Durham   12 BA-370
    See also 3 HA-28.
Hellen, James, 5 Jan. 1778, Lydia Blackburn   1 CA-1
Hellery, Jere., 16 July 1796, Mary Cordroy   1 AL-53
Helm, Leonard, 1791, Mary Horsman   50 BA-391
Helmes, James, 7 Jan. 1787, Betsie Shriebek   10 BA-188
Helmesh, Heinrich, 19 Nov. 1799, Catharina Schwelk   10 BA-198
Helms, Dan'l, 28 Dec. 1794, Louisa Opferrbucher   50 BA-396
Helms, John, 2 Oct. 1793, Catharine Clark   3 BA-275
Helsby, Samuel, 4 March 1795, Margaret Newton   2 DO
Helsby, Thomas, 7 April 1790, Sarah Saunders   2 DO
Helt, Christ'n, 30 Jan. 1796, Julian Schriver   29 BA-7
Hembe, Henry, 6 March 1787, An. Marg. Dofler   2 FR-1134
Hemphill, William, 10 Nov. 1779, Margaret Ashmore   3 HA-1
Hempston, Christian, 10 Sept. 1792, Darcus Fardy   4 FR
Hemsley, William, 26 Dec. 1797, Anna Maria Tilghman   4 KE-68
Hancock, William, 26 July 1798, by Rev. Ridgely; Elizabeth
    Waters   4 AA
Hender, Thomas, 29 June 1797, Nancy Townsend   3 BA-346
Henderson, Barneby, 23 Oct. 1797, Margaret Knox   1 WO
Henderson, Ezekiel, 22 Dec. 1795, Hannah Timons   1 WO
Henderson, Geo., 4 May 1786, Jemima Griffin   11 BA-9
Henderson, George, 17 June 1800, Charity Cole   3 HA-29
    2 HA-352 gives the date as 19 June 1800.
Henderson, Gilbert, 8 Oct. 1782, Esther Dyer   11 BA-5
Henderson, Griffith, 7 Jan. 1797, Hannah Richardson   4 FR
    2 FR-1136 gives the date as 10 Jan. 1797.
Henderson, Isaac, 22 Feb. 1797, Sally Davis   1 WO
Henderson, Jacob, 25 Nov. 1800, Elizabeth Abbott   1 WO
Henderson, Jacob, 17 Dec. 1800, Sarah Bennett   1 WO
Henderson, Jesse, 22 Dec. 1800, Molly White Long   1 WO
Henderson, John, 17 April 1783, Michal Barton   3 BA-184
Henderson, John, 8 Feb. 1796, Sally Henderson   1 WO
Henderson, Nathaniel, 12 Sept. 1792, Elizabeth Berryman
    3 HA-22
Henderson, Wm. H., 19 Sept. 1800, Tabitha Dixon   1 WO
Henesy, Michael, 18 Sept. 1791, Elizabeth Warrington   3 BA-254
    See also 18 BA-3.
Heney, Wm., 1788, Susanna Hay   50 BA-388
Henley, Robert, 15 July 1794, Eleanor Flood   3 BA-291
Henner, William, 9 Jan. 1794, Mary Gertr. Kuhns   2 FR-1135
Henning, John, 5 Sept. 1781, Mary Abell   3 SM-59
Henninger, Philip, 22 July 1797, Henrietta Dillhelm   29 BA-8
Henninger, Philip, 2 Feb. 1799, Lydia Flanigan   29 BA-10
Henray, Michael, 18 July 1795, Rachel Wooden   5 BA-7
Henricks, Geo., 4 Dec. 1800, Rebecca Boys   29 BA-12
Henry, Elex. Ashton, 25 May 1777, Mary Dent   2 CH-453
Henry, Ezekiel, 16 Feb. 1781, Sarah Ganze   2 DO
Henry, Isaac, 29 March 1796, Nancy Medford   2 DO
Henry, James, 15 Feb. 1796, Lurana Medford   2 DO
Henry, James, 29 June 1800, Polly Dailey   6 BA
Henry, John, 6 March 1787, Margaret Campbell   2 DO
Henry, John, 17 April 1796, Elizabeth Wright   6 BA
Henry, Jno., 2 Aug. 1798, Margaret Shipley   29 BA-8

Henry, Levin, 25 Feb. 1800, Nancy Bradley   2 DO
Henry, Osburn, 23 June 1779, Ann Tompson   2 CH-453
Henry, Robert Jenkins, 18 Sept. 1778, Martha Stevenson 5 BA-7
Henry, Samuel, 15 Nov. 1797, Bridget Cross   3 BA-352
Henry, Wm., 1790, M. Camel; blacks, married by permission
   50 BA-390
Hepbourne, Thomas, 18 Dec. 1797, Margaret Duger   4 KE-68
Her, John. See Pier, John.
Herback, Henry, 4 Dec. 1792, Cath. Reisz   2 FR-1135
Herbert, Benjamin, 15 Aug. 1795, Sarah Crabson   3 HA-24
Herbert, James, 27 Feb. 1795, Ann Crabston   7 BA-2
Herbert, Jeremiah, 15 Nov. 1796, Mary Hill   4 FR
Herd, Wm., 14 March 1799, Phoebe Waltz   2 FR-1136
Hering, Ludewig, 13 April 1789, Catharina Maurern   1 FR-59
Herman, Jacob, 31 March 1799, Marg. Zeiler   2 FR-1136
Herman, Nicholas, 29 Dec. 1800, Marg. Kennedy   2 FR-1136
Herman, Philip, 23 Aug. 1785, Barbara Freimiller   10 BA-184
Hernmyer, Jacob, 10 May 1779, Catherine Steiner   4 FR
Heron, Charles, 20 Feb. 1786, Scarborough Stokeley   2 DO
Heron, Cuthbert, 18 May 1781, Hannah Minor   2 DO
Heron, Thomas, 31 Jan. 1797, Mary Abbitt   2 SO
Herpster, Frederick, 7 May 1793, Mary Shollison   4 FR
Herrick, Frederick, 26 Feb. 1797, by Rev. Ridgely; Mary
   Dove   4 AA
Herrick, Thomas, 2 Oct. 1797, Margaret Wooden   6 BA
Herring, Henry, 1 April 1799, Mary Sailer   4 FR
Herring, Langford, 24 April 1794, Ann Cromwell   18 BA-6
Herring, Robert, 4 Sept. 1794, Susanna Lavely   6 BA
Herron, Timothy, 4 Sept. 1783, Ann O'Brian   11 BA-6
Hershberger, Henry, 7 May 1787, Catherine Ramspergh 4 FR
Herstons, Charles, 5 Nov. 1797, Delilah Sprigg   6 BA
Hert, Eneas, 22 Jan. 1781, Jane Robinson   3 HA-3
Hert, Jeremiah, 4 June 1785, Susanna Braeghle   4 FR
Hertinger, Christian, 28 April 1789, Julianna Bayer 2 FR-1135
Hertzerfer, John, 21 Nov. 1785, Mary Reichart   4 FR
Herzog, Pet., 11 Jan. 1785, Cath. Lea   2 FR-1134
Heselett, Wilhelm, 15 Nov. 1789, Elizabeth Schumacher 6 FR-202
Hess, Johannes, 6 Jan. 1788, Maria Margaretha M. Maurer
   10 BA-190
Hess (Hehs), Joseph, 9 Nov. 1800, Catherine Busch   9 BA-143
Hester, William, 6 May 1787, Rachel Bart   2 FR-1134
Hettinger, Mich'l, 29 Sept. 1793, Barb. Muma   50 BA-393
Hetton, James, 10 April 1800, Maryan Hickey   6 BA
Heugh, John, 20 Feb. 1792, Anne Munro   4 FR
Hewer, Jacob, 14 Nov. 1791, Mary Bonham   1 AL-52
Hewett, Caleb, 24 Aug. 1799, Mary Morton   8 BA-1
Hewitt, Eli, 25 March 1797, Martha Dennis   3 BA-343
Hewitt, Thomas, 6 Feb. 1791, by Rev. Green; Margaret Chalmers
   4 AA
Hianiss, Benjamin, 20 Jan. 1791, Lucy Swain   3 PG-258
Hickerson, Samuel, 13 Nov. 1788, Mary Thrap   1 BA-1
Hickey, James, 14 Sept. 1789, Mary Ann Linch   4 FR
Hickey, Peter, 25 Oct. 1797, Margaret Aires   3 BA-352
Hickholt, Henry, 3 Aug. 1784, Rachel Bret   11 BA-7
Hickman, Abel, 17 Dec. 1798, Sally Bratten   1 WO
Hickman, Christopher, 23 Jan. 1786, Christena Davis 4 FR
Hickman, Joseph, 19 Sept. 1780, Margaret Jenkins   2 PG-3
Hickman, William, 11 March 1800, Nelly White   2 SO
Hicks, Ab'm, 13 March 1781, Sarah Gorsuch   11 BA-2
Hicks, Abram, 13 May 1781, Sarah Gorsuch   2 CH-453
Hicks, Denwood, 21 Sept. 1793, Mary Owens   2 DO
Hicks, Henry, 14 Nov. 1795, Polly Sewell   2 DO
Hicks, John, 24 May 1794, Lucy McCollister   2 DO
Hicks, John, 22 May 1800, Ann Ford   4 SM-184
Hicks, Joshua, 22 Nov. 1796, Rebecca Sollers   29 BA-8

```
Hicks, Robert, 7 Sept. 1788, Elizabeth Henry          3 BA-218
Hicks, Thomas, 31 Jan. 1784, Sarah Wall               2 DO
Hicks, Thomas, 12 May 1789, Amelia Newton             2 DO
Hicks, Thomas, 16 Feb. 1791, Nelly Hodson             2 DO
Hicks, Thomas, 19 Jan. 1792, Sarah Stewart            2 DO
Hickson, Thomas, 14 May 1785, Mary Black              4 FR
    2 FR-1134 gives the date as 15 May 1785, and the bride's
    name as Mary Swartz.
Hiede, Gecrge, 3 May 1792, Rachel Griffith            6 BA
Hiege, Johannes, 7 July 1788, Cathrina Schworz       10 BA-190
Hiett, Wm., 4 Feb. 1783, Susanna McKie               11 BA-6
Higdon, Ignatius, 1781, Elizabeth Taylor              2 CH-453
Higdon, John, 27 Jan. 1798, Eleanor Gaunt             4 FR
Higdon, Peter, 20 Dec. 1792, Anna Pierce              4 FR
Highfield, John, 31 Aug. 1795, Catherine Metz         4 FR
Higginbotham, Ralph, 28 Feb. 1799, Isabella Presbury  2 HA-351
Higgins, Clark, 21 Feb. 1797, Margaret Thomas         5 MO-114
Higgins, Edward, 24 Sept. 1793, Anne Ellerton         3 BA-275
Higgins, Francis, 30 May 1795, Temperance Hughes      2 DO
Higgins, James, 3 Aug. 1797, Verlinda Wilcoxen        5 MO-114
Higgins, Jno., 4 Jan. 1798, Eliz. Fisher              5 MO-114
Higgins, Langford, 23 Dec. 1798, Nancy Applegarth     1 TA-321
Higgins, Patrick, 22 Sept. 1793, Mary Ann Page        6 BA
Higginson, John H., 2 May 1799, Brittanica Bennett    4 SM-184
Higgs, Jonathan, 20 June 1779, Elizabeth Ford         2 CH-453
Higham, Andrew, 1 Feb. 1788, Elizabeth Morgan        29 BA-1
Highjoe, Philip, 4 Dec. 1791, Elizabeth Dunkin        6 BA
Higinbotham, Ralph, 23 Feb. 1799, Isabella Presbury   3 HA-28
Higinbothom, Thomas, 21 Jan. 1800, Susanna Blundell   3 BA-382
Higson, George, 26 June 1789, Sarah Hubbard          21 BA-1
Hiland, George, 30 May 1782, Catherine Smith          3 BA-183
Hilary, John, 4 Aug. 1791, Elizabeth Ferrell          3 PG-258
Hildebeitel, Salomon, 31 May 1784, Cathr. Hercherotherein
    1 CL-29
Hildebrand, Jacob, 26 July 1789, Cathrine Pomp       10 BA-194
Hildebrand, John, 3 April 1798, Margaret Myers        4 FR
Hildebrand, Jos., 31 Aug. 1788, Magd. Eliz. Haffner   2 FR-1135
Hilderbrick, George, 26 April 1785, Mary Ann Koontz   4 FR
Hilke, Christian, 4 Sept. 1788, Barbary Thomas        4 FR
Hill, Abram, 3 April 1779, Judy Clabaugh              4 FR
Hill, Benj'n, 5 Sept. 1778, Sarah Scaggs              4 FR
Hill, Ebenezer, 22 Nov. 1782, Mary Ball               2 DO
Hill, Elisha, 25 Nov. 1799, Elizabeth Taylor          1 WO
Hill, Harmon, 10 Dec. 1780, Fra's Dever               3 HA-3
Hill, Henry Roby, 25 Sept. 1788, Ann Tolbert          4 FR
    2 FR-1135 gives the date as 28 Sept. 1788.
Hill, James, 4 Nov. 1784, Frances Collins            11 BA-7
Hill, James, Jr., 9 Oct. 1797, Nancy Williss          2 SO
Hill, John, 7 Sept. 1788, Deborah Wallace            18 BA-1
Hill, John, 22 June 1798, Mary McDaniel               2 DO
Hill, John, 8 June 1800, Jane Bowland                 3 BA-386
Hill, John C., 18 March 1799, Mary Fenner             3 BA-369
Hill, John H., 28 Jan. 1800, Nancy Johnson            1 WO
Hill, Joseph, Jr., 16 Sept. 1778, Margaret Row        4 FR
Hill, Joseph, son of Abel, Feb. 1782, Susannah Hill   3 AA-418
Hill, Joses, 22 Jan. 1784, Jane High                 11 BA-7
Hill, Josiah, 28 Feb. 1798, Polly Franklin            1 WO
Hill, Levin, 2 May 1796, Margaret Robertson           2 DO
Hill, Levin, 20 Dec. 1797, Margaret Hodson            2 DO
Hill, Levin, Jr., 17 April 1798, Catherine Johnson    1 WO
Hill, Levin, 16 Feb. 1799, Milley Molock              2 DO
Hill, Nathan, 12 Sept. 1786, Drucilla Davis           4 FR
Hill, Reuben Henry, 4 March 1800, Polly Jones         2 SO
Hill, Richard, 11 Nov. 1797, Ann Adams                6 BA
Hill, Richard, 26 June 1800, Anna Willis              3 BA-387
```

```
Hill, Robert, 21 Dec. 1786, Eleanor Hyfield          4 FR
Hill, Robert, 4 April 1790, Maily Fitzgerald         2 FR-1135
Hill, Robert, 13 Nov. 1798, Sarah Ellis              4 KE-68
Hill, Sephania, 22 Sept. 1795, Barb. Leshner         2 FR-1136
Hill, Thomas, 16 April 1783, Sarah Howard            4 FR
Hill, Thomas, 7 Sept. 1783, Hannah Sullivan          4 FR
Hill, Thomas, 19 Feb. 1793, Elizabeth Wharton        4 FR
Hill, Thomas, 1 March 1794, Elizabeth Blackston     39 BA-1
Hill, William, 3 April 1779, Mary Perkinson          4 FR
Hill, Wm., 14 April 1795, Kiturah Baker              6 BA
Hill, William, June 1795, Elizabeth Charleton        5 BA-8
Hill, William, 22 Oct. 1798, Rebecca Hill            1 WO
Hillary, Jeremiah, 21 Dec. 1786, Ann Clary           2 FR-1134
Hillary, John, 24 Feb. 1791, Verlinda Williams       3 PG-257
Hilleary, George, 29 Nov. 1781, Sarah Smith          2 PG-5
Hilleary, Oglon, 30 April 1783, Elizabeth Purdy      4 FR
Hilleary, Tilghman, 15 Jan. 1782, Ann Wheeler        2 PG-3
Hillen, Thomas, 14 Dec. 1794, Robinie Kennedy McHaffie
     44 BA-1
Hillen, William, 4 Feb. 1779, Dorcas Johnson         1 CA-2
Hillery, Thomas, 9 Feb. 1782, Ann Murphey            4 FR
Hillery, Wm., 6 Sept. 1781, Drusey Evans             4 FR
Hilman, Alexander, 30 July 1800, Elisabeth Whipple   3 BA-388
Hilton, Abraham, 20 Oct. 1789, Elizabeth Grimes      1 BA-2
Hilton, Abraham, 22 May 1794, Catherine Thompson; free
     blacks                                          3 BA-287
Hilton, Andrew, 14 Jan. 1789, Catherine Spalding     4 FR
Hilton, James, 21 Dec. 1789, Priscilla Harris        4 FR
Hilton, Jno., 15 Aug. 1782, Lydia Sicamore          11 BA-5
Hilton, John, 30 March 1798, by Rev. Wyatt; Rebecca Gardiner
     4 AA
Hilton, Luke, 16 June 1792, Margaret Wilson          4 FR
Hilton, Matthew, 28 Jan. 1791, Susanna Wheeler       4 FR
     2 FR-1135 gives the date as 29 Jan. 1791.
Hilton, Thomas, 13 Jan. 1795, Lely Griffin           3 AA-424
Hilton, Trueman, 27 Oct. 1780, Christena Patrick     4 FR
Hilton, Wm., 13 Dec. 1781, Eliz. Hannah             11 BA-5
Hilton, Wm., 26 Jan. 1782, Elizabeth Nicholls        4 FR
Hinamon, Geo., 11 Oct. 1785, Elizabeth Howard        4 FR
Hinckel, John, 22 May 1799, Mary Rennels             2 FR-1136
Hinckle, John, 18 July 1799, Rachel Grove            4 FR
Hinckle, Jns. (sic), 25 March 1781, Mussey Brightwell 4 FR
Hindes, Rudolph, 3 June 1778, Sarah Haff             4 FR
Hindman, James, 20 March 1797, Eliz. Hamilton        1 TA-321
Hindon, Benjamin, (7 June 1788), Sophia Marsh       15 BA-1
Hiner, Joseph, 4 Feb. 1796, Ann Holloway             6 BA
Hines, John, 9 March 1795, Mary Roderick             4 FR
Hines, Nathaniel, 4 Nov. 1796, Elizabeth Penn        4 FR
Hines, Patrick, 10 Jan. 1792, Esther Bankard         4 FR
Hines, William Bois, 16 Nov. 1800, Elizabeth Lawrence 1 BA-9
     4 BA-78 gives the groom's name as William Rose
     Lawrence.
Hinghay, Hugh, 11 April 1800, Susan Hannard          3 HA-29
Hignson, Thomas, 4 Nov. 1790, Ann Hodson             2 DO
Hinkle, Anthony, 13 March 1800, Kitty Bond           3 BA-383
Hinkle, George, 13 Oct. 1798, Elizabeth Hinkle       4 FR
Hinkley, Fred'k, 10 Feb. 1792, Mary Hilton           4 FR
Hinks, William, 6 Oct. 1791, Jemmiah Fisher          6 BA
Hinman, James, 3 Jan. 1798, Sarah Scarborough        1 WO
Hinton, Charles Boyd, 31 Dec. 1780, Mary Feller      2 PG-5
Hinton, John, 23 Sept. 1786, Susan McClain           4 FR
Hinton, Josias, 23 Dec. 1799, Elizabeth Crosby       3 AA-415
Hinton, Masharuk, 29 Jan. 1788, Eliz. Joseph         2 FR-1135
Hinton, Richard, 18 March 1779, Ruth Cash            4 FR
Hinton, Thomas, c.July 1778, Mary Watson             3 AA-414
```

```
Hinton, Thomas, 18 Oct. 1798, Eleanor Turner          6 BA
Hipkins, Charles, 10 May 1789, Elizabeth Myres        1 BA-2
Hipsilly, Joshua, 21 April 1778, Elizabeth Goodman   11 BA-1
Hipsley, Benjamin, 20 Nov. 1788, Elizabeth Bishop     3 BA-219
Hiplsey, Charles, 17 April 1786, Sarah Poole          4 FR
Hipsly, Jno., 25 Oct. 1787, Eleanor Bishop           11 BA-10
Hirshberger, Henry, 13 May 1787, Cath. Remsperger     2 FR-1135
Hiseler, Michael, 25 Sept. 1784, Mary Hoffman         4 FR
Hiser, David, 16 July 1795, Charlotte Sweeting        3 BA-307
Hiss, Jacob, 6 June 1786, Elizabeth Gatch            11 BA-9
Hissey, Charles, 9 Nov. 1797, Hannah Zimmerman        6 BA
Hissey, James, 18 Sept. 1800, Mary Miller             3 BA-392
Hissey, William, 6 Jan. 1784, Mary Kettle            11 BA-7
Hitch, John, 23 Jan. 1797, Jane Polk                  2 SO
Hitch, John, 21 Feb. 1797, Milly Disharoon            2 SO
Hitch, John, 23 Feb. 1797, Amanda Disharoon           3 SO
Hitch, Joseph, 24 Sept. 1799, Sarah Muir              2 SO
Hitchcock, Jesse, 9 May 1792, Mary Falls              3 HA-21
Hiud, John, 7 April 1788, Ann Shields                 6 BA
Hixenbaugh, John, 8 Jan. 1794, Ann Snook              2 AL-700
Hobbs, Beall, Sept. 1790, Eleanor Smith               4 AA
Hobbs, Charles, 13 Jan. 1785, Elizabeth Ogle          4 FR
Hobbs, Charles Ridgely, 19 Oct. 1793, by Rev. Dorsey; Comfort
    Elizabeth Bagford                                 4 AA
Hobbs, Elie, 4 Oct. 1782, Elizabeth Hamilton          4 FR
Hobbs, Hanson, 22 Jan. 1791, by Rev. Chalmers; Mary Shipley
    4 AA
Hobbs, James, 25 Dec. 1790, Anne Knox                 5 BA-7
Hobbs, John, Jr., 22 Jan. 1794, Onner Burgess         4 FR
Hobbs, Joseph, 1 Sept. 1785, Nancy Randall           11 BA-8
Hobbs, Joseph, 17 June 1793, Susanna Bare             4 FR
Hobbs, Joshua, 17 April 1788, Rachel Hobbs            4 FR
Hobbs, Matthias, 11 Feb. 1800, Esther Whitney         2 SO
Hobbs, Thomas, 18 Feb. 1798, Arith Owings             4 FR
Hobbs, William, of Samuel, 13 Dec. 1786, Henrietta Dorsey
    4 FR
Hobbs, William C., 30 May 1796, Christina Schnertzell 4 FR
Hobbs, Zachariah, 30 Oct. 1797, Susanna James         4 FR
Hockensmith, John, 8 June 1799, Barbara Sluss         4 FR
Hodge, Henry, 3 Sept. 1799, by Rev. Ridgely; Mary Sappington
    4 AA
Hodge, Thomas, 31 Dec. 1797, Deborah Berry            3 PG-443
Hodges, James, 20 June 1797, Mary Claypoole           4 KE-68
Hodges, John, 26 Sept. 1793, Mary Bryan               3 BA-275
Hodges, Joseph, 15 Jan. 1784, Eliza Shields          11 BA-7
Hodges, William, 9 Aug. 1783, Rachael Denton         11 BA-6
Hodgkiss, Michael, 12 May 1794, Sarah Dewees          4 FR
Hodgson, George, 30 Dec. 1799, Nancy Jenkins          2 CH-453
Hodson, Charles, 5 July 1793, Ann Smith               2 DO
Hodson, Charles, 9 Dec. 1797, Nancy Manning           2 DO
Hodson, Henry, 16 July 1781, Elizabeth Hodson         2 DO
Hodson, John, 9 Dec. 1786, Sarah Whittington          2 DO
Hodson, John, 29 Dec. 1790, Charlotte Hodson          2 DO
Hodson, John Hooper, 27 May 1784, Peggy Stokeley      2 DO
Hodson, Levin, 28 Jan. 1792, Hannah Hayward           2 DO
Hodson, Levin, 12 May 1797, Liddy Sherwood            2 DO
Hodson, Thomas, 23 Dec. 1798, Rebecca Jones           2 DO
Hoff, Peter, 24 April 1790, Mary Boyer                4 FR
Hoffer, John, 30 July 1794, Ann Peterson             18 BA-6
Hoffert, Jacob, 15 Nov. 1799, Catherine Baker         4 FR
Hoffman, Adam, 20 Jan. 1786, Elizabeth Lane          29 BA-1
Hoffman, David, 4 June 1796, Eve Margaret Heck         4 FR
Hoffman, Geo., 2 April 1786, Eva Marg. Jantz          2 FR-1134
Hoffman, George, 8 Oct. 1791, Eleanor Phillips        4 FR
Hoffman, Heinr., 8 Sept. 1793, Elis. Williams        50 BA-393
```

Hoffman, Heinr., 10 March 1794, Maria Gallentin   50 BA-394
Hoffman, Jacob, 15 April 1784, Mary McClain   4 FR
Hoffman, Jacob, 23 June 1790, by Rev. Cooper; Hester
   Ashmead   4 AA
Hoffman, Jacob, 14 Nov. 1799, Margaret Beck?   3 AL-6
Hoffman, Peter, 16 May 1799, Deborah Owings   1 BA-9
   4 BA-74 names the groom as Peter Hoffman, Jr.
Hoffman, Philip, 14 June 1789, Elizabeth Gitzadanner   4 FR
   2 FR-1135 states the bride was a widow.
Hoffman, Valentine, 5 July 1791, Elizabeth Doll   4 FR
Hoffner, Michael, 23 Nov. 1794, Catherine Waughter   4 FR
Hogan, Dennis, 1 Sept. 1791, Elizabeth Lucas   18 BA-3
   See also 3 BA-253.
Hogan, John, 27 Oct. 1797, Eleanor Keaton   5 BA-7
Hogen, Abraham, 13 June 1797, Rebecca Buchanan   5 BA-7
Hogg, Charles, 8 Aug. 1786, Elenor Anderson   4 AA
   The ceremony was performed by Rev. Pigman.
Hoggins, John, 3 Nov. 1787, Tamar Branson   4 FR
Hoggins, Richard, 19 Aug. 1794, Elizabeth Knott   4 FR
Hogue, Jonathan, 16 July 1799, Sally Lee Brady   2 DO
Hohtmann, Jacob, 27 Feb. 1784, Barbara Schwinger   10 BA-180
Hoit, Israel, 22 Nov. 1798, Sarah Megaff   5 BA-7
Holbrook, Samuel, 23 Oct. 1798, Nelly D. Gillis   2 SO
   3 SO gives the date as 24 Oct. 1798, and the
   bride's name as Nelly O. Gillis.
Holbrooks, Jacob, 29 Dec. 1793, Eliza Banzle   18 BA-6
Holding, Peter, 4 May 1788, Sarah Hair   1 BA-1
Hole, John, 22 Nov. 1798, Dorcus Knott   4 FR
Hole, John, 29 Jan. 1780, Catherine Hollan   4 FR
Holland, Charles, 9 Oct. 1783, Ann Joyce   11 BA-6
Holland, Daniel, 24 April 1788, Rachel Cottrell   6 BA
Holland, Edward, 19 Nov. 1794, by Rev. Joseph Wyatt;
   Mary Simson   4 AA
Holland, Francis, 25 May 1797, Sybell West   1 BA-8
Holland, George, 2 Aug. 1778, Margaret Allender   11 BA-1
Holland, Isaac, 24 April 1790, by Rev. Cooper; Jane   :
   Steward   4 AA
Holland, James, 3 March 1792, Sarah Welsh   4 FR
Holland, James, 17 Feb. 1793, Sarah Weeks   3 BA-258
Holland, Jesse, 18 Feb. 1799, Nancy Wilkins   2 SO
Holland, John, 26 Feb. 1783, Ann Ensor   11 BA-6
Holland, Jno., 11 Aug. 1795, Polly Richardson   1 WO
Holland, John, 26 Sept. 1799, Elisabeth Ethrington   3 BA-378
Holland, Jonathan, 12 Sept. 1778, Drusilla Ridgely   4 FR
Holland, Jonathan, 7 March 1789, Urith Ridgely   23 BA-1
   4 FR gives the date as 10 March 1789.
Holland, Nehemiah, 12 Feb. 1796, Martha Richardson   1 WO
Holland, Otho, 25 Feb..1782, Jane Ridgely   4 FR
Holland, Samuel, 7 Jan. 1792, Nackey Phillips   4 FR
Holland, Solomon, 23 Jan. 1800, Margaret Gatton   5 MO-116
Holland, Thomas, 21 Dec. 1797, Margaret O'Connor   3 BA-353
Holland, Wm., 12 Feb. 1781, Ann Wayman   4 FR
Holland, Wm., 31 Dec. 1799, Sally Bowen   1 WO
Holland, Zadock, 25 Dec. 1798, Priscilla Mockbee   4 FR
Hollandshead, John, 25 Dec. 1783, Mary Wilkinson   3 AA-420
Hollar, Michael, 19 Feb. 1787, Catherine Dorff   4 FR
Hollar, Michael, son of Godfrey, 26 Aug. 1798, Catherine
   Rabourn   4 FR
Holler, Christopher, 6 May 1783, Barbara Lutz   4 FR
Holler, Tobias, 29 Sept. 1792, Elizabeth Hiseler   4 FR
Holleren, Bartholomew, 22 Jan. 1798, Ann Caldwell   2 SO
Holles, James, 8 April 1798, Sarah Osborne   2 HA-350
Holliday, John, 10 Dec. 1778, by Rev. Magowan; Sarah Child
   4 AA
Holliday, John, 9 May 1796, Margaret Rareton   5 BA-7

```
Holliday, Jno., 16 Aug. 1800, Mary Breimen          29 BA-11
Holliday, Leonard, 14 Dec. 1799, Sarah Holland       3 AA-415
Hollingsworth, Abel, 12 Aug. 1797, Sarah Ponder      4 KE-68
Hollingsworth, Henry, 13 Jan. 1793, Levinah Cross    3 BA-258
Hollingsworth, Jesse, 30 Sept. 1790, Rachel Lyde Parkin
    1 BA-3
Hollingsworth, Jonah, son of Isaac and Rachel, 15th day, 1 mo.
    (Jan.), 1778, Hannah Miller, dau. of Solomon and Sarah
    3 SF
Hollingsworth, Thomas, 29 May 1800, Ann Orrick       8 BA-2
Hollingsworth, Zebulon, 22 April 1790, Eliza Ireland 11 BA-13
Hollins, John, 31 Dec. 1785, Janit Smith             5 BA-7
Hollins, John, 24 Sept. 1794, Charlotte Mahoney      3 BA-293
Hollis, Benjamin, 30 Oct. 1784, Elizabeth Hursby     3 HA-9
Hollis, James, 2 June 1795, Jane Beatty              3 HA-24
    7 BA-2 gives the date as 4 June 1795.
Hollis, W., 15 Nov. 1785, Elizabeth Howard           3 HA-10
Holliwell, Jas., 17 July 1785, Hannah Aspin         11 BA-8
Hollock, James, 30 Dec. 1793, Sarah Thomas           2 DO
Holloway, Armel Showell, 17 Dec. 1798, Ann Maria Godfrey
    1 WO
Holloway, Daniel, 26 June 1792, Sarah Rodwell       18 BA-4
Holloway, Wil'm, 16 Aug. 1791, by Rev. Chalmers; Anna
    Wilson                                           4 AA
Hollowell, William, 28 Aug. 1784, Mary Coaleman      3 HA-8
Hollyday, Leoanrd, 7 Oct. 1783, Amelia Weems         3 AA-420
Holman, Adam, 21 Jan. 1793, Elizabeth Matthews       4 FR
Holmes, Anthony, 7 July 1795, Marg't Reeves         40 BA-1
Holmes, Francis, 12 Feb. 1798, Eliz'th Cox           1 TA-321
Holmes, Gabriel, 17 Feb. 1793, Mary Bacon            1 BA-5
Holmes, Isaac, 28 Aug. 1791, Christiana Johnston     3 BA-253
    See also 18 BA-3.
Holmes, Joshua, 25 Dec. 1783, Arit Sellman           3 BA-186
    & 234
Holmes, Lenhard, 7 June 1791, Mary Horsman          29 BA-2
Holmes, Solomon, 30 Nov. 1798, Mary Skinner          2 DO
Holmes, William, 5 Dec. 1796, Jane Cook              3 HA-25
    2 HA-349 gives the date as 7 Dec. 1796.
Holmes, William James, 1 June 1786, Anna Wells      10 BA-186
Holms, Robert, 30 Aug. 1799, Sarah Insley            2 DO
Holston, Robert, 27 Oct. 1783, Marg't Gardiner      11 BA-6
Holt, John, 28 June 1799, Polly Carson              29 BA-10
Holton, Jno., 25 June 1793, Sarah Burns             50 BA-393
Holton, William, 31 Dec. 1779, Eliz'th Craghill      3 SM-58
Holtz, Nicholas, 17 June 1785, Susannah Simmerman    4 FR
    2 FR-1134 gives the date as 19 June 1785.
Holtzman, Conrad, 17 March 1795, Eve Darr            4 FR
Holtzman, Henry, 22 March 1781, Mary Smith           4 FR
Holtzman, Jacob, 6 May 1786, Molly Shell             4 FR
Holtzman, John, 10 July 1793, Ann Alexander          4 FR
Hon, Lewis, 7 May 1789, Eliz. Hagan                  2 FR-1135
Honore, Jno. Anthony, 31 May 1787, Maria McMakin     6 BA
Honrich, Albrecht, 4 June 1786, Maria Margaret Landondin
    10 BA-186
Hood, Isaac, 11 Dec. 1794, Martha White              4 FR
Hood, James, 22 July 1784, Kitty Franklin           11 BA-7
Hood, Thomas, 5 Dec. 1799, Rachel Wayman             5 MO-116
Hoofman, Daniel, 11 April 1788, Bridget O'Brien      3 BA-217
    & 219
Hoofman, Dan'l, 1793, Mary Shrote                   50 BA-393
Hoofman, William, 30 Aug. 1784, Catherine Smith      3 HA-9
Hook, Dan'l, 19 Feb. 1787, Sarah Burgess             4 FR
Hook, Frederick, 18 Sept. 1794, Sarah Keyser         6 BA
Hook, Jacob, 23 Nov. 1784, Eliza Campbell           11 BA-8
Hook, Jacob, 13 March 1791, Sus. Boone              29 BA-2
```

```
Hook, John, 20 April 1795, Sophia Starke?          40 BA-1
Hook, John Snowden, 12 Aug. 1778, Elizabeth Ward    4 FR
Hook, Joseph, 8 Oct. 1780, Sophia Jones            11 BA-4
Hook, Joseph, (5 June 1790), Margaret Harvey       15 BA-3
Hook, Joseph, 22 May 1794, Barb. Hodge             29 BA-5
Hook, Rudolph, 15 Jan. 1778, Catherine Ritter      11 BA-1
Hook, Stephen, 14 Nov. 1784, Sarah Thrasher         4 FR
Hook, William, 28 June 1794, Sarah Dunkin           3 BA-287
Hooker, James, 31 Aug. 1799, Rebecca Robb          29 BA-10
Hooker, Joshua, 8 Dec. 1796, Ruth Brothers?        45 BA-1
Hooker, Richard, 13 April 1797, Jemima Lynch       50 BA-401
Hooker, Samuel, 15 Dec. 1784, by Rev. West; Rachael Belt
  51 BA-29
Hooper, Henry, 14 April 1783, Mary Ennalls          2 DO
Hooper, Henry, 5 July 1796, Catherine Hooper        2 DO
Hooper, Henry, 13 Jan. 1797, Peggy Creighton        2 DO
Hooper, Isaac, 2 Nov. 1797, Jane Kirkwood           3 BA-352
Hooper, Jacob, 30 Dec. 1783, Mary Cord             11 BA-7
Hooper, James, 19 Dec. 1798, Priscilla Pattison     2 DO
  1 DO-40 gives the date as 20 Dec. 1798.
Hooper, James, 30 Jan. 1800, Mahala Traverse        2 DO
  1 DO-40 gives the date as 11 Feb. 1800.
Hooper, John, 4 May 1781, Elizabeth Scott           2 DO
Hooper, John, 8 July 1788, by Rev. Claggett; Elizabeth
  Brown                                             4 AA
Hooper, John, 16 April 1791, Amelia Barns           2 DO
Hooper, Joseph, 13 Feb. 1783, Ann Bibby             2 DO
Hooper, Joseph, 4 Aug. 1799, Susanna Benton         3 BA-375
Hooper, Joshua, 13 Feb. 1800, Comfort Dunnock       1 DO-40
  2 DO gives the date as 11 Feb. 1800.
Hooper, Richard, 25 March 1797, Nancy Robson        2 DO
Hooper, Roger, 9 June 1800, Polly Newton            2 DO
Hooper, Samuel, 19 Jan. 1786, Ann Whiteley          2 DO
Hooper, Sam'l, 20 Dec. 1796, Mary Kitely            7 BA-3
Hooper, Thomas, 17 Aug. 1785, Sarah Hooper          2 DO
Hooper, Thomas, 17 June 1788, Mary Hooper           2 DO
Hooper, Wm., 5 Feb. 1794, Mary Crowley             29 BA-5
Hooper, William, 21 Dec. 1799, Rebecca Arnett       2 DO
Hooper, William, 4 Oct. 1800, Priscilla Gadd        2 DO
Hoopes, Robert, 21 Aug. 1782, Martha James          3 HA-7
Hoopman, Christian, 6 Aug. 1792, Eliz. Baughman    29 BA-3
Hoops, Arthur, 6 Nov. 1782, Sarah Bay               3 HA-7
Hoover, Adam, 3 May 1794, Catherine Weaver          4 FR
Hope, Wm., 16 Jan. 1786, Bridget Warner             2 FR-1134
Hopkins, Benj., 5 Feb. 1795, Nancy Briscoe          4 FR
  2 FR-1135 gives the date as 12 Feb. 1795.
Hopkins, Charles, 22 July 1793, Ann Jenkins         3 HA-22
  1 BA-5 gives the date as 23 July 1793.
Hopkins, Denny, of Francis, 5th day, 5 mo., 1785, Ann
  Bartlett, dau. of James                           4 SF-175
Hopkins, Elisha, son of Gerard, of A. A. Co., dec.; 24th
  day, 11 mo., 1796, Sarah Snowden, dau. of Samuel
  Snowden of P. G. Co.                              6 SF
Hopkins, Gerard, of Balto. Town, joiner, son of Samuel and
  Sarah, 19th day, 12 mo., 1778, Rachel Harris, widow,
  dau. of Henry and Priscilla                       6 SF
Hopkins, Gerrard, 19 April 1789, Elizabeth Luci    10 BA-192
Hopkins, Gerard, son of Johns and Elizabeth, 6th day, 4 mo.,
  1796, Dorothy Brooke, dau. of Roger and Mary      6 SF
Hopkins, Isaac, 16 Jan. 1798, Martha Harris         2 SO
  3 SO gives the date as 24 Jan. 1798.
Hopkins, James (born 11 Sept. 1757), June 1796, Lucany
  Cook                                              1 TA-318
Hopkins, James, 7 Dec. 1797, Esther R. Hopkins      1 TA-321
Hopkins, John, 7 Nov. 1797, Leah Dickerson          2 SO
  3 SO gives the date as 9 Nov. 1797.
```

```
Hopkins, John, 15 April 1798, Eleanor Morgan         3 HA-27
  1 BA-8 gives the date as 19 April 1798.
Hopkins, John, 21 Jan. 1800, Nancy Foxwell           2 SO
Hopkins, John, 30 July 1800, Elizabeth Hendley       4 SM-184
Hopkins, John Wallis, 9 Oct. 1800, Susannah Dallam   3 HA-30
Hopkins, Joseph, 20 Jan. 1780, Rebecca Bret          11 BA-4
Hopkins, Joseph, 29 Nov. 1791, Sally Hopkins         6 BA
Hopkins, Joseph, 7 Nov. 1796, Mary Hughes            3 BA-333
Hopkins, Joseph, 17 Nov. 1796, Sarah Downey          3 BA-333
Hopkins, Joseph, 12 April 1799, Sarah Morgan         3 HA-28
  1 BA-9 gives the date as 18 April 1799.
Hopkins, Josiah, 30 July 1800, Polly Burbage         1 WO
Hopkins, Matthias D., 16 March 1799, Nelly Dashiell  2 SO
  3 SO gives the date as 19 March 1799.
Hopkins, Nicholas, 12 May 1791, Mary Bryan           6 BA
Hopkins, Nicholas, 16 April 1795, Rebecca Duke       3 BA-301
Hopkins, Philip, 21st day, 3 mo., 1787, Mary Boon, dau.
  of Isaiah                                          6 SF
Hopkins, Richard, 13 Dec. 1796, Elizabeth Twilly     2 SO
Hopkins, Richard, 23 April 1799, Sally Airse         2 SO
Hopkins, Samuel, 24 Oct. 1799, Jemima Moore          2 SO
Hopkins, Thomas, son of Francis, 14th day, 10 mo., 1780,
  Sarah George, dau. of Joseph                       4 SF-165
Hopkins, Thomas, 3 Aug. 1797, Hetty Reddish          2 SO
Hooper, Benjamin, 22 April 1798, by Rev. Ridgely; Amelia
  White                                              4 AA
Hoppermill, John, 29 Aug. 1791, Margaret Warble      4 FR
Horn, Abraham, 1786, Eliz. Lenhard                   50 BA-387
Horn, Richard, 27 July 1780, Martha Tunis            3 HA-2
Hornblower, Wm., 29 Sept. 1790, Ann Aves             4 FR
Horne, John S., 2 May 1799, Mary Ridgely             3 BA-371
Horner, Nathan, 9 Dec. 1794, Sarah Wheeler           3 HA-23
  7 BA-1 gives the date as 18 Dec. 1794.
Horner, Nathan, 3 April 1799, Delia Carroll          3 HA-28
  1 BA-9 gives the date as 2 May 1799.
Hornes, Michael, 29 Nov. 1788, Flora Wansole         11 BA-12
Horney, William, 21 Sept. 1798, Nelly McCarte        4 KE-68
Hornsley, John, 12 April 1797, Unity Wilson          6 BA
Horseman, Boozley, 6 Jan. 1800, Levina Hurley        2 DO
Horseman, Luke, 26 Nov. 1787, Ann Riggin Elliott     2 DO
Horseman, William, 19 April 1791, Elizabeth Gootee   2 DO
Horseman, William, 2 May 1799, Polly Stanford        6 BA
Horsey, Anthony Smith, 10 Dec. 1789, Sarah Horsey, dau.
  of Samuel                                          1 SO-138
Horstman, John, 3 Feb. 1787, Elis. Riddle            29 BA-1
Hosher, Wm., 29 Aug. 1797, Nancy Trader              1 WO
Hoshier, Lemual, 22 Jan. 1799, Elizabeth Truitt      1 WO
Hoskinson, George, son of Hugh, 25 Feb. 1800, Mary Read
  7 MO-29
Hoskinson, Thomas, 6 Jan. 1795, Mary Bird            4 FR
Hossleton, Edward, 30 Aug. 1780, Magdalena Welton    4 FR
Host, Mich'l, 10 Feb. 1789, Eliza Hannan             11 BA-12
Hotchkiss, Solomon, 20 Jan. 1794, Alasanna Hall      18 BA-6
Houck, John, 11 March 1797, Elizabeth Sin            4 FR
Houck, Matthias, 1 May 1797, Magdalen Engle          4 FR
Houcks, Jacob, 29 March 1782, Catherine Shultz       4 FR
Houcks, Mathias, 20 Sept. 1781, Susanna Morningstar  4 FR
Houk, John, 9 March 1796, Eliz.Fiere                 3 WA-60
Houlton, Jno., 17 Jan. 1786, Eleanor Sorle           11 BA-9
Hourigan, Patrick, 14 May 1797, Sarah Barry          47 BA-1
Hous?, Michael, 1788, Cath. Ansel                    50 BA-388
House, Caleb, 11 Aug. 1783, Sarah Pearpoint          4 FR
House, Daniel, 4 Feb. 1782, Elizabeth Long           4 FR
House, John, 7 July 1796, Ann Hazlewood              1 AL-53
House, Thomas, 2 Nov. 1780, Hannah Sullivan          11 BA-4
```

```
House, William, 26 Dec. 1795, Modelena Harmon          4 FR
Houser, Jacob, 13 Oct. 1787, Cath. Bander              4 FR
Houston, Caleb, 14 Dec. 1797, Betsey Mill              1 WO
Houston, George, 15 Dec. 1796, Rhoda Bratten           1 WO
Houston, Joseph, 12 June 1795, Bridget Patterson       1 WO
Houston, Joseph, 21 Feb. 1797, Anne Revell             2 SO
Houston, William J., 8 Dec. 1800, Sally Chaille        1 WO
Howard, Benjamin, 30 Jan. 1781, Mary Ann Buckly        2 CH-453
Howard, Benjamin, 17 April 1792, Susanna Knight        3 BA-257
Howard, Brice, 16 April 1783, Respaw? Hobbs            4 AA
Howard, Cornelius, 26 April 1792, Mary Campbell        4 FR
Howard, Edward, 20 March 1795, Sara Miller             1 AL-53
Howard, Edward Aquila, 10 Dec. 1798, Charlotte Rumsey  3 HA-27
   1 BA-8 gives the date as 11 Dec. 1798.
Howard, Elisha, 19 March 1794, Chloe McAtee            4 FR
Howard, Francis, 7 Oct. 1796, Margaret Fitzgerald      3 BA-329
Howard, George, 17 Nov. 1782, Elizabeth Fisher         4 FR
Howard, George, 21 Nov. 1799, Leah Kersey              2 SO
Howard, Henry, 23 July 1785, Ann Purdey                4 FR
Howard, Henry, 31 Dec. 1793, Mary Brown                3 BA-279
Howard, Jas., 18 Oct. 1779, Casiah Veatch              4 FR
Howard, John, 16 Nov. 1778, Mary Crale                 4 FR
Howard, Jno., 8 June 1797, Ann Henry                   29 BA-8
Howard, Joseph, 25 Jan. 1783, Sarah Killkup            4 FR
Howard, Joseph, 13 Dec. 1787, Darcus Howard            4 FR
Howard, Jos., (5 Feb. 1789), Ann Cramlet               15 BA-2
Howard, Joseph Ford, 11 March 1799, Mary Walden        3 BA-368
Howard, Joshua, 1792, Rachel Roh                       50 BA-392
Howard, Joshua, 24 Aug. 1792, Elizabeth Warfield       4 FR
Howard, Leonard, 4 Sept. 1793, Rebecca Etherington     3 HA-23
Howard, Levin, 30 Aug. 1785, Mary Lee                  2 DO
Howard, Philip, 24 Feb. 1797, Mary Crosby              29 BA-8
   50 BA-401 gives the date as 24 March 1797.
Howard, Sam'l, 10 June 1797, Elizabeth Lyles           4 FR
Howard, Samuel, 19 Nov. 1798, Ellenor Fort             45 BA-3
Howard, Severn, 14 March 1790, Leah Addams             1 SO-137
Howard, Thomas, 23 April 1791, Ann Hughes              4 FR
Howard, Thomas, 26 April 1791, by Rev. Forrest; Ann
   Hughes                                              3 FR
Howard, Thomas, 23 Dec. 1800, Rachel Trundle           7 MO
Howard, Thomas Gassaway, 2 April 1793, Martha Susanna
   Tolley                                              1 BA-5
Howard, William, 28 Jan. 1779, Mary Barnes             2 PG-2
Howe, Edward, 6 Oct. 1787, M. Sprenkel                 29 BA-1
Howe, John, 2 April 1782, Lowery Rop                   4 FR
Howe, Thomas Charles, 28 June 1800, Martha Ensor       3 BA-387
Howe, William, 23 Oct. 1784, Elizabeth Maxwell         3 BA-190
Howe, William Rob't, 13 June 1778, Ann Strider         4 FR
Howel, Samuel, 11 July 1781, Rebecca Price             3 HA-4
Howell, James, 10 May 1784, Mary Trotten               11 BA-7
Howes, Charles, 8 Dec. 1779, Tamar Gibbons             2 PG-7
Howes, Zachariah, 6 Oct. 1782, Elizabeth Busey         3 AA-418
Howith, Sewell, 25 Dec. 1786, Elizabeth Harper         2 DO
Howland, David, 16 Aug. 1799, Sally Glover             29 BA-10
Howland, John Wilks, 3 Dec. 1795, Mary Gudgeon         3 BA-313
Howlett, John, 2 May 1793, Drusilla Johnson            6 BA
Howling, Daniel, 23 Aug. 1787, Cornelia McMyer         5 BA-7
Howlman, Abr'm, 7 Oct. 1784, Margaret Lampre           3 HA-9
Howsley, Thomas, 27 March 1796, Mary Danaway           6 BA
Hoy, Nicholas, 1 June 1798, Rachel Umstead             4 FR
Hoye, William W., 26 May 1796, Eleanor Slicer          1 AL-53
Hubbard, Andrew, 2 Dec. 1796, Elizabeth Smith          2 DO
Hubbard, James, 13 Jan. 1800, Fanny Marshall           2 DO
Hubbard, John, 25 Sept. 1783, Sarah Harrington         2 DO
Hubbard, Lemuel, 9 Dec. 1783, Keziah North             2 DO
```

Hubbard, Levin. 16 Dec. 1789, Lydia Marshall   2 DO
Hubbard, William, 1 Aug. 1781, Ann Adams   2 DO
Hubber, Henry, 29 April 1787, Mary Gardner   11 BA-10
Hubbert, Charles, 30 June 1791, Mary Matkin   2 DO
Hubbert, Edward, 6 Dec. 1793, Anne Wright   2 SF
Hubbert, Henry, 26 March 1792, Amelia Marshall   2 DO
Hubbert, Hugh, 23 April 1789, Lotty Lee   2 DO
Hubbert, Job, 28 Oct. 1785, Fanny Eaton   2 DO
Hubbert, Jno., 23 June 1782, Eliza Mewshaw   11 BA-5
Hubbert, John, 17 Sept. 1795, Mary Hooper   2 DO
Hubbert, Michael, 11 Dec. 1797, Elizabeth Payne   2 DO
Hubbert, Samuel, 22 Aug. 1785, Nelly Phillips   2 DO
Hubbert, Samuel, 1 May 1797, Nancy Woolford   2 DO
Hubbert, Solomon, 2 Jan. 1781, Mary Lee   2 DO
Hubbert, Thomas, 8 May 1781, Sarah Littleton   2 DO
Hubbert, Wm., 11 June 1796, Eliz. Neiss   29 BA-7
Hubeland, George, 1791, Elis. Gilbert   50 BA-391
Huber, (John) Jacob, 20 Jan. 1787, Susanna Harbaugh   5 FR-53
Huber, Philip, 12 Oct. 1800, Sus. Borckhardy   2 FR-1136
Huble, George. See Stuble, George.
Hudson, Annanias, 27 Dec. 1800, Luretta Benson   1 WO
Hudson, Arthur, 22 Feb. 1797, Nancy Taylor   1 WO
Hudson, Benjamin, 25 March 1796, Elizabeth Williams   1 WO
Hudson, Dennis, 16 July 1795, Polly Melvin   1 WO
Hudson, Edward, 30 Oct. 1791, Providence Porter   6 BA
Hudson, Eli, 13 Jan. 1800, Nancy Ennis   1 WO
Hudson, James, 10 Feb. 1781, Catharine Hubbard   2 DO
Hudson, James, 22 Feb. 1789, Dorothea Batten   1 BA-2
Hudson, Jesse, 10 May 1800, Mary Collins   1 WO
Hudson, John, 9 Feb. 1798, by Rev. Dorsey; Catherine
    Cord   4 AA
Hudson, Jonathan, 22 Dec. 1798, Sarah Kirk Townsend   1 WO
Hudson, McKenny, 25 Dec. 1795, Hannah Dymock   1 WO
Hudson, Richard, 25 June 1778, Jane James   1 CA-1
Hudson, Robert, 31 May 1796, Mary Atkinson   1 WO
Hudson, Tom, Aug. 1800, Sarah Walter   3 WA-70
Hudson, Wm., 7 March 1798, Comfort Knox   1 WO
Hudson, William, 7 May 1799, Peggy Hudson   1 WO
Hufford, Daniel, 23 Aug. 1779, Eliz'th Cassell   4 FR
Huggins, Joseph, 30 Jan. 1782, Margaret Carnes   3 HA-6
Hugh, William, 24 Dec. 1796, Mary Houston   1 WO
Hughes, Abraham, 1 May 1796, Belinda Norris   6 BA
Hughes, Benjamin, son of Edward, of Burks Co., Pa.
    (sic), 26th day, 12 mo., 1781, Elizabeth Boone, dau.
    of Isaiah   6 SF
Hughes, Christopher, 20 Jan. 1779, Peggy -(?)-   3 BA-213
Hughes, Daniel, 26 Oct. 1780, Susanna Schlater   5 BA-7
Hughes, Elijah, 14 Feb. 1799, Fanny Daugherty   6 BA
Hughes, Esrem, 1 April 1800, Elizabeth Whiteford   3 HA-29
Hughes, Francis, 1 Jan. 1782, Mary Mildews   11 BA-5
Hughes, Francis, 31 May 1796, Mary Dyer   4 FR
Hughes, George, 25 Jan. 1795, Cassandra Jones   6 BA
Hughes, George, 9 Nov. 1797, Eleanor Hardey   3 PG-443
Hughes, Henry, 20 Sept. 1794, Mary Carr   6 BA
Hughes, Hugh, 6 Nov. 1794, Ann Bond   29 BA-6
Hughes, Jacob, 9 March 1780, Rachael Langdol   11 BA-4
Hughes, James, 18 Dec. 1783, Frances Cottral   11 BA-7
Hughes, James, 27 Aug. 1799, Anna Allen   1 WO
Hughes, Jesse, son of Samuel and Elizabeth, 1st day, 6 mo.,
    1780, Elizabeth Wood, dau. of Wm. and Margaret   3 SF
Hughes, John, 25 May 1782, Elizabeth Grey   3 AA-418
Hughes, Jno., 26 Oct. 1787, Sarah Baily   11 BA-10
Hughes, John, 13 March 1792, Elizabeth Gudgeon   1 BA-4
Hughes, John, 15 May 1796, Rachel Todd   6 BA
Hughes, John, 21 July 1798, Elizabeth Voss   2 DO

```
Hughes, Jno., 22 April 1800, Mary Hill                   29 BA-11
Hughes, John W., 5 Nov. 1785, Ann Durbin                  3 HA-10
Hughes, Joseph, 25 April 1792, Mary Buchanan              4 FR
Hughes, Levi, 5 Dec. 1800, Jemima Cannon                  2 DO
Hughes, Roland, 8 Oct. 1781, Susannah Griffee             3 HA-5
Hughes, William, 16 Sept. 1783, Lydia Jones               3 HA-8
Hughes, William, 2 May 1786, Ann Cantwell                 6 BA
Hughes, William, 19 Nov. 1789, Elizabeth McKirdy          6 BA
Hughes, William, 22 June 1791, Margaret Vinson            2 DO
Hughes, William, 24 Aug. 1800, Patience Rush              3 BA-390
Hughs, John, 29 Nov. 1797, Sally Voss                     2 DO
Hughs, William, 24 July 1791, Margaret Vinson            28 BA-1
Hugston, Joseph, 27 Aug. 1781, Hannah Purnell             3 HA-4
Hull, Brittingham, 6 June 1799, Sally McClester Sterling
                                                          2 SO
Hull, Joshua, 25 July 1798, Elizabeth Miles               2 SO
Hull, Richard, 6 April 1794, Susanna Potter               3 BA-285
Hull, Samuel, 5 July 1779, Frances Mahew                  2 PG-3
Hull, Samuel, 27 Oct. 1782, Margaret Hollis               3 BA-184
Hulse, Samuel, 4 Aug. 1779, Margaret Knight               4 FR
Humbert, Peter, 23 April 1778, Rebecca Bunn               4 FR
Humecke, Fred'k, 20 Nov. 1794, Anna Schroder             50 BA-396
Humphrey, Andrew, 16 Aug. 1780, Agnes Henderson           3 HA-2
Humphreys, Nathan, 16 May 1793, Susanna Gilley           18 BA-5
Humphris, John, 14 Jan. 1800, Matty Vance                 2 SO
Humphris, Joseph, 28 Jan. 1800, Dolly Jackson             2 SO
Hund, John, 15 Jan. 1789, Priscilla Brown                 3 PG-255
Hundley, Joseph, 6 Aug. 1793, Sophia Stevens              6 BA
Hungerford, John, 24 Nov. 1778, Mary Cowen                1 CA-2
Hungerford, Thomas, 17 Nov. 1778, Violetta Gwinn          2 CH-453
Hunley, John, 4 Nov. 1798, Anne Perry                     3 BA-365
Hunt, James, 13 Jan. 1793, Unice Loveless                 3 PG-437
Hunt, James, 9 Nov. 1795, Elizabeth Rogers                6 BA
Hunt, Jno., 28 April 1782, Alice Burgess                 11 BA-5
Hunt, John Wilkeson, 3 May 1778, by Rev. Magowan; Sarah
     Swanstead                                            4 AA
Hunt, Thos., 18 April 1782, Eliza Rush                   11 BA-5
Hunt, Wm., 6 Jan. 1785, Eliza Whaland                    11 BA-8
Hunt, Wm., 1 July 1787, Elizabeth Wright                  6 BA
Hunter, Andrew, 2 Feb. 1783, Ann Poole                    3 SM-60
Hunter, James, 4 Oct. 1796, Jemima Inloes                 1 BA-7
Hunter, John, 14 Aug. 1796, by Rev. Ridgely; Margaret
     Mahony                                               4 AA
Hunter, Richard, 20 Jan. 1782, Rachel Whiting             2 PG-3
Hunter, Thomas, 9 Dec. 1796, Ann Quynn                    4 FR
Hunter, William, 30 Dec. 1798, Sarah Nichols              6 BA
Huntington, Nathaniel, 4 June 1794, Mary White            2 DO
Hurd, William, 13 March 1799, Pheby Waltz                 4 FR
Hurley, Constantine, 24 July 1798, Elizabeth Huggins      2 DO
Hurley, Cornelius, 4 April 1795, Lenney Wade              3 PG-441
Hurley, Daniel, 10 Sept. 1797, Mary Jones                 3 PG-443
Hurley, Elijah, 6 Jan. 1800, Polly Hurley                 2 DO
Hurley, Isaac, 6 Sept. 1794, Sally McCredy                2 DO
Hurley, James, 9 Sept. 1800, Margaret Gambell             2 DO
Hurley, Job, 24 Oct. 1792, Polly Dyal                     2 DO
Hurley, John, 15 Aug. 1789, Caty Norman                   2 DO
Hurley, Jno., 28 May 1797, Eliz. Benton                   5 MO-114
Hurley, Michael, 29 Oct. 1793, Joanna Gwinn               3 BA-275
Hurley, William, 13 Aug. 1778, Mary Evans                 2 PG-3
Hurley, William, 30 Nov. 1784, Jemima McCready            2 DO
Hurley, William, 20 Aug. 1799, Rhoda Walton               2 SO
Hurly, Basil, 8 Feb. 1789, Mary Soper                     3 PG-255
Hurly, John, 20 Dec. 1787, Sarah Evans                    3 PG-253
Hurly, Wm., 5 Jan. 1790, Sarah Taylor                     3 PG-256
Hurly, William, 25 Dec. 1790, Rebecca Soaper              3 PG-257
```

```
Hurman, Henry, 21 Oct. 1799, Sally Wilson          29 BA-10
Hurogan, Thomas, 21 July 1799, Ruth Patty           3 BA-374
Huron, Thomas, Feb. 1797, Polly Abbott              3 SO
Hurst, John, before 20 July 1793, by Rev. Bloodgood; Eliza
   Broome                                           4 AA
Hurst, John, 20 Oct. 1793, Elizabeth Brown          4 FR
Hurst, Joseph, 9 Oct. 1798, Levice Harper           2 DO
Hurst, Samuel, 20 Nov. 1786, Lavinia Littleton      2 DO
Hurst, Thomas, 22 Sept. 1800, Nancy Williams        2 DO
Hurst, William, 25 Dec. 1794, Ann Minor             4 FR
Hurst, William, 20 Sept. 1795, Lydia Clacknor       6 BA
Hurt, John, 15 Nov. 1796, Mary Tilden               4 KE-68
Hurthley, John, 21 July 1789, Elisabeth Earaus     10 BA-194
Hurton, John, 9 June 1795, Elizabeth Peck           5 BA-7
Hurtt, John, 31 Dec. 1794, Martha Dunn, dau. of James
   and Elizabeth                                    1 KE-292
Hush, John, 23 Jan. 1800, Elizabeth Ford            6 BA
Hush, Peter, 21 June 1787, El. Goldsmith           29 BA-1
Husker (Hunter?), George, 12 Feb. 1794, Ann Tyrel   2 AL-700
Husker (Husher, Hunter), James, 5 June 1794, Barbara Sigler
   2 AL-700
Husleton, William, 17 June 1787, Lydia Griffith     6 BA
Hussey, George, 11 Jan. 1781, Rachael Hayward       3 BA-180
Hust, Thomas, 19 May 1797, Polly Higgins            2 DO
Hustman, Mich'l, 7 June 1799, Cath. Delle          50 BA-405
Huston, John, 2 Dec. 1800, Sarah Dashiell           2 SO
Hutchings, James, 26 Sept. 1799, Margaret Given     1 BA-9
Hutchings, Thomas, 1 Jan. 1778, Elizabeth Hellen    1 CA-1
Hutchins, Bennett, 7 Nov. 1779, Jane Stone          3 SM-57
Hutchins, Joseph, 5 Jan. 1779, Mary Hardesty        1 CA-2
Hutchins, Samuel, 9 June 1796, Mary Justis          3 BA-323
Hutchins, Thomas, 3 Oct. 1780, Catherine Mitchell   3 HA-2
Hutchins, William, 11 March 1781, Eleanor Miles     2 CH-453
Hutchins, William, 7 March 1782, Eleanor Miles      3 HA-6
Hutchins, Wm., 19 July 1790, D.? Jackson           29 BA-1
Hutchinson, Archibald, 20 April 1780, Barbara Bruher 4 FR
Hutchinson, George, 18 Nov. 1781, Rachel Lowe       2 PG-5
Hutchinson, James, 23 Nov. 1799, Rosanna Button     2 DO
Hutchinson, Samuel, 4 June 1786, Ann Brown          3 PG-251
Hutchinson, Will'm, Jr., 18 April 1780, Christian Willet
   2 PG-7
Hutchison, Francis, 25 Jan. 1798, Sarah Ball        5 MO-114
Hutchison, George, 13 Aug. 1778, Mary Harrison      2 PG-2
Hutson, John, 23 April 1800, Leah Briddle           1 WO
Hutson, Joshua, (16 Feb. 1789), Susanna Hooker     15 BA-2
Hutson, Richard, 10 March 1800, Polly Collins       1 WO
Hutton, Charles, 22 April 1794, Mary Gardner        3 AA-424
Hutton, Henry, 17 July 1783, Elizabeth Gott         3 AA-419
Hutton, Henry, 21 June 1796, Sarah Sadler          14 BA-18
Hutton, Samuel, son of Thomas and Katherine (dec.) of
   Penna., 5th day, 11 mo., 1783, Elizabeth Needles, dau.
   of Edward and Elizabeth                          4 SF-174
Hutzell, Michael, 10 Dec. 1791, Susanna Miller      4 FR
   2 FR-1135 gives the date as 11 Dec. 1791.
Huzel, Georg, 14 Nov. 1797, Elisabeth Michelsen     1 FR-59
Hyatt, Aquilla, 25 Jan. 1798, by Rev. Ridgely; Rachel
   Hyatt                                            4 AA
Hyatt, Jesse, 14 Jan. 1792, Nancy Riggs             4 FR
Hyland, John, 31 Oct. 1799, Nancy Johnson           3 BA-380
Hyman, John, 26 Sept. 1799, Nancy Orrick            3 BA-378
Hyner, Joseph, 14 Dec. 1783, Elizabeth Sthall      11 BA-7
Hyner, Joseph, 19 Aug. 1798, Elizabeth Sherard      3 BA-362
Hynes, Philip, 7 Feb. 1782, Mary Myers              4 FR
Hynson, John C., 27 June 1797, Ann Cosden           4 KE-68
Hynson, Nathaniel, 26 May 1796, Kitty Owings        6 BA
```

Hynson, Ringgold, 30 Jan. 1797, Avarillere Maria Griffith
  4 KE-68
Hynum, Thos., 4 March 1784, by Rev. Mr. Robison; Mary
  White   11 BA-7
Hyse, John, 1 May 1781, Rachel Ford   3 HA-4

Iam, Thomas, 1 Nov. 1778, Sarah Merriet   11 BA-1
Icoff, Adolph, 17 Jan. 1784, Mary Thomas   4 FR
Iglehart, Richard, 19 Jan. 1800, by Rev. Ridgely; Nancy
  Hammond   4 AA
Iglehart, William, 27 March 1781, Susanna Soaper 2 PG-5
Iiams, Benjamin, 24 May 1798, by Rev. Ridgely; Mary Mitchell
  4 AA
Iiams, Isaac, 6 Aug. 1795, by Rev. Ridgely; Elizabeth Beach
  4 AA
Iiams, John, 23 June 1778, Susanna Taylor   2 PG-2
Iiams, John, 21 March 1782, Mary Waters   4 FR
Iiams, John, 27 Feb. 1794, by Rev. G. Ridgely; Rachel
  Marriott   4 AA
Iiams, Samuel, 4 Feb. 1779, Mary Ratcliff   3 AA-415
Iiams, Thomas, 22 Nov. 1780, Ann Neal   3 AA-416
Ijams, Thomas Plummer, 10 Feb. 1794, Sarah Duvall 4 FR
Imbleton, Edward, 28 June 1790, Ann Bryan   11 BA-13
Impford, Titus, 9 Oct. 1793, Elizabeth Thomas   3 BA-275
Ingham, Robert, 18 April 1800, Lydia Yorke   3 HA-29
  2 HA-352 gives the date as 20 April 1800.
Ingle, John, 18 July 1795, Anne Witcomb   3 BA-307
Ingle, John, 30 Aug. 1798, Achsah Fell   6 BA
Ingle, Wm., 12 April 1787, Dorcus Hendrickson   6 BA
Inglebrecht, John Conrad, 1 Oct. 1785, Margaret Houx 4 FR
Ingles, Silas, 3 Dec. 1786, Margaret Harris   5 BA-8
Ingram, Clark, 4 Dec. 1795, Mary Dorsey   5 BA-8
Ingram, John, 27 April 1779, Sarah Hutcheson   5 BA-8
Ingram, John, 26 May 1785, Sarah Howard   2 DO
Ingram, Robert, 19 Dec. 1785, Henrietta Coulbourne 2 DO
Ingram, Sam'l, 10 Oct. 1786, Mary McKnight   11 BA-9
Inkster, Jas., 1 Nov. 1789, Eliz. Mahone   11 BA-12
Inloes, David, (c.1791), Mary Cole   15 BA-4
Inloes, James, 5 March 1794, Barsheba Hacket   3 BA-285
Inlose, Samuel, 27 Nov. 1800, Eliz. Stone   5 MO-116
Inlows, Thomas, (date not given), Catherine Inlows 15 BA-4
Inseler, Volerius, 14 March 1778, Catherine Fresh 11 BA-1
Inser, William, 2 March 1800, Nancy Headington 6 BA
Insley, Daniel, 22 Jan. 1781, Clara Andrews   2 DO
Insley, Elijah, 5 Aug. 1799, Rachel Lowe   2 DO
Insley, Esau, 5 June 1793, Sarah Fallen   2 DO
Insley, Francis, 27 Oct. 1785, Keziah Willey   2 DO
Insley, Gabriel, 17 Jan. 1785, Elizabeth Andrews 2 DO
Insley, James, 22 March (or May) 1794, Arcady Willey 2 DO
Insley, John, 19 Sept. 1781, Rachel Moore   2 DO
Insley, John, 10 Oct. 1797, Amelia Jones   2 SO
Insley, Thomas, 1 Feb. 1793, Polly Elliott   2 DO
Insley, Valentine, 30 Aug. 1791, Grace Creighton 2 DO
Insley, William, 10 Nov. 1784, Rosanna Foxwell 2 DO
Ireland, George, 11 April 1779, Mary Dare   1 CA-2
Ireland, Rev. Jno., 20 Sept. 1787, Joanna Giles Waters
  11 BA-10
Ireland, Jonathan, 23 June 1783, Elizabeth Rice 4 FR
Ireland, Richard, 1 May 1790, Linday Cecil   6 BA
Ireland, William, 12 Dec. 1784, Susana Reyner   2 KE-316
Irish, John, 2 April 1782, Mary Hall   3 BA-183
Irons, Michael, 29 May 1792, Eve Stripe   2 FR-1142
Irons, Thomas, 3 Dec. 1795, by Rev. Ridgely; Delilah
  Scott   4 AA

```
Irons, Timothy, 22 June 1798, Sarah Dormon        1 WO
Irvin, James, 5 Feb. 1799, Sarah Cunningham       5 BA-8
Irvine, James, 24 Feb. 1789, Mary Cole            2 FR-1142
Irvine, John, 17 June 1799, Catherine Oldham      8 BA-1
Irving, George, son of Thomas, 10 Nov. 1785, Ann Irving,
    dau. of John                                  3 SO
Irving, James, 29 Nov. 1796, Sally Fountain       2 SO
Irving, John, 26 Jan. 1798, Nelly Shiles          2 SO
Irwin, Henry, 14 Aug. 1798, by Rev. Ridgely; Frances
    Jones                                         4 AA
Irwine, John, 4 Feb. 1786, Nancy Keene            2 DO
Isaac, Richard, 26 Sept. 1779, by Rev. Magowan; Susannah
    Freeland                                      4 AA
Isaac, Thomas, 25 Feb. 1799, Elizabeth Freeland   3 AA-417
Isaacs, Isaac, 7 Oct. 1798, Henrietta Mulakin     3 BA-364
Isabey, Francis, 21 April 1796, Martha Wilson     6 BA
Isac, Sutton, 14 Feb. 1795, by Rev. Ridgely; Elizabeth
    Clark                                         4 AA
Isamminger, Peter, 6 Feb. 1794, Rebecca Henderson 1 AL-52
Isenberger, Henry, 18 Nov. 1788, Catherine Medtert 4 FR
Isenberger, Jacob, 15 Feb. 1780, Margaret Hospelhaun 4 FR
Isenberger, Peter, 12 Sept. 1796, Marg't Smouse   4 FR
Isenbergh, Nicholas, 12 Dec. 1780, Mary Smouse    4 FR
Isentrey, George, 7 Nov. 1795, Ann Goodman        4 FR
Iser, Nicholas, 22 Jan. 1795, Sophia Rutter       6 BA
Iser, Philip, 26 Oct. 1779, Anna Albaugh          4 FR
Iser, Richard, 17 Oct. 1779, Barbara Shall        11 BA-3
Isgrig, John, 15 April 1786, by Rev. Turner; Hellen Demmitt
    51 BA-29
Isgrig, Wm., 4 May 1780, Temperance White         11 BA-4
Isour, Joshua, 3 April 1786, by Rev. West; Sarah Dougherty
    51 BA-30
Israel, Basil, 26 June 1780, Eleanor Mansfield    4 FR
Israel, Eli, 5 May 1785, Ann Goslin               11 BA-8
Israel, John, 8 May 1788, Rachel Clary            4 FR
Israel, Joseph, 22 Jan. 1788, Hester Thompson     6 BA
Israel, Lakin, 13 June 1791, Leah Hall            2 FR-1142
Isterlox, Caspar, 18 July 1784, Mary Wily         10 BA-182
Itzgan, Philip, 1791, Pfe. Hartman                50 BA-390
Ivory, Charles, 19 Jan. 1779, Ruth Neale          2 PG-3
Ivory, John, 1 Feb. 1796, Anne Graves             3 BA-317
Ivy, John, 12 Nov. 1780, Elizabeth Powell         1 CA-3


Jabson, Jonathan, 13 May 1795, Charity Walter     3 WA-58
Jack and Easter, property of David Crawford, were married
    24 Dec. 1797; Jack's mother Cicila a witness  8 MO-16
Jack and Peggy, negroes; June 1791                3 PG-258
Jackson, Collin, 25 Feb. 1796, Jane Nicoll        5 BA-8
Jackson, Ezekial, 4 Jan. 1794, Eliza. Jackson     3 CH-161
    "disp. for consang. in 2nd to 3rd degree."
Jackson, Henry, 3 Jan. 1797, Ann Hynson           4 KE-69
Jackson, Hezekiah, 7 May 1795, Frances Heiner     3 BA-305
Jackson, James, Aug. 1798, Betsy Floyd            2 SO
Jackson, John, 18 Oct. 1796, Elizabeth Burbage    1 WO
Jackson, John, 4 Sept. 1797, Rebecca Hill         3 BA-349
Jackson, Joseph, son of Isaac, 27th day, 2 mo., 1794,
    Gulielma Maria Waters, dau. of Samuel         6 SF
Jackson, Nathan, 4 Feb. 1796, Mary Hemton         3 WA-60
Jackson, Nathaniel, 14 Sept. 1799, Nelly Curtis   5 BA-8
Jackson, Samuel, 9 March 1797, Elizabeth Crowder  1 TA-321
Jackson, Thomas, 19 March 1794, Mary O'Brian      6 BA
Jackson, Thomas, 2 Feb. 1796, Elizabeth Allender  3 BA-317
Jackson, Thomas, 8 Sept. 1797, Anne Riley         3 BA-349
Jackson, Thomas, 25 May 1799, Elizabeth Smoot     2 DO
```

Jackson, Wm., 3 Feb. 1789, Jane Vermeer   2 PG-4
Jackson, William, 9 Oct. 1794, Sarah Smith   36 BA-1
    4 BA-77 gives the date as 12 Oct. 1794.
Jackson, William, 19 April 1795, Margaret Butler   3 BA-301
Jackson, William, 8 Sept. 1798, Elizabeth Nicholson   4 KE-69
Jackson, William, 23 June 1799, Mary Blaydon   4 BA-75
    1 BA-9 gives the date as 23 June 1800.
Jacob, Adam, 16 Aug. 1791, Eliz. Spannseiler   2 FR-1142
Jacob, Ezekiel, 15 March 1781, Ann Davies   2 PG-5
Jacob, Mordecai, 1 Nov. 1789, Mary Coe   3 PG-255
Jacob, Richard, 9 April 1778, Susanna Wells   2 PG-2
Jacob, Samuel, son of Richard, 25 July 1780, Elizabeth
    Gray, dau. of Joshua   2 AA-114
Jacob, William, son of Zach'a, 27 March 1781, Mary Godfrey,
    formerly of Portsmouth, VA.   3 BA-180
Jacob, William, 7 Nov. 1785, Rachael Williams   11 BA-8
Jacob, Wm., 4 July 1786, Jane Fitzgerald   11 BA-9
Jacobie, John, 2 March 1779, Catherine Weane   4 FR
Jacobs, -(?)-, 30 April 1778, Ann Grahame   2 CH-453
Jacobs, Benj., 3 Nov. 1787, Elizabeth Bilbert   4 FR
    2 FR-1142 gives the date as 4 Nov. 1787, and the bride's
    name as Gilbert.
Jacobs, Benjamin, 8 Sept. 1798, Elizabeth Ousler   45 BA-2
Jacobs, Charles, 4 Feb. 1799, Mary Maloney   3 BA-368
Jacobs, Constantine, 15 Sept. 1785, Nancy Turpin   2 DO
Jacobs, George, 23 Feb. 1791, Ann Perrill   4 FR
Jacobs, Geo., 9 June 1796, Jane Moore   29 BA-7
Jacobs, Henry, 21 April 1790, Catherine Willard   4 FR
Jacobs, Jacob, 13 March 1788, Rachel Payne   2 DO
Jacobs, Jeremiah, c.1792 in Washington Co., by Rev. Chal-
    mers; Sarah Larimond   4 AA
Jacobs, John, 17 Dec. 1799, Margaret Carroll   3 AA-416
Jacobs, Jonathan, 16 March 1786, Elizabeth Reed   2 DO
Jacobs, Joseph, 22 Feb. 1782, Elizabeth Griffen   4 FR
Jacobs, Joseph, 29 Nov. 1794, by Rev. Joseph Wyatt;
    Delinda? Little   4 AA
Jacobs, Richard, 19 Oct. 1789, Eleanor Hilleary   4 FR
    2 FR-1142 gives the date as 20 Oct. 1789.
Jacobs, Samuel, 30 April 1778, Catharine Maskers   11 BA-1
Jacobs, Wm., 16 Nov. 1778, Dorcas Stokes   4 FR
Jacobs, Wm., 28 April 1781, Sarah Thomas   4 FR
Jacobson, Lawrence, 2 Oct. 1799, Sarah Vinson   29 BA-10
Jacques, Denton, 2 June 1780, Eliza Powell   4 FR
Jacquett, John Paul, 18 Oct. 1798, Rebecca Stran   3 BA-364
Jaenzy, Michael, 22 Nov. 1785, Christina Schmit   2 FR-1142
Jaffries, John, 17 Sept. 1793, Sarah Lea   5 BA-8
Jalland, John, 19 Jan. 1786, Ruth Jane Bungy   11 BA-9
James and Hannar, property of John Medley, were married
    20 April 1800, with permission of their proprietor,
    "on their way to Kentucky"   8 MO-24
James, slave of Bernard O'Neill, 2 March 1795, Eleanor, slave
    of Mr. Voldenire   8 MO-9
James, negro of Mr. Crabb, 15 May 1796, Clary, negro   5 MO-113
James, Abraham, 20 July 1797, Maria Dicks   6 BA
James, Absolom, 26 Dec. 1798, Elizabeth Harrington   2 DO
James, Amos, son of Thomas and Ann, 2nd day, 6 mo., 1791
    Mary Lee, dau. of Samuel and Mary   1 SF
James, Charles, 2 March 1797, Elizabeth Engle   2 AL-700
James, Henry, 7 Jan. 1796, Elizabeth Ross   6 BA
James, Isaac, 27 Feb. 1782, Frances Deaver   3 HA-6
James, John, 11 Oct. 1783, Henrietta Maria Davey   11 BA-6
James, John, 10 April 1786, Martha Haff   4 FR
    2 FR-1142 gives the date as 13 April 1786.
James, John, (29 July 1789), Letitia Dilworth   20 BA-1
James, John, 9 May 1795, Mary Johns   3 BA-305

James, John, 17 Oct. 1798, Liddy Hays   3 AL-5
James, John, 9 June 1799, Jane Taylor   6 BA
James, Joseph, 28 July 1795, Nancy Long   2 DO
James, Joseph, 23 Aug. 1798, Elizabeth Sherwood   1 BA-8
James, Levi, 4 Sept. 1798, Rachel Houck   4 FR
   2 FR-1142 gives the bride's name as Hough.
James, Obadiah, 7 April 1785, Anne Bird   2 DO
James, Obediah, 19 March 1798, Mary Breerwood   2 DO
James, Samuel, 29 May 1793, Frances Randolph   1 AL-52
   2 AL-700 gives the date as 30 May 1793.
James, Samuel, 18 March 1799, Sarah Hughes   7 BA-4
James, Thomas, 15 Nov. 1780, Mary Eager   2 CH-453
James, Thomas, 16 Aug. 1781, Elizabeth Mace   2 DO
James, Thomas, 11 Nov. 1781, Mary Cagon   3 HA-5
James, Thomas, 29 Nov. 1785, Catherine Gilhampton   6 BA
James, Thomas, 30 Jan. 1800, "his second wife (name
   not given)"   7 MO-29
James, William, 15 Aug. 1781, Rachel Bull   3 HA-4
James, William, 24 Aug. 1781, Margaret Thompson   3 HA-4
James, William, 24 Nov. 1785, Susanna Landon   5 BA-8
James, Wm., 29 Nov. 1785, Mary Gilhampton   6 BA
James, William, 13 Nov. 1794, Janet Hay   5 BA-8
James, William, 14 Feb. 1797, Flora Alexandria   5 BA-8
James, William, 16 Nov. 1797, Elizabeth James   5 BA-8
Jameson, Francis, 25 Dec. 1790, Ann Thompson   4 FR
Jameson, Samuel, 19 Jan. 1795, Jane Boarman   3 CH-162
   "disp. for consang. in 3rd to 4th degree"
Jameson, Thomas, 15 Feb. 1798, Ann Gardiner   3 CH-162
Jamison, Henry, 26 Dec. 1793, Mary Queen   3 CH-161
   "disp. for consang."
Jamison, Ignatius, 28 March 1796, Lucy Luckett   4 FR
Jamison, John, 17 April 1794, Ann Jackson   6 BA
Jamison, Leonard, 18 Nov. 1790, Mary Smith   4 FR
Janes, Thomas, 20 Dec. 1792, Mary Waters   4 FR
Janes, William, 12 Feb. 1793, Sabret King   3 PG-438
Janney, Israel, son of Jacob and Hannah, 17th day, 8 mo.,
   1780, Anna Plummer, dau. of Joseph and Sarah   3 SF
Janney, Jacob, son of Jacob and Hannah, 14th day, 10 mo.,
   1780, Sarah Harris, dau. of Moses and Elizabeth   3 SF
Janney, John, of Alexandria, Va., son of Joseph, Jr.,
   and Hannah, of London, 26th day, 3 mo., 1795, Eliza-
   beth Hopkins, dau. of Jno. and Elizabeth   6 SF
Jarboe, Bennet, 27 July 1798, Elizabeth Frazier   4 FR
Jarboe, Peter, 16 Jan. 1779, Nancy Jarboe   3 SM-57
Jarman, Belitha, 18 Feb. 1796, Rachel Adkins   1 WO
Jarman, Benj., 13 Dec. 1796, Elizabeth Timmons   1 WO
Jarrett, James, 20 July 1791, Elizabeth Foxwell   2 DO
Jarrett, Matthew, 21 Nov. 1785, Polly King   2 DO
Jarvis, Abraham, 10 Dec. 1799, Letty Doyle   50 BA-406
Jarvis, Aquila, 9 Dec. 1787, Elizabeth Rowles   3 BA-214
Jarvis, Edward, 25 Dec. 1793, Nancy Oram   3 BA-279
Jarvis, John, Jan. 1780, Ann Richards   3 AA-416
Jarvis, John, 4 June 1795, Nancy Williams   5 BA-8
Jarvis, Joseph, 28 Sept. 1780, Margaret Jamison   3 HA-2
Jarvis, Joseph, 10 Dec. 1796, Elizabeth Barnaby   4 KE-69
Jarvis, Orman, 31 Dec. 1786, Hannah Cole   11 BA-10
Jarvis, Philip, 4 June 1778, Sarah Alguire   11 BA-1
Jarvis, Robert, 20 April 1794, Rebecca Stinchcomb   36 BA-1
   See also 4 BA-76.
Javins, Dan'l, 21 May 1778, Anne Welsh   2 MO-1
Jay, Joseph, 19 June 1796, Anne Williams   3 BA-323
Jeager, Joh., 17 June 1798, Cath. Forbech   50 BA-403
Jean, William, 15 Jan. 1786, Ruth Miller   11 BA-9
Jefferies, Joshua, 31 July 1791, Charlotte Hobbs   3 PG-258
Jeffers, Joseph, 16 Aug. 1796, Elizabeth Robertson   4 FR

Jeffers, Thomas, 22 Dec. 1798, Ann Reynolds — 4 KE-69
Jefferson, Benjamin, 6 Jan. 1783, Prescilla Jefferson — 4 FR
Jefferson, Henry, 16 Dec. 1780, Mary Howard — 4 FR
Jefferson, John, 5 Jan. 1779, Masey? Gray — 1 CA-2
Jeffery, Thomas, 24 May 1778, Catherine Barkhouse — 11 BA-1
Jeffery, Thomas, 5 Jan. 1799, by Rev. Ridgely; Rachel
    Litchfield — 4 AA
Jeffery, William, 5 May 1791, Mary Puntenay — 30 BA-1
Jefferys, Benj., 15 May 1785, Eliz. Schmit — 2 FR-1142
Jeffords, George, 28 Jan. 1796, Catherine Robinson — 5 BA-8
Jeffrey, Thomas, 27 Jan. 1791, Hally Baney Robey — 3 PG-258
Jeffries, Benjamin, 20 Oct. 1791, Eleanor Berry — 3 PG-258
Jeffries, William, son of Samuel and Margaret, 2nd day,
    12 mo., 1783, Priscilla Amos, dau. of William and
    Hannah — 1 SF
Jegley, Hennerich, 28 May 1795, Marg. Le sig. — 3 WA-59
Jegly, Jacob, April 1798, Sus. Vogelgesang — 3 WO-64
Jekenol?, Henry Clemens, 1792, Biddy Logan — 50 BA-392
Jembers, Robert, Nov. 1800, Cath. Heiss or Heist — 3 WA-70
Jemison, Charles, 9 March 1780, Mary Molley — 4 FR
Jendes, George, 25 Dec. 1795, A. Mary Roth — 2 FR-1142
Jendes, Henry, 20 May 1798, Cath. Jendes — 2 FR-1142
Jendes, John, 9 April 1792, Cath. Sauer — 2 FR-1142
Jenings, Richard, 19 July 1786, Lucy Brawner — 4 FR
Jenkins, David, 26 June 1798, Rebecca Shermon — 2 SO
Jenkins, Enoch, 9 April 1795, Hannah Dougherty — 7 BA-2
Jenkins, George, 31 March 1782, Margaret Wise — 3 SM-60
Jenkins, Isaac, 5 June 1787, Mary Galwith — 3 PG-252
Jenkins, James, 6 May 1800, Sarah Asher — 6 BA
Jenkins, Job, 19 Aug. 1778, Sarah Tucker — 4 FR
Jenkins, John, 26 July 1794, Eleanor Crampton — 4 FR
Jenkins, Joseph, 28 June 1780, Margery Wilson — 2 PG-3
Jenkins, Joseph, 21 Oct. 1780, Ann Perry — 11 BA-4
Jenkins, Philip, 8 June 1779, Elizabeth Hungerford — 2 CH-453
Jenkins, Richard, 2nd day, 1 mo., 1779, Ann Kelly — 2 SF-288
Jenkins, Thomas, 13 Jan. 1780, Mary Mackall — 3 SM-58
Jenkins, William, 5 Jan. 1779, Darcus Mastres — 3 PG-450
Jenkins, William, 23 Dec. 1787, Elizabeth Simpson — 2 CH-453
Jenkinson, John, son of Amanuel, 5th day, 11 mo., 1783,
    Elizabeth Cox, dau. of Isaac — 4 SF-172
Jenks, Henry, 16 Sept. 1798, Jane Webb — 3 BA-363
Jennings, James, 28 Sept. 1797, Eleanor McGowan — 3 BA-351
    47 BA-1 gives the date as 23 Sept. 1797.
Jennings, John, 2 Nov. 1793, Elizabeth Keough — 3 BA-279
Jennings, Jno., 5 Dec. 1793, Rachel Shryock — 29 BA-5
Jennings, Peter, 20 Jan. 1794, by Rev. G. Ridgely; Jemima
    Waters — 4 AA
Jennings, Peter, 9 June 1794, Eliz. Lombard — 29 BA-5
Jenny, Ebenezer, 4 Feb. 1790, R. Telheln — 29 BA-1
Jeours, George, 31 May 1800, Hannah Parrott — 8 BA-2
Jerry, negro of Mrs. Johns, May 1796, Molly -(?)- — 5 MO-113
Jerry, slave of Mr. Theldkeld, 16 Nov. 1800, Margaret,
    slave of Ann Sanders — 8 MO-26
Jervis, James, 15 Aug. 1793, Elizab. Plumer — 2 FR-1142
Jessop, Abraham, 12 Oct. 1797, Achsah Wells — 6 BA
Jessop, Charles, 13 April 1786, Mary Gorsuch — 5 BA-8
Jessop, Nicholas, 15 Jan. 1799, Lydia Bosley — 6 BA
Jewell, William, 29 June 1785, Mary M. Thomas — 3 HA-9
Jimeson, Samuel, 27 May 1793, Mary Elizabeth Overtosh — 4 FR
Jinkins, Francis, 10 Oct. 1781, Mary Durham — 3 HA-5
Jinney, Thomas, 3 Nov. 1799, Sarah Wilson — 3 HA-28
Jinnings, William, 16 May 1795, Mary Hoppon — 6 BA
Johagan?, William, 23 Feb. 1778, Darkus Loveless — 2 MO-1
John, James, 10 Aug. 1797, Mary Anne Alexandria — 3 BA-348
Johns, Aqualia, 12 Jan. 1792, Mary Bayly — 3 PG-436

```
Johns, Henry, 22 Feb. 1785, Sarah Brown              3 HA-10
Johns, Hosea, 23 Dec. 1794, Penelope Slade           1 BA-6
Johns, Richard, 14 April 1789, Mary Luce             6 BA
Johnson, Absalom, 24 Jan. 1782, Ruth Wooden          11 BA-5
Johnson, Adam, 17 Aug. 1797, Johanna Gilbert         3 HA-26
   2 HA-350 gives the date as 17 Aug. 1797.
Johnson, Archibald, 23 Sept. 1784, Elizabeth Usshall  3 HA-9
Johnson, Barnet, 27 April 1791, Jane Thomas          3 HA-21
Johnson, Basil, 3 Sept. 1778, Sarah Tracey           4 FR
Johnson, Benja.; 12 Oct. 1779, Lucy Todd             4 FR
Johnson, Benjamin, 29 Dec. 1798, Mary Hammond        4 FR
Johnson, Benjamin, 23 Nov. 1799, Sarah Dashiell      1 WO
Johnson, Caleb, 31 July 1794, Mary Cross             5 BA-8
Johnson, Casper, 29 April 1799, Martha Gulick        4 FR
Johnson, Charles, 24 Feb. 1779, Mary Ann Jemison     4 FR
Johnson, Charles, 20 Feb. 1794, Elizabeth Robinson   6 BA
Johnson, Charles, 19 March 1794, Molly Horton        2 DO
Johnson, Charles, 10 Jan. 1796, Mary Fugate          1 BA-7
Johnson, Charles, 6 Nov. 1799, Molly Pritchett       2 DO
Johnson, David, 21 June 1796, Bridget Lanon          3 BA-323
Johnson, Edward, 20 Jan. 1798, Margaret Wallace      2 DO
Johnson, Edward, 31 May 1798, Elizabeth McCubbin     3 BA-359
Johnson, Eliakem, 28 Dec. 1798, Charlotte Waters     1 WO
Johnson, Elijah, 14 Aug. 1790, Margaret Gamble       5 BA-8
Johnson, Elijah, 20 March 1794, Elizabeth Oram       37 BA-1
Johnson, Ezekiel, 26 June 1795, Ann Ferguson         2 DO
Johnson, Ezekiel, 15 Oct. 1799, Sarah Keene          2 DO
Johnson, Francis, 14 Sept. 1795, Margaret Crocket    5 BA-8
Johnson, Frederic, 11 Dec. 1796, Mary Weisner        29 BA-8
Johnson, George, 11 June 1795, Catherine Selby       1 WO
Johnson, George, 22 July 1800, Elisabeth Burnham     3 BA-388
Johnson, Harsford?, 15 March 1796, Mary Soward       2 DO
Johnson, Hofley, 15 May 1798, Ann Mansfield          4 KE-69
Johnson, Horatio, 20 Nov. 1794, Eliza'th Warfield    6 BA
Johnson, Ignatius Sims, 8 Jan. 1798, Ann Spalding    3 CH-162
Johnson, Isaac, 23 Jan. 1798, Hannah Poland          2 AL-700
Johnson, Israel, 14 Oct. 1798, Margaret Whiteford    6 BA
Johnson, Israel Hendrick, 29 Dec. 1784, Merab Daws   11 BA-8
Johnson, Jacob, Jr., 22 Dec. 1796, Keturah Wiley     6 BA
Johnson, Jacob, 7 Feb. 1798, Nancy Armstrong         1 WO
Johnson, James, 28 April 1790, Leah Rumbley          2 DO
Johnson, James, 26 March 1793, Ann Wrotten           2 DO
Johnson, Jas., 29 Nov. 1794, Cath. Orval             29 BA-6
Johnson, James, 31 Jan. 1797, Patty Baker            1 WO
Johnson, Jas., 7 April 1798, Eliz. Kirk              29 BA-9
Johnson, Jesse, 30 Feb. 1799, Betsy Johnson          2 SO
Johnson, John, 14 Nov. 1781, Catherine Turner        3 HA-5
Johnson, John, 27 Oct. 1786, Susanna West            4 FR
Johnson, John, 7 June 1791, Rebecca Dean             2 DO
Johnson, John, 15 April 1795, Darky Jones            2 DO
Johnson, John, 21 Dec. 1796, Sally Crapper           1 WO
Johnson, John, c.1798, by Rev. Riggin; Ary Robertson 4 AA
Johnson, Jno., 31 Jan. 1799, Ann Curry               29 BA-10
Johnson, John, 2 Jan. 1800, Elizabeth Magnes         3 HA-29
Johnson, John, 14 Aug. 1792, Ann Elbert              2 DO
Johnson, Joseph, 28 May 1778, Catherine Miller       4 FR
Johnson, Joseph, 10 July 1780, Letitia Cross         3 HA-2
Johnson, Joseph, 23 Oct. 1781, Barbara Yost          4 FR
Johnson, Joseph, 30 Dec. 1795, Rebekah Askley        3 HA-24
   7 BA-2 gives the date as 31 Dec. 1795, and the bride's
   name as Ashley.
Johnson, Josias, 10 Jan. 1792, Peggy Morgan          3 HA-21
   1 BA-4 gives the date as 12 Jan. 1792.
Johnson, Launder, 6 Dec. 1798, by Rev. Ridgely; Sarah
   Williams                                          4 AA
```

```
Johnson, Leonard, 11 Sept. 1795, Aralanta Brittingham    1 WO
Johnson, Levin, 24 Aug. 1790, Lovey Parkerson            2 DO
Johnson, Levin Y., 28 April 1797, Nelly Stafford         2 DO
   1 DO-39 gives the date as 29 April 1797.
Johnson, Luke, 18 June 1795, Elizabeth Shirrud           6 BA
Johnson, Matthew, before 4 May 1798, by Rev. Stewart;
   Anney Tica Vashon                                     4 AA
Johnson, Noah, 13 March 1794, Rachel Spencer             4 FR
Johnson, Peter, 1 Nov. 1797, Priscilla White             3 BA-352
Johnson, Richard, 29 Sept. 1799, by Rev. Wyatt; Sarah
   Henwood                                               4 AA
Johnson, Richard, 22 Oct. 1799, Mary Herbert             3 HA-28
   2 HA-351 gives the date as 23 Oct. 1799.
Johnson, Robert, 3 Sept. 1777, Alice Peterkin            3 BA-173
Johnson, Robert, 30 Oct. 1790, Ann Sprigg                4 FR
Johnson, Roger, 1 Feb. 1781, Elizabeth Thomas            4 FR
Johnson, Sam'l, 1791, Rachel Dorsey; blacks              50 BA-391
Johnson, Sander, before 20 July 1793, by Rev. Bloodgood;
   Rebecca Robinson                                      4 AA
Johnson, Thomas, 15 Aug. 1779, Mary Odle                 11 BA-3
Johnson, Thomas, 17 June 1792, Elizabeth Cord            1 BA-4
Johnson, Thomas, 29 May 1793, Ann Love                   3 HA-22
Johnson, Thomas, 22 May 1794, Ann Giles                  1 BA-6
Johnson, Thomas, 1 Oct. 1795, Eliza Russell              4 BA-77
Johnson, Thomas, 12 Nov. 1796, Elizabeth Taylor          3 HA-25
   1 BA-7 gives the date as 17 Nov. 1796.
Johnson, Whittington, 1 April 1783, Alice Todd           2 DO
Johnson, Whittington, 3 March 1786, Lovey Wingate        2 DO
Johnson, Wm., 12 June 1783, Cath'e Clarke                11 BA-6
Johnson, William, 11 Jan. 1787, Sarah Brock              6 BA
Johnson, William, 23 Feb. 1797, Ann Hope                 3 HA-25
Johnson, William, 23 Aug. 1797, Eleanor Ashley           47 BA-1
Johnson, William, 5 April 1798, Ann Johnson              2 SO
Johnson, William, 5 May 1798, Frances Bird               4 KE-69
Johnson, William, 29 June 1798, Elizabeth Fitzpatrick    3 BA-359
Johnson, William, 30 Nov. 1799, Cassandra Thomas         4 FR
Johnson, William, 9 Dec. 1799, Catherine Cost            4 FR
Johnson, William, 4 Aug. 1800, Mary Nooner               2 DO
   1 DO-40 gives the date as 7 Aug. 1800.
Johnson, William, 5 Nov. 1800, by Rev. Wyatt; Mary Davis
   4 AA
Johnston, Barney, 14 Jan. 1796, Catherine Smith          3 BA-317
Johnston, Daniel, 21 Feb. 1800, Sarah Davison            3 AL-6
Johnston, Edward, (31 March 1791), Ann Ploughman         31 BA-1
Johnston, Edward, 24 Nov. 1795, Maria Coffal             5 BA-8
Johnston, Henry Augustine, 22 Feb. 1781, Sarah Wells     2 PG-5
Johnston, James, 24 Feb. 1797, Mary Cole                 3 BA-342
Johnston, Jeremiah, 29 Nov. 1786, by Rev. Turner; Eleanor
   Sollers                                               51 BA-30
Johnston, Jno., 18 Aug. 1796, Sus. Smith                 29 BA-7
Johnston, Joseph, 18 Nov. 1796, Maria Agnew              3 BA-333
Johnston, Roger, 3 April 1790, Lydia Bennett             27 BA-1
Johnston, William, 8 March 1797, Grace Piper             3 BA-342
Joice, Nathan, 23 July 1789, Hannah Bahsage              10 BA-194
Joice, Pierce, 31 July 1794, Mary Cross                  5 BA-8
Joice, Stephen, 22 Dec. 1782, Eliza Kinkade              11 BA-6
Joines, Joseph, 10 March 1798, Ann Taylor                4 KE-69
Joker, Thomas, 13 Dec. 1790, Kitty Handly                6 BA
Jolley, John, 20 April 1797, Elizabeth Dallam            2 HA-349
Jolly, John, 19 April 1796, Elizabeth Dallam             3 HA-25
Jolly, William, 28 May 1793, Sarah Chew                  3 HA-22
Jones, Aaron, 13 Sept. 1785, Priscilla Pagan             2 DO
Jones, Aaron, 2 March 1793, Elizabeth Dove               2 DO
Jones, Abraham, 28 Oct. 1788, Mary Gittings              1 BA-1
Jones, Abraham, 27 Oct. 1796, Mary Butler                45 BA-1
```

Jones, Abraham, 13 Dec. 1796, Elizabeth Ann Harwood   7 MO-29
Jones, Alexis, 4 Feb. 1796, Susanna Martin   3 PG-442
Jones, Antony Peter, 25 Oct. 1778, Patience -(?)-   11 BA-1
Jones, Aquila, son of Evan and Susanna, 1st day, 2 mo.,
  1791, Elizabeth Dillon, dau. of Moses and Hannah   1 SF
Jones, Benjamin, 1 Feb. 1778, Sarah Gibson   1 CA-1
Jones, Benjamin, 25 March 1783, Sarah Jones   1 BA-1
Jones, Benjamin, 13 Dec. 1786, by Rev. Turner; Providence
  Odle   51 BA-30
Jones, Benjamin, 13 Sept. 1791, Charity Taylor   3 HA-21
Jones, Benjamin, 27 Jan. 1800, Sarah Wallace   2 SO
Jones, Butler, 9 Feb. 1790, Eliz. Linsay   3 PG-256
Jones, Charles, 16 Feb. 1797, Temperance Spicer   6 BA
Jones, Charles, 27 Nov. 1798, Hetty Fleming   2 SO
Jones, Charles Offutt, 24 Jan. 1799, Rebecca Offutt   5 MO-115
Jones, Cloudesberry, 23 July 1787, Elizabeth Hayward   2 DO
Jones, Dan'l, 30 Aug. 1794, Cath. Messersmith   29 BA-5
Jones, Daniel, 30 Oct. 1799, Mary Ann Goldsmith   29 BA-10
Jones, David, 8 Jan. 1781, Jemima Robosson   2 AA-114
Jones, David, 21 July 1799, Rachel Shorter, sister of Peggy
  and James Shorter   8 MO-21
Jones, Denwood, 25 May 1800, Nancy Hubbert   2 DO
Jones, Edmund, 22 Sept. 1799, Catherine Elmore   3 BA-378
Jones, Edward, 23 April 1797, Hanna Jenkins   2 AL-700
Jones, Elisha, 16 Nov. 1784, Sarah White   11 BA-8
Jones, Ezekiel, before 12 Dec. 1792, by Rev. John Long;
  Ruth Warfield   4 AA
Jones, Ezekiel, 17 Sept. 1799, Isabella Bryan   2 DO
  1 DO-40 gives the date as 19 Sept. 1799.
Jones, Francis, 18 March 1791, Rachel Coventry   4 FR
Jones, George, 31 Jan. 1788, Elizabeth Wilson   3 PG-254
Jones, George, 7 Nov. 1793, Elizabeth Crow   2 AL-700
Jones, Hambury, 23 May 1794, Elizabeth Poole   4 FR
Jones, Hanbury, 13 April 1787, Sarah Viers   4 FR
Jones, Handy, 16 Dec. 1800, Leah Hammond   1 WO
Jones, Henry, 1 July 1797, Elizabeth Jones   2 SO
Jones, Henry, 6 July 1797, Elizabeth Jones   3 SO
Jones, Isaac, 9 July 1780, Elizabeth Deaver   3 HA-2
Jones, Isaac, 2 April 1793, Mary Hearn   16 BA-4
Jones, Jacob, 29 May 1784, by Rev. Robison; Eliza Earp
  11 BA-7
Jones, Jacob, 13 Sept. 1795, Rachel Striebeck   29 BA-6
Jones, Jacob, 30 Oct. 1798, Mary Hughes   6 BA
Jones, James, 29 May 1795, Mary Stockdale   2 HA-349
  3 HA-24 gives the date as 29 May 1795.
Jones, James, 14 Dec. 1796, Ann Hurtt   4 KE-69
Jones, Jas., 10 Sept. 1797, Fanny Murphy   7 BA-3
Jones, James, 24 Jan. 1799, Ann Bennett   4 SM-184
Jones, James Hall, 6 June 1797, Margaret Dale   1 WO
Jones, James Mc., 8 Aug. 1785, Sarah Roe, dau. of Nicholas
  1 WI-115
Jones, James Merrican, 26 Nov. 1791, Helen Baker   3 BA-254
Jones, Jason, 25 Nov. 1799, by Rev. Roberts; Elizabeth
  Thompson   4 AA
Jones, Jeremiah, 23 Dec. 1800, by Rev. Ridgely; Sarah Waters
  4 AA
Jones, John, 20 Sept. 1780, Betty Dashiell   1 WI-116
Jones, John, 20 Dec. 1783, Sarah Frazier   2 DO
Jones, John, 21 Oct. 1785, Cassandra Johns   11 BA-8
Jones, John, 26 Nov. 1785, Eleanor Bestpitch   2 DO
Jones, John, 5 Aug. 1786, Rachel Young   29 BA-1
Jones, John, 25 Sept. 1789, Elizabeth Edwards   2 DO
Jones, John, c.1792, by Rev. Hutchinson; Rachel Atkinson
  4 AA
Jones, John, 22 May 1792, Uphamy Walter   2 DO

```
Jones, John, 23 May 1794, Ann Norman                    2 DO
Jones, John, 6 Oct. 1794, Betsey Tregoe                 2 DO
Jones, John, 17 June 1795, Mary Fooks                   2 DO
Jones, John, 9 March 1797, by Rev. Ridgely; Mary Roberts
   4 AA
Jones, John, 14 Aug. 1797, Nancy Bishop                 6 BA
Jones, John, 6 Sept. 1797, Sarah Moore                  2 SO
   3 SO gives the date as 7 Sept. 1797.
Jones, John, 2 Jan. 1798, Elizabeth Cannon              2 DO
Jones, John, 7 Jan. 1798, Sarah Younger                 4 KE-69
Jones, John, 16 March 1798, Tallitha Jones              2 DO
Jones, John, 28 May 1799, Eleanor Taylor                3 BA-371
Jones, John, 11 Feb. 1800, Patty Taylor                 2 SO
Jones, John Bowls, 2 Dec. 1792, Mary Padgett            3 PG-437
Jones, John Hambleton, 1 Sept. 1784, Betsy Howard       3 HA-9
Jones, Jos., 28 Jan. 1790, Vileter Padgett              3 PG-256
Jones, Joseph, 27 Feb. 1794, Henrietta Cash             2 FR-1142
Jones, Joseph, 6 Nov. 1800, by Rev. Ridgely; Mary Clarke
   4 AA
Jones, Joshua, 7 Dec. 1796, Ann Warfield                4 FR
Jones, Joshua Merrican, 26 Nov. 1791, Helen Baker      18 BA-3
Jones, Joseph, 24 Feb. 1794, Henrietta Cash             4 FR
Jones, Levi, 25 Dec. 1795, Rachell Long                 1 WO
Jones, Levin, 20 Aug. 1789, Nancy Jones                 2 DO
Jones, Levin, 24 May 1791, Mary Jackson                 5 BA-8
Jones, Levin, 10 Dec. 1796, Elizabeth James             2 SO
Jones, Lewis, 2 Sept. 1800, Betsy Follin                2 SO
Jones, Littleton, 29 May 1798, Leah Heath               2 SO
Jones, Matthew, 16 Feb. 1798, Joanna Johnson            1 WO
Jones, Matthias, 5 Aug. 1797, Milcah Gale Cha-(?)-      2 SO
Jones, Morgan 21 Sept. 1793, Julia Philison             2 DO
Jones, Morgan, 25 Jan. 1798, Cordelia Baker             1 BA-8
Jones, Moses, 2 Dec. 1790, Druscilla Baker              3 PG-257
Jones, Nathan, 21 Jan. 1800, Anna Ruxton                5 MO-116
Jones, Nicholas, 4 April 1799, Susanna Gorsuch         45 BA-3
Jones, Paul, 18 July 1795, Elizabeth Beasley            4 PG-157
Jones, Perry, 17 Feb. 1793, Liney Gantbe                3 PG-438
Jones, Philip, 7 July 1787, by Rev. Reed; Deborah McCauley
   4 AA
Jones, Richard, 1 April 1786, Sarah Brewer              4 FR
   16 BA-1 gives the date as 4 April 1786.
Jones, Richard, 10 Nov. 1786, Elizabeth Allen           4 FR
Jones, Richard, 15 Sept. 1796, Mary Durbin              3 HA-25
Jones, Richard, 5 Jan. 1797, Marg't Lagell              1 TA-321
Jones, Richard, 22 Sept. 1797, Mary Durbin             47 BA-1
Jones, Robinson, 3 Aug. 1780, Mary Burgess             11 BA-4
Jones, Roger, 7 Dec. 1789, Sarah Woolford               2 DO
Jones, Roger, 14 Jan. 1793, Ann Jones                   2 DO
Jones, Solomon, 19 June 1781, Deborah Spedden           2 DO
Jones, Stephen, 29 April 1780, Sarah Bennington         3 HA-1
Jones, Thomas, 25 Nov. 1779, Elizabeth McLure           5 BA-8
Jones, Thomas, 1 Feb. 1781, Sarah Lamb                  2 DO
Jones, Thomas, 15 Dec. 1781, Hannah Furney             11 BA-5
Jones, Thomas, 27 Dec. 1789, Winiferd Thorn             3 PG-256
Jones, Thomas, 19 Dec. 1797, Priscilla Dunn             2 SO
   3 SO gives the date as 21 Dec. 1797, and the bride's
   name as Priscilla Done.
Jones, Thomas, 28 Feb. 1799, Sarah Leith               45 BA-3
Jones, Thomas, 11 Nov. 1799, Elizabeth Woolford         2 DO
Jones, Thomas, 18 Nov. 1799, Patty Woolford             2 DO
Jones, Thomas, 24 Dec. 1799, Nelly Leatherbury          2 SO
Jones, Walter, 15 Jan. 1799, Elizabeth Harwood          7 MO-29
Jones, Wiley, 30 June 1785, Jane Clark                  3 HA-9
Jones, William, 28 Jan. 1779. Mary Smith                2 PG-2
Jones, William, 29 Nov. 1781, Elizabeth Vickers         2 DO
```

```
Jones, Wm., 26 Jan. 1786, Mary McKinsy              11 BA-9
Jones, William, 16 July 1788, Rebecca Ball           2 DO
Jones, Wm., 13 Nov. 1790, Ann Thomas                29 BA-2
Jones, William, 26 June 1791, Darkey Mocber          3 PG-258
Jones, William, 13 May 1794, Eleanor Harp            3 BA-287
Jones, William, 22 Feb. 1796, Mary Applegarth        2 DO
Jones, William, 26 Nov. 1796, Elizabeth Woolford     2 DO
Jones, William, 4 Oct. 1797, Sarah Laws              2 SO
   3 SO gives the date as 8 Oct. 1797, and the bride's
   name as Lawes.
Jones, Wm., 9 Jan. 1798, Catherine Hadder            1 WO
Jones, William, 5 Oct. 1798, Rebecca Hurley          2 DO
Jones, William, 15 Dec. 1798, Nelly Hayward          2 SO
Jones, William, 4 April 1799, Margaret Peck          5 BA-8
Jones, William, 9 Feb. 1800, Eliza Leary             5 BA-8
Jordan, Frederic, 14 Aug. 1797, Mary Bornet?        29 BA-8
Jordan, George, 14 Sept. 1791, Elizabeth Felrix      1 AL-52
Jordan, Henry, 26 Oct. 1778, Elizabeth Murfort      11 BA-1
Jordan, Hugh, 24 March 1798, Susanna Pollock        29 BA-9
Jordan, James, 29 Aug. 1792, Sarah Smith             3 BA-257
Jordan, Samuel, 25 Nov. 1790, Sarah Gurner           6 BA
Jordon, Alexander, 9 March 1797, Agnes Hughes        4 FR
Jordon, David, 9 Oct. 1784, Margaret Bruner          4 FR
Jordon, Samuel, 31 July 1788, Eliza Thompson         2 CH-453
Joseph, property of Mr. Threlkeld, 16 Nov. 1800, Susanna,
   property of Mr. Keech                             8 MO-26
Joseph, Francis, 24 March 1800, Elizabeth Shock      3 BA-384
Joss, George, 15 Jan. 1791, Catherine Zimmerman      4 FR
Josse, Anthony, 16 Sept. 1797, Mary Greenwood        4 FR
Jost, John, 5 Aug. 1792, Julianna Jung               2 FR-1142
Jostman, Mich'l, 7 June 1799, Cath. Delly           29 BA-10
Joy, John, 10 June 1798, Elizabeth Smith             4 FR
Joy, Stephen, 7 Dec. 1796, Mary Shively              4 FR
Joyce, Elisha, 4 Jan. 1795, Elizabeth Raven          6 BA
Joyce, Jacob, 6 Jan. 1794, Susanna Moore             6 BA
Joyce, Joshua, 30 April 1793, Elizabeth Johnson      5 BA-8
Joyce, Nicholas, 8 Oct. 1791, Deborah Sanders Lansdale 3 BA-254
   See also 18 BA-3.
Joyce, Richard, 23 Feb. 1786, Eliza Turner          11 BA-9
Joyce, Thomas, 4 Jan. 1795, by Rev. Ridgely; Sarah Watts
   4 AA
Joyce, Wm., 3 March 1791, Jane Sindall               6 BA
Jub, William, 17 June 1792, Avis Hammond             3 BA-256
Judey, Jacob, 21 March 1788, Priscilla Howard        4 FR
Juit, Jacob, 19 Aug. 1779, Eliz'th Boyrley           4 FR
Juley, Michael Heddinger, 11 July 1793, Catherine Herman
   35 BA-1
Julien, Rene, 7 Dec. 1799, Anna Hedges               4 FR
Jumper, Christian, 10 Oct. 1783, Elizabeth Orem      4 FR
Jung, Chasper, Dec. 1798, Susanna Josten             1 FR-59
Jung, Dewald, 30 Jan. 1793, Eliz. Hirshberger        2 FR-1142
Jung, Georg, 23 Feb. 1784, Elizabeth Eberhardin     10 BA-180
Jung, Georg, 16 May 1787, Maria Renner              10 BA-188
Jung, George, 9 April 1798, Mary Jost                2 FR-1142
Jung, Jacob, 17 March 1795, Cath. Kern               2 FR-1142
Jung, Nicholas, 4 June 1788, Eva Simons              6 FR-201
Jury, Richard, 23 Nov. 1780, Nancy Stallion          2 CH-453
   3 HA-5 gives the date as 22 Nov. 1781, and the bride's
   name as Stallions.
Justice, Ezekiel, 10 June 1790, Ann Hall             4 FR
Justice, Moses, 3 March 1795, Sophia Snal            2 FR-1142
Justice, Nicholas, 17 Jan. 1787, Elizabeth Dotson    4 FR
Justin (or Tustin), Septimus, 8 Oct. 1791, Eliz. Paul 29 Ba-2
```

Kadle, Gibson, 14 March 1796, Martha Lemaster   4 FR
Kain, Timothy, 8 April 1784, Easther Cownover   3 HA-8
Kall, Theodore, 17 May 1798, Florentina Hahn   50 BA-403
Kallender, Thomas, 26 Jan. 1785, Catherine Woolford   2 DO
Kallman, Jacob, 24 Dec. 1797, (bride's name not given) 1 FR-59
Kannaday, John, 11 July 1779, Ann Perry   3 BA-178
Kannaday, Joseph, 10 June 1800, Clemency Denbow   3 HA-29
Kannyman, Moses, 15 Dec. 1786, Hannah Barrel   2 FR-1144
Karn, Jacob, 21 Feb. 1799, Mary Thomas   4 FR
Karper, Philip, 9 Oct. 1798, Cath. Drill   2 FR-1145
Karr, Walter, 2 Feb. 1798, Mary Harrison   4 FR
Karson (Parson), John, 24 June 1799, Charlotta Bankson 9 BA-143
Kast, Georg, 6 Jan. 1799, Ann Marie Herschmennen   1 FR-59
Kast, Jacob, 3 Dec. 1799, M. Magd. Grosz   2 FR-1145
Kately, Barney, 24 March 1799, Catherine Toole   6 BA
Katultigh, Henry, 3 Dec. 1795, Mary Boden   4 FR
Kauterer, Christian, 18 Sept. 1798, Nancy McComas   50 BA-404
Kavanagh, William, 21 May 1791, Mary Toofoot   4 FR
Kayhawley, David, 30 March 1780, Elizabeth Kerrick   2 PG-3
Kaywood, Isaac, 12 July 1797, Ann Talbott   4 FR
Keadle, Gibson, 8 Feb. 1794, Rebeckah Jacobs   4 FR
Keraney, Richard, 27 Aug. 1797, Ann McCaskey   5 BA-8
Kebble, George, 25 Jan. 1798, Rosetta Collins   3 SO
Keeble, Humphry, 1 Oct. 1794, Lucy Berry   3 BA-293
Keech, Timothy, 27 Feb. 1783, Araminta Uldra   3 SM-61
Keech, William, 7 Sept. 1780, Jane Williams   2 PG-3
Keefauver, Nicholas, 15 April 1784, Margaret Peckepaugh 4 FR
Keefaver, Peter, 18 Dec. 1786, Catherine Yost   4 FR
Keefer, Henry, 20 Aug. 1795, Rachel Reed   4 FR
Keefour, Jacob, 25 July 1783, Mary Iseminger   4 FR
Keen, Wm., 1790, Ab. Moore   50 BA-390
Keene, Benjamin, III, 15 Feb. 1792, Nancy Woolford   2 DO
Keene, Benjamin, 26 March 1798, Mary Aaron   2 DO
Keene, Benjamin, 24 Jan. 1799, Ann Keene   1 DO-40
    2 DO gives the date as 23 Jan. 1799.
Keene, Ezekiel, 2 March 1790, Sarah Foreman.   2 DO
Keene, Henry, 19 Jan. 1797, Mary Tubman   1 DO-39
    2 DO gives the date as 18 Jan. 1797.
Keene, Henry, 16 Aug. 1798, Ann LeCompte   1 DO-40
    2 DO gives date as 23 July 1798.
Keene, John, 8 Oct. 1800, Catherine Dean   2 DO
Keene, Levin, 23 Dec. 1797, Ann Spedden   2 DO
Keene, Matthew, 18 Sept. 1782, Sarah Mister   2 DO
Keene, Matthew, 26 April 1788, Esther Lee   2 DO
Keene, Matthew, 13 Jan. 1790, Nancy Bramble   2 DO
Keene, Matthew, 24 May 1791, Keziah Bramble   2 DO
Keene, Matthew, 12 July 1791, Mary Bramble   28 BA-1
Keene, Richard, 5 April 1784, Amelia Woodard   2 DO
Keene, Richard, 15 June 1791, Sarah Woodard   2 DO
    28 BA-1 gives the date as 16 June 1791.
Keene, Samuel, 31 Dec. 1795, Charlotte Robson   2 DO
Keene, Samuel Lake, 13 Dec. 1780, Hilliary Griffin   2 DO
Keene, Shadrach, 16 May 1800, Priscilla Dunnock   1 DO-40
    2 DO gives the date as 14 May 1800.
Keene, Vachel, 26 June 1794, Keziah Robertson   2 DO
Keene, William, 30 Jan. 1797, Britania Willey   2 DO
Keene, William, 6 Feb. 1797, Kitty Barnes   2 DO
    1 DO-39 gives the bride's name as Betty Barnes.
Keener, Andrew, 20 Sept. 1785, Fredericka Amelung   4 FR
Keener, John, 7 Oct. 1790, Mary Condon   4 FR
Keephirt, Michael, 30 July 1779, Ann Sutton   11 BA-3
Keese, Joseph, 27 March 1797, Elizabeth Tucker   2 DO
Keese, Levin, 7 May 1794, Sarah Hayward   2 DO
Kefer, Martin, Jan. 1800, Mary Varner   3 WA-68
Keifel, Nich's, 17 May 1794, Mary Morfilius   29 BA-5

```
Keighler, Daniel, 14 July 1798, Mary Ashburner        3 BA-360
Keil, Adam, 22 March 1791, Elizab. Martin             2 FR-1144
Keil, Christoph., 2 June 1799, Ally Wilkin            29 BA-10
Keil, Jacob, 28 Nov. 1786, Abigail Gallman            2 FR-1143
Keil, Nicholas, 4 Jan. 1791, Mary Baggerly            2 FR-1144
Keilholtz, Heinr., 20 Aug. 1797, Maria Haus          50 BA-402
Keilholtz, Jno., 18 July 1795, Cath. Shaller         50 BA-397
Keinpf, Adam, 1791, Rachel Donaldson                 50 BA-391
Keirsted, Luke, 23 Nov. 1779, Elizabeth Simmons       3 AA-415
Keith, Patrick, 26 June 1780, Mary Godfrey            5 BA-8
Keith, Price, 5 Jan. 1797, Ann Cruthers               4 FR
Keith, William, 20 April 1795, Mary Stillford         6 BA
Kelhoffer, Hennrich, April 1799, Elis. Kukus          3 WA-67
Kell, Thomas, 25 Oct. 1797, Mary Anne Goldsmith       3 BA-352
Kellem, Curtis, 15 Nov. 1798, Leah Dunton             1 WO
Keller, Conrad, 30 Jan. 1790, Elizabeth Stallings     4 FR
Keller, George, 17 March 1786, Sarah Hedges           4 FR
    2 FR-1143 gives the date as 21 March 1786.
Keller, Jacob, 18 Nov. 1781, Rebecca Thompson         4 FR
Keller, Jacob, 11 Oct. 1786, Susannah Smith           4 FR
    2 FR-1143 gives the date as 17 Oct. 1786.
Keller, Jacob, 22 July 1797, Elizabeth Slagle         4 FR
    2 FR-1144 gives the date as 30 July 1797, and the
    bride's name as Eliz. Schlegel.
Keller, John, 25 April 1778, Mary Yost                4 FR
Keller, John, 23 Nov. 1790, Cath. Koblentz            2 FR-1144
Keller, Jno., 21 Sept. 1797, Eliz. Clouer            29 BA-8
Keller, Michael, 22 March 1796, Eliz. Ebbert          2 FR-1144
Kelley, Dennis, 5th day, 4 mo., 1783, Sarah Jenkins   2 SF-288
Kelley, Dennis, 18 Dec. 1794, Hannah Wilson           2 SF
Kelley, Joseph, (4 May 1789), Rachel Bagford         15 BA-2
Kelley, Thomas, 15 July 1799, Martha Hartley          3 HA-28
Kellow, Thomas, 13 Jan. 1782, Ann Roswell             2 CH-453
Kelly, Benj., 25 Dec. 1800, Eliz. Moore               5 MO-117
Kelly, Butler, 24 March 1793, Ann Kitely              3 BA-265
Kelly, Dennis, 17 Jan. 1793, Priscilla Grimes         4 FR
Kelly, Edmund, 14 Jan. 1794, Mary Tucker              3 AA-424
Kelly, Edward, 12 Nov. 1789, Delilah Pocock           1 BA-2
Kelly, Edw'd, 30 Dec. 1794, Grace Taylor             29 BA-6
Kelly, Edward, 25 May 1795, Mary Thompson             4 FR
Kelly, Emanuel, 14 Sept. 1794, Sarah Leach            6 BA
Kelly, Hugh, 22 July 1778, Mary Hudless              11 BA-1
Kelly, James, 7 Oct. 1794, Rachel Hove or Hore       10 BA-196
Kelly, James, 1 April 1799, Sarah Jordan              3 BA-369
Kelly, John, 12 Aug. 1790, Charlotte Chadwick         6 BA
Kelly, Jno., 28 July 1794, Nancy Smith               50 BA-395
Kelly, John, 31 Jan. 1797, Sarah White                2 SO
    3 SO gives the date as 2 Feb. 1797.
Kelly, Lawrence, 20 July 1796, Margaret Chamberlain   3 BA-327
Kelly, Moses, 10 Aug. 1788, Ruth Rolls                6 BA
Kelly, Thomas, 19 Aug. 1792, Rachel Arters           29 BA-3
Kelly, Thomas, 23 Dec. 1797, Honor Capen              3 BA-353
Kelly, William, 11 Dec. 1799, Mary Miller            11 BA-4
Kelso, James, 3 Jan. 1793, Mary Walker                3 BA-258
Kelso, Jas., 1 Aug. 1793, Elis. Standiford           50 BA-393
Kelty, Cornelius, 26 March 1796, Ann Livers           4 FR
Kemp, Frederick, 31 Aug. 1780, Susanna Ritter         4 FR
Kemp, Frederick, 21 March 1782, Dorathy Hershberger   4 FR
Kemp, Henry, 19 July 1779, Modelane Ritter            4 FR
Kemp, Henry, 10 March 1781, Margaret Mathews          4 FR
Kemp, Henry, 19 May 1794, Susanna Miller              4 FR
Kemp, Jacob, 11 Nov. 1793, Marg't Getzendanner        4 FR
Kemp, James, 8 Nov. 1791, Elizabeth Noll              2 DO
Kemp, John, 24 April 1778, Barbara Huff               4 FR
Kemp, John, 12 June 1782, Elizabeth Snow              4 FR
```

Kemp, John, son of John (dec.), and Mary, 4th day, 11 mo.,
   1790, Sarah P. Troth, dau. of Henry and Sarah (dec.)
   4 SF-197
Kemp, Ludwig, 6 Sept. 1785, Barbara Norris   4 FR
Kemp, Peter, (date not given), Mary Seaman or Leaman   4 FR
Kemp, Quinton, son of William, 4th day, 12 mo., 1782, Lovey
   Charles, dau. of Solomon   4 SF-169
Kempf, Jacob, 12 Nov. 1793, Marg. Getzendanner 2 FR-1144
Kempf, Solomon, 28 Nov. 1790, Barb. Hirshberger 2 FR-1144
Kendal, John, 11 Nov. 1787, Mary Barnes   6 BA
Kendall, Aaron, 6 Nov. 1798, Sarah Kirk   4 FR
Kendrick, Benjamin, 31 Dec. 1779, Mary Smith   3 SM-58
Kenley, Lemuel, 7 Dec. 1797, Elizabeth Baylis 3 HA-26
Kenley, Samuel, 5 Sept. 1780, Jane Willson   3 HA-2
Kennard, Ebenezer, 6 April 1791, Elizabeth White 2 DO
Kennard, Mathew, 29 July 1794, Polly Haithorn 3 HA-23
Kennedy, Dennis, 2 March 1799, Eleanor Richards 4 FR
Kennedy, George, 30 June 1795, Eleanor Scott   4 FR
Kennedy, Henry C., 2 Nov. 1799, Elenor Rawlings 2 DO
Kennedy, John, 26 May 1783, Bridget Pearson   3 BA-185
Kennedy, Jno., 24 Sept. 1787, Mary McCannon 11 BA-10
Kennedy, John, 15 Dec. 1792, Mary Ann Sauffer 4 FR
Kennedy, Martin, 31 July 1782, Mary Callahan 11 BA-5
Kennedy, Thomas, M., 10 April 1785, Christianna Lancaster
   3 HA-10
Kennedy, William, 6 Feb. 1796, Cath. Daily   3 WA-60
Kennedy, William, 20 April 1797, Eleanor Peake 6 BA
Kennerly, Peter, 23 April 1799, Anne Kennerly 2 SO
Kennett, William, 9 July 1799, Sally Riggan   1 WO
Kenny, John, 9 Oct. 1790, Sally Sewell   2 DO
Kenott, Conrad, 30 Oct. 1783, Sarah Brendlinger 4 FR
Kenseder, Joh., 9 April 1796, Cath. Wolf   3 WA-60
Kensell, Jacob, 11 May 1794, Catherine Smith   4 FR
Kent, Emanuel, 19 June 1788, Eleanor Burneston 18 BA-1
Kent, Rob't, 8 Jan. 1798, Marg. Meyer   29 BA-9
Kephart, Simon, 7 Aug. 1782, Susannah Leipley 4 FR
Keplinger, John, 29 April 1787, Cath. Poley   2 FR-1144
   4 FR gives the bride's name as Bolie.
Keplinger, Mich'l, 11 May 1799, Rose Nice   29 BA-10
Kerby, Jno., 22 March 1790, Arianna Porter   11 BA-13
Kerl, Mich'l, 22 March 1790, M. Marvel   29 BA-1
Kern, Adam, 24 May 1785, Rosina Willjahr   2 FR-1143
Kern, Jacob, 26 Feb. 1799, Magd. Thomas   2 FR-1145
Kern, Jacob, 1 June 1797, Marg. Schnook   2 FR-1144
Kerns, John, 19 Aug. 1799, Alice Gready   3 BA-376
Kerr, George, 13 Aug. 1792, Mary Crom   4 FR
Kerr, John, 29 July 1793, Ann Rogers   4 FR
Kersey, Robert, 22 March 1800, Mary Rawlings 2 DO
Kersner, Michael, 24 Aug. 1782, Mary Ann Engles 4 FR
Kessler, George, 22 Oct. 1798, Elizabeth Jacob 4 FR
Kessler, John, 8 March 1794, Nancy Waskey   4 FR
Kessler, Peter, 18 March 1786, Elizabeth Power 4 FR
Kessuck, Roger, 16 Nov. 1795, Milcah Thomas 3 BA-313
Kettinger, Mich'l, 21 Oct. 1789, Elis. Lower 29 BA-1
Ketzindanner, John, 5 Sept. 1785, Rebeckah Fout 4 FR
Key, Abner, 17 Nov. 1796, Catherine Eagan   6 BA
Key, James Elvin, 24 April 1794, Elizabeth Smith 3 BA-285
Key, Philip, 9 June 1796, Sophia Hall   3 BA-323
Key, William, 4 March 1797, Sally Deakins   3 AL-4
Keys, Elijah, 25 Dec. 1795, Elizabeth Evans 2 DO
Keys, John, 19 Sept. 1787, Sarah Brumagem   2 DO
Keys, John, 23 Sept. 1795, Polly Wheeler   2 DO
Keys, Levin, 25 May 1800, Nancy Wheeler   2 DO
Keys, Robert, 2 Aug. 1798, Margary Noble   2 DO
Keys, Thomas, 24 Sept. 1796, Sarah Evans   2 DO

Keys, William, 13 March 1786, Tolly Addison   2 DO
Keys, William, 24 Jan. 1789, Rosanna Hodson   2 DO
Kezlinger, Jacob, Aug. 1800, Elis. Highshoe   3 WA-69
Kibble, George, 23 Jan. 1798, Rosetta Collins   2 SO
Kibby, Joseph, 25 Aug. 1795, Eleanor Hays   4 FR
Kid, Henry, 19 Oct. 1780, Eleanor Berry   11 BA-4
Kidd, John, 15 March 1780, Sarah Roiston   3 HA-1
Kidwell, Matthew, 25 Dec. 1781, Priscilla More   2 CH-453
Kiefer, Henry, 20 Aug. 1795, Rachel Ried   2 FR-1144
Kiersted, Luke, 7 Sept. 1797, Jane Allison   6 BA
Kigar, John, 23 March 1791, Esther Shitzen   4 FR
Kile, Adam, 18 March 1791, Elizabeth Martin   4 FR
Kile, Nicholas, 3 Jan. 1791, Mary Baggarly   4 FR
Kiler, Daniel, 15 May 1799, Elizabeth Ward   4 FR
Kilgow?, James, 9 Dec. 1779, Rebecca Bradford   11 BA-4
Killen, John, 21 Dec. 1783, Polly Tripolet   11 BA-7
Killion, Jacob, 28 Sept. 1795, Mary Newman   40 BA-1
Killman, John, 21 Nov. 1791, Jane Joyce   6 BA
Killman, Levin, 24 Sept. 1799, Henrietta Worth   2 DO
Killman, Martin, 24 May 1785, Elizabeth Jones   2 DO
Kilman, James, 28 April 1798, Sarah Green   6 BA
Kilman, John, 7 Nov. 1795, Alice Riley   3 BA-313
Kilner, James, 15 May 1796, Catherine Burgoyne   3 BA-323
Kimbel, -(?)-, 3 Dec. 1795, Polly Stephenson   7 BA-2
Kimberley, John, 28 April 1796, Elizabeth Tomlinson 1 AL-53
Kimble, Elijah, 22 June 1795, Elizabeth Jackson   3 HA-24
Kimble, Elijah, 2 Dec. 1795, Polly Stephenson   3 HA-24
Kimble, Giles, 19 March 1780, Eleanor Groves   3 HA-1
     5 HA gives the date as 21 March 1779.
Kimble, Stephen, 11 Feb. 1793, Hannah Taylor   3 HA-22
Kimble, William, 8 Sept. 1792, Nelly Kimble   3 HA-22
Kimboley, Bond James, 11 Sept. 1787, Mary Mills   1 BA-1
Kimister, John, 17 Oct. 1789, Elizabeth Green   6 BA
Kindscaper, Robert, 28 March 1799, Pricilla Cramford 6 BA
King, Alexander, 14 Jan. 1798, Anne Stonestreet   3 PG-440
King, Basil, 28 Sept. 1783, Deborah Waters   1 CH-206
King, Charles, 30 March 1779, Elizabeth Risener   4 FR
King, Charles, 3 April 1779, Mary Middagh   4 FR
King, Edward, 6 March 1789, Susanna Keene   2 DO
King, Edward, 20 March 1792, Nancy Woolford   2 DO
King, Edward, 11 Sept. 1799, Polly Gosley   2 DO
King, George, 6 Dec. 1788, Rachal Perry   4 FR
King, James, 10 May 1797, Nancy Kennett   1 WO
King, John, 23 June 1779, Keziah Upton   2 PG-3
King, John, 10 Feb. 1780, Susannah Norvel   3 AA-416
King, John, 30 Dec. 1788, by Rev. Forrest; Elenor Hardisty
     4 AA
King, John, 8 April 1789, Dorothy Meekins   2 DO
King, John, 2 Aug. 1791, Elizabeth McDarall   3 PG-258
King, John, 24 Nov. 1791, Elizabeth Meekins   2 DO
King, Dr. John, 14 Sept. 1796, Harriet H. Bell   3 SO
King, John, 23 July 1798, Marg. Daub   2 FR-1144
     4 FR gives her name as Margaret Toup.
King, Lennard, 16 Nov. 1780, Susannah Watson   2 PG-7
King, Michael, 16 Dec. 1787, Mary Gordon   3 BA-216
King, Nicholas, 17 July 1797, Peggy Gaunt   4 FR
King, Rt. Rev. Reuben, 3 Feb. 1787, Mary Ann Vinc   2 CH-453
King, Richard, 17 Dec. 1778, Sarah Rawlings   1 CA-2
King, Richard, 15 Feb. 1795, Elizabeth Brown   3 PG-440
King, Richard, 8 March 1795, Anamina Weaver   3 PG-440
King, Samuel, 2 Sept. 1779, Elizabeth Waggaman   1 WI-107
King, Thos., 22 June 1780, Sarah Gice or Gree   11 BA-4
King, Thomas, 4 Sept. 1783, Ann Barnes   11 BA-6
King, Townley, 16 Dec. 1782, Rebeckah King   2 CH-453
King, William, (date not given), Eliz'th Wright   4 FR

King, William, 30 Dec. 1781, Ann Ware   2 CH-453
King, William, 23 Oct. 1796, Susanna Holland   3 PG-440
King, William, 9 July 1799, Polly Taylor   2 SO
King, William, 24 Feb. 1800, Sarah Redyard   2 DO
Kingan, John, 18 Oct. 1798, Martha Allcraft   3 BA-364
Kingston, Nathaniel, 8 May 1787, Abigail McMakin   6 BA
Kinnedy, Joseph, 3 Oct. 1778, Christianna King   4 FR
Kinney, David, 24 Dec. 1787, Betsy Kirk   2 FR-1144
Kinney, Solomon, 1 June 1780, Sarah Mezick   1 WI-117
Kinny, Daniel, 24 July 1796, Mary Higgins   6 BA
Kinsel, Jacob, 11 May 1794, Cath. Schmit   2 FR-1144
Kinsey, Isaac, son of Joseph and Hannah, 7th day, 2 mo.,
     1789, Rachel Matthews, dau. of Thomas and Rachel   1 SF
Kinter, Charles Fred'k, 29 Oct. 1799, Eliza Griffith   6 BA
Kinzil, Charles, 8 Feb. 1798, Ann Johnson   3 HA-27
     See also 1 BA-8.
Kipp, Jno., 15 June 1800, Polly Wollslager   29 BA-11
Kirby, Anthoney, 14 May 1793, Drusilla Roberts   3 BA-267
Kirby, Edward, 17 Dec. 1788, Judith Landrews   6 BA
Kirby, Francis, 1 Jan. 1782, Millburn Hagar   3 SM-59
Kirby, George, c.1799, by Rev. Steuart; Ann Randall   4 AA
Kirby, Godfrey, 4 May 1791, Nancy Hahn or Hohn   29 BA-2
Kirby, John Baptist, 23 Sept. 1799, Sarah Elson   2 PG-3
Kirby, Joshua, 29 July 1790, Eliza Murray   11 BA-13
Kirchhoff, Johann Christian, 20 Feb. 1785, Eleanora Wood
     1 FR-59
Kirfman, Adam, 20 Jan. 1798, Doraty Randall   4 FR
Kirk, Elisha, son of Caleb and Elizabeth; 5th day, 4 mo.,
     1780, Ruth Miller, dau. of Solomon and Sarah   3 SF
Kirk, James, 31 Dec. 1799, Jane Wiles   3 HA-29
Kirk, Richard, 28 Jan. 1796, Mary Davidge Jones   4 FR
Kirkland, Edward, 24 Feb. 1791, by Rev. Green; Sarah Glover
     4 AA
Kirkman, Jacob, 29 Aug. 1799, Susanna Hall   5 MO-116
Kirkman, Levin, 30 March 1791, Leah Harper   2 DO
Kirkman, Thomas, 18 May 1795, Margaret Thompson   2 DO
Kirkman, Thos., 29 June 1795, Mary Fisher   29 BA-6
Kirkman, Thos., 14 Aug. 1799, Rose Vickers   29 BA-10
Kirkwood, John, 22 Nov. 1796, Elizabeth Rupert   6 BA
Kirkwood, John, 9 Aug. 1799, Maria Powers   3 BA-375
Kirshaw, James, 25 Dec. 1788, Kesya Vansweringen   2 CA-114
Kirwan, Andrew, 7 Aug. 1790, Sarah Wood   2 DO
Kirwan, Bryan, 3 March 1797, Jane Mills   6 BA
Kirwan, Frederick, 21 Dec. 1795, Elizabeth Jarrett   2 DO
Kirwan, John, 28 Oct. 1790, Elizabeth Meekins   2 DO
Kirwan, John, 30 March 1796, Elizabeth Phillips   2 DO
Kirwan, Peter, 19 July 1782, Elizabeth Keene   2 DO
Kirwan, Peter, 10 May 1792, Mary Edgers   2 DO
Kirwan, Peter, 8 Aug. 1798, Molly Pearson   2 DO
Kirwan, Thomas, 4 Feb. 1797, Kesiah Foxwell   2 DO
Kirwan, Thomas, 8 Nov. 1798, Betsy Robinson   2 DO
Kissinger, Francis, 3 April 1790, Sarah Leroy   4 FR
Kist, Philip, 3 Aug. 1798, Anne Holt   4 FR
Kitchen, John, 5 May 1797, Mary McCulloh   3 WA-62
Kitely, Abraham, 14 Nov. 1797, Sarah Tinnis   6 BA
Kitsmiller, Jacob, Nov. 1796, Rosina Wolford   3 WA-61
Kitsmiller, Joh., Sept. 1800, Elis. Wolford   3 WA-70
Kitten, John, 7 Nov. 1799, Rachel Towson   6 BA
Kitters, John, 12 July 1791, Rachel Tawson   5 BA-8
Kittinger, Jacob, 20 Jan. 1798, Barbara Shafer   4 FR
Kittinger, John, 25 April 1795, Margaret Houck   4 FR
Kittle, William, 6 April 1782, Nancy Brown   4 FR
Kitton, Theophilus, 9 July 1795, Mary Cochran   6 BA
Kitzadanner, Geo., 22 April 1780, Eliz'th Darr   4 FR
Kitzadanner, Thos., 13 Oct. 1787, Mary Ann Koontz   4 FR

Latour, John, 23 Oct. 1795, Grace Smith   3 BA-311
Laudeman, Frederick, 6 Sept. (1790), M. Wisman or Wyman
     29 BA-1
Lauder, William, 3 Jan. 1792, Rachel Fowler   3 HA-21
Lauderman, George, 20 April 1794, Sarah Joyce   6 BA
Lauman, (?), 10 Aug. 1794, Marg. Bellin   3 WA-57
Laurence, James, 5 April 1778, Elizabeth Taylor   11 BA-1
Lausser (or Lauffer), Mitch'l, 15 Jan. 1799, Eva Hirsh-
     berger   2 FR-1148
Lavely, George, 9 Nov. 1780, Sarah Rees   11 BA-4
Lavely, William, 18 April 1797, Tracy Livers   4 FR
Lavender, Levin, 12 Feb. 1795, Mary Beatty   3 BA-299
Laverty, James, 12 Jan. 1790, Catherine Holland   11 BA-13
Lavigne, Augustine, 13 Feb. 1794, Cassandra Andrew   3 BA-281
Law, Anthony, 3 Dec. 1799, Kitty Bausman   5 BA-9
Law, James, 9 July 1795, Elizabeth Davies   3 BA-307
Law, William, 25 April 1796, Polly Miller   1 WO
Lawder, Benjamin, 14 Aug. 1800, Ann French   6 BA
Lawler, William, 31 Aug. 1780, Mary Sacke   2 CH-453
Lawles, John, 29 Sept. 1780, Rachel Allen   3 AA-416
Lawless, Benjamin, 28 June 1784, Elizabeth Samuel   2 CH-453
Lawrence, James, 1 May 1782, Ann Taff   3 HA-7
Lawrence, James, 31 March 1794, Mary Taylor   36 BA-1
Lawrence, John, 12 Feb. 1780, Eliza Ellit   11 BA-1
Lawrence, John, 5 July 1795, Rebecca Yarley   1 BA-7
Lawrence, Richard, 6 March 1780, Ann Warfield   4 FR
Lawrence, Rich'd, 22 March 1780, Ann Warfield   2 PG-3
Lawrence, Rich'd, 20 Dec. 1786, Eliza McMyer   11 BA-10
Lawrence, Samuel, 22 June 1790, Sarah Hobbs   4 FR
Lawrence, Thomas, 29 Aug. 1797, Mary Mitchell   35 BA-5
     See also 3 BA-349.
Lawrence, Wendel, 28 Feb. 1797, Ann Steele   44 BA-2
Lawrence, William, 23 March 1793, Mary Shields   3 BA-264
Lawrints?, Peter, 8 Sept. 1794, Nancy Lecaze   6 BA
Lawson, Charles, 8 April 1798, Eliz'th Green   5 BA-9
Lawson, James, 6 Feb. 1796, Elizabeth Middle   7 BA-3
Lawson, John, 18 Dec. 1798, Mary Sterling   2 SO
Lawson, Richard, 29 Oct. 1791, Diana Parkinson   3 BA-254
     See also 18 BA-3.
Lawson, Richard, 21 Feb. 1795, Isabella Bestpitch   2 DO
Lawson, Samuel, 13 April 1779, Rachel Daugherty   1 SO-163
Lawson, William, 4 Dec. 1778, Eleanor Simpson   2 PG-3
Lawson, William, 8 Oct. 1782, Susanna Beall   2 PG-3
Layfield, Levin, 16 Jan. 1798, Nancy Brittingham   1 WO
Layfield, William, 22 March 1800, Amelia Dryden   1 WO
Laying, Alexander, 25 Sept. 1795, Henrietta Dawson   3 BA-311
     35 BA-1 states that in the marriage license the
     groom's name is given as Thomas.
Layport, George, 21 Jan. 1793, Sarah Poling   2 AL-700
Leach, Ebenezer, (20 April 1791), Rebecca McNeal   31 BA-1
Leach, John, 1 Oct. 1780, Susanna Hinton   2 PG-3
Leach, Jno., 15 April 1784, by Rev. Mr. Robison; Sarah
     Holton   11 BA-7
Leach, Jno., 25 Dec. 1796, Rachel Bowman   5 MO-113
Leach, Walter, 2 Oct. 1796, Charlotte Lynch   4 FR
Leader, Charles, 3 Dec. 1799, Hannah Smith   5 BA-9
Leadley, Isaac, 26 Dec. 1793, Nancy McCubbins   1 BA-6
Leaf, Henry, 20 Feb. 1798, Ann Tipton   45 BA-2
Leaf, John, 22 Nov. 1781, Rachel Campbell   11 BA-5
Leagers, Geo., 26 March 1792, Elizabeth Pittinger   4 FR
League, Abraham, 1 Jan. 1798, Elizabeth Moore   6 BA
League, Aquila, 17 May 1785, Nancy Davis   11 BA-8
League, John, 6 May 1790, Sarah Fowler   3 BA-228
League, John, 25 Oct. 1798, Elizabeth Taylor   6 BA
League, Laban, 15 June 1796, Elizabeth Kilbourn   19 BA-11

```
League, Moses, 9 Jan. 1800, Elizabeth Tasker          6 BA
League, Reuben, 29 July 1795, Marg. Segasley         29 BA-6
   50 BA-397 gives the date as 18 July 1795, and the
   bride's name as Margaret Sigesey.
Leahry, John, 25 Nov. 1790, Esther Duncan             5 BA-9
Leak?, Samuel, 11 Jan. 1798, Ann Warfield             6 MO
Leake, Richard Henry, 2 Jan. 1800, Joanna Loeffler    3 BA-382
Leakin, Daniel, 8 Feb. 1787, Ann Shekle               2 FR-1148
Leakin, Jno., 5 Oct. 1784, Eliza H. Irvin            11 BA-7
Leakins, Thomas, 1 May 1798, Sarah Smith              3 BA-358
Leakins, William, 1 April 1790, Martha Mumford        2 FR-1148
Leapingcott, Samuel, 29 Jan. 1799, Polly Smith        2 SO
Lear, Dan'l, 24 Jan. 1781, Mary Pancartson            4 FR
Lear (or Tear), Daniel, 17 April 1797, Charlotte McCoy 3 BA-343
Lear, Fred'k, 17 Oct. 1795, Catherine Miller          4 FR
Lear, Michael, 27 Oct. 1796, Mary Crist               4 FR
Lease, George, (date not given), Elizabeth Tice       4 FR
Lease, Jacob, 18 May 1789, Casandra Thompson          4 FR
Leasher, Jacob, 14 Dec. 1791, Mary Caufman            4 FR
Leashorn, Conrad, 16 Nov. 1783, Mary Easton           4 FR
Leatch, Benjamin, 11 Sept.?, 1781, Mary Wells         3 AA-417
Leatch, Jesse, 18 April 1799, Mary Letton             5 MO-116
Leatherland, Wm., 16 Jan. 1781, Eliza Kirby           3 SM-59
Leatherman, John, 20 Nov. 1798, Catherine Miller      4 FR
Leatherman, Peter, 25 Aug. 1786, Mary Swigart         4 FR
Leatherwood, Samuel, 3 Aug. 1778, Hannah Buckingham   4 FR
   11 BA-1 gives the date as 13 Aug. 1778.
Leatherwood, Thos., 3 Feb. 1784, Mary Porter         11 BA-7
LeBaron, Lenard, 26 Oct. 1795, Marg. Elkins          29 BA-6
Leberson, Thomas, 21 Sept. 1790, Sarah Mercer         1 CE-23
Lechte, Ferdinand, 25 Feb. 1799, Nancy Brown         29 BA-10
LeCompte, Charles, 18 Dec. 1790, Drucilla Traverse    2 DO
LeCompte, Edmund, 22 March 1797, Eleanor Cope         2 DO
Lecompte, Isaiah, 28 May 1793, Sarah Geoghegan        2 DO
LeCompte, James, 23 Dec. 1782, Elizabeth Stewart      2 DO
LeCompte, Joseph, 24 Dec. 1794, Esther LeCompte       2 DO
LeCompte, Levin, 30 Nov. 1784, Sarah LeCompte         2 DO
LeCompte, Moses, 11 June 1782, Elizabeth Wheeler      2 DO
LeCompte, Peter, 24 May 1800, Sarah Busick            2 DO
LeCompte, Stephen, 17 July 1792, Rebecca LeCompte     2 DO
LeCompte, Thomas, 11 May 1799, Rebecca Buckley        2 DO
LeCompte, William, 10 Aug. 1790, Elizabeth Webster    2 DO
LeCompte, William H., 5 Oct. 1793, Elizabeth Sewars   2 DO
Ledley, John, 10 Jan. 1793, Sarah Speer               6 BA
Ledue, Laurant, 9 Oct. 1792, Susanna Mifford          3 BA-257
Lee, Abraham, 11 Nov. 1791, Elizabeth Harrington      2 DO
Lee, Charles, 16 Jan. 1792, Martha Wilson             3 HA-21
Lee, Charles, 20 Sept. 1792, by Rev. Parrott; Alla Nowell
   4 AA
Lee, Charles, 8 Oct. 1799, Nancy Bently               3 BA-379
Lee, David, 20 May 1797, Daphne Bishop                2 DO
Lee, Garret Fitzgerald, 3 Jan. 1790, Ann C. Bannister 2 FR-1148
Lee, George, 1 Jan. 1792, Rosanna Peterkin            3 BA-255
Lee, Hall, 29 Jan. 1795, Kesiah Stansbury             6 BA
Lee, James, 8 April 1780, Sarah Elliott               3 HA-1
   5 HA gives the date as 8 April 1779.
Lee, James, 29 March 1792, Nancy Riley               18 BA-4
Lee, James, 25 Sept. 1799, Elizabeth Manley           4 SM-184
Lee, James, 24 Feb. 1800, Elizabeth Lee               3 HA-29
   2 HA-351 gives the date as 25 Feb. 1800.
Lee, John, 29 Dec. 1784, Rebecca McGregory            3 HA-9
Lee, John, son of Samuel and Mary, 4th day, 11 mo., 1790,
   Sibylla Lee, dau. of William and Elinor             1 SF
Lee, Joseph, 2 Aug. 1781, Belinda Vernon              3 AA-417
Lee, Joshua, 7 Sept. 1796, Priscilla Malkins          3 BA-329
```

```
Lee, Marshall, 12 Jan. 1799, Sarah Blake            3 HA-27
  2 HA-351 gives the date as 13 Jan. 1799, and the
  bride's name as Rachel Blake.
Lee, Michael, 17 Oct. 1799, Susanna Welsh           6 BA
Lee, Parker Hall, 10 April 1782, Elizabeth Dallam   3 HA-6
Lee, Robert, 26 Dec. 1779, Mary Ambler              2 PG-7
Lee, Samuel, 10 April 1794, Mary Jackson            3 BA-285
Lee, Samuel W., 2 Feb. 1795, Mary Gover             3 HA-24
Lee, Stephen, 19 Feb. 1789, by Rev. Claggett; Rachel Welch
  4 AA
Lee, William, 14 Jan. 1781, Elizabeth Rogers        2 DO
Lee, William, 4 Jan. 1789, Margaret Day             1 BA-1
Lee, William, 8 Sept. 1790, Sarah Greenfield        2 DO
Lee, William, 12 Aug. 1792, Priscilla Roberts       6 BA
Lee, William, 24 Aug. 1797, by Rev. Ridgely; Rebeckah
  Conaway                                           4 AA
Lee, Willoughby, 17 April 1786, Fanny Cryer         2 DO
Leech, Jeremiah, 13 July 1789, Jenny West           2 DO
Leech, Jno., 13 Dec. 1795, Elizabeth Howard        29 BA-7
Leeply, George, 20 Oct. 1791, Elizabeth Nicholls    4 FR
Leeply, John, 29 July 1789, Luch. Beamer            4 FR
Leeson, Francis, 10 Nov. 1793, Elizabeth Mackanerney 3 BA-279
Lefaver, Daniel, 4 June 1796, Margaret Sulser       4 FR
Lefebre, David, Jan. 1799, Sus. Crissinger          3 WA-66
Lefever, Elias, 9 Oct. 1798, Catherine Craver       4 FR
Le Fort, Louis Francis Isidore, 12 July 1799, Frances
  Deschamps                                         3 BA-373
Legand, Peter Marie Guelie De K., 15 Dec. 1792, Genevieve
  Emili Grembolt                                    4 FR
Legard, John, 8 Feb. 1780, Mary Cilestin            3 BA-179
  See also 11 BA-4.
Leggit, Samuel, 15 Dec. 1787, Jane Parker           4 FR
Lehman, Abraham, 30 March 1790, Eliz. Fluck         2 FR-1148
Lehman, Gebhard, 17 July 1790, Martha Willert      11 BA-13
Lehmann, Jacob, 23 Nov. 1793, Phillipine Meyer     10 BA-196
Lehnherr, Friederich, 23 Dec. 1797, Maria Yuncker   3 WA-63
Lehr, Henry, 1 Jan. 1799, Mary Dien                 2 FR-1148
Leibrandt, Johannes, 28 June 1794, Mary Speck      10 BA-196
Leiel, Andreas, 1791, Cath. Bryan                  50 BA-391
Leigh, John, 24 Jan. 1798, Ann (?)                  1 TA-323
Leighter, Abaram, July 1798, Elis. Dusinger         3 WA-65
Leinbach, Christian, son of Frederick and Elizabeth,
  30 April 1782, Anna Rosina Paus, dau. of Christian
  and Magdalena (Frey)                              5 FR-73
Lemane, James, 31 March 1794, Mary Taylor           3 BA-285
Lemaster, Richar, 25 March 1799, Rebecca Johnson    4 FR
Lemmer, Valentine, 30 Dec. 1795, Mary Eirich       29 BA-7
Lemmon, William, 7 Dec. 1794, Susanna Penn          3 BA-296
Lemon, John, 10 Nov. 1799, Esther Lawrence          6 BA
Lemon, Lemuel, (17 Nov. 1787), Sarah Burke         15 BA-1
Lemon, Nicholas, 12 April 1795, Ruth Mills          3 BA-301
Lencker, Georg, 18 Oct. 1791, Susanna Methenal      2 WA-16
Leneveu, Lewis, 15 July 1783, Hannah Sullivan      11 BA-6
Lenhard, Jacob, 1 Nov. 1792, Mary Snyder           50 BA-392
Lennehan, Charles, 9 March 1790, Sarah Joiner      11 BA-13
Lentz, Conrad, 1786, Maria Neuser?                 50 BA-387
Lentz, John, 24 Oct. 1786, Mary Magd. Wagner        2 FR-1148
Leonard, and Sale, slaves of David Crawford, m. 24 Dec.
  1797, Sale's mother Cicila was a witness.         8 MO
Leonard, Christian, 27 Aug. 1781, Catherine Baugher 4 FR
Leonard, James, 24 Dec. 1786, Ann Harris            6 BA
Leonard, James, (8 July 1791), Catherine Lemmon    15 BA-4
Leonard, John, 1 Feb. 1781, Mary Watson             1 SO-146
Leonard, Philip, 18 July 1793, Mary Ann Gray        3 BA-270
Leppert, Heinr., 26 May 1799, Elizab. Fornals      50 BA-405
```

```
Lepresh, Joseph, 13 Oct. 1794, Elizabeth Geugler        10 BA-196
Lept, Henry, 4 Jan. 1798, Johanna Brown                 29 BA-9
Lerew, Abraham, 18 Oct. 1800, Mary Gartner              50 BA-408
Lerue, James, 15 Oct. 1799, Elizabeth Counns             3 BA-379
Lester, Peter, 16 Sept. 1799, Annaretta Taylor           1 WO
Lester, William, 10 Aug. 1797, Elizabeth Johnson         3 BA-348
Lester, William, 19 Nov. 1799, Elizabeth Fawcett         2 HA-351
   3 HA-28 gives the date as 15 Nov. 1799.
Lethsbury, John, 19 Jan. 1798, Henrietta Price           4 KE-69
Letick, George, 17 March 1792, by Rev. Dorsey; Sarah
   Sadler                                                4 AA
Letter, George, 13 May 1788, Christina Laufer            2 FR-1148
Lettig, Dan'l, 26 April 1785, Marg. Deckson              2 FR-1148
Levering, Enoch, 28 Jan. 1800, Hannah Brown              5 BA-9
Levering, Peter, 22 May 1798, Hannah Wilson             29 BA-9
Leverton, Moses, 15th day, 1 mo., 1785, Rachel Wright    2 SF-288
Levillain, Michael, 22 Feb. 1795, Cath. Hose            29 BA-6
Levy, Christ., 18 Nov. 1786, Sus. Ream                  29 BA-1
Levy, David, 25 Sept. 1791, Mary Sturm                   2 FR-1148
   4 FR gives the groom's name as David Levy, Jr., and
   the bride's name as Mary Sturrum.
Levy, Jacob, 21 Nov. 1789, Mary Shroiner                 4 FR
Lewis, Abraham, 21 Feb. 1785, Lovey Wright               2 DO
Lewis, Abraham, 28 Aug. 1796, Emilia Twogood             3 BA-327
Lewis, Charles, 23 May 1784, Hannah Oram                11 BA-7
Lewis, Charles, 16 Nov. 1797, Margaret Barns             6 BA
Lewis, Daniel, 10 May 1778, Margery Waters               4 MO-1
Lewis, Elisha, 17 March 1788, Elizabeth Kellum Melalla   2 DO
Lewis, George, 16 March 1791, Katy Phillips              2 DO
Lewis, George, 24 Dec. 1796, Henrietta Beems             3 BA-333
Lewis, Hugh, 14 Jan. 1790, Susannah Gregory              3 PG-256
Lewis, Isaac, 9 June 1800, Nancy Rain                    1 WO
Lewis, James, 2 July 1778, Hannah Carter                11 BA-1
Lewis, James, 24 Jan. 1795, Bridget Christie             3 BA-299
Lewis, Jno., 16 Nov. 1779, Verlinda Gatton               4 FR
Lewis, John, 23 Oct. 1783, Eliza Parnell                11 BA-6
Lewis, Jno., 6 Aug. 1784, Eliza Seabrooks               11 BA-7
Lewis, Jno., 16 Feb. 1789, Mary Young                   11 BA-2
Lewis, John, 30 April 1789, Sarah Kirby                  5 BA-9
Lewis, John, 11 April 1797, Elizabeth Gardiner           3 BA-343
Lewis, John, 2 May 1799, Nancy Silverthorn               3 BA-371
Lewis, Joseph, 30 March 1777, Ruth Holmes                2 PG-2
Lewis, Kendal, 9 Feb. 1796, Margaret Bestpitch           2 DO
Lewis, Levin, 23 April 1796, Rachel Kirwan               2 DO
Lewis, Levy, 25 May 1797, Nancy Booker                   1 TA-323
Lewis, Nicholas, 25 Dec. 1800, Mary Mackie               2 HA-352
   4 HA gives the date as 23 Dec. 1800.
Lewis, Richard, 4 Sept. 1783, Hannah Warrell            11 BA-6
Lewis, Richard, 21 Nov. 1793, Elizabeth Myers            6 BA
Lewis, Samuel, 30 Jan. 1796, Rachel Reems; free mulattoes
   3 BA-317
Lewis, Stephen, 4 July 1794, Juley Barnett               2 DO
Lewis, Teackle, 18 Feb. 1800, Polly Cooper               2 SO
Lewis, Thomas, 18 March 1794, Mary Ellis                 4 FR
   See also 2 FR-1148.
Lewis, Thomas, 2 July 1798, Sophia Teshner               4 FR
Lewis, William, 30 Aug. 1796, Catherine Gardon           2 DO
Lewis, William, 28 Oct. 1797, Catherine Porter          47 BA-1
   See also 3 BA-352.
Lewis, William, 4 Jan. 1798, Elizabeth Jessop            6 BA
Lewis, William Y., 8 May 1798, Rachael Stewart           3 BA-358
Lewthwaite, Christopher, 9 July 1797, Agness Carlisle    5 BA-9
Leypold, Fred'k, 18 Oct. 1798, Eliz. Breitenbach        29 BA-9
Lichtold, Andreas, 24 June 1784, Catharine Steiger      10 BA-182
Licklider, George, 23 Feb. 1797, Susanna Beavers         4 FR
```

```
Lidiard, John, 26 March 1793, Mary Garty            5 BA-9
Lieberknecht, Christoph, 22 Nov. 1791, Mar. Marg't Miller
   2 WA-16
Liesz, George, 26 April 1795, Eliz. Liesz           2 FR-1148
Lieth, Samuel, 12 Oct. 1782, Cassiah Thrasher       4 FR
Liggat, Samuel, 15 Dec. 1787, Jane Parker           5 BA-9
Lightner, John, 21 July 1797, Mary Warner           4 FR
Lighty, John, 17 May 1796, Elizabeth Miller         4 FR
Lilley, John, 1 Jan. 1779, Sarah Whitehead          4 FR
Lilley, John, 16 May 1799, Hannah Rummey            6 BA
Lilley, Robert, 9 April 1800, Nancy Baker           6 BA
Limes, Christopher, 29 April 1794, Mary Litton      3 BA-285
Limes, Harman, 4 Jan. 1783, Ann Burnett            11 BA-6
Linahan, William, 15 Nov. 1795, Mary Young          6 BA
Linam, William, 17 Dec. 1797, Sarah Pinix           1 BA-8
Linberger, Philip, 21 April 1794, Cath. Lauthauzer 50 BA-394
Linck, Adam, 14 April 1783, Jane Ogle               4 FR
Lincoln, Reuben, 8 July 1800, Rachel Oliver         3 BA-387
Lindenberger, Charles, 21 Nov. 1790, Susannah Randall  6 BA
Lindenberger, George, 8 Jan. 1795, Anne Henry Stevenson
   3 BA-299
Lindey, John, 8 Aug. 1797, Eliz. Cutchall           3 AL-5
Lindsay, Adam, 30 Dec. 1783, Jane Bennett          11 BA-7
Lindsay, George, 22 Sept. 1789, Eliz. McDonald      2 FR-1148
Lindsay, Michael, 16 Dec. 1794, Catharine Porter    3 BA-296
Lindsay, Thomas, 3 Sept. 1782, Margaret Trentor     4 FR
Lindsey, Alexander, 27 Nov. 1790, Rebecka Merstiller  4 FR
   2 FR-1148 gives the date as 30 Nov. 1790, and the
   bride's name as Marsteller.
Lindsey, Charles, 15 Dec. 1796, Hannah Moody        3 PG-442
Lindsey, George, 18 Sept. 1789, Elizabeth McDonald  4 FR
Lindsey, Thomas, 19 Sept. 1790, Rebecca Frazier     3 PG-257
Lindsy, Mager, 16 Jan. 1799, Hetty Townsend         1 WO
Lindzey, Matthias, 12 Dec. 1798, Nancy Brown        1 WO
Line, Henry, 14 Feb. 1786, Margaret Bents           4 FR
Linebach, Joseph, 13 Dec. 1795, Maria Schaw         3 WA-59
Ling, Robert, 12 April 1797, Anne Chapman           3 BA-343
Linganfelder, John, 12 Aug. 1797, Ann Mount         4 FR
Lingenfelder, Phil., 24 Jan. 1796, Cath. Schrich   50 BA-398
Lingrall, Nehemiah, 23 March 1789, Rosanna Paul     2 DO
Linham, John, 1 Jan. 1792, Elizabeth Baxter         3 BA-255
Linhart, Frederick, 6 June 1793, Mary Isler         3 BA-268
Link, Jacob, 19 April 1788, Elizabeth Creager       4 FR
Link, Stephen, 12 Feb. 1782, Mary Denton           11 BA-5
Link, Thomas, 22 March 1790, Ann Maria Fout         4 FR
Link, Thomas, 27 April 1794, Eleanor Preston        4 BA-76
Link, Thomas, 16 May 1796, Elisab. Dunwoody        50 BA-399
Linkin, Abraham, 30 Jan. 1781, Eleanor Borden       2 CH-454
Linkins, Henly, 28 Oct. 1780, Chleah Allin          2 CH-454
Linn, Isaac, 9 March 1799, Eve Jacobs               4 FR
Linstead, John, 7 April 1796, by Rev. Samuel Hill; Susanna
   Grey                                            46 BA-1
Linstead, Joseph, 22 May 1800, by Rev. Wyatt; Rebecca
   Reeves                                           4 AA
Linthicum, Amasa, 13 Oct. 1799, Rachel Johnson      6 BA
Linthicum, Ancas, 10 Jan. 1792, Sarah Cromwell     18 BA-4
Linthicum, Benjamin, 3 May 1797, Charity Muir       2 DO
Linthicum, Joshua, 19 May 1800, Elizabeth Beard     1 AA-162
Linton, Isaac, 4 Feb. 1793, Susanna Richards        4 FR
Linton, Zachariah, 20 May 1778, Mary Maynard        4 FR
Linvill, John, 16 June 1791, Martha McAllister      6 BA
Lipscombe, Spotswood, 7 July 1799, Eliza Smith Pendleton
   2 CH-454
Liskey, Jacob, Feb. 1782, Priscilla Swan            3 AA-418
Litman, John, 29 Jan. 1782, Elizabeth Bennett       2 PG-3
```

Littel, Samuel, 12 April 1796, Sydney Roberts   3 WA-60
Little, David, 30 April 1795, Elis. Wolz   3 WA-58
Little, John, 20 July 1794, Elizabeth Adams   1 BA-6
Little, John, before 31 Aug. 1796, by Rev. Mills; Sarah
     Swann   4 AA
Little, John, 24 June 1800, Margaret Daugherty   3 HA-29
Little, Michael, 25 July 1778, Mary Quinner   4 FR
Little, Peter, 24 Aug. 1797, Annabella Hughes   6 BA
Little, Robert, 13 Sept. 1791, Lucy Connelly   18 BA-3
     3 BA-254 gives the bride's name as Connolly.
Littlejohn, Miles, 26 Sept. 1792, Sarah Paine   5 BA-9
Littlejohn, Thomas, 28 March 1796, Sarah McCarter   3 BA-321
Litzinberger, John, 31 Dec. 1793, Martha McClintick 5 BA-9
Livingston, Benj., 10 April 1797, Sarah Jones   1 WO
Livingston, Geo., 23 Sept. 1800, Susannah Ennis   1 WO
Livingston, Paul Bartholomy Heineman, 19 April 1795,
     Letitia Smith   40 BA-1
Lloyd, Daniel, 24 Aug. 1780, Charity Shaw   2 PG-3
Lloyd, James, 24 Dec. 1798, Priscilla Russell   2 SO
Lloyd, John, 8 Sept. 1791, Mary Marther   3 PG-258
Lloyd, John, 24 Dec. 1798, Sarah Kersey   2 SO
Lloyd, Samuel, 26 Nov. 1798, Henny Hows   4 FR
     See also 2 FR-1148.
Lobe, Joseph, 12 March 1787, Jemima Loveall   6 BA
Lock, John, 22 March 1780, Sarah Bastian   4 FR
Lock, Thomas, 16 Feb. 1783, Catherine Estep   2 CH-454
Lock, Thomas, 10 Dec. 1793, Sarah Dunkan   18 BA-6
Locker, David, 31 July 1794, Sarah Payn   3 PG-440
Locker, Isaac, 15 Jan. 1795, Sarah Miles   3 PG-440
Locker, Shadrick, 30 April 1778, Eleanor Gentle   2 MO-1
Lockerman, Hill, 17 Feb. 1792, Lovey Jones   2 DO
Lockerman, Stanley B., 22 Oct. 1799, Elizabeth Sparhawk
     2 DO
Lockerman, Stanley Byus, 8 Dec. 1796, Sophia Dickinson 2 DO
Lodge, William, 26 Sept. 1783, Mary King   4 FR
Lodge, William O., 17 Jan. 1797, Frances Porter   5 MO-113
Loeman, Mich'l, 27 Nov. 1797, Elizabeth Bale   4 FR
Logan, Jas., 1791, Polly Casper   50 BA-391
Logan, John N., 22 Nov. 1781, Sarah Wedding   2 CH-454
Logan, Mich'l, 10 Jan. 1782, Hamutal Kirkland   11 BA-5
Logan, William, 19 March 1778, Margaret Shebar   4 FR
Logan, William, 27 Sept. 1797, Mary Carmichael   4 KE-69
Logsdon, Bennett, 17 Dec. 1796, Abigail Lewis   3 AL-4
Logsdon, John, of William, 11 Nov. 1799, Patience Arnold
     3 AL-6
Logsdon, Ralph, 31 Oct. 1795, Mary Arnold   1 AL-53
Logsdon, William, 22 June 1797, Susanna Williams   3 AL-4
Logue, Joh., Sept. 1799, Anna Martin   3 WA-67
Logue, Richard, 19 Feb. 1789, Mary Stansbury   11 BA-12
Lohr, Johann Carl, 27 Nov. 1791, Cathrina Elisabeth Weeton
     10 BA-194
Loker, William, 6 Feb. 1800, Elizabeth Thomas   4 SM-184
Lokey, Benj'm., 14 March 1800, Polly Taylor   1 WO
Lomax, John, 23 Sept. 1781, Chloe Posey   2 CH-454
Lomax, Zeth, 29 March 1778, Eleanor Gray   2 CH-454
Lombright, Philip, 28 Dec. 1797, Mary Hole   4 FR
Londreagrin, Dennis, 25 Dec. 1781, Mary Casse   3 HA-5
Loney, Amos, 28 Nov. 1782, Mary Donellan   11 BA-6
Loney, William, 21 Dec. 1783, Mary Frisby   3 HA-8
Long, Charles, 16 Dec. 1793, Catherine Firestone   4 FR
Long, Coulbourn, 28 Aug. 1799, Mary Davis   1 WO
Long, Coulbourn, 30 Dec. 1800, Sarah Price   1 WO
Long, Hugh, 15 Dec. 1788, Margareth Musin   10 BA-192
Long, Isaac, 13 Dec. 1797, Charlotte Griffen   1 WO
Long, Isaac, 31 Dec. 1799, Mary Lefory   2 AL-701

```
Long, John, 21 Feb. 1780, Ann Scott                    3 HA-1
Long, John, 12 Nov. 1791, Elizabeth Partridge          6 BA
Long, Josias, 13 Jan. 1793, Ann Friend                 2 CH-454
Long, Peter, 30 Aug. 1791, Margaret Carr               1 BA-3
Long, Robert, 4 May 1784, Sarah Wilson                 5 BA-9
Long, Robert Cary, 12 Oct. 1797, Sarah Carnaghan       6 BA
Long, Rosamon, 18 Dec. 1792, Sarah Divian              2 AL-700
Long, Sam'l, 21 May 1780, Ann Smith                   11 BA-4
Long, Samuel, 28 June 1797, Mary Cummins               3 BA-346
Long, Thomas, 5 Sept. 1779, Mary Conner                2 PG-2
Long, Thomas, 20 July 1791, Mary Holley                3 PG-258
Long, Zadock, 13 Oct. 1796, Leah Whittington           1 WO
Longberry, Charles, 15 April 1779, Mary Van Buskirk    2 AL-701
Longdon, Arthur, 25 Jan. 1792, Mary Lewis              1 BA-4
Longfield, George, 13 June 1793, Ann Crawford          3 BA-269
Longhead, Adam, 15 July 1790, Sarah Connelly           3 BA-235
Longley, Edmund, 12 Aug. 1794, Sarah Cromwell         18 BA-6
Longley, James, c.1786/7, Elizab. Starck              50 BA-387
Longly, Jno., 17 Jan. 1797, Marg. Cain                29 BA-8
Longly, Samuel, 28 July 1797, Catharina Husk          10 BA-198
Longshore, Mahlon, 2 Oct. 1800, Sarah Ragan            2 AL-701
Longsworth, Solomon, 6 June 1785, Lucretia McElfresh   4 FR
   2 FR-1148 gives the date as 7 June 1785, and the
   bride's name as M'Elfish.
Lookingpeel, John, 4 Sept. 1790, Sarah Worman          4 FR
Lord, Henry, 12 Sept. 1781, Rachel Lowe                2 DO
Lord, Jesse, 15 Dec. 1800, Milcah Jones                2 DO
Lord, Leonard, 26 Jan. 1795, Rebecca Adams             2 DO
Lord, Stephen, 19 Jan. 1790, Ruth Stevenson            6 BA
Lord, Thomas, 17 Jan. 1797, Betty -(?)-                2 SO
Lorens, Joh. Adam, 26 -(?)- 1797, Elisabeth Behren     1 FR-59
Lorman, William, 3 April 1794, Mary Fulford            3 BA-285
Lostater, Wm., 5 Aug. 1795, Lamar Parr                 7 BA-2
Loten, Daniel, 18 May 1790, Annie Ross                 2 DO
Lott, Jacob, 14 May 1785, Cath. Michael                4 FR
Loubies, Philip, 25 April 1785, Mary Helm             11 BA-8
Louderman, George, 20 June 1792, Ann Jameson          29 BA-3
Louis, John, 16 Feb. 1779, Mary Keplinger              4 FR
Lovat, Jonas, 4 Aug. 1793, Sarah Jacobs                2 AL-700
Love, David, 7 Nov. 1784, Nancy Ramsey                 4 FR
Love, John, 8 Nov. 1791, Susannah Green                3 HA-21
Love, Samuel, 6 Feb. 1798, Sarah Jones                 5 MO-113
Loveitt, Wm., 3 June 1798, Sarah Holmes                6 BA
Lovejoy, Josias, 19 Feb. 1789, Sarah Campbell          2 PG-4
Lovelace, Elisha, 8 Jan. 1789, Anne Jones              3 PG-255
Loveless, Bartin, 11 June 1778, Lucy Watson            2 MO-1
Loveless, Isaac, 9 Jan. 1794, Sarah Barrtt             3 PG-439
Loveless, James, 15 Nov. 1789, by Rev. Reed; Willimina Pool
   4 AA
Lovet, John, 13 April 1783, Ann Jones                  3 HA-7
Lovett, Daniel, 11 Sept. 1794, Polly James             1 AL-53
   2 AL-700 gives the date as 23 Sept. 1794.
Low, Alexander, 10 July 1797, Nancy Brewington         1 WO
Low, Andrew, 2 July 1788, Polly Griffin                2 DO
Low, Charles F., 27 Oct. 1795, Mary Sutton             3 PG-441
Low, David, 14 Jan. 1796, Margaret Demmitt             4 BA-77
Low, Henry, 8 April 1792, Peggy Low                    3 PG-437
Low, Isaac, 26 Sept. 1790, Jemima Hitchcock            1 BA-3
Low, John, 16 March 1787, Margaret Bromwill            2 DO
Low, Reason, 16 Feb. 1792, Sarah Cole                  3 PG-436
Lowderslager, Solomon, 30 April 1799, Anne Sykes      45 BA-3
Lowe, Andrew, 19 July 1778, Mary Peckenpaugh           4 FR
Lowe, Barton, 12 Feb. 1782, Susanna Wallingsford       2 PG-3
Lowe, Cornelius, 11 May 1793, Elizabeth Bevan          5 BA-9
Lowe, Henry, 18 Oct. 1796, Ann Macbee                  5 MO-113
```

```
Lowe, Isaac, 4 Aug. 1787, Rebecca Wheatley          2 DO
Lowe, Isaac, 29 Aug. 1787, Margaret Burn            2 DO
Lowe, Isaac, 28 Sept. 1791, Jemima Hitchcock        3 HA-21
Lowe, Isaac, 3 July 1793, Sarah Hooper              2 DO
Lowe, Jacob, 1 Nov. 1799, Susannah Rep              4 FR
Lowe, James, 10 July 1781, Ann Wilcoxon             2 PG-5
Lowe, James, 5 April 1784, Jane Kelly               11 BA-7
Lowe, James, 31 July 1790, Elizabeth Wig            3 PG-257
Lowe, John, 1 July 1782, Sarah Darnall              2 PG-3
Lowe, John, 24 July 1784, Eliza Debligey            11 BA-7
   3 BA-213 gives the bride's name as Deblegy.
Lowe, John, 7 Sept. 1797, Mary Jones                3 BA-349
Lowe, John Hawkins, 3 Jan. 1788, Barbara Magruder   3 PG-254
Lowe, Nicholas, 7 April 1787, by Rev. West; Ketura Baker
   51 BA-30
Lowe?, Tubman, 9 April 1789, by Rev. Claggett; Elizabeth
   Bond                                             4 AA
Lowes, Tubman, son of Henry and Esther, 9 April 1789,
   Elizabeth Birkhead Bond, dau. of Thomas and Elizabeth
   Bond of Cal. Co.                                 1 WI-183
Lowman, Basil, 24 Jan. 1790, Ann Frazier            18 BA-2
Lowman, Henry, 27 April 1797, Martha Downes         4 KE-69
Lowman, James, c.1792, in Washington Co., by Rev. Chalmers;
   Rachel Downing                                   4 AA
Lowman, Michael, 27 Nov. 1797, by Rev. Dorsey; Elizabeth
   Bale                                             4 AA
Lowman, Richard, 6 Oct. 1798, Rachel Harris         4 KE-69
Lowndes, Benja., 28 Oct. 1790, Dorithy Buchanan     11 BA-13
Lowrey, Ceazer, 17 May 1794, Mary Cooper            4 FR
Lowrie, James, 22 Aug. 1786, Marg't McCawly         11 BA-9
Lowry, Sam'l, 13 Sept. 1798, Agnes Cooper           7 BA-4
Lowry, William, 22 Sept. 1796, Rebecca Groome       5 MO-113
Lowton, Benson, 29 Oct. 1800, by Rev. Wyatt; Susanna
   Maddox                                           4 AA
Loyd, John, 23 Aug. 1793, Catherine Rear            3 BA-271
Loyd, William, 8 Dec. 1794, Cath. O'Donnell         29 BA-6
Lucas, James, 20 Aug. 1780, Ruth Lewis              2 PG-3
Lucas, James, 15 Dec. 1791, Mary Free               3 PG-436
Lucas, John, 16 Dec. 1780, Mary Simmons             2 PG-5
Lucas, John, 7 Feb. 1793, Sarah Divins              1 BA-5
Lucas, John, 1 Dec. 1797, Christena Waters          4 FR
Lucas, John D., 11 June 1796, Jane Benick           1 AL-53
Lucas, Parker, 6 Oct. 1796, Rhoda Bowen             1 WO
Lucas, Thos., 1789, Sarah Orton                     50 BA-388
Lucas, Thomas, 28 Dec. 1793, Elizabeth Simmons      4 FR
Luckett, Benjamin, 10 Jan. 1790, Elizabeth Semmes   2 CH-454
Luckett, David, 28 June, 1798, Susanna Luckett      4 FR
Luckett, John, 31 Jan. 1781, Kitty Munro            4 FR
Luckett, John, 29 April 1800, Jenet Hickman         7 MO-29
Luckett, Philip, 7 May 1796, Mary Harding           4 FR
Lude, Nichlas, 4 Aug. 1799, Eva Schmelzern          1 FR-59
Ludwick, Jacob, 6 June 1786, Elizabeth Gaudden      2 DO
Lumbert, Richard, 19 June 1792, Elizabeth Davison   3 BA-256
Lung, Jacob, 6 Nov. 1799, Susanna Rep               4 FR
Lunin, Edward, 11 April 1790, Grace Bethorn         6 BA
Lunt, Henry, 29 Dec. 1790, Sarah Stewart            3 BA-235
Lurly, John, 2 Jan. 1783, Hephsehe Harris           2 CH-454
Lurty, John, 30 April 1780, Susanna Nugent          3 SM-58
Lusby, John, 23 Nov. 1794, by Rev. Joseph Wyatt; Patience
   Fennell?                                         4 AA
Lushey, Francis, 29 April 1800, Anne Cromwell       3 BA-385
Lustater, Jacob, 31 July 1795, Fannie Parr          3 HA-24
Luten?, King, 19 Aug. 1784, Providence Baker        11 BA-7
Luter, Michael, 19 Dec. 1789, Mary Kindle           4 FR
Luther, Christ'n, 16 Nov. 1779, Alley Sewell        4 FR
```

```
Luther, Michael, 20 Dec. 1789, Mary Kindle          2 FR-1148
Luttig, John C., 21 Jan. 1798, Sally Pratt          3 BA-354
Lutz, Andreas, 25 Nov. 1784, Susanna Mumma         10 BA-184
Lutzell, Mich'l, 8 May 1784, Sophia Grove           4 FR
Lux, Darby, 21 Feb. 1798, Mary Nicholson            6 BA
Lux, Robert, 16 Feb. 1779, Debora Hobs              4 AA
  The ceremony was performed by Rev. Magill.
Lyder, Henry, 27 May 1780, Catherine Staley         4 FR
Lyles, Richard, 4 April 1787, Elizabeth Jones       4 FR
Lyles, Thomas, 22 April 1779, Eleanor Duckett       2 PG-2
Lyles, Will., 15 Aug. 1779, by Rev. Magowan; Martha William-
  son                                               4 AA
Lyman, Joseph, 3 Sept. 1799, Eleanor Rix            3 BA-377
Lynch, Abraham, 28 Dec. 1795, Mary Hannahe          4 FR
Lynch, Anthony, 21 June 1792, Mary Barton           1 BA-4
Lynch, Hugh, 19 Oct. 1780, Rebecca Owings          11 BA-4
Lynch, James, 12 Sept. 1795, Marg't Hurley         44 BA-1
Lynch, John, 13 Feb. 1799, Mary Ridgely             4 FR
Lynch, Joshua, 8 May 1798, Henrietta Maria Stansbury 6 BA
Lynch, Kidd, 21 Aug. 1791, Sarah Sumarts            1 BA-3
Lynch, Matthias, 20 Dec. 1780, Elizabeth Saunders   3 HA-3
Lynch, Patrick, 30 Oct. 1783, Eliza Welsh          11 BA-6
Lynch, Patrick, 7 Dec. 1786, Elizabeth Howlett      6 BA
Lynch, Robuck, 22 Nov. 1800, Priscilla Cole         6 BA
Lynch, Samuel, 24 March 1785, Mary Leager           3 HA-9
Lynch, William, 17 June 1779, Elisabeth Regan       5 BA-9
Lynch, William, 15 Nov. 1795, Mary Young            6 BA
Lyne, John, 26 Aug. 1786, Mary Huff                 4 FR
Lynham, George, 16 Sept. 1799, Mary De Pang         3 BA-377
Lynn, John, 26 Feb. 1784, Eleanor Edelin            4 FR
Lynthicum, Joseph, 9 May 1787, Sarah Spedden        2 DO
Lyon, James, 16 July 1797, Anna Spencer             5 BA-9
Lyon, Patrick, 8 Dec. 1793, Jane Bailey             3 BA-279
Lyon, Robert, 2 Dec. 1783, Susanna Hall             5 BA-9
Lyon, Samuel, (7 March 1789), Hanna Thomas         20 BA-1
Lyon, Samuel, 8 Aug. 1797, Linny Davis              5 MO-113
Lyondon, Jno., 13 June 1782, Lindy Beard           11 BA-5
Lyons, John, 6 Jan. 1784, Grace Miller              3 AA-420
Lyons, John, 24 Jan. 1797, Joanna Ragan            44 BA-2
Lyons, Thomas, 7 Aug. 1799, Mary Silverthorn        3 BA-375
Lyons, William, 10 March 1795, Rachel McCoy         5 BA-9


Mc-(?)-, Thomas, 5 Nov. 1795, by Rev. Joseph Wyatt; Elizabeth
  Foreman or Freeman                                4 AA
McAboy, Thomas, 21 Feb. 1797, Rachel Rilet          2 FR-1152
McAdam, James, 1 May 1794, Sarah Cottigan           3 HA-23
McAdue, Samuel, 1 Sept. 1795, Anne Spencer          3 BA-311
McAllister, Charles, 21 Oct. 1786, Ann Sampson     11 BA-9
  See also 3 BA-191.
McAtee, Francis X., 17 March 1787, Mary Reeder      4 FR
McAtee, George, 2 March 1799, Mary Hardy            4 FR
Macatee, Henry, 28 Jan. 1799, Theresa Wheeler       3 HA-28
McAtee, Ignatius, 17 Jan. 1798, Mary Magruder       4 FR
McAtee, Thomas, 3 Nov. 1778, Sarah Maddox           2 PG-2
McAtee, Thomas, 17 Oct. 1795, Jane Bradey           4 FR
McBride, Roger, 11 Feb. 1793, Mary Phile            3 BA-258
McBroom, Jno., 31 Jan. 1782, Karenhappuck Elltt    11 BA-5
McCabe, James, before 25 Nov. 1789 in Harford Co., Mary
  Golloher                                         20 BA-1
McCabe, Thomas, 18 Oct. 1796, Mary Neass            6 BA
McCabe, Thomas, 1 Jan. 1800, Constant Love Peacock  5 BA-11
McCafarty, Thom-s, 1789, Cath. Klein               50 BA-388
McCain, Wm., 25 Sept. 1780, Mary McDonnaugh         4 FR
McCaine, James, 24 Dec. 1793, Priscilla Davis      18 BA-6
```

```
McCallam, Duncan, 2 July 1797, Temperance Stokes        6 BA
McCalle, James, 17 June 1784, Betzie Berney            10 BA-182
McCallister, Daniel, 2 Jan. 1783, Sarah Brinsfield      2 DO
McCallister, Henry, 5 May 1781, Elizabeth Williams      2 DO
McCallister, Roger, 1 June 1781, Patience Tilghman      2 DO
McCallister, William, 20 Jan. 1781, Elizabeth Covey     2 DO
McCammon, Joseph, 30 Nov. 1793, Sarah Burk              5 BA-10
McCan, Jno., 4 Jan. 1790, Ann Johnson                  11 BA-13
McCandley?, John, 10 Feb. 1787, Jane Ewen               6 BA
     The groom's name may also be read as McCandhy.
McCannon, Jas., 24 Feb. 1780, Ann Worthington          11 BA-4
McCartee, Samuel, 23 Oct. 1787, Elizabeth Lane          2 DO
McCarter, Wm., 9 June 1780, Sarah Keith                11 BA-13
McCarty, Cornelius, 27 Sept. 1792, Sarah Pitcher        5 BA-10
McCarty, Darby, 1786, Ann Williamson                   50 BA-387
McCarty, James, 17 Aug. 1792, Barsheba Dean             2 DO
McCarty, John, 24 Nov. 1785, Elisabeth Sawbright        5 BA-10
McCarty, Owen, 8 April 1779, Eliz. Flannighan           5 HA
     3 HA-1 gives the date as 7 April 1780, and the bride's
     name as Flannagan.
McCarty, William, 5 Dec. 1790, Margaret Peasely         5 BA-10
McCauly, John, 18 Nov. 1798, by Rev. Ridgley; Ann Miller
     4 AA
McCauly, Thos., 26 Dec. 1779, Eleanor Gettero          11 BA-4
McCausland, Marcus, 2 Dec. 1784, Polly Presstman        6 BA
Macceney, Zacharias, 24 Feb. 1789, by Rev. Claggett; Martha
     Symmons                                            4 AA
McClain, Daniel, 2 March 1791, Anna Mosteller           4 FR
McClain, John, 14 Jan. 1782, Elizabeth Clarke           3 SM-60
McClain, John, 20 Sept. 1782, Ann Ardings               3 AA-418
McClain, John, 4 Aug. 1783, Eliz'th Yates               4 FR
McClain, Joshua, 3 Nov. 1796, Elizabeth Bennet          4 FR
McClain, William, 30 April 1790, Mary Brishe            4 FR
McClain, William, 2 May 1790, Mary Breusch              2 FR-1151
McClanan, John, 21 Dec. 1788, Ann MacGill               3 PG-255
McClaskey, James, 28 July 1790, Henrietta Riggs         2 FR-1151
McClaskey, James, 19 Nov. 1795, Elizabeth Meads         6 BA
McClaskey, John, 7 May 1797, Mary Wheeler               3 BA-344
McClasky, Joseph, 11 Sept. 1788, Else Jewce            10 BA-190
McClean, Andrew, 2 Dec. 1800, Esther Israel             2 BA-17
McClean, Daniel, 3 March 1791, Anna Marstellar          2 FR-1151
McClean, Joseph, 12 Jan. 1790, Sus. Gossling            2 FR-1151
McClean, Robert, 1 July 1790, H. Grove                 29 BA-1
McClean, Samuel, 19 Jan. 1797, Filey Hickman            4 KE-69
McCleary, Andrew, 1 Dec. 1800, Esther Israel            3 HA-30
     12 BA-37 gives the date as 2 Dec. 1800.
McClery, John, 7 March 1799, Sarah Hendrickson          3 AL-5
McCloskey, James, 28 July 1790, Henrietta Riggs         4 FR
McCloskey, Wm., 1 Feb. 1791, Hannah Hopsin              2 FR-1151
McClugher, James, 3 July 1778, Margaret Kelly          11 BA-1
McCollic, A., 11 May 1781, M. McDonnell                 3 HA-4
McCollister, David, 25 May 1791, Lucy Bradley           2 DO
McCollister, Jacob, 11 Aug. 1799, Peggy Young           2 DO
McCollister, James, 24 Dec. 1798, Elizabeth Rosell      2 DO
McCollister, Nathan, 5 June 1798, Nancy Jones?          2 DO
McCollister, Robert, 20 Aug. 1794, Mary Harper          2 DO
McCollister, William, 19 May 1791, Ann Trice            2 DO
McCollom, David, 27 Dec. 1778, Mary Crips               4 FR
McColm, Dennis, 21 July 1789, Ann Dunkin                6 BA
McColn, John, 13 Jan. 1796, Sarah Smith                 1 AL-53
McComas, Aaron, 7 July 1785, Margaret McClure           3 HA-9
McComas, Aaron, 19 Feb. 1798, Martha Gilbert            3 HA-27
McComas, Alexander, 19 April 1785, Clemency Presbury    3 HA-9
McComas, Aquila, 10 or 14 Jan. 1797, Martha Amoss       3 HA-25
McComas, Charles, 11 June 1800, Mary Gilbert            3 HA-29
     2 HA-352 gives date as 15 June 1800.
```

McComas, Daniel, 17 Oct. 1782, Martha Johnson   3 HA-7
McComas, Daniel, 18 Feb. 1796 (sic), Elizabeth Scott   3 HA-26
  See also 1 BA-7.
McComas, Edward D., 14 Nov. 1780, Sarah Selby   2 CH-454
McComas, Frederick, 17 Nov. 1789, Susanna Onion   1 BA-2
McComas, James, 3 Dec. 1781, Ann Amos   3 HA-5
McComas, James, 29 March 1794, Sarah Howard   1 BA-6
  3 HA-23 gives the date as 27 May 1794.
McComas, N. D., 23 July 1794, Elizabeth Connor   3 HA-23
McComas, Nathaniel, 5 June 1800, Susanna Bradford   3 HA-29
McComas, Nicholas Day, 24 July 1794, Elizabeth Onion   1 BA-6
McComas, William, 11 June 1785, Elizabeth Gilbert   3 HA-9
McComas, William, 14 Feb. 1797, Mary McComas   12 BA-370
McComsey, Robert, 18 April 1785, Catherine Warner   4 FR
McComesky, Moses, (6 Jan. 1790), Mary Bosley   15 BA-3
McComsy, Robert, 18 April 1785, Cath. Warner   2 FR-1151
McConchie, William, 25 Sept. 1777, Elizabeth Muncaster 2 CH-454
McConel, Alex'r, 17 Nov. 1789, M. Linton   29 BA-1
McCongall, Daniel, 7 Oct. 1799, Mary McLaughlin   3 HA-28
McConkey, James, 13 Dec. 1795, Agness Nichol   5 BA-10
McConkie, James, 5 Nov. 1795, Hetebilia Baylis   3 HA-24
McConnel, Jno., 27 June 1789, Christiana Karr   11 BA-12
McConnell, John, 16 June 1799, Sarah Leret   3 BA-372
McConnell, Samuel, son of Samuel and Ann, 2nd day, 11 mo.,
  1797, Frances Maulsby, dau. of David and Mary   1 SF
McConnikin, William, 9 Nov. 1793, Rachel Stevens   39 BA-1
McCormack, Thos., 9 Oct. 1798, Eleanor Walter   1 WO
McCormick, Francis, 31 Jan. 1799, Martha Moore   3 BA-367
McCormick, James, 14 June 1788, Nancy Moore   4 FR
  See also 2 FR-1151.
McCormick, Joh., 10 Aug. 1794, Elizabeth M'Cormick   3 WA-57
McCormick, John, 13 Aug. 1798, Jane Graydy   3 BA-362
McCorty, Darby, 28 May 1787, A. Williamson   29 BA-1
McCotter, Henry, 12 July 1791, Sarah Robertson   2 DO
McCotter, John, 26 Sept. 1786, Euphanar Bell   2 DO
McCoy, Charles, 24 Dec. 1795, by Rev. Ridgely; Elizabeth
  Pumphrey   4 AA
McCoy, James, 9 Feb. 1797, Eliz. Brown   5 MO-114
McCoy, John, 21 July 1790, Sarah Wade   5 BA-10
McCoy, John, 24 May 1794, Eliza Alley   18 BA-6
McCoy, Richard, 18 July 1796, Catherine Higan   3 BA-327
McCoy, Robert, 26 Feb. 1782, Hanna Pile   11 BA-5
McCoy, Robert, 9 Jan. 1797, Cassandra Cole   3 HA-25
McCoy, Wm., 30 May 1793, Rachel Joice   18 BA-5
McCoy, William, c.1799, by Rev. Stewart; Rachel Read   4 AA
McCracken, John, 4 Nov. 1784, Elizabeth Wood   4 FR
McCracken, John, 7 Nov. 1792, Sarah Smith   3 HA-22
  1 BA-5 gives the date as 12 Nov. 1792.
McCracken, Jno., 22 Jan. 1792, Ann Northermond (or
  Northerwood)   11 BA-5
McCray, Farquire, 22 April 1781, Susanna Ferguson   2 PG-5
McCray, John, 6 Oct. 1795, Mary Ellis   3 BA-311
McCrea, William, 1 Feb. 1792, Elizabeth Thompson   4 FR
McCready, Andrew, 31 Aug. 1796, Sarah Hopkins   3 SO
McCready, James, 26 July 1793, Nelly Holland   2 DO
McCready, John, 6 Sept. 1791, Rebecca Ellensworth   2 DO
McCreary, Nathaniel, 6 May 1794, Lane Corbin   6 BA
McCreddy, Isaac, 28 March 1797, Mathew White   2 SO
McCredy, Andrew, 29 Aug. 1796, Sarah Hopkins   2 DO
MacCreery, Thomas, 21 April 1792, Susanna Nelson   3 BA-256
McCreery, William, 16 Sept. 1785, Letitia Neilson   11 BA-8
McCubbin, John, 27 Dec. 1791, Polly Tudor   1 BA-4
Maccubbin, John H., 10 July 1790, by Rev. Cooper; Ann
  Gray   4 AA
McCubbin, Samuel, 6 Nov. 1797, by Rev. Ridgely; Frances
  Williams   4 AA

McCubbin, Thomas, 8 March 1778, Anne Lingan	4 MO-1
McCubbin, Zachariah, 22 Jan. 1778, Ann Ottay	11 BA-1
McCubbin, Zachariah, 17 March 1787, Marg't Brooke	11 BA-10
McCulloch, James, 27 April 1788, Margaret Bryan	2 DO
McCulloh, William, 27 Jan. 1797, Betsy Merchant	2 SO
McCullough, William, 4 Feb. 1796, Rachel Sheredine	3 HA-25
McCully, John, 26 Feb. 1800, Margaret Logan	6 BA
McCurdy, Hugh, 17 June 1794, Grace Allison	5 BA-10
McCurley, Patrick, 23 Feb. 1781, Sarah Webb	3 HA-3
McCusey, John, 19 Dec. 1782, Sarah Simpson	4 FR
McDade, Charles, 25 March 1796, Elizabeth Reed	4 FR
McDaid, James, 25 Nov. 1780, Mary Barnett	4 FR
McDaniel, David, 14 Jan. 1797, Elizabeth Carey	1 WO
McDaniel, David, 18 March 1800, Sebrew White	2 SO
McDaniel, Francis, 15 Aug. 1798, Elizabeth Hopkins	4 FR
McDaniel, John, 16 Dec. 1783, Mary Berry	11 BA-7
McDaniel, John, 3 May 1799, Rachel Smallwood	1 WO
McDaniel, Nathan, 7 May 1793, Milly Lowe	2 DO
McDermot, Thomas, 26 May 1799, Jane Cunningham	5 BA-11
McDermott, John, 18 Sept. 1797, Catherine Joyce	40 BA-3
McDermott, Thos., 2 May 1788, Etty Bryan	6 BA
McDoe, William, 21 Oct. 1793, Elizabeth Riddle	3 BA-275
McDonald, Andrew, 6 July 1785, Ruth Seabrook	11 BA-8
McDonald, Alexander, 19 June 1797, Polly Davis	3 BA-346
McDonald, Angus, 31 Dec. 1798, Annie Doyle	3 AL-5
McDonald, Francis, 20 July 1789, Eleanor Hamilton	4 FR
See also 2 FR-1151.	
McDonald, George, 8 May 1780, Catherine Sutherland	4 FR
McDonald, Hugh, 19 June 1778, Rebecca McDonald	11 BA-1
McDonald, James, 10 Oct. 1799, Elizabeth Schriner	4 FR
McDonald, Jno., 26 Jan. 1794, Barb. Baum	29 BA-5
McDonald, Jonathan, 15 Dec. 1782, Violetta Wedding	2 CH-454
McDonald, Joseph, 17 April 1778, Anna Neill	4 FR
McDonald, Joseph, 6 Feb. 1800, Sinah Dew	3 AL-6
McDonald, Michael, 20 April 1784, by Rev. Robison; Dinah	
Selman ⌐	11 BA-7
McDonald, William, 26 March 1796, Elizabeth Condon	4 FR
McDonalson, Joseph, 25 May 1778, Margaret Ross	11 BA-1
McDonell, Cornelius, 26 Sept. 1778, Unity Corbin	11 BA-1
McDonnell, John, 18 May 1798, Mary Hood	6 BA
McDorman, George, 3 March 1800, Rebecca White	2 SO
Mackdouall, Joseph, July 1787, Rachel Showels	2 FR-1151
McDowel, Hugh, 1792, Elizab. Bauer	50 BA-392
McDowel Thos., 25 Feb. 1798, Cath. Chesroe	29 BA-9
McDowell, John, 13 April 1779, Mary Willen	1 CA-2
McDugle, James, 28 June 1798, Sarah Richards	2 AL-701
McElderry, Thomas, 16 June 1787, Elizabeth Parks	17 BA-9
5 BA-10 gives the bride's name as Parker.	
McElderry, Patrick, 7 June 1789, Mary Clagett	3 PG-255
McElfresh, Charles, 25 Nov. 1789, Ann Smith	4 FR
McElfresh, David, 13 Dec. 1789, Lucey Neilson	4 FR
McElfresh, John, Jr., 4 May 1778, Rachel Dorsey	4 FR
McElfresh, John, 17 March 1780, Jane Cumming	4 FR
McElfresh, Joseph, 19 Jan. 1792, Sarah Howard	4 FR
McElfresh, Philip, 22 Feb. 1781, Lydia Griffith	4 FR
McElhenny, Michael, 2 April 1795, Cassandra Jones	7 BA-2
McElroy, James, 28 Sept. 1799, Sarah Winn	5 BA-11
McElroy, Patrick, 9 Feb. 1793, Prisey Thompson	4 FR
McElroy, William, 26 Feb. 1794, Elizabeth Hagerty	5 BA-10
McEntire, Alexander, 10 Feb. 1793, Nanny Chamberlane	4 FR
MacEttas, Luceas, 10 Oct. 1784, Catharina -(?)-	10 BA-182
McEvoy, James, 3 July 1800, Mary Anne Hickley	3 BA-387
McFaddin, James, 25 May 1783, Rebecca Sligh	11 BA-6
McFaden, Henry, 4 Aug. 1793, Bridget Murphy	6 BA
McFaden, John, 20 Dec. 1798, Priscilla Wilson	5 BA-10

```
McFall, John, 15 March 1796, Margaret Hayes          3 BA-321
McFeadon, William, 4 Aug. 1792, Ann Ellick           5 BA-10
McGalvain, John, 3 Dec. 1778, Eliz'th McKinley       4 FR
McGarey, Barnabas, 16 April 1796, Mary McGary        4 FR
McGaughy, Edward, 25 June 1799, Jane Wilson          3 BA-373
McGaully, John, 1 Dec. 1779, Catherine Gill          11 BA-4
McGehen, John, 29 July 1794, Ann Carroll             3 HA-23
McGill, Arthur, 12 Oct. 1778, Ann Stone              1 SM-137
McGill, John, 9 Nov. 1796, Martha Brazier            3 HA-25
     2 HA-349 gives the date as 10 Nov. 1796.
McGill, Patrick, 28 Nov. 1789, Eleanor West          4 FR
McGill, Robert, 28 April 1789, Eleanor Bell          2 PG-4
McGlachlan, Wm., 25 Aug. 1785, Isobel Primrose       6 BA
McGoneron, Thomas, 30 Aug. 1778, Mary Clark          1 MO-1
M'Gonogall, Rowland, 9 Oct. 1797, Araminthe DeBreelen 29 BA-8
McGookin, Dan'l, 15 June 1794, Eliz. Major           29 BA-5
McGowan, Sam'l, 15 June 1779, Agnes Griffey          4 FR
McGrath, David, 25 June 1800, Eliza Dorman           2 SO
McGrath, John, 14 Feb. 1797, Anne Smith              2 SO
     3 SO gives the date as 16 Feb. 1797.
McGroggen, Patrick, 27 Dec. 1794, Charlotte Owings   3 BA-296
McGuigan, Arthur, 1 Nov. 1796, Elizabeth Good        4 FR
McGuire, John, 27 Nov. 1782, Sarah Bailey            2 DO
McGuire, John, 1 Sept. 1797, Mary Rickard            4 FR
McGuire, John, 3 Aug. 1799, Rebecca Hurst            2 DO
McGuire, Nathan, 5 Aug. 1778, Anne Taylor            11 BA-1
McGuire, Patrick, 18 March 1780, Margaret Saunders   3 HA-1
McGuire, Roger, 22 Oct. 1795, Eleanor Casey          44 BA-1
McGuire, Thomas, 15 April 1779, Mary Stevenson       5 BA-9
McGuyre, John, 2 Dec. 1798, Hanner Shoff             4 FR
McGwinn, William, 27 Feb. 1797, Eliz'th Ransford     44 BA-2
McHarry, John, 1 April 1799, Margaret Fitzgibbon     3 BA-369
     3 BA-371 gives the date as 1 June 1799.
McHenry, Dennis, 28 Aug. 1797, Joyce Whilton         3 BA-349
M'Hiver, Daniel, 8 Aug. 1793, Sarah Ramsey           2 FR-1152
McIlvain, Andrew, 15 March 1778, Elizabeth Cloud     11 BA-1
Macimky, William, 19 Jan. 1789, Rebecca Treldrior    10 BA-192
McInnally, John, 7 July 1799, Grace Taylor           5 BA-11
McIntire, Alexand., 17 Feb. 1793, Nancy Chamberlane  2 FR-1152
McIntire, Daniel, 12 Sept. 1794, Margaret Weaver     4 FR
McIntire, John, 19 Jan. 1792, Mary Dunkin            4 FR
McIntire, Paul, 14 Oct. 1796, Deborah Yates          2 DO
McIntosh, Michael, 18 July 1795, Elizabeth Hickman   4 FR
Mackall, John, 9 April 1780, Sarah Lane              3 AA-416
Mackall, Levin, 24 Feb. 1784, Margaret Weems         3 AA-421
McKardile, Isaac, 8 April 1785, Sarah DeCoine        4 FR
McKardill, Isaac, 12 April 1785, Sarah De Coin       2 FR-1151
McKay, Benj'n, 17 Jan. 1797, Rebecca Briscoe         2 FR-1152
Mackbee, William, 25 April 1790, Jemima Grover       1 BA-2
McKeag, William, 8 Aug. 1797, Peggy Naley            3 BA-348
McKean, John, 4 April 1795, Ann Helm                 5 BA-10
MacKean, Peter, 6 Nov. 1792, Ann Hall                1 AL-52
Mackee, Alexander, 17 April 1794, Margaret Murray    3 BA-285
McKeel, Thomas, 25 Sept. 1783, Betsy Ross            2 DO
McKeen, Jas. (or Jos.), 10 Sept. 1798, Eliz. Wells   29 BA-2
Mackelfresh, Thomas, 30 Sept. 1784, Martha Phelps    10 BA-182
McKenley, Roger, 3 Sept. 1781, Elizabeth Johnson     3 HA-4
McKenly, Aaron, 11 Aug. 1789, Rachael Harp           11 BA-12
MacKenney, Alexander, 18 Feb. 1787, Margaret Kirshaw,
     dau. of Francis and Rebecca                     2 CA-113
McKenny, John, 23 Aug. 1793, Mary Hanna              3 HA-23
McKenny, Roddey, 8 Aug. 1790, Eliz. Hickenbothom     18 BA-2
McKenzee, James, 1 April 1781, Casandra Magruder     3 SM-59
McKenzie, Alexander, 8 Nov. 1781, Sarah Anderson     3 SM-59
McKenzie, Archibald, 24 May 1798, Elizabeth Doyle    3 BA-359
```

```
McKenzie, Benjamin, 30 June 1799, Rebecca Beetle         3 BA-373
McKenzie, Colin, 23 May 1799, Sarah Pinkerton            5 BA-11
McKenzie, Dan'l, 25 May 1799, Nancy Jones               29 BA-10
McKenzie, George, 22 Nov. 1798, Mary Jackson             3 BA-365
McKeough, Patrick, 7 Jan. 1792, Elizabeth Collins        4 FR
McKey, George, 26 Nov. 1799, Martha Dilworth             5 BA-11
Mackey, William, 4 Nov. 1786, Margaret Glover            2 DO
Mackie, Ebenezer, 30 July 1786, Ann Ashton              11 BA-9
McKim, Alexander, 20 July 1785, Cath. Sarah Davy        11 BA-8
McKim, Thomas Mc. (20 May 1789), Rosanna Mc(Ken)        15 BA-2
McKinley, Michael, 30 March 1800, Elisabeth Elbert       3 BA-384
McKinley, Neale, 2 Dec. 1794, Marg't King               44 BA-1
McKinlie, Robert, 18 Oct. 1792, Elizabeth McLaughlin     3 BA-257
McKinly, Joh., Aug. 1800, Nancy Lett                     3 WA-70
McKinsee, John, 11 Jan. 1792, Ann Strauble               5 BA-10
McKinsey, John, 4 Aug. 1795, Eliz'th Warner             44 BA-1
McKinzey, John, 20 March 1794, Solomy Tolbert            3 PG-439
McKinzey, John, 23 Feb. 1797, Elizabeth Bramble          2 DO
McKiver, Dan, 3 Aug. 1793, Sarah Ramsey                  4 FR
McKubbin, James, 5 Feb. 1795, Lydia Collins             44 BA-1
McLain, Hugh Charles, 17 May 1795, Mary French           3 BA-305
McLain, James, 15 Sept. 1785, Eliza Cowan               11 BA-8
McLane, Robert, 11 Oct. 1793, Elizabeth Wheeler          3 BA-275
McLaran, John, 26 Aug. 1792, Ann Taylor                  3 BA-257
McLaughlin, Charles, 6 Feb. 1799, Margaret Armstrong     2 HA-351
McLaughlin, Daniel, 11 Feb. 1779, Frances Debruler       5 HA
     3 HA-1 gives the date as 10 Feb. 1780.
McLaughlin, David, 6 Sept. 1794, Cassandra Steele        3 HA-23
McLaughlin, Dennis, 18 Dec. 1788, Mary Dawson            1 BA-1
McLaughlin, Patrick, 28 Sept. 1785, Catherine Campbell   3 HA-9
McLaughlin, Patrick, 8 Nov. 1798, Ann Chandley           2 HA-351
McLaughlin, Wm., 20 Feb. 1787, Mary Plowman             11 BA-10
McLaughlin, Wm., 23 May 1799, Lucy French                3 AL-5
McLean, Adam, 16 June 1799, Demaris Harry                3 BA-372
McLean, Alexander, 1 Nov. 1785, Kesiah Haslet            5 BA-10
McLellan, Jno., 4 Sept. 1783, Mary Hargan              ᴸ 11 BA-6
Maclevain, Alexander, 28 June 1791, Sarah Poutenay       5 BA-10
McLine, John, 6 Dec. 1798, Mary Ann Thornburgh           5 BA-10
McLinsey, Michael, 28 Feb. 1797, Mary Hackey             3 BA-342
McLuy?, George, 12 May 1793, Eleanor Read                6 BA
Macmachle, Joseph, 28 May 1797, Ann Masters              6 BA
McMahan, Charles, 9 Aug. 1788, Nancy Conner              2 DO
Macmahan, John, 10 Jan. 1782, Sarah Bartlett             1 TA-294
McMahan, Solomon, 25 Dec. 1798, Eliz'th Burridge         3 TA-324
     1 TA-308 states the bride was born 29 Sept. 1778, and
     was a dau. of William and Grace Berridge.
McMahon, James, 16 Dec. 1790, Jane Lilly                 3 BA-229
McMahon, James, 3 April 1796, Bridet Mahoney             3 BA-321
McMahon, Michael, 13 Dec. 1800, Elisabeth Boyd           3 BA-396
McMahon, William, 31 Dec. 1795, Sally Vanlear            1 AL-53
MacMas, Lucas, 26 July 1785, Cathrina Schmid            10 BA-184
McMasters, William, 30 June 1799, Anne Sadler            3 BA-373
McMath, Samuel, 19 June 1792, Mary Curry                 1 BA-4
McMath, William, 11 Dec. 1792, Sarah Moores              3 HA-22
     See also 1 BA-5.
McMechen, Hugh, 1 Nov. 1795, Amelia Hewett               3 BA-313
McMechen, Thomas, 21 July 1799, Sarah Raven              3 BA-374
McMechen, William, 20 Feb. 1800, Eleanor B. Armistead    3 BA-383
McMillan, Hugh, 5 May 1785, Mary Hicks                   2 FR-1151
McMillan, Wm., 11 Dec. 1800, Sally Counsil               6 BA
McMin, George, 3 March 1785, Sarah Campbell              2 FR-1151
     4 FR gives the groom's name as McMinn.
McMullan, James, 31 Oct. 1791, Jane Adair                2 WA-16
McMullen, John, 8 April 1791, Ann Unglesby               2 FR-1151
McMullen, Robert, 30 Oct. 1785, Ann Touchstone           3 HA-10
```

```
McMyers, John, 16 Jan. 1794, Elizabeth Pit          5 BA-10
McNair, John B., 26 July 1798, Mary Pumphrey        3 BA-361
McNamara, Gabriel, 11 Jan. 1790, Mary Wingate       2 DO
McNamara, Hugh, 14 March 1795, Anne Williams        3 BA-301
McNamara, John Stuart, 21 Jan. 1784, Lovey Lake     2 DO
McNamara, Patrick, 15 Aug. 1780, Sarah Gleson       3 BA-180
McNamee, John, 3 May 1788, Elizabeth Justice        5 BA-10
McNeal, John, 17 Dec. 1797, Hannah Mahn             2 FR-1152
McNeale, Archibald, 19 Oct. 1786, Sarah Whitmore    4 FR
McNear, George, 9 June 1797, Charlotte Little       4 KE-69
McNulty, William, 8 April 1795, Esther Cummins      2 DO
McPherson, Dan'l, 22 Sept. 1780, Kitty McKensey     11 BA-4
McPherson, Isaac, of Alexandria, Va., son of Daniel (dec.),
    and Mary, 1st day, 2 mo., 1793, Hannah Ellicott of
    Balto. Co., dau. of John and Leach (sic)        6 SF
McPherson, John, 25 June 1782, Elizabeth Readen     2 CH-454
McPherson, John, 12 May 1783, Elizabeth Thompson    2 CH-454
McPherson, John, 11 Sept. 1783, Sarah Smith         4 FR
McPherson, Thomas, 21 April 1795, Mary Tongue       3 AA-424
McPherson, William, 16 July 1782, Mary Smoot        2 CH-454
McQuillan, William, 30 Dec. 1780, Hester Cowman     3 AA-416
McReden, Abraham, 15 Aug. 1800, Rosanna Punteny     6 BA
McRoberts, Andrew, 17 March 1787, Nancy Garret      6 BA
McRire, William, 25 Dec. 1796, Rachel Warner        6 BA
McVicker, John, 26 Nov. 1795, Elizabeth Hazlewood   2 AL-700
McWilliams, John, 21 Feb. 1793, Elizab. Hagan       2 FR-1152
Mace, Edmund, 17 April 1797, Elizabeth King         2 DO
    1 DO-39 gives the date as 18 April 1797.
Mace, John, 16 July 1787, Elizabeth Brannock        2 DO
Mace, John, 4 Nov. 1787, Ann Nicholson              4 FR
Mace, Landon, 9 March 1796, Elizabeth Abbott        2 DO
Mace, Moses, 4 Nov. 1798, Chloe Jones               3 BA-365
Mace, Thomas, 9 May 1798, Dolly Wallace             2 DO
Mace, Thomas, 21 June 1800, Lydia Smith             2 DO
Mace, William, 30 Jan. 1781, Rachel Ross            2 DO
Mace, Wingate, 9 April 1795, Delilah Brannock       2 DO
Macher, Benjamin, 6 July 1800, Anna Catherine Kessler  9 BA-143
Mack, John, 22 March 1795, Mary Ann Brian           6 BA
Mackey, Robert, 30 April 1796, Sarah Ragan          4 FR
    2 FR-1152 gives the date as 1 May 1796.
Madden, James, 4 Aug. 1778, Rebecca Harrison        1 MO-1
Madden, James, 18 Jan. 1795, Elizabeth Chance       7 BA-2
Madden, Joseph, 14 Feb. 1781, Eliz'th Hillery       4 FR
Maddon, Dennis, 15 Sept. 1799, Mary Cumming         3 AL-6
Maddon, Jacob, 8 April 1780, Dolly Steward          4 FR
Maddon, John, 13 Dec. 1783, Margery Falconer        4 FR
Maddox, Benjamin, 23 Dec. 1782, Benedicta Fernandis 2 CH-454
Maddox, John, 22 April 1788, Martha Harris          2 CH-454
Maddox, John, 20 June 1779, Sarah Farnandis         2 CH-454
Maddox, Richard, 31 Dec. 1797, Hannah Franklin      6 BA
Maddox, Samuel, 9 July 1780, Ann Wardde             2 CH-454
Maddox, William, 21 Aug. 1794, Eliz. Hughes         18 BA-6
Maddox, William, 25 March 1797, Ann Hughes          6 BA
Maddux, William, 9 Dec. 1798, Leah Miles            2 SO
Madkin, Stanley, 29 Oct. 1788, Elizabeth Tregoe     2 DO
Madkins, Hill, 27 April 1792, Priscilla Dickeson    3 BA-258
Madera, Nicholas, 15 April 1786, Susanna Adamson    4 FR
Madon, Joseph, 25 Feb. 1781, Elizabeth Hilleary     2 PG-5
Magan, John, 22 March 1792, Sarah Hutchins          1 BA-4
Magens, Abraham, 6 Oct. 1796, Eliz. Frey            2 FR-1152
Maggs, Thomas, 1 Jan. 1797, Marg't Price            1 TA-323
Maginnis, John, 10 Aug. 1778, Hetty Moran           4 FR
Magness, James, 12 Aug. 1787, Hannah Wise           3 PG-253
Magness, James, 24 Dec. 1799, Ann Baxter            3 HA-29
Magness, John, 30 July 1799, Martha Norris          3 HA-28
```

```
Magness, William, 23 Dec. 1790, Sarah Waters        1 BA-3
Magnus, John, 1 Aug. 1799, Martha Morris           12 BA-370
Magowan, Walter, 28 Oct. 1780, Elizabeth Harrison   3 AA-416
Magrath, Bartholomew, 12 Dec. 1796, Mary Wilkinson  6 BA
Magruder, D. Ninian, 7 Oct. 1795, Lydia Beatty      4 FR
Magruder, Dennis, 30 Sept. 1779, Anne Contee        2 PG-2
Magruder, Isaac, 1 Feb. 1779, Sophia Baldwin        2 PG-2
Magruder, Jas., 10 Dec. 1799, Eliz. Linthicum       5 MO-116
Magruder, Jno., 5 Nov. 1799, Mary Linthicum         5 MO-116
Magruder, John R., 21 March 1799, Susanna M. Butler 4 FR
Magruder, Joseph, 25 June 1778, Cath. Flemming      2 MO-1
Magruder, Nath. B., 28 May 1797, Mary Bearins       3 AL-4
Magruder, Nathan, 15 Aug. 1790, Eliz. Bevin         2 PG-4
Magruder, Nathaniel, 4 May 1783, Mary Billingsley   2 CH-454
Magruder, Nathe. B., 1 June 1797, Mary Barnes       2 AL-700
Magruder, Zach., 10 Feb. 1797, Ann Dawson           3 AL-4
Mahan, William, 25 Nov. 1800, Agnes Jones           3 HA-30
Mahaney, Daniel, 10 July 1782, Elizabeth Baltzell   4 FR
Mahew, Brian, 15 April 1782, Ann Dossey             2 PG-3
Mahew, Sam'l, 18 Nov. 1786, Marg't Mackal          11 BA-10
Mahn, Adam, 14 Aug. 1791, Marg. Janzy               2 FR-1151
Maholl, Thomas, 13 Nov. 1796, Elizabeth Burnside    5 BA-10
Mahon, William, 27 Nov. 1800, Anne Jones            2 HA-352
Mahoney, Barnabas, 29 April 1796, Mary Reel         4 FR
Mahoney, Daniel, 1792, Juliet Smith                50 BA-392
Mahoney, James H., 6 Jan. 1794, Sarah Williams      4 FR
Mahoney, John, 21 Nov. 1790, Henny Brashears        4 FR
Mahony, Clement, 17 July 1780, Sarah Ann Oakley     2 CH-454
Mahony, Thomas, 8 June 1796, Sarah Cashman         29 BA-7
Maidwell, Alex'r, 27 April 1795, Eliz. Winick      29 BA-6
Maidwell, Alexander, 18 June 1795, Catherine Summerman?
   6 BA
Maidwell, Jas. (or Jos.), 23 Feb. 1797, Rachel Bennix  29 BA-8
Maidwell, John, 24 May 1798, Ann Green              6 BA
Main, Henry, 18 Oct. 1787, Mary Berries Ford        3 PG-253
Mainard. Ezra, 28 Oct. 1800, Hannah Robertson       2 FR-1152
Mainster, Jacob, 1 Dec. 1796, Mary Gardiner        29 BA-8
Major, John, 14 Nov. 1784, Barbara Mayer           10 BA-182
Major, ·John, 22 March 1797, Sarah Rawley           2 DO
Malcolm, John, 30 July 1789, Elizabeth Douglas      3 BA-227
Malcomb, Thomas, 1780, Bridget Henson               3 SO
Males, John, 8 June 1794, Catherine Wease           4 BA-76
Maley, Patrick, 11 Nov. 1792, Grasey Nickell        3 BA-257
Mallet, Wm., 21 Nov. 1784, Sophia Randall          11 BA-8
Malloy, Patrick, 11 Nov. 1792, Gressey Nickell      3 BA-258
Malone, Barth. Murphy, 27 Dec. 1795, Lydia Bradie   2 FR-1152
Malone, Hugh, 8 June 1779, Ann Cox                  5 HA
Malone, Hugh, 7 June 1780, Ann Coy                  3 HA-2
Malone, William, 5 Nov. 1779, Frances Coslee        2 SO
Maloney, Dan'l, 18 May 1795, Mary Lydia (sic)      29 BA-6
Maloney, John, (28 June 1788), Lucy Belt           15 BA-1
Maloney, Peter, 9 Oct. 1785, Villey Aston          11 BA-8
Man, Vert, 16 Aug. 1795, Susanna McCarty           50 BA-398
Manchan, John, 24 Dec. 1793, Mary Hains             2 FR-1152
Manders, Basil, 5 July 1781, Mary Piles             2 PG-5
Mangard, George, 6 June 1795, Katy Hawz             3 WA-59
Manies, Joseph, 13 Oct. 1791, Elizabeth Aber        6 BA
Manix, Timothy, 10 Feb. 1782, Bridget Spellice     11 BA-5
Mankin, Isaiah, 16 Jan. 1800, Nancy H. Gardner      6 BA
Manley, William, 8 Jan. 1789, Sarah Brown           3 PG-255
Manly, John, 26 March 1799, Patty Crew              3 BA-369
Mann, Friedh., 23 April 1797, Nancy Camel          50 BA-401
Mann, Georg, 12 April 1796, Maria Gabhart           3 WA-60
Mannell, James, 5 Sept. 1799, Mary Doly             3 BA-377
Mannen, Joseph, 17 Nov. 1785, Mary Gone             6 BA
```

Manning, Abraham, 20 Feb. 1784, Jane Barker   3 AA-421
Manning, Anthony, 15 Nov. 1794, Sarah White   2 DO
Manning, Jno., 5 June 1786, Ann McGuinnis   11 BA-9
Manning, Joseph, 15 March 1780, Elizabeth Dunnington   2 CH-454
Manning, Nathaniel, 5 May 1798, Betsy McGuire   2 DO
Manro, Nathan, 6 Nov. 1788, Catherine Welsh   19 BA-3
Mansell, George, 5 Nov. 1784, Ann West Lawrence   4 FR
Mansfield, Thomas, 24 Feb. 1796, Elizabeth Lawrance   4 BA-78
Manson, William, 3 Aug. 1797, Catharine Daugherty   3 BA-348
Mansparager, Daniel, 25 Aug. 1794, Catherine Hyne   4 FR
Mantz, David, 27 Oct. 1782, Elizabeth Miller   4 FR
Mantz, John, 25 June 1796, Susanna Krugg   4 FR
Mantz, Major Peter, 23 April 1778, Catherine Hauer or
    Howard   4 FR
Marater, John, 1 Aug. 1798, Elizabeth Nicholson   4 FR
Marcan, James, 24 Dec. 1795, Mary Gardner   50 BA-398
Marchant, John, 31 March 1796, Elizabeth Harrison   3 BA-321
Marche, John, 5 June 1794, Hannah Onion   1 BA-6
Marger, William, 17 Jan. 1793, Mary Anderson   3 BA-258
Margrader, Lacanah, 13 Feb. 1797, Ann Dawson   2 AL-700
Marica, William, 1 Nov. 1778, Ruth Duvall   2 PG-3
Marine, William, 4 Dec. 1787, Mary Fletcher   2 DO
Mariner, Joseph, 8 May 1796, Mary Rappold   29 BA-7
Markel, Adam, 18 Sept. 1779, Mary Dickensheets   4 FR
Markell, William, 24 Feb. 1781, Mary Boyer   4 FR
Marker, Daniel, 6 May 1797, Christena Beckenbaugh   4 FR
Marker, Henry, 28 Feb. 1780, Clory Shotts   4 FR
Markey, David, 19 March 1796, Catherine Hummel   4 FR
Markin, Sam'l, 30 Oct. 1780, Rachel Larkin   4 FR
Markle, George, 7 Dec. 1796, Catherine Smith   4 FR
Markley, Gabriel, 3 or 8 Jan. 1782, Cathe. Dickensheets 4 FR
Markley, John, 24 July 1791, Susannah Reidenour   2 WA-16
Marks, Henry, 8 Sept. 1793, Mary King   6 BA
Marlow, Edward, 27 Sept. 1791, Rebeckah Rice   4 FR
Marlow, Horatio, 9 Aug. 1794, Elizabeth Burgee   4 FR
Marlow, Samuel, 19 Jan. 1797, Mary Richards   3 PG-442
Marlow, Thomas, 14 Dec. 1789, Elizabeth Grazier   4 FR
Marlow, William Berry, 18 Feb. 1796, Delilah Strong   3 PG-442
Marr, Francis, 26 June 1787, by Rev. Reed; Mary Ross   4 AA
Marr, Joshua, before 30 Nov. 1779, Joanna Speak   2 PG-1
Marr, Thomas, 20 June 1779, by Rev. Magowan; Barbara Poole
    4 AA
Marr, Walter, 13 May 1783, Ann Ross   3 AA-419
Marr, William, 17 June 1784, Arey Owings   3 BA-188
Marriett, Thomas, 11 Feb. 1800, by Rev. Roberts; Elener
    White   4 AA
Marriott, Caleb, 17 Dec. 1797, by Rev. Ridgely; Margaret
    Wheeler   4 AA
Marriott, Ephraim, 14 Feb. 1795, by Rev. Ridgely; Mary
    Chaney   4 AA
Marriott, James, 2 Dec. 1792, by Rev. G. Ridgely; Rachel
    Waters   4 AA
Marriott, Joseph, 27 March 1796, by Rev. Ridgely; Rebeckah
    Iiams   4 AA
Marriott, Joshua, 3 Jan. 1793, by Rev. G. Ridgely; Anne
    Waters   4 AA
Marriott, Komward (sic), 24 March 1799, Mary Ridgely   4 AA
Marriott, Thomas, 28 Jan. 1796, by Rev. Ridgely; Mary
    White   4 AA
Marsh, Beal, 2 May 1797, Eleanor Corbin   29 BA-8
Marsh, Clement, 17 Jan. 1799, Jemima Elliot   1 BA-9
Marsh, David, 15 Jan. 1791, Nancy Bosley   6 BA
Marsh, John, 3 May 1784, Cathe. Hewit   11 BA-7
Marsh, John, 15 March 1797, Nancy Gale   4 KE-70
Marsh, Nath'l, 28 Feb. 1782, Ann Miller   11 BA-5

```
Marsh, Philip, 12 May 1797, Polly Selby              1 WO
Marsh, Richard, c.1792, by Rev. Hutchinson; Sarah Delauder
  4 AA
Marsh, William, 26 June 1783, Lurana Ashley         11 BA-6
Marsh, William, c.1798, by Rev. Riggin; Martha Smith  4 AA
Marsh, Wm., 14 Aug. 1799, Ann Naylor                29 BA-10
Marshall, Alex'd'r, 30 Dec. 1799, Susanna Pearl      4 FR
Marshall, Andrew, 24 Sept. 1787, Ann Frazier         2 DO
Marshall, Benjamin, 5 April 1791, Kitty Keese        2 DO
Marshall, Daniel, 18 Jan. 1794, Sarah LeCompte       2 DO
Marshall, Elijah, 24 Aug. 1789, Nancy Smith          2 DO
Marshall, Elijah, 12 Sept. 1797, Mary Tregoe         2 DO
Marshall, Elijah, 24 Nov. 1797, Cassy Seward         2 DO
Marshall, Ephraim, 30 July 1798, Polly Noble         2 SO
Marshall, Henry, 18 Nov. 1779, Mary Dowell           3 AA-415
Marshall, Henry, 14 April 1798, Eve Rothrock         3 BA-357
Marshall, Isaac, 5 Feb. 1798, Polly Collyer          1 WO
Marshall, James, 16 Aug. 1799, Nancy Jones           2 DO
Marshall, John, 25 April 1781, Sarah Soward          2 DO
Marshall, John, 26 May 1787, Johanna Douglas         2 CH-454
Marshall, John, 27 Dec. 1787, Rachel Wigfield        3 PG-253
Marshall, John, 10 Dec. 1788, Lina Lee               2 DO
Marshall, John, 9 Feb. 1790, Eliz. Fendal Fry Ford   3 PG-256
Marshall, John, 13 May 1800, Mary Dean               2 DO
Marshall, John D., 9 May 1793, Delilah Purnell       1 SO-210
Marshall, Joseph, 9 Jan. 1794, Elizabeth Proctor     6 BA
Marshall, Josias, 13 April 1797, Sarah Harriss       3 PG-443
Marshall, Levin, 30 April 1785, Rosanna Stokes       2 DO
Marshall, Levin, 13 Dec. 1790, Mary Hooper           2 DO
Marshall, Nicholas, 4 Sept. 1799, Keziah Arnold      2 DO
Marshall, Richard, 5 March 1782, Margaret Handy      2 PG-3
Marshall, Samuel, 11 Jan. 1798, Elizabeth McGeihan   4 FR
Marshall, Skinner, 4 July 1797, Margaret Bennett     1 DO-39
Marshall, Thomas, 6 Dec. 1782, Sarah Maddox          2 CH-454
Marshall, Thomas, 24 Dec. 1789, Sarah Soward         2 DO
Marshall, Thomas, 29 Oct. 1795, Ann Clagett          3 PG-441
Marshall, Thomas, 7 Sept. 1796, Britania Robinson    2 DO
Marshall, Valliant, 31 Oct. 1789, Nancy Willoughby   2 DO
Marshall, William, 22 Jan. 1781, Elizabeth Hanson    2 CH-454
Marshall, William, 19 Dec. 1790, Louisa Brent        5 BA-10
Marshall, Zadock, 25 Nov. 1796, Peggy Costen         1 WO
Marsham, James, 23 Oct. 1779, Rebecca Gordon         2 PG-3
Marston, Thomas, 15 Aug. 1800, Nancy Olders          6 BA
Mart, Christian, 24 March 1793, Magd. Helbort        2 FR-1152
Martheny, Wm., 7 Nov. 1791, Uness Eastburn           4 FR
Martin, Andrew, 23 July 1799, Elizabeth Evatt        3 HA-28
  2 HA-351 gives the date as 24 July 1799, and the
  bride's name as Evett.
Martin, Andrew, 20 May 1800, Elizabeth Boyse         8 BA-1
Martin, Charles, 4 Feb. 1800, Rachel Black           6 BA
Martin (or Mastin), Cornelius, 17 Dec. 1799, Jane Kennedy
  6 BA
Martin, David, 1 Dec. 1789, Catherine Reible         4 FR
Martin, Edward, 15 April 1798, Elizabeth Dawson      2 AL-701
Martin, Elijah, 21 Dec. 1780, Mary Tall              2 DO
Martin, Elijah, 21 June 1786, Sarah Chapman          2 DO
Martin, Elijah, 20 Feb. 1792, Bazy Adams             2 DO
Martin, George, 31 May 1795, Ann Jackson             5 BA-10
Martin, George, 15 April 1798, Elizabeth Davis       4 FR
Martin, H. A., 12 Feb. 1782, Elizabeth Boswell       2 CH-454
Martin, Henry, 2 June 1785, Mary Moore              11 BA-8
Martin, Isaac, 27 Aug. 1785, Sarah Dudley           16 BA-3
Martin, Jacob, 18 Jan. 1783, Elizabeth Tabler        4 FR
Martin, Jacob, 28 Oct. 1799, Catherine Koontz        4 FR
Martin, James, 8 Sept. 1794, Sarah Rouse             3 BA-293
```

```
Martin, James, 22 May 1800, Araminta Hart            3 BA-386
Martin, John, 18 Feb. 1787, Anna Barb. Finfrock, widow 2 FR-1151
Martin, John, 24 May 1787, Lydia Hickman             2 CH-454
Martin, John, 19 Sept. 1795, Peggy Rhinehart         4 FR
Martin, John, 20 Feb. 1799, Elizabeth Correll        4 FR
Martin, John, 18 June 1799, Betsy Lindsay            3 BA-372
Martin, John, 4 June 1800, Margaret Townsley         3 HA-29
Martin, Joseph, 22 Dec. 1783, Elisabeth Foy         10 BA-178
Martin, Peter, 1 Feb. 1783, Fanny King              11 BA-6
Martin, Peter, 2 June 1796, Lydia Ramey              4 FR
Martin, Richard, 2 Jan. 1780, Ann Russell            2 PG-3
Martin, Samuel, 25 Dec. 1796, Annia Peacock          3 PG-442
Martin, Thomas, 23 March 1788, Milcah, dau. of Rev. Thomas
   Airey                                             1 TA-298
Martin, Tristram, 13 May 1799, Mary Oldham           1 TA-325
Martin, William, 26 April 1779, Margaret Crawley     5 BA-9
Martin, William, 3 Feb. 1780, Anne Thompson          3 SM-58
Martin, Wm., 3 Sept., 1780, Catherine Laybold       11 BA-4
Martin, William, 13 April 1784, Mary Ingram         11 BA-7
Martin, William, 17 June 1795, Nancy Mahoney         3 BA-305
Martin, William, 18 July 1800, Rebecca Geoghegan     2 DO
Martin, Zephaniah, 30 Dec. 1795, Sarah Eliz'th Ferd.
   Robinson                                          3 PG-441
Martini, Henrich, 9 May 1787, Margareth Beckin       1 FR-1
Martz, Peter, 9 Nov. 1783, Eliz'th Shroiner          4 FR
Martz, Peter, 26 Oct. 1785, Mary Horine              4 FR
Maryartie, Jacob, 21 June 1796, Susanna Schoen       2 FR-1152
Maslin (or Mastin), Francis, 10 Jan. 1778, Charity Cooksey
   4 CH-1
Mason, Abram, 19 Sept. 1782, Sarah Hays             11 BA-5
Mason, Archibald, 1 Dec. 1793, Mary Conner           2 FR-1152
Mason, Benja., 14 Aug. 1784, Sus'a Newman           11 BA-7
Mason, Benjamin, 9 Dec. 1797, Sarah Cooper           3 BA-353
Mason, Edward, 10 Oct. 1787, Mary Evans              6 BA
Mason, Geo., 12 March 1799, Mary Taylor             29 BA-10
Mason, James, son of George and Jane, 2nd day, 3 mo.,
   1780, Rachel Scott, dau. of Abraham and Elizabeth 1 SF
Mason, James, 27 April 1796, Betsey Terry            2 DO
Mason, John, 10 Sept. 1789, Ann Condon               1 BA-2
Mason, John, 5 March 1797, Sarah Reding              3 BA-342
Mason, Lot, 12 Jan. 1780, Sally Haselip              2 CH-454
Mason, Martin, 25 June 1796, Margaret Leonard        4 FR
Mason, Richard, 13 Oct. 1792, Mary Stear             6 BA
Mason, Thomas, 25 Dec. 1798, Sarah Davis             6 BA
Mass, Adam, 24 Jan. 1796, Nancy Dyer                50 BA-398
Massen, Hyland, 20 Dec. 1798, Susannah Murphy       50 BA-404
Massey, John, 24 Nov. 1798, Ann Brickhead            3 HA-27
Massey, Noah, 7 June 1797, Rebecca Toulson           4 KE-70
Massey, Robert, 3 May 1782, Sarah Warren             2 CH-454
Masters, Ezekiel, 13 Sept. 1789, Casandra Norton     3 PG-255
Masters, John, 7 June 1778, Priscilla Bayne          2 PG-3
Masters, Joshua, 3 April 1791, Elizabeth Selbey      3 PG-257
Masters, Thomas, 6 Oct. 1796, Elizabeth Ball         6 BA
Mastres, Nathan, 14 Jan. 1794, Winifirt Jinkins      3 PG-439
Matern, Philip, 22 Sept. 1791, Barb. Thomas          2 FR-1151
Matham, John, 1790, Rachel Gee; blacks              50 BA-389
Mathany, Daniel, 16 May 1799, Frances Bean           4 SM-184
Mather, Jno., 11 May 1789, Kitty Neale              11 BA-12
Mathern, Philip Mich's., 13 Aug. 1791, Barbara Thomas 4 FR
Mathers, Thomas, 28 March 1793, Eliz. Cummings       2 FR-1152
Mathers, William, 6 June 1799, Anne Farris           6 BA
Mathews, Josiah, 19 Jan. 1792, Jane Forwood          1 HA-396
Mathews, Roger, 9 Oct. 1800, Constant Forwood        3 HA-30
Mathiot, George, son of Jno. M., of Lancaster Co., Penna.,
   31st day, 10 mo. 1787, Ruth Davis, dau. of Joshua 6 SF
```

```
Mathison, John, 15 March 1799, Mary Gilberthorp        3 BA-369
Matkins, Levin, 18 March 1799, Molley Todd             2 DO
Matthew, Jacob, 20 April 1794, Sophia Strubel          2 FR-1152
Matthews, Bennet, 1 Dec. 1778, Eliz. Wilmot            5 HA
Matthews, Carvel, 25 Jan. 1796, Nancy Matthews         3 HA-24
    2 HA-349 gives the date as 28 Jan. 1796.
Matthews, Daniel, son of Daniel and Ann, 6th day, 4 mo.,
    1779, Mary Rowls, dau. of Hezekiah and Elizabeth   1 SF
Matthews, Daniel, son of Thomas (dec.), and Rachel, 7th day,
    2 mo., 1788, Susanna (Thatcher) Bartlett, widow of John
    Bartlett, and dau. of Richard and Abigail Thatcher, dec.,
    of Kennet Twp., Chester Co., Penna.                4 SF-185
Matthews, Edw'd, 1 Jan. 1782, Sarah Tracy             11 BA-5
Matthews, Eli, son of Thomas and Rachel, 30th day, 4 mo.,
    1800, Mary Cooper, dau. of Thomas and Catherine    1 SF
Matthews, Francis, 13 Dec. 1799, Margaret O'Donnell    3 BA-381
Matthews, Jacob, 14 Dec. 1798, Mary Boyds              4 FR
Matthews, Jacob, 8 Oct. 1799, Susannah Lowman          4 FR
Matthews, Jesse, 30 July 1792, Ann Conn                3 HA-21
    1 BA-4 gives the date as 1 Aug. 1792.
Matthews, Jesse, son of Thomas and Rachel, 29th day, 1 mo.,
    1794, Milcah Belt, dau. of Richard and Ketura      1 SF
Matthews, John, son of Thomas and Rachel, 8th day, 12 mo.,
    1790, Leah Price, dau. of Aquila and Ann           1 SF
Matthews, John, son of Thomas and Rachel, 8th day, 9 mo.,
    1794, Martha Yarnall                               1 SF
Matthews, John, son of Thomas and Rachel, 18th day, 9 mo.,
    1794, Martha (Edmondson) Yarnall, widow of Uriah
    Yarnall, and dau. of Joshua and Mary Edmondson     4 SF-203
Matthews, John, 1 June 1796, Susannah Kelly            6 BA
Matthews, Josiah, 16 Jan. 1792, Jane Forwood           3 HA-21
Matthews, Levin, 26 May 1798, Charlotte Willis         1 WO
Matthews, Oliver, son of William and Ann, 28th day, 11 mo.,
    1798, Phebe Wright, dau. of Jonathan and Susanna   1 SF
Matthews, Peter, 6 Feb. 1795, Mary Harris              4 FR
Matthews, Roger, 23 Nov. 1783, Elizabeth Maxwell       3 HA-8
Matthews, Roger, 16 Oct. 1800, Constant Forwood        2 HA-352
Matthews, Samuel, son of George and Dorothy, 1st day, 12
    mo., 1779, Ann Price, dau. of Mordecai and Rachel  1 SF
Matthews, Thomas, 24 Dec. 1780, Anna Poston            1 CH-205
Matthews, Thomas, 2 Feb. 1795, Anne Gill               3 BA-299
Matthews, Wm., 17 March 1779, Catherine Burchell       4 FR
Matthews, William, 9 April 1786, Elizabeth Shorters    3 BA-191
Matthews, William, son of Oliver and Hannah, 2nd day, 1 mo.
    1794, Elizabeth Hanway, dau. of Thomas and Elizabeth
    1 SF
Matthews, William, 21 Feb. 1797, Ebby Mills            2 SO
Matthews, Wm. P., 3 Oct. 1794, Eliza Sterett           5 BA-10
Matthias, Joh., 17 Nov. 1797, Gertraud Hasselbach     50 BA-402
Mattick, Gottfried, March 1799, Sus. Miller            3 WA-66
Mattingly, Edw'd, 17 Sept. 1779, Martha Syms           7 CH-1
Mattingly, John, 11 Sept. 1796, Onea Arnold            1 AL-53
Mattingly, Ralph, 29 Dec. 1788, Winifred Higdon        2 CH-454
Mauan, Daniel, 25 Dec. 1791, Dorothea Schnatter        2 WA-17
Mauder, William, 24 July 1783, Lavinia Walter          2 DO
Maugins, Matthias, 9 March 1792, Mary Frey             4 FR
Maulsby, Maurice, 22 March 1792, Eleanor Maulsby       3 HA-21
    See also 1 BA-4.
Maulsby, John, son of David and Mary, 21st day, 2 mo. 1781, Mary
    Starr, dau. of John and Mary                       3 SF
Maund, J. James, 13 July 1789, Lucy Carter            29 BA-1
Maurer, Martin, 26 June 1796, Marg. Lenhardt           2 FR-1152
Maurer, Peter, 2 March 1799, Marg. Hosselbach         29 BA-10
Maurer, Peter, 24 March 1799, Catherine Foltz          9 BA-142
Maxwell, Jacob, 25 May 1795, Eleanor Eliz'th Wilmer    3 HA-24
    7 BA-2 gives the date as 28 May 1795.
```

Maxwell, James, 12 Dec. 1782, Ann Grant   11 BA-6
Maxwell, John, 28 Jan. 1792, by Rev. Dorsey; Sarah Stinch-
  comb   4 AA
Maxwell, Moses, 10 Dec. 1793, Sally Charity Bond   1 BA-6
Maxwell, Moses, 7 March 1796, Ann Wilmer   3 HA-25
  7 BA-3 gives the date as 10 March 1796.
Maxwell, Thomas, 24 Oct. 1786, Mary Stickle   4 FR
  2 FR-1151 gives the bride's name as Steckel.
May, Benja., 31 Dec. 1781, Marg't Councilman   11 BA-5
May, Frantz P., 22 Dec. 1791, Cath. Gross   2 FR-1151
May, Henry, 7 Jan. 1778, by Rev. Love; Elizabeth Brooks 4 AA
May, James, 26 Sept. 1799, Sarah Corbett   3 BA-378
May, Richard, 24 Jan. 1780, Mary Pitman   4 CH-3
May, Thomas, 27 Dec. 1781, Cathrine Biamer   3 BA-182
Mayberry, Jesse, 10 Oct. 1792, Mary Houser   4 FR
Maycock, William, 5 Sept. 1784, Phebe Miles   3 BA-189
Mayer, Heinrich, 15 Nov. 1784, Cathrine Gardner   10 BA-182
Mayhew, Elisha Norton, 1 Nov. 1795, Elizabeth West   6 BA
Mayhew, John Love Wm., 26 Feb. 1778, Eliza Self   2 MO-1
Mayhew, William, 7 Jan. 1790, Eleanor McKenzie   3 BA-227
Maynadier, Henry, 26 July 1781, Eliza Key   3 AA-417
Maynard, Henry, 21 Dec. 1788, Elenor Howard   2 FR-1151
Mayo, George, 23 Sept. 1791, Eleanor Jones   2 DO
Mayo, Thomas, son of Thomas, 13 June 1790, Anne Evans,
  dau. of David   2 AA-114
Mead, Horatio, 3 Feb. 1784, Catherine Whittington   3 AA-420
Meads, Benjamin, 13 April 1797, Margaret Jessop   6 BA
Meads, Mordecai, 20 Nov. 1799, Mary Baker   3 HA-28
Meak, William, 4 Aug. 1785, Mary Gold   11 BA-8
Meakins, Joseph, 30 Sept. 1799, Milley Johnson   2 DO
Meaks, William Bell, 21 March 1792, Lydia James   3 BA-255
Meale, Samuel, 25 April 1791, Kessia Cross   3 BA-229
Measel, Frederick, Jr., 11 June 1794, Rosanna Frey   4 FR
Measell, Jacob, 5 Aug. 1780, Eleanor Boogher   4 FR
Medcalf, Edward, 11 Feb. 1796, Cloe Butt   5 MO-113
Medcalf, Hesekiah, 17 March 1793, Clarissa Lindon   2 FR-1151
Meddis, Godfrey, 5 June 1798, Polly Walker   2 DO
Medford, Charles, 27 Aug. 1800, Ruth Perry   2 DO
Medford, George, 22 April 1798, Araminta Anizer   4 KE-70
Medford, James, 26 April 1796, Amelia Henry   2 DO
Medford, John, 15 March 1796, Margaret Brodess   2 DO
Medford, Peter, 25 Jan. 1797, Betsey Medford   2 DO
Medford, William, 1 Jan. 1791, Charlotte Grainger   2 DO
Medley, Henry, 7 Feb. 1779, Margaret Ford   1 SM-137
Medley, Isaac, 7 March 1797, Mary Peters   2 FR-1152
Medlicat, Samuel, 26 Sept. 1796, Anne Carter   3 BA-329
Medlicoat, Sam'l, 24 Sept. (1796), Ann Carter   29 BA-7
Meed, Samuel, 6 Dec. 1794, by Rev. Joseph Wyatt; Ann
  Richardson   4 AA
Meek, Christopher, 20 March 1792, Betsey Summers   4 FR
Meek, David, 17 March 1793, by Rev. G. Ridgely; Anne Bos-
  tick   4 AA
Meek (or Meck), Western, 13 Nov. 1800, by Rev. Ridgely;
  Susanna Perkins   4 AA
Meekins, Abraham, 12 April 1797, Elizabeth Pool   2 DO
Meekins, Dennis, 22 April 1784, Mary Meekins   2 DO
Meekins, Henry, 14 Aug. 1781, Elizabeth Meekins   2 DO
Meekins, John, 12 April 1796, Charlotte Dunnock   2 DO
Meekins, John Denwood, 23 April 1796, Mary Meekins   2 DO
Meekins, John Pritchett, 18 Jan. 1800, Eleason Meekins 2 DO
Meekins, Joseph, 11 Aug. 1791, Sarah Busick   2 DO
Meekins, Joshua, 5 Feb. 1795, Jemima Hall   2 DO
Meekins, Mark, 13 June 1799, Sally Shenton   2 DO
Meekins, William, 11 Sept. 1797, Elizabeth Busick   2 DO
  1 DO-39 gives the date as 21 Sept. 1797.

```
Meekins, William, 23 May 1800, Keziah Creighton        2 DO
Meeks, William, 4 Feb. 1797, Temperance Wood           4 KE-69
Meelhouse, John, 7 Feb. 1786, Polly Taylor             4 FR
Meem, Jno., 25 Aug. 1795, Martha Moore                29 BA-6
Megarrity, Thomas, 27 Feb. 1798, Elisabeth Gray        5 BA-10
Mein, Michael, 4 Aug. 1794, Catharina Noppa           10 BA-196
Meiner, John, 29 Nov. 1796, Mary Kuhl                  2 FR-1152
Melcher, Philip, 6 Sept. 1789, Esther Fluck           2 FR-1151
Meldrum, James, 12 Dec. 1787, Hannah Cook              3 BA-203
Mellinger, Georg, 20 Nov. 1796, Maria Forbech         50 BA-400
Melone, Alexander, 8 April 1798, Mary Jennings         3 BA-357
Meloy, John, 29 June 1793, Anna Decker                 4 FR
Melvell, Alexander, 10 June 1780, Elioner Evans        3 BA-180
Melvin, John, 24 Nov. 1800, Mary Redden                1 WO
Melvin, William, 30 Sept. 1800, Sarah Tull             1 WO
Menace, Robert, 18 April 1783, Eleanor Young           2 CH-454
Menas, Robert, 27 Nov. 1788, Hannah Coe                6 BA
Mencer, George, 24 April 1792, Eliz. Cramer           29 BA-3
Mennot, William, 1786, Eliz. Sparrow; blacks; married
    by permission of their masters                    50 BA-387
Menser, John, 20 Dec. 1791, Catharina Solomon          2 WA-17
Menson, Gabriel, 15 June 1795, Margaret Deiter         3 BA-305
Mercer, Benja. James, 18 May 1790, Anna Stophel       11 BA-13
Mercer, John, 11 June 1799, Elizabeth Pierpoint        3 BA-372
Mercer, Peregrine, 18 Feb. 1786, Rebecca Dorsey       11 BA-9
Merchant, James, 7 March 1798, Elizabeth Mullikin      3 TA-324
Merchant, John, 22 Dec. 1798, Nancy Hudson             1 WO
Merchant, John, 2 June 1799, Sabery Smith              1 TA-325
Merchant, William, before 12 Dec. 1792, by Rev. John
    Long; Eliza Jefferson                              4 AA
Mercier, Luke, 22 Dec. 1800, Nancy Liddid              6 BA
Mercier, Richard, 9 May 1779, Cassandra Tevis         14 BA-1
    5 BA-9 gives the date as 9 May 1772, and the bride's
    name as Jevis.
Meredith, Absalom, 14 May 1798, Mary Cyus              4 KE-70
Meredith, Davis, 9 Nov. 1800, Ann Pritchard            2 AL-701
Meredith, Norris, 19 Aug. 1790, Mary Norris            4 FR
Meredith, Pritchett, 10 May 1793, Ann Jackson          2 DO
Meredith, Thomas, 16 Feb. 1795, Peggy Bealer           1 AL-53
Meredith, Thomas, 17 Sept. 1798, by Rev. Dorsey; Ruth
    Welch; 4 FR gives the date as 28 Sept. 1798.       4 AA
Merican, John, 29 Nov. 1798, by Rev. Wyatt; Elizabeth
    Moss                                               4 AA
Merick, John, 9 Feb. 1797, Polly Stears                4 FR
Merker, Daniel, 9 May 1797, -(?)- Beckebach            3 WA-62
Meroll, Philip, 14 Feb. 1798, Monica Truman            3 CH-162
Merrick, John, 12 Sept. 1791, Rachel Foreman           2 DO
Merrick, John, 26 Dec. 1797, Catherine Sweeny          1 TA-324
Merrick, Michael, 22 May 1800, Verlinder Bowman        5 MO-116
Merrick, William, 4 Oct. 1800, Sarah Reedy             2 DO
Merriken, John, son of Jacob, 4 July 1786, Sarah Jacob,
    dau. of Samuel                                     2 AA-114
Merriken, Joseph, c.1799, by Rev. Higgins; Ann Gray    4 AA
Merriken, Richard, before 12 Dec. 1792, by Rev. John
    Long; Mary Duvall                                  4 AA
Merrill, Esme, 29 Feb. 1792, Gertrude Addams, dau. of
    Jacob and Ann                                      1 SO-141
Merrill, Levi, 23 Jan. 1798, Elizabeth Wheeler         1 WO
Merriwether, Nicholas, 21 Dec. 1797, Eliz. Hood        5 MO-114
Merryman, -(?)-, 18 Aug. 1787, M. Merryman            29 BA-1
Merryman, Benjamin, of William, 29 April 1786, by Rev.
    Davis; Cynthia Doyle                              51 BA-29
Merryman, Caleb, 1786, Mary Merryman                  50 BA-387
Merryman, Elijah, 15 Nov. 1785, Elizabeth Cromwell    16 BA-1
Merryman, Job, 4 Aug. 1791, Ann Neal                  23 BA-2
```

Merryman, Jno., 13 March 1785, Nancy Treakle   11 BA-8
Merryman, John, 14 Dec. 1790, Sarah Johnson   1 BA-3
Merryman, Nicholas, 21 Feb. 1792, Mary Comley   6 BA
Merryman, Nicholas, of Benjamin, 26 June 1798, Sarah
     Anderson   1 BA-8
Merryman, William, 6 Feb. 1800, Anne Presbury   3 BA-382
Mesmith, Isaac, 29 Dec. 1791, Ann Johnson   2 FR-1151
Messer, John, 19 July 1793, Mary Werner   4 FR
Messer, Wm., 26 Nov. 1778, Eleanor Fenton   4 FR
Messersmith, George, 30 April 1799, Nancy Thompson   6 BA
Messersmith, Wm., 10 Jan. 1794, Frances Cromwell   29 BA-5
Messert, Abraham, 11 Dec. 1798, Ana Ehehalden   1 FR-59
Messick, Covington, 14 Oct. 1788, Leah Willis   2 DO
Messick, Daniel, 21 Feb. 1797, Priscilla Winright   2 SO
Messick, John, 31 Dec. 1792, Dolly Vincent   2 DO
Messick, Zadock, 4 Aug. 1790, Dorothy Paul   2 DO
Mezzick, George, 10 Sept. 1787, Tamer Whiteley   2 DO
Messing, Christian, 21 Dec. 1789, Sophia Nagle   4 FR
Metcalfe, Thomas, 28 March 1794, Rachel Hodgkiss   4 FR
Metz, Christ., 5 June 1797, Elis. Bergdoll   3 WA-62
Metz, Frederick, 2 June 1800, Christiana Keelan   3 AL-6
Metzen, Henry, 6 Aug. 1792, Hanna Lamecole?   29 BA-3
Metzler, Dan'l, 3 Nov. 1793, Marg. Bozman   50 BA-393
Mewshaw, Nathan, 16 Sept. 1794, Ann Holloway   18 BA-6
Meyer, Jacob, 7 Nov. 1795, Louisa Spieser   29 BA-7
Meyer, Jacob, 21 Dec. 1797, Ann Hanke   29 BA-9
Meyer, Johannes, 13 Aug. 1793, Elizabeth Speilern   10 BA-196
Meyerhof, Almer, 21 Dec. 1797, A. Maria Dorrin   50 BA-402
Meyers, Frederick, 18 Feb. 1779, Mary Fine   4 FR
Meyers, Henry, 17 July 1796, Ann Davis   2 FR-1152
Meyers, Jacob, March 1800, Mary Schoenefeld   3 WA-69
Meyers, Joh., March 1800, Cath. Albreith   3 WA-68
Meyers, Joseph, 28 May 1796, Mary Schuck   29 BA-7
Meyers, Martin, 19 April 1797, Cath. Angle   3 WA-62
Mezeck, James, 7 July 1796, Nelly Covington   3 SO
Mezick, Daniel, 22 Feb. 1797, Priscilla Winright   3 SO
Mezick, Jewell, 24 Sept. 1799, Katharine Larramore   2 SO
Mezick, John, 15 July 1800, Sarah Dorman   2 SO
Mezzick, George, 10 Sept. 1787, Tamer Whiteley   2 DO
Michael, Adam, 2 June 1792, Susanna Gisebert   4 FR
Michael, Jacob, 12 Nov. 1795, Mary Everett   2 HA-349
Michael, Jacob, 7 March 1798, Sarah Giestbert,   4 FR
Michael, James, 25 Oct. 1794, Neomi Taylor   3 HA-23
Michael, William, 16 April 1783, Barbara Peckenbaugh   4 FR
Michael, William, 14 Feb. 1797, Rachael Brian   3 AL-4
Michael, William, 8 July 1797, Ann Judd   3 HA-26
     2 HA-350 gives the date as 9 July 1797.
Michael, William, 18 Dec. 1798, Margaret Razor   4 FR
Micmen, Nathaneel, 26 Oct. 1778, Mary Galleger   11 BA-1
Mick, John, 24 Dec. 1795, Priscilla Grover   2 FR-1152
Mickle, Robert, 24 Dec. 1795, Eliza Etting   5 BA-10
Middleton, James, 23 April 1789, Nancy Corry   2 CH-454
Middleton, John, 15 Sept. 1793, Mary Cowan   1 BA-5
Middleton, Joseph, 5 March 1795, by Rev. Joseph Wyatt;
     Kitty Whitcroft   4 AA
Miercken, David, 2 Aug. 1792, Louisa Hicks   29 BA-3
Mifflin, James, 8 July 1790, Catherine Potter   26 BA-1
Milbourn, Thomas, 8 Jan. 1799, Tibitha Selby   1 WO
Milbourne, Cotton, 2 Sept. 1795, Sarah Lavely   6 BA
Milbourne, Gilbert, 11 Jan. 1798, Susan Parks   2 SO
Milburn, James, 23 Sept. 1783, Elizabeth Collins   3 HA-8
Milder, Jacob, 9 March 1788, Elisabeth Brugerin   10 BA-190
Mildew, Aquila, 7 July 1791, Zena German   3 BA-234
Miles, Charles, 21 Nov. 1795, Elizabeth Beall   4 PG-157
Miles, Daniel, 20 Nov. 1788, Mary German   3 BA-212
     3 BA-218 gives the date as 28 Oct. 1788.

```
Miles, Edward, 23 June 1795, Margaret Estep          3 CH-162
Miles, Frederick, 3 Jan. 1782, Elizabeth White       2 PG-3
Miles, George, 13 Aug. 1799, Mary Feldman            1 WO
Miles, Henry, 10 March 1798, Rachel Ward             2 SO
Miles, Henry T., 19 Sept. 1797, Ann Osburn           3 CH-162
Miles (or Mules), James, 2 March 1790, by Rev. Reed; Martha
    Guest                                            4 AA
Miles, John, 24 June 1780, Patty Parnold             11 BA-4
Miles, Jno., 7 Feb. 1799, Eliz. Snell                29 BA-10
Miles, John, 26 Dec. 1799, Mary Dewees               6 BA
Miles, Jonathan, 16 Dec. 1796, Leah Tull             1 WO
Miles, Levi, Feb. 1788, Mary Ward                    1 SO-211
Miles, Richard, 12 April 1789, Mary Pindel           4 AA
    The ceremony was performed by Rev. Forrest.
Miles, Samuel, 8 June 1778, Margaret Sizer           11 BA-1
Miles, Thomas, 11 Feb. 1784, Margaret Gover          3 AA-420
Miles, Whittington, 3 Nov. 1796, Elizabeth Hart      2 DO
Milford, James, 9 Oct. 1797, Mary Ann Stone          5 BA-10
Milholland, Rawley, 1790, Mary Gooseberry            50 BA-389
Millar, William, 15 July 1780, Elizabeth Smith       3 BA-180
Millard, Henry, 22 Sept. 1799, Rebecca Work          8 BA-1
Millard, Joseph Lee, 3 May 1800, Anne Parren White   3 BA-385
Millard, William, 24 June 1780, Elizabeth Webb       2 PG-3
Miller, Andrew, 18 July 1780, Rachel Fontz           4 FR
Miller, Charles, 24 Dec. 1797, Anne Steward          6 BA
Miller, Ch's. Bernh., 20 March 1785, Marg. Gross     2 FR-1151
Miller, Christian, 3 Oct. 1791, Elizabeth Wissinger  4 FR
Miller, Christian, 9 Dec. 1794, Mary Cromly          3 BA-296
Miller, Christopher, 26 July 1783, Wismey McIntosh   2 CH-454
Miller, Conradt, 9 Aug. 1789, Elizab. McDonald       2 FR-1151
Miller, David, 23 April 1778, Catherine Heffner      4 FR
Miller, David, 4 May 1790, Cath. Kast                2 FR-1151
Miller, Dewalt, 14 June 1791, Eleanor Hansey         4 FR
Miller, Frederic, 6 June 1794, Eliz. Lehr            29 BA-5
Miller, Frederick, 13 July 1778, Cartrouch Lown      11 BA-1
Miller, George, 28 Sept. 1786, Sarah Oyston          11 BA-9
Miller, George, 22 Feb. 1787, Cath. Englebrecht      2 FR-1151
Miller, Henry, 9 May 1797, Caroline Brooks           29 BA-8
Miller, Isaac, 2 April 1800, Elizabeth Culver        2 SO
Miller, Jacob, 8 Oct. 1778, Margaret Dentlinger      4 FR
Miller, Jacob, 13 Nov. 1779, Uliana Long             4 FR
Miller, Jacob, 20 Nov. 1787, Catherine Walter        4 FR
Miller, Jacob, 27 Jan. 1795, Mary Walter             29 BA-1
Miller, Jacob, 26 Jan. 1800, Ann Rice                2 FR-1152
Miller, James, 26 Oct. 1780, Linda Hamilton          11 BA-4
Miller, John, 17 Oct. 1782, Mary Sollers             11 BA-5
Miller, John, 15 Aug. 1786, Barb. Schmidt            2 FR-1151
Miller, John, 3 Oct. 1786, Elizabeth Street          4 FR
Miller, John, 27 April 1789, Christena Gunn          4 FR
Miller, John, 19 June 1791, by Rev. Forrest; Mary Vanferson
    3 FR
Miller, John, 11 Oct. 1791, Cath. Bayer              2 FR-1151
Miller, John, 24 March 1792, Susanna Kemp            4 FR
Miller, John, 31 Jan. 1793, Eliz. Hellman            2 FR-1151
Miller, John, of Dan, 3 Nov. 1795, Magdalen Foutz    4 FR
Miller, Jno., 16 Sept. 1796, Peggy Reed              29 BA-7
Miller, Joh., March 1799, Peggy Schreiber            3 WA-66
Miller, John, 11 May 1799, Sally Fisher              2 SO
Miller, Joh., April 1800, Mary Robey                 3 WA-69
Miller, Jno., 31 Dec. 1800, Cath. Frick              29 BA-12
Miller, Joh. Jacob, 7 April 1799, An. Cath. Ries     50 BA-405
Miller, Joseph, 5 Sept. 1780, Sus. Chew              3 HA-2
Miller, Joseph, 16 Sept. 1785, Frances Wilson        3 HA-10
Miller, Joseph, 2 July 1795, Elizabeth Prue          4 PG-157
Miller, Joseph, 24 Feb. 1798, Ann Pennington         4 KE-70
```

```
Miller, Joseph, 2 March 1798, Priscilla Robinet        3 HA-27
Miller, Joseph, 31 March 1800, Susanna Bell            3 BA-384
Miller, Joshua, 23 March 1798, Deborah Plummer         4 FR
Miller, Michael, 4 June 1795, Elizabeth Hankin         41 BA-1
Miller, Michael, 12 April 1796, Mag. Timmern           3 WA-60
Miller, Nathaniel, 13 Feb. 1797, Sarah Hatcheson       4 KE-69
Miller, Nehemiah, 20 Feb. 1791, Margaret Downes        23 BA-2
Miller, Nicholas, 18 Oct. 1781, Mary Musgrove          4 FR
Miller, Nicholas, 14 Aug. 1797, Ann Criswell           45 BA-1
Miller, Richard, 8 Sept. 1796, Eleanor Fielas          3 BA-329
Miller, Robert, son of Solomon and Sarah, 21st day, 10
    mo., 1779, Cassandra Wood, dau. of William and
    Margaret                                           3 SF
Miller, Robert, son of Robert and Sarah, 26th day, 11 mo.,
    1788, Jane Williams, dau. of Jacob and Ruth        3 SF
Miller, Robert, 23 Jan. 1793, Mary Highfield           4 FR
Miller, Samuel, 2 April 1790, Rachel Marriott          4 AA
Miller, Samuel, of David, 10 July 1791, Catherine Dieter,
    dau. of Jacob                                      2 WA-16
Miller, Walter Tulley, 1786, Mary Hodges               1 KE-307
Miller, Wm., 18 March 1786, Susanna Gordon             11 BA-9
Millerman, George, 7 May 1795, Rosy Ann Coleman        6 BA
Milles, James, 30 Oct. 1781, Mary Martin               3 HA-5
Milligan, John, 1 Jan. 1799, Sally Stevens             2 SO
Million, Patrick, 8 May 1800, Hannah Owings            3 BA-386
Mills, Andrew, 25 June 1795, Catherine Stofell         4 FR
Mills, Cornelius, 12 Jan. 1800, by Rev. Roberts; Ann Wise-
    ham                                                4 AA
Mills, David, 16 Aug. 1784, Leah Cole                  2 DO
Mills, David, 26 Dec. 1792, Sarah Barron               2 DO
Mills, Edward, 29 March 1797, Elizabeth Ennalls        2 DO
Mills, Henry, 18 May 1793, Sarah Beckwith              2 DO
Mills, Henry, 14 March 1795, Marg't Haher              50 BA-397
Mills, James, 7 May 1788, Nancy Cannon                 2 DO
Mills, James, 13 July 1790, Margaret Bane              2 DO
Mills, James, 14 Feb. 1796, Susanna Lawrence           6 BA
Mills, James B. (or P.), 28 Jan. 1797, Betsy Lankford  2 SO
Mills, John, 3 Jan. 1778, Ruth Jacobs                  2 PG-3
Mills, John, 26 Nov. 1781, Betsy Staples               2 DO
Mills, John, 20 Jan. 1782, Elizabeth Waters            2 PG-3
Mills, Jno., 19 March 1797, Marg. Woolford             50 BA-401
Mills, John, 14 April 1800, Keziah Jones               2 DO
Mills, Richard, 16 Oct. 1781, Mary Keller              4 FR
Mills, Robert, 18 Nov. 1789, Amelia Vickers            2 DO
Mills, Theodore, 3 Sept. 1797, Cath. Zellers           29 BA-8
Mills, Thomas, 28 Dec. 1785, Eleanor Vickers           2 DO
Mills, Thomas, 25 March 1786, by Rev. William Tench
    Ringgold; Mary Thomas                              3 FR
Mills, William, 29 Aug. 1792, Elizabeth Tregoe         2 DO
Millykin, John, 3 Jan. 1799, Sally Stevens             3 SO
Milstead, Thomas, 16 Sept. 1780, Elizabeth Ratcliffe   2 CH-454
Mimdorf, David, 17 May 1797, Juliana Schweitzer        50 BA-401
Mincher, William, 25 Dec. 1791, Elizabeth Haney        3 BA-255
Minetree, Paul, 1 Aug. 1786, Nancy Dorset              2 CH-455
Minetree, Paul, 6 April 1782, Eleanor Smoot            2 CH-455
Mingo, negro; 16 Nov. 1799, Jenny Stanley              2 DO
Minish, Levin, 3 Dec. 1796, Mary McDaniel              2 DO
Minner, Christopher, 11 June 1792, Frances Bryan       3 BA-256
Minnick, George, 18 March 1797, Mary Foutch            4 FR
Minnish, Richard, 28 July 1797, Eleanor Gilliss        2 SO
Minor, John, 29 Nov. 1796, Mary Kale                   4 FR
Minor, Thomas, 15 Sept. 1778, Eliza Turley             2 MO-1
Minstalld, Nicholas, 28 Feb. 1797, Mary Allison        5 MO-114
Mintsch, John, 22 May 1797, Marg. Reed                 3 WA-62
Mintz, Abraham, 9 Sept. 1792, Nory Jones               6 BA
```

Mishaw, David, 31 Dec. 1796, Achsah Mewshaw   3 BA-333
Mister, Lowder, 15 Oct. 1791, Rhoda Ross   2 DO
Mitchel, George, before 15 Sept. 1796, by Rev. Green;
    Hannah Seidriss?   4 AA
Mitchel, John, 31 March 1796, by Rev. Ridgely; Anne Burgee
    4 AA
Mitchel, Michael, 22 June 1786, Mary Botts   11 BA-9
Mitchel, Middleton, 21 April 1792, Rebecca Reston   3 PG-437
Mitchel, Walter, by 12 Feb. 1778, Christiana Browning 2 PG-6
Mitchel, William, 30 Dec. 1784, Susanna Handly   11 BA-8
Mitchel, William, 24 May 1787, Eliza Calver   11 BA-10
Mitchel, Zadock, 25 Jan. 1797, Sarah Venables   3 SO
Mitchell, Alexander, 26 Nov. 1799, Elizabeth Scott   4 FR
Mitchell, Alexander, 19 Dec. 1799, Eliza Torrance   5 BA-11
Mitchell, Andrew, 29 May 1790, Nancy Wing   2 DO
Mitchell, Arthur, 1 Jan. 1795, Elizabeth Cannon   3 BA-299
Mitchell, Cyrus, 24 Oct. 1793, Betsy Richardson   2 DO
Mitchell, Edward, 17 Nov. 1791, Charlotte Valentine 5 BA-10
Mitchell, Elijah, 1 June 1795, Ann Boardman   3 HA-24
Mitchell, Ezekiel, 13 May 1796, Mary Mitchell   2 DO
Mitchell, Gideon, (19 April 1788), Margaret Frizzell 15 BA-1
Mitchell, John, 9 Feb. 1777, Sarah Baldwin   2 PG-2
Mitchell, Jno., 16 May 1782, Mary Daffin   11 BA-5
Mitchell, John, 5 Sept. 1786, Henny Marshall   2 DO
Mitchell, John, 9 Feb. 1790, Amelia Jones   2 DO
Mitchell, John, 1 Dec. 1793, Peggy Downing   6 BA
Mitchell, John, 13 May 1797, Jane Murphy   6 BA
Mitchell, John, 11 April 1798, Susanna M. Jacobs   3 AL-5
Mitchell, John, 6 Sept. 1798, Martha Matticks   2 HA-350
Mitchell, Lazarus, 17 Nov. 1794, Adelaide Roberts   3 BA-296
Mitchell, Levin, 29 Aug. 1792, Mary Murray   2 WO-26
Mitchell, Levin, 25 Jan. 1797, Catherine Seward   2 DO
Mitchell, Mordecai Miles, 28 Nov. 1779, Sarah Wilson 2 PG-3
Mitchell, Richard, 12 Feb. 1798, Priscilla Gilbert   3 HA-27
    2 HA-350 gives the date as 15 Feb. 1798.
Mitchell, Robert, 18 Aug. 1797, Elizabeth Mumford   1 WO
Mitchell, Theodore, 10 Feb. 1793, Cabey Gittinger   4 FR
Mitchell, Thomas, 23 Aug. 1781, Elizabeth Wood   2 PG-5
Mitchell, Thomas, 7 Dec. 1796, Eleanor Morgan   3 HA-25
    47 BA-1 gives the date as 8 Dec. 1796.
Mitchell, Thomas, 2 Jan. 1798, Nancy Jackson   2 SO
Mitchell, Thomas Lee, 30 Sept. 1792, Elizabeth Wilson 3 PG-437
Mitchell, William, 11 Dec. 1792, Mary White   3 PG-437
Mitchell, William, 20 Dec. 1796, Sarah Mitchell   3 HA-25
Mitchell, William, 22 Dec. 1796, Sarah Mitchell   2 HA-349
Mitchell, William, 18 Dec. 1798, Sally Smullen   2 SO
Mitchell, Zadoc, 17 Jan. 1797, Sally Venables   2 SO
Mitchell, Zebulon, 1 Feb. 1792, Sarah Glover   2 DO
Mitchell, Zebulon, 2 Dec. 1800, Fanny Thomas   2 DO
Mitcheson, Henry, 21 Sept. 1788, Mary Hingdon   3 BA-212
Mix, Thomas Bell, 11 Feb. 1799, Anna Maria Hanson   5 BA-11
Moak, John, 5 March 1796, Eleanor Wooden   6 BA
Moale, John, 5 Oct. 1790, by Rev. Reed; Lucy Morton 4 AA
Moale, Richard N., 16 April 1797, Judith Carter Armistead
    47 BA-1
Moale, Thomas, 21 March 1793, Eleanor Owings   4 BA-75
Moale, Thomas, 21 March 1793, Elenor Owings   35 BA-1
Moals, Nicholas, 23 Aug. 1791, Elizabeth Price   6 BA
Mobberly, Bazil, 8 Feb. 1782, Marg't Brewer   11 BA-5
Mobley, Edward, 20 Nov. 1788, Rachel Griffith   4 FR
Mobley, Hezekiah, 6 Dec. 1796, Elizabeth Kidwell   3 PG-442
Mobley, Lewis, 23 Nov. 1780, Trusilla Dorsey   4 FR
Mobley, Mordecai, 23 April 1789, Elizabeth Brown   6 BA
Mobley, William, 30 June 1799, Sophia Phillips   45 BA-3
Mockbee, Basil, 6 Nov. 1779, Ann Mockbee   2 PG-3

```
Mockbee, William, 5 March 1780, Ann Clark                2 PG-3
Mockbee, William, 24 Dec. 1780, Margaret Henniss         2 PG-5
Mockbey, Mirean, 30 Dec. 1788, Elizabeth West           23 BA-1
Mockebay, Humphrey, 24 April 1791, Verlinder Stalions    3 PG-257
Moens, Francis, 14 Oct. 1779, Ann Beckitt                2 PG-3
Moffatt, Thomas, 30 Jan. 1783, Hannah Presbury           5 BA-10
Moffett, Jacob, 9 Sept. 1797, Rachel Newcomb             4 KE-70
Moffett, Jesse, 5 Oct. 1797, Rachel Bryan                4 KE-70
Moffett, John, 7 Aug. 1783, Susanna Curtis               4 FR
Moffett, John, 14 Jan. 1784, Olive Ford                 11 BA-7
Moffitt, George, Jr., 22 Aug. 1779, Ann Little, widow     2 KE-314
Mohler, Jacob, 23 July 1789, Sarah Mathers               2 FR-1151
Mohon, Jno., 21 Sept. 1795, Mary Callhoun               29 BA-6
Mohr, Henry, 6 June 1800, Peggy Wilson                  29 BA-11
Molesworth, Joseph, 31 March 1778, by Rev. Magill;
     Rebecca Molineux                                    4 AA
Molft, Tobias, 2 March 1784, Susanna Ulrich             10 BA-180
Molikin, Basil, 5 Dec. 1778, by Rev. Magill; Rachel
     Gaterel                                             4 AA
Molledor, John, 7 Sept. 1794, Julianna Kast              2 FR-1152
Moller, Adolph, 5 April 1798, Elizabeth McGlathers       4 FR
Moller, John Ludwig, son of Joseph, 31 May 1784, Gertrude
     Protzman                                            5 FR-81
Molick, Moses, 18 Dec. 1784, Sarah Tregoe                2 DO
Molton, Martha (sic), 17 June 1798, Sarah Boyd           2 HA-350
Molton, Wilfred, 10 April 1795, Frances Brown Davis      4 FR
Monahan, John, 26 Jan. 1781, Darcas Waldrin              3 HA-3
Mongar, Zorobable, 12 Nov. 1800, Peggy Martin            2 SO
Monjar, William, 9 Jan. 1793, Mary Jones                 3 HA-22
Monk, William, 15 March 1781, Bathia Hairs               2 CH-455
Monk, William, 27 Dec. 1792, Elizabeth Simpson           3 HA-22
Monker, William, 20 April 1800, Polly Fry                6 BA
Monroe, Solomon, 16 Dec. 1794, Margaret Spicer           2 AL-700
Montecue, Thomas, 23 Nov. 1800, Anne Watson              3 BA-395
Montgomery, Isaac, 1 Oct. 1798, Ruth Hargrove            3 HA-27
Montgomery, James, 7 June 1789, Susanna Whitaker         1 BA-2
Montgomery, John, 10 April 1792, Joshan Sedwick          4 FR
Montgomery, John, Jr., 25 Sept. 1798, Eliza Murphy       2 AL-701
Montgomery, Thomas, 16 Dec. 1781, Rebecca Southwell      2 CH-455
Mooberry, William, 9 Oct. 1785, Elizabeth Reardon        3 HA-10
Mooberry, William, 19 Sept. 1796, Elizabeth Morris       3 HA-25
     7 BA-3 gives the date as 20 Sept. 1796.
Moock, Samuel, Nov. 1798, Christ. Humbert                3 WA-65
Moody, John, 27 Jan. 1791, Brillicina Thomas             3 PG-257
Moody, Robert, 6 June 1799, Christian Butler             3 BA-372
Moody, Thomas, 24 March 1796, Mary Berry                 5 MO-113
Moody, William, 26 Nov. 1797, Mary Brackett              6 BA
Moon, Geo., 25 Dec. 1793, Elizabeth Rider               38 BA-1
Moor, Nicholas Evens, 6 March 1796, Nancy Collins        3 SO
Moore, Adam, 11 May 1797, Nancy Mullen                  50 BA-401
Moore, Alex'r, 1790, -(?)- Watts                        50 BA-390
Moore, Asa, 8 March 1791, Elizabeth Thomas               3 PG-257
Moore, Charles, 17 April 1781, Alethe Henry              2 DO
Moore, Christopher, 21 Nov. 1799, Priscilla Lee          3 BA-380
Moore, David, 28 Nov. 1791, Rhoda Edgar                  2 DO
Moore, George, 25 Dec. 1790, Lydia Winchester            6 BA
Moore, George, 17 Dec. 1795, Sarah Bayne                 3 PG-441
Moore, Isaac, 28 Nov. 1782, Judah Short                  1 SO-209
Moore, Isaac, 1 Jan. 1798, Nancy Langrall                2 DO
     1 DO-39 gives the date as 7 Jan. 1798.
Moore, Jacob, 1 Jan. 1789, Kitty Fremiller              11 BA-12
Moore, James, 20 July 1781, Elizabeth Walks              3 HA-4
Moore, James, 3 June 1791, Sarah Harper                  2 DO
Moore, James, 7 May 1793, Mary Tregoe                    2 DO
Moore, James, 20 April 1794, Elizabeth Plunkett          3 BA-285
```

```
Moore, James, 18 Jan. 1797, -(?)- Brewer              4 KE-69
Moore, James, 25 Aug. 1798, Rachel Wales              4 KE-70
Moore, James, 26 Aug. 1800, Rizpah Wallace            2 DO
  1 DO-40 gives the date as 28 Aug. 1800.
Moore, Jas. Augustus, 30 March 1797, Elizabeth Rook   6 BA
Moore, Jason, 30 April 1799, Deborah Woolsey          3 HA-28
Moore, Jehu, son of John and Hannah, 23rd day, 3 mo., 1796,
  Hannah Hibberd, dau. of Joseph and Jane             3 SF
Moore, John, 11 Sept. 1781, Elizabeth Brown           3 HA-5
Moore, John, 10 Dec. 1793, Mary Rockenbrod            50 BA-393
Moore, John, 16 Nov. 1795, Rachel Beard               2 DO
Moore, John, 3 Aug. 1797, Mary Scarborough            3 HA-26
  See also 1 BA-8.
Moore, John, 21 Oct. 1799, Sally Bowen                2 SO
Moore, John Gay, 3 Aug. 1786, Averilla Allender      24 BA-1
Moore, John Smith, 20 Sept. 1778, Margaret Musgrove   2 CH-455
Moore, Jos., 2 July 1791, Sus. Waters                29 BA-2
Moore, Joseph, 24 July 1798, Elizabeth Dun            8 MO-16
Moore, Levin, 15 Oct. 1783, Rachel Lee                2 DO
Moore, Levin, 2 June 1788, Phebe Moore                2 DO
Moore, Nicholas Ruxton, 21 July 1779, Eliz. Orrick   11 BA-3
Moore, Nicholas Ruxton, 25 Dec. 1793, Sarah Kelso     5 BA-10
Moore, Philip, 30 April 1799, Delia Hall              1 BA-9
Moore, Richard, 23 Oct. 1792, Sarah Moore             1 AL-52
Moore, Robert, 23 July 1782, Ruth Chapman             5 BA-9
Moore, Robert, 20 April 1790, L. Reynolds            29 BA-1
Moore, Robert, 19 Nov. 1791, Elizabeth Holmes         6 BA
Moore, Robert, 13 May 1793, Jane Galloway             3 BA-267
Moore, Robert, 22 Oct. 1795, by Rev. Ridgely; Lucy White
  4 AA
Moore, Robert, 18 Dec. 1797, Molly Hart               2 DO
Moore, Thomas, 30 June 1785, Mary Moore               2 DO
Moore, Thomas, Jr., of Loudon Co., Va., 21st day, 9 mo.,
  1791, Mary Brooke, Jr. (sic)                        6 SF
Moore, Thomas, 3 Jan. 1792, Ann Trice                 2 DO
Moore, Thomas, 2 Nov. 1795, Saby Wheatley             2 DO
Moore, Thomas, 19 Jan. 1797, Ruth Richardson          6 BA
Moore, Thomas, 27 Dec. 1800, Catherine Buckley        6 BA
Moore, Wm., 20 March 1779, Catherine Grimes           4 FR
Moore, Wm., 10 March 1789, Jane Young                 2 FR-1151
Moore, William, 27 May 1789, by Rev. Hagerty; Susannah
  Sanders                                             4 AA
Moore, William, 10 Nov. 1791, Sarah Allender          6 BA
Moore, William, 29 March 1797, Elizabeth Clarke       2 DO
Moore, William, 13 May 1798, Mary Kline               2 AL-701
Moore, William, 24 Sept. 1799, Anna Jones             3 BA-378.
Moore, Wm., 24 Nov. 1800, Margaret Robinette          3 AL-7
Moore, William Stephen, 6 March 1794, Catherine Leypold
  3 BA-285
Moore, Zachariah, 4 Nov. 1788, -(?)- Bourne           4 FR
Moore, Zadock, 23 Sept. 1779, Mary Soaper             2 PG-3
Moorehead, Joh., Jan. 1799, Esther Toncray            3 WA-66
Moorehead, Thomas, 28 May 1798, Eleanor Broadburn     3 BA-359
Moores, Daniel, 3 Dec. 1792, Sally Budd               3 HA-22
  1 BA-5 gives the date as 1 Jan. 1793.
Moores, John, 11 Sept. 1787, Mary Lee                 1 BA-1
Moraign, Thomas, 1 Feb. 1798, Rebecca Hayward         2 DO
More, Charles, c.Nov. 1778, Margaret Tibbs            3 AA-415
More, James, 12 April 1798, Rebecca Crabson           2 HA-350
More, Josiah, 12 Dec. 1778, Charity Duckett           2 PG-3
Moreign, Henry, 6 Nov. 1790, Eleanor Layton           2 DO
Moreign, Moses, 31 Dec. 1789, Elizabeth Harvey        2 DO
Moreign, Moses, 9 Jan. 1796, Milly Middleton          2 DO
Moreland, Isaac, 20 Nov. 1781, Elizabeth Stephens     2 CH-455
Moreton, Nathaniel, 1 March 1798, Sarah Copeland      2 HA-350
```

Moreton, Robert, 17 Dec. 1800, Anne Groves   3 BA-396
Moreton, William, 10 Nov. 1785, Sarah West   3 HA-10
Morfoot, John, 15 Feb. 1786, by Rev. West; Nancy Kelly
    51 BA-30
Morgan, Henry, 30 June 1793, Ann Collins   3 BA-269
Morgan, James, 21 Nov. 1782, Nancy Travers   5 BA-10
Morgan, Jesse, 19 Aug. 1795, Sarah Scott   29 BA-6
Morgan, Joel, 19 Nov. 1797, Elizabeth Norris   6 BA
Morgan, John, 25 April 1779, Hannah Wood   2 PG-3
Morgan, John, 24 May 1788, Susanna Higler   4 FR
Morgan, John, 26 March 1799, Priscilla Jeffries   6 BA
Morgan, Robert, 1 June 1780, Martha Hamilton   2 PG-7
Morgan, Robert, 15 Dec. 1791, Elizabeth McComas   3 HA-21
Morgan, Stephen, 17 April 1797, Anna Williamson; blacks,
    married by permission   50 BA-401
Morgan, Thomas, 20 March 1794, Sarah Mullen   3 BA-285
Morgan, Thomas, son of John and Mary, 1st day, 10 mo.,
    1795, Sarah Amos, dau. of William and Susanna   1 SF
Morgan, Thomas, 22 Jan. 1798, Polly Baker   2 DO
Morgan, William, son of Benjamin and Jane, 30th day, 3 mo.,
    1791, Sarah Price, dau. of Mordecai and Rachel   1 SF
Morgan, William, 17 Jan. 1793, Mary Anderson   35 BA-1
Morgan, William, 20 Feb. 1797, Catharine Scanlan   3 BA-342
Morgan, Zorobabel, 13 Nov. 1800, Peggy Martin   3 SO
Morie, Joseph, 14 Oct. 1793, Josephine Scrote   3 BA-275
Moriston, John, 15 Sept. 1798, Catherine Harvy   2 SF
Morningstar, Philip, 23 Nov. 1781, Solema Morningstar 4 FR
Morossa, John Joseph, 25 Dec. 1796, Mary Payne   3 BA-333
Morrin, James, 21 Nov. 1796, Ann Lasher   6 BA
Morris, Augustus, 24 Jan. 1797, Christina Kurn?   6 BA
Morris, Benjamin, 27 Sept. 1792, Rebecca Simpkins   1 AL-52
    2 AL-700 gives the date as 12 Oct. 1792.
Morris, Edward, 1 April 1783, Sarah Scott   5 BA-10
Morris, Edward, 21 June 1785, Elizabeth LeCompte   2 DO
Morris, Edward, free black, 8 Jan. 1792, Frances Ferrel,
    slave of John Hammonds   3 BA-255
Morris, Edward, 13 Aug. 1795, Sarah Roberts   1 WO
Morris, Israel, son of William and Sarah, 2nd day, 3 mo.,
    1780, Sarah Bond, dau. of Joshua and Ann   1 SF
Morris, James, 29 May 1778, Jane Burk   11 BA-1
Morris, James, 10 April 1782, Patience Collins   3 HA-6
Morris, James, 9 April 1792, Elizab. Pittinger   2 FR-1151
Morris, John, 5 Jan. 1784, Catherine Hogg   4 FR
Morris, Jno., 28 March 1785, Rachael Hammond   11 BA-8
Morris, John, 22 Sept. 1790, Rachel Paul   2 DO
Morris, John, 27 July 1792, Margaret White   18 BA-4
Morris, John, 26 March 1797, Hannah Campbell   4 FR
Morris, Jonathan, 9 March 1782, Mary Kimbell   4 FR
Morris, Jonathan, 8 Nov. 1789, Mary Fraisier   4 FR
Morris, Joshua, 8 Feb. 1796, Eliz. Simpson   3 CH-162
Morris, Paul, 11 Nov. 1797, Priscilla Priestman   6 BA
Morris, Philip, 12 Sept. 1795, Nancy Mumford   1 WO
Morris, Philip, 16 Oct. 1798, Eleanor Burbage   1 WO
Morris, Thos. B., 19 Jan. 1790, Casandra Thrall   3 PG-256
Morris, William, 4 June 1784, Hermi Cannon (or Carmon)
    10 BA-182
Morris, Wm., 8 Jan. 1786, Ann Hugar   3 PG-251
Morris, William, 10 Sept. 1800, Rebecca Rock   6 BA
Morrison, James, 21 March 1795, Cassandra Gittings   4 FR
Morrison, James, 26 March 1795, Clariss Gittings   2 FR-1152
Morrison, James, 13 Aug. 1796, Elizabeth Heisson   10 BA-198
Morrison, James, 4 Oct. 1797, Eleanor Riggen   2 SO
Morrison, John, 1 Sept. 1791, Frances Webster   3 HA-21
Morrison, John, 16 Aug. 1797, Mary Jackson   2 AL-700
Morrison, John, 3 April 1798, Elizabeth Hort   4 FR

Morrison, Robert, 30 Dec. 1792, Margery Morrison   3 BA-259
Morrison, William, 5 July 1794, Elizabeth Lane   39 BA-1
Morrow, Archebald, 24 March 1778, Margaret Hilton   4 FR
Morrow, Kennedy, 21 July 1795, Mary Wilson   5 BA-10
Morrow, Thomas, 22 Feb. 1789, Catherine McCurdy   3 BA-219
Morrow, Thomas, 22 Feb. 1789, Catherine Micrordy   6 BA
Morrow, William, 1 July 1799, Ann Hazleton   3 BA-373
Morry, Henry, 31 Jan. 1797, Elizabeth Walker   6 BA
Morse, Benedictus, 30 Sept. 1798, Elizabeth Ferren   3 BA-363
Morsel, Benjamin, 3 Feb. 1788, Esther Cornwall   18 BA-1
Morson, John. See Morrison, John.
Mortar, Valentine, 14 April 1786, Susanna Ingles   4 FR
Morton, David, 23 June 1791, Amy May   6 BA
Morton, John, 26 Dec. 1800, Eleanor Hawkins   8 BA-2
    See also 48 BA-2.
Morton, John Andrew, 26 Jan. 1795, Mary Grandget   6 BA
Morton, Nathaniel, 23 Feb. 1798, Sarah Copeland   3 HA-27
Moser, Benjamin, 18 April 1796, Mary Letherman   3 WA-61
Mosher, Philip, 11 Sept. 1793, Johanna Robinson   5 BA-10
Mosier, James, 29 Dec. 1787, Nancy Ridgely   6 BA
Moss, Abraham, 15 Aug. 1779, Isabella Sollers   11 BA-3
Moss, David, 19 Nov. 1797, Hannah Welsh   29 BA-9
Moss, Frederick, 27 July 1784, Nancy Wheeler   11 BA-7
Moss, Philip, 15 Aug. 1779, Sarah Sculd   11 BA-3
Moss, William, 9 Jan. 1798, Sarah Holden   4 KE-70
Mosser, Hyland, 20 Dec. 1798, Susanna Murphy   29 BA-10
Mosseter, Mich'l, 7 May 1793, Philippina Jacob   2 FR-1152
Mott, Benjamin, 22 Nov. 1798, Ann Proctor   4 KE-70
Mottis, Peter, 2 June 1778, Philopena Heckathorn   4 FR
Motz, Martin, 28 March 1797, Cath. Tard   3 WA-62
Mount, John, 12 May 1794, Margaret Smith   4 FR
Moutree, James, 30 June 1795, Phiby Jones   6 BA
Mowbrary, James, 2 Dec. 1790, Nancy McGowing   6 BA
Mowbray, Cook, 19 Dec. 1791, Margaret Breerwood   2 DO
Mowbray, Henry, 14 April 1791, Mary Hooper   2 DO
Mowbray, James, 24 Dec. 1798, Sarah Applegarth   2 DO
Mowbray, John, 26 April 1796, Nancy Thomas   2 DO
Mowbray, Levin, 3 June 1794, Dolly Vinson   2 DO
Mowerer, Adam, 27 Sept. 1790, Magdl. Win   4 FR
Mowton, John, 25 Nov. 1783, Cathe. Plackroot   11 BA-7
Mox, Joh., Sept. 1792, Eliz. Rockenbrod   50 BA-392
Moxley, Nehemiah, 26 Nov. 1794, Elizabeth Norwood   4 FR
Moxley, Samuel, 25 Aug. 1783, Agnes Cox   4 FR
Muccava, Martin, 27 June 1778, Susanna Caley   11 BA-1
Mud, Joseph, 29 April 1783, Williamina Weems   3 AA-419
Mudd, Alexius, 26 Jan. 1794, Jane Edelin   3 CH-161
    "disp. for consang. in 3rd degree"
Mudd, Andrew, 17 Jan. 1797, Eleanor Green   5 MO-114
Mudd, Ezekiel, 12 May 1779, Elizabeth Edelin   2 CH-455
Muds, James, 10 April 1798, Ann Comegys   4 KE-70
Mugg, John, 13 Jan. 1797, Elizabeth Greenwell   4 FR
Muir, James, 9 March 1791, Charity Shaw   2 DO
Muir, Robert, 28 Jan. 1795, Anney Keene   2 DO
Muir, Samuel, 13 Feb. 1798, Senah Vansickle   2 DO
Mulakin, James, 14 Jan. 1796, Elizabeth Hardey   3 PG-442
Mulhall, Patrick, 2 Nov. 1797, Barbara Scull   3 BA-352
Mulholland, Christ. 5 Jan. 1790, Eliz. Riddel   29 BA-1
Mulhorn, George, 11 July 1781, Nancy Bratcher   3 HA-4
Mulican, Joseph, 12 Oct. 1797, Massey Ann Mitchell   3 PG-443
Mullen, John W., 18 April 1791, Ann Unglesby   4 FR
Mullen, Patrick, 29 Dec. 1782, Sarah Askew   11 BA-6
Mullen, Samuel, 6 March 1800, Rachel Botner   3 BA-383
Mullendore, David, 29 April 1790, Catherine Cost   4 FR
Muller, Adam, 24 Oct. 1797, Sophia Henry   10 BA-198
Muller, Conrad, 2 July 1796, Nancy Robinson   10 BA-196

Muller, Nicolaus, 28 July 1779, Catharina Wagenheimerin
   10 BA-178
Mullett, Jno., 21 Jan. 1794, Mary Lenhard   29 BA-5
Mullican, Arch'd, 19 March 1778, Elizabeth Vincent   2 MO-1
Mullican, Wm., 30 Dec. 1800, Eliz. Dowden   5 MO-17
Mullikin, James, 15 April 1781, Eleanor Beanes   2 PG-5
Mullikin, John, 16 Nov. 1789, Mary Hamston   4 FR
Mullikin, Samuel, 23 Aug. 1788, Sarah Stewart   2 DO
Mullikin, William, 28 March 1780, Ann Barrett   2 PG-3
Mullindore, Jacob, 28 March 1785, Susanna Swisher   4 FR
Mullindore, John, 30 Aug. 1794, Uhly Cost   4 FR
Mullinger, Friedr., 29 May 1794, Cath. Enders   50 BA-394
Mulloy, James, 13 Aug. 1789, Sarah Weeks   1 BA-2
Mumford, James, 20 March 1792, Nancy Fuller   2 FR-1151
   4 FR gives the groom's name as James Mumford, Jr., and
   the date as 29 March 1792.
Mumford, Jesse, 11 July 1782, Elizabeth Freeman   2 WO-24
Mumford, Jesse, 10 Feb. 1797, Betsy Richardson   1 WO
Mumford, William, 18 Oct. 1796, Catherine Hartsoke   4 FR
Mumma, Christopher, 27 Jan. 1787, by Rev. Turner; Sarah
   Wright   51 BA-30
Mummy, Thomas, 13 July 1797, Cath. Fishburn   29 BA-8
Munday, Wm., 6 Feb. 1786, Leah Simpson   11 BA-9
Mungaret, Jno., 8 Nov. 1786, Nancy Latitur (sic)   11 BA-9
Munk, William, 23 March 1782, Susanna Heirs   3 HA-6
Munnickhuysen, John, 28 Feb. 1799, Mary Howard   3 BA-368
Munro, Jonathan, 15 Jan. 1795, Sarah Connor   6 BA
Munro, Nathan, 6 Nov. 1788, Catherine Welsh   6 BA
Munro, William, 28 Sept. 1799, Jane McConkey   3 BA-378
Munroe, Thomas, 25 Sept. 1796, Milly Wilkerson   3 PG-442
Munson, Joel M., 13 Aug. 1797, Ann Swan   6 BA
Munstan, Charles, 20 Nov. 1779, Ann Fitzgerald   3 BA-178
Muran, James, 14 May 1780, Jane Helling   2 PG-7
Murdoch, Walter, 28 May 1797, Sarah Beavins   3 AL-4
Murdock, Benjamin, 22 Dec. 1781, Mary Ann Magruder 4 FR
Murdock, James, (date not given), Phebe Delasien   2 CH-455
Murdock, Walter, 31 May 1797, Rachel Beavens (or Barnes)
   2 AL-700
Murdock, William, 27 May 1783, Jane Contee Harrison 4 FR
Murphey, Daniel, 20 Feb. 1798, Charlotte Weaver   6 BA
Murphey, Duncan, 7 Sept. 1790, Prethenia Siars   4 FR
Murphey, James, 13 Feb. 1792, Eleanor Smith   4 FR
Murphey, John, 3 April 1790, Grace Marshall   4 FR
Murphey, Joshua, 26 Oct. 1797, Ann Peck   4 FR
Murphey, Thomas, 30 July 1778, Sidney Folkner   11 BA-1
Murphey, Timothy, 5 Jan. 1786, Martha Gallion   16 BA-1
Murphey, Zephaniah, 4 Jan. 1778, Eleanor Gray   1 CH-206
Murphy, Amon, 13 Nov. 1792, by Rev. Dorsey; Mary Ward 4 AA
Murphy, Daniel, 5 April 1800, Sarah Rutter   3 BA-384
Murphy, Henry, 3 April 1781, Elizabeth Norris   2 CH-455
   3 HA-6 gives the date as 30 March 1782.
Murphy, James, 8 June 1778, Mary Craddock   2 MO-1
Murphy, Jas., 23 Feb. 1794, Debora Deaver   50 BA-394
Murphy, Jno., 3 Jan. 1790, Eleanor Lynch   11 BA-13
Murphy, Owen, 15 Sept. 1797, Catherine Hawes (or Haves)
   8 MO-16
Murphy, Thomas, 29 March 1797, Elizabeth Cristfield 4 KE-70
Murphy, William, 3 Oct. 1783, Mary Pritchett   2 DO
Murphy, William, 17 March 1788, Ruth Heather   2 DO
Murphy, Wm., 11 June 1793, Ann Wilmore   18 BA-5
Murphy, William, 2 Dec. 1794, Marg. Moore   2 FR-1152
Murphy, William, 22 Dec. 1800, Celia Vansickle   2 DO
Murray, Anthony, 7 June 1791, Keziah Andrew   2 DO
Murray, Archibald, 23 Feb. 1788, Mary McFarrin   5 BA-10
Murray, Charles, 21 Feb. 1799, Catherine Goulding 6 BA

Murray, Elam, 18 Dec. 1788, Ann Hickens   11 BA-12
Murray, Francis, 16 Oct. 1795, Jane Hutton   44 BA-1
Murray, James, 27 Nov. 1785, Margaret Raney   11 BA-9
Murray, James, 18 Aug. 1800, Margaret Guyton   3 HA-29
Murray, John, 7 Dec. 1779, Sarah Turner   11 BA-4
Murray, John, 10 April 1792, Elizabeth Ayres   3 BA-257
Murray, John, 14 Nov. 1795, Sophia Smith   2 DO
Murray, Joshua, 1792, Mary Powel   50 BA-392
Murray, Michael, 9 April 1797, Polly Sims   3 SO
Murray, Nich's, 13 May 1794, Sus. Bandle   29 BA-5
Murray, William, 13 Feb. 1800, Jane Simpson   3 BA-383
Murray, William Vans, 15 Oct. 1789, Charlotte Hugins 2 DO
Murrel, Robert, 10 March 1797, Rachael Lee   4 FR
Murry, Elias, 3 April 1795, Ellender Freeborn   3 WA-58
Murry, Francis, 27 March 1800, Hetty Tull   1 WO
Murry, James, 29 Sept. 1793, Susanna Swann   1 BA-5
Murry, John, 20 Jan. 1783, Sarah Forwood   3 HA-7
Murry, Joseph, 31 March 1795, Rachel Crawford   2 FR-1152
Murry, Michael, 3 April 1797, Polly Sims   2 SO
Murry, Thomas, 17 Dec. 1795, by Rev. Joshua Jones; Keziah
    Rollins   46 BA-1
Murry, William, 14 Jan. 1800, Lydia Weeks   6 BA
Muschert, John, 17 Jan. 1795, Hetty Eastburn   5 BA-10
Muse, Joseph E., 2 July 1797, Sophia Kerr (born 16 May
    1778), dau. of David and Rachel   1 TA-322
Musgrove, Anthony, 22 April 1783, Sarah Flook   4 FR
Musgrove, Gilbert, 11 Oct. 1797, Dorcas Whittington 4 FR
Musgrove, Nathan, 26 Feb. 1784, Ann Selby   4 FR
Mussetter, Christian, 27 April 1792, Regina Sauffer 4 FR
Mussetter, Christopher, 17 Dec. 1799, Ruth Ijams   4 FR
Mushberg, David, 25 June 1787, El. Galent   29 BA-1
Musson, John, 28 May 1788, S, Turner   29 BA-1
    50 BA-388 gives the bride's name as Elis. Turner,
    and states that the parties are blacks.
Muviar, Henry?, March 1798, Mary Coon   3 WA-64
Myer, Henry, 8 May 1784, Anne Goodman   ,   4 FR
Myer, Jacob, 24 Aug. 1782, Susannah Kirk   4 FR
Myer, Sam, 13 April 1796, Catherine Need   4 FR
Myers, Benjamin, 28 Aug. 1794,Susanna Kelly   3 BA-291
Myers, Charles, 30 Dec. 1786, Elizabeth Garrols   5 BA-10
Myers, George, 12 June 1783, Margaret Zimmerman   4 FR
Myers, Henry, 12 July 1796, Ann Davis   4 FR
Myers, Jacob, 4 July 1782, Rebecca Burniston   4 FR
Myers, Jacob, of Yost, 8 Oct. 1785, Barbara Beames 4 FR
Myers, Jacob, 15 July 1795, Mary Payne   1 AL-53
    2 AL-700 gives the date as 16 July 1795.
Myers, Jacob, 3 Dec. 1800, Sarah Warren   8 BA-2
Myers, John, 5 Sept. 1782, Mary Ann Adams   4 FR
Myers, John, 30 Jan. 1792, Hannah Dehoff   4 FR
Myers, John, 5 June 1793, Sarah Reeves   6 BA
Myers, John, 17 March 1796, Ann Anderson   2 FR-1152
Myers, Michael, 6 Oct. 1792, Elizabeth Fout   4 FR
Myers, Nicholas, 18 Nov. 1795, Mary Daley   6 BA
Myers, Patrick, 15 July 1794, Anne Haley   3 BA-291
Myers, Robert, 14 Feb. 1795, Mary James   5 BA-10
Myler, Mathew, 25 Sept. 1778, Eliz'th Fowler   4 FR
Myles, Zachariah, 18 June 1793, Rebecca Bell   16 BA-4
Myles, Zachary, 11 Sept. 1799, Jane McMechers   8 BA-1
Myrehaver, Peter, 2 Feb. 1783, Catherine Hart   4 FR
Myrick, Joseph, 27 March 1796, Lilly Reese   3 BA-321

Nabb, Richard, 16 Feb. 1797, Margaret Saunders   4 KE-70
Nabbs, Thomas, 26 Aug. 1778, Mary Goodwin   11 BA-1
Nace, John, 22 March 1796, July Roco?   6 BA

Nagle, Edward, 7 March 1792, Margaret Miller   3 BA-255
Nagle, Jacob, 12 July 1794, Mary Selby   1 AL-53
Nagle, Sebastian, 4 March 1800, Magd. Shafer   2 FR-1157
Naile, Henry, 7 May 1787, Mary Rogers   4 FR
Nairne, Robert, 6 Feb. 1799, Polly Oston   1 WO
Nally, Nathan Barton, 6 Jan. 1778, Sarah Taylor   2 CH-455
Nally, Rich'd, 23 April 1778, Keziah Tanneyhill   2 MO-1
Nanvorruck, John, 2 Feb. 1798, Mary Nobs   3 BA-355
Nash, Thomas, 25 Dec. 1788, Lucretia Weeks   1 BA-1
Naugle, Peter, 12 May 1793, Mary Conrad   6 BA
Navey, Brigs, 29 May 1793, Keziah Riggin   2 DO
Navey, John, 1 June 1786, Amelia Jones   2 DO
Navey, John, 2 March 1793, Ally Murphy   2 DO
Nayler, William, 22 May 1779, Clementia Abercrombie   5 BA-11
Naylor, Alexander, 9 March 1786, Mary Mills   2 FR-1157
Naylor, Batson, 8 Nov. 1778, Eleanor Austin   5 CH-1
    2 CH-455 gives date as 8 Nov. 1781.
Naylor, Isaa, Jones, 17 March 1779, Barbara Goodman   4 FR
Naylor, Wm., 2 Oct. 1800, Nancy Sanford   3 AL-7
Neace, William, 13 July 1797, Elizabeth Murray   45 BA-1
Neal, John, 14 April 1789, Mary Scofield   1 BA-2
Neal, Theodore, 7 May 1778, Sarah Kirby   2 PG-3
Neale, Bernard, 18 Aug. 1800, Elizab. Christian   2 FR-1157
Neale, George, 8 Dec. 1799, Mary Lee   2 SM-138
Neall, Francis, son of Solomon and Ruth, 1st day, 12 mo.,
    1790, Susanna Kemp, dau. of James and Elizabeth   4 SF-199
Nealy, James, c.1786/7, Eva Widman   50 BA-387
Neary (or Weary), Peter, 1 Aug. 1784, Polly Shamms   11 BA-7
Needham, John, 9 Nov. 1800, Nancy Cole   3 BA-395
Needham, William, 30 Aug. 1795, Jane Pogue   7 BA-2
Needles, Edward, 4th day, 2 mo., 1789, Sarah Berry,
    dau. of Joseph   4 SF-194
Needles, Stephen, 17 April 1796, Nancy Martin   5 BA-11
Needles, Tristram, 1st day, 12 mo., 1779, Anna Buckbee 4 SF-158
Neff, Conrad, 20 Feb. 1798, Sus. Creighbaum   2 AL-700
Neff, Jacob, 10 Dec. 1796, Margaret Getzendanner   4 FR
Neff, John, 15 Feb. 1798, Elizabeth Harriade   4 FR
Neidham, William, 28 Aug. 1795, Jane Rogue   3 HA-24
Neighbours, Nathan, 22 March 1799, Sarah Price   4 FR
Neild, Abraham, 22 May 1798, Nancy Reed   2 DO
Neild, Hugh, 30 Jan. 1798, Mary Shehawn   2 DO
Neill, James, 28 Sept. 1784, Susanna Ellicott   5 BA-11
Neill, William, 2 Nov. 1797, Mary Sheredine   1 BA-8
    See also 3 HA-26.
Neith, Samuel, 24 April 1795, Elis. Bruns   3 WA-58
Nellson, George, 24 April 1779, Jemimah Bonham   4 FR
Nellson, Henry, 24 Dec. 1779, Sophia Polle   4 FR
Nelson, Aquila, 14 Feb. 1792, Frances Vansickle   3 HA-21
Nelson, Basil, 21 Oct. 1787, Sarah Maynard   2 FR-1157
Nelson, David, 16 Nov. 1780, Rachel Baker   2 CH-455
    3 HA-5 gives the date as 16 Nov. 1781.
Nelson, Elijah, 4 Jan. 1798, Sophia Melvin   1 WO
Nelson, George, 19 June 1782, Sarah Watt   3 HA-6
Nelson, James, 16 Sept. 1778, Mary Brown   11 BA-1
Nelson, James, 1 Aug. 1786, Anne Summers   11 BA-9
Nelson, John, 9 April 1780, Elizabeth Burgess   2 CH-455
Nelson, John, 31 May 1784, Mary Morren (or Morrer)   11 BA-7
Nelson, John, 20 Sept. 1800, Rebecca Ann Munroe   3 HA-30
    2 HA-352 gives the date as 23 Sept. 1800.
Nelson, Josiah, 15 March 1796, Margaret Smith   1 WO
Nelson, Levi, 5 Dec. 1797, Hannah Mills   1 WO
Nelson, Peter, 29 Oct. 1798, Eleanor Muckel   4 FR
Nelson, Robert, 23 April 1782, Sarah Johnson   3 HA-6
    3 HA-6 gives the date as 20 June 1782.
Nelson, Roger, 26 Feb. 1788, Mary Sim   4 FR

```
Nelson, Capt. Roger, 2 Feb. 1797, Elizabeth Harrison      4 FR
Nelson, Thomas, 9 May 1793, Matilda Johnson               3 BA-267
Nelson, William, 13 April 1779, Sally Smallwood           2 CH-455
Nelson, William, 31 Jan. 1797, Sally Sturgis              1 WO
Nelson, Wm., 20 Dec. 1797, Sarah Brothery                 1 WO
Nelson, William, 12 Nov. 1798, Ann McDonald               4 FR
Nesmith, Isaac, 27 Dec. 1791, Ann Johnson                 4 FR
Nettle, Thomas Dutton, 20 July 1779, Muriel Dutton        4 CH-2
     2 CH-455 gives the date as 5 July 1779.
Nettles, James, 29 Jan. 1795, Tomsey Phips                3 AA-424
Neuschwanger, Henry, 15 March 1787, Cath. Beltz           2 FR-1157
Nevel, Samuel, 10 Aug. 1785, Elizabeth Mitchell           3 HA-9
Nevett, Charles, 18 Jan. 1790, Levinah Bowling            2 PG-1
Nevil, Ralph, 7 Feb. 1797, Sarah Greenwood                4 KE-70
Nevit, John, 2 Jan. 1800, Susanna Milton                  2 SM-138
Newbald, William, 2 May 1797, Elizabeth Cottingham        2 SO
Newbay, Godfrey, 29 Jan. 1797, Rachel Blond               29 BA-8
Newbold, Thos., 22 May 1798, Polly Taylor                 1 WO
Newcomb, William, 20 Dec. 1780, Sarah Beckett             2 PG-5
Newcomb, William, 7 Aug. 1798, Hannah Tedron              4 KE-70
Newel, William, 1 April 1794, Susanna Morehead            3 BA-285
Newhouse, John, 31 Dec. 1791, Ann Statia Connelly         4 FR
Newjent, David, 9 March 1787, Mary Ann Dramon             6 BA
Newman, Henry, (23 Aug. 1791), Sarah James                31 BA-1
Newman, Isaac, 16 Jan. 1798, Mary Shipham                 2 SO
Newman, John, 28 Nov. 1787, Leah Lord                     1 SO-156
Newman, John, 10 Jan. 1797, Rebecca Burgan                4 KE-70
Newman, John, 30 April 1798, Polly Davis                  2 SO
Newman, John, 13 April 1800, Elizabeth Cole               6 BA
Newman, Stacy, 24 Dec. 1799, Sarah Davis                  2 FR-1157
     4 FR gives the date as 29 Dec. 1799.
Newton, Ebenezer, 8 Oct. 1800, Mary Traverse              2 DO
Newton, Edward, 25 Feb. 1790, Mary Bowdle                 2 DO
Newton, Jobe, 17 March 1779, Nansey Riggin                1 SO-156
Newton, Nathan C., 27 Jan. 1800, Margaret Nichols         2 DO
Newton, Thomas, 21 Aug. 1797, Polly Gadd                  2 DO
Newton, Thomas, 23 June 1800, Peggy Fitchett              2 DO
Newton, William, 24 Dec. 1782, Rachel Lawrence            5 BA-11
Newton, William, 25 March 1795, Margaret Helmsby          2 DO
Nice, David, 7 Oct. 1789, Cath. Peck                      29 BA-1
Nicewonger, John, 21 Dec. 1780, Ann Noffsinger            4 FR
Nicholas, George, 28 Dec. 1778, Mary Smith                5 BA-11
Nicholas, John, 4 June 1787, Sally Raines                 2 CH-455
Nicholas, John, 26 April 1800, Mary Bear                  3 BA-385
Nicholas, Nathaniel, 25 Oct. 1790, Elizabeth Harris       1 BA-3
Nicholas, Philip N., 18 Feb. 1799, Mary Spear             5 BA-11
Nicholas, Wilson Cary, 29 Jan. 1785, Margaret Smith       5 BA-11
Nicholls, Benj., 30 Aug. 1796, Drusilla Culver            5 MO-113
Nicholls, James, 11 Jan. 1785, Sarah Ips                  4 FR
Nicholls, James, 26 Feb. 1787, Ann James                  4 FR
Nicholls, John Haymond, 28 Nov. 1785, Cassandra Wilcoxon
     4 FR
Nicholls, Thos., April 1800, Priscilla Mackey             5 MO-116
Nicholls, William, 24 Sept. 1782, Charity Offutt          4 FR
Nichols, Daniel, 29 Aug. 1781, Mary Kirkman               2 DO
Nichols, Edw'd, 15 Aug. 1780, Wilhelmina Hamilton         2 PG-7
Nichols, Henry, 14 Dec. 1790, Elizabeth Blake             3 PG-257
Nichols, James, 28 July 1785, Charlotte Saunders          3 HA-9
Nichols, James, 26 Feb. 1787, Ann James                   2 FR-1157
Nichols, Rozel, 22 Feb. 1800, Lotty Hitch                 2 SO
Nichols, Thomas, 16 June 1796, Martha Carter              3 HA-25
     See also 7 BA-3.
Nichols, William, 1 Feb. 1778, Martha Smith               2 PG-2
Nichols, William, 24 Dec. 1780, Elizabeth Bird            2 PG-5
Nicholson, Benja., 9 Sept. 1783, Mary Merson              11 BA-6
```

Nicholson, Charles, 2 Jan. 1797, Ebby Hitch   2 SO
Nicholson, Edward, 14 Nov. 1797, Ann Wilkins   4 KE-70
Nicholson, James, 1 Sept. 1786, Hannah Aires   6 BA
Nicholson, Jeremiah, 10 March 1796, Hester Nicholson 5 MO-113
Nicholson, Jno., 11 April 1799, Tabitha Oden   5 MO-116
Nicholson, John Ridgely, 25 March 1794, Matilda Heath Smith
    1 BA-6
Nicholson, Richard, (13 or 18) Oct. 1777, Bridget Farclong
    1 MO-2
Nicleson, John, 16 Jan. 1796, by Rev. Ridgely; Mary
    Mobley   4 AA
Nicodemus, John, 24 Dec. 1784, Ann Neff   4 FR
Nicol, George, 22 March 1798, Eliz. Wallis   2 FR-1157
Nicoll, David, 26 June 1797, Dorcas Allen   29 BA-8
Nicols, Henry, Jr., son of William and Henrietta, 26 Oct.
    1786, Elizabeth Robins, dau. of Stanley and Mary 1 TA-325
Nicols, Henry, 5 Dec. 1793, Rebecca Smith   3 BA-279
Nicols, Samuel, son of Wm. and Henrietta, 3 Feb. 1794,
    Mary Blake, dau. of Chas. and Mary   1 TA-325
Nicols, Samuel, 15 Feb. 1800, Elizabeth Smith, dau. of
    Thomas   1 TA-325
Niehoff, Balser, 19 May 1795, Eliza Groce   4 FR
Niehoff, John Daniel, 25 June 1796, Catherine Ramsberg 4 FR
Niehoff, Nicholas, 8 Jan. 1793, Eva Yowler   4 FR
Nield, Richard, 8 Oct. 1788, Elizabeth Byus   2 DO
Niemayer, John, 21 Feb. 1787, Barb. Stohr   2 FR-1157
Nierle, Johannes, 24 June 1800, Peggy Bery   10 BA-200
Niger, Michael, 18 Jan. 1793, Sarah Morgan   1 BA-5
Night, Peter, 5 March 1798, Sarah Cline   2 HA-350
Nigill, Adam, 2 Feb. 1790, Ann Barnes   3 PG-256
Ninde, James, 26 Feb. 1797, Catharine Blyth   6 BA
Nippert, John, 1791, Cath. Hiessman   50 BA-390
Nixon, William, 22 Feb. 1790, Mary Pettit   6 BA
Noble, Anthony, before 12 Dec. 1792, by Rev. John Long;
    Sarah Hill   4 AA
Noble, James, 12 Dec. 1781, Mary West   3 HA-5
Noble, James, 11 Jan. 1799, Hatty Johnson   1 WO
Noble, John, 13 April 1781, Ann Hooper   2 DO
Noble, Joseph, 1 Feb. 1800, Eliz. Schock   29 BA-11
Noble, Joshua, (date not given), Sarah Twiford   2 SF
Noble, Levin, 7 Feb. 1799, Margaret Adley   2 DO
Noble, Thomas, 14 March 1800, Nancy Miller   2 SO
Noble, Thomas, 27 June 1800, Sarah Ballard   2 SO
Noble, William, 9 April 1788, Mary Vickers   2 DO
Noble, William, 27 April 1789, Molly Noble   2 DO
Nock, Joseph, of Ezekiel, 18th day, 10 mo., 1798, Rachel
    Regester, dau. of John   4 SF-217
Nolan, Wm., 19 April 1795, Barb. Silzel   29 BA-6
Noland, Barney, 16 Dec. 1781, Rosanna Mungin   4 FR
Noland, Bernard, 16 Oct. 1787, Elizabeth Beall   4 FR
Noland, Gregory, 23 Aug. 1798, Eliz. Dowdle   2 FR-1157
Noland, John, 22 July 1787, Ann Watkins   2 FR-1157
Noland, Michael, 18 April 1786, Mary Sickman   4 FR
Noland, Thomas, 30 Oct. 1783, Ann Moore   11 BA-6
Noland, Thomas, 16 June 1796, Mary Bayne   3 PG-442
Noles, Joseph, 16 May 1797, Biddy Ryan   47 BA-1
Noll, James, 11 June 1793, Sophia Noll   2 DO
Norfolk, William, 15 Jan. 1782, Dorcas Hutchings   3 AA-418
Norgate, James, 1 Jan. 1800, Elizabeth Waters   2 DO
Norget, James, 13 July 1793, Sarah Norman   2 DO
Norman, Christopher, 17 Aug. 1794, Elizabeth Hammond 2 DO
Norman, Levy, 17 April 1797, Mary Godfrey   6 BA
Norman, Thomas, 11 April 1798, Bathana Hurley   2 DO
Norquay, Magness, 17 July 1795, Jane Trotman   5 BA-11
Norquay, Magnus, 6 Feb. 1797, (Marie Charlotte) "Charl."
    Gitte   29 BA-8

Norris, Augustus, 25 Nov. 1779, Sarah Norris　　　　　3 HA-1
Norris, Barnabas, 1 June 1790, Barbara Oatner　　　　4 FR
Norris, Benjamin, 11 Dec. 1788, Margaret Butler　　　6 BA
Norris, Daniel, 23 Aug. 1791, Frances Hughes　　　　　1 BA-4
　　3 HA-21 gives the date as 18 Aug. 1792.
Norris, Edward, 14 Dec. 1799, Rebecca Lee　　　　　　3 HA-28
Norris, George, 14 April 1796, Eleanor Talbot　　　　4 FR
Norris, Henry, 3 April 1790, Margaret Gorden　　　　 1 BA-2
Norris, Jacob, 30 March 1785, Avarilla Gallion　　　 3 HA-9
Norris, James, 19 April 1783, Anne Worth　　　　　　 3 HA-7
Norris, James, 30 Sept. 1794, Margaret James　　　　 2 DO
Norris, James, 31 May 1798, Mary Willoughby　　　　　6 BA
Norris, John, 13 Jan. 1784, Rachel Norris　　　　　　4 FR
Norris, John, 18 Feb. 1785, Sarah Richardson　　　　 3 HA-9
Norris, John, 18 March 1795, Elizabeth Rigdon　　　　4 FR
Norris, John, 10 May 1798, Mary Daughaday　　　　　　6 BA
Norris, John, 10 Sept. 1799, Ann Wadsworth　　　　　 3 HA-28
Norris, Lloyd, 7 Nov. 1799, Jane Peterkin　　　　　　3 BA-380
Norris, Martin, 12 Feb. 1784, Mary Williamson　　　　3 AA-420
Norris, Martin, before 12 Dec. 1792, by Rev. John Long;
　　Margaret Dorsey　　　　　　　　　　　　　　　　　 4 AA
Norris, Richard, 5 Oct. 1780, Elizabeth Harris　　　 3 AA-416
Norris, Samuel, 5 May 1778, Catherine Miller　　　　 4 FR
Norris, Thomas, son of Thomas, 22nd day, 11 mo., 1792,
　　Ann Cowman, dau. of John and Sarah　　　　　　　 6 SF
Norris, Thomas, 2 Oct. 1797, Susanna Irons　　　　　 4 FR
Norris, William, 22 Nov. 1778, Dorothy White　　　　 3 SM-57
Norris, William, 24 Dec. 1800, Martha Norris　　　　 3 HA-3
Norris, William, 12 Feb. 1791, Elizabeth Margaret Silver　4 FR
Norris, William, 26 Dec. 1799, Sarah Schaffer　　　　5 BA-11
Norriss, William, 24 Sept. 1782, Mary Hayes　　　　　4 FR
North, James, 13 Oct. 1783, Elizabeth Howell　　　　 2 DO
North, James, 28 Aug. 1790, Elizabeth Phillips　　　 2 DO
North, Moses, 17 Dec. 1798, Nancy Harrington　　　　 2 DO
North, Pollard, 6 Oct. 1791, Mary Rogers　　　　　　 2 DO
North, Richard, 1 Jan. 1783, Nancy Rogers　　　　　　2 DO
North, Richard, 30 June 1786, Nancy Dawson　　　　　 2 DO
North, Robert, 25 Aug. 1797, Nancy Frazier　　　　　 2 DO
North, Rubin, 9 June 1798, Elizabeth Woollen　　　　 2 DO
Northon, Benja., 8 March 1790, Mary Pansier　　　　　11 BA-13
Norton, Dennis, 12 March 1797, Marg't Murphy　　　　 40 BA-3
Norton, John, 20 Sept. 1789, Sarah Jones　　　　　　 1 BA-2
Norvel, John, 30 April 1778, by Rev. Magowan; Sarah Askey
　　4 AA
Norvel, William, Aug. 1778, Elizabeth Mace　　　　　 3 AA-414
Norvel, William, 11 Feb. 1779, Mary Stevens　　　　　3 AA-415
Norwood, Elijah, 6 Oct. 1787, Rachel Price　　　　　 6 BA
Norwood, James, 30 Dec. 1793, Drusilla Murphey　　　 4 FR
Norwood, Jno., 18 June 1782, Mary Haile　　　　　　　11 BA-5
Norwood, Samuel, 11 Dec. 1787, Rebecca Brown　　　　 3 BA-214
Nouls, James, 6 Aug. 1783, Ann Linard　　　　　　　　11 BA-6
Novey, William, 25 Feb. 1792, Sarah Mills　　　　　　2 DO
Nowell, John, 29 May 1788, by Rev. Claggett; Sarah
　　Addington　　　　　　　　　　　　　　　　　　　　4 AA
Nower, Alexander, 13 Feb. 1794, Martha Morrison　　　3 HA-23
　　See also 7 BA-1.
Nowland, Peregrine, 10 Feb. 1787, Rebecca Savin, dau.
　　of William　　　　　　　　　　　　　　　　　　　 1 CE-23
Nowland, Peregrine, 5 Oct. 1798, Elizabeth Combess　 7 BA-4
Nowland, Peter, 9 Nov. 1794, Eliza Collins　　　　　 50 BA-396
Nuner, Jehu, 10 Feb. 1795, Meome Pearson　　　　　　 2 DO
Nuner, William, 29 Nov. 1781, Anna Hall　　　　　　　2 DO
Nunum, Lawson, 6 Oct. 1800, Betsey Whiteley　　　　　2 DO
Nusbaum, David, 21 Feb. 1792, Eve Waltz　　　　　　　4 FR
Nuss, Frederick, 7 Oct. 1797, Caty Doeffer　　　　　 4 FR

```
Nusz, Fred-rick, 5 Oct. 1797, Cath. Dofler        2 FR-1157
Nute, James, 11 Jan. 1798, Sarah Price            4 KE-70
Nutter, Charles, 19 Nov. 1792, Sophia LeCompte    2 DO
Nutter, Thos. E., 21 June 1799, Nancy Nelms       1 WO
Nutter, William, 13 Nov. 1800, Sarah Rogers       2 SO
Nuttwell, Elias, 13 May 1781, Deborah Sheckells   2 PG-5


Oakly, John Scroggan, 15 June 1778, Mary Ann Mahoney   4 CH-1
Oatner, John, 16 Feb. 1790, Elizabeth Conrad      4 FR
Ober, John, 18 Nov. 1795, Elizabeth Woodward      3 BA-313
Oberfeld, Mathias, 11 Sept. 1779, Anna Maria Hardman   4 FR
Oberholzer, Jno, 1791, Cath. Jarvis              50 BA-391
Obermayer, Joh., Sept. 1798, Feni Carter          3 WA-65
Obhold, Johann Andreas, 29 Dec. 1783, Elisabeth Ordenbach
    10 BA-178
Obleman, John, 10 Nov. 1792, Catherine Kephart    4 FR
O'Brian, Patrick, 31 July 1782, Eliza Stewart    11 BA-5
O'Brien, Daniel, 31 June 1795, Mary Askew        29 BA-6
O'Bryan, Daniel, 29 Sept. 1778, Mary Ann Fin     11 BA-1
O'Bryan, Daniel, 12 Oct. 1790, Mary Ann Perry     2 FR-1158
O'Bryan, Dennis, 9 Oct. 1790, Mary Ann Perry      4 FR
O'Callahan, James, July 1778, Catherine McFerlin 11 BA-1
O'Daniel, Peter, 7 April 1791, Ruthey Boyd        4 FR
Odell, John, 22 Jan. 1795, Anney Cooper           6 BA
Oden, Nathan, 24 Sept. 1778, Ann Norfut           2 MO-1
Odenbaugh, Charles, 2 July 1785, Martha Dean     16 BA-3
O'Donnell, John, 12 Oct. 1785, Sarah Chew Elliott 11 BA-8
Oechslein, John, 29 March 1796, Mary Bossert      2 FR-1158
O'Ferrel, Thomas, 8 July 1790, Hannah Norris      6 BA
Offutt, Barak, 26 Feb. 1799, Virlinder Offutt     5 MO-115
Offutt, Thos. Odle, 17 July 1800, Charity Benton  5 MO-116
Ogburn, Archibald, 26 Sept. 1789, Rachel Longly   3 PG-255
Ogden, Robert, 22 Oct. 1778, Anne Wynn            2 PG-3
Ogg, Alexander, 29 March 1781, Jane Hellen        3 AA-417
Ogg, Alexander, 15 Feb. 1784, Ann Skinner         3 AA-420
Ogg, Benjamin, 19 Dec. 1789, Mary Hooker          6 BA
Ogg, James, (25 March 1791), Sarah Baseman       15 BA-4
Ogier, John, 4 Jan. 1797, Margaret Reese          3 BA-354
Ogle, Alexander, 28 Nov. 1783, Mary Beatty        4 FR
Ogle, Geo., 25 Nov. 1784, Alazane Flanagan       11 BA-8
Ogle, George, 11 Dec. 1798, Mary Smothers         6 BA
Ogle, Mordecai, 29 Sept. 1793, Leanora Linton     2 AL-700
Ogle, Robert, 23 Jan. 1800, Polly Foster          3 BA-382
Ogle, William, 4 Jan. 1794, Susanna Jackson       4 FR
Ogle, William, 18 Jan. 1799, Margaret Ogle        4 FR
Ogle, William, 20 July 1800, Eleanor Clarke       3 BA-388
Ogleby, Francis, 5 Feb. 1794, Charlotte McCoy    14 BA-16
O'Haro, Samuel, 9 Nov. 1795, Juliana Rolors       3 BA-313
Oharrough, John, 12 Feb. 1796, Eliz. Huiez        3 WA-60
O'Hauer, David, 13 April 1797, Rebecca Gregory   50 BA-401
O'Haver, David, 13 April 1797, Rebecca Gregory   29 BA-8
O'Henry, Henry, 27 July 1791, Ann Price           1 BA-8
    3 HA-26 gives the date as 27 July 1797.
O'Laughlin, Bryan, 8 June 1797, Kitty Mumma      29 BA-8
Olberry, John, 28 Oct. 1794, Mary Myers           2 AL-700
Oldham, Jno., 12 April 1795, Hannah Albright     29 BA-6
Oliver, Francis, 24 Oct. 1782, Wilhelminah Scott  3 AA-419
Oliver, John, 4 Nov. 1781, Sophia Thralls         2 PG-5
Oliver, John, 5 Jan. 1790, Catherine Hughes       6 BA
Oliver, Levi, 28 Oct. 1799, Polly Reed            1 WO
Oliver, Robert, 29 Nov. 1800, Susanna Whitney     6 BA
Oliver, William, 13 Dec. 1780, Frances Cook       2 DO
Oliver, William, 16 Feb. 1785, Nancy Blackstock   2 CH-455
Ollip, Adam, 6 Jan. 1787, Margaret Foutz          4 FR
```

```
Olliser, George, 6 Sept. 1796, Molly Johnson            4 FR
Ollive, John Bapt., 12 Oct. 1795, Louisa Thiron        44 BA-1
Olliver, James, 25 Feb. 1781, Susannah Armstrong        3 HA-3
O'Mara, Patrick, 7 May 1797, Mary Rettig               29 BA-8
Oneal, Jno., 29 July 1794, Mary Conners                29 BA-5
O'Neale, Barton, 9 Jan. 1786, Mary Dyson                4 FR
O'Neale, David, 15 Oct. 1798, Rebecca Lane              5 MO-115
Onion, Stephen, 26 June 1783, Kitty Crone              14 BA-5
Onions, William, 29 Oct. 1795, Catherine Manakey        4 FR
Or, Michael, 13 Dec. 1796, Rosanna Sheltnecht           4 FR
Oram, Arnold, 2 April 1795, Elizabeth League            6 BA
Oram, Benjamin, 1790, by Rev. Green; Sarah Runnells     4 AA
Oram, Henry, 8 Jan. 1778, by Rev. Magill; Anne Ridgely  4 AA
Oram, Jno., 20 April 1784, by Rev. Robison; Ann Lewis  11 BA-7
Oram, Levy, 21 Sept. 1789, Mary Hurley                  2 DO
Oram, Thomas, 17 May 1797, Rebecca Jones                2 DO
Orme, James, 18 Nov. 1797, Rebecca Orme                 6 MO
Orme, Moses, 23 Oct. 1781, Elizabeth Davis              2 CH-455
Orme, Nathan, 21 Jan. 1800, Polly Beall                 5 MO-116
Orme?, Nathan, 25 May 1800, Elizabeth Clark             8 MO-25
Orme, Dr. Richard J., 18 Nov. 1800, Ann Crabb           5 MO-116
Ormond, Edward, 13 Aug. 1778, Sarah Marsh              11 BA-1
Orn, Edward, 22 June 1799, Rhoda Brewer                 3 BA-372
Orndorff, Peter, 2 July 1795, Margaret Allen           14 BA-17
Orr, James, 5th day, 3 mo., 1789, Angelina Malsby       1 SF
Orr, Robert, 9 Aug. 1794, Ruth Crawford                 3 HA-23
Orrick, John, 25 Dec. 1794, Mary Garvey                 3 BA-296
Orsborn, David, 14 March 1783, Sarah Bagerly            4 FR
Orsler, Charles, 5 Feb. 1778, Martha McCandlay         11 BA-1
Ort, Johannes, 31 Oct. 1798, Cathrina Klein            10 BA-198
Ort, Wilhelm, 1788, Christina Heyer                    50 BA-388
Osband, Peter, 8 Nov. 1795, Rebecca Rowland             4 PG-157
Osborn, Benjamin, 8 April 1781, Elizabeth Garrison      3 HA-3
Osborn, Cyrus, 25 Nov. 1795, Martha Warfield            3 HA-24
Osborn, Daniel, 4 Dec. 1797, Rebecca Coplan             2 FR-1158
Osborn, James, 9 April 1786, Eleanor Haley         ı   11 BA-9
Osborn, Jno., Jr., 19 May 1785, Mary Armigost          11 BA-8
Osborn, John, 27 Oct. 1794, Elizabeth Stewart           3 HA-24
Osborn, Richard, 14 Dec. 1796, Mary Humphrey            2 FR-1158
Osborn, William, 16 Dec. 1781, Ann Lytle                3 HA-5
Osborn, Wm., 21 Dec. 1799, Christiana Stonecifer        3 AL-6
Osborne, Cyrus, 26 Nov. 1795, Martha Warfield           2 HA-349
Osborne, William, 19 Dec. 1780, Nancy Lytle             2 CH-455
Osburn, Henry, 23 June 1779, Ann Timpson                7 CH-1
Osburn, Michael, 7 June 1798, Susanna Christopher       6 BA
Osburn, Samuel, 21 March 1790, Susanna Akels            3 BA-227
Osburn, Thos., 25 Sept. 1794, Diana Askins             50 BA-395
Osburn, Walter, 8 Oct. 1782, Mary Miles                 2 CH-455
Osler, William, 18? Jan. 1778, Mary Parker             11 BA-1
Ostertag, Jacob, 11 Sept. 1796, Rachel Landers          2 FR-1158
Ot, Michael, 23 April 1786, Eliz. Wirtenbacher          2 FR-1158
Othe, Chas., 14 March 1796, Ann Green; blacks          50 BA-399
Otley, James, 24 Jan. 1780, Elizabeth Richardson        3 SM-58
Otley, Jehu, 22 March 1796, Lydia Dean                  3 HA-25
Otley, John, 22 March 1796, Lydia Dean                  2 HA-349
Ott, John, 11 May 1794, Mary Schafer                    2 FR-1158
Ott, Mich'l, 22 April 1786, Eliz'th Wertenbaker         4 FR
Otto, Anthony, 31 Oct. 1796, Ursula Lose               29 BA-7
Otto, Derrick, 17 Dec. 1800, Cath. Schmoktenberg       29 BA-12
Otto, Georg Nich's, 18 March 1800, Susanna Young       50 BA-407
Ourey?, Samuel, 18 Feb. 1792, Sarah Boyer               4 FR
Ousler, Jno., 30 April 1782, Sarah Baker               11 BA-5
Owen, Hezekiah, 10 May 1787, Eliz. Dewall               2 FR-1158
     4 FR gives the bride's name as Elizabeth Duvall.
Owen, John, 4 Sept. 1783, Abigail Cullom                4 FR
```

Owen, Joseph, 19 June 1781, Rebecca Latten   2 PG-5
Owen, Thomas, 8 May 1793, Ann McAtee   3 PG-438
Owen, William, 4 Jan. 1785, Frances Shekell   4 FR
Owen, William, 12 Oct. 1799, Mary Inright   6 BA
Owens, Edward, 19 March 1786, Hannah Jones   6 BA
Owens, Edward, 10 April 1792, Mary Meekins   2 DO
Owens, Henry, 25 March 1780, Priscilla Owens   3 AA-416
Owens, Isaac, 26 March 1792, Rebecca Swett   2 DO
Owens, Jacob, 19 Oct. 1797, Rachel Groves   1 AA-162
Owens, James, 22 Dec. 1796, Sally Matthews   2 SO
Owens, John, 3 Oct. 1779, Sarah Saunders   3 SM-57
Owens, John, 9 March 1780, Sarah Howerton   2 PG-3
Owens, Joshua, 23 July 1799, Hetty Brooks   2 SO
Owens, Robert, 6 Jan. 1800, Susannah Green   3 HA-29
Owens, Samuel, 7 Jan. 1783, Ann Grey   3 AA-419
Owens, William, 15 May 1783, Mary Norvell   3 AA-419
Owings, Archibald, 10 Sept. 1796, Priscilla Hays   4 FR
Owings, Beale, (18 Feb. 1790), Ruth Dorsey   15 BA-3
Owings, Beale, 20 Dec. 1795, Cornelia Harriss   2 FR-1158
    4 FR gives the bride's name as Cordelia Harris.
Owings, Benj., 1792, Cath. Zimmerman   50 BA-392
Owings, Christopher, 15 March 1799, Charlotte Worthington
    4 FR
Owings, Edward, 27 Aug. 1782, Cath. Milligan   11 BA-5
Owings, Isaac, 13 March 1794, Achsah Dorsey   36 BA-1
    4 BA-76 gives the date as 18 March 1794.
Owings, Joshua, 26 Oct. 1790, Ruth Frost   11 BA-13
Owings, Leavin, 15 Feb. 1779, Sarah Wonnel   1 SO-58
Owings, Nicholas, 22 Jan. 1786, Frances Risteau   16 BA-1
Owings, Samuel, 4 Nov. 1779, Mercy Turner   2 PG-3
Owings, Sam'l, 22 March 1791, Ruth Cockey   4 BA-75
Owings, Thomas, 27 March 1796, Sarah Squires   35 BA-4
Owins, Samuel, (15 May 1788), Arianna Dorsey   15 BA-1
Oyer, Francis, 20 Jan. 1798, Peggy Coock   3 WA-64
Oyer, Wendel, 26 Oct. 1797, Cath. Coock   3 WA-63
Oyster, Henry, 25 Oct. 1797, Barb. Waitman   3 WA-63
Oyston, Henry, 1 Feb. 1785, Margaret Pontenay   3 BA-189
Oyston, William, 4 May 1800, Ann Hamm   6 BA
Ozard, Robert, 5 Nov. 1796, Anne Johnston   3 BA-333
Ozbern, John, 15 Jan. 1788, Sarah Magruder   3 PG-254
Ozburn, John, 4 May 1794, Elizabeth Gibbs   3 PG-440
Ozier, Joseph, 1 May 1798, Elizabeth Stuart   4 KE-70

Padgett, Benjamin, 25 March 1778, Ann Green   4 FR
Padgitt, Wm. Ward, 16 Dec. 1788, Mary Grover   2 FR-1159
Pagan, Henry, 28 Dec. 1790, Keziah Travers   2 DO
Page, Daniel, 18 June 1795, Polly Hughes   3 BA-346
Page, John, 22 July 1799, Sarah Wheeler   2 DO
Page, Thomas, 6 April 1781, Catherine Willson   4 FR
Pagett, Josias, 8 Jan. 1797, Johanna Lovelace   3 PG-441
Pain, Michael, 4 March 1780, Peggy Cartery   4 FR
Paine, John, 1 Jan. 1797, Christina Formar   6 BA
Painell, James, 27 Feb. 1800, Nackley Stoxdale   8 BA-1
Painter, George, 18 Dec. 1800, Nancy Thompson   3 BA-396
Pall, Zachariah, 20 Dec. 1797, Polly Hart   2 DO
Palmer, Christian, Feb. 1799, Mary Welty   3 WA-66
Palmer, Edward, 4 Sept. 1788, Mary Nowlan   3 BA-211
Palmer, George, 23 Aug. 1797, Ann Comegys   4 KE-70
Palmer, Horace, 18 April 1795, Elizabeth Bodry   6 BA
Palmer, Jno., 2 May 1785, Ann Curtain   11 BA-8
Palmer, Thomas, 21 May 1779, Margaret English   5 BA-11
Palmer, William, 7 July 1781, Memory Walker   2 DO
Palmer, Wm., 29 Sept. 1796, Aravilla Jarvis   29 BA-7
Pamphilon, Thomas, 7 Oct. 1790, Rebecca Weary   5 BA-11

```
Parish, Aquila, (6 June 1798), Rebecca Tipton        15 BA-2
Parish, Benjamin, 1 March 1792, Nancy Hunter          1 BA-4
Parish, Edward, (11 March 1789), Delia Norris        15 BA-2
Parish, Gilbert, 29 May 1792, Ruth Hall               2 FR-1159
Parish, Joshua, 13 Jan. 1799, Sarah Rolan            45 BA-3
Parish, Mathew, 19 April 1800, by Rev. Roberts; Elener
     Goodwin                                           4 AA
Parish, Nicholas, 3 March 1793, Elizabeth Johnson     1 BA-5
Parish, Solomon, 4 Feb. 1794, Mary Parish             2 FR-1159
Park, James, 13 Oct. 1798, Elizabeth Copper           4 KE-70
Parke, Arthur, 13 Aug. 1781, Keziah Foxwell           2 DO
Parker, Aq'e, 3 March 1780, Sarah Amos                3 HA-1
Parker, Bavquilla, 19 Dec. 1798, Sally Wright         1 WO
Parker, Charles, 10 Jan. 1797, Tabitha Johnson        1 WO
Parker, Daniel, 28 Sept. 1798, Emaria Vein            2 DO
Parker, Evan, 5 July 1787, Barbara Iams               6 BA
Parker, Gilbert, 15 April 1790, Susanna Grimes        4 FR
Parker, James, 22 March 1792, Mary Pampillion         5 BA-11
Parker, John, 26 Aug. 1780, Sarah Jones               3 HA-2
Parker, John, 11 July 1795, Rebecca Lamb              6 BA
Parker, John, 6 Aug. 1796, Nancy Parker               1 WO
Parker, John, 24 Nov. 1800, Elizabeth Neptor          3 AL-7
     2 AL-701 gives the date as 27 Nov. 1800, and the
     bride's name as Neptine.
Parker, Robert, 29 Jan. 1800, Ann Stephenson          3 HA-29
Parker, Samuel, 27 Oct. 1798, Margaret Pinder         4 KE-70
Parker, Thomas, 29 July 1799, Catherine Lewis         2 DO
Parker, William, 23 Dec. 1781, Susanna Peacock        3 AA-418
Parker, William, (8 March 1788), Rachel Gosnel       15 BA-1
Parker, William, 5 Nov. 1800, Betsy Roach             2 SO
Parkerson, Abraham, 5 Oct. 1783, Jeane Norman         3 AA-420
Parkhouse, Wm., 27 July 1784, Sus. McKinnan          11 BA-7
Parkinson, Edw'd, 17 July 1785, Dinah James          11 BA-8
Parkinson, Edward, 20 Oct. 1796, Mary Ward            3 BA-329
Parkinson, John, 27 June 1778, Ann Leisle             4 FR
Parkinson, Rev. William, 3 Jan. 1799, Henrietta Beatty  6 BA
     See also 4 FR.
Parks, Abraham, 28 Sept. 1797, Eleanor Waller         6 BA
Parks, Archibald, 1 Sept. 1789, Ann Bosley           11 BA-12
Parks, Benjamin, 2 Oct. 1783, Eleanor Jones          11 BA-6
Parks, David, 15 April 1794, Eliza Towson            18 BA-6
Parks, Elisha, 17 March 1785, Rachael Brannon        11 BA-8
Parks, Frederick, 13 Dec. 1787, Rachel Parks          3 BA-216
Parks, Job, 1 Sept. 1798, Nancy Hart                  2 DO
     1 DO-40 gives the date as 6 Sept. 1798.
Parks, John, 4 Sept. 1788, Ruth Henricks              3 BA-218
Parks, John, 1 May 1796, Mary Stewart                 3 BA-323
Parks, Mack, 25 Aug. 1789, Delia Busick               2 DO
Parks, Mayberry, 26 June 1796, Mary Collins           3 BA-323
Parks, Nathan, 15 June 1794, Elizabeth Williams       6 BA
Parks, Nathan, 20 Nov. 1796, Rachel Griffith         45 BA-1
Parks, Nathan, 7 Dec. 1800, Mary Freeberge            6 BA
Parks, Peter, 11 Sept. 1790, P. Jones                29 BA-1
Parks, Planner, 21 June 1792, Priscilla Cole          2 DO
Parks, William, 15 Aug. 1784, Mary Mildews           11 BA-7
Parks, William, 9 Oct. 1798, Ellenor Corbin          45 BA-3
Parks, William, 13 Aug. 1799, Mary Travers            2 DO
Parks, Zebulum, 3 April 1799, Charlotte Walston       2 SO
Parlet, David, 1 April 1784, Rosanna German          11 BA-7
Parlet, William, 26 Feb. 1778, Elizabeth Gorman      11 BA-1
Parlett, Joshua, 8 March 1785, Cath. Price           11 BA-8
Parley, David, 26 June 1796, Sarah Wright             5 BA-12
Parnell, Bedwell, 19 July 1778, Ruth Easton           4 FR
Parnnion?, Henry, 27 Jan. 1799, Eliz. Sanders         5 MO-115
Parran, Alexander, 10 Feb. 1778, Mary King            1 CA-1
```

Parran, Benjamin, 15 Jan. 1778, Dorcas Hellen   1 CA-1
Parran, Charles Somerset, 17 Dec. 1782, Margaret Ireland
     3 SM-60
Parran, Thomas, 6 Feb. 1783, Jane Mackall   3 SM-61
Parratt, Aaron, son of Aaron, dec.; 22nd day, 3 mo., 1797,
     Rachel Bowers, dau. of John   4 SF-211
Parratt, Benjamin, son of Aaron and Mary (dec.), 19th day,
     6 mo., 1799, Sarah Parvin, dau. of Benjamin and
     Sarah (dec.)   4 SF-219
Parrish, Aquilla, 5 April 1796, Eleanor Condon   4 FR
Parrish, James, 23 Oct. 1786, Priscilla Street   2 FR-1159
Parrot, Thomas, 5 March 1795, Mary Smith   3 AA-424
Parrott, Thomas, 3 Sept. 1778, by Rev. Magowan; Letta Brown
     4 AA
Parry, James, c.1792, by Rev. Chalmers, in Fred. Co.; Sarah
     Warfield   4 AA
Parsley, Jonas, 30 Nov. 1799, Eleanor Clayton   5 MO-116
Parsons, Abner, son of John and Rebecca, 29th day, 4 mo.,
     1790; Rachel Dyer, dau. of Joseph and Joanna   1 SF
Parsons, George, 18 May 1797, Prissey Disharoon   2 SO
     3 SO gives the date as 19 May 1797, and the bride's
     name as Priscilla.
Parsons, James, 1 Nov. 1799, Mary Davis   1 WO
Parsons, Joseph, son of Thomas, 1st day, 8 mo., 1782,
     Elizabeth Neall, dau. of Solomon   4 SF-168
Parsons, Joseph, son of Thomas (dec.); 5th day, 3 mo.,
     1788, Elizabeth Parrott, dau. of Aaron (dec.)   4 SF-187
Parsons, Joseph, son of Bernard, 24 July 1798, Ann Chatham
     8 MO-16
Partridge, Jonathan, 22 Sept. 1781, Mary Reed   2 DO
Partridge, Robert, 8 Jan. 1784, Cathe. Randall   11 BA-7
Pasco, William, 14 Oct. 1780, Ann Flaxton   2 CH-455
Passapa, Moses, 13 Oct. 1784, Polly Bacon   2 DO
Passey, James, 17 May 1794, Anariah McGuire   3 BA-287
Paster, Francis, 8 June 1794, Stacy Beall   2 FR-1159
Paston, William, 27 Dec. 1797, Elizabeth Gardner   3 PG-441
Paterson, William, 2 July 1795, Nancy Craig   3 BA-307
Patesell, John, 28 Feb. 1795, Christena Ramsberg   4 FR
Patrick, George, 18 Feb. 1790, Ruth Montgomery   1 BA-2
Patrick, Hugh, 2 June 1799, Nancy Gill   5 BA-12
Patrick, John, 8 Aug. 1789, S. (or J.) Durbin   29 BA-1
Patridge, Daubney B., 4 March 1785, Elizabeth Porter   6 BA
Patridge, Isaac, 9 Jan. 1796, Mary Stewart   2 DO
Patridge, Job, 31 July 1800, Sarah Wilson   6 BA
Patridge, Jonathan, 25 Aug. 1786, Sarah Breerwood   2 DO
Patridge, Jonathan, 22 Oct. 1796, Celia Staplefort   2 DO
Patridge, Wm., 8 Jan. 1795, Ann Wells   6 BA
Pattan, Thomas, 9 May 1779, Mary Hern   11 BA-3
Patterson, Benjamin, 11 Sept. 1784, Jemima Price   4 FR
Patterson, George, 20 Dec. 1799, Elizabeth Merrill   1 WO
Patterson, Jacob, 7 June 1795, Elizabeth Ware   3 AA-424
Patterson, James, 13 May 1787, Jane Keath   5 BA-11
     3 BA-221 states that the marriage was performed by
     the Rev. Patrick Allison of the Presbyterian Congre-
     gation on 13 May 1789 (sic), and gives the bride's name
     as Heath.
Patterson, Jeremiah, 9 Dec. 1784, Nancy Barns   2 DO
Patterson, John, 8 Feb. 1781, Avarilla Hall   3 HA-3
Patterson, John, 21 July 1784, Sarah Hicks   2 DO
Patterson, John, 29 Oct. 1796, Nancy Bradshaw   3 BA-329
Patterson, John, 30 March 1799, Elizabeth Wire   3 AL-5
Patterson, John, 19 Aug. 1800, Peggy Hatch   6 BA
Patterson, Joseph, 9 March 1797, Elizabeth Let   2 FR-1160
Patterson, Lawrence, 18 July 1784, Nancy Lepton   11 BA-7
Patterson, William, 15 May 1779, Dorcas Spear   5 BA-11

Patterson, William, 9 Dec. 1779, Mary Jones   2 PG-3
Patterson, Wm., 9 April 1799, Susannah Griffin   2 FR-1160
Pattison, Jeremiah, 28 May 1800, Amelia Hooper   2 DO
Pattison, John, 29 May 1794, Elizabeth Pattison   6 BA
Pattison, Richard, 4 March 1788, Mary McKeel   2 DO
Paul, Isaac, 25 Jan. 1798, Susannah Brown   6 BA
Paul, Jabus, 7 Oct. 1800, Polly Willey Mequena   2 DO
Paul, James, 26 Dec. 1781, Elizabeth Lankford   2 DO
Paul, John, 27 Dec. 1790, Mary Wroten   2 DO
Paul, Zachariah, 12 March 1798, Polly Hart   1 DO-39
Pauly, Dan'l, 2 Sept. 1800, Caroline Roth   50 BA-408
Pauscault, Lewis, 8 Jan. 1784, Mary Schligh   10 BA-180
Paxson, Joseph, 20 July 1797, Mary Lusty   2 FR-1160
Paxton, Thomas, 22 Dec. 1799, Elizabeth Miller   4 FR
Payne, Alkana, 8 Dec. 1781, Delither Harper   2 DO
Payne, George, 13 Aug. 1792, Mary Sapp   1 AL-52
Payne, Jacob, 8 Jan. 1799, Elizabeth Payne   1 WO
Payne, James, 15 June 1785, Elizabeth Hudson   2 DO
Payne, James, 11 July 1795, Letitia Milward   3 BA-307
Payne, John, 1 Feb. 1791, Elizabeth Locker   3 PG-257
Payne, John, 29 May 1792, Mary Glenn   3 BA-256
Payne, John, 23 July 1799, Sally Pruitt   1 WO
Peach, William Elson, 23 Feb. 1797, by Rev. Ridgely; Sarah
      Duvall   4 AA
Peachy, William, 4 Jan. 1794, Amelia Reynolds   6 BA
Peacock, George, 13 Dec. 1796, Sarah Peacock   4 KE-70
Peacock, Jacob, 27 June 1793, Mary Gardiner   3 BA-269
Peacock, John, 5 July 1781, Elizabeth Smith   3 BA-181
Peacock, John, 20 Nov. 1793, Cloe Downing   3 PG-438
Peak, John, 29 Jan. 1798, Ann Barber   4 FR
Peak, Robert, 27 Sept. 1789, Elizabeth Murry   1 BA-2
Peale, William, 24 Dec. 1793, Polly Berry   5 BA-11
Peale, William, 20 Oct. 1796, Elizabeth Berry   3 BA-329
Pearce, Charles, 3 Sept. 1793, Drusilla Stansbury   6 BA
Pearce, Ezekiel, 26 Feb. 1781, Eleanor Powell   2 PG-5
Pearce, Jno., 3 May 1786, Eliza Lawrence   11 BA-9
Pearce, John, 29 June 1795, Frances Cunningham   2 BA
Pearce, Samuel, 28 Jan. 1796, by Rev. Ridgely; Margaret
      Shellhammon   4 AA
Pearce, Thomas, 20 April 1795, Elizabeth Cummins   3 BA-301
Pearl, James, 16 April 1799, Priscilla Adkins   2 FR-1160
Pearre, Alexander, 4 Jan. 1791, Tabitha Brashears   4 FR
Pearson, Andrew, 31 May 1796, Patty Smith   3 BA-323
Pearson, Daniel, 27 Jan. 1799, Sally Anastatia Holden   3 BA-367
Pearson, David, 30 Jan. 1798, Mary Ann Kimbo   5 BA-12
Pearson, Laban, 24 Sept. 1794, Polly Holmes   2 DO
Pearson, Noah, 9 Feb. 1796, Triphena Thomas   2 DO
Pearson, Richard, 12 Feb. 1783, Nelly Shehawn   2 DO
Pearson, Thomas, of Benjamin, of Reading, Berks Co., Pa.;
      19th day, 5 mo, 1798, Lydia Cox, dau. of Aaaron (dec.)
      4 SF-216
Pease, Dennis, 15 Aug. 1795, Marg. Edwards   29 BA-6
Peasee?, Charles, 5 Sept. 1780, Ann Peasee?   2 PG-7
Peat, Clude?, 25 Aug. 1782, Mary Hurly   11 BA-5
Pebble, Abraham, 15 Nov. 1786, Elizabeth Waggoner   4 FR
Pebble, Peter, 15 June 1778, Mary Cepharton   4 FR
Peck, David, 13 Jan. 1797, Elizabeth Clark   4 FR
Peck, John, 1788, Charlotte Brown   50 BA-388
      29 BA-1 gives the date as 18 Nov. 1788.
Peck, John, 27 Dec. 1793, Betty -(?)-; blacks   2 FR-1159
Peck, John, 23 June 1795, Cath. Biard   3 WA-59
Peck, John, 7 May 1796, Lotty Owings   6 BA
Peck, Thomas, 2 July 1796, Kitty Williams   4 FR-
Peck, William, 12 Sept. 1796, Sus. Glasscock   2 FR-1159
Peckard, Wm., 26 Dec. 1796, Mary Jackson   29 BA-8

```
Peddicoart, Jasper, 23 Oct. 1785, Amelia Hobbs        11 BA-8
Peddicoat, Adam, 25 Feb. 1783, Eliza Zimmerman        11 BA-6
Peduzi?, Peter, 5 Sept. 1797, Sally Shaw              40 BA-3
Peers, George, 28 Feb. 1793, Mary Ledley              6 BA
Peerson, Henry, 19 Oct. 1795, Mary Childs             5 BA-12
Peirce, John, 21 Feb. 1786, by Rev. Pigman; Elizabeth
     Hines                                            4 AA
Peit, -(?)-, 1790, -(?)- Nuidig                       50 BA-389
Pellen, Boyne, 11 Oct. 1796, Sara Clarke              1 AL-53
Pelling, Jonathan, 29 May 1785, Margaret Keys         3 BA-190
Pelly, Solomon, 8 Aug. 1799, Massy Holland            5 MO-116
Pemberton, William, 11 Jan. 1796, Mary Maxwell        3 BA-317
Pemberton, William, 14 April 1796, Sarah Odle         6 BA
Pence, George, 5 April 1788, Elizabeth Gombare        4 FR
Pender, Georg, 23 May 1795, Rebecca Alter             3 WA-58
Pendergrass, -(?)-, 25 Sept. 1787, Marg't Cummins     11 BA-10
Pendergrass, Robert, 28 Dec. 1800, Johanna Rogan      5 BA-12
Peniston, Samuel, 30 Aug. 1798, Ariana Renaud         7 BA-4
Penn, John, 20 July 1779, Eleanor Dutton              2 CH-455
Penn, John, 8 June 1794, Margaret Fountz              50 BA-395
Penn, Roby, 3 Jan. 1799, Lucrecra Howse               5 MO-115
Penn, Sam'l, 25 Aug. 1781, Eliz'th Ostler             4 FR
Penn, Shadreck, 23 May 1779, Ann Chaney               2 PG-3
Penn, Stephen, 28 Oct. 1798, Eleanor Scrivnor         6 MO
Penn, William, 8 April 1788, Mary Iiams               6 BA
Penn, William, 25 Sept. 1794, Deborah Connoway        3 BA-293
Penn, William, 1 March 1797, Sarah Penn               4 FR
Pennel, John, 10 Jan. 1792, Ann Saunders              6 BA
Pennel, John, 20 Dec. 1795, Peggy Schmok?             10 BA-196
Pennell, Richard, 22 Feb. 1798, Sally Tully           3 SO
Pennington, Henry, 21 March 1793, Jane Neale          6 BA
Pennington, John, 26 May 1791, Martha Miller          6 BA
Pennington, Nathan, 20 Sept. 1794, Eliza Clerage      18 BA-6
Pennington, William, 17 Sept. 1799, by Rev. Wyatt; Elizabeth
     Stevens                                          4 AA
Penny, Alexander, 27 Jan. 1791, Susannah Lord         6 BA
Penny, Thomas, 4 Jan. 1778, Amelia Adams              2 CH-455
Pennybaker, Samuel, 25 July 1783, Susannah Plunck     4 FR
Penrice, Thomas, 5 Nov. 1795, Mary Webb               3 BA-313
Peot, Peter, 11 March 1793, Louisa Avelin             3 BA-264
Pepper, Frederick, 17 Aug. 1797, Catherine Neill      6 BA
Pepper, Frederick, 22 Nov. 1798, Debro Gisburts       4 FR
Pepperman, Anthony, 18 Sept. 1798, Mary Clayton       3 BA-363
Perchariot (sic), Peter, 6 Sept. 1794, Guida Richard? 6 BA
Perego, Joseph, 9 May 1783, Jemima Woodward           5 BA-11
Peregrine, Henry, 25 Dec. 1800, Elizabeth Gardner     6 BA
Peret, Valentine, 6 Nov. 1791, Elizabeth Earce        18 BA-3
Perine, Maulden, 22 Oct. 1793, Hephzibah Brown        6 BA
     See also 19 BA-8.
Perine, Peter, 19 Nov. 1797, Mary Howard              6 BA
Perine, Peter, 2 Dec. 1798, Margaret Perine           6 BA
Perine, William, 19 March 1799, Susanna Fowler        6 BA
Perkins, Benjamin, 13 March 1796, Susannah Nice       6 BA
Perkins, Edmund, 8 Dec. 1798, Rebecca Steel           4 KE-70
Perkins, Joel G., 9 Oct. 1798, Eliz. Matsin           29 BA-9
Perkins, Samuel, 6 April 1780, Ann -(?)-              11 BA-4
Perkins, William, 15 Jan. 1779, Susanna Knight        5 HA
     3 HA-1 gives the date as 9 Jan. 1780, and the bride's
     name as Samuel (sic) Knight.
Perkins, William, 4 Dec. 1799, Eliza Flinn            6 BA
Perregoy, Charles, 23 June 1785, Ruth Gorsuch         16 BA-3
Perrett, Valentine, 6 Nov. 1791, Elizabeth Earee      3 BA-254
Perrigoy, Joseph, 13 Jan. 1788, Susanna Green         6 BA
Perril, Alexander, 29 May 1792, Grace Beaumont        2 FR-1159
     4 FR gives the groom's name as Perrill.
```

Perrill, Thomas, 5 March 1791, Zilpha Calliman   4 FR
Perrill, William, 14 June 1783, Sarah Padgett   4 FR
Perry, Andrew, 28 Sept. 1793, Martha Murray   3 BA-275
Perry, Ishmael, 23 Nov. 1797, Peggy Anderson   2 SO
Perry, James, 10 May 1792, Sarah Warfield   4 FR
Perry, John, 6 Nov. 1783, Barbara Hoffman   11 BA-6
Perry, John, 16 April 1786, Margaret Mannen   6 BA
Perry, Jno., 19 Dec. 1799, Jane Alnutt   5 MO-116
Perry, Peter, 27 Dec. 1797, Phoebe Henderson   6 BA
Perry, Richard, 8 Oct. 1789, Sophia Thomas   3 BA-228
Perry, Samuel, 19 May 1793, Rebecca Pennington   3 BA-267
Perry, Samuel, 9 June 1798, Mary Langwell   6 BA
Perry, Thomas, 4 Jan. 1778, Aurelia Adams   5 CH-1
Perry, William, 13 Aug. 1779, Mary Griffith   3 HA-28
    2 HA-351 gives the date as 15 Aug. 1799.
Perryman, Isaac, 21 Feb. 1786, Ann Jolley   16 BA-1
Perryman, John, 17 Oct. 1791, Cassandra Horner   3 HA-21
Peter, Black, April 1794?, (wife's name not given)   7 BA-1
Peter, John, 23 April 1786, Cath. Haller   2 FR-1159
Peter, John, 18 Nov. 1799, Polly Porter   3 BA-380
Peters, Conrad, 11 Nov. 1794, Lydia Haile   29 BA-6
Peters, George, 25 March 1796, Polly Trimble   29 BA-7
Peters, Henry, 10 Jan. 1790, by Rev. Reed; Sarah Powel
    4 AA
Peters, James, 3 Nov. 1792, Sarah Heavend   3 PG-437
Peters, Jno., 27 Jan. 1792, Mary Steitz   29 BA-2
Peters, Jno., 28 April 1796, Phebe Healds   29 BA-7
Peters, John, 30 March 1800, Hetty Pike   3 BA-384
Peters, Thomas, 30 Oct. 1783, Rebecca Johnson   11 BA-6
Peterson, Laurence, 13 Oct. 1798, Mary Couisins   6 BA
Peterson, William, 13 Jan. 1783, Rachel Heughs   4 FR
Pettebone, Charles, c.1798, by Rev. Riggin; Rebecca Elliott
    4 AA
Petterie, Aaron, 10 Aug. 1783, Jane Walker   11 BA-6
Petticoart, George, 6 Dec. 1797, Sophia Dorsey   4 FR
Petticoat, James, 28 April 1793, Mary Belt   6 BA
Pettingall, Jonathan, 26 Dec. 1797, Elizabeth Steward   6 BA
Pettingill, James, 2 Dec. 1797, Rebecca Green   6 BA
Petty, Jesse, 4 Jan. 1797, Mary Pryer   2 SO
Petty, Jno., 2 Jan. 1786, Margery Fauster   11 BA-9
Pew, Joseph, 21 Oct. 1787, Peggy King   6 BA
Pewdgard, Robard, 4 June 1795, Peggy Dowler   3 WA-59
Pewsy, Planner, 30 March 1797, Sarah Hayman   3 SO
Peyday, Thomas, 10 Jan. 1778, Eleanor Roberts   11 BA-1
Pfalzgraf, Joh. Georg, 4 April 1795, Elis. Miller   3 WA-58
Pfeffer, John, 3 Nov. 1789, Cath. Schafer   2 FR-1159
Pfistler, Valentin, "beide von Balto. Co.," 9 Oct. 1783,
    Mary Keam   10 BA-178
Phalan, Jesse, 7 Jan. 1790, Lydia Dean   11 BA-13
Phebus, John, 14 March 1792, Margaret Muir   2 DO
Phelps, Benjamin, 13 Dec. 1795, Priscilla Wheat   3 PG-441
Phelps, Ezekiel, 11 May 1794, by Rev. G. Ridgely; Margaret
    Watkins   4 AA
Phelps, Jesse, 3 Sept. 1795, Sarah Pumphrey   3 PG-441
Phelt, Matthew, 15 Dec. 1796, Margaret McBlaherty   3 BA-333
Phile, Charles, 5 Sept. 1792, Cath. Hershberger   29 BA-3
Philan, Richard, 12 Dec. 1791, Elizabeth Parkinson   6 BA
Philher, Joseph, 24 Jan. 1782, Chloe Griffin   2 CH-455
Philips, Humphrey, 15 April 1798, by Rev. Wyatt; Elizabeth
    Weston   4 AA
Philips, Jason, 10 April 1797, Ann Majers   4 FR
Philips, John, 7 Feb. 1797, Susanna Funk   2 FR-1160
Philips, Nich., 15 Feb. 1798, Mary Wilson   2 FR-1160
Philips, Philip, 15 April 1781, Sarah Hopkins   3 AA-417
Philips, Samuel, 27 Oct. 1778, Mary Steel   11 BA-1

```
Philips, Sam., 14 Jan. 1790, Eleanor Ball              3 PG-256
Philips, Stephen, 12 Nov. 1795, Rechall Pumphrey       3 PG-441
Philips, Thomas, 10 Dec. 1789, Margaret Welsh          6 BA
Philips, Thomas, 21 Dec. 1797, Elizabeth Lynn          4 FR
Philips, William, 10 July 1787, Lucretia Davis         4 FR
Phillips, Benjamin, 10 Oct. 1787, Jemima Kirwan        2 DO
Phillips, Caleb, 3 Feb. 1780, Sarah Darbey             4 FR
Phillips, Elie, 22 Feb. 1796, Catherine Harris         4 FR
Phillips, Elliott, 10 April 1782, Margaret Meekins     2 DO
Phillips, Henry, 4 Feb. 1788, Amelia Lane              2 DO
Phillips, Henry, 27 July 1790, Nancy Meekins           2 DO
Phillips, Isaac, 30 May 1784, Sarah Phillips           3 HA-8
Phillips, James, 4 July 1797, Henrietta Christopher    2 DO
Phillips, Jesse, 19 Feb. 1784, Mary Hardy              4 FR
Phillips, John, 21 Dec. 1784, Mary Lee                 2 DO
Phillips, John?, 20 Sept. 1792, by Rev. Parrott; Jean
   Beaven or Beaver                                    4 AA
Phillips, Joseph, 26 April 1782, Elizabeth Traverse    2 DO
Phillips, Joseph, 18 May 1785, Lovey Dawson            2 DO
Phillips, Levin, 24 May 1792, Nancy Keene              2 DO
Phillips, Levin, 21 March 1793, Elizabeth Meekins      2 DO
Phillips, Levin, 22 March 1796, Violety Meekins        2 DO
Phillips, Levy, 13 March 1791, Eleanor Swearingen      2 FR-1159
Phillips, Major, 7 Dec. 1791, Hilary Hooper            2 DO
Phillips, Nehemiah, 16 Oct. 1797, Nancy Clark          2 DO
Phillips, Reuben, 31 July 1790, Henrietta Elliott      2 DO
Phillips, Reuben, 2 Nov. 1792, Nancy Seward            2 DO
Phillips, Reuben, 9 July 1795, by Rev. Ridgely; Elizabeth
   Cromwell                                            4 AA
Phillips, Samuel, 27 July 1793, Rosanna Harris        18 BA-5
Phillips, Samuel, 10 June 1794, Betsy Wallace          2 DO
Phillips, Thomas, 16 Oct. 1794, Mary Wheatley          2 DO
Phillips, Thomas, 20 Oct. 1797, Mary Reed              2 DO
Phillips, William, 12 April 1796, Ann Creighton        2 DO
Phillpott, Chas. Thos., 14 Feb. 1780, Eliz'th Mockaboy 4 FR
Philpot, Benjamin, 3 Aug. 1786, Eliza Smoot            2 CH-455
Philpot, Bryan, 17 Nov. 1796, Elizabeth Johnson   ·    1 BA-7
Philpot, Charles, 14 Jan. 1799, Elizabeth Gwinn        4 FR
Philpott, Zachariah, 3 Dec. 1781, Cassandra Garrott    4 FR
Philps, Parker, 31 Dec. 1789, Anna Jacobs              6 BA
Phipps, Austin, 1 March 1798, Elizabeth Stansbury      6 BA
Phipps, Benjamin, 30 July 1778, by Rev. Magowan; Luana
   Kilman                                              4 AA
Phipps, Nathan, 29 Jan. 1788, Rebecca Davies           1 BA-1
Phipps, Thomas, 4 March 1778, Sarah Forster            3 AA-415
Phips, Benj'n, 4 Feb. 1789, by Rev. Claggett; Ann Hopkins
   4 AA
Phison, John, 16 June 1780, Martha Armstrong           3 HA-2
Phoebus, James, 26 March 1799, Betsy Muir              2 SO
Pickerin, Peter, 24 Nov. 1786, by Rev. West; Elisab. Hook
   51 BA-30
Pickering, Samuel, 20 Sept. 1781, Sophia Slater        2 DO
Pickesgill, John, 2 Oct. 1795, Mary Young              3 BA-311
Picket, Francis, 13 May 1781, Catherine Larkin         3 HA-4
Pickett, John, 4 Aug. 1779, Ann Gannon                 4 FR
Picking, Robert, 25 May 1783, Margaret Cost            4 FR
Pidden, Thos., 20 March 1790, P. Brown                29 BA-1
Pier (or Her), John, 31 July 1798, by Rev. Ridgely; Mary
   Reed                                                4 AA
Pierce, Dan'l, 5 Feb. 1782, Ann Ankers                11 BA-5
Pierce, Humphrey, 6 Aug. 1789, Anne Williamson         5 BA-11
Pierce, Joseph, 9 Jan. 1799, Mary Cables               3 BA-367
Pierce, Joseph Purdue, 19 June 1800, Margaret Cole     6 BA
Pierce, Levy, 12 Sept. 1798, Elisabeth Williamson      5 BA-12
Pierce, Thomas, 9 March 1793, Mary Wilson              3 HA-22
```

Pierpoint, Benedict, 22 Oct. 1792, Milky Griffith   29 BA-3
Pierpoint, Henry, 25 Sept. 1783, Sissin Randell   11 BA-6
Pierpoint, Joseph, 18 April 1783, Catherine Show   4 FR
Pierpoint, Thos., 28 Sept. 1794, Marg. Wells   29 BA-5
Pigott, Charles, 25 June 1782, Lidia Shipler   4 FR
Pike, Daniel, 15 May 1796, Ketty Nixon   35 BA-4
     See also 3 BA-323.
Pike, James, 9 Jan. 1794, Alice Butler   3 BA-281
Pilch, James, 19 July 1795, Elizabeth Butler   6 BA
Pilchard, Moses, 29 Jan. 1799, Elizabeth Blades   1 WO
Piles, Richard, 26 May 1784, Mary Lowman   4 FR
Pilkington, Tho., 31 March 1785, Mary Workman   11 BA-8
Pinckerton, James, 22 Oct. 1800, Mary Short   3 BA-394
Pindall, Charles Ridgely, 21 Oct. 1800, Mary Lauderman   3 BA-394
Pindel, Gassay, 18 May 1783, Mary Watkins   3 AA-419
Pindel, John Larkin, 6 Aug. 1791, Sus. Louderman   29 BA-2
Pindle, Thomas, (30 June 1790), Margaret Gorsuch   15 BA-3
Pindle, Thomas, 15 Dec. 1791, Eleanor Watkins   1 AA-169
Pine, Thomas, 11 Oct. 1797, Susanna Cremar   3 BA-351
     See also 47 BA-1.
Pines, Wm., 20 May 1784, Temperance Carback   11 BA-7
Pines, William, 24 Nov. 1786, Eliza Farman   11 BA-10
Pining (or Tining), John, 23 Dec. 1783, Sarah Rigdon   3 HA-8
Pinter, James, 8 March 1794, Comfort Burgess   18 BA-6
Piper, Jacob, 29 July 1797, Polly Amen   3 WA-63
Piper, Philips, 1 July 1780, Eliz'th Huffman   4 FR
Pippinger, William, 11 Nov. 1790, Mary James   2 FR-1159
Pitt, Archibald, 7 April 1795, Susanna Newton, dau. of
     Arnold and Elizabeth. Thomas Pitt, bro. of Archi-
     bald was a witness.   8 MO-11
Pitt, John, 23 June 1781, Mary Mills   2 DO
Pitt, Samuel Willson, 14 Feb. 1793, Mary Scott   2 DO
Pitts, Hillary, 5 July 1781, Salley Parker   2 WO-35
Pitts, Hillary, 21 Dec. 1790, Catherine Purnell   2 WO-36
Pitts, John, 28 Sept. 1797, Sally Truitt   1 WO
Pitts, William, 28 Jan. 1800, Sally Hill   1 WO
Pitzer, Richard, 21 Feb. 1797, Ann Green   2 AL-700
Pixler, Jacob, 23 Nov. 1795, Barbara Grable   4 FR
Place, Jno., 26 Sept. 1794, Mary Herbert   29 BA-5
Placide, Paul, 19 Sept. 1797, Louisa Duvenois   40 BA-3
Plasterer, Joseph, 11 Nov. 1790, Nancy Porter   2 FR-1159
Platford, David, 23 April 1778, Sarah Cotton   1 CA-1
Platt, John, 28 Dec. 1783, Levinah Williams   3 HA-8
Pleasant, James, 7 Aug. 1790, Deborah Brooke   26 BA-1
Plisho, Nicholas, 23 Dec. 1779, Mary Miller   3 BA-184
     See also 11 BA-4.
Ploom, William, 8 June 1800, Rachael Garvey   3 BA-386
Plowman, Jonathan, 21 Feb. 1785, by Rev. Turner; Hannah
     Loveall   51 BA-29
Plowman, Richard, 19 Jan. 1789, Ruth Kelly   6 BA
Plumb, George, 31 Jan. 1781, Mary Magdalen Eater   4 FR
Plumber, Charles, 13 Jan. 1796, Jane Hendricks   6 BA
Plumer, Abednego, 11 Oct. 1796, Anna Redman   2 FR-1159
Plumley, Oliver, 1 April 1795, Phebe Myers   4 FR
Plummer, Abraham, 26 Feb. 1784, Mary Swamley   4 FR
Plummer, Ebenezer, 1792, by Rev. Parrott; Eleanor Childs
     4 AA
Plummer, Isaac, son of Thomas and Eleanor, 25th day, 5 mo.,
     1785, Grace Taylor, dau. of Israel and Elizabeth
     3 SF
Plummer, Israel, son of Samuel and Mary, 29th day, 10 mo.,
     1795, Rebeckah Morsell, dau. of William and Mary   3 SF
Plummer, James, 10 Dec. 1783, Dorcas Cash   4 FR
Plummer, Jesse, 18 July 1786, by Rev. Pigman; Ruth Griffith
     4 AA

```
Plummer, John, 28 Nov. 1780, Ann Digges              2 PG-1
Plummer, John, 26 Sept. 1782, Sarah Hodge            2 PG-3
Plummer, Jonathan, 21 Dec. 1789, Ann Ward            4 FR
Plummer, Joseph, 12 May 1789, Mary Cash              4 FR
Plummer, Meshac, 13 Jan. 1795, Anna Elliott          2 FR-1159
Plummer, Moses, son of Joseph and Sarah, 3rd day, 11 mo.,
   1785, Elizabeth Webb                              3 SF
Plummer, Robert, son of Abraham and Sarah, 3rd day, 10
   mo., 1793, Rachel Talbott, dau. of John and Mary  3 SF
Plummer, Thomas, son of Joseph and Mary, 24th day, 7 mo.,
   1800, Susanna Talbott, dau. of John and Mary      3 SF
Plummer, Wm., 27 Nov. 1779, Margaret Jones           4 FR
Plummer, Wm., 11 Jan. 1791, Linney Ann Hoggins       4 FR
Plummer, William, son of Thomas and Eleanor, 1st day,
   11 mo., 1792, Rachel Morsell, dau. of William and
   Mary                                              3 SF
Plummer, William, 22 Jan. 1795, Rachel Hobbs         2 FR-1159
Plummer, Zephaniah, 15 Jan. 1791, Charity Hempstone  4 FR
Pocock, Abraham, 30 March 1799, Lydia Foster         3 BA-369
Pocock, David, 14 Aug. 1794, Mary Smith              3 HA-23
   1 BA-6 gives the date as 26 Aug. 1794.
Pocock, George Adwell, 2 August 1795, Anne Liston    3 BA-307
Pocock, John, 6 Nov. 1788, Temperance Isgrig         3 BA-218
Pogue, James, 24 July 1790, Elisabeth McDonough      5 BA-11
Poits, William, of Sussex Co., Del., 4 April 1786, Adah
   Berry                                             2 SF
Poland, James, 28 Aug. 1798, Margaret Hill           2 AL-701
Poland, William, 2 Feb. 1797, Ann Poland             2 AL-700
Poland, William, 25 May 1797, Rachel Poland          2 AL-700
Polk, David, 10 Nov. 1797, Margaret Cooper           5 BA-12
Polk, Whittington, 5 Dec. 1797, Rebecca Chapman      2 SO
Pollitt, Levin, 9 Jan. 1797, Sarah Sloan             2 SO
Pollitt, Samuel, 18 Dec. 1798, Nancy Disharoon       2 SO
Pollock, Thomas, 19 May 1777, Susanna Curd           2 CH-455
   4 CH-1 gives the date as 19 May 1778.
Polson, Andrew, 21 Nov. 1799, Susannah McCabe        2 AL-701
Polson, James, 12 July 1778, Rachel Durbin           4 FR
Pomeroy (or Lowery), Edward, c.1799, by Rev. Higgins; Eliza
   Carville                                          4 AA
Pomfrey, Gabriel, 27 Feb. 1794, Rachel Brashears     3 AA-424
Pomphrey, James, 27 Dec. 1786, Usley Osbern          3 PG-252
Pomphrey, William, 5 Feb. 1792, Mary Rollings        3 PG-436
Ponder, William, 9 Oct. 1797, Sarah Harris           4 KE-70
Ponsiby, Thos., 20 Sept. 1795, Ann Philips           44 BA-1
Ponteney, James, 18 Oct. 1798, Achsah Wood           6 BA
Pontier, Anty, 19 Feb. 1795, Mary Cath. Duplan       44 BA-1
Pool, Charles, 16 Dec. 1799, Susanna Pool            4 FR
Pool, Dennis, 2 Feb. 1794, Henrietta Gather          2 FR-1159
Pool, George, 28 Oct. 1796, Ann Blackburn            4 FR
Pool, Henry, 9 March 1790, Margaret James            2 FR-1159
Pool, John, Jr., 2 Jan. 1800, Miss Sprigg            7 MO-29
Pool, Levin, 18th day, 1 mo., 1797, Elizabeth Emmerson  2 SF-289
Pool, Samuel, 15 April 1787, Jemima Norwood          2 FR-1159
Pool, William, 12 Dec. 1782, Lilee Hall              4 FR
Pool, William, 21 Feb. 1793, Rachel Derbin           3 BA-258
Poole, Brice, 13 Dec. 1795, Achsah James             2 FR-1159
Poole, George, 25 April 1780, Catherine Raberdoe     4 FR
Poole, James, 12 July 1778, Rachel Shipley           4 FR
Poole, John, 20 Dec. 1783, Mary Norwood              4 FR
Poole, John, 31 Dec. 1799, Prissa W. Sprigg          4 FR
Poole, Joseph, 9 June 1792, Eleanor Glaze            4 FR
Poole, Samuel, 7 April 1787, Jemima Norwood          4 FR
Poole, William, 19 Aug. 1784, Ann Onion              4 FR
Poole, William, Jr., 23 Jan. 1797, Ann Dickson       4 FR
Pope, Joseph, Jr., 18 Dec. 1787, Amelia Pope         3 PG-253
```

```
Pope, Levi, 26 Dec. 1793, Eleanor Stone              3 PG-438
Porkes (or Porter), Laurence, before 12 Feb. 1778, Mary
   Kelley                                            2 PG-6
Porter, Alexander, 14 Sept. 1794, Honour Parish      6 BA
Porter, Augustine, 16 Jan. 1800, Frances Stansbury   6 BA
Porter, Caleb, 30 Jan. 1794, Priscilla Hudson        6 BA
Porter, Chas., 27 Sept. 1800, Temperance Roberts    29 BA-11
   See also 50 BA-408.
Porter, David, 16 Dec. 1800, Mary Ray                5 MO-116
Porter, Edward, 21 Jan. 1800, Mary Heiter            5 MO-116
Porter, Gabriel McKinsey, 11 May 1797, Rebecka Frost 2 AL-700
Porter, Hast (?), 17 Jan. 1793, Kitchuel Messick     1 WI-122
Porter, Hugh, 20 Nov. 1797, Peggy Winright           3 SO
   2 SO gives the date as 14 Nov. 1797.
Porter, Isaiah, 18 Oct. 1796, Eleanor Marcus         4 FR
Porter, James, 2 May 1782, Ann Barnes               11 BA-5
Porter, John, 3 Feb. 1798, Elizabeth Burk            6 BA
Porter, John, 3 Feb. 1798, Phillis Sexton           19 BA-3
Porter, Joseph, 30 June 1784, Mary Patridge          2 DO
Porter, Joseph, 20 Feb. 1797, Sarah Ashley           4 KE-70
Porter, Kelita, 15 Nov. 1792, Catherine Trimble      2 AL-700
Porter, Levin, 25 Aug. 1786, Susanna Reed            2 DO
Porter, Levin, 24 Aug. 1799, Nancy Moore             2 DO
Porter, Lewis, 18 Jan. 1795, Catharine Brown         3 BA-299
Porter, McKemmy, 18 July 1797, Nancy Parker          1 WO
Porter, Nathan, 10 Jan. 1793, Pamella Scott         18 BA-5
Porter, Nathaniel, 31 Aug. 1784, Rebecca Mason       3 BA-188
Porter, Peregrine, 3 May 1798, Mary Raven            6 BA
Porter, Philip, 28 July 1793, Kitty Baughman         6 BA
Porter, Robert, 17 Dec. 1793, Susanna Buck           3 BA-279
Porter, Thomas, 24 Aug. 1778, Susanna McDonald       4 FR
Porter, Thomas, 21 Nov. 1796, Mary Logsdon           1 AL-53
Porter, William, 14 Jan. 1796, Naomi Sturgis         1 WO
Porter, William, 1 Nov. 1796, Anne Johnson           2 SO
Porter, Wrixham Lewis, 30 July 1798, Priscilla Riggen 2 SO
Posey, George, 9 Aug. 1778, Mary Roby                2 PG-2
Posey, Thomas, 25 March 1788, Mary Dutton            2 CH-455
Posey, Uriah, (date not given), Catherine Skinner    2 CH-455
Posey, Zachariah, 10 April 1792, Elizabeth Hamilton  3 PG-437
Poslyn, William, 27 Aug. 1782, Sarah Hammel          2 CH-455
Post?, Daniel, (27 March 1789), Isabella Barclay    20 BA-1
Pots, Jonas, 22 Nov. 1798, Martha Dowlen             2 FR-1160
Potter, David, 9 May 1797, Mary Adams                2 SO
Potter, John, 2 Feb. 1796, Sarah McKinsey            2 AL-7-0
Potter, Thomas, 16 Jan. 1797, Charity Wilson         2 SO
Potter, Thomas Wood, 27 July 1786, Issabella Conner  1 SO-159
Potts, Jacob, 31 Oct. 1782, Susanna Coard            3 HA-7
Potts, Jonas, 22 Nov. 1798, Martha Dowlen            4 FR
Potts, Richard, 19 Dec. 1799, Eleanor Murdock        4 FR
Pouly, Daniel, 2 Sept. 1800, Caroline Roth          29 BA-11
Poulson, Cornelius, 3 April 1797, Rachel Baxter      4 FR
Poulteney, Thomas, son of Thomas and Elizabeth of Phila-
   delphia, 21st day, 4 mo., 1790, Ann Thomas, dau. of
   Evan and Rachel                                   6 SF
Povey, Christian, 8 Sept. 1788, Catherine Smeltzer   4 FR
Powe, Christian, 9 Sept. 1788, Catharina Schmeltzer  1 FR-59
Powel, Caleb, 29 Jan. 1796, Elizabeth Bethards       1 WO
Powel, Elijah, 25 Nov. 1779, Elizabeth Pepper        1 SO-159
Powel, Peter, 7 Oct. 1794, Elisabeth Foster          5 BA-12
Powel, William, 18 Nov. 1779, Brigett Hill           1 SO-159
Powel, William, 25 April 1791, Martha Jordan         6 BA
Powell, George, 26 Nov. 1800, Jemima Able            3 BA-395
Powell, Henry, 20 April 1779, Sarah Purnell          3 AA-415
Powell, Howell, 7th day, 9 mo., 1780, Ann Troth      4 SF-163
Powell, Howell, 17th day, 4 mo., 1793, Ann Regester  4 SF-202
```

Powell, Jeremiah, 14 April 1793, Sarah Nicolson   3 BA-265
Powell, Jesse, 1 June 1799, Caty Whittington   1 WO
Powell, John, before 20 July 1793, by Rev. Bloodgood;
    Elizabeth Gardner   4 AA
Powell, John, 24 Oct. 1799, Isabella Nesbitt   12 BA-370
Powell, Joshua, 12 Jan. 1800, by Rev. Ridgely; Peggy Jacob
    4 AA
Powell, Levi, 5 June 1798, Betsy Powell   2 SO
Powell, Thomas, 10 Oct. 1790, Margaret Doyle   3 BA-228
Powell, William, 12 Feb. 1778, Alice Evans   1 CA-1
Powell, William, 11 Jan. 1799, Mary Edwards   4 FR
Powell, William, 19 Oct. 1780, Elizabeth Mead   3 AA-416
Powers, Barnet, 24 Nov. 1794, Rachel Bennet   3 BA-296
Powers, John, 19 Jan. 1799, Elizabeth Slaun   3 BA-367
Powil, William, 29 June 1784, Suhsannah Carter   10 BA-182
Pownal, Thomas, 17 Dec. 1780, Rachel Deale   3 AA-416
Prat, James, 13 Jan. 1791, Sarah Shaw   5 BA-11
Prater, Zephaniah, 12 May 1791, Nancy Jinkins   3 PG-257
Prather, Baruch, 12 Dec. 1799, Casandra Swearingen   5 MO-116
Prather, Benjamin, 27 Jan. 1782, Rachel Walker   2 PG-3
Prather, John, 9 Aug. 1785, Amelia Philips   2 FR-1159
Prather, John, 8 Dec. 1796, Mary Moore   6 BA
Prather, John Garrot, 3 March 1791, by Rev. Forrest; Mary
    Ann Sargant   3 FR
Prather, Joseph, 12 June 1781, Elizabeth Welsh   2 PG-5
Prather, Walter, 9 April 1778, Ann Higgins   4 MO-1
Prather, William, 2 June 1798, Elizabeth Adamson   6 MO
Pratt, Henry, 9 July 1780, Ann Wright, dau. of Solomon   1 CR-75
Pratter?, Zachariah, 2 March 1778, Rosamond Callahane   2 PG-2
Prauff, Jacob, 11 May 1779, Ann M. Buckey   4 FR
Presbury, George, 6 Nov. 1793, Betsy Lytle   3 HA-23
    7 BA-1 gives the bride's name as Little.
Presbury, George Gouldsmith, 27 July 1786, Eliza Ferguson
    11 BA-9
Presbury, James, 23 Dec. 1800, Martha Baker   3 HA-30
Presbury, Joseph, 20 April 1778, Mary Waters   11 BA-1
Presbury, Walter, 31 Aug. 1797, Mary Galloway   47 BA-1
Prestman, Thomas, 9 March 1797, Phebe Kelly   6 BA
    19 BA-12 gives the bride's name as Phebe Miller.
Preston, George, 3 Jan. 1798, Sarah Pulley   2 AL-700
Pretty, George, 11 Sept. 1800, Hannah Brown   48 BA-1
    See also 8 BA-2.
Pretty, Wm., 1792, Lucretia Nash   50 BA-392
Price, Arthur, 9 April 1800, Sally Bradford   1 WO
Price, Bennet, 18 May 1780, Sarah Lane   3 AA-416
Price, Charles, 6 Dec. 1792, Fancy McFall   2 DO
Price, Edward, 28 April 1796, Elizabeth Crist   4 FR
Price, Ephraim, 17 July 1798, Nancy Bloodworth   2 SO
Price, James, 29 Jan. 1779, Elizabeth Boteler   2 PG-2
Price, James, 31 Jan. 1782, Elizabeth St. George   2 CH-455
Price, James, 17 June 1795, Elizabeth Lewis   5 BA-12
Price, James, 2 July 1797, Ann Ennalls   1 TA-325
    2 DO gives the date as 1 July 1797.
Price, James, 2 May 1798, Avariller Jones   4 KE-70
Price, John, 29 Nov. 1792, Providence Kirby   6 BA
    Other sources give the groom's name as John Price
    Gill.
Price, John, 20 Feb. 1796, Elizabeth Lefaver   4 FR
Price, John, 28 Dec. 1796, Rebecca Pritchard   2 FR-1159
Price, John, 5 Feb. 1799, Jane Sanner   4 SM-184
Price, John, 16 Feb. 1799, Betsy Colvin   6 BA
    See also 19 BA-14.
Price, Joseph, 18 June 1797, Hannah Fisher   29 BA-8
Price, Nath., 26 Feb. 1797, Mary Elbin   3 AL-4
Price, Nathan, 17 Feb. 1785, Ruth Thomas   11 BA-8

```
Price, Peter, 22 April 1783, Mary Harcourt           3 BA-185
Price, Peter, 6 Dec. 1787, Jane Wedgerworth          3 PG-253
Price, Philip, Jr., 3 Nov. 1798, Mary Sulser         4 FR
Price?, Richard, 17 Sept. 1795, Mary Evans          43 BA-1
Price, Samuel, son of Mordecai and Elizabeth, 5th day,
    12 mo., 1787, Mary Parrish, dau. of William and
    Keturah                                          1 SF
Price, Samuel, Jr., son of Samuel and Ann, 7th day, 1 mo.,
    1795, Frances Moore, dau. of John and Rebecca    1 SF
Price, Solomon K., 10 Oct. 1797, Elizabeth Harris    1 WO
Price, Stephen, 2 Jan. 1783, Susanna Rolls          11 BA-6
Price, Capt. Thomas, 10 Nov. 1785, Susanna Mackall   4 FR
Price, Warrick, son of Samuel and Ann, 1st day, 11 mo.,
    1792, Susanna Coates, dau. of Jonathan and Jane  1 SF
Price, William, 3 Oct. 1779, Elizabeth Carter        3 SM-57
Price, Wm., 11 Sept. 1788, Eliza Brown              11 BA-11
Price, William, 3 Dec. 1793, Elizabeth Vermilion     3 PG-438
Price, William, 10 Nov. 1798, Jemima Wilson          1 WO
Prichard, John, 25 Feb. 1787, Elisabeth Whitacar     5 BA-11
Prill, Samuel, 3 Jan. 1797, Catherine Auman          4 FR
Primrose, John, 24 May 1787, Mary White              6 BA
Primrose, Robert, 28 Nov. 1795, Sidney Clement       3 BA-313
Prin, William, 8 Feb. 1797, Mary Williams            4 KE-70
Pringle, James, 10 Nov. 1785, Sarah Forsyth         11 BA-8
Pringle, Mark, 12 June 1794, Frances Russell         4 BA-76
Pringle, Mark, 12 June 1794, Frances Russell        36 BA-1
Pringle, Mark, 7 July 1797, Lucy Stith              47 BA-1
Prist, George, 5 Oct. 1784, Cath. Kizer              4 FR
Pritchard, Arthur, 9 July 1794, Sally Bell           2 DO
Pritchard, Jesse, 3 May 1779, Eliz'th Stoner         4 FR
Pritchard, John, 15 Feb. 1791, Sarah Airey           2 DO
Pritchard, Obadiah, 22 Oct. 1783, Sarah Baley        3 HA-8
Pritchard, Thomas, 2 Jan. 1796, Nancy Tichenal       1 AL-53
Pritchard, William, 21 Oct. 1795, Eliza Flinn        3 BA-311
Pritchett, Arthur, 16 Dec. 1790, Mary McNamara       2 DO
Pritchett, Arthur, 24 Oct. 1798, Judah Coward .      1 DO-40
    2 DO gives the date as 1 Sept. 1798.
Pritchett, Edward, 10 Aug. 1799, Henrietta Voss      2 DO
Pritchett, Elijah, 6 May 1789, Esther Norman         2 DO
Pritchett, Elijah, 12 Jan. 1792, Rachel Coward       2 DO
Pritchett, Henry, 28 April 1792, Seney Frames        2 DO
Pritchett, John, 23 Dec. 1796, Jeminy Parks          2 DO
Pritchett, John, 2 Dec. 1797, Sarah Jinkins          2 SF
Pritchett, John, 4 Oct. 1798, Nancy Dean             1 DO-40
    2 DO gives the date as 14 Oct. 1798.
Pritchett, John, 3 Sept. 1787, Elizabeth Wingate     2 DO
Pritchett, Planner, 7 Jan. 1798, Leah Moore          1 DO-39
    2 DO gives the date as 18 Dec. 1797.
Pritchett, Thomas, 24 Dec. 1788, Leah Thomas         2 DO
Pritchett, Zebulon, 1 Aug. 1798, Dolly Brown         2 DO
Pritchett, Zebulon, 10 Jan. 1800, Hannah Woodland    2 DO
Probart, James, 13 June 1799, Mary Veale             3 BA-372
Proctor, Hugh, 7 Dec. 1797, Priscilla Grover         6 BA
Proctor, Isaac, 29 Sept. 1794, Eliz. Butler          3 CH-162
    "disp. for consang. in 2nd degree"
Proctor, Isaiah, 15 July 1798, Margaret Chaney       6 BA
Proctor, Levy, 15 June 1800, Ruth Horton             6 BA
Proctor, William, 24 May 1786, Susanna Clarridge     2 DO
Proser, John, 9 Feb. 1798, Sarah Hall                3 HA-27
Prosser, John, 13 Feb. 1798, Sarah Hall              2 HA-350
Protzman, Ludwig, shoemaker, 1787, Maria Elizabeth Rauser,
    dau. of Martin and Sarah                         5 FR-92
Prout, Richard, 16 Oct. 1784, Hannah -(?)-; negroes 11 BA-7
Pruitt, Elijah, 24 Nov. 1797, Betsy Bishop           1 WO
Pruitt, Selby, 1 May 1795, Rebecca Pepper            1 WO
```

```
Pruitt, Severn, 16 Feb. 1797, Polly Merrill           1 WO
Pryan, Peter, 19 March 1796, Margaret Cole            3 BA-321
Prye, Christopher, 3 Aug. 1784, Hannah Thrasher       4 FR
Pryor, Henry, 10 Nov. 1797, Kitty Rochester           4 KE-70
Puff, Peter, 28 July 1781, Catherine Heffner          4 FR
Puffinberger, Adam, 7 Feb. 1791, Oner Dorsey          4 FR
Pugh, Jacob, 16 Sept. 1798, Elizabeth Morgan          6 BA
Puhly, Paul, 26 March 1794, Mary Ross                 29 BA-5
Pulling, Jonathan, 29 May 1785, Marg't Keys           11 BA-8
Pumel, Joh. Arnold, 8 Jan. 1797, Elisab. Ehurs        50 BA-401
Pumphrey, Joseph, 22 Oct. 1793, Sarah Stewart         3 BA-275
Pumphrey, Joshua, 9 July 1785, Dinah Stewart          11 BA-8
Pumphry, Wm., 24 Sept. 1782, Mary Cromwell            11 BA-5
Punteny, Edward, 22 Oct. 1778, Elizabeth Reed         11 BA-1
Purden, Michael, 7 Jan. 1796, Alice Kinsley           3 BA-341
Purdon, William, 23 Aug. 1795, Susanna Esseck         3 BA-307
Purdum, James, 19 Nov. 1785, Elizabeth Browning       4 FR
Purdy, Edmund, 18 Dec. 1792, Rebecca Burgee           4 FR
Purdy, Henry, 3 Oct. 1782, Mary Philips               3 AA-418
Purdy, William, 12 Jan. 1795, Mary Bucey              4 FR
Purdy, William, before 4 May 1798, by Rev. Stewart; Sarah
    Pierce                                            4 AA
Purnell, Esme, 7 May 1799, Dolly Chaille              1 WO
Purnell, John, 8 Nov. 1797, Patty Burnell (sic)       1 WO
Purnell, John J., 10 Jan. 1797, Dolly Bennett         1 WO
Purnell, Milby, 8 Dec. 1795, Amelia Parker            1 WO
Purnell, Robert, 29 Oct. 1800, Betsey Reed            1 WO
Purper, Carl, 1788, An. Maria Leysin                  50 BA-388
Purse, Thomas, 9 May 1795, Mary Pilkington            3 BA-305
Pursel, Joseph, 7 May 1796, June Jans                 3 WA-60
Purtel, Robert, 4 Aug. 1796, Catherine Sitler         3 BA-327
Purviance, James, 23 Nov. 1797, Eliza Young           5 BA-12
Purviance, John, 3 Jan. 1799, Abigail Dugan           5 BA-12
Puzey, Planner, 14 March 1797, Sally Hayman           2 SO

Quail, Robert, 1793, Agnes Ramkin                     50 BA-393
Quarles, John, 13 May 1797, Elizabeth Husbands        3 HA-26
    1 BA-8 gives the date as 18 May 1797, and states the
    groom was from Virginia.
Quay, Jno., 4 April 1790, Sarah Perry                 11 BA-13
Quay, Thomas, 13 April 1800, Sarah Murphy             6 BA
Quay, William, 7 Nov. 1795, Mary Burk                 5 BA-12
Queen, Henry, 15 Feb. 1779, Margaret Pye              6 CH-1
Queen, Joseph, 2 Dec. 1787, Eddie Jerningham          2 CH-455
Quesang, John, 15 April 1798, Elisa Whipple           3 BA-357
Quidaman, Francis, 6 July 1799, Jane Crow             3 BA-373
Quimby, John, 1 Nov. 1796, Ann Daws                   4 KE-70
Quinlan, James, 7 April 1798, Susannah Cooper         3 HA-27
Quinley, Wm., 26 Nov. 1787, Mary Causey               6 BA
Quinlin, Benjamin, 6 Dec. 1800, Patty Green           3 HA-30
Quinlon, Patrick, 6 Jan. 1799, Mary Graham            5 BA-12
Quinton, William, 17 Jan. 1799, Sarah Houston         1 WO
Quynn, Allen, Jr., 12 Dec. 1790, Mary Mantz           4 FR
Quynn, John, 27 March 1782, Elizabeth Padgett         4 FR

Raab, Diedrich, 9 Aug. 1796, Helena Ficke             50 BA-399
    See also 29 BA-7.
Rabba, John, 15 May 1799, Sarah (Hyer?) Tinges?       29 BA-10
Rabitt, John, 5 May 1778, Elenor Miles                2 PG-2
Raborg, Mich'l, 25 Jan. 1788, Cath. Lent              29 BA-1
Rachel, Daniel, 5 Nov. 1791, Catherine Myers          4 FR
Rachob, Fred'k, 18 June 1785, Susanna Shafert         4 FR
Racine, Daniel, 9 Oct. 1794, Harriot Perry Gentille   3 BA-293
```

```
Radish, John, 22 March 1799, Elr.? Johnson           1 WO
Rady, Joshua, 14 June 1790, Eliza Hughes            11 BA-13
Raff, William, 8 Aug. 1778, Mary Barry              11 BA-1
Ragan, Andrew, 18 Dec. 1796, Susanna Maule           4 FR
Railey, Basil, 28 Dec. 1780, Dorothy Hutchins        3 SM-58
Raitt, Hammond, 30 Oct. 1797, Eleanor Norris         4 FR
Rallston, William, 13 Oct. 1790, Martha McMasters    6 BA
Ramsay, Andrew, 14 April 1779, Jemima Bailess        5 HA
Ramsay, John, 1 Feb. 1780, Susanna Wood              1 CA-3
Ramsay, William, 7 Jan. 1779, Rebecca Jefferson      1 CA-2
Ramsay, William, 31 Oct. 1780, Rebecca Bond          1 CA-3
Ramsberg, George, 24 Nov. 1797, Caty Culler          4 FR
Ramsberg, Jacob, Jr., 16 April 1796, Charlotte Grosh 4 FR
Ramsberg, Stephen, 9 July 1796, Elizabeth Brunner    4 FR
Ramsbergh, George, 7 April 1789, Christena Perknen   4 FR
Ramsbergh, John, 13 Jan. 1789, Catherine Thomas      4 FR
Ramsbergh, John, son of Adam, 23 April 1787, Elizabeth
  Miller                                             4 FR
Ramsey, David, 28 Dec. 1785, Elizabeth LeCompte      2 DO
Ramsey, John, 26 Dec. 1796, Priscilla Smith          4 FR
Ramsey, Robert, 26 Dec. 1785, Lucy Alexon            2 DO
Ramsey, William, 2 Jan. 1800, Margaret Herren        5 MO-116
Ramsour, Adam, 23 Aug. 1795, Mary Purdie             2 FR-1163
Ramsower, Henry, 19 June 1785, Mary Smith            2 FR-1162
Rand, Thomas, 5 May 1799, Mary Burns                 2 HA-351
Randal, David, 9 Dec. 1780, Mary Philips             3 AA-416
Randal, Nathan, 21 Oct. 1790, Ruth Davis            11 BA-13
Randall, Aquila, 8 June 1779, Rebecca Cord          14 BA-1
  5 BA-12 gives the bride's name as Cad.
Randall, Christopher, 15 Nov. 1788, by Rev. Claggett; Ann
  Crandell                                           4 AA
Randall, Israel, 23 June 1796, Dalilah Lee           3 BA-323
Randall, John, 20 Sept. 1796, Ann Willess            3 BA-329
Randall, John, 10 Nov. 1800, Nancy Simms             3 BA-395
Randall, Nich's, 25 May 1780, Marg't Worthington    11 BA-4
Randall, Robert, 6 June 1792, Henrietta Medford      3 KE
Randall, Roger, 6 July 1788, Elizabeth Burgess      18 BA-1
Randell, William, 29 Nov. 1792, Sarah James         18 BA-5
Randolph, Isaac F., 16 Aug. 1800, Elizabeth Hughes  49 BA-1
Raney, Joseph, 25 July 1799, Rebecca Frincham        3 BA-374
Rankin, Hugh, 2 Nov. 1797, Margaret Hughes           5 BA-12
Rankins, William, 22 July 1783, Rebeckah Gatton      4 FR
Ransdale, Stephen Chilton, 22 May 1795, Margaret Dowdle 4 FR
Ranter, John, 13 Dec. 1778, Sarah Ann Humphrey       2 PG-3
Ratakle, Adam, 16 Dec. 1779, Mary Arnold            11 BA-4
Ratcliff, James, 14 Aug. 1791, Elizabeth Cook       28 BA-1
  2 DO gives the date as 13 Aug. 1791.
Ratcliff, John, 13 March 1788, Sarah Henry           2 DO
Ratcliff, John, 3 July 1791, Frances Griffin         2 DO
Ratcliff, Joseph, 6 March 1798, Mary Lloyd           3 BA-356
Ratcliff, Thomas, 7 Feb. 1781, Sarah Wheeler         2 DO
Ratcliffe, James, 26 Jan. 1796, Polly Meddis         2 DO
Rathers, James, 20 Sept. 1782, Abigail Henderson     3 HA-7
Ratlief, Thomas, 23 Oct. 1794, Elizabeth Cannon      3 BA-293
Rauert, George, 25 Oct. 1791, Susanna Gerlach        2 WA-16
Rauhort, Michael, 5 June 1786, Anna Maria Ligt      10 BA-186
Rawleigh, Levin, 18 April 1800, Betsy Dail           2 DO
Rawley, Benjamin, 3 Oct. 1797, Leah Walter           2 DO
Rawley, Daniel, 18 May 1790, Mary Robb               1 BA-2
Rawley, James, 22 Dec. 1800, Polly Covey             2 DO
Rawley, John, 19 Jan. 1796, Trephema Willey          2 DO
Rawley, Robert, 13 Feb. 1799, Leah Pitt              2 DO
Rawley, William, 20 Feb. 1790, Rosanna Stewart       2 DO
Rawlings, Benj., 21 Nov. 1792, Elizab. Garrott Gittings 4 FR
Rawlings, Edward, 6 June 1799, Ann Parks             6 BA
```

```
Rawlings, Isaac, 2 June 1798, Ann Warrington          6 BA
Rawlings, John, 29 Aug. 1793, Margaret Smith          3 BA-272
Rawlings, John, 11 May 1794, Sophia Duvall            3 AA-424
Rawlings, Richard, 26 April 1781, Sarah Thornton      2 PG-5
Rawlings, Richard, 13 Feb. 1800, Elizabeth Taylor     1 AA-163
Rawlings, Solomon, 6 Aug. 1781, Ann Donaldson         4 FR
Rawlinson, Benjamin, 7 June 1792, Margaret Brisco     3 KE
Ray, Basil, 20 Jan. 1782, Rebecca Walls               2 PG-3
Ray, James, 8 Dec. 1796, Eliz. Warfield               5 MO-113
Ray, Miles, 30 June 1799, Rachel Hardy                3 BA-373
Ray, Walter, 3 Jan. 1792, Rebecca Bershears           3 PG-436
Rayling, John Ludwick, 20 May 1783, Anne Marg't. Snydern  4 FR
Raymer, Jacob, 22 June 1797, Maria Zimmerman          4 FR
Raymer, Michael, 22 Jan. 1791, Susanna Margaret Fultz 4 FR
Raymond, John W., 12 Nov. 1800, Sarah Garnons         3 BA-395
Rayner, Benjamin, 26 Sept. 1778, Anne Hodges         11 BA-1
Raynor, John, 30 Oct. 1783, Rachael Watts            11 BA-6
Raysee, Johannes, 7 Sept. 1788, Magdalena Doderno    10 BA-190
Rea, Thomas, 30 Oct. 1800, Elizabeth Wallis           6 BA
Read, Jacob, 20 Oct. 1789, Elizabeth Russel           3 BA-221
Read, Joseph, 24 Feb. 1789, Agnes Smith               3 BA-219
Read, Larkin, 5 May 1796, Edith Perigo                6 BA
Read, Philip, 1 Oct. 1781, Eleanor Tawney             3 SM-59
Reader, Daniel, 13 Dec. 1794, Cavy Luxon              3 PG-440
Reading, Maurice, 14 Feb. 1796, Prudence Rolls        3 BA-317
Reagan, Morris, 19 Dec. 1786, Eleanor Brasinham      11 BA-10
Ream, John, 5 Dec. 1780, Esther Plunk                 4 FR
Reaves, Leon, 5 March 1783, Juliana Boley             4 FR
Reaves, Richard, 6 April 1784, Margaret West          3 BA-186
Reblogel, Philip, 5 Oct. 1788, Elenor McClean         2 FR-1162
Redden, George, 2 July 1793, Elenor Thompson          3 BA-269
Redden?, John, 29 Nov. 1797, Hesse Taylor             1 WO
Redden, John, 29 March 1800, Sarah Schoolfield        1 WO
Reddick, James, 17 June 1778, Elizabeth Chaplin      11 BA-1
Reddish, Robert, 29 Jan. 1800, Mary Kelly             2 DO
Redhead, Peter, 14 June 1800, Ann Benson              2 DO
Redig, John, 15 March 1791, Barb. Zimmerman           2 FR-1162
Reding, Teagle, 1 Aug. 1799, Peggy Puss               2 SO
Redman, Jno., 25 Jan. 1800, Harriot Ward              5 MO-116
Redman, Joseph, 24 April 1778, Sarah Windsor          4 MO-1
Redman, Zachariah, 18 Dec. 1800, Catherine Gibbons    4 SM-184
Redmond, Matthew, 8 April 1799, Margaret Anne Flinn   3 BA-370
Reed, Abraham, 27 Oct. 1798, Elizabeth Brubecher      4 FR
Reed, Alexander, 3 Feb. 1794, Elizabeth Miller        4 FR
Reed, Archibald, 16 June 1792, Catherine Talbot       4 FR
Reed, Benjamin, 6 February 1797, Elizabeth Brown      2 DO
Reed, Emanuel, 8 Feb. 1789, Ann Hunt                  1 BA-1
Reed, George, 7 Nov. 1790, Dinah Lane                18 BA-2
Reed, Hugh, 26 Feb. 1781, Martha Hamby                3 HA-3
Reed, Hugh, 28 Nov. 1792, Mary Elfry                  5 BA-12
Reed, James, 13 April 1790, Eleanor Urrick            5 BA-12
Reed, James, 10 Oct. 1794, Cath. Ringer               3 WA-57
Reed, James, 17 June 1800, Barsheba Meredith          2 DO
Reed, Jno. Gillis, 12 Oct. 1786, Mary Allen          11 BA-9
Reed, Jonathan, 27 July 1799, Catherine Handlen       3 BA-374
Reed, Joseph, 30 Aug. 1797, Elizabeth Hurtt           4 KE-71
Reed, Nelson, 8 June 1790, Nancy Steyer              26 BA-1
Reed, Peter, 23 July 1796, Jane Caton                 3 BA-327
Reed, Robert, 13 March 1782, Mary Carr                3 HA-6
Reed, Robert, 12 Sept. 1796, Catherine Conner         6 BA
Reed, Samuel, 26 Dec. 1793, Eleanor Morrison          5 BA-12
Reed, Sam'l, 5 Aug. 1794, Bezy Forter                 3 WA-57
Reed, Samuel, son of William and Letitia, 3rd day, 3 mo.,
      1796, Elizabeth Wilson, dau. of John and Deborah  1 SF
Reed, Thomas, 2 Dec. 1793, Sarah Howard               4 FR
```

```
Reed, William, 1 Dec. 1781, Mary Mills                    2 DO
Reed, William, 14 Nov. 1792, Rosanna Woolford             2 DO
Reed, William, 20 January 1796, Nancy Woolford            2 DO
Reed, William, 30 June 1799, Rachel Davis                 8 BA-1
Reeder, Benjamin, 29 Sept. 1782, Susannah Bond            3 SM-60
Reeder, Benjamin, 23 Dec. 1786, Eleanor Slaughton         2 CH-456
Reeder, Benjamin, 14 Oct. 1797, Ann Hungerford            5 MO-114
Reeder, John, 22 Oct. 1779, Chloe Green                   2 CH-456
Reedy, Lewis, 4 Jan. 1800, Eliz. Miller                   29 BA-11
Reel, Frederick, 7 March 1799, Margaret Lucorsh           4 FR
Reel, George, 20 Sept. 1788, Elizab. Snyder               4 FR
Rees, George, 29 March 1778, Anne Rees                    11 BA-1
Reese, Daniel, 29 July 1790, Elizabeth Bond               6 BA
Reese, George, 22 Feb. 1784, Eliza Eagleston              11 BA-7
Reese, Henry, 19 May 1791, Mary Burtell                   6 BA
Reese, Hezekiah, 8 Dec. 1798, Eleanor McMullan            5 BA-12
Reese, John, 23 Aug. 1781, Elizabeth Brown                3 HA-4
Reese, Jno., 27 Sept. 1789, Mary Steenes                  11 BA-12
Reese, John, 3 Feb. 1799, Elizabeth Rusk                  3 BA-367
Reese, John, 23 Nov. 1799, Mary Zachariah                 4 FR
Reese, Joseph, 26 July 1798, Elizabeth Jervis             6 BA
Reese, Joshua, 18 Nov. 1799, Mary Hayward Cale            2 SO
Reese, William, 17 Nov. 1783, Eliza Hurly                 11 BA-7
Reeves, Anthony, 2 May 1793, Elizabeth McKenzie           3 BA-266
Reeves, Robert, 15 Aug. 1790, Rachel Shields              5 BA-12
Reeves, Thomas C., 8 Aug. 1779, Rebecca Ratcliffe         2 CH-456
Reeves, William, 23 April 1795, Abigail Grate             40 BA-1
Rehkop, Fred., 19 June 1785, Sus. Schaeffer               2 FR-1162
Reichard, Johannes, 9 April 1799, Anna Maria Kuhner       10 BA-198
Reichter, Henry, 22 July 1783, Catherine Zerrick          4 FR
Reid, James, 24 Nov. 1797, Betsy Davis                    1 WO
Reid, John, 22 Nov. 1792, Ann Millan                      4 FR
Reid, Matthew, 1 Feb. 1790, Ellender Riggs                4 FR
Reidenauer, Christoph, March 1800, Elis. Bauers           3 WA-69
Reidenauer, Daniel, March 1798, Barb. Kershner            3 WA-64
Reif, Jno., 3 May 1800, Cath. Miller                      29 BA-11
Reiley, Thomas, 25 April 1800, Eleanor Schaeffer          3 BA-385
Reilly, John, 25 Sept. 1797, Mary Lundragan               44 BA-2
Reilman, George, 1791, Mar. Wolf                          50 BA-390
Reily, Michael, 27 July 1800, Mary Roucher                6 BA
Reily, Peter, 9 Jan. (1794?), Money Fisher                50 BA-393
Reily, William, 28 Dec. 1794, Mary Foosle                 4 BA-77
Rein, John, 4 Sept. 1796, Priscilla Wilson                2 FR-1163
Reinecker, Conrad, 7 Jan. 1790, E. Fite                   29 BA-1
Reinhart, Philip, 2 May 1793, Susanna Richardson          16 BA-4
Reintzel, Daniel, 20 Dec. 1800, Ann Robertson             5 MO-116
Reintzel, Valentine, 26 Feb. 1799, Mary Waughop           4 SM-184
Relly, Christian, 19 May 1778, Mary Thomas                11 BA-1
Remage, Nicholas, 14 June 1794, Ann Deverce               18 BA-6
Remsberger, George, 27 March 1789, Cathe. Sulser          4 FR
Remsperger, Geo., 7 April 1789, Christina Peckner         2 FR-1162
Remsperger, George, 31 March 1789, Cath. Sulzer           2 FR-1162
Remsperger, Georg, 26 Nov. 1797, Catharina Coller         1 FR-59
Remsperger, John, 24 April 1787, Elizab. Miller           2 FR-1162
Remsperger, John, 13 Jan. 1789, Cath. Thomas              2 FR-1162
Remsperger, Michael, 29 March 1791, Cath. Wolff           2 FR-1163
Rencher, William, 10 Dec. 1799, Polly Wright              2 SO
Renddy, John, 22 May 1788, Deborah Bowen                  6 BA
Renick, Wm., 12 Oct. 1798, Eliz. Walton                   3 AL-5
Renner, Abraham, 27 Nov. 1798, Elizabeth Overholtzer      4 FR
Renner, John, 7 Dec. 1782, Mary Wine                      4 FR
Renner, Wm., 21 March 1782, Charity Coleman               4 FR
Reno, Jesse, 29 May 1793, Prudence Randolph               1 AL-52
      2 AL-700 gives the date as 30 May 1793.
Renous, Trope, 1 Jan. 1794, Detestamona Mince             6 BA
```

Renshaw, James, 24 Jan. 1796, Eleanor Cole   6 BA
Renshaw, Martin, 19 Nov. 1788, Magdalen Jones   1 BA-1
Renshaw, Martin, 4 Oct. 1795, Jane Park   6 BA
Renshaw, Philip, 12 March 1784, Ruth German   3 BA-187
  11 BA-7 gives the date as 21 March 1784.
Renshaw, Robert, 12 Feb. 1782, Mary Anderson   3 HA-6
Reo, Peter, 26 June 1797, Mary de Boysene   3 BA-346
Retter, John, 29 March 1786, N. Shreyer   10 BA-186
Reu, Joh., 3 April 1796, Elisab. Hosner   50 BA-399
Reuthart, Bernhard, 19 Feb. 1795, Elisab. Fisher   50 BA-396
Revell, John, 29 Jan. 1799, Sally Abbott   2 SO
  3 SO gives the date as 31 Jan. 1799.
Revell, William, 27 Feb. 1798, Nancy Mills   2 SO
Rew, James, 15 July 1794, Nancy Ashmore   3 BA-291
Reybergh, William, 6 April 1784, Mary Ann Evilleng   4 FR
Reydenauer, David, 20 June 1796, Cath. Fiscus   3 WA-61
Renold, James, 17 May 1793, Sarah Johnson   3 BA-267
Renolds, -(?)- (sic), 25 Sept. 1787, Rachael Owens   11 BA-10
Reynolds, Edward, 21 June 1781, Mary Wilkinson   3 AA-417
Reynolds, George, 30 July 1795, Elizabeth Sparks   2 DO
Reynolds, Heugh, 13 Oct. 1780, Alley Flemming   4 FR
Reynolds, John, 19 Jan. 1778, Ann French   1 SM-137
Reynolds, John, 29 Oct. 1796, Sarah Owings   6 BA
Reynolds, John, 1 April 1800, Mary Thomas   3 BA-384
Reynolds, Robert, 7 June 1778, Mary Carter   11 BA-1
Reynolds, Thomas, 29 Jan. 1789, Elizabeth Tomlin   4 FR
Reynolds, Thomas, 9 Dec. 1796, Dolly Bowen   1 WO
Reynolds, Tobias, 28 July 1785, Sarah Griffith   11 BA-8
Reynolds, William, 28 July 1780, Sarah Smith   3 AA-416
Reynolds, William, 12 March 1796, Sus. Brendlinger   3 WA-60
Rhea, William, 1 Jan. 1789, Ann Puntenay   11 BA-12
Rhine, Casper, 3 April 1784, Margaret Hinkle   4 FR
Rhine, Rudy, 14 Aug. 1793, Barbara Conner   4 FR
Rhoads, Adam, 12 July 1798, Sarah Hill   2 AL-701
Rhode, Jacob, 20 Feb. 1792, Rachel King   4 FR
Rhodes, Abraham, 26 Nov. 1799, Mary Newmyer   2 AL-701
Rhodes, Andrew, 7 Dec. 1797, Anne Pinfield   3 BA-353
Rhodes, Ebenezer, 6 Dec. 1798, Mary Starr (or Stair)   2 AL-701
Rhodes, John, 31 Jan. 1782, Mary Bennett   2 PG-3
Rhodes, Joshua, 17 May 1791, Cath. Spielman   2 FR-1163
  4 FR gives the bride's name as Spealman.
Rice, Andrew, 5 May 1785, Mary Need   4 FR
Rice, Benjamin, 4 Feb. 1782, Mary Purnell   4 FR
Rice, George, 5 Aug. 1795, Mary Ann Smith   1 WO
Rice, George, 21 Dec. 1800, Elizab. Dofler   2 FR-1163
Rice, James, 3 Oct. 1783, Nancy Dern   4 FR
Rice, James, 21 April 1790, Catherine Dern   4 FR
Rice, John, 4 Jan. 1790, Margaret North   2 DO
Rice, John, 28 Dec. 1796, Rebeckah Pritchard   4 FR
Rice, Joseph, 15 Jan. 1788, Eliz. Melvin   2 FR-1162
  4 FR gives the date as 12 Jan. 1788.
Rice, Joseph, 16 Feb. 1788, Ann Gray   3 BA-216
Rice, Joseph, 6 Nov. 1794, Rebecca Leatch   2 FR-1163
  4 FR gives the bride's name as Leaton.
Rice, Mathias, 31 May 1783, Margaret Powerin   4 FR
Rice, Michael, 7 June 1790, Elizabeth Baltzell   4 FR
Rice, Perry, 20 Aug. 1794, Patty Duttero   4 FR
Rice, Robert, 13 June 1793, Eleanor Lawrence   6 BA
Rice, William, 17 Dec. 1790, Mary Hedges   4 FR
Rich, Peter, 29 Oct. 1800, Elizabeth Lane   2 DO
Richard?, Edward, before 12 Dec. 1792, by Rev. John Long;
  Sarah Lewis   4 AA
Richard, May (sic), 24 Jan. 1780, Mary Pitman   2 CH-456
Richards, Basil, 10 Oct. 1794, Elizabeth Richards   4 FR
Richards, Benjamin, 14 June 1795, Elizabeth Howard   3 HA-24

```
Richards, Brice, 17 Oct. 1796, Elizab. Hart        2 FR-1163
Richards, Daniel, 19 May 1783, Jane Cochran        4 FR
Richards, Dutton, 11 Dec. 1800, Margaret Bowen     3 BA-396
Richards, Elisha, 5 Dec. 1782, Sarah Worald        3 AA-419
Richards, Edward, 13 March 1779, Jane Root         4 FR
Richards, George, 21 Dec. 1795, Anna Penn          4 FR
Richards, Godfrey, 1 Aug. 1791, Tempe Knight       1 AL-52
Richards, James, 20 Dec. 1796, Ann Marlow          3 PG-442
Richards, John, 22 Nov. 1781, Catherine Arnold     4 FR
Richards, John, 12 Nov. 1788, Aberella Norriss     2 FR-1162
Richards, John, 9 Feb. 1796, Ann Waters Williams   2 FR-1163
   4 FR gives the bride's name as Ann Waters.
Richards, John, 13 June 1797, Sarah Riggan         1 WO
Richards, John, 6 May 1800, Mary Truitt            1 WO
Richards, Joseph, 27 Oct. 1791, Ann Burger         6 BA
Richards, Joseph, 3 June 1797, Marg't Berbine     44 BA-2
Richards, Joseph, 18 Dec. 1798, Eleanor Purdey     4 FR
Richards, Joshua, 22 March 1789, Sarah Coward      6 BA
Richards, Richard, 9 Aug. 1780, Eliz'th Nevin      4 FR
Richards, Samuel, 15 Feb. 1790, Elizabeth Biddle   6 BA
Richards, Thomas, 25 Feb. 1787, Eliza Alguier     11 BA-10
Richards, William, 29 Sept. 1778, Tabitha Litton   4 MO-1
Richards, William, 18 Jan. 1787, Leviney Hyatt     4 FR
Richards, William, 31 Dec. 1789, Cath. Cooper      2 FR-1162
Richards, Wm., 24 Jan. 1790, Cloe Smallwood        3 PG-256
Richardson, Arnold, 9 Sept. 1800, Polly Barry      6 BA
Richardson, Benjamin, 2 Feb. 1797, Elizabeth Eaton 3 HA-25
Richardson, Benj., 26 June 1798, Catharine Bratten 1 WO
Richardson, Daniel, 5 May 1797, Betsy Gibbs        2 DO
Richardson, Edward, 29 Nov. 1796, Hanna Durbin     3 AL-4
   2 AL-700 gives the date as 1 Dec. 1796.
Richardson, Fielder, son of Richard and Mary, 31st day, 10
   mo., 1798, Mirriam Griffith, dau. of Abraham and Mary
   1 SF
Richardson, Henry, 20 March 1783, Elizabeth Morgan 3 HA-7
Richardson, James, 16 Nov. 1797, Eleanor Sullivan  3 BA-352
Richardson, John, 19 Oct. 1778, Mary Noble         4 FR
Richardson, John, 18 June 1794, Mary V. Hayes      3 BA-287
Richardson, Joseph, 13 July 1778, Bridget Burk    11 BA-1
Richardson, Joseph, 27 June 1789, Elizabeth Noel   2 DO
Richardson, Joseph, 15 Aug. 1799, Delilah Stanfust 4 SM-184
Richardson, Josias Winn, 23 March 1790, Eleanor Vermilion
   3 PG-257
Richardson, Richard, 15 April 1800, Sarah Richardson 2 FR-1163
Richardson, Robert, 21 July 1793, Mary Moore       6 BA
Richardson, Robert, 27 March 1796, Elizabeth Ridgly 3 BA-321
Richardson, Sam'l, 8 April 1800, Elizab. Mobberly  2 FR-1163
Richardson, Thomas, 14 Nov. 1777, by Rev. Magill; Katherine
   Calahone                                        4 AA
Richardson, Thos., 31 July 1785, Eliza Botts      11 BA-8
Richardson, Wm., 9 Feb. 1779, Nancy Davis          4 FR
Richardson, William, 16 July 1782, Jane Bramhall   2 CH-456
Richardson, William, 11 Feb. 1790, Mary Morgan     1 BA-2
Richmond, John, 2 Jan. 1782, Eleanor Maccabay     11 BA-5
Richmond, William, 12 Nov. 1799, Hannah Neale      6 BA
Richter, Abraham, 31 Sept. 1795, Cath. Uthern     29 BA-6
Richter, Peter, 18 Aug. 1789, Cath. Grof           2 FR-1162
Ricketts, Benja., 1 Feb. 1779, Ruth Wells          4 FR
Ricketts, Benjamin, 29 Sept. 1791, Cassandra Forrester 18 BA-3
   See also 3 BA-254.
Ricketts, Hugh, 21 April 1794, Mary Carr          18 BA-6
Ricketts, Robert, 4 Oct. 1778, Ellia'r Allison     2 MO-1
Ricketts, Robert, 1 June 1797, Kezia Ricketts      5 MO-114
Ricketts, Thomas, 7 June 1778, Ruth Adamson        2 MO-1
Ricketts, Zadock, 20 July 1797, Ann Groome         5 MO-114
```

Riddell, James, 10 March 1794, Jane Adams   5 BA-12
Riddell, William, 22 April 1797, Sarah Bendall   1 DO-39
  2 DO gives the date as 19 April 1797.
Riddle, John, 20 June 1791, Ann Muir   2 DO
Riddle, Jno., 1 Dec. 1796, Susanna Porter   5 MO-113
Riddle, Robert, 23 March 1782, Mary McNeill   11 BA-5
Riddle, Robert, 12 March 1786, Mary Hawksworth   11 BA-9
Ridenauer, Adam, March 1798, Cath. Tice (or Tin)   3 WA-64
Ridenhour, Henry, 23 Sept. 1779, Mary Smith   4 FR
Ridenhour, Jacob, 3 May 1785, Susanna Haas   4 FR
Rideout, Samuel, 23 Dec. 1790, Mary Grafton Addison 3 PG-257
Rider, Benj'n, 12 Aug. 1792, Charlotte Burke   6 BA
Ridge, Cornelius, 8 Feb. 1783, Elizabeth Brawner   4 FR
Ridge, Edward, 21 Oct. 1780, Catherine Creager   4 FR
Ridge, Wm., 28 Nov. 1780, Barbara Flemming   4 FR
Ridge, Wm., of Benja., 31 March 1781, Rebecca Springer 4 FR
Ridgely, Charles, 2 Dec. 1800, Ruth Ingram Smith   6 BA
Ridgely, Edward, 9 Feb. 1793, by Rev. Dorsey; Martha Worthing-
  ton   4 AA
Ridgely, Henry, 7 June 1787, Matilda Chase   11 BA-10
Ridgely, Mordecai, 14 April 1789, by Rev. Hagerty; Mary
  Cromwell   4 AA
Ridgely, Mordecai, 19 Nov. 1795, by Rev. Ridgely; Patience
  Johnson   4 AA
Ridgely, Peregrine, 3 Aug. 1789, Mary Lewis   4 AA
Ridgely, Richard, 15 Oct. 1778, by Rev. Magill; Elizabeth
  Dorsey   4 AA
Ridgely, Richard, 24 Sept. 1782, Rebeckah Templing 4 FR
Ridgely, Richard, 28 Aug. 1798, Mary Hyme   4 FR
Ridgely, Westall, 1 July 1791, Sarah Templing   4 FR
Ridgely, Westall, 24 Dec. 1799, Elizabeth Hyme   4 FR
Ridgeway, Benjamin, 16 Dec. 1779, Mary Hardy   2 PG-3
Ridgeway, James, 26 Feb. 1797, Rebecca Hurdle   5 MO-114
Ridgly, William, 8 Dec. 1779, Ann Worthington   11 BA-4
Ridgway, Basil, 21 Jan. 1779, Elizabeth Brashears 2 PG-3
Ridgway, John, 8 Dec. 1778, Rachel Mocbee   2 PG-2
Ridgway, Mordecai, 30 Nov. 1794, Eleanor Soper   3 PG-440
Ridley, George, 28 June 1781, Mary Tucker   3 AA-417
Ridout, Horatio, son of John and Mary (born 27 April 1769),
  1 Dec. 1791, Rachel Goldsborough, youngest dau. of
  Robert and Sarah; see also 2 DO.   2 AA-121
Ried, Abraham, 28 Oct. 1798, Eliz. Brubacher   2 FR-1163
Riehl, Frederick, 7 March 1799, Marg. Lukhorst   2 FR-1163
Riely, John, 27 June 1796, Lucy Scantlan   3 BA-323
Rieman, Daniel, 30 June 1785, Catharina Peter   10 BA-184
Riepart, Martin, 25 Dec. 1796, Mary Robinson   6 BA
Rieston, Samuel, 31 July 1787, Sarah Deberry   4 FR
Riff, John, 27 Nov. 1782, Eliza Moss   11 BA-6
Rigbie, Robert, 9 June 1796, Eliz. Robinson   29 BA-7
Rigby, Alexander, 31 Oct. 1799, Esther Mimm   3 BA-380
Rigby, George, 10 Sept. 1789, Eleanor Smith   1 BA-2
Rigby?, John, 3 Sept. 1799, by Rev. Wyatt; Elizabeth
  Colter   4 AA
Rigdon, Alexander, 11 Dec. 1781, Ann Johnson   3 HA-5
Rigdon, James, 30 Dec. 1781, Rebecca Jarvis   3 HA-3
Rigg, Charles, 28 Dec. 1781, Elizabeth Andrews   2 CH-456
Riggen, David, 12 March 1799, Eleanor Collins   6 BA
Riggen, Edmond, 12 March 1797, Elisabeth Coleman   3 BA-342
  See also 47 BA-1.
Riggen, Isaac, 5 Feb. 1799, Nelly Lawson   2 SO
Riggen, Pierce, 16 Jan. 1798, Betsy Harris   2 SO
Riggen, Robert, 30 Oct. 1798, Peggy Costen   2 SO
Riggin, Nehemiah, 7 April 1784, Betty Daugherty   1 SO-72
Riggin, Roads, 28 Jan. 1788, Sarah Bestpitch   2 DO
Riggins, Edward, 17 Dec. 1790, Henrietta Hooper   2 DO

```
Riggs, Edmund, 23 May 1799, Jane Willson            5 MO-116
Riggs, Erasmus, 31 Jan. 1797, Eleanor Wilcoxon      5 MO-114
Riggs, John, 12 Dec. 1782, Mary Elligan             4 FR
Riggs, John, 5 Feb. 1785, Mary Hardy                4 FR
Riggs, Jno. H., 26 June 1800, Rebecca Howard        5 MO-116
Riggs, Thomas, 17 Nov. 1796, Mary Riggs             5 MO-113
Righe, John, 22 Nov. 1792, Phebe Stoner             4 FR
Righter, Peter, 14 Aug. 1789, Catherine Grove       4 FR
Rights, Ludwick, 9 Nov. 1795, Margaret Cramer       4 FR
Rightstine, William, 8 March 1794, Catherine Chopper 4 FR
Riley, Camden, 16 Jan. 1800, Anna Ray               5 MO-116
Riley, Henry, 4 June 1798, Elizabeth Brown          4 FR
Riley, John, 14 Feb. 1791, Mary Steel               4 FR
Riley, John, 1 Oct. 1791, Alley Sadler              2 DO
Riley, Little, 23 April 1796, Sally Townsend        1 WO
Riley, Michael, 3 Nov. 1800, Mary Waters            3 BA-394
Riley, Stephen, 2 Jan. 1783, Mary Hooks            11 BA-6
Riley, Thomas, 5 Jan. 1781, Mary Campbell           3 HA-3
Riley, Wm., 7 Oct. 1784, Sarah Dukehart            11 BA-7
Riley, William, 28 Sept. 1791, Barbara Hodgkin     18 BA-3
     See also 3 BA-254.
Rily, John, 20 Feb. 1791, Mary Steel                2 FR-1162
Rimmer, William, 8 July 1798, Mary Stone            3 BA-360
Rine, John, 3 Sept. 1796, Priscilla Wilson          4 FR
Rine, Valentine, 23 Jan. 1795, Mary Clay            4 FR
Rineberger, Henry, 13 June 1796, Sarah Thomas       4 FR
Rineheart, George, 1 March 1780, Priscilla Weaver   4 FR
Riney, James, 27 Dec. 1785, Anne Semes              2 CH-456
Riney, John, 28 Oct. 1794, Nancy Dunnaway           3 BA-293
Ring, Richard, 12 Feb. 1797, Anne Gardiner          6 BA
Ringer, Jacob, 21 March 1780, Ann Beamer            4 FR
Ringer, Mathias, 5 March 1779, Eliz'th Plank        4 FR
Ringer, Philip, 3 Aug. 1794, Elizabeth Bayer or Boyer 3 WA-57
Ringgold, Tench, 16 April 1799, Mary Christian Lee, dau.
     of Thomas Sim and Mary Lee                     8 MO-21
Ringgold, William T., 10 June 1797, Martha Truman   4 KE-71
Ripley, Lewis, 11 Nov. 1788, Mary Miller            2 FR-1162
Risen, Chandley, 14 May 1779, Mary Hamilton         2 CH-456
     See also 2 PG-2.
Risses?, John, 21 June 1799, Elizabeth Glasgow      4 SM-184
Risteau, George, 3 April 1787, Ann Lux             11 BA-10
Risteau, John Talbot, 25 Jan. 1785, Elizabeth Denny 4 BA-79
Riston, Allen, 8 April 1779, Elizabeth Easton       2 PG-3
Riston, Basil, 6 Dec. 1787, Ann Bonafield           3 PG-253
Riston, Elisha, 12 Jan. 1779, Aminta Selby          2 PG-3
Riston, Elisha, 7 Feb. 1790, Ann Mayoh              3 PG-256
Ritchie, Abner, 19 Dec. 1785, Mary Ann Jenkins      4 FR
Ritchie, John, 18 Feb. 1787, Catherine Beatty       2 FR-1162
Ritchie, Niel, 28 Jan. 1783, Sarah Tull, dau. of John 1 SO-163
Ritemeyer, Conrad, 8 Dec. 1789, Susanna Shroiner    4 FR
Ritshie, William, 8 Dec. 1785, Patty Hooper        11 BA-9
Ritter, Abrah., April 1798, Cath. Bayer             3 WA-64
Ritter, Edward Hanson, 5 March 1795, Margaret McClure 3 BA-301
Ritter, Jno., 22 Feb. 1784, Eleanor Burk           11 BA-7
Ritter, Michal, 30 June 1799, Chatarina (sic) Baulusen 1 FR-59
     4 FR gives the bride's name as Catherine Powlas.
Ritter, Thomas, 28 Oct. 1786, by Rev. West; Elizabeth
     Leaf                                          51 BA-29
Ritz, Jacob, 28 Dec. 1789, Mary Stull               4 FR
Riyor, Heinrich, 28 Sept. 1785, Barbara Lora       10 BA-186
Rizeing, George, 31 Jan. 1780, -(?)- Whitehair      4 FR
Rizer, Martin, 4 June 1799, Rosina Gephart          3 AL-5
Roach, Edward, 17 Nov. 1783, Martha Huff            4 FR
Roach, Georg, 1792, Rebecca Watkins                50 BA-392
Roach, James, 24 Sept. 1789, Ruth Jordan            6 BA
```

```
Roach, Micaiah, 4 April 1786, Ruth Rice           4 FR
Roach, Michael, 3 Jan. 1783, Tabitha Bryan       11 BA-6
Roach, Richard, 6 Jan. 1783, Drusey Lanham        4 FR
Roach, Stephen, 17 Aug. 1797, Mary Lamden         1 WO
Roach, Stephen, 20 Nov. 1799, Eleanor Cullen     29 BA-11
Roach, William, 29 Oct. 1787, Sarah Batten        2 DO
Roach, William, 27 Jan. 1793, Elizabeth Hambleton 1 BA-5
Road, George, 14 Nov. 1778, Mart. Mugg            4 FR
Roads, Andrew, 27 Nov. 1788, Sussana Jones        3 BA-219
Roads, Charles, 4 May 1779, Abigail Pursley       4 FR
Roads, George, 2 June 1796, Cath. Fasnacht        3 WA-61
Roads, Jacob, 8 April 1780, Nancey Cash           4 FR
Roads, John, 4 Dec. 1791, Mary Baxter             6 BA
Roads, Thomas, 23 May 1782, Rachel West           3 HA-6
Roan, John, 23 Nov. 1798, Jane Robinson           5 BA-12
Roar, Jacob, 23 Oct. 1779, Catherine King         4 FR
Roaus, Georg, 5 June 1793, Rosina Watts          50 BA-393
Robb, John, 25 Dec. 1791, Susanna Dunkin          3 BA-255
Robb, William, 15 April 1791, Elizabeth Gartz     5 BA-12
Robbins, Roger, 3 Oct. 1793, Rebecca Freeland?   14 BA-15
    5 BA-12 gives the bride's name as Keeland.
Robee, Patrick Moreland, 30 July 1782, Rebecca Johnson  4 FR
Robert, Conr'd, 2 March 1784, Mar. Magdl. Frankfurtherin
    2 CL-82
Roberts, Archibald, 24 Sept. 1787, Mary Ann Bosley  4 FR
Roberts, Benja., 22 Dec. 1785, Terry Stansbury   11 BA-9
Roberts, George, 17 June 1781, Mary Taylor        2 DO
Roberts, George, 26 July 1798, Ann Foster        29 BA-9
Roberts, Henry, of Richard and Mersey, 24th day, 11 mo.,
    1784, Ann Farquhar, dau. of William and Rachel  3 SF
Roberts, James, 27 Dec. 1795, Ann Bain            7 BA-2
Roberts, John, 11 Nov. 1780, Susannah Mason       2 CH-456
Roberts, John, 12 Aug. 1781, Sarah Barrett        2 PG-5
Roberts, John, 15 Oct. 1789, Susannah Orrick      6 BA
Roberts, Jno., 24 Jan. 1797, Eliz. Heater         5 MO-114
Roberts, John, 7 May 1797, Elizabeth Holmes       3 BA-344
Roberts, John, 24 Dec. 1797, Tamer Williams      35 BA-6
Roberts, John, 12 Aug. 1799, Martha Coleman       3 BA-375
Roberts, Joshua B., Sept. 1799, Sally Russell     2 SO
Roberts, Levy, 9 July 1778, Elizabeth Flood      11 BA-1
Roberts, Moses, 6 April 1795, Mary Webb           2 DO
Roberts, Nathan, 1 March 1792, Mary Saunders      3 BA-255
Roberts, Owen, 13 June 1795, Marg. Pawson        29 BA-6
Roberts, Owen, 2 June 1798, Jane Vansickle        3 HA-27
    2 HA-350 gives the date as 3 June 1798, and the bride's
    name as Vansick.
Roberts, Peter, 17 May 1780, Mary Slown           3 HA-2
Roberts, Peter John, 23 April 1792, Maria Sanderson  1 BA-4
Roberts, Richard, 17 Nov. 1789, by Rev. Reed; Sarah Owens
    4 AA
Roberts, Richard, 27 April 1794, Daphne Johnson   3 BA-285
Roberts, Robert, 30 Aug. 1797, Rebecca Heggins    4 FR
Roberts, Sylvanus Uriah, 1 Oct. 1796, Sarah Gillett  1 WO
Roberts, Thomas, 27 Jan. 1780, Rebecca Brashears  3 AA-416
Roberts, Thomas, 7 Feb. 1792, Elizabeth Toole    28 BA-2
Roberts, Thomas, 3 Jan. 1798, Susannah Stevenson  4 FR
Roberts, Wm., 25 Oct. 1790, Sarah Hodgkiss        6 BA
Roberts, William, 11 Jan. 1798, by Rev. Wyatt; Elizabeth
    Hall                                          4 AA
Roberts, William, 23 Jan. 1798, Sarah Rencher     2 SO
    3 SO gives the date as 29 Jan. 1798.
Robertson, Dan'l, 9 Aug. 1797, Esther Miller      4 FR
Robertson, George, 2 Oct. 1781, Virlinda Johnston 2 PG-5
Robertson, George, 19 July 1782, Rosanna Chapman  2 DO
Robertson, Hezekiah, 25 Jan. 1798, Polly Hurley   2 DO
```

Robertson, James, 8 Jan. 1789, Amelia Long   1 SO-162
Robertson, James, 11 June 1799, Rhoda Claywell   1 WO
Robertson, John, 16 Dec. 1793, Maria Willson   3 BA-279
Robertson, John, 1 July 1798, Margaret Lashley   3 BA-260
Robertson, John, 17 Sept. 1799, Philliss Bird   2 SO
Robertson, John, 9 Dec. (1800?), Elizabeth Dorithy 2 SO
Robertson, John Babtist, before 4 May 1798, by Rev. Stewart;
    Sarah Stewart   4 AA
Robertson, Joseph, 12 Aug. 1794, Nancy Gray   3 BA-291
Robertson, Joseph, 12 July 1800, Mary Andrews   8 BA-2
    See also 48 BA-1.
Robertson, Mitchell, 24 Dec. 1780, Rose Mastin   2 CH-456
Robertson, Robert, 11 June 1798, Anne Hack Waters   2 SO
Robertson, Robert, 28 July 1798, Abigail Fonder   3 BA-361
Robertson, Samuel, 27 Dec. 1799, Rachel Howard   4 FR
Robertson, William M., 27 Sept. 1794, Henrietta Murray 2 DO
Robertson, Zachariah, 15 May 1786, Mary Smith   4 FR
Robey, John Osburn, 22 Feb. 1797, Verlinda Luckett 3 CH-162
Robey, Michael, 27 Dec. 1790, Elizabeth Jarman   3 PG-257
Robinett, Richard, 18 Nov. 1800, Mary Shaw   5 BA-12
Robinette, Amos, 27 Nov. 1800, Darkey Willison   3 AL-7
Robinson, And'w, 30 May 1780, Margaret Knave   4 FR
Robinson, Benjamin Talbot, 9 June 1778, Martha Deaver 11 BA-1
Robinson, Charles, 29 June 1787, by Rev. Davis; Miss Lytica
    Galloway   51 BA-30
Robinson, Charles, 11 Feb. 1790, Vilitter Jones   3 PG-256
Robinson, Chiles, 19 Nov. 1779, Elizabeth Robinson 4 FR
Robinson, David, 9 April 1800, by Rev. Wyatt; Kitty Johnson
    4 AA
Robinson, Edward, 22 Aug. 1779, Catherine Methard   4 FR
Robinson, Elijah, 24 Nov. 1788, by Rev. Hagerty; Ann
    Talbot   4 AA
Robinson, George, 7 Sept. 1785, Mary Phillips   2 DO
Robinson, George, 24 Sept. 1794, Mary Graves   18 BA-6
Robinson, George, 8 July 1799, Elizabeth Hobbs   3 BA-373
Robinson, George, 25 Aug. 1800, Charlotte Deal   2;DO
Robinson, Giles (or Chiles), 19 Nov. 1799, Elizabeth
    Robinson   4 FR
Robinson, James, 25 Sept. 1783, Mary Nelson   11 BA-6
Robinson, James, 17 Feb. 1795, Mary Lynch   6 BA
Robinson, John, 30 Oct. 1790, Joanna Greenfield   6 BA
Robinson, Johnm 3 Jan. 1792, Amelia Keene   2 DO
Robinson, John, 7 May 1797, Elizabeth Holmes   35 BA-5
Robinson, John, 30 May 1797, Mary Baker   44 BA-2
Robinson, Jno., 22 June 1797, Cath. Rothrock   29 BA-8
Robinson, John, 24 Dec. 1797, Tamar Williams   3 BA-353
Robinson, Joseph, 1 Oct. 1795, Elizabeth Smith   7 BA-2
Robinson, Joseph, 26 Aug. 1799, Mary Traplin   29 BA-10
Robinson, Joshua, 25 Dec. 1781, Mary Taylor   3 AA-416
Robinson, Lawrence, 1 May 1800, by Rev. Wyatt; Sharon?
    Potter?   4 AA
Robinson, Lott, 15 Nov. 1800, Ann Moore   3 AL-7
Robinson, Michael, 13 April 1790, Jenette Lee   2 DO
Robinson, O'Neill, 14 May 1782, Delilah Ridgely   11 BA-5
Robinson, Richard, 13 Aug. 1778, Sarah Penn   11 BA-1
Robinson, Robert, 28 July 1798, Abigail Fonder   35 BA-6
Robinson, Samuel, 2 Aug. 1789, Anna Holmes   10 BA-194
Robinson, Seth, 20 Nov. 1800, Nancy Moor   2 AL-701
Robinson, Thomas, 6 April 1798, by Rev. Wyatt; Milly Foreman
    4 AA
Robinson, Wm., 9 Oct. 1794, Mary Price   50 BA-396
Robinson, William, 20 July 1798, Ann Burrows   4 KE-71
Robison, William, 8 April 1779, Mary Sims   2 CH-456
Robson, Roger, 30 Aug. 1798, Mahala Cator   1 DO-40
    2 DO gives the date as 28 Aug. 1798.

Robson, Thomas, 16 Aug. 1790, Hannah Denny   3 BA-228
Roby, Aquila, 8 Jan. 1782, Mary Cole   2 CH-456
Roby, James, 5 Jan. 1796, Mary Walker   3 PG-442
Roby, Theophilus, 2 Feb. 1796, Ann Willett   5 MO-113
Roby, Zachariah, 16 Jan. 1783, Elizabeth Pickrell   2 CH-456
Rochester, James, 15 Dec. 1797, Elizabeth Esget   4 KE-71
Rochester, Nathaniel, 19 April 1788, Sophia Beatty   4 FR
Rochester, Samuel, 22 Dec. 1797, Mary Price   4 KE-71
Rock, John, 14 June 1797, Polly Mitchell   1 WO
Rock, Thomas, 29 May 1791, Rebecca Reed   1 BA-3
Rock, William, 23 Feb. 1778, Charity Adams   4 CH-1
Rockhold, Charles, 15 April 1791, Eleanor Pocock   1 BA-4
  3 HA-21 gives the date as 2 Dec. 1791.
Rockhold, John, 2 Feb. 1790, Martha Waters   1 BA-2
Rode, Henry, 6 Oct. 1800, Marg. Pfalzgraf   29 BA-11
Rode, John, 7 Jan. 1796, Sally Mincher   6 BA
Rodes, Jonathan, 25 Dec. 1790, Henrietta Ingram   4 FR
Rodgers, George, 4 Dec. 1778, Jane Patten   4 FR
Rodgers, John, 6 Oct. 1779, Mary Tannihill   4 FR
Rodgers, John, 6 Feb. 1782, Mary Blair   4 FR
Rodgers, Rowland, 3 Dec. 1800, Kitty Rodgers   3 HA-30
Rodgers, William, 20 March 1800, Mary Hanna   3 HA-29
  See also 2 HA-351.
Roe, William Clayton, 31 Jan. 1782, Juliana Thomas   1 CR-76
Rogers, Allen, 11 April 1792, Rebecca Evans   5 BA-12
Rogers, Jacob, 10 Aug. 1790, Elizabeth Lymes   26 BA-1
Rogers, Jeremiah, of Thomas and Katherine, 7th day, 6 mo.,
  1797, Anna Brown, of Jeremiah and Anna   11 SF-244
Rogers, John, son of Evan and Margaret, 6th day, 3 mo.,
  1783, Susanna Hicks, dau. of James and Mary   1 SF
Rogers, Joseph, 9 Sept. 1781, Sarah Scarborough   3 HA-5
Rogers, Joseph, 16 Sept. 1783, Sarah Halbert   11 BA-4
Rogers, Joseph, 14 April 1796, Sarah Sheperd   3 BA-321
Rogers, Joseph, son of Thomas and Catherine, 1st day, 2 mo.,
  1798, Meriam King, dau. of Thomas and Ann   11 SF-247
Rogers, Joseph, 23 July 1799, Deborah Stansbury   3 BA-374
Rogers, Thomas, 23 June 1781, Sarah Young   3 HA-4
Rogers, Thomas, 1 Jan. 1795, Maggie Hanna   3 HA-24
Rogers, William, 19 Nov. 1786, Elizabeth Dawson   5 BA-12
Rogers, William, son of Thomas and Catherine, 10th day,
  6 mo., 1790, Katherine Brown, dau. of Jeremiah and
  Anna   11 SF-222
Rogers, William, 8th day, 12 mo., 1796, Catherine Churchman
  11 SF-243
Roh, Fried'k, 3 Jan. 1790, Rebecca Roles   50 BA-390
Rohr, Rudolph, 27 Nov. 1791, Cath. Lausser   2 FR-1163
  4 FR gives the groom's name as Rudolph Rohr, Jr., and
  the bride's name as Cathe. Runner.
Rohrbach, George, 10 March 1790, H. Smith   29 BA-1
Roiston, Joshua, 2 Sept. 1786, by Rev. Turner; Mary Hooker
  51 BA-30
Roland, Gaidon, 29 Jan. 1780, Elizabeth Dawson   4 FR
Roland, George, 25 March 1783, Martha Slater   2 CH-456
Roles, Jno., 19 July 1785, Eliza Jacob   11 BA-8
Roll, John, 6 June 1779, by Rev. Magowan; Sarah Friland 4 AA
Roll, Joh., 17 Jan. 1797, Cath. Oysterbuhn   50 BA-401
Rolle, Robert, 30 March 1780, Martha Freeland   1 CA-3
Rollins, Aaron, 9 Aug. 1783, Eliza Pritchett   11 BA-6
Rolph, William, 24 May 1797, Elizabeth Sands   4 KE-71
Rolzer, -(?)-, 5 Oct. 1794, Christina Haus   50 BA-395
Ronals, Joh., 12 March 1795, Marg. Wolz   3 WA-58
Rook, Thos., 13 Aug. 1800, Jane Porter   29 BA-11
Roos, Frederick, 27 March 1796, Mary Froshauer   2 FR-1163
Root, Daniel, 14 May 1782, Elizabeth Cowell   4 FR
Root, James, 10 Aug. 1779, Mary Umstatt   4 FR

```
Root, Lemuel, 22 Jan. 1793, Magd. Schmit             2 FR-1163
Root, Richard, 7 Feb. 1797, Agnes Stoner             4 FR
Rorker, Abraham, 13 Jan. 1799, Jane Dew              6 BA
Rose, Frederick, 26 March 1796, Mary Frushour        4 FR
Rose, John, 7 Jan. 1795, Catherine Lemon             4 FR
Rose, William, 7 July 1778, Mary Welsh              11 BA-1
Rosell, Charles, 18 June 1795, Margaret Holston      6 BA
Rosenhazard, Casper, 20 April 1797, Patty Riddle     6 BA
Ross, Abraham, 24 July 1783, Elizabeth Barker        3 AA-419
Ross, Andreas, 16 July 1794, Rachel Endesson        50 BA-395
Ross, Cain, 19 Feb. 1788, Mary Brown                 2 DO
Ross, Charles, 8 Nov. 1781, Jestanna Ross            2 DO
Ross, Charles, 24 April 1794, Mary Smith             6 BA
Ross, Daniel, 31 July 1783, Elizabeth --ioa--        3 AA-419
Ross, Daniel, 29 May 1785, Mary West                11 BA-8
Ross, David, 9 Aug. 1784, Nancy Walston Miles        2 DO
Ross, Edward, 11 Feb. 1794, Lucy Flemming            2 DO
Ross, Francis, 12 Jan. 1797, Nancy Long              3 SO
Ross, George, 26 Oct. 1799, Betsy Caple              6 BA
Ross, Ham, 11 Oct. 1792, Mary Stocks                28 BA-2
Ross, James, 31 Jan. 1788, Nancy Skinner             2 DO
Ross, John, 21 Feb. 1780, Margery Spelman           11 BA-4
Ross, John, 18 Nov. 1788, Hannah Smith               6 BA
Ross, Jno., 6 Oct. 1791, Mary Smith                 29 BA-2
Ross, Joshua, 24 Sept. 1787, Rosanna Cook            2 DO
Ross, Lazarus, 27 Nov. 1780, Jane Cox                3 SM-58
Ross, Peter, 14 Aug. 1800, Arabella Cantler          2 HA-352
Ross, Reuben, 29 July 1795, Henny Holland            2 DO
Ross, Richard, 4 Nov. 1789, Sarah Brereton          11 BA-12
Ross, Roberson, 6 Nov. 1788, Sarah Tregoe            2 DO
Ross, Robert, 7 Dec. 1781, Rebecca Wingate           2 DO
Ross, Robert, 19 Aug. 1785, Betsy Elliott Todd       2 DO
Ross, Robert, 13 March 1787, Sarah Gotier?          11 BA-10
Ross, Robert Lockhart, 26 Jan. 1792, Elisabeth McLure 5 BA-12
Ross, Thomas, 19 May 1781, Sarah Madkins             2 DO
Ross, Thomas, 29 Aug. 1787, Barthula Hogans          2 DO
Ross, Thomas, 20 May 1795, Dolly Webster             2 DO
Ross, Thomas (Wm,?), 8 Jan. 1793, Mary Price         3 BA-258
Rosseau, John, 1790, Mary Curtis                    50 BA-389
Rossinot, Michael, 27 Dec. 1796, Mary Rose Ballerin 40 BA-3
Rosson, Wm., 12 Aug. 1786, Ann Wright               11 BA-9
Roth, Jno. A., 15 June 1800, Susanna Gladman        29 BA-11
Rothrock, Abr., 26 Jan. 1785, Elizab. Roberts Antietam 2 FR-1162
Roualet?, Francis, 20 Aug. 1782, Margaret Celeston   3 BA-183
Roulison, Moses, 6 Feb. 1784, Sarah Collins         11 BA-7
Round, Jacob, 1 Nov. 1799, Martha Richardson         1 WO
Rousseau, Charles, 20 Sept. 1797, Theresa Debrauder  6 BA
Routzong, Henry, 29 April 1793, Mary Magdalena Colman 4 FR
Routzawn, Jacob, 26 Dec. 1795, Christena Synn        4 FR
Roux, Peter, 3 June 1798, Anne McCoy                 3 BA-359
Rouzahn, Jacob, 27 Dec. 1795, Christina Sinn         2 FR-1163
Row, Edward, 8 March 1791, Abigail Miles             6 BA
Rowe, Jacob, 22 Aug. 1797, Susanna Conrod            4 FR
Rowens, Alexander, 13 Nov. 1788, Sarah Grainger      2 DO
Rowenzaum, Benjamin, 30 April 1799, Pheby Shriver    4 FR
Rowland, Henry, 21 Nov. 1799, Mary Carr              3 HA-1
Rowland, Robert, 20 Oct. 1790, Agnes McClary         6 BA
Rowles, Ely, 28 Sept. 1788, Sarah Cord               6 BA
Rowles, Hezekiah, son of Lacy and Mary, 17th day, 5 mo.,
    1781, Margaret England, dau. of Samuel and Sarah 11 SF-197
Rowles, Jacob, 20 July 1794, Elizabeth Dungan        3 BA-291
Rowles, Thos., 2 Feb. 1787, Chis (sic) Branson      29 BA-1
Rowlings, John, 5 Jan. 1796, Catherine Smallwood     3 PG-442
Rowls, Elihu, son of Hezekiah and Elizabeth, 7th day, 12
    mo., 1798, Esther White, dau. of John and Sarah 11 SF-253
```

```
Rows, Thomas, 21 May 1795, Martha Adams                 6 BA
Rowser, Henry, 21 June 1782, Eve Shiteaire              4 FR
Royal, John, 15 March 1792, Mary Sheels or Skeels       3 BA-255
Rozen, Henry, 19 Aug. 1798, Mary Chivers               29 BA-9
Ruark, Henry, 22 May 1788, Rosanna Meekins              2 DO
Ruark, Henry, 26 Sept. 1797, Mary Parker                2 DO
Ruark, James, 8 Nov. 1791, Patty Travers                2 DO
Ruark, John, 25 June 1792, Elizabeth Traverse           2 DO
Ruark, Johnson, 25 July 1800, Sally Westerhouse         1 WO
Ruark, Matthew, 25 Nov. 1794, Grace Wallace             2 DO
Ruark, Seth, 6 May 1800, Sally Anderson                 1 WO
Rubbet, Peter, 7 Feb. 1798, Sophia Miller               6 BA
Ruber, Joh., 13 May 1799, Cath. Rist                   50 BA-405
Ruby?, William, 9 Oct. 1796, Mary Lunn?                46 BA-1
Ruck, James, 1 Sept. 1782, Ann Balos                    3 HA-7
Rudecill, Jacob, 6 Feb. 1789, Catherine Moser           4 FR
    6 BA gives the date as 15 Feb. 1789.
Rudricks, Anthony, 1 Oct. 1790, Margaret Nabours       18 BA-2
Rue, John, 30 Dec. 1798, Ephamia Summers                2 SO
Rue, Levi, 23 Dec. 1799, Sally Bird                     2 DO
Rue, Southey, 2 Feb. 1790, Sarah Oram                   2 DO
Rue, Southy, 26 Sept. 1797, Sarah Keene                 2 DO
Ruff, Henry, 26 April 1781, Mary Marthars               3 HA-4
Ruff, Henry, 1 June 1788, Anna Preston                  1 BA-1
Ruley, Philip, 10 Aug. 1792, Amelia Cooms               3 HA-21
Ruley, William, 9 Oct. 1796, by Rev. Zebulon Kankey;
    Mary Lunn                                          46 BA-1
Ruliff, Gilbert, 1 Jan. 1778, Mary Curran              11 BA-1
Rumage, Nicholas, 5 Nov. 1797, Mary Slater              6 BA
Rummage, Nich's, 28 April 1785, Priscilla Mildues      11 BA-8
Rummel, George, 27 Nov. 1800, Hannah Foreman           29 BA-12
Rummelles, William, before 12 Dec. 1792, by Rev. John
    Long; Lydia Whitaker                                4 AA
Runkle, Joseph, 7 July 1794, Susanna Bussard            4 FR
Runnells, Stephen, 27 Oct. 1799, by Rev. Roberts; Lucy
    Harris                                              4 AA
Runner, Christian, 23 Feb. 1790, Eliz'th Thomas         4 FR
Runner, Michael, Jr., 11 Jan. 1799, Eve Hershberger     4 FR
Rupart, Martin, 25 Dec. 1795, Mary Robinson            19 BA-12
Rush, Arnold, 27 Aug. 1792, Janett Conn                 1 BA-4
Rush, Elam, 29 Oct. 1800, Eleanor Sadler                6 BA
Rusk, John, 20 Jan. 1799, Kitty Lightner                6 BA
Rusk, Robert, 4 Sept. 1794, Barb. Balspach             29 BA-5
Russel, James, March 1799, Sarah Lepton                 3 WA-66
Russel, Thomas, 12 Oct. 1780, Rebecca Moale             3 BA-192
Russel, Thomas, 3 May 1800, Elizabeth Townsend          3 BA-386
Russel, William, 22 March 1793, Eliz. Randall           2 FR-1163
Russell, Charles, 29 Jan. 1786, Priscilla King          2 DO
Russell, Henry, 3 Nov. 1782, Chloe Smallwood            2 CH-456
Russell, James, 24 June (1800?), Molly Twilley          2 SO
Russell, Job, 4 July 1796, Mary Whiteley                2 DO
Russell, Levi, 28 July 1797, Nancy Groves               2 SO
Russell, Levin, 1 Dec. (1800?), Liza Selvey             2 SO
Russell, Philip, 18 Feb. 1781, Elizabeth Dove           2 PG-5
Russell, Richard, 18 Oct. 1778, Margaret Tumbleterd    11 BA-1
Russell, Robert, 30 July 1798, Elizabeth Hobbs          3 BA-361
Russell, Thomas, 12 Oct. 1780, Rebecca Moale           11 BA-4
Russell, Thomas, 22 March 1791, Sarah Wheatley          2 DO
Russell, Thomas, of John and Hannah, 31st day, 10 mo.,
    1793, Sarah Roberts, dau. of Richard and Mercy      3 SF
Russell, William, 8 April 1788, Leah Roads              2 DO
Russell, William, 22 Jan. 1795, Elizabeth Williamson    3 BA-299
Russell, William, 16 Dec. 1795, Catharine Deagan        5 BA-12
Rust, Charles, 6 Jan. 1785, Mary Sharmiller            11 BA-8
Rust, Jno., 9 July 1782, Mary Patterson                11 BA-5
```

Rust, John, 11 Aug. 1797, Elizabeth Marshall   4 FR
Rust, Jonathan, 1790, Eliz. Isaac   50 BA-389
Ruth, George, 30 Sept. 1779, Ann Harris   11 BA-3
Ruth, John, 2 June 1795, Charlotte Barton   7 BA-2
Rutherford, Wm., 27 Aug. 1797, Eliz. Harper   3 AL-5
Rutledge, Jacob, 1 April 1799, Monica Wheeler   3 HA-26
Rutledge, Joshua, 11 Nov. 1792, Augustine Biddle   1 BA-5
Rutledge, Thomas, 5 Jan. 1794, Ann Burton   1 BA-6
Rutledge, Zachariah, 9 Nov. 1780, Isabella Sinclair   11 BA-4
Rutter, Edward, 3 Aug. 1800, Mary Anne Ripper   3 BA-389
Rutter, Edward Hanson, 5 March 1795, Margaret McClure   3 BA-301
Rutter, Henry, 22 Nov. 1779, Christiana Nice   11 BA-4
Rutter, Jno., 16 Feb. 1786, Eliza Askew   11 BA-9
Rutter, Jonathan, 16 May 1778, Martha Longwell   11 BA-1
Rutter, Josias, 24 May 1796, Mary Pennington   3 BA-323
Rutter, Moses, 30 March 1790, Elizabeth Hubbert   26 BA-1
Rutter, Richard, (c.1791), Mary Key   15 BA-4
Rutter, Solomon, 9 Dec. 1788, Magd. Reidenouer   29 BA-1
Rutter, Thomas, Jr., 17 Nov. 1787, Mary Gray   11 BA-10
Ryan, George, 27 Sept. 1794, Sarah Steward   4 FR
Ryan, John, 29 July 1799, Eleanor Murphy   3 BA-374
Ryan, Philip, 22 Sept. 1798, Sarah Dickson   6 BA
Ryan, Timothy, 11 Feb. 1800, Elizabeth Pannell   3 BA-383
Rye, John, 13 Sept. 1797, Mary Barbary   3 BA-350
Rye, Warren, 23 Jan. 1780, Sarah Smith   2 CH-456
Ryland, John Burke, 15 April 1797, Sarah Jones   3 BA-343
Ryland, Joseph, 24 July 1795, Mary Mathews   6 BA
Ryland, William, 5 Dec. 1796, Joanna Mather   3 HA-25
Ryle, John, 26 Aug. 1790, Willey Clarke   3 PG-257
Ryley, Patrick, 22 May 1778, Elizabeth Cringland   4 FR
Ryley, Patrick, 22 Sept. 1778, Hanna Price   4 FR
Ryne, Mich'l, 8 Feb. 1779, Eleanor Smith   4 FR
Ryon, Darby, 31 Dec. 1779, Ann Sim   2 PG-1
Ryson, Lancelot, 26 March 1778, Clara Cash   2 CH-456

Sadler, John, 20 Dec. 1785, Priscilla Clarridge   2 DO
Sadler, John, 12 Sept. 1791, Milcah Harrington   2 DO
Sadler, John, 23 Aug. 1794, Catherine Devilbiss   4 FR
Sadler, Joseph, 5 Nov. 1794, Elsey Reynolds   29 BA-6
Sadler, Samuel, 4 April 1780, Sarah Lewin   3 AA-416
Sadler, Thomas, 7 Nov. 1793, Elizabeth Howard   1 BA-6
Sadler, Thomas, 30 Sept. 1799, Christiana Foss   6 BA
Saider, John, 3 Feb. 1788, Catherine Ann Penn   2 CH-456
St. Clair, George, 4 Jan. 1794, Celia Ann Connolly   3 BA-299
St. Clair, James, 29 June 1797, Susanna Bosley   1 BA-8
    3 HA-26 gives the date as 12 June 1797.
St. Clair, John, 18 Dec. 1799, Temperance West   3 HA-29
    2 HA-351 gives the date as 19 Dec. 1799.
St. Clair, Thomas, 3 July 1800, Mary Blaney   3 HA-29
Saintclere, Robert, 30 Nov. 1791, Sinthy Hill   6 BA
Saker, Wm., 31 July 1793, Cath. Scott   50 BA-393
Salisbury, William, 31 Jan. 1786, Mary Bradley   2 DO
Salkill, John, 25 Sept. 1797, Lucy Smith   4 FR
Sallaway, Thomas, 7 July 1794, Sarah Sugar   39 BA-1
Salman, John, 8 April 1780, Ann Slack   11 BA-4
Salmon, George, 21 Oct. 1779, Rebecca Mercer   5 BA-13
Salter, Thomas, 22 July 1797, Charlotte Glebe   6 BA
Sampson, George, 19 July 1794, Catherine Dysert   18 BA-6
Sampson, Richard, 7 March 1781, Hannah Amoss   2 CH-456
    3 HA-6 gives the date as 3 March 1782.
Samsell, John, 1 Dec. 1795, Cath. Bott   2 FR-1169
Samsell, Peter, 17 Aug. 1800, Marg. Gilaspie   2 FR-1170
Samson, Aquila, 12 Sept. 1790, Mary Inlows   1 BA-3
Sanbach, Francis, 23 July 1789, Lydia Selman   11 BA-12

```
Sancer, John, 24 Jan. 1797, Ann Caster              3 PG-443
Sanders, Francis, 23 Oct. 1793, Marg. Schley        2 FR-1169
Sanders, James, 11 Feb. 1782, Ruth Andrews          3 BA-188
Sanders, Jno., 24 April 1794, Mary Harker           29 BA-5
Sanders, Joseph (c.June 1778), Mary Phaley          3 AA-414
Sanders, Joseph, 29 Jan. 1795, Ann Branson          8 MO-9
Sanderson, Francis, 24 Oct. 1793, Margaret Schley   4 FR
Sandes, James, 18 Oct. 1797, Sarah Sandes           4 FR
Sandison, Alexander, 13 July 1799, Jane Alexander   5 BA-13
Sands, Alexander, 13 April 1788, Delilah Burk       3 BA-217
Sands, Benjamin, 13 Dec. 1798, Rebecca Jackson      4 KE-71
Sands, John, 21 July 1798, by Rev. Wyatt; Delila Phillips
    4 AA
Sanford, Nich's, 10 April 1798, Cath. Ritter        29 BA-9
Sanger, Seth, 7 Aug. 1794, Catherine Elkins         5 BA-13
Sank, George, 25 Aug. 1799, Hannah Vansandt         3 BA-376
Sanner, Isaac, 12 Dec. 1782, Eleanor Price          3 SM-60
Sanner, Matthias, 13 Feb. 1800, Ann Cissell         4 SM-184
Sanner, Thomas, 23 Dec. 1783, Mary Collason         3 SM-61
Sansom, Henry, 23 Sept. 1799, Anna Kins             3 BA-378
Sap, George, 6 March 1797, Polly Stops              6 BA
Sapet, Jno. Francis, 18 Oct. 1793, Mary Kettler     6 BA
Sapp, Daniel, 1 Oct. 1796, Mary Roboson             1 AL-53
Sapp, George, 23 June 1797, Cath. Arnold            3 AL-5
Sappanton, Thomas, 22 Jan. 1800, by Rev. Wyatt; Susanna
    Allen                                           4 AA
Sappington, Jacob, 15 Oct. 1790, E. Brown           29 BA-1
Sappington, James, 27 May 1789, Rachel Clark        4 FR
Sappington, Richard, 2 Oct. 1785, Cassandra Durbin  3 HA-9
Sappington, Thomas, 16 Aug. 1790, by Rev. Cooper; Elizabeth
    Lewis                                           4 AA
Sard, Thomas, 25 Dec. 1794, Elizabeth Williams      2 DO
Sarge, Peter, 26 May 1788, Nancy Marine             2 DO
Sargent, George, 4 Oct. 1796, Ann Wells             2 FR-1169
Sargent, James, 29 June 1794, Mary Young            3 BA-287
Sargent, John, 20 Nov. 1787, Esther Campden         4 FR
Sargent, Samuel, 28 March 1796, Mary Silvey         6 BA
Satchell, Henry, 2 January 1795, Dolly Husk         2 DO
Satchell, Thomas, 4 December 1800, Sarah Satchell   2 DO
Sater, Charles, 30 June 1799, Ruth Beasman          6 BA
Sauer, David, 24 March 1793, Eliz. Kreibel          2 FR-1169
Sauer, Jacob, 26 Jan. 1790, Catherine Morckel       6 FR-202
Sauer, Philip, 10 Dec. 1793, Sarah Hobelmann        2 FR-1169
Sauer, Samuel, 7 June 1795, Elizabeth Samuth        10 BA-196
Saul, Christopher, 14 Aug. 1798, Sarah Davis        3 BA-362
Saunders, James, 2 June 1789, Nancy Newton          2 DO
Saunders, John, 19 Aug. 1780, Fria's Perry          3 HA-2
Saunders, John, 3 Oct. 1792, Dorcas Allen           3 BA-257
Saunders, John, 15 July 1796, Charlotte Day         3 HA-25
Saunders, Levin, 8 August 1792, Amelia Woodland     2 DO
Saunders, Thomas, 26 Dec. 1780, Leah Waters         2 DO
Saunders, William, March 1790, Elizabeth Rawlings   4 AA
Saunders, William, 4 August 1800, Polly Carroll     2 DO
Savage, Patrick, 26 May 1796, Elizabeth Corrie      3 BA-323
Savage, William, 8 Sept. 1794, Hester Dennis        2 DO
Savery, William, 28 July 1787, Rosannah Robinson    6 BA
Savoy, Francis, 16 Feb. 1795, Mary Courtes          3 CH-162
Sawyer, Anthony, 10 March 1799, Sarah Spalding      3 BA-368
Sawyer, Peter, 12 July 1792, Margaret Buckey        4 FR
Saxe, Henry, 10 Jan. 1783, Rennes Denton            3 SM-60
Sayler, Martin, 29 Jan. 1798, Elizabeth Wilson      4 FR
Saylor, Daniel, 7 April 1798, Barbara Raitt         4 FR
Scaggs, James, 20 Sept. 1790, Cath. Raszer          2 FR-1168
    4 FR gives the bride's name as Reaser.
Scaggs, Richard, 22 Dec. 1795, Susanna Holtzman     4 FR
```

```
Scags, Thomas, 7 Sept. 1791, Lydia Hillen            3 BA-254
Scanlan, Jas., 25 Nov. 1797, Mary Pearson           29 BA-9
Scarborough, Edward, 2 May 1797, Nancy Selby         1 WO
Scarborough, John, 8 July 1796, Elizabeth Smullen    1 WO
Scarborough, Nathan, 23 April 1795, Mary Webster     3 HA-24
Scarf, James, 20 April 1780, Mary Hollandshead       1 CA-3
Scarf, William, 1 Jan. 1795, Hannah Taylor          29 BA-6
Schaaf, Jacob, 5 Sept. 1797, Marg. Weber             2 FR-1170
Schaefer, George, 25 Dec. 1785, Cath. Stoll          2 FR-1167
Schaeffer, Jacob, 18 Nov. 1782, Juliana Teffnerin    2 CL-82
Schafer, John, 14 May 1799, Sus. Ott                 2 FR-1170
Schags?, Thomas, 7 Sept. 1791, Lydia Killen         18 BA-3
Schally, Jacob, 3 Aug. 1788, Susanna Horner         10 BA-190
Schally, John, 9 Aug. 1794, Eva Revers              10 BA-196
Schan, Henry, 28 April 1795, Mary Kessler            2 FR-1169
Schatz, John, 18 Sept. 1791, Eliz. Leschorn          2 FR-1168
Schatz, Philip, 6 (Oct.?) 1793, Cath. Bergesser      2 FR-1169
Schauer, Harvey, 20 March 1796, Martha Lowman        3 WA-60
Schaun, John, 26 April 1789, Rebecca Whitcraft       2 FR-1168
Schaun, Peter, 6 Sept. 1789, Sarah Whitcraft         2 FR-1168
Schaup, Christian, 24 Jan. 1786, Elizab. Fister      2 FR-1168
Schaup, John, 12 July 1785, Barb. Mayer              2 FR-1167
Scheckel, John, 10 Sept. 1795, Mary Burges           2 FR-1169
Scheel, George, 6 June 1795, Rebecca Molloth         3 WA-59
Scheister, Philip, 1790, An. Miller                 50 BA-390
Scheithauer, Hein., 1788, Marg. Simon               50 BA-388
Schell, Henry, 24 Feb. 1789, Elizabeth Ollex         4 FR
Schenck, John, 26 April 1797, Lydia Reynolds         2 FR-1169
Schenerfeld?, Joh., March 1799, Barbara Schneider    3 WA-66
Schenkel, Johannes, 24 Nov. 1793, Margaretha Huchber 10 BA-196
Scherch, Joseph, 2 May 1795, Eliz. Bezmar            3 WA-58
Scherrick, John, 13 February 1798, Ann Weyand        3 WA-64
Schester, Franz, 24 April 1795, Elis. Schain         3 WA-58
Scheydecker, Mich'l, 22 Aug. 1786, Mary Marg. Roth   2 FR-1168
Schick, Lorenz, July 1800, Eliz. Ebbert              3 WA-69
Schielhausz, Philip, 8 May 1790, Julian Hempe        2 FR-1168
Schilling, William, 29 March 1787, Cath. Gilbert     2 FR-1168
Schlegel, Frederick, 6 March 1796, Eliz. Buteler     2 FR-1169
Schlegel, Joh., Sept. 1800, Rebarbara (sic) Gelwichs 3 WA-70
Schlegel, John Frederick, minister, son of John Frederick,
     9 May 1785, Anna Rosina Mack                    5 FR-100
Schley, John, 24 April 1792, Mary Schreiber          2 FR-1168
Schley, Mathias, 15 Oct. 1797, Mary Drill            2 FR-1170
Schmahl, John, 11 Oct. 1785, Philippina Plank        2 FR-1167
Schmeltzer, Nedreu, 2 Dec. 1794, Cath. Can (or Cau)  3 WA-57
Schmid, Johannes, 13 Oct. 1789, Elizabeth Hertzog    6 FR-201
Schmidt, Christ., March 1798, Eva Flori              3 WA-64
Schmidt, Friedr., 28 April 1794, Christina Comin    50 BA-394
Schmidt, Jac., 20 Dec. 1785, Julianna Jung           2 FR-1167
Schmidt, Joh., Jan. 1799, Cath. Bar                  3 WA-66
Schmidt, Joh., August 1800, Sovia Vogelgesang        3 WA-69
Schmidt, John, 8 Nov. 1785, Sarah Gardiner          10 BA-186
Schmidt, Michael, 23 December 1797, Cath. Tim (or Dim) 3 WA-63
Schmit, Abraham, 4 Sept. 1789, Esther Lefeber        2 FR-1170
Schmit, Andrew, 21 Oct. 1792, Mary Eliz. Stein       2 FR-1168
Schmit, Daniel, 17 June 1798, Barb. Stephanus        2 FR-1170
Schmit, Henry, 13 Dec. 1796, Anna Mary Stehly        2 FR-1169
Schmit, Jacob, 23 March 1794, Cath. Lafewer          2 FR-1169
Schmit, Jacob, 14 Jan. 1798, Eliz. Butman            2 FR-1170
Schmit, Mathew, 3 Jan. 1786, Eliz. Beckenbach        2 FR-1167
Schmit, Mich'l, 21 Feb. 1786, Sus. Steckel           2 FR-1168
Schmit, Philip, 1 May 1788, Kerrenhappuck Brothers   2 FR-1168
Schmit, Philip, 31 May 1791, Mary Fuchs              2 FR-1168
Schmit, William, 28 Feb. 1797, Sus. Renner           2 FR-1169
Schmitt, Jac., 5 April 1785, An. M. Benter           2 FR-1167
```

Schmittenberger, Casper, 29 Dec. 1799, Christina Henninghaus
    50 BA-406
Schmutz, Abraham, Sept. 1799, Cath. Fye   3 WA-67
Schneider, Abraham, 25 Oct. 1791, Maria Hammel, dau. of
    John   2 WA-16
Schneider, Andrew, 28 April 1794, Christina Trorbach   29 BA-5
Schneider, Christian, 2 Dec. 1794, Sarah Miller   2 FR-1169
Schneider, George, 27 Jan. 1800, Cath. Brunner   2 FR-1170
Schneider, John Adam, 15 Nov. 1791, Catherine Minnich, dau.
    of Henry   2 WA-16
Schnock, Adam, 1 April 1789, Maria Butterbachen   6 FR-201
Schnook, Peter, 15 March 1791, Polly Pippinger   2 FR-1168
Schock, Jacob, 20 March 1795, Elis. Deal   3 WA-58
Schofield, William, 22 June 1795, Sarah Layfield   1 WO
Schon, Conrad, 21 Aug. 1791, Marg't Leissinger   2 WA-16
Schooley, Reuben, son of John and Mary, 1st day, 11 mo.,
    1785, Esther Lacey, dau. of Thomas and Esther   1 SF
Schoolfield, John, Nov. 1788, Mary Schoolfield   1 SO-168
Schoolfield, Joseph, 28 Feb. 1797, Esther Gunby   1 WO
Schoolfield, Wm., 8 Sept. 1797, Rosanna Merrill   1 WO
Schoolmyer, John Peter, 6 March 1779, Mary Eve Rineheart 4 FR
Schop, Jacob, 22 Nov. 1791, Elizab. Brengle   2 FR-1168
Schortel, Wm., 26 Aug. 1800, Martha Wilson   29 BA-11
Schrader, Joh., April 1800, Rebecca Lane or Laue   3 WA-69
Schreiber, John H., 8 Sept. 1800, Maria F. Yeiser   3 BA-391
Schreiner, Adam, 25 Dec. 1785, Mary Geissinger   2 FR-1167
Schreyack, Dan'l, 2 Nov. 1787, Mary Kassel   2 FR-1168
Schreyer, David, 18 Nov. 1798, Cathy Fleck   2 FR-1170
Schreyer, Henry, 21 Sept. 1790, Mary Ludy   2 FR-1168
Schreyner, Pet., 19 May 1789, Eva Biddel   2 FR-1168
Schrigly, Enoch, 22 Oct. 1799, Mary Murry   2 FR-1170
Schroder, John, 12 April 1796, Rosey Killy   2 FR-1169
Schroeder, Godfrey, 22 Aug. 1799, Ann Cath. Stephan (or
    Stiffler)   29 BA-10
Schroeder, Henry, 4 April 1795, Mary Schley   4 FR
Schroeder, Herm. Hy, 30 Oct. 1785, Sus. Schwartz   2 FR-1167
Schroeter, Chas., 23 May 1799, Cath. Hauptman   29 BA-10
    See also 50 BA-405.
Schrom, George, July 1800, Sarah Aitch   3 WA-69
Schug, Conrad, 22 Jan. 1785, Elisabeth Heller   10 BA-184
Schuh, Solomon, 13 Oct. 1799, Magd. Kern   2 FR-1170
Schuler, Joh., 10 March 1793, Widow Jaffry   50 BA-393
Schultz, Alexander, 10 Oct. 1786, Mary Price   2 FR-1168
Schuman, Mich'l, 1792, Cath. Wegeran   50 BA-392
Schwab, Michael, 27 Oct. 1797, Polly Braun   3 WA-63
Schwarz, Heinrich, 3 Oct. 1783, Barbara Schmidt   10 BA-178
Schwatner, Adam, 7 April 1799, Anna Cox   2 FR-1170
Schwedtner, Adam, 11 July 1797, Eva Lehman   2 FR-1170
Schweitzer, Lorentz, 2 Nov. 1797, Sarah Niecky   2 FR-1170
Schweitzer, Matthew, 6 Dec. 1796, Cath. Schenck   2 FR-1169
Schwengel, Benjamin, 6 Oct. 1794, Eva Schmedtin   3 WA-57
Schwenk, Jno., 22 Feb. 1798, Polly Hoffman   29 BA-9
Schwingel, George, 2 April 1793, Maria Householder   10 BA-196
Scoby, Robert, 11 June 1795, Elizabeth Baughan   4 FR
Scollard, Anthony, 11 Dec. 1787, Ann Campbell   3 BA-203
Scors, John A., 24 Feb. 1795, Elizabeth Summers   3 BA-299
Scot, James, 4 Feb. 1796, Mary Williams   2 FR-1169
Scot, John, 2 May 1786, Cath. Boon   2 FR-1168
Scot, John, 12 May 1788, Mary Cramphen   3 PG-254
Scot, Samuel, 25 Sept. 1787, Ann Tarlton   3 PG-253
Scotland, Robert, 8 July 1781, Hannah Ramsay   3 HA-4
Scott, Alexander, 17 Oct. 1780, Martha Roads   3 HA-2
Scott, Amos, 18 April 1789, R. Price   29 BA-1
Scott, Amos, 11 Sept. 1798, Anne West   5 MO-115
Scott, Andrew, 21 Feb. 1786, Rosanna Watson   11 BA-9

```
Scott, Andrew, 13 July 1786, Mary Calvin           29 BA-1
Scott, Aquila, 14 (or 17) April 1779, Henrietta Semmes  2 CH-456
Scott, Benjamin, 23 Sept. 1800, Sally Anderson      1 WO
Scott, Burrage, 6 Nov. 1788, Ann Davies             3 BA-218
Scott, Daniel, 6 April 1797, Margaret Short         1 BA-7
   See also 3 HA-26.
Scott, David, 8 Oct. 1797, by Rev. Ridgely; Eby Hilbreath
   4 AA
Scott, Edward, 9 Feb. 1790, Mary Claggett           2 PG-4
Scott, Geo., 15 July 1785, Eliza Napear            11 BA-8
Scott, George, 4 Dec. 1800, by Rev. Ridgely; Margaret Cole
   4 AA
Scott, James, 26 Dec. 1786, Elizabeth Thompson      6 BA
Scott, James, 5 Feb. 1797, Mary Humphreys           3 PG-443
Scott, John, 10 April 1779, Mary Strane             4 FR
Scott, John, 15 Nov. 1780, Sarah Smith              1 SO-175
Scott, John, 5 Feb. 1782, Agnes Hadden              2 CH-456
Scott, John, Jr., 15 May 1788, Elizabeth Goodwin Dorsey
   3 BA-217
Scott, John, 25 Dec. 1790, Anne Baise               5 BA-13
Scott, Jno., 10 Oct. 1793, Elis. Saker             50 BA-393
Scott, John, 17 May 1798, Ann Wood                  6 BA
Scott, John, 20 June 1799, Ann Hillery              2 AL-701
Scott, John, 15 Sept. 1799, Sally Coleby            3 BA-377
Scott, Joseph, Jr., 5 March 1795, Hannah Norris     1 BA-7
Scott, Joseph, 15 March 1796, Marg. M'Carman       29 BA-7
Scott, Robert, 6 March 1778, Anne Thrift            2 MO-1
Scott, Samuel, 24 Aug. 1793, Nancy Duncan           6 BA
Scott, Thomas, 9 July 1782, Alice Philpot           2 CH-456
Scott, Thomas, son of Abraham and Elizabeth, 27th day, 2 mo.,
   1793, Elizabeth Matthews, dau. of Thomas and Rachel
   1 SF
Scott, William, 6 Oct. 1784, Mary Mitchel          11 BA-7
Scott, William, 8 Dec. 1787, Sarah Merryman         6 BA
Scott, William, 22 Feb. 1792, Rebecca Hardey        3 PG-436
Scott, William, 3 Feb. 1794, Rebecca Ball           2 DO
Scoven, Edward, 22 Aug. 1799, Sidney Robinson       8 BA-1
Scrivener, Lewis, 16 Jan. 1781, Kisriah Trott       3 AA-417
Scrivener, William, 31 Sept. 1779, Henrietta Dixon  3 AA-415
Scrivenor, Vincent, 11 Dec. 1788, by Rev. Hagerty; Mary
   Griffith                                         4 AA
Scroggs, Alexander, 20 Feb. 1794, Nancy McElroy     5 BA-13
Scurlock, Wm., 11 Dec. 1785, Charity Norman         2 FR-1167
Scut, Edward, 13 July 1779, Mary Wilson             2 PG-3
Scutchall, George, 18 April 1778, Catherine Cline   4 FR
Seaborn, Benedict, 11 Oct. 1788, Sarah Linstead    18 BA-1
Seaders, Henry, 23 Dec. 1799, by Rev. Wyatt; Ruth Seaders
   4 AA
Seargent, Elijah, 7 Feb. 1783, Margaret Frasier     4 FR
Sears, James, 16 Oct. 1783, Rosanna Foster          2 DO
Sease, Paul, 1 Oct. 1787, Magdaline Birely          4 FR
Sebatian, Samuel, 23 Oct. 1800, Catrina Dally       8 BA-2
   48 BA-1 gives the bride's name as Dalby.
Sechrist, Charles, 17 Oct. 1778, Eliz'th Castle     4 FR
Sedgwick, Benjamin, 2 June 1788, Mary Albert        1 BA-1
See, Daniel, 9 June 1794, Ann Longhary              2 AL-700
Seekamp, Albert, 1789, Mary Kimel                  50 BA-388
Sefton, Charles, 21 July 1797, Mary Campbell        4 FR
Sefton, William, 27 May 1794, Sarah Taylor          2 DO
Segur, Stephen, 29 May 1780, Elizabeth Richards     3 BA-184
Sehon, John, 30 March 1782, Lucy Burrow             4 FR
Seitenstricker, Dan'l, 19 Feb. 1795, Elisab. Bernhard  50 BA-396
Selby, Charles W., 26 March 1797, Elizabeth Selby   2 AL-700
Selby, George, 20 Dec. 1797, Betsy Curtis Sturgis   1 WO
Selby, James, 26 March 1799, Mary Rankin            1 WO
```

Selby, John Smith, 16 April 1780, Sabina Orme   2 PG-7
Selby, Lemuel, 10 May 1799, Sally Selby   1 WO
Selby, Samuel, III, 26 Jan. 1796, Jane Thistle   1 AL-53
    2 AL-700 gives the date as 14 Feb. 1796.
Selby, Thomas, 25 Dec. 1796, Ann Haslewood   2 AL-700
Selby, William, 21 May 1799, Mary Button   6 BA
Selfe, John, 4 March 1783, Rebecca Watson   4 FR
Sellerne, Louis, 23 June 1795, Margaret Daily   3 BA-305
Sellers, James, 15 May 1800, Elizabeth Joices   3 BA-386
Sellers, William, 18 Dec. 1785, Eliza Webster   11 BA-9
Sellman, Gassaway, 16 Sept. 1779, Catherine Davis   4 FR
Sellman, Johnzee, 9 Feb. 1792, Sarah Rawlins   29 BA-3
Sellman, Jonathan, 27 May 1794, Ann E. Harwood   3 AA-424
    1 AA-162 describes the groom as Jonathan Sellman
    of Sellman.
Selman, Mordecai, 4 April 1782, Lydia Franklin   11 BA-5
Selman, Thomas, 6 May 1798, Ruth Harris   4 FR
Selmon, John Reason, 23 April 1800, Kitty Sowers   3 BA-385
Semmes, Mark, 9 Aug. 1790, Catherine Simpson   2 CH-456
Semmes, Thomas, Feb. 1779, Mary Ann Brawney   2 CH-456
Semple, John, 30 Oct. 1800, Mary Lamb   3 BA-394
Senibach, Peter, 20 Feb. 1798, Magdalena Schmelzern   1 FR-59
Sennebaugh, Peter, 12 Feb. 1798, Mary Smeltzer   4 FR
Serjeant, William, 2 July 1782, Margaret Tucker   4 FR
Serman, Anthony, 5 April 1796, Ann Manning   29 BA-7
Serman, Isaac, 31 Jan. 1797, Elizabeth -(?)-   2 SO
Sermon, Anthony, 15 April 1796, Ann Manning   50 BA-399
Sertimeyer, Christoph, 20 Nov. 1783, Eva Schmidt   10 BA-178
Sewal, Andrew, 27 Feb. 1798, Eleanor Beale   4 FR
Sewalt, Jacob, 17 Dec. 1780, Barbara Curtz   4 FR
Seward, John, 27 Oct. 1800, Elizabeth Griffith   2 DO
Sewel, James, 20 Oct. 1785, Ann Watts   11 BA-8
Sewell, Vachel, before 15 Sept. 1796, by Rev. Green; Sarah
    Anglen   4 AA
Seybrand, Jno., 15 Dec. 1797, Eliz. Smith   29 BA-9
Shackells, Cephas, 17 Sept. 1780, Eleanor Pratt   2 PG-3
Shackells, Francis, 16 Oct. 1783, Rebecca Cherry   3 AA-420
Shaefer, Ludwig, 29 Oct. 1798, Rosina Valentine   10 BA-198
Shafer, George, 19 Dec. 1785, Catherine Stull   4 FR
Shafer, Jacob, 21 May 1798, Susanna Ramsberg   4 FR
Shafer, John, 11 May 1799, Susanna Oat   4 FR
Shafer, Tobias, 24 Oct. 1794, Catherine Comfer   4 FR
Shaffer, Jacob, 11 Nov. 1784, Peggy Radley   11 BA-8
Shahan, Samuel, 5 May 1796, Jane Burn   3 BA-323
Shanassy, John, 28 Nov. 1789, Rebecca Yeiser   6 BA
Shane, Joseph, 6 Sept. 1795, Mary Cutfield   3 BA-311
Shaneman, Jno., 31 Dec. 1795, Martha Ross   29 BA-7
Shaney, John, 20 April 1795, Elizabeth Chester   3 BA-301
Shank, John, 20 April 1797, Lydia Reynolds   4 FR
Shanks, Abner, 7 Jan. 1783, Mary Hurley   2 DO
Shannon, George, 3 June 1779, Eliza Touchstone   5 HA
    3 HA-2 gives the date as 3 June 1780.
Shannon, Michael, 29 Dec. 1785, Eliza Strawbridge   11 BA-9
Sharms, Jno., 6 Sept. 1800, Polly Lucas   50 BA-408
Sharp, John, son of Thomas and Susanna, 3rd day, 6 mo., 1795,
    Elizabeth Walton, widow of William, and dau. of Anthony
    and Elizabeth Kennard   9 SF-72
Sharp, Peter, 27 March 1783, Anne Dickinson   5 BA-13
Sharp, William, 10 March 1796, Susanna Cowan   3 BA-321
Sharp, William, 19 June 1797, Elizabeth Greenwood   4 KE-71
Sharpe, Jacob, 7 July 1794, Mary Tomey   6 BA
Sharper, Enoch, 22 July 1783, Mary Beard, free negroes   11 BA-6
Sharrats, John, 8 June 1793, Catherine Crouse   4 FR
Shartel, Jacob, 1 Jan. 1796, Eliz. Simon   29 BA-7
Shartel, Wm., 26 Aug. 1800, Martha Wilson   50 BA-407

```
Shauman, Michel, March 1799, Polly Kepling              3 WA-66
Shaver, John, 4 Oct. 1783, Elizabeth Stull              4 FR
Shaver, Tobias, 21 July 1783, Mary Currance             4 FR
Shaw, Basil, 17 Dec. 1783, Catherine Eck                4 FR
Shaw, Hugh, 23 Oct. 1790, Ann McKay                     4 FR
Shaw, Edward, 15 April 1800, Cloe Posey                 2 CH-456
Shaw, John, 14 May 1778, Mary Hawkins                  11 BA-1
Shaw, John, 3 Jan. 1788, Sarah Vincent                  2 CH-456
Shaw, John, 20 March 1800, Priscilla G-(?)-             6 BA
Shaw, Dr. Louis Dene, 16 Sept. 1779, Jenny Clements     2 CH-456
Shaw, Samuel, 4 June 1799, Eliza Farr                   2 CH-456
Shaw, Thomas, 24 May 1778, Anne Norton                 11 BA-1
Shaw, Thomas Nightsmith, 6 Jan. 1778, Sarah Stansbury  11 BA-1
Shaw, William, 19 Oct. 1784, Rachael Rowles            11 BA-7
Shaw, William, 21 Jan. 1796, Sophia Wood                6 BA
Shaw, William, 16 March 1797, Rebecca Davis             6 BA
Shaw, William, 9 May 1799, Sarah Raven                  6 BA
Shead, John, 30 Oct. 1783, Mary Boyd                   11 BA-6
Shean, Dennis, 31 July 1786, Bridget Kidd              11 BA-9
Shearly, Thomas, 19 Feb. 1797, Sarah Harris            29 BA-8
Shearman, Benjamin, 7 Dec. 1783, Rebecca Spencer        3 BA-186
Shearman, Samuel, 21 April 1790, Mary Cummins           2 DO
Shearman, Solomon, 18 May 1794, Deborah Barnett         2 DO
Shearman, Stephen, 24 Feb. 1789, Charlotte Phillips     2 DO
Shearman, Stephen, 16 June 1798, Rosanna Vane           2 DO
Shears, John, 26 June 1783, Mary Johnson                3 AA-419
Shearstrand, David, 28 Feb. 1799, Kitty Fonbaker        3 BA-368
Shearwood, Job, 8 Aug. 1781, Cassandra Shreeves         2 PG-5
Sheats, Henry, 5 Sept. 1789, Rachel Ellis               4 FR
Sheats, Jacob, 27 March 1790, Hannah Harple             4 FR
Sheaves, William, 17 Dec. 1790, Elizabeth Lawrence      4 FR
Sheckels, John, 12 April 1785, Ruth Story               4 FR
Sheehan, Cornelius, 8 Sept. 1794, Catharine Thompson    3 BA-293
Sheehan, Henry, 31 Aug. 1797, Martha Perry              3 BA-349
Sheehan, William, 24 December 1791, Mary Mace           2 DO
Sheely, Andrew, 1 May 1781, Mary Heffner                4 FR
Shees, Sebastian, 5 Sept. 1784, Pheby Burckhart         4 FR
Sheet, Samuel, 20 Nov. 1779, Elizabeth Halmonay         3 BA-178
Sheets, Christian, 21 April 1794, Margaret Wetsell      4 FR
Sheets, Martin, 24 December 1793, Sarah Aldridge        4 FR
Shehawn, Mason, 29 June 1791, Elizabeth Hooper          2 DO
Shehawn, Thomas, 6 May 1785, Sarah Hinson               2 DO
Shehawn, Thomas, 22 June 1799, Catherine Hooper         2 DO
Shehee, Dabiel, 24 Dec. 1790, Allafair Green            2 DO
Shehee, John, 19 December 1800, Sarah Layton            2 DO
Sheiy, John, 3 Jan. 1786, Cathrina Ballram             10 BA-186
Shekel, John, 9 Sept. 1795, Mary Burges                 4 FR
Shekells, Francis, 7 June 1787, by Rev. Reed; Ann Wells 4 AA
Sheldecker, Joseph, 10 Dec. 1793, Barb. Brown          29 BA-5
Shell, Charles, 30 Oct. 1783, Mary Plonk                4 FR
Shellhouse, Peter, 8 May 1790, Juliana Hemp             4 FR
Shellmon, Jacob, 30 March 1778, Catherine Bentz         4 FR
Shelmerdine, Stephen, 9 Jan. 1794, Eunice Philips       4 FR
Shelook, William, 20 May 1782, Mary Bennett            11 BA-5
Shenton, Charles, 18 November 1793, Betty Booze         2 DO
Shenton, Joseph, 28 April 1800, Mary Dunnock            2 DO
Shenton, Raymond, 20 April 1799, Nancy Johnson          2 DO
Shepard, John, 25 Dec. 1794, by Rev. Ridgely; Rebecca Forrest
     4 AA
Shepburn, Thomas, 7 April 1796, Mary Woolhouse          3 BA-321
Shephard, Wm., 13 May 1780, Mary Bryan                 11 BA-4
Shepherd, John, 24 Feb. 1781, Mary Anne Galloway        5 BA-13
Shepherd, John, 17 May 1781, Eliz'th Wiseman            4 FR
Shepherd, John, 13 Oct. 1787, Eleanor Melony            6 BA
Shepherd, John, 6 June 1799, Rebecca NcDougal           3 AL-6
```

```
Shepherd, Nathan, 12 Dec. 1799, Mary Bennet              8 BA-1
Shepherd, Nath'l, 31 Oct. 1783, Mary Owens               3 AA-420
Shepherd, Samuel, 28 April 1792, Sarah Orrick            3 BA-258
    Parties described as free blacks.
Shepherd, Samuel, c.1798, by Rev. Riggin; Margaret Thum-
    bert                                                 4 AA
Shepherd, Solomon, son of William and Richmonda, 27th day,
    10 mo., 1779, Susanna Farquhar, dau. of William and
    Ann Miller                                           3 SF
Shepherd, William, son of William and Richmonda, 21st
    day, 8 mo., 1782, Phebe Way, dau. of William and Mary
    3 SF
Sheppard, John, 3 Dec. 1797, Eliz. Hemphauser           2 FR-1170
Sheppard, Thomas, 1 Nov. 1795, Nancy Amos                6 BA
Shepperd, Alden, 10 Aug. 1799, Mary Allen                6 BA
Shepperd, Thomas, 4 May 1797, Anne Weary                 3 BA-344
Sheredine, Daniel, 23 March 1797, Ann Russell           47 BA-1
Sheredine, James, 4 Dec. 1794, Elizabeth Gawthrop        7 BA-1
Sheredine, Thomas, 9 March 1797, Ann Neill               1 BA-7
    3 HA-25 gives the date as 19 March 1797.
Sheredine, Upton, 1 Aug. 1799, Sophia Dorsey             4 FR
Sherer, Elias, 31 Aug. 1794, Elizabeth Hargood          10 BA-196
Sheridan, James, 4 Dec. 1794, Elizabeth Gorthrop         3 HA-23
Sheridan, Thomas, 23 April 1785, Mary Locust             3 HA-9
Sheriff, Joshua, 30 June 1781, Rhoda Shearwood           2 PG-5
Sherlock, John, 25 Oct. 1798, Eliza Gilmor               3 BA-364
Sherman, Jeman, 26 Aug. 1783, Eliza Minnahan            11 BA-6
Sherrod, Henry, 27 Jan. 1780, Sarah Miller              11 BA-4
Sherwood, William, son of Henry, 24th day, 12 mo., 1795,
    Elizabeth Corse, dau. of David                       4 SF-208
Sherwood, William, 5 March 1799, Elizabeth Coleman       2 DO
Shetinghellerm, Jacob, 25 Sept. 1798, Mary Walter        4 FR
Shettleworth, Allen, 9 Feb. 1792, Anne Withering         2 CH-456
Shibeler, Geo., 20 March 1779, Eliz'th Everley           4 FR
Shidle, William, 28 July 1796, Mary M. Gill              3 HA-25
Shidle, William, 28 July 1796, Mary McGill               2 HA-349
Shields, John, 30 Jan. 1780, Marg't McFadden            11 BA-4
Shields, Zachariah, 30 June 1798, Anne Bailey            3 BA-360
Shiller, Jacob, 1 Nov. 1796, Catherine Rodenheiser       6 BA
Shilling, Jacob, 6 April 1784, Christina Gergerin        2 CL-82
Shilling, Michael, 18 Feb. 1778, Catherine Weister      11 BA-1
Shilling, Murray, 18 July 1793, Rebecca Brown            4 FR
Shilling, William, 27 March 1787, Catherine Gilbert      4 FR
Shimer?, Isaac, 16 Jan. 1798, Eliz. Delashmutt           2 FR-1170
    4 FR gives the bride's name as Sarah.
Shindler, Adam, 8 June 1783, Christena Queary            4 FR
Shineflue, Conrad, 27 June 1797, Elizabeth Longe         3 HA-26
Shinemann, Abraham, 25 May 1784, Juliana Shultz         10 BA-180
Shingletaker, Jacob, 1 May 1797, Catherine Hellenberger  4 FR
Shipley, Absolom, 6 Sept. 1792, Providence Shipley       6 BA
Shipley, Basil, 18 Aug. 1781, Susanna Knox               4 FR
Shipley, Benjamir, 16 Aug. 1791, Amelia Webster         18 BA-3
    See also 3 BA-253.
Shipley, Brice, 30 Jan. 1792, Elizabeth Beasman          6 BA
Shipley, Chs., 31 Oct. 1782, Jenny Grymes               11 BA-5
Shipley, Eli, 16 Feb. 1782, Elizabeth Kingston           3 HA-6
Shipley, Elijah, 10 Nov. 1785, Hannah Selby             11 BA-8
Shipley, Elijah, Sept. 1790, Milcah Dean                 4 AA
Shipley, George, 2 March 1784, Susanna Frost            11 BA-7
Shipley, Henry, 19 Sept. 1782, Ruth Howard              11 BA-5
Shipley, Hezekiah, 4 April 1796, Ruth Picket             4 FR
Shipley, John, 17 Dec. 1791, by Rev. Dorsey; Sarah Kendall
    4 AA
Shipley, Levin, 20 Oct. 1791, Mary Loyd                 18 BA-3
    See also 3 BA-254.
```

Shipley, Lloyd, 9 Jan. 1783, Marg't Frost   11 BA-6
Shipley, Richard, 10 Sept. 1795, by Rev. Ridgely; Anne
  Rowles   4 AA
Shipley, Robert, 5 March 1789, Providence Elder   6 BA
Shipley, Talbot, 26 Aug. 1779, Rachel Chew   5 BA-12
Shipley, Vachel, 13 June 1782, Ann Garner   11 BA-5
Shippey, David, 23 August 1800, Catherine Hodson   2 DO
Shipton, Henry, 25 June 1778, Mary Broderick   11 BA-1
Shiron, Thomas, 11 Dec. 1796, Nancy Sadler   6 BA
Shirrid, Matthew, 23 June 1795, Elizabeth Hall   3 BA-305
Shivell, Adam, 5 May 1796, Catherine Riggs   4 FR
Shively, Bernard, 22 Sept. 1777, Eleanor Longford   2 CH-456
Shlips, William, 19 Aug. 1795, Elizabeth Zimmer   6 BA
Shoars, Rich'd, 25 Sept. 1783, Sarah Evans   11 BA-6
Shock, Georg, 1789, Mary Heilman   50 BA-388
Shock, Jacob, 15 Oct. 1794, Eliza O'Donnell   18 BA-6
Shockey, Valentine, 23 Dec. 1799, Elizabeth Climer   3 AL-6
Shockley, John, 15 May 1798, Nancy Richardson   2 SO
Shockly, Eli, 27 April 1798, Betsy Colebourn   1 WO
Shockly, Jonathan, 5 July 1799, Polly Savage   1 WO
Shockly, Thomas, 27 April 1798, Nancy Colebourn   1 WO
Shoe, Solomon, 12 Oct. 1799, Modelena Carn   4 FR
Shoemaker, Abr., 15 Oct. 1798, Phoeb. Baldwin   2 FR-1170
Shoemaker, Adam, 16 Jan. 1790, Eliz. Switzer   29 BA-1
Shoemaker, Frederick, 14 March 1787, Mary Cotrel   11 BA-10
Shoemaker, Ignatius, 15 Feb. 1795, Louisa Shaffer   44 BA-1
Shoemaker, Jacob, 4 Feb. 1800, Catherine Woodrung   2 AL-701
Shoghan, Cornelius, 5 May 1793, An. Mary Mahn   2 FR-1169
Shontz, Mich., 18 March 1782, Cath. Jones   4 FR
Shook, Jacob, 14 Dec. 1795, Elizabeth Zimmerman   4 FR
Shook, Jacob, 7 Jan. 1799, Catherine Clem   4 FR
Shook, Walter, 18 July 1795, Ann Mary Miller   4 FR
Shope, Jacob, 21 Nov. 1791, Elizabeth Brengle   4 FR
Shope, William, 13 Dec. 1785, Eliza Barnaby   11 BA-9
Shores, Edward, 10 May 1799, Nelly Austen   2 SO
Shorms, Jno., 6 Sept. 1800, Polly Lucas   29 BA-11
Short, Abraham, 22 March 1797, Annie Coleman   2 DO
Short, Abraham, 21 Feb. 1799, by Rev. Ridgely; Patience
  Deaver   4 AA
Short, George, 9 March 1780, Martha Henry   2 PG-3
Short, James, 11 Feb. 1779, Mary Grimes   2 PG-3
Short, John, 3 Feb. 1780, Ann Lloyd   11 BA-4
Short, John, 14 Dec. 1780, Ann Early   2 PG-3
Short, John, 27 Feb. 1794, by Rev. G. Ridgely; Anne Wood
  4 AA
Short, Richard, 27 Jan. 1786, Rebeckah Pue   4 FR
Short, Richard, 5 Oct. 1797, by Rev. Ridgely; Susanna
  Chaney   4 AA
Shorte, James, 14 Dec. 1791, Mary McCaslin   3 PG-436
Shorter, Roger, 21 May 1793, Bridgett Booze   2 DO
Shorter, Roger, 28 December 1796, Sally Robinson   2 DO
Shortridge, Sam'l, 25 Jan. 1778, Anne Roberts   2 MO-1
Shots, John, 17 Sept. 1791, Elizabeth Leashorn   4 FR
Shots, Philip, 5 Oct. 1793, Catherine Bargesser   4 FR
Shott, Philip, 5 Dec. 1789, M. Myers   29 BA-1
  See also 50 BA-390.
Shoup, George, 18 Sept. 1778, Charlotte Loy   4 FR
Shoup, John, 12 July 1785, Barbara Moyer   4 FR
Shoup, Peter, 20 Oct. 1780, Rebecca Goodman   4 FR
Shoup, Samuel, 23 Jan. 1793, Dolley Grove   4 FR
Shover, Henry, 31 Dec. 1779, Rosanna Baker   4 FR
Show, Conrad, 6 March 1789, Elizabeth Runner   4 FR
Showalker, Adam, 6 Feb. 1787, Barbara Snowdagle   4 FR
Showe, Henry, 25 April 1795, Mary Kessler   4 FR
Showes, Sam'l, 26 Aug. 1780, Catherine Hargishmyer   4 FR

```
Showne, Peter, 5 Sept. 1789, Sarah Whitcroft          4 FR
Shrader, Henry, 18 Sept. 1778, Susanna Horine         4 FR
Shrader, James, 7 April 1798, Jemima Johnson          3 BA-357
Shreaves, Wm., 14 Dec. 1790, Elizab. Lawrence         2 FR-1168
Shriebeck, -(?)-, 1790, -(?)- Paul                    50 BA-389
Shrier, John, 29 Aug. 1782, Anne Oldis                3 BA-188
Shrigly, Enoch, 22 Oct. 1799, Mary Murry              4 FR
Shrimplin, William, 26 March 1795, Fanny Barkus       2 AL-700
Shriner, Adam, 23 Dec. 1785, Mary Kisinger            4 FR
Shriner, Peter, 12 May 1789, Eve Biddle               4 FR
Shriock, Dan'l, 26 Nov. 1787, Mary Gossell            4 FR
Shriver, Frederick William, 21 July 1794, Elizabeth Seesman
    4 FR
Shriver, Henry, 19 March 1779, Barbara Welfley        4 FR
Shriver, Joseph, (date not given), Mary Score         4 KE-71
Shroad, John, 12 Jan. 1790, M. Word                   29 BA-1
Shroder, Herman Hinrich, 29 Oct. 1785, Susanna Schwartz  4 FR
Shrote, Mathias, 11 June 1799, Cath. Stembe           29 BA-10
Shroud, Jno., 26 Sept. 1799, Sarah Lynch              29 BA-10
Shrouds, Thomas, 9 July 1794, Sally Dean              2 DO
Shroyer, David, 2 June 1797, Catherine Shafer         4 FR
Shroyer, David, 15 Nov. 1798, Catherine Fleck         4 FR
Shryer, John, 1 June 1795, Christiana Fetter          1 AL-53
Shryner, Michael, 20 March 1797, Ann Worman           4 FR
Shryock, Christian, 3 Sept. 1794, Mary Shingle        4 FR
Shryock, Jacob, 26 Sept. 1793, Elis. Dutro            50 BA-393
Shryock, Mathias, 6 April 1798, Elizabeth Gaugh       4 FR
Shryock, Valentine, 2 Aug. 1783, Christena Derr       4 FR
Shuck, Peter, 10 Feb. 1795, Elizabeth Shoup           4 FR
Shule, Henry, 19 Oct. 1795, Mary Hislet               3 BA-311
Shule, John, Dec. 1797, Catherine Brengle             4 FR
Shull, Christian, 27 May 1797, Elizabeth Brenner      4 FR
Shull, Frederick, 30 Nov. 1782, Catherine Shell       4 FR
Shull, Peter, August 1800, Elis. Shacke               3 WA-69
Shults, Andrew, 15 Aug. 1778, Mary Miller             11 BA-1
Shultz, Alex'd'r, 31 May 1779, Eleanor Freeman        4 FR
Shultz, David, 27 Sept. 1783, Eve Myers               4 FR
Shultz, Joh., 1789, Mar. Kemp                         50 BA-388
Shultz, Peter, 31 Aug. 1794, Sophia Meyer             29 BA-5
Shuman, Jacob, 22 Dec. 1787, Polly Templing           4 FR
Shupp, John, 10 Nov. 1797, Elis. Conrad               3 WA-63
Shurbert, George, 23 April 1793, Eliza Alvey          22 BA-2
Shurr, John, 26 Aug. 1783, Eliz'th Akin               4 FR
Shutter, Daniel, 22 May 1796, Margaretha Collodin     10 BA-198
Sibury, William, 4 Jan. 1784, Rebecca Taylor          11 BA-7
Siclar, William, 18 Dec. 1800, Nancy Morrow           8 BA-2
    48 BA-2 gives the groom's name as Sickler.
Sidall, Philip, 9 April 1789, Addiosa Linton          2 PG-4
Sidle, Gudlip, 8 Aug. 1778, Eve Shively               4 FR
Sidwell, Abraham, son of Richard and Ann, 10th day, 6 mo.,
    1789, Hannah Brown, dau. of Joseph and Hannah     11 SF-220
Sidwell, Henry, son of Henry and Margaret, 3rd day, 2 mo.,
    1791, Cinah Plummer, of Thomas and Phebe          11 SF-224
Sidwell, Job, son of Hugh and Ann, 4th day, 11 mo.,
    1790, Rebecca Wilson, dau. of Benjamin and Lydia  11 SF-223
Sidwell, Job, son of Richard and Ann, 5th day, 3 mo., 1795,
    Sarah Trimble, dau. of Joseph and Ann             11 SF-236
Sidwell, Levi, son of Hugh and Ann, 1st day, 9 mo., 1791,
    Margaret Perry, dau. of Thomas and Sarah          11 SF-227
Sidwell, Samuel, son of Hugh and Ann, 10th day, 5 mo.,
    1787, Sarah Wilson, dau. of Benjamin and Lydia    11 SF-214
Sieg, Charles, 15 Sept. 1793, Mary Faut               2 FR-1169
Siegfried, Charles Louis, 26 March 1798, Charlotte
    Frazer                                            3 BA-356
Siesz, Jacob, 28 Sept. 1790, Mary Schreyer            2 FR-1168
```

Sifert, Mathias, 12 July 1790, Elizabeth Durff   4 FR
Siffert, Martin, 1790, by Rev. Green; Elizabeth Madewell 4 AA
Sifton, Edward, 7 May 1778, by Rev. Magowan; Elizabeth
    Seagall   4 AA
Sigafoose, Jacob, 9 May 1793, Mary Werner   4 FR
Siglekin, Jno., 11 Dec. 1796, Cath. Hashogen   29 BA-8
Sigler, John, 8 Aug. 1798, Rachal Pitzer   2 AL-701
Sigler, Philip, 30 Sept. 1795, Ann Glaze   2 AL-700
Sillinger, Andrew, 11 May 1795, Amelia Robars   3 WA-58
Silver, George, 12 April 1783, Ann Griffin   4 FR
Silver, John, 7 April 1778, Ann Springer   4 FR
Silvers, John, 30 Jan. 1798, Elizabeth Dinsel   6 BA
Silvidore, Samuel, 20 Feb. 1799, Margaret Richardson   6 BA
Silzee, George, 12 June 1800, Rebecca Sims   6 BA
Sim, Anthony, 4 Dec. 1790, Christiana Smith   4 FR
Sim, Thomas, 19 Sept. 1793, Marg. Reily   50 BA-393
Simm, Thomas, 25 Nov. 1794, Catherine Lewis Thomas   4 FR
Simmon, Joseph, 26 July 1798, Wilhelmina Brown   50 BA-403
Simmonds, George, 14 Aug. 1783, Rebeckah White   4 FR
Simmonds, Samuel, 16 Sept. 1797, Ann Canady   4 KE-71
Simmons, Aaron, 2 Feb. 1783, Sarah Thompson   2 CH-456
Simmons, Basil, 15 May 1783, Mary Laurence   3 AA-419
Simmons, Edward, 27 February 1794, Teresa Tollev   2 DO
Simmons, Isaac, 22 Feb. 1784, Ann Childs   3 AA-421
Simmons, Jacob, 27 May 1780, Eleanor Cross   2 PG-3
Simmons, James, 2 July 1787, Margaret Griffith   6 BA
Simmons, James, 18 Sept. 1794, Mary Drury   3 AA-424
Simmons, James, 4 June 1799, Lydia Armstrong   3 BA-372
Simmons, Jesse, 18 Sept. 1781, Rachel Wells   2 PG-5
Simmons, Jno., 2 Nov. 1784, Jane Bouden   11 BA-7
Simmons, John, 28 Jan. 1800, Sus. Knie   2 FR-1170
Simmons, John H., 4 Feb. 1796, Eleanor Howard   4 FR
Simmons, Joseph, 15 May 1780, Mary Deacons   2 CH-456
Simmons, Levin, 25 Jan. 1792, Elizabeth Foster   2 DO
Simmons, Moses, 23 June 1798, Nancy Aaron   1 DO-39
    2 DO gives the date as. 8 June 1798.
Simmons, Philemon, 20 Nov. 1794, Elizabeth Pagan   2 DO
Simmons, Philemon, 23 Feb. 1798, Nancy Edmondson   2 DO
Simmons, Richard, 8 March 1779, Mary Willet   2 PG-2
Simmons, Richard, 17 Feb. 1795, Susanna Nowell   3 AA-424
Simmons, Richard, 10 May 1781, Catherine Baldwin   2 PG-5
Simmons, Samuel, 15 Feb. 1791, Elizabeth Ward   4 FR
Simmons, Thomas, 23 July 1778, Mary Adams   4 FR
Simmons, Thos., 17 June 1790, Eleanor McBride   11 BA-13
Simmons, Thomas, 28 Feb. 1794, Nancy Clarridge   2 DO
Simmons, Thomas, 13 March 1795, Margaret Harris   2 DO
Simmons, Thomas, 2 June 1795, Elizabeth Lyles   3 AA-424
Simmons, William, 24 April 1781, Margaret Chaulk   3 AA-417
Simmons, William, 9 Aug. 1796, Sarah Dorton   5 BA-13
Simms, J. Cleborn, 5 Dec. 1789, Mary Ann Beall   4 FR
Simon, -(?)-, 1790, -(?)- Tamer; blacks   50 BA-389
Simon, Jacob, 21 Jan. 1798, Cath. Wagner   29 BA-9
Simon, Joseph, 26 July 1798, Wilhelminah Brown   29 BA-9
Simoney, Henry, 28 April 1799, Catherine Kilmeyer   9 BA-142
Simpson, Amos, 19 Aug. 1783, Rebecca Strong   11 BA-6
Simpson, Andrew, 28 Feb. 1798, Patty Holland   1 WO
Simpson, Andrew, 31 July 1799, Mary Lindsy   29 BA-10
Simpson, Basil, 5 Jan. 1797, Henrietta Worthington   4 FR
Simpson, Benj., 2 Jan. 1785, Elisab. Dewall   2 FR-1167
    4 FR gives the bride's name as Duvall.
Simpson, Charles, 19 Nov. 1786, Sarah Bentels   2 CH-456
Simpson, Erasmus, 20 July 1782, Lucy Willson   4 FR
Simpson, George, 24 Dec. 1799, Margaret Bateman   2 CH-457
Simpson, George, 14 July 1800, Nancy Edwards   3 BA-388
Simpson, James, 27 Oct. 1794, Anne Yates   3 BA-293

```
Simpson, John, 22 April 1788, Mary Dent Morris          3 PG-254
Simpson, Jno., 13 Feb. 1794, Elizabeth Durbin Wm. Andrew  6 BA
Simpson, John, 9 Dec. 1794, Elizabeth Hobbs             3 BA-296
Simpson, Jno., 4 Sept. 1799, Eliz. Grant              29 BA-10
Simpson, John, 2 Aug. 1800, Anne Robinson              3 BA-389
Simpson, Joseph, 19 Aug. 1782, Mary Ann Montgomery     2 CH-457
Simpson, Joseph, 3 Feb. 1788, Rachel Galworth          3 PG-254
Simpson, Josias, 8 Dec. 1789, Sarah Phillips           3 PG-256
Simpson, Lucien, 18 Nov. 1794, Elizabeth Burch         3 PG-440
Simpson, Rezan, 15 March 1795, Elizab. Sheckles        2 FR-1169
Simpson, Rich'd, 22 May 1780, Catherine Cumming        4 FR
Simpson, Thomas, 23 May 1782, S. M. Kidwell            2 CH-457
Simpson, Thomas, 10 April 1787, Ruth King              3 PG-252
Simpson, Thomas, 12 Nov. 1789, Judith Wathen           2 CH-457
Simpson, Walter, 12 Jan. 1784, Jane Stewart           11 BA-7
Simpson, Walter, 7 Jan. 1796, Eliz. Morres             3 CH-162
Simpson, Walter, 10 Jan. 1799, Eliz. Thomas            2 FR-1170
Sims, James, 9 June 1781, Sarah Key                    2 CH-457
Sin, Edward, Nov. 1785, Ann Condren                   11 BA-8
Sinard, John, 9 Nov. 1797, Tany Cook                   5 BA-13
Sincgin?, John, 7 May 1784, Mary King                 10 BA-180
Sinclair, Moses, 29 Dec. 1782, Mary Jennison           3 BA-185
Sinclair, Robert, 6 Sept. 1795, Kitty Pancoss          6 BA
Sinclaire, Robert, 17 March 1796, Ann Cromwell         1 AL-53
Sindall, David, 4 Dec. 1791, Urith Cook                6 BA
Sindall, Solomon, 25 Aug. 1798, Nancy Oneale           6 BA
Sindall, William, 20 May 1799, Mary Clayton            6 BA
Sindle, Philip, 24 Sept. 1778, Elizabeth Horton       11 BA-1
Singleton, John, from Whitehaven, Eng.; 14 Feb. 1774,
    Bridget Goldsborough                               1 TA-328
Singleton, John, from Whitehaven, Eng.; 30 Dec. 1790,
    Anna Goldsborough, dau. of Nicholas and Mary, (born
    25 Feb. 1765); see also 1 TA-328                   1 TA-317
Singleton, William, 20 March 1793, Elizabeth Slater    3 BA-264
Sinix, Wm., 2 June 1793, Hannah Wilson                50 BA-393
Sinklac, Geo., 14 Feb. 1790, Cloe Rhyon                3 PG-256
Sinklair, James, 20 Aug. 1789, Kezia McLain            6 BA
Sinn, Philip, 3 Oct. 1798, Eliz. Lehr                  2 FR-1170
    4 FR gives the bride's name as Loehr.
Sinnals, Thomas, 5 May 1799, Anna Kerns                3 BA-371
Sinners, Elijah R., 24 Dec. 1795, Elizabeth Jones      6 BA
Sintz, Adam, 23 Dec. 1797, Mary Metz                   4 FR
Sire, James, 10 Aug. 1786, by Rev. Turner; Ann Hart   51 BA-30
Sisler, Philip, 19 Jan. 1797, Polly Burk              29 BA-8
Sissel, Hazil, 5 Jan. 1797, Lyde Ball                  2 FR-1169
Sissell, Philip, 2 April 1793, Juliet Juluck           4 FR
Sissler, Samuel, 29 June 1800, Kitty Smith             3 BA-387
Sisson, Richard, 18 July 1795, Mary Ingram             3 BA-307
Sittlemire, Christopher, 8 July 1783, Marg't Butler   11 BA-6
Sixsmith, Simeon, 8 Aug. 1789, Mary Groves             5 BA-13
Skeel, William, 26 Nov. 1791, Ann Staple              18 BA-3
    See also 3 BA-254.
Skillman, Robert, 24 Dec. 1797, Hannah Sailors         5 BA-13
Skils, Joh., 28 June 1795, Chris. Bez                  3 WA-59
Skinner, Frederick, 4 Oct. 1778, by Rev. Magowan; Betty
    Johns                                              4 AA
Skinner, Henry Smith, 6 Dec. 1796, Sarah Hilleary      4 FR
Skinner, Thos., 3 Oct. 1786, Eliz. Crockett           11 BA-9
Skinner, William, 22 Dec. 1781, Elizabeth Stewart      2 DO
Skinner, Thomas, 22 Oct. 1799, Sarah Lee               2 DO
Skipper, Thos., 3 Nov. 1791, Isabel Barry             29 BA-3
Slack, Jacob, 22 Dec. 1781, Elizabeth Ramsay           3 HA-5
Slack, John, 22 Sept. 1789, Mary Auman                 2 FR-1168
Slacom, Job, 23 April 1788, Susanna Keene              2 DO
Slacom, Marcellus, 23 Dec. 1788, Mary Keene            2 DO
```

Slacum, Barzilla, 3 Jan. 1794, Mary Hart   2 DO
Slacum, Marcellus, 1 June 1798, Sarah Staplefoot   1 DO-39
  2 DO gives the date as 1 June 1798.
Slade, Ezekiel, 28 Jan. 1783, Mary Hcdgskin   11 BA-6
Sladen, James, 21 July 1788, Eleanor Murphy   3 BA-205
Sladsman, Mich'l, 27 April 1794, Mary Harp   29 BA-5
Slagle, John, 10 Dec. 1798, Cathrine Slagle   45 BA-3
Slater, David, 30 May 1790, Sarah Contee   2 PG-4
Slater, Joseph, 15 Sept. 1793, Sarah Smith   5 BA-13
Slater, Wm., 30 Aug. 1787, Hannah James   11 BA-10
Slaughter, Thomas, 27 June 1800, Susanna Jones   3 BA-387
Slaven, William, 22 Aug. 1794, Elizabeth Essex   4 FR
Slegle, Frederick, March 1796, Elizabeth Boteler   4 FR
Slemaker, Jacob, 1791, Clar. Zuille   50 BA-391
Slemaker, Jas., 3 May 1791, Clarinda Zuile   29 BA-2
Sleter, James, 29 March 1795, Mary Formar   3 WA-58
Sligh, John, 18 Jan. 1785, Maria Elisabeth Carpseton   10 BA-184
Slimmer, Christian, 11 Dec. 1796, Elizabeth Vaughan   6 BA
Sliney, Nathaniel, 31 May 1794, Susanna Spalding   39 BA-1
Sloan, John, 30 Nov. 1789, Sarah Jeffery   18 BA-2
Sloan, Rev. Samuel, 16 June 1781, Mrs. Elizabeth Moore   1 SO-167
Sloan, William, 4 Oct. 1795, Betsey Ashman   3 HA-24
Slocomb, John, 25 Oct. 1796, Polly McCreddy   1 WO
Slohn, Samuel, July 1798, Elis. Hason   3 WA-65
Sloppy, Jacob, 24 Feb. 1789, by Rev. J. Pogue   29 BA-1
Slown, Andrew, 3 June 1780, Rachael Roberts   3 HA-2
Slunger, John, 24 April 1797, Margaret Gross   4 FR
Smack, Holland, 2 Jan. 1798, Betsey Williams   1 WO
Smack, Holland, 10 Oct. 1799, Ann Williams   1 WO
Smack, Jesse, 19 Dec. 1797, Sally Truitt   1 WO
Smack, Levi, 7 Jan. 1799, Andesiah Crapper   1 WO
Small, Elijah, 21 Feb. 1799, Rebecca Jemmison   2 HA-351
Small, Elijah, 21 Feb. 1799, Rebecca Jameson   3 HA-28
Small, Jacob, 25 March 1794, Eliza Hopkins   6 BA
Small, Jacob, 11 Dec. 1794, Nancy Fleetwood   3 BA-296
Small, James, 3 Aug. 1797, Mary Ann Riddan   .6 BA
Small, John, 6 Oct. 1785, Philipena Plonk   4 FR
Small, Mich'l, 15 Nov. 1794, Catherine Smith   4 FR
Smallwood, Basil, 13 May 1787, Mary Gariff   3 PG-252
Smallwood, Bayne, 3 Dec. 1782, Chloe McAtee   2 CH-457
Smallwood, John, 16 Dec. 1787, Cloe Wilson   3 PG-253
Smallwood, Robert, 25 Aug. 1796, Margaret Keitholtz   3 BA-327
Smallwood, Samuel, 29 March 1795, Leonora Sexton   3 PG-441
Smallwood, Walter B., 30 April 1796, Elizabeth Noble   3 PG-442
Smallwood, William, before 12 Dec. 1792, by Rev. John
  Long; Sarah Philpot   4 AA
Smart, Zachariah, 22 Aug. 1799, Esther Dunn   3 BA-376
Smedley, Aaron, 11 Oct. 1785, Rebecca Lear   2 FR-1167
Smedley, Jacob, 23 March 1778, Elizabeth Cline   4 FR
Smewin, John, 3 Oct. 1790, Drusilla Felt   6 BA
Smith, Abraham, 1 Sept. 1798, Hester Lafaver   4 FR
Smith, Adam, 17 Sept. 1791, Sarah Dodds   4 FR
Smith, Alexander, 6 Sept. 1800, Mary League   3 BA-391
Smith, Alexander Lawson, 28 Aug. 1792, Martha Griffith   3 HA-22
Smith, Amos, 13 July 1794, (bride not named!)   3 BA-291
Smith, Andrew, 1 Dec. 1796, Rachel Beard   2 DO
Smith, Aquila, 6 Sept. 1785, Cathe. Connoway   11 BA-8
Smith, Anthony, 9 July 1786, Mary Battey   11 BA-9
Smith, Archibald, 18 Dec. 1795, Mary Hammond   1 WO
Smith, Arthur, 30 Jan. 1794, Mary Anderson   5 BA-13
Smith, Balser, 26 Dec. 1795, Catherine Caufman   4 FR
Smith, Barnett, 19 Oct. 1798, Charlotte Glover   6 BA
Smith, Basil, 3 May 1781, Ann Cunningham   2 CH-457
Smith, Bazill, 1 May 1782, Ann Cunningham   3 HA-6
Smith, Bazil, 14 Aug. 1783, Elizabeth Dooley   3 HA-8

Smith, Benjamin, 16 May 1795, Ann Hardy   4 FR
Smith, Benjamin, 5 Aug. 1797, Sarah Ann Newman   2 SO
   3 SO gives the date as 6 Aug. 1797.
Smith, Benjamin Dingly, 29 July 1800, Nancy Coard   1 WO
Smith, Caleb, 4 May 1784, Eliza Oyston   11 BA-7
Smith, Casper, 26 Aug. 1794, Mary Weaver   29 BA-5
Smith, Charles, 13 April 1779, Mary Ringer   4 FR
Smith, Charles, 15 Decmber 1792, Leah Airey   2 DO
Smith, Christ., 31 April 1795, Magd. Bollhouse   29 BA-6
Smith, Curtis, 26 Dec. 1798, Nancy Jones   2 DO
Smith, Daniel, 31 May 1783, Mary Shull   4 FR
Smith, Daniel, c.1792, by Rev. Linton; Hannah Gallop   4 AA
Smith, Daniel, 5 June 1794, Elizabeth Yates   6 BA
Smith, David, 29 Oct. 1787, Polly Campbell   2 DO
Smith, David, 27 Feb. 1796, Isabella Campbell   2 DO
Smith, David, 31 Oct. 1799, Cassandra Branham   6 BA
Smith, David, 29 Jan. 1800, Elizabeth McCollum   3 AL-6
Smith, David, 22 Sept. 1800, Hannah Nelson   1 WO
Smith, Edward, 24 March 1782, Ann Warfield   2 PG-3
Smith, Edward, 4 April 1787, Betsy Ball   2 DO
Smith, Edward Horsey, 4 June 1799, Nancy Waller   2 SO
Smith, Elijah, 30 Aug. 1788, Martha Jenkins   4 AA
   The ceremony was performed by Rev. Reed.
Smith, Elijah, 30 Aug. 1797, Ann Start   4 KE-71
Smith, Elijah, 6 Dec. 1799, Sally Dailey   1 WO
Smith, Emory, 23 Dec. 1797, Sophia Smith   4 KE-71
Smith, Ephraim, 30 May 1786, Beddy Smith   3 BA-191
   10 BA-186 gives the date as 30 May 1786, and the
   bride's name as Biddy Schmidt.
Smith, Ephraim, 3 July 1799, Martha Edwards   29 BA-10
Smith, Fairfax, 1 May 1796, Rebecca Erobe? Wobbleton   3 SO
Smith, Francis, 22 Nov. 1799, Eliza Thornton   11 BA-3
Smith, Frederick, 26 Dec. 1785, Sarah Pringle   11 BA-9
Smith, George, 1792, Mary Frick   50 BA-392
Smith, George, free; 19 Feb. 1797, Nancy Grant, slave   3 BA-342
Smith, George, 9 July 1799, Rebecca Landen   2 SO
Smith, George, 1 June 1800, Mary Leach   6 BA
Smith, Henry, 6 Sept. 1778, Sarah Conaway   11 BA-1
Smith, Henry of Geo., 26 Jan. 1784, Sarah Buckman   4 FR
Smith, Henry, 15 July 1787, Mary Ramsower   2 FR-1168
Smith, Henry, 21 May 1798, Mary Grove   4 FR
Smith, Isaac, 20 March 1793, Polly Jones   2 DO
Smith, Isaac, 18 March 1800, Eliz. McKinley   29 BA-11
Smith, Jacob, 16 Feb. 1779, Solomy Koontz   4 FR
Smith, Jacob, 27 Sept. 1783, Christena Iseminger   4 FR
Smith, Jacob, 23 Feb. 1797, Sarah Nash   45 BA-1
Smith, Jacob, 23 Nov. 1798, Mary Norwood   4 FR
Smith, James, 2 Aug. 1777, Barbara White   1 CA-5
Smith, James, 7 Aug. 1781, Rachel Perkins   2 PG-5
Smith, James, 4 March 1782, Cassandra Tucker   4 FR
Smith, James, 1 May 1784, Constantia Ford   2 CH-457
Smith, James, 3 May 1791, Rosanna Reed   2 DO
Smith, James, 5 March 1792, Rosanna Edmondson   2 DO
Smith, James, 17 Feb. 1794, Nancy Roberts   2 DO
Smith, James, 24 May 1794, Elizabeth Tucker   3 BA-287
Smith, James, 8 May 1795, Frankey Nehms   1 WO
Smith, James, 7 Sept. 1795, Mary Vickers   2 DO
Smith, James, 8 Aug. 1797, Sarah Haley   1 BA-8
Smith, James, 11 Sept. 1797, Atty Evans   2 FR-1170
   4 FR gives the bride's name as Alty Evans.
Smith, James, 20 Sept. 1797, Sarah Haley   3 HA-26
Smith, James, 2 Aug. 1798, Mary Magher   3 BA-361
Smith, James, 16 Sept. 1800, Betsey C. Rounds   2 SO
Smith, Jeremiah, 21 Oct. 1784, Rebecca Asheton   5 BA-13
Smith, Jeremiah, 2 May 1791, Leticia Kenly   6 BA

```
Smith, Job, 27 Dec. 1781, Marg't Orrick                 11 BA-5
Smith, Job, 29 June 1784, Marg't Smith                  11 BA-7
Smith, Job, 27 Dec. 1798, Martha Bussey                  6 BA
Smith, Joel, 13 Dec. 1793, Elizabeth Sugar              39 BA-1
Smith, John, 3 Sept. 1777, Elizabeth Rawlings            2 CH-457
Smith, Jno., 15 July 1779, Margaret Pindel               4 AA
    The ceremony was performed by Rev. Magowan.
Smith, John, 13 Nov. 1780, Rebecca Jewel                 2 CH-457
Smith, John, 30 Jan. 1781, Mary Whitler                  3 AA-417
Smith, John, 22 April 1781, Edith Pyle                   3 HA-4
Smith, John, 27 Jan. 1782, Mary Laveale                  3 AA-418
Smith, John, 15 Jan. 1784, Sarah Maddox                  4 FR
Smith, John, 10 Jan. 1787, Margaret Woolfe               4 FR
Smith, John, 23 Dec. 1787, Ann King                      2 CH-457
Smith, John, 21 Jan. 1788, Nancy Tolly                   2 DO
Smith, John, 4 Feb. 1789, Ann Highfield                  4 FR
Smith, John, 28 Sept. 1789, S. Arnold                   29 BA-1
Smith, John, 8 Oct. 1789, by Rev. Hagerty; Elizabeth
    Eden                                                 4 AA
Smith, John, 29 Aug. 1792, Ann Jackson                  29 BA-3
Smith, John, 9 May 1793, Margaret Beard                  4 FR
Smith, John, 10 Oct. 1794, Elizabeth Downs               7 BA-1
    3 HA-23 gives the date as 9 Sept. 1794.
Smith, Jno., 23 Dec. 1794, Cath. Etter                  29 BA-6
Smith, John, 27 March 1795, Mary Fout                    4 FR
Smith, Jno., 21 May 1795, Susanna Maidwell              29 BA-6
Smith, John, 30 May 1795, Jane Conner                    6 BA
Smith, John, 26 July 1795, Mary Ann Mills, dau. of
    Joseph and Mary                                      8 MO-11
Smith, John, 14 April 1796, Nelly McGrath                3 SO
Smith, John, 12 Oct. 1797, Sarah Chiddick                6 BA
Smith, John, c.1798, by Rev. Riggin; Ruth Gray           4 AA
Smith, John, 18 Jan. 1798, Mary Pritchards               3 AL-5
Smith, John, 1 Feb. 1798, Elizabeth Pritchard            2 AL-700
Smith, John, 9 Feb. 1798, Anna Smith                     1 WO
Smith, John, 25 May 1799, Abby Thomas; free mulattoes    3 BA-371
Smith, John, 17 Aug. 1799, Sarah Askew                   8 BA-1
Smith, John, 16 Dec. 1799, Mary Jones                    1 WO
Smith, John, of John, 15 Dec. 1795, Mary Keefer          4 FR
Smith, John Addison, 4 Nov. 1800, Elizabeth Gardner      3 BA-394
Smith, John H., 12 May 1788, by Rev. Claggett; Elizabeth
    Chew                                                 4 AA
Smith, John Henry, 21 Jan. 1794, Elizabeth Kutz (or Perrick)
    4 FR
Smith, John Jacob, 9 Feb. 1789, Jane Parran Hellen      11 BA-12
Smith, Dr. John T., 26 Feb. 1789, Eliza Price            4 FR
Smith, John William, 5 March 1788, Rachel Low            3 PG-254
Smith, Joseph, 21 April 1778, Sarah Hutchison            3 AA-414
Smith, Joseph, 26 Feb. 1789, by Rev. Forrest; Milly
    Watson                                               4 AA
Smith, Joseph, 2 May 1790, Teresa Jameson                4 FR
Smith, Joseph, 11 April 1799, Winifred McCarty           3 BA-370
Smith, Joshua, 23 June 1799, Rebecca Johnson             6 BA
Smith, Lambert, 6 Nov. 1792, Elizabeth Gittings          1 BA-4
Smith, Larkin, 6 July 1796, Rachel Nicholson             3 BA-327
Smith, Lewis, 29 Jan. 1796, Barbara Glance               4 FR
Smith, Marshall, 10 Dec. 1799, Anna Timmons              1 WO
Smith, Mathias, 14 Sept. 1790, Ann Shuttice              4 FR
Smith, Mathias, 7 Jan. 1793, Mary Buckey                 4 FR
Smith, Mich'l, 26 April 1794, Cath. Hauck               29 BA-5
Smith, Middleton, 28 Aug. 1785, Julian Keller            2 FR-1167
Smith, Moses, 15 Jan. 1795, Mary Berry                   7 BA-2
    3 HA-24 gives the date as 8 Jan. 1795.
Smith, Nathaniel, 21 Nov. 1794, by Rev. Joseph Wyatt;
    Elizabeth Leech                                      4 AA
```

```
Smith, Nathaniel, 11 Feb. 1796, by Rev. Ridgely; Sarah
    Wood                                              4 AA
Smith, Nicholas, 28 Oct. 1783, Rebecca Hissey        11 BA-6
Smith, Paca, 7 Feb. 1799, Sarah Phillips             2 HA-351
    3 HA-28 gives the date as 4 Feb. 1799.
Smith, Peter, 21 Feb. 1789, Elizabeth Hart           4 FR
Smith, Peter, 4 Oct. 1790, Elizabeth Albaugh         4 FR
Smith, Peter, 29 Dec. 1795, Elizabeth Gitts          4 FR
Smith, Peter, 18 March 1799, Catherine Albaugh       4 FR
Smith, Philip, 31 Oct. 1795, Mary Storey             29 BA-6
Smith, Philip, of Philip, 2 Nov. 1795, Catherine Shroyer  4 FR
Smith, Richard, 25 Sept. 1791, Mary Bevan            5 BA-13
Smith, Richard, 4 Nov. 1798, Sinah Truman            3 BA-365
Smith, Robert, 7 Dec. 1790, Margaret Smith           5 BA-13
Smith, Robert, 2 Jan. 1798, Sarah Martin             1 WO
Smith, Samuel, 31 Dec. 1778, Margaret Spear          5 BA-12
Smith, Samuel, 10 June 1783, Tabitha Wheeler         11 BA-6
Smith, Samuel, 1 Jan. 1800, Mary Dutton              2 CH-457
Smith, Samuel R., 19 May 1796, Ann S. Sitler         6 BA
Smith, Simon, 20 Dec. 1796, Sarah Garrett            4 KE-71
Smith, Solomon, 25 Sept. 1790, Letitia Nixhon        6 BA
Smith, Stephen, 20 June 1789, J. Burns               29 BA-1
Smith, Stoutten, 12 Feb. 1799, Elizabeth Parmore     1 WO
Smith, Tetrick, 30 May 1789, Mary Smith              4 FR
Smith, Thos., 15 June 1779, by Rev. Magowan; Mary Deale  4 AA
Smith, Thomas, 15 Sept. 1785, Mary Dashiell          1 WI-117
Smith, Tho., 22 March 1789, Sarah Rawlison           11 BA-12
Smith, Thos., 22 March 1789, Verlinda Leach          2 PG-4
Smith, Thomas, (8 Feb. 1791), Sarah Brooks           15 BA-4
Smith, Thomas, 7 July 1798, Ann McKinley             4 KE-71
Smith, Walter, 19 Sept. 1779, Mary Hendley           3 SM-57
Smith, William, 4 Aug. 1778, Alice Stallings         1 CA-1
Smith, William, 13 Jan. 1779, Rachel Miller          4 FR
Smith, William, 17 Feb. 1780, Jane Daugherty         3 HA-1
Smith, William, 25 April 1780, Frances Greene        3 BA-182
Smith, William, 14 Dec. 1780, Pheby Bodington        4 FR
Smith, William, 22 April 1781, Martha Bond           3 HA-4
Smith, William, 2 Sept. 1783, Mary Brown             4 FR
Smith, William, 11 April 1784, Margaret Spence       3 HA-8
Smith, William, 29 Aug. 1785, Sarah Bateman          11 BA-8
Smith, William, 14 May 1791, Mary Webster            3 PG-258
Smith, William, 12 Oct. 1792, Catherine Sinn         4 FR
Smith, William, 26 Nov. 1792, Susannah Phillips      3 HA-22
Smith, William, 12 March 1793, Sarah Visetworth      3 HA-23
Smith, William, 24 May 1794, Mary Bryan              3 BA-287
Smith, William, 3 Feb. 1795, Mary Miles              3 AA-424
Smith, William, 25 Feb. 1796, Elizabeth Rowland      3 BA-317
Smith, Wm., 2 July 1796, Phillis Sexton              29 BA-7
Smith, William, 12 Dec. 1796, Elis. Smith            3 WA-62
Smith, William, 6 July 1797, Elizabeth Mahon         2 HA-350
    3 HA-26 gives the date as 5 July 1797.
Smith, William, 19 March 1798, Ann Howard            4 KE-72
Smith, William, 29 July 1800, Rebecca Batts          1 WO
Smith, Wm., 16 Sept. 1800, Polly Gunn                1 WO
Smith, William B., 10 July 1794, Frances Steele      3 BA-291
Smith, William Rogers, 2 Oct. 1798, Margaret Dugan   3 BA-364
Smith, Winston, 26 Oct. 1796, Cassandra Dallam       47 BA-1
    See also 3 HA-25.
Smith, Zachariah, c.1792, by Rev. Hutchinson; Eliza Ann
    Harrowood                                        4 AA
Smithson, Benjamin, 24 Dec. 1792, Ann Howard         3 HA-22
Smithson, Daniel, 10 Dec. 1782, Marg't Anderson      11 BA-6
Smithson, Daniel, 3 Feb. 1785, Susanna Taylor        3 HA-9
Smithson, Nathaniel, 24 Jan. 1780, Mary Bull         3 HA-1
Smithson, William Eaton, 1 Sept. 1777, Rhoda Robey   2 CH-457
```

```
Smoot, Henry, 23 Dec. 1781, Elizabeth Warren         2 CH-457
Smoot, Horatio, 7 July 1799, Heathy Smoot            2 CH-457
Smoot, Isaac, 28 Oct. 1779, Mary Lock                2 CH-457
Smoot, John, 6 April 1779, Anny Ford                 4 CH-2
     2 CH-457 gives the date as 8 April 1779.
Smoot, John, 10 April 1790, Elizabeth Parker         2 DO
Smoot, Josiah, 22 Dec. 1781, Ann Douglas             2 CH-457
Smother, Thomas, 14 Dec. 1788, Silvia P. Devall; free
     negroes                                         2 FR-1168
Smythe, Samuel, 15 Oct. 1791, Elizabeth Wignell     18 BA-3
     See also 3 BA-254.
Snavely, Jacob, May 1799, Elis. Stoner               3 WA-67
Snead, Edward, 10 Nov. 1796, Jane Webb               3 BA-333
Snead, Richard, 10 Nov. 1796, Jane Webb             35 BA-4
Snedeker (or Deneker), Peter, 7 May 1794, Elizabeth Frost
     2 AL-700
Sneider, George, 19 Oct. 1784, Christiane Lora      10 BA-182
Snides, John, 15 Sept. 1796, Ann Parkin              5 BA-13
Snivner, John, 1 July 1797, Susanna Maconner         4 KE-71
Snook, John, 8 Dec. 1783, Catherine Ambrose          4 FR
Snook, John, 14 April 1794, Nancy Ayers              2 AL-700
Snowdagle, Peter, 22 March 1779, Christena Eckman    4 FR
Snowden, Philip, son of Samuel, 1st day, 12 mo., 1791,
     Patience Hopkins, dau. of Joseph                6 SF
Snowden, Richard, son of Samuel and Elizabeth, 2nd day,
     8 mo., 1782, Hannah Moore Hopkins, dau. of William
     and Rachel                                      9 SF-43
Snowden, Richard, 13 Feb. 1798, Eliza Warf'd         5 MO-115
Snowden, Samuel, son of Samuel, 1st day, 12 mo., 1796,
     Elizabeth Cowman, dau. of Jno.                  6 SF
Snuggrass, William, 7 Dec. 1797, Catherine Hart      5 BA-13
Snuke, Peter, 30 March 1780, Ulianna Mottis          4 FR
Snyder, John, 6 April 1780, Dorothy Waltz            4 FR
Snyder, John, 21 June 1780, Charity Barrick          4 FR
Snyder, Mathias, 17 Oct. 1800, Eliz. Dayly          29 BA-11
Snyder, Valentine, 18 Dec. 1800, Eliz. Jones        29 BA-12
Sollers, Basil, 6 Feb. 1800, Susanna Owings          4 BA-78
     1 BA-9 gives the date as 25 March 1800.
Sollers, Dennis, 22 Nov. 1779, Priscilla Randall     4 FR
Sollers, Elisha, 3 May 1798, Sarah Partridge         6 BA
Sollers, James Mackall, 25 April 1779, Rebecca Elt   1 CA-2
Sollers, Thomas, 25 April 1797, Sarah Pennington     3 BA-344
Sollman, Adam, 9 Oct. 1778, Susanna Isenbergh        4 FR
Somervel, William, 7 Sept. 1779, Elizabeth Chisley   3 SM-57
Somervell, James, 27 Jan. 1787, Anne Relp            5 BA-13
Sommerkemp, Philip, 22 May 1795, Frederica Keener    4 FR
Sommers, Philip, 19 Oct. 1798, Cath. Sauer           2 FR-1170
Soper, Benon, 24 July 1792, Elizabeth Ridgway        3 PG-437
Soper, Mareen Duvall, 15 Feb. 1798, Margret Pope     3 PG-443
Soper, Nathan, 26 Nov. 1791, Ann Dercey              3 PG-436
Soper, Philip, 31 July 1794, Elizabeth Pope          3 PG-440
Soper, Samuel, 9 April 1793, Margaret Kirk           4 FR
Soreis, John, 25 April 1791, Gertrude Weingartner    6 FR-202
Sotherin, William, 20 Aug. 1795, Judah Meekins       2 DO
Sothern, Henry, 27 Nov. 1796, Elizabeth Marbury      3 PG-442
Sothorn, Thomas, 2 Jan. 1798, Mary McPherson         3 PG-443
Soulsby (or Salisbury), Matthew, 30 Nov. 1794, Prudence
     Travis                                          3 BA-296
Southean, Richard, 15 Oct. 1783, Catherine Southean  2 CH-457
Southerland, Alexander, 31 Jan. 1795, Ann Taylor     4 FR
Southword, William, 24 June 1800, Mary Speck         3 BA-387
Soward, Richard, 23 July 1791, Jenny Bane            2 DO
Soward, Thomas, 19 Dec. 1782, Millicent Mills        2 DO
Soward, Thomas, 18 Aug. 1798, Rachel Burkley         4 KE-71
Soward, William, 12 Jan. 1785, Leah Lee              2 DO
```

```
Soward, William, 21 Dec. 1789, Nancy Lee              2 DO
Sower, John, 28 Feb. 1797, Jane Mahar                 6 BA
Spafferd, Jacob, 8 Aug. 1799, Celior Sinclair         6 BA
Spaks, Abraham, 6 Feb. 1794, by Rev. Benton Riggen; Mary
     Ore                                              4 AA
Spalden, Benedict, 21 Dec. 1779, Anna Stone           1 SM-137
Spangler, Christian, 17 Jan. 1795, Ann Harvey         4 FR
Spangler, John, 20 Dec. 1788, Mary Adams              4 FR
Spanseiler, Michael, 6 Dec. 1785, Sarah Price         2 FR-1167
Sparkes, Simon, 18 June 1794, Sarah Nute             39 BA-1
Sparks, Millington, 23 May 1797, Rebecca Brooks       4 KE-71
Sparks, Sluyter, 21 Oct. 1797, Elizabeth Walls        4 KE-71
Sparrow, Jonathan, 17 June 1796, Priscilla Smith      5 MO-113
Speak, James, 14 Sept. 1793, Margaret Higdon          4 FR
Speak, William, 16 Feb. 1782, Molly Hanlope           2 CH-457
Spear, George, 24 May 1795, Catharine Renner          1 BA-7
Spear, John, 14 Sept. 1779, Elisabeth Smith           5 BA-13
Spear, Joseph, 10 Jan. 1798, Barbara Spear            5 BA-13
Spearaugh, George, Nov. 1800, Sarah Eakle             3 WA-70
Specht, Conrad, 21 April 1795, Eliz. Schaffer         2 FR-1169
Specht, Lewis, 7 Aug. 1798, Elizabeth Cramer          4 FR
Specknall, Basil, 7 Sept.? 1781, Eliza Stamp          3 AA-417
Sped, Johannes, 27 July 1788, Anna Maria Mayauer     10 BA-190
Spedden, Hugh, 29 Oct. 1787, Nancy Spedden            2 DO
Spedden, Hugh, 18 Dec. 1797, Catherine Spedden        2 DO
Spedden, Hugh, 23 May 1798, Betsy Spedden             2 DO
Spedden, Impy, 8 Oct. 1794, Ann Lynthicum             2 DO
Spedden, John, 25 Dec. 1792, Ann Bromwell             2 DO
Spedden, John, 24 May 1799, Mary Cook                 2 DO
Spedden, Ralph, 21 Sept. 1795, Sarah Mitchell         2 DO
Spedden, Ralph, 18 Dec. 1800, Judy Marshall           2 DO
Spedding, Robert, 23 June 1781, Elizabeth Taylor      2 DO
Speek, William, 29 Oct. 1778, Eve Barbary Onbreham   11 BA-1
Speelman, Henry, 11 Dec. 1798, Lotty Gabler           4 FR
Spellard, Mathias, 24 Sept. 1797, Winifred Gleeson   44 BA-2
Spence, James, 7 Jan. 1779, Ann McClure               5 HA
Spence, James, 6 Jan. 1780, Ann McClure               3 HA-1
Spence, John, 6 Aug. 1791, Mary Jaffray               5 BA-13
Spence, Peter, 12 Nov. 1799, Elizabeth Jarvis         3 BA-380
Spencer, Edward, 16 March 1796, Rebecca Wildman       4 FR
Spencer, Stephen, 11 July 1797, Ali Hener            10 BA-198
Spessard, David June 1798, Eva Hoise                  3 WA-65
Spicer, Abraham, 13 Jan. 1791, Sarah Sulivan          6 BA
Spicer, Burden, 27 Jan. 1791, Sarah Travers           2 DO
Spicer, James, 25 Sept. 1783, Elizabeth Scovey        3 BA-185
Spicer, Jeremiah, 23 Dec. 1791, Crissy Travers        2 DO
Spicer, John, 22 Dec. 1791, Rachel Lee               29 BA-3
Spicer, Thomas, 17 Aug. 1782, Elizabeth Lloyd         3 BA-183
Spicer, Thomas, 10 June 1800, Anne Cadle              3 BA-387
Spicer, Valentine, 4 April 1791, Sarah Bowers        29 BA-2
Spicer, William, 2 Jan. 1783, Hanna Traverse          2 DO
Spickner, Henry, 2 May 1797, Eliz. Kupferschmit       2 FR-1169
Spiers, Thomas, 31 July 1800, Elisabeth Kemp          3 BA-388
Spiker, Jo-n, 28 May 1799, Mary Miller                2 AL-701
Spiller, Timothy, 9 Aug. 1792, Mary Collins          29 BA-3
Spires, Zephaniah, 1 March 1779, Catherine Walker     4 FR
Spitzenburgh, Henry, 28 Jan. 1799, Mary Ann Bell      4 FR
Spitznagel, Jacob, 12 Aug. 1794, Mary Schreyer        2 FR-1169
Spoont, Joseph, 5 Oct. 1798, Mary Smith               4 FR
Spray, John, 31 July 1788, Mary Summers               3 BA-205
Sprigg, John, 14 Dec. 1795, Elizabeth Wyvil           4 FR
Sprigg, Joseph, 8 April 1781, Margaret Elezy          3 AA-417
Sprigg, Josiah, 26 Dec. 1791, Mary Crawford           3 PG-436
Sprigg, Osborn, 26 May 1788, by Rev. Claggett; Mary Smith
     4 AA
```

```
Sprigg, Osburn, 8 April 1779, Sarah Gantt            2 PG-3
Sprigg, Sam'l, 21 June 1783, Mary Harding            4 FR
Sprigg, Thomas, 13 May 1793, Lucy Dorsey             4 FR
Springer, Edward, 12 Aug. 1787, Eliz. Krieger        2 FR-1168
Springer, Gamaliel, 21 May 1786, Araminta Walker     11 BA-9
Springer, Jacob, 6 Jan. 1799, Eliz. Kaufman          2 FR-1170
Springer, Peter, 26 Sept. 1786, Jane Fulton          2 FR-1168
Springer, Wm., 18 Nov. 1792, Mary Hauer              4 FR
Sprucebanks, Jackson, 29 Dec. 1796, Betsy Body       7 BA-3
Spry, David, 3 Nov. 1798, Martha Price               4 KE-71
Spurrier, Edward, 16 June 1785, Ann Griffith         11 BA-8
Spurrier, Henry, 17 Aug. 1800, by Rev. Ridgely; Ruth
  Spurrier                                           4 AA
Spurrier, John, of Wm., 22 Aug. 1785, Anne Coale, dau.
  of Wm.                                             1 HO-225
Spurrier, Joseph, 9 April 1789, Eleanor David        4 FR
Spurrier, Levin, 7 March 1780, Eleanor Carey         4 FR
Spurrier, Revin, 2 Jan. 1790, Deba W. Burgess        4 AA
Squire, Michael, 26 Aug. 1788, Judith Merkel         2 FR
Squire, Wm., 9 Nov. 1782, Sarah Parker               11 BA-5
Squires, Daniel, 21 March 1786, Sophia Lysby         16 BA-1
Squires, Thomas, 6 Nov. 1794, Lucy Tumblestone       4 FR
Sroark (sic), Samuel, 16 March 1780, Hannah Carter   3 HA-1
Staab, Daniel, 11 Sept. 1798, Eliz. Berg             2 FR-1170
Stacey, Robert, 18 May 1778, Rebecca Carter          11 BA-1
Stack, Newton, 3 Oct. 1797, Mary Kinnamon            2 DO
Stack, Sam'l, 21 Oct. 1790, Susanna Sadler           11 BA-13
Stad, Jacob, March 1799, Baggy Davis                 3 WA-66
Staffee, Hurman, 12 May 1790, Rebecca Griffith       6 BA
Stafford, John, 3 July 1799, Nelly Roach             6 BA
Stahl, Andrew, 22 Nov. 1791, Rhunna Overry           29 BA-3
Stahl, Chas., 25 March 1794, Mary Sewitt             29 BA-5
Staines, William, 29 March 1798, Susanna Hughes      3 BA-356
Staley, Jacob, 10 June 1780, Ann Castle              4 FR
Staley, Jacob, 10 May 1794, Elizabeth Staley         4 FR
Staley, Melchor, 27 May 1790, Barbara Fluke          4 FR
Staley, Melchor, 14 Aug. 1790, Eve Margaret Bare     4 FR
Staley, Peter, 24 April 1797, Elizabeth Shafer       4 FR
Stalions, Joseph, 26 March 1789, by Rev. Forrest; Ann Smith
  4 AA
Stalions, Perry, 4 Jan. 1789, by Rev. Forrest; Elizabeth
  Hinton                                             4 AA
Stalions, Thos., 1 Dec. 1791, -(?)- Michell          3 PG-258
Stall, Edward H., 17 Dec. 1800, Martha Aitken        3 BA-396
Stallings, Benj'n, 22 Sept. 1788, Elizabeth Thompson 4 FR
Stallings, Newman, 27 Jan. 1798, Catherine Kolb      4 FR
Stallings, (Norman?), 28 Jan. 1789, by Rev. Claggett;
  Verlinda Harvey                                    4 AA
Stallings, William, 18 Sept. 1792, by Rev. Parrott;
  Elizabeth Stamp                                    4 AA
Stallins, William, 7 Sept. 1797, Susanna Dern        4 FR
Stallions, Absalom, 27 May 1781, Barbara Winfield    3 AA-417
Stallions, Thomas, 23 June 1783, Dorothy Franey      3 AA-419
Staltcop, William, 17 Oct. 1793, Mary Shockness      4 FR
Stamer, Ulric Bernhard, 25 March 1794, Mary Bamberger 29 BA-5
Stamp, Thomas, 28 Aug. 1797, Catherine Curtin        3 PG-443
Standfast, Wm., 4 April 1784, Eliza Wilson           11 BA-7
Standford, Edmond, 18 Oct. 1787, Hannah Gray         1 BA-1
Standiford, Benjamin, 9 Jan. 1798, Rachel Amoss      3 HA-27
Standiford, James, 27 Dec. 1782, Sarah Stewart       3 HA-7
Stanford, John, 24 Dec. 1799, Leah Breerwood         2 DO
Stanley, John, 1 Oct. 1783, Margaret Maxwell         3 BA-188
Stanley, Thos., 15 Nov. 1785, Cath. Kise             2 FR-1167
Stanley, Thomas, 19 Dec. 1789, Caroline Elizabeth?
  Cabler                                             4 FR
```

```
Stanly, Charles, 4 August 1800, Louisa Gore          49 BA-1
Stansbury, Abraham, 21 Feb. 1794, Rebeckah Stevenson  4 FR
Stansbury, Caleb, 31 Oct. 1778, Rebecca Cook         11 BA-1
Stansbury, Chas., 3 Dec. 1796, Mary Ann Thompson     29 BA-8
Stansbury, Daniel, 1 May 1788, Elizabeth Stansbury    6 BA
Stansbury, Daniel, 14 Sept. 1793, Sarah Mitchell      6 BA
Stansbury, Daniel, 16 Nov. 1797, Rebecca Perrigo      6 BA
Stansbury, Dan'l, 9 Aug. 1800, Jemima Davis          29 BA-11
Stansbury, David, 13 April 1786, Henrietta Maria Fowler
    6 BA
Stansbury, Elijah, 27 Dec. 1779, Sarah Gorsuch       11 BA-4
Stansbury, Emanuel, 12 May 1778, Rachel Pumphrey     11 BA-1
Stansbury, James, 7 Feb. 1789, Jemima Gorsuch         6 BA
Stansbury, John, 9 Dec. 1779, Ruth Crook             11 BA-4
Stansbury, Jno. Dixon, 30 Dec. 1794, Elizabeth Johnson 6 BA
Stansbury, John E., 8 Dec. 1796, Mary Proctor         3 BA-333
Stansbury, Joseph, 8 May 1788, Ruth Chineth           6 BA
Stansbury, Joseph, 1 May 1794, Frances Phillips Gough  3 BA-287
Stansbury, Richard, 27 Jan. 1785, Eleanor French     11 BA-8
Stansbury, Richard, 20 Feb. 1787, Elizabeth Garritson  6 BA
Stansbury, Richardson, 14 April 1791, Sarah Raven      6 BA
Stansbury, Samuel, Sr., 24 May 1777, Anne Cullison     3 BA-173
Stansbury, Tobias, 2 May 1784, Mary Buffington        11 BA-7
Stansbury, Tobias, 10 Dec. 1799, Ariana Sollers        6 BA
Stansbury, Wm., 29 Jan. 1782, Ruth Welsh              11 BA-5
Stanton, Beachamp, 3 Nov. 1787, Chloe Chilcutt         2 SF
Stanton, Beachamp, 6 Oct. 1791, Deborah Murpha         2 SF
Stanton, John, 9 Aug. 1785, Sus. Murphy                2 FR-1167
Stanton, Thomas, 9 May 1796, Hannah Elliott            2 DO
Staplefort, Nathan, 15 Oct. 1783, Hagar Staplefort     2 DO
Stark, Peter, 29 Oct. 1798, Nancy Hollock              2 DO
Stark, Richard, 23 Aug. 1782, Elizabeth Gatewood       2 CH-457
Starkins, Thomas, 18 Jan. 1797, Catherine Cossett      3 BA-341
Starr, Henry, 20 Oct. 1799, Catherine Grimes           6 BA
Starr, James, 24 Oct. 1786, Ann Grovier                6 BA
Starr, Obadiah, 8 Aug. 1795, Ruth Boyd                 5 BA-13
Starr, Thomas, 3 May 1798, Charlotte Jones             2 DO
Starr, Wm., 21 June 1799, Anna Fisher                 50 BA-405
Statien, George, 17 April 1797, Rachel Turner          1 WO
Stattlemayer, Dewalt, 22 July 1794, Sabery Downey      2 FR-1169
Stattlemayer, Jac., 25 Jan. 1785, Hetwig Schumacher    2 FR-1167
Stattlemayer, John, 30 July 1798, Sarah Michael        2 FR-1170
Staub, Adam, 20 Nov. 1797, Ann Freet                   2 FR-1170
Staup, Peter, 28 June 1800, Magd. Eler                 2 FR-1170
Stavsley, James, 2 May 1798, Elizabeth Moore           4 KE-71
Stayton, William, 28 July 1798, Rebecca Wright         2 SO
    3 SO gives the date as 29 July 1798.
Stearnes, William, 11 Jan. 1795, Catherine Asterman    3 BA-299
Steck, Wilhelm, Sept. 1799, Ester Zweckman (or Zeeckman)
    3 WA-67
Steckel, Solomon, 18 Nov. 1798, Charlotte Doll         2 FR-1170
Steckel, Valentine, 19 Jan. 1794, Cath. Remsperger     2 FR-1169
Steel, James S., 24 March 1798, Elizabeth Norris       4 FR
Steel, John, 18 April 1789, Mary Hays                  6 BA
Steel, Joseph, 17 Jan. 1795, Margaret Porter           3 HA-24
Steel, Solomon, 6 Sept. 1794, Mary McDonald            4 FR
Steele, Edward, 16 June 1787, Clore Purviance         10 BA-188
Steell, John, 28 March 1797, Nancy Payson              3 BA-343
Stehly, Jacob, 11 May 1794, Elizab. Stehly             2 FR-1169
Stehly, John, 8 May 1800, Margaret Adams               2 FR-1170
Stehly, Joseph, of Jac., 30 July 1800, Elizabeth Stehly,
    dau. of Jos.                                       2 FR-1170
Stehly, Joseph, of Jos., 13 Nov. 1800, Cath. Guthman   2 FR-1170
Stehly, Peter, 25 April 1797, Eliz. Schafer            2 FR-1169
Steiger, Jno., 9 Oct. 1794, Cath. Keplinger           29 BA-5
```

```
Steinbeck, George, 1790, -(?)- Resen          50 BA-390
Steinbeck, George, 23 Sept. 1790, M. Refrew?   29 BA-1
Steiner, Christian, 3 May 1800, Sus. Remsperger  2 FR-1170
Steiner, Frederick, 16 May 1788, Klarissa Reb    2 FR-1168
    4 FR gives the bride's name as Clarissa Rape.
Steiner, Frederick, 16 Feb. 1800, Marg. Sinn     2 FR-1170
Steiner, Henry, 14 Oct. 1787, Elizab. Brengel    2 FR-1168
Steiner, Jacob, 21 Sept. 1786, Eliz. Hauer       2 FR-1168
    4 FR gives the groom's name as Jacob Steiner, Jr.
Steiner, John, 19 July 1785, Eliz. Plank         2 FR-1167
Steinmetz, Mich'l, 31 July 1798, Mary Ann Williams  29 BA-9
Steits, Lorentz, 25 Dec. 1783, Maria Heilmann   10 BA-178
Stempel, Henrich, 11 March 1798, (bride's name not given)
    1 FR-59; 4 FR gives the bride's name as Christiana
    Harman.
Steowt, Jno., 4 Feb. 1790, Mary Dove             3 PG-256
Stephen, Daniel, 30 Sept. 1799, Mary Lemar (or Lemmon)  6 BA
Stephens, Edward, 30 Nov. 1786, Sarah Dingle     2 DO
Stephens, Levin, 30 Dec. 1798, Sally Sanders     2 DO
Stephens, Messer, 24 Dec. 1795, Ruth Jacobs     35 BA-4
Stephens, Stephen, 30 Aug. 1798, Mary Cosden     4 KE-71
Stephens?, Thomas, 19 Dec. 1797, Nancy Warfield  6 MO
Stephens, William, 13 Dec. 1794, Ann Pigman      1 AL-53
Stephenson, James, 30 J-ly 1799, Priscilla Hopkins  3 HA-28
Stephenson, Jonah, 10 May 1799, Rachel Hughes    3 HA-28
Stephenson, Jonas, 16 July 1800, Mary Dunsheath  3 HA-29
    2 HA-352 gives the date as 2 Oct. 1800.
Stephenson, Moses, 2 Oct. 1790, Margret McCarthy  3 BA-228
Stephenson, Nathan, 25 Sept. 1789, Mary Evans    4 FR
Stephenson, Richard, 18 Oct. 1789, Usilia Wood   6 BA
    See also 4 FR.
Sterling, Ephraim, Aug. 1783, Esther Sterling    1 SO-175
Sterling, Ephraim, 3 Dec. 1799, Molly Bird       2 SO
Sterling, Jas., 19 May 1782, Eliza Gibson       11 BA-5
Sterling, Southy, 14 Nov. 1797, Rachel Dryden    1 WO
Sterling, Travers, 26 March 1789, Grace Sterling  1 SO-175
Sterrett, Joseph, 16 Oct. 1800, Mary Harris      3 BA-393
Steuart, Charles, 15 June 1780, Eliz. Calvert    2 PG-7
Steuart, Philip, 15 May 1787, Mary Marshall      3 PG-252
Stevens, Ambrose, 24 July 1780, Marg't Burke    11 BA-4
Stevens, Benjamin, 11 April 1798, Prissy Vanderwolf  2 SO
Stevens, Charles, 10 Aug. 1796, Marg. Waltz      2 FR-1169
Stevens, Cola, 15 Oct. 1792, Rebecca Rooks       2 DO
Stevens,· Edward, son of William and Sarah, 22 June 1783,
    Eleanor Robinson, dau. of Richard and Judith  1 TA-329
Stevens, Edward, 22 May 1796, Keziah Coale       2 FR-1169
Stevens, James, 28 Jan. 1798, Sarah Bodfield     1 TA-330
Stevens, John, 10 Oct. 1779, Mary Reardon        5 BA-13
Stevens, John, 28 Sept. 1780, Agnes Whiteford   11 BA-4
Stevens, John, 28 July 1785, Frances Marshall    2 DO
Stevens, John, 23 April 1791, Rachel Richards    4 FR
Stevens, John, 5 June 1793, Jane Nailer          2 FR-1169
Stevens, John, 20 Nov. 1794, Achsah Owings       3 BA-296
Stevens, John, 9 Sept. 1800, Elizabeth Marshall  2 SO
Stevens, Joseph, 21 July 1797, Nancy Ingram      6 BA
Stevens, Levin, 15 Jan. 1796, Mary Thomas        2 DO
Stevens, Levin, 1 July 1796, Mary Thomas         2 DO
Stevens, Nathan, 15 Sept. 1781, Vina Smith       2 DO
Stevens, Nath'l, 13 Feb. 1783, Sarah Hatton     11 BA-6
Stevens, Nathan, 21 June 1799, Ann Simmons       2 DO
Stevens, Rich'd, 23 Dec. 1783, Jane Keisterd    11 BA-7
Stevens, Robert, 1 Feb. 1797, Elizabeth Wright   2 DO
Stevens, Thomas, 6 Dec. 1790, Sally Griffith     2 DO
Stevens, Thomas, son of Peter and Hannah, 14 Dec. 1790,
    Sally Griffith, dau. of John and Sarah       1 TA-329
```

```
Stevens, Thomas, 23 Nov. 1796, Ann Ferguson          2 DO
  1 DO-39 gives the date as 24 Nov. 1796.
Stevens, Wm., 12 June 1779, Lidia Ouria              4 FR
Stevens, William, 25 Dec. 1781, Viney Whittington    3 AA-418
Stevens, William, 8 Sept. 1791, Nancy McKeel         2 DO
Stevenson, Andrew, 30 Nov. 1793, Isabella Smith      1 BA-6
Stevenson, Charles, 28 Jan. 1800, Mary Boyd          3 BA-382
Stevenson, Edward, 14 June 1791, Mary Stevenson      6 BA
Stevenson, Edward, 6 April 1799, Nancy Williams      1 WO
Stevenson, George, 5 Oct. 1791, Sarah Botts          3 HA-21
Stevenson, George, 10 April 1794, Elizabeth McCracken 6 BA
Stevenson, George, 11 Dec. 1798, Rose Hainy          6 BA
Stevenson, George P., 3 Feb. 1791, Esther Smith      5 BA-13
Stevenson, Henry, 9 Oct. 1794, Anne Caulk            3 BA-293
Stevenson, John, 25 June 1778, Sarah Gott            11 BA-1
Stevenson, John, 23 Feb. 1779, Jane Stewart          5 HA
  3 HA-1 gives the date as 25 Feb. 1780.
Stevenson, John, 12 Oct. 1780, Sarah Carey           5 BA-13
Stevenson, Jno., 29 Dec. 1783, Eliza Cowan           11 BA-7
Stevenson, John, 9 Nov. 1786, Mary Habner            24 BA-1
Stevenson, John, 19 Dec. 1798, Elizabeth Towsend     1 WO
Stevenson, John, 25 Sept. 1799, Eleanor Hall         6 BA
Stevenson, John, 10 Dec. 1799, Sarah Hawkins         4 FR
Stevenson, Jonas, 12 May 1799, Rachel Hughes         12 BA-370
Stevenson, Jonathan, 27 May 1795, Lydia Mills        1 WO
Stevenson, Joseph, 30 Nov. 1797, Elizabeth Stevenson 1 WO
Stevenson, Joshua, 18 May 1800, Mary Spencer         8 BA-1
Stevenson, Josiah, 21 May 1791, Margaret Wells       4 FR
Stevenson, Josias, 1 March 1795, Urath Stevenson     6 BA
Stevenson, Merryman, 19 Jan. 1790, Ruth Stevenson    6 BA
Stevenson, Meshach, 21 April 1794, Esther Jones; free
  negroes or mulattoes                               3 BA-285
Stevenson, Mordecai, 13 Aug. 1778, Sarah Barnesberry 11 BA-1
Stevenson, Moses, 21 April 1789, Eleanor Shaw        3 BA-219
Stevenson, Samuel, 18 Nov. 1788, Lucy Dorsey         2 FR-1168
Stevenson, Samuel, 5 July 1795, Elizabeth Peathers   3 BA-307
Stevenson, Thomas, 7 June 1781, Susanna Safferty     3 HA-4
Stevenson, Thomas, 4 Aug. 1800, Sally Ward           2 SO
Stevenson, Wm., 20 April 1784, Eliza Brant           11 BA-7
  The ceremony was performed by Rev. Robison.
Stevenson, William, 7 March 1796, Kitty Parker       7 BA-3
Stevenson, William, 4 Aug. 1796, Hester Parker       3 HA-25
Stevenson, Wm., 8 May 1799, Nancy Navin              1 WO
Stevenson, William, 27 Feb. 1800, Ann Foster         6 BA
Steward, Edward, 21 Nov. 1786, Susanna Klee          2 FR-1168
Steward, Henry, 7 Sept. 1783, Catherine Mumford      3 BA-185
Steward, James, 22 Feb. 1789, Eleanor Dunes          1 BA-2
Steward, John, 28 Oct. 1780, Mary King               11 BA-4
Steward, John, 30 Jan. 1799, Catherine Walter        4 FR
Steward, Mark, 18 Oct. 1797, Priscilla Hillman       7 BA-3
Steward, William, 25 June 1788, Elizabeth Guyton     1 BA-1
Steward, William, 18 Nov. 1793, Marg't Ricketts      4 FR
Stewart, Archibald, 26 Nov. 1791, Sarah Nelson       5 BA-13
Stewart, Charles, 12 Feb. 1784, Mary Waters          3 AA-420
Stewart, Charles, 5 Feb. 1785, Mary Woolford         2 DO
Stewart, Charles, 1 Oct. 1793, by Rev. G. Ridgely; Eliza-
  beth Stewart                                       4 AA
Stewart, Charles, 22 May 1794, Cloey Ann Newton      8 MO
Stewart, David C., 16 May 1799, Jane Purviance       5 BA-13
Stewart, Ezekiel, 19 Dec. 1799, Elizabeth Yieldhall  3 BA-381
Stewart, James, 15 March 1778, Catherine Milstead    2 CH-457
Stewart, James, 2 Jan. 1791, Massey Burgess          3 PG-258
Stewart, James, 9 Feb. 1796, Grace Clarke            5 MO-113
Stewart, James, 24 Nov. 1799, Elizabeth Hannah       5 BA-13
Stewart, James, 15 Jan. 1782, Phoebe Marshall        11 BA-5
```

Stewart, John, 24 June 1782, Elizabeth Jackson   2 DO
Stewart, John, Jr., 27 July 1786, Jane Robertson   1 WI-119
Stewart, John, 16 Dec. 1791, Ariana Ross   3 PG-436
Stewart, John, 6 Jan. 1798, Sarah Hodson   2 DO
Stewart, John, 1 Dec. 1799, Catherine Ensor   3 BA-381
Stewart, John Cowder, 28 Dec. 1790, Mary Barnett   5 BA-13
Stewart, Joseph, 13 Dec. 1800, Rebecca Wade   3 BA-396
Stewart, Joshua, 12 Sept. 1780, Sarah Cartwright   11 BA-4
Stewart, Mordecai, before 4 May 1798, by Rev. Stewart;
     Ann Pitts   4 AA
Stewart, Rich'd, 26 Dec. 1799, Eliz. Remmeton   5 MO-116
Stewart, Robert H., 21 April 1796, Frances Roberts   2 DO
Stewart, Thomas, 23 Sept. 1793, Lilly Lee   2 DO
Stewart, William, 3 Oct. 1779, Sarah Nicholson   2 PG-2
Stewart, William, 23 Oct. 1792, Mary Scott   18 BA-4
Stewart, William, 22 Dec. 1800, Jemima Paul   2 DO
Stewart, Woolford, 27 July 1790, Elizabeth Tregoe   2 DO
Stickle, Valentine, 18 Jan. 1794, Catherine Ramsbergh   4 FR
Stidger, William, 5 March 1800, Sophia Davis   2 AL-701
Stiehl, Abraham, 24 Sept. 1788, Mary Albach   2 FR-1168
Stigar, John, 23 Dec. 1786, by Rev. Turner; Clare Osborn
     51 BA-30
Stikeleader, Peter, 2 April 1796, Eva Leighter   3 WA-60
Stiles, George, 27 Jan. 1787, Anne Steel   5 BA-13
Stilwell, Elias, 21 May 1792, Catherine Morgan   1 AL-52
Stillwell, John, 7 July 1789, Deborah Allender   6 BA
Stimmel, Ebenezer, 29 April 1794, Barb. Bossert   2 FR-1169
Stimmel, Jacob, 15 Nov. 1785, Eliz. Bossert   2 FR-1167
Stimmell, Peter, 29 May 1794, Barbara Buzzard   4 FR
Stimmell, Yost, 28 Oct. 1784, Magdalena Stoker   4 FR
Stinchcomb, Christopher, 17 Oct. 1793, Magdalena Zimmerman
     18 BA-5
Stinchcomb, George, 21 June 1783, Aberilla Andrews   11 BA-6
Stinchcomb, Larkin, 25 Nov. 1792, Rachel Stocksdale   6 BA
Stinchcomb, McLain, 19 Sept. 1778, Nackey Merryman   11 BA-1
Stinchcomb, Thomas, 23 April 1778, Ruth Owings   11 BA-1
Stinchcomb, Victor, 14 March 1790, Ann Cord   6 BA
Stinchicomb, Ch's, 28 Jan. 1783, Sarah Stevens   11 BA-6
Stipe, James, 21 March 1778, Mary Donn   4 FR
Stipe, John, 10 May 1794, Barbara Burckhartt   4 FR
Stobo, Capt. Jacob, 12 Oct. 1783, Sarah Hughes   3 BA-185
Stockdale, Edm'd, 26 Nov. 1789, Naomi Evans   6 BA
Stockdale, Edward, Feb. 1778, Eleanor Bennett   11 BA-1
Stockdale, Thomas, 18 Dec. 1797, Sarah Baxter   3 HA-26
     See also 1 BA-8.
Stockett, Henry, 26 Dec. 1794, Barbara McKenzie   6 BA
Stockett, Richard Galen, 28 March 1799, Margaret Hall   1 HO-221
Stockett, Thomas Williams, 31 Jan. 1797, by Rev. Green;
     Susannah Beard   4 AA
Stockett, William Thomas, before 17 Oct. 1793, by Rev.
     Blodgood; Sarah Beard   4 AA
Stockman, John, 27 July 1797, Elizabeth Thomas   4 FR
Stockston, Warner, 14 Oct. 1787, Nancy Gladdon   2 FR-1168
Stoffleman, Henry, 1 Jan. 1800, Catherine Bartlemay   3 BA-382
Stokeham, Isaac, 14 Nov. 1780, Mary McGregory   3 BA-180
Stoker, Michael, 21 June 1778, Mary A-(?)-   4 FR
Stokes, David, 9 May 1800, Sarah Johns   3 HA-29
Stokes, James, 23 April 1789, Priscilla Harper   2 DO
Stokes, Jno., 20 Oct. 1784, Marg't Savage   11 BA-7
Stokes, Robert Young, 24 May 1781, Sarah Brooke, dau. of
     Clement Brooke   1 HA-392
Stolinger, George, 23 Jan. 1800, Ann Deaver   12 BA-371
     See also 2 BA-17.
Stoll, John, 9 May 1790, Marg. Dottero   2 FR-1168
Stonall (or Stovall), William, 13 March 1796, Mary Ensor
     3 BA-321

```
Stone, Edward, 25 Jan. 1796, Nancy Chattle          29 BA-7
Stone, Henry, 11 Dec. 1798, Rebecca Porter           6 BA
Stone, John, 10 May 1778, Sarah Raredon              2 MO-1
Stone, John, 15 July 1780, Mary Timmyons             2 PG-7
Stone, John, 8 Dec. 1792, Barbara Binger             4 FR
Stone, John, 30 July 1796, Mary Shroyer              4 FR
Stone, Joseph, 21 Feb. 1779, Eliz. More              1 SM-137
Stone, Joseph, 28 Nov. 1780, Winifred Hutchins       3 SM-58
Stone, Joseph, 5 Nov. 1784, Eliz. Swailes            1 SM-137
Stone, Marshall, 30 March 1791, by Rev. Chalmers; Betty
  Harris                                             4 AA
Stone, Nehemiah, 3 March 1778, Sarah Willson         2 PG-2
Stone, Thomas, 19 Nov. 1782, Catherine Stevens       3 AA-419
Stone, Walter Hanson, 27 March 1785, Ann Muncaster   2 FR-1167
  See also 4 FR.
Stone, William, 21 April 1778, Hannah Cockey        11 BA-1
Stone, William, 1 Jan. 1795, Elizabeth Watkins       3 PG-440
Stone, Zephaniah, 24 Dec. 1789, Prisilla Pope        3 PG-256
Stoneburner, Jacob, 9 Aug. 1798, Margaret Harschell  4 FR
Stoneman, William, 29 Jan. 1793, Elizabeth Gormond   2 AL-700
Stoner, Daniel, 9 Feb. 1792, by Rev. Forrest; Mary Deaghee
  3 FR
Stoner, David, 20 Oct. 1787, Mary Fleagle            4 FR
Stoner, Henry, 13 Oct. 1787, Elizabeth Pengle        4 FR
Stoner, Jacob, 11 Oct. 1792, Mary Bucey              4 FR
Stoner, John, Jr., 27 June 1785, Elizabeth Plonk     4 FR
Stoner, John, 21 March 1795, Susanna Ramsberg        4 FR
Stoner, Stephen, 11 Oct. 1795, Barbara Ramsberg      4 FR
Stoops, James, 5 April 1797, Susanna Lockerman       4 KE-72
Stoops, Peregrine, 22 May 1798, Sarah Henry          4 KE-71
Stophel, Jacob, 21 July 1798, Elizabeth Burkhartt    4 FR
Storey, Joseph, 25 Nov. 1796, Ann Hollis             4 KE-71
Storm, Mich'l, 27 March 1796, Cath. Koller           2 FR-1169
Storm, Peter, 17 April 1796, Susanna Wright          2 FR-1169
Storms, Isaac, 26 Feb. 1793, Sarah Wright            4 FR
Storms, Peter, 29 Nov. 1796, Rebeckah Thompson       4 FR
Storr, William, 21 June 1799, Anne/Unni Fisher      29 BA-10
Stortzman, Martin, May 1798, Molly Keller            3 WA-65
Story, George L., 4 Aug. 1795, Christy Dashiell      3 BA-307
Story, Jno., 18 July 1796, Mary Geoghegan           29 BA-7
Stottlemier, John, 27 July 1798, Sarah Michael       4 FR
Stottlemire, George, 6 Nov. 1779, Catherine Calon    4 FR
Stottlemyer, Jacob, 25 Jan. 1785, Hedwick Shoemaker  4 FR
Stoub, Adam, 20 Nov. 1797, Ann Freet                 4 FR
Stouffer, Henry, 22 July 1799, Ann Mitchell          4 FR
Stover, John, 15 Oct. 1792, Margaret Hauer           4 FR
Stover, Philip, 4 Feb. 1799, Susanna Welt            4 FR
Stovet, Jacob, 1792, Actius Marsh                   50 BA-392
Strain, Robert, 23 Aug. 1800, Priscilla Hopkins     50 BA-407
Strasberger, John, 13 May 1785, Ann Walling          4 FR
Strassburger, Fred'k, 10 April 1796, Eliz. Vanderburg 2 FR-1169
Stratton, Will'm, 21 Feb. 1797, Mary Howard         44 BA-2
Stratz, Christian, 23 Oct. 1787, Margaret Strein     6 FR-201
Straughan, Jno., 30 Sept. 1790, Rebecca Johnson     11 BA-13
Strauss, Hennerich, 6 Oct. 1794, Christina Glassbrenner
  3 WA-57
Strawbridge, Abram, 15 May 1794, Rebecca Mantle     50 BA-394
Strawbridge, Theophilus, 17 Feb. 1796, Abigail Edger 29 BA-7
Strawsberger, John, 21 Jan. 1796, Barbara Fundiberg  4 FR
Strebech, Wm., 16 Oct. 1796, Marg. Kline            29 BA-7
Streeker, John, 21 March 1797, Catherine Wilson      3 HA-26
Street, Benja., 11 Dec. 1782, Martha Cambridge      11 BA-6
Street, Daniel, 12 March 1784, Eliza Amos           11 BA-7
Street, Edward, 18 April 1798, Sarah Meekins         2 DO
Street, George, 29 Jan. 1779, Elizabeth Cotton       4 FR
```

```
Street, John, 13 Dec. 1790, Hannah Todd              2 DO
Street, Mansfield, 27 Nov. 1795, Anne Wainwright     2 DO
Street, Mansfield, 23 Sept. 1799, Betsy Wainwright   2 DO
Streets, William, 8 Oct. 1785, Sarah Ross            2 DO
Streett, Thomas, 29 May 1800, Sarah Kennaday         3 HA-29
Streett, William, 15 Dec. 1799, Sarah Cox            3 HA-28
Stretch, Samuel, 13 Oct. 1799, Elizabeth Cook        6 BA
Stricker, John, 30 March 1797, Catherine Wilson      2 HA-349
Strickland, John, 30 June 1793, Alice Perry          1 BA-5
Strickland, Joseph, 22 Jan. 1789, Verlinda Page      2 PG-4
Stricklin, John, 8 Jan. 1781, Eliza Simpson          2 CH-457
Strickling, John, 4 Jan. 1782, Elizabeth Timmons     3 HA-5
Striebech, Christ'r, 9 Jan. 1790, N. Paul            29 BA-1
Strike, Nicholas, 4 Jan. 1794, Eleanor Fann          6 BA
Strike, Nicholas, 2 Jan. 1797, Margaret Phenix       3 BA-341
Stroble, Zachariah, 7 Jan. 1794, Cassandra Ann Amos  3 HA-23
Stroman, John, 8 June 1778, Mary Sitler              11 BA-1
Strong, George, 27 Oct. 1797, Elizabeth Crabbs       4 FR
Strong, Joseph, 1 Nov. 1789, Rachael Hale            11 BA-12
Strong, Joseph, 23 May 1795, Mary Allender           7 BA-2
Strong, Ludwick, 30 Oct. 1785, Mary Hill             11 BA-8
Strongware, Simon, 10 May 1798, Nancy Bishop         2 SO
Strop, Jas., 4 Feb. 1798, Mary Louderman             29 BA-9
Stroud, Thomas, 16 March 1780, Mary Barnhouse        3 HA-1
Stuardt, Lenard, 25 Dec. 1792, Elizab. Perril        2 FR-1168
Stuart, Hugh, 24 Feb. 1795, Margaret Wooden          6 BA
Stuart, Philip, 16 Dec. 1792, Mary Tell Baynes       3 PG-437
Stubbins, Charles, 6 July 1800, Johanna Dye          49 BA-1
Stubbles, Samuel, 20 Sept. 1800, Jane Reanser        3 BA-392
Stubbs, John, 7 April 1794, Sarah Quay               3 BA-285
Stubbs, Joseph, son of Daniel and Ruth, 4th day, 5 mo.,
    1786, Ruth Pyle, dau. of Moses and Mary          11 SF-210
Stuble, (or Huble), George, Nov. 1799, Cath. Oxx     3 WA-68
Stud, Caspar, 16 Jan. 1787, Margareth Schull         10 BA-188
Studor, Martin, 2 April 1792, Mary Wertenbaker       4 FR
Stull, Adam, 15 April 1788, Elizabeth Ramsbergh      4 FR
Stull, Daniel, 19 Dec. 1789, Mary Beatty             4 FR
Stull, John, 6 May 1790, Margaret Duttero            4 FR
Stull, Lawrence, 11 May 1778, Rebecca Gassaway       4 FR
Stump, Harman, 19 June 1793, Elizabeth Dallam        3 HA-22
Stump, John, 17 Oct. 1779, Cassandra Wilson          5 BA-13
Stump, Joseph, 15 March 1798, Eliz. Bogges           2 FR-1170
    4 FR gives the bride's name as Boggass.
Stumpf, George, 29 March 1795, Elis. Walter          3 WA-58
Stuntzer, Henry, 22 May 1796, Elizab. Roth           2 FR-1169
Sturgis, James, 3 Dec. 1799, Caty Purnell Jones      1 WO
Sturgis, John, 24 Jan. 1797, Tabitha Brumbly         1 WO
Sturgis, John, 25 Jan. 1797, Nancy Bishop            1 WO
Sturgis, Levin, 29 Nov. 1799, Nancy Taylor           1 WO
Sturgis, Richard, 18 Dec. 1798, Leah Gunn            1 WO
Sueman, John, 14 May 1791, Margaret Snyder           4 FR
Sueman, Peter, 25 June 1791, Anna Templing           4 FR
Suffrace, Charles, 10 Oct. 1785, Eliz. Liscomb       11 BA-8
Suhman, Adam, 23 Nov. 1790, Cath. Koblentz           2 FR-1168
Suit, Walter, 26 Aug. 1777, Susanna Davis            2 CH-457
Sulavane, Owen, 10 Dec. 1800, Elizabeth Fidamon      2 SF
Sulivan, James B., 9 April 1795, Eliza Ennalls       2 DO
Sulivan, John, 15 Feb. 1791, Elizabeth Collings      6 BA
Sulivane, Joseph, 20 May 1795, Ann Hooper            2 DO
Sullivan, Andrew Moore, 24 March 1798, Araminta Burnham
    3 BA-356
Sullivan, Daniel, 15 Oct. 1784, Mary Gray            10 BA-182
Sullivan, Dennis, 8 June 1778, Mary Henderson        11 BA-1
Sullivan, Jeremiah, 5 June 1783, Ann Hoy             11 BA-6
Sullivan, John, 13 April 1788, Rebeckah Widdon       18 BA-1
```

```
Sullivan, John P., 13 Oct. 1799, Harriot Linnaway      6 BA
Sullivan, Philip, 21 Sept.? 1781, Ann Shears           3 AA-417
Sullivan, Sylvester, 5 Aug. 1797, Rosanna Hawse        5 MO-114
Sullivan, Thomas, 23 Jan. 1783, Sarah Wood             3 AA-419
Sullivan, Thomas, (c.1791), Jemima Heir               15 BA-4
Sullivan, William, 12 Feb. 1782, Henrietta Wood        3 AA-418
Sullivan, William, 10 Aug. 1799, Mary Harryman         6 BA
Sullivane, Owin, 26 Dec. 1792, Ester Stanton           2 SF
Sullivant, Dennis, 25 Aug. 1782, Martha Griffin        3 AA-418
Sumblin, William, 23 Sept. 1794, Harriot Davis        18 BA-6
Summers, Alex'r, 25 March 1797, Mary Vinagar           4 FR
Summers, Andrew, 19 July 1795, Catherine Harp          6 BA
Summers, Benjamin, 11 Oct. 1798, Virlinder Beckwith    5 MO-115
Summers, Elijah, 11 April 1798, Rachel Shorter         2 DO
Summers, Elijah, 23 Aug. 1799, Betsy Crosswell         2 SO
Summers, James, 20 Jan. 1800, Martha Perry             3 BA-382
Summers, John, 17 Sept. 1778, Elizabeth Spear         11 BA-1
Summers, John, 27 Feb. 1794, Rebecca Scarce            3 PG-439
Summers, John, 12 Feb. 1795, Ann Workman               6 BA
Summers, Levin, 31 Dec. 1786, Elizabeth Willcoxon      3 PG-252
Summers, Nathaniel, 2 Jan. 1793, Sarah Scarce          3 PG-437
Summers, Paul, 14 April 1789, Susanna Ranter           2 PG-4
Summers, Peter, 2 Jan. 1783, Christena Hefner          4 FR
Summers, Philip, 19 Oct. 1798, Barbara Sower           4 FR
Summers, Stephen, 24 July 1787, Elizabeth Summers      1 SO-169
Summers, Thomas, 8 Feb. 1779, Mary Ann Brawney         2 CH-457
Summers, Thomas, of Thos., July 1789, Sophia Ward      1 SO-175
Summers, Thomas, 17 Oct. 1789, Patsy Harris            2 DO
Summers, William, 1 Oct. 1778, Rebecca Jacobs          2 MO-1
Summervill, Henry, 7 Aug. 1789, Priscilla Ball         2 DO
Summerville, Jno., 18 March 1783, Eleanor Malaphant   11 BA-6
Sumwald, George, 17 Oct. 1784, Mary Wort              11 BA-7
Sumwald, Phillip, 8 Jan. 1784, Elizabeth Krebs        10 BA-180
Sunafranck, George, 17 April 1799, Elizabeth Roof      4 FR
Sunday, Matthias, 19 May 1790, Elizabeth Lewis         3 BA-228
Sunderland, Benj'n, 20 July 1788, by Rev. Claggett; Mary
    Everet                                             4 AA
Sunpower, Adam, 5 Feb. 1781, Susanna Cronise           4 FR
Super, Joh., 4 April 1796, Elisab. Cart               50 BA-399
Suss, Godfrey, son of John George and Catherine, 16 Nov.
    1791, Anna Maria Kramer, dau. of Michael and Eliza-
    beth                                               5 FR-111
Suss, John George, son of John George and Maria Catherine,
    13 Feb. 1781, Maria Barbara Eigenbrod, dau. of John
    Yost and Eva Maria                                 5 FR-113
Suss, Paul, son of John George and Catherine, 4 Oct. 1787,
    Maria Magdalena Beyerle, dau. of Jacob             5 FR-114
Sute, Nath'l, 30 Dec. 1792, Elizab. Grover             2 FR-1169
Suter, Jacob, 25 May 1794, Margaretha Gortner         50 BA-394
Sutfin, William, 21 June 1783, Rachel Owin             4 FR
Sutherland, John, 23 Dec. 1777, Nelly Frazer           2 PG-3
Sutherland, John, 4 Dec. 1780, Margaret Murray         2 PG-5
Sutter, Peter, April 1799, Cath. Urban                 3 WA-67
Sutton, Isaac, 2 Nov. 1780, Ann Grimes                11 BA-4
Sutton, John, 21 Dec. 1797, Elizabeth Fenley           3 PG-443
Sutton, Jonathan, 16 Nov. 1791, Sally McCracken        3 HA-21
Sutton, Mathias, 13 Feb. 1799, Sally Dunnock           2 DO
Sutton, Nathan, 9 March 1800, Mary Fossee              6 BA
Sutton, Thos., 20 Jan. 1785, Ann Gotsil               11 BA-8
Swaidner, Adam, 25 March 1797, Eve Lamon               4 FR
Swaidner, Adam, 5 April 1799, Anne Cox                 4 FR
Swain, Benjamin, 4 Feb. 1794, Hannah Ellison           3 AA-424
Swain, Jacob, 2 May 1796, Mary Ambrose                 4 FR
Swain, Jeremiah, 24 July 1785, Rebecca Herbert        16 BA-3
Swamley, Jacob, 19 Jan. 1799, Eleanor Fulkes           5 MO-115
```

```
Swan, George, 13 Dec. 1796, Emmy Redman            2 FR-1169
Swan, Henry, 10 Jan. 1789, by Rev. Claggett; Minty Davis
     4 AA
Swan, Joseph, 7 Oct. 1790, Agnes Maxwell          11 BA-13
Swan, Matthew, 7 Sept. 1784, Ann McKean           11 BA-7
Swaney, John, 11 Feb. 1791, Phebe Berrier          4 FR
Swann, Joshua, 26 Dec. 1795, Nancy Helm            6 BA
Swann, Samuel, 7 May 1778, Susannah Punteney      11 BA-1
Swarz, John, 2 Nov. 1784, Mary Elizabeth Sholl    10 BA-182
Swayne, Charles, 14 Dec. 1799, Catherine Gire      4 FR
Swayne, Joseph Spires, 17 Aug. 1786, Amelia Ann Hutton  3 PG-251
Sweadner, Adam, 10 June 1797, Eve Lemmon           4 FR
Swearingen, George, 18 Jan. 1798, Ruth Wilcoxon    6 MO
Swedner, Henry, 27 June 1786, Elizabeth Sensor     4 FR
Sweeny, Loyd, 11 Feb. 1790, Mary Mangun            2 PG-4
Sweeting, John, 28 March 1793, Susanna (Hiser?)   18 BA-5
Sweeting, John, 12 Nov. 1799, Tabitha Bowen        6 BA
Sweeting, Thomas, 14 Nov. 1799, Catherine Wineman  5 BA-13
Sweringen, Thos., 7 Jan. 1790, Els Pope            3 PG-256
Swift, David, 23 Feb. 1796, Lettice Biggs          3 HA-25
     7 BA-3 gives the date as 25 Feb. 1796.
Swigett, John, 19th day, 3 mo., 1780, Mary Breeding  2 SF-288
Swiggate, Benjamin, 29 Oct. 1787, Nancy Tregoe     2 DO
Swiggate, James, 30 Nov. 1790, Fama Adams          2 DO
Swindall, Peter, 6 April 1786, Catherine Hisdale   5 BA-13
Swisher, Matthias, 23 Nov. 1796, Catherine Shank   4 FR
Switzer, Jno., 18 Oct. 1798, Patty Kimble         29 BA-9
Switser, Lawrence, 31 Oct. 1797, Sarah Nickey      4 FR
Sydel, Hennrich, May 1799, Mary Weaddle            3 WA-67
Sykes, James, 4 Aug. 1784, Eliza Goldsborough      2 DO
Sylvester, George, 7 Jan. 1798, Rachel Rumage      6 BA
Syme, Nicholas, 25 July 1777, Elizabeth Johnson    2 CH-457
Synnott, Edward, 3 Sept. 1785, Ann Coudren         3 BA-190


Tabbs, Barton, 20 June 1779, Elizabeth Bond.       1 CA-2
Tabbs, George C., 17 Feb. 1799, Lucretia Hopewell  4 SM-184
Tabler, Adam, 21 May 1779, Philepeana Yesterday    4 FR
Tabler, Melchor, 7 April 1779, Philipeana Berger   4 FR
Tabler, Michael, 13 April 1783, Catherine Coonce   4 FR
Tabler, Michael, 20 Jan. 1789, Mary Roberts        4 FR
Tabler, Wm., 16 June 1780, Margaret Yesterday      4 FR
Tagert, John, 12 Oct. 1790, Mary Williamson        5 BA-14
Tague, Thomas, 13 July 1793, Rebecca Henley        6 BA
Talbert, John, 19 Oct. 1777, Ann Davis             2 CH-457
Talbot, James, 5 Dec. 1789, Mary Hilton            4 FR
Talbot, John, 17 June 1784, Henrietta Philips     11 BA-7
Talbot, Richard, 20 Aug. 1778, Achsa Wells        11 BA-1
Talbot, Richard, 29 Oct. 1792, by Rev. Dorsey; Rachel Todd
     4 AA
Talbot, Thomas, 15 April 1780, Susanna Rhodes      1 CA-3
Talbott, Basil, 19 June 1788, Keziah Lowe          3 PG-254
Talbott, Benjamin, son of John and Mary, 6th day, 10 mo.,
     1785, Susanna Chandlee, dau. of William and Mary  3 SF
Talbott, Charles, 28 Oct. 1789, Ann Ramsower       4 FR
Talbott, Edmund, 10 Oct. 1780, Elizabeth Parker    3 HA-2
Talbott, James, 5 Jan. 1788, by Rev. Forrest; Ann Poulson
     4 AA
Talbott, John, son of John and Mary, 30th day, 12 mo., 1790,
     Elizabeth Plummer, dau. of Samuel and Mary    3 SF
Talbott, John, 19 Oct. 1796, Sarah Taylor          6 BA
Talbott, Joseph, son of John and Mary, 1st day, 11 mo.,
     1786, Mary Farquhar, dau. of Allen and Sarah  3 SF
Talbott, Kinsey, son of John and Mary, 21st day, 8 mo.,
     1800, Deborah Plummer, dau. of Joseph West and
     Mary                                          3 SF
```

```
Talbott, Paul, 6 March 1791, Sarah Ann Bryan          3 PG-257
Talbott, Thomas, 29 Jan. 1795, Elizabeth Rutledge     1 BA-7
Talbutt, George, 6 Aug. 1778, Mary McDaniel,          2 MO-1
Tall, Anthony, 23 Dec. 1783, Lina Webb                2 DO
Tall, Anthony, 17 April 1800, Nancy Harrington        3 BA-385
Tall, Bruffitt, 13 Feb. 1798, Elizabeth Woodland      2 DO
Tall, Daniel, 17 April 1798, Henney Tall              2 DO
    1 DO-39 gives the date as 21 June 1798, and the
    bride's name as Henrietta.
Tall, John, 25 Oct. 1781, Elizabeth White             2 DO
Tall, John, 1 April 1790, Hagar Havergail             2 DO
Tall, John, 26 Jan. 1795, Henny Frazier               2 DO
Tall, Walter, 25 Nov. 1794, Ann Drill                 2 FR-1178
Tall, William, 29 Jan. 1790, Elizabeth Navey          2 DO
Tall, William, 16 Sept. 1799, Sarah Harrington        2 DO
    1 DO-40 gives the date as 17 Sept. 1799.
Tall, Young, 1 Feb. 1796, Sarah Lamb.                 2 DO
Talley, Ebenezer, 30 May 1794, Margaret Philips       4 FR
Tamplin, Richard, 17 Oct. 1795, Eve Runner            4 FR
Tamplin, William, 20 June 1793, Susanna Gire          4 FR
Tannehill, William, 9 Dec. 1785, Elizabeth Simmons    4 FR
Tanner, Henry, 10 Dec. 1778, Mary Games               1 CA-2
Tanner, Isaac, 11 Nov. 1784, Marg't Reese             11 BA-8
Tanyhill, Leonard, 2 Oct.? 1778, Ann Anly             5 CH-1
Tappan, Abner, 30 Jan. 1792, Elizabeth Stanford       2 DO
Tarlton, Elisha, 18 Aug. 1799, Ann Greenwell          2 SM-138
Tarlton, Ignatius, 9 March 1783, Mary Adams           3 SM-61
Tarlton, Jeremiah, 29 June 1786, Mary Harbert Briscoe 4 FR
Tarman, Benj'n, 8 March 1791, Lettee Fields           3 PG-257
Taron, Wm., 16 July 1797, Susannah Cook               29 BA-8
Tarr, James, 14 Sept. 1799, Mary Skinner              2 DO
Tarr, John, 31 Jan. 1797, Peggy Allen                 1 WO
Tarr, Major, 3 Dec. 1799, Betsey Johnson              1 WO
Tarr, Samuel, before 31 Aug. 1796, by Rev. Mills; Rachel
    Isaac                                             4 AA
Tarr, William, 22 Sept. 1797, Hannah Guthery          1 WO
Tate, James, 29 Jan. 1782, Elizabeth Coulter          5 BA-14
Tatom, John, 1 March 1797, Temperance Holding         4 KE-72
Tawes, John, March 1782, Catherine Ward               1 SO-174
Taws, John, 27 Aug. 1799, Leah Boston                 2 SO
Taylor, Amasa, 1 Jan. 1781, Jemimah Kimble            3 HA-3
Taylor, Aquila, (4 Feb. 1789), Sarah Holland          20 BA-1
Taylor, Aquilla, 6 March 1798, Rachel Knight          4 FR
Taylor, Arthur, 31 July 1798, Polly Lester            1 WO
Taylor, Ezekiel, 14 May 1799, Charity Foxwell         2 SO
Taylor, George, 24 Nov. 1792, Martha Goldsmith        6 BA
Taylor, George, 5 Sept. 1796, Polly Timmons           1 WO
Taylor, Henry, 3 May 1790, Ann Griffith               4 FR
Taylor, Henry H., 30 April 1786, Ann Benneham (or Renneham)
    11 BA-9
Taylor, Hezekiah, 20 Oct. 1799, Mary Brown            6 BA
Taylor, Hope, 23 Oct. 1798, Rachel Burnett            1 WO
Taylor, Hugh. 13 Sept. 1786, Elizabeth Currey         3 BA-191
Taylor, Ignatius, 13 May 1780, Margaret Jordan        3 SM-58
Taylor, Jacob, 21 March 1799, Sarah Thompson          6 BA
Taylor, James, 7 June 1784, Mary Jones                3 BA-203
    3 BA-192 gives the date as 17 June 1784.
Taylor, James, 24 Jan. 1785, Eliza Lucas              11 BA-8
Taylor, James, 13 Oct. 1792, Margaret Murry           3 BA-257
Taylor, James, 26 Aug. 1795, Jane White               3 HA-24
    7 BA-2 gives the date as 27 Aug. 1795.
Taylor, James, 11 Dec. 1795, Peggy Aydelott           1 WO
Taylor, James, 6 Nov. 1796, Jemima Coward             6 BA
Taylor, James, 21 Nov. 1797, Elizabeth Reams          6 BA
Taylor, James, 25 Jan. 1800, Sarah Aitkin             3 HA-29
    2 HA-351 gives the date as 6 Feb. 1800.
```

```
Taylor, Jenifer, 24 March 1799, Elizabeth Milburn      4 SM-184
Taylor, Jesse, 26 May 1784, Ruth Bale                  4 FR
Taylor, Jessee, 8 Dec. 1796, Mary Thomas               7 BA-3
Taylor, John, 20? June 1780, Aliceanna Melikin         3 HA-2
Taylor, John, 29 July 1780, Mary Griffin              11 BA-4
Taylor, John, 6 Nov. 1780, Rebecca Jones               2 PG-7
Taylor, John, 13 May 1783, Elizabeth Tarlton           3 SM-61
Taylor, Jno., 5 Oct. 1784, Sarah Dean                 11 BA-7
Taylor, Jno., 25 March 1787, Eleanor Leaf             11 BA-10
Taylor, Jno., 10 Oct. 1790, Eleanor Hooper            11 BA-13
Taylor, John, 12 Sept. 1791, Sarah West                2 DO
Taylor, John, 1 July 1795, Rebecca Sendrum             3 HA-24
Taylor, John, 10 May 1796, Polly Powell                1 WO
Taylor, John, 11 Dec. 1797, Temperance Acworth         2 SO
   3 SO gives the date as 30 Nov. 1797.
Taylor, John, 21 June 1798, Hanna Cassol               3 AL-5
Taylor, John, 18 Oct. 1799, Elisabeth Catlin           3 BA-379
Taylor, John, 4 Nov. 1799, Mary Kirwan                 2 DO
Taylor, John Gibbs, Jr., 12 Oct. 1797, Hannah Aydelott 1 WO
Taylor, Joseph, 10 July 1778, Eleanor Ryley            4 FR
Taylor, Joseph, 22 Sept. 1789, Hester Dunkin          11 BA-12
Taylor, Levin, 24 March 1785, Ruth Hoppin             11 BA-8
Taylor, Mathias Costen, 14 June 1793, Betsey Fitchett  2 DO
Taylor, Matthew, 26 Nov. 1798, Mary Topham             3 BA-365
Taylor, Moses, 27 Dec. 1792, Nancy Durban              1 BA-5
Taylor, Nathaniel, 15 May 1795, Mary Collins           7 BA-3
Taylor, Reuben, 29 June 1797, Jane Henderson           2 AL-700
Taylor, Richard, 6 Feb. 1777, Margaret Welsh           3 BA-172
Taylor, Richard, 9 Jan. 1785, Eleanor Spicer          11 BA-8
Taylor, Richard, 4 Dec. 1788, Mary Johnson             4 FR
Taylor, Richard, 2 Feb. 1789, Clemency Thomson         1 BA-1
Taylor, Richard, 24 Nov. 1796, Sus. Riddle             2 FR-1178
Taylor, Richard, 27 July 1797, Mary Thomas            47 BA-1
Taylor, Richard, 25 Dec. 1798, by Rev. Ridgely; Martha
   Druce?                                              4 AA
Taylor, Richard, 19 Dec. 1800, Eleanor Courtney        3 HA-30
   2 HA-352 gives the date as 25 Dec. 1800.
Taylor, Robert, 1 April 1794, by Rev. Benton Riggen; Margaret
   Wheeler                                             4 AA
   3 HA-23 gives the date as 1 April 1794.
Taylor, Samuel, 11 April 1793, Rhody Hurley            3 PG-438
Taylor, Samuel, 24 April 1797, Sally Taylor            1 WO
Taylor, Samuel, 13 Jan. 1798, Milicent Wilson          4 KE-72
Taylor, Solomon, 27 Jan. 1780, Eleanor Cheney          3 AA-416
Taylor, Thomas, 21 May 1795, Barbara Hook              6 BA
Taylor, Thomas, 31 Jan. 1799, Ruth Stansbury           6 BA
Taylor, Thomas Stubbs, 5 Oct. 1797, Anne Fox Lindsay   3 BA-351
   See also 47 BA-1
Taylor, Wm., 20 Feb. 1781, Rugzear (sic) Walcove       4 FR
Taylor, William, 9 Jan. 1783, Hannah Judah             5 BA-14
Taylor, William, 9 May 1790, Rebekah Hines            18 BA-2
Taylor, William, 19 July 1790, Barbara Lymes          26 BA-1
Taylor, William, 19 June 1794, Mary Lee                2 DO
Taylor, William, 30 Dec. 1795, Elizabeth Townshand     3 PG-441
Taylor, William, 31 Aug. 1796, Elizabeth Garey         1 AL-53
Taylor, William, 17 Aug. 1797, Priscilla Furnice       3 SO
Taylor, Wm., 13 Feb. 1799, Nancy Sturgis               1 WO
Taylor, William H., 18 Dec. 1799, Sally Johnson        1 WO
Tayman, Joseph, 3 Feb. 1778, Susanna Clow              3 AA-414
Taynobb, Thomas, 12 March 1794, Martha Haithorn        3 HA-23
Teague, Jacob, 22 Dec. 1796, Zaporah Rounds            1 WO
Teague, Laban, 15 June 1796, Elizabeth Kilbourn        6 BA
Teal, Henry, 12 Nov. 1785, Margaret Nollert            4 FR
Teal, Jacob, 30 June 1791, by Rev. Forrest; Elizabeth
   Lininger                                            3 FR
```

Tear, Daniel, 17 April 1797, Charlotte McCoy   35 BA-5
Tearse, Andrew, 15 May 1799, Cloe Everit   3 HA-28
Teer, Owen, 17 Oct. 1790, Patty Greenfield   18 BA-2
Tenant, Thomas, 8 Nov. 1796, Mary Waters   3 BA-333
Tench, Leonard, 17 Feb. 1795, Sarah Langley   3 CH-162
Tennis, Jacob, 26 Sept. 1796, Sarah Williams   5 BA-14
Tensfelt, Zach's, 15 June 1800, Cath. Marg. Goldenberg
    50 BA-407
Terral (or Fairall), Mathew, 19 Jan. 1797, Helhan Barnes
    2 AL-700
Terry and Charlot, slaves of Notley Young, 5 June 1797 8 MO-14
Terry, John, 29 May 1800, Sarah Abbott   2 DO
Terry, William, 8 Nov. 1800, Mary Moor   6 BA
Tertzbaugh, John, 7 June 1783, Catherine Keplinger   4 FR
Tesh, Peter, 3 Sept. 1797, Polly Bankard   50 BA-402
Tesh, Philip, 3 Sept. 1797, Polly Bankert   29 BA-8
Tevis, Benjamin, 19 Dec. 1786, Helen Elder   6 BA
Tevis, Daniel, 26 Jan. 1792, Eliz. Woolery   29 BA-3
Tevis, Nathaniel, 23 Oct. 1787, Kesiah Simpson   6 BA
Tevis, Thomas, 7 Oct. 1790, Elizabeth Mackelfresh   27 BA-1
Tharsher, John, 29 Sept. 1783, Elizabeth Tutterer   4 FR
Thatcher, Ignatius, 16 July 1780, -(?)- Saporly   2 CH-457
Theobald, Robert, 27 March 1796, Nancy Francis Wood   3 BA-321
Thomas, Anthony, 31 Jan. 1782, Lucy Seissell   2 PG-3
Thomas, Aquilla, 11 Sept. 1797, Ruthy Ellis   4 FR
Thomas, Archibald, 2 June 1778, Sarah Trammell   4 FR
Thomas, Charles, 25 Nov. 1786, Sarah Tall   2 DO
Thomas, Dan'l, 29 Jan. 1780, Peggy Dannelly   4 FR
Thomas, David, 1 Jan. 1795, Philip, negro slave of Eliza-
    beth Doyle   8 MO-9
Thomas, David, 8 June 1800, Sarah Johnson   3 HA-29
Thomas, Evan, 27 Feb. 1781, Ruth Arnold,   3 BA-180
Thomas, Evan, 6 March 1785, Sarah Phesay   3 HA-9
Thomas, Gabriel, 11 March 1779, Mary Ramsbergh   4 FR
Thomas, George, 11 May 1783, Rosanna Peck   4 FR
Thomas, Griffith, 10 Oct. 1793, Elizabeth Grove   4 FR
Thomas, Henry, 25 Oct. 1790, Deborah Abbott   2 DO
Thomas, Henry, 23 Nov. 1790, Marg. Remsperger   2 FR-1178
    4 FR gives the bride's name as Ramsbergh.
Thomas, Hezekiah, 27 June 1780, Jane White   2 CH-457
    2 PG-3 gives the date as 27 June 1784.
Thomas, Isaac, 17 Nov. 1796, Mary Flack   4 FR
Thomas, James, 8 April 1778, Margaret Crow   11 BA-1
Thomas, James, 14 Aug. 1790, Elizabeth Vickers   2 DO
Thomas, James, 27 April 1791, Henretta Cryer   2 DO
Thomas, James, 1 Feb. 1796, Arabella Barnes   3 HA-24
    47 BA-1 gives the date as 4 Feb. 1796.
Thomas, John, 23 June 1778, Martha Henderson   11 BA-1
Thomas, John, 2 May 1781, Rachel Theft   3 HA-4
Thomas, John, 22 Aug. 1782, Biddy Smith   11 BA-5
Thomas, John, 5 April 1783, Catherine Wortz   4 FR
Thomas, John, 30 April 1786, Eliz. Remsperger   2 FR-1178
Thomas, John, 16 March 1787, Catherine Thomas   4 FR
Thomas, John, 9 June 1789, Eleanor McGill   4 FR
Thomas, John, 14 July 1789, Sarah Barber   2 FR-1178
Thomas, John, 25 November 1792, Mary Tuness   2 DO
Thomas, John, 11 Dec. 1798, by Rev. Wyatt; Elizabeth
    Gausar?   4 AA
Thomas, John, 5 Sept. 1799, Nancy Spansby   3 BA-377
Thomas, John, 3 June 1800, Polly Roach   2 SO
Thomas, Jonah, son of John, 29th day, 5 mo., 1787, Rebecca
    Parrish, dau. of John   1 SF
Thomas, Joseph, 12 May 1797, Polly Willson   2 DO
Thomas, Joseph, 27 Oct. 1799, Hannah Carty   3 HA-28
    2 HA-351 gives the date as 29 Oct. 1799.

Thomas, Leonard, 18 March 1785, Barbara Yose   4 FR
Thomas, Leonh., 20 March 1785, Barb. Johs   2 FR-1178
Thomas, Levey, 1 Dec. 1789, Elizabeth Reeves   2 FR-1178
Thomas, Levi, 1 Dec. 1787, Delilah Noble   2 DO
Thomas, Levin, 28 July 1785, Nancy Ward   2 DO
Thomas, Levin, 17 Oct. 1797, Margaret Satchell   2 DO
Thomas, Lewis, 10 Aug. 1789, Mary Lasque   3 BA-227
Thomas, Moses, 29 Dec. 1799, Nancy McClain   2 HA-351
Thomas, Nathan, 10 May 1782, Clarissa Edelen   4 FR
Thomas, Nicholas, 12 Oct. 1796, Margaret Hogans   2 DO
Thomas, Notley, 7 Jan. 1798, Ann Nolley   3 PG-443
Thomas, Peter, 7 May 1799, Barb. Schafer   2 FR-1179
Thomas, Philip, 7 March 1782, Sarah Margaret Weems 3 AA-418
Thomas, Richard, 6 March 1799, Polly Hallock   2 DO
Thomas, Richard Snowden, son of Samuel, 13th day, 12 mo.,
  1784, Mary Mifflin, dau. of Southey   7 SF-121
Thomas, Robert, 29 Aug. 1799, Eve Reese   3 BA-376
Thomas, Samuel, 15 Dec. 1796, Hannah Ewalt   4 KE-72
Thomas, Thomas, 27 April 1781, Jane Abell   3 SM-59
Thomas, Thomas, 26 Dec. 1799, Margaret Thomas   2 DO
Thomas, Tristram, 11 April 1797, Eleanor Bendall   2 DO
Thomas, Trustram, 23 Oct. 1787, Eleanor Langfitt   2 DO
Thomas, Tyler, 9 May 1799, Rachael Thomas   3 SM-57
Thomas, Valentine, 17 March 1799, Eliz. Keller   2 FR-1179
Thomas, William, 14 April 1779, Henrietta Briscoe   3 SM-57
Thomas, William, 2 May 1780, Anne Allen   3 SM-58
Thomas, Wm., 16 Oct. 1783, Marg't Baxter   11 BA-6
Thomas, Wm., 24 June 1785, Sarah Purkins   2 FR-1178
Thomas, William, son of Tristram and Elizabeth, 7 March
  1787, Elizabeth Thomas, dau. of William and Rachel
  1 TA-330
Thomas, William, 5 Aug. 1790, Mary Soward   2 DO
Thomas, William, 30 Jan. 1794, Janet Anne Foure   3 BA-281
Thomas, William, 6 Sept. 1796, Mary Whealton   2 DO
Thomas, William, 15 Jan. 1798, Catherine Bradshaw   3 BA-354
  35 BA-6 gives the date as 15 Feb. 1798.
Thomas, William, 14 Nov. 1799, Martha Patrick   6 BA
Thomason, William, 16 Oct. 1783, Margaret Baxter   3 BA-185
Thompson, Alexander, 20 Nov. 1798, Margaret Arnest 3 BA-365
Thompson, Ambrose, 10 Dec. 1791, Mary Ann Thompson 4 FR
Thompson, Amos, 12 July 1793, Elizabeth Hays   6 BA
Thompson, Amos, 10 Oct. 1799, Nancy Deagane   6 BA
Thompson, Andrew, 30 Jan. 1795, Rachel Lawrence   4 FR
Thompson, Anthony, 24 Oct. 1786, Mary King   2 DO
Thompson, Aquila, Feb. 1778, Elizabeth Wallingford 11 BA-1
Thompson, Aquila, 2 Oct. 1782, Hannah Woolsey   3 HA-7
Thompson, Basil, 5 March 1780, Cloe Brown   1 SM-137
Thompson, Benjamin, 31 Dec. 1795, Charlotte Tripolet 4 FR
Thompson, Benj., 26 Jan. 1799, Eliz. Haney   5 MO-115
Thompson, Charles, 19 April 1796, Elizabeth Timms   8 MO-12
Thompson, Clement, 23 March 1788, Sarah Davis   18 BA-1
Thompson, David, 6 April 1779, Sarah Drew   5 HA
  3 HA-1 gives the date as 1 April 1780.
Thompson, Edward, 19 Nov. 1778, Mary Fitzgerald   11 BA-1
Thompson, Edward, 8 Feb. 1781, Elizabeth Hanson   3 HA-3
Thompson, Edward, 20 Oct. 1793, Mary Dunn   3 BA-275
Thompson, Ephraim, 13 April 1781, Mary Williams   2 DO
Thompson, George, 18 Sept. 1789, by Rev. Hagerty; Mary
  McCabe   4 AA
Thompson, Henry, 13 May 1796, Elizabeth Leese   4 FR
Thompson, Henry, 29 March 1798, Anne Lux Bowley   3 BA-357
Thompson, Ingree, 7 Nov. 1789, Mary Smith   18 BA-2
Thompson, Jack, 27 Sept. 1800, Becca Benson; blacks 7 BA-4
Thompson, Jas., 18 April 1782, Johanna Hicky   11 BA-5
Thompson, James, 30 Nov. 1788, Rhoda Athey   3 PG-255

```
Thompson, Jas., 20 March 1794, Maria Munnings        29 BA-5
Thompson, James, 22 May 1794, Elizabeth Cleaves       3 BA-287
Thompson, Jas., or Jos., 24 Jan. 1799, Polly Hoss    29 BA-10
Thompson, James Frazier, 7 June 1778, Sarah Moore     2 PG-3
Thompson, John, 3 Dec. 1778, Sarah Brown              5 HA
Thompson, John, 5 July 1782, Susanna Luckey           3 HA-6
Thompson, John, 1 Dec. 1785, Deborah Test            11 BA-9
Thompson, Jno., 14 June 1787, Eliza Parks            11 BA-10
Thompson, John, 12 Sept. 1787, Barbara Cross          4 FR
Thompson, John, 12 Oct. 1790, by Rev. Green; Mary Rawlings
     4 AA
Thompson, John, 22 Aug. 1791, Ann English            18 BA-3
Thompson, John, 22 Aug. 1791, Ann English, formerly McFee
     3 BA-235
Thompson, John, 9 Dec. 1792, Catherine Cotter         3 BA-259
Thompson, John, 17 Dec. 1795, by Rev. Ridgely; Anne
     Marriott                                         4 AA
Thompson, John, 21 Dec. 1796, Hannah Neftland         3 BA-333
Thompson, Joseph, 1 April 1779, Ann Eliz'th Brooke    4 FR
Thompson, Joseph, 5 Sept. 1786, Jane Black            3 BA-191
Thompson, Joseph, 28 June 1797, Sophia Turner?       29 BA-8
Thompson, Josias, 19 Nov. 1795, Jane Forsyth          5 BA-14
Thompson, Lesly, 19 June 1791, Elizabeth Holbrook     6 BA
Thompson, Macky, 2 Aug. 1785, Elizabeth Cope          2 DO
Thompson, Moses, 1 May 1793, Mary Eyres               5 BA-14
Thompson, Nathaniel G., 28 July 1792, Elizabeth Jackson
     14 BA-14
Thompson, Richard, 6 March 1796, Eliz. Pelly          5 MO-113
Thompson, Richard, 24 July 1799, Elizabeth Kirk       4 SM-184
Thompson, Rob't, 22 May 1789, Marg't Manley          11 BA-12
Thompson, Thomas, 28 Jan. 1780, Elizabeth Willmott    3 HA-1
Thompson, Thomas, 2 Nov. 1780, Elizabeth Jones        1 CA-3
Thompson, Thomas, 23 Sept. 1782, Priscilla Mace       2 DO
Thompson, Thomas, 29 July 1784, Catharine Faller      4 FR
Thompson, Thomas, 15 Feb. 1786, Mary Harper           2 DO
Thompson, Thomas, 4 Jan. 1800, Rebecca Rawley         2 DO
Thompson, Wm., 11 May 1797, Mary Miltenberger        29 BA-8
Thompson, William, 10 Aug. 1797, Elizabeth Anderson   3 BA-348
Thompson, William, 3 Feb. 1798, Margaret Ward         2 DO
Thompson, William, 28 June 1798, Jane Summers         3 BA-359
Thompson, Robert, 20 Dec. 1794, Catherine Askew       3 BA-296
Thompson, Wm., 15 April 1800, Eliz. Snyder           29 BA-11
Thomson, Benj'n, 31 Dec. 1795, Charl. Tripolett       2 FR-1178
Thomson, David, 25 Dec. 1794, Sarah Eagleston         6 BA
Thomson, Henry, 15 May 1796, Elizab. Liess            2 FR-1178
Thomson, John, 29 April 1790, Mary Sellers            2 FR-1178
Thomson, John, 14 June 1796, Eve Shaw                 6 BA
Thomson, Sam'l, 11 Feb. 1790, Ann Walker              3 PG-256
Thomson, Wm., 12 March 1791, Mary Poe                29 BA-2
Thorn, Henry, before 30 Nov. 1779, Elizabeth Wilson   2 PG-1
Thorn, Henry B., 28 Feb. 1790, Mary Thorn             3 PG-257
Thorn, William, 16 Oct. 1799, Sarah Sater             1 BA-9
     See also 4 BA-75.
Thornberry, John, 25 Dec. 1786, Sarah Bentley         4 FR
Thornburgh, Joseph, 11th mo., 21 day, 1798, Cassandra
     Ellicott                                         6 SF
Thornburgh, Robert, 10 Nov. 1793, Elizabeth Kittleman
     (or Giderman)                                    3 BA-279
Thornbury, John, 26 Dec. 1786, Sarah Bently           2 FR-1178
Thornbury, Thomas, 18 Nov. 1788, Prudence Collins     4 FR
Thorne, Stephen, 22 Jan. 1799, Sally Owens            3 SO
Thornell, Robert, 1 Dec. 1789, J. Tate               29 BA-1
Thorns, Stephen, 15 Dec. 1798, Sally Owens            2 SO
Thornton, Henry, 16 March 1798, Euphame Townsend      1 WO
Thornton, John, 10 April 1780, Jane Dunstone          3 HA-1
```

Thorp, Isac, 15 May 1798, Mary Taylor					2 AL-701
Thrall, Sam'l, 21 July 1785, Ann Collins					11 BA-8
Thralls, Jacob, 18 Feb. 1797, Eleanor Prather				3 PG-443
Thralls, Richard, 3 Jan. 1788, Lucy Mullikin				3 PG-254
Thrap, Wm., 29 Dec. 1785, Frances Baker					11 BA-9
Thrasher, Eli, 26 Oct. 1791, Henrietta Lamar				4 FR
Thrasher, Elias, 4 Nov. 1788, Sarah Lamar				2 FR-1178
Threll, Nathan'l, 4 Aug. 1799 Barbara Menzern				1 FR-59
Thurston, Samuel, 23 Oct. 1800, Maria Norris				3 BA-394
Tibbels, Thomas, 17 Aug. 1799, Mary Bradshaw				3 BA-376
Tibbles, John, 27 Nov. 1796, Mary Alter					1 TA-330
Ticklin, Jeremiah, 6 Nov. 1781, Mary Raily				3 SM-59
Tidings, Heley?, 31 Jan. 1782, Mary Read					2 PG-3
Tidings?, Kiley or Adey, 31 March 1793, Frances Atwil			22 BA-2
Tilden, Charles, 17 Aug. 1797, Anna Buchanan				4 KE-72
Tilden, John, 20 Nov. 1800, Eliza Barriere				3 BA-395
Tile, Solomon, 15 Oct. 1796, Christina Farmar				3 WA-61
Tilghman, James, 18 Feb. 1778, by Rev. Love; Elizabeth
	Johns									4 AA
Tilghman, Col. Tench, 9 June 1783, Anna Maria Tilghman,
	dau. of Matthew and Anna						1 TA-331
Tillard, Col. Edward, 15 Sept. 1782, Ann Lyles				3 AA-418
Tillen, Thomas, 27 June 1797, Elizabeth Joyce				3 BA-346
Tilliard, Col. Edward, 17 Nov. 1792, Sarah Estep			4 FR
Tillingham, George, 12 Nov. 1796, Mary Dawlin				4 KE-72
Tilyard, William, March 1778, Mary Conner				11 BA-1
Timmons, Belitha, 6 Sept. 1799, Rebecca Taylor				1 WO
Timmons, Charles, 11 Sept. 1793, Mary Furney				4 FR
Timmons, Edward, 5 Dec. 1796, by Rev. Green; Margaret Morriss
	4 AA
Timmons, Ephriam, 16 Dec. 1796, Patty Holloway				1 WO
Tinges, Henry W., 28 April 1795, Sarah Ilger				29 BA-6
Tinges, John, 5 July 1795, Barbara Worthberger				6 BA
Tingle, William, 4 Feb. 1796, Sarah Long					1 WO
Tinnely, Charles Brooke, 27 Dec. 1797, Elizabeth Janes			4 FR
Tinsdale, Thomas, 29 Dec. 1796, Agnes Melvin				1 WO
Tipton, Jarret, 11 Jan. 1787, by Rev. Pigman; Rachel
	Wilson									4 AA
Tipton, Micajah, 20 Dec. 1798, Anne Leaf					45 BA-3
Tipton, Solomon, 1 Nov. 1793, Mary Randall				3 BA-279
Tison, Isaac, son of Elisha and Mary, 8th day, 11 mo., 1797,
	Elizabeth Thomas, dau. of Evan and Rachel			6 SF
Titloe, Abraham, 17 Aug. 1782, Susanna Tertsbaugh			4 FR
Titlow, Christian, 24 Sept. 1782, Barbara Rowe				4 FR
Titus, Tunis, 7 March 1798, Monarchy Kelly				4 FR
Toben, John, 2 Jan. 1799, Jane Lodge					3 BA-367
Tobin, James, 21 April 1787, Eliza Pearson				11 BA-10
Todd, Andrew, 29 Aug. 1782, Elizabeth Sipes				4 FR
Todd, Basil, 29 Aug. 1782, Sarah Grimes					4 FR
Todd, Benjamin, 17 July 1789, Mary Andrews				2 DO
Todd, Benjamin, Jr., 3 Dec. 1798, Nancy Travers				2 DO
Todd, David, 23 June 1791, Jane Coward					2 DO
Todd, Jacob, 9 April 1785, Comfort Ross					2 DO
Todd, John, 1 Dec. 1791, Mary German					6 BA
Todd, Joseph, 1 Jan. 1798, Nancy Dean					2 DO
Todd, Joshua, 29 Oct. 1792, Sophia Hyatt					4 FR
Todd, Lancelot, 20 Aug. 1775, Mary Leakins				11 BA-1
Todd, Levin, 6 May 1800, Keziah Bramble					2 DO
Todd, Naboth, 18 Dec. 1797, Betsy Ross					2 DO
Todd, Nicholas, 29 May 1783, Ann Leaken					11 BA-6
Todd, Owen, 20 April 1800, Mary Bissett					6 BA
Todd, Philip, 22 Oct. 1795, Elizabeth Goulding				6 BA
Todd, Thomas, 4 June 1799, by Rev. Wyatt; Christian Marshall
	4 AA
Todd, Warfield, 22 Nov. 1796, Elenor Ball				2 FR-1178

```
Tolbert, Benjamin, 6 Dec. 1787, Hannah Combs          6 BA
Tolburt, James, 2 Jan. 1788, Ann Paulson              4 FR
Tolburt, Josias, 5 June 1796, Milly Bayne             3 PG-442
Tolburt, Levi, 27 Feb. 1794, Jamima Smith             3 PG-439
Tolbut, Jesse, 16 Nov. 1794, Mildred Lanham           3 PG-440
Tolley, James Walter, 21 May 1799, Susanna Howard    12 BA-370
Tolly, Thomas, 23 Dec. 1790, Elizabeth Bell           2 DO
Tolper, Zephaniah, 23 Dec. 1799, Ann Jones           29 BA-11
Tolson, Francis, 2 March 1794, Elizabeth Simms        3 PG-439
Tolson, Isaac, 1 July 1781, Nearnia? Lord             3 HA-4
Tolson, Isaac, 22 July 1781, Nancy Stallions          3 HA-4
Tolson, Isaac, 20 Oct. 1781, Ann Collins              3 HA-5
Tomelty, Henry, 5 Jan. 1783, Eliza Flemmon           11 BA-6
Tomkins, John, 27 Sept. 1787, Nancy Norwood           2 CH-457
Tomkins, John, son of Benjamin and Mary, of Fawn Twp.,
    York Co., Penna., 20th day, 5 mo., 1789, Sarah
    Burgess, dau. of Joseph and Deborough             9 SF-53
Tomlinson, James, 25 July 1795, Mary Paulson          4 FR
Tomlinson, Joseph, 28 April 1791, Margaret Noel       6 BA
Tomlinson, Richard, 3 Nov. 1793, Phoebe Neff          1 AL-52
Tomlinson, Samuel, 21 March 1796, Hannah Fox          3 BA-321
    See also 35 BA-4.
Tompkins, William, 26 Dec. 1800, Mary Farr            2 CH-457
Tompson, Baptist, 7 Nov. 1779, Mary Lancaster         2 CH-457
Tompson, James, 30 Dec. 1790, Mary Philips            3 PG-258
Tool, James, 8 June 1782, Elizabeth Cecil             4 FR
Toole, James, 9 Aug. 1788, Susanna Moore              5 BA-14
Toon, John, 2 Dec. 1800, Mary McCrea                  6 BA
Toon, Samuel, 20 March 1799, Hetty Tenant             3 BA-369
Topham, Matthew, 2 June 1796, Mary Jacobs             5 BA-14
Tornbach, Wm., 3 Dec. 1786, M. Hahn                  29 BA-1
Tornquist, Geirge, 7 Aug. 1800, Anna Margaretha Elkins
    1 BA-9
Totten, Joseph, 21 July 1792, Elizabeth Ihlin        14 BA-14
Totten, Joseph, 28 July 1792, Elizabeth Jackson       5 BA-14
Touchstone, Richard, 7 Jan. 1800, Sarah Touchstone   12 BA-371
    See also 2 BA-17.
Toughman, Frederick, 27 Aug. 1790, Sarah Kyser        4 FR
Towbridge, John, 8 Dec. 1788, Mary Holtzman           4 FR
Towers, Capt. George, 8 Jan. 1794, Mary Aikins        6 BA
Towers, John, 18 Aug. 1792, Elizabeth Hannan          3 BA-256
Towner, John, 5 March 1795, Frances Tobert            4 FR
Townley, Thomas, 26 Jan. 1782, Henrietta Stewart      2 PG-3
Townsand, James, son of Danford, 5 March 1778, Mary Brumbly
    1 SO-86
Townsend, Benjamin, 29 April 1797, Christena Coore    4 FR
Townsend, Elijah, 29 Sept. 1793, Nancy Coglian        3 BA-275
Townsend, Ephraim, 22 Oct. 1796, Rachel Cutler        1 WO
Townsend, Gilbert, 22 Nov. 1798, Nancy Handy          1 WO
Townsend, James, 12 Sept. 1781, Catharina Jones       3 HA-5
Townsend, James, 14 Nov. 1798, Mary Smullen           2 SO
Townsend, Joseph, son of John, 31st day, 5 mo., 1787,
    Mary Matthews, dau. of George and Dorothy         1 SF
Townsend, Levin, 12 June 1799, Nancy Townsend         1 WO
Townsend, Levin, 22 July 1799, Anne Dorman            2 SO
Townsend, Rives R., 24 July 1795, Sarah Scarborough   1 WO
Townsend, Robert, 1 Sept. 1787, Margaret Willson      3 BA-192
    See also 3 BA-203.
Townsend, Robert, 19 Jan. 1794, Juliet Freeland       3 BA-281
Townsend, Robert, 14 April 1795, Nancy Kernyl         1 WO
Townsend, Samuel, 30 Aug. 1781, Mary Hodgkins         2 PG-5
Townsend, Stephen, 20 June 1796, Esther Benson        1 WO
Townsend, William, 10 May 1778, Sarah Townsend       11 BA-1
Townsend, Wm., 7 June 1800, Betsey Hooke              1 WO
Townsend, Zadock, 10 June 1799, Mary Townsend         1 WO
```

Townshand, Leonard, 18 Dec. 1796, Elizabeth Parker   3 PG-442
Townshend, Leonard, 22 Dec. 1789, Sarah Eleanor Young   3 PG-256
Townshend, (or Taungham), William, 13 Oct. 1795, Keziah
          Bonafant   3 PG-441
Townsley, Joseph, 4 Jan. 1785, Margaret Mahan   3 HA-10
Towser, Jonathan, 16 Nov. 1798, Mary McAllister   5 BA-14
Towson, Abraham, 12 Feb. 1794, Jane Gates   3 BA-281
Towson, Jacob T., 19 April 1788, Jane Boyd   5 BA-14
Towson, Jacob, 13 Nov. 1798, Margaret Towson   3 HA-27
Towson, James, 13 May 1786, by Rev. Turner; Cary Osborn
          51 BA-30
Toy, Isaac, 18 March 1793, Frances Dallam   3 HA-22
Toy, John, 11 Feb. 1793, Mary Carlon   3 HA-22
Tracey?, George, 14 Aug. 1797, Sarah Cox   45 BA-1
Trafford, Edward, 24 May 1789, Rebecca Parker   23 BA-1
Tramain, Wm., 16 Aug. 1795, Catherine Billson   7 BA-2
Trant, Caspar, 12 Dec. 1787, Mary Ament   2 FR-1178
Trapnall, William, 14 Oct. 1779, Honor Wheeler   5 BA-14
Traughten, George, 16 April 1800, Charlotte Airy   3 BA-385
Traut, Wendel, 25 July 1794, Sarah Gebhart   2 FR-1178
Travelet, Francis, 27 March 1796, Betty Hines   35 BA-4
Travers. Hicks, 30 Dec. 1798, Polly Phillips   2 DO
Travers, Jacob, 19 July 1781, Jane Pagan   2 DO
Travers, Jacob, 31 Jan. 1798, Priscilla Woolford   2 DO
Travers, Joseph, 15 Nov. 1791, Jinney Travers   2 DO
Travers, Levin, 5 Oct. 1791, Mary Hill   2 DO
Travers, Matthews, 19 Sept. 1784, Jane Biays   5 BA-14
Travers, Thomas A., 22 Sept. 1799, Alcie R. Neale   4 SM-184
Travers, William Briscoe, 9 Nov. 1791, Sarah Flanteroy
          18 BA-3; see also 3 BA-254.
Travers, Zadock, 28 Sept. 1793, Elizabeth Beckwith   2 DO
Traverse, Frederick, 4 April 1786, Nancy Traverse   2 DO
Traverse, George, 13 August 1798, Polly Nevitt   2 DO
          1 DO-40 gives the date as 30 Aug. 1798, and the bride's
          name as Nevett.
Traverse, Henry, 18 July 1787, Lovicouad Traverse   2 DO
Traverse, Jacob, 3 Feb. 1798, Priscilla Woolford   1 DO-39
Traverse, John C., 5 April 1797, Polly Dove   2 DO
Traverse, Joseph, 17 Nov. 1788, Rebecca Gadd   2 DO
Traverse, Major, 16 June 1794, Betsey Creighton   2 DO
Traverse, Mathew, 1 Jan. 1796, Betsey Hooper   2 DO
Traverse, Matthias, 31 May 1782, Letitia Aaron   2 DO
Traverse, Shadrack, 19 Oct. 1787, Rachel Elliott   2 DO
Traverse, Thomas, 20 May 1784, Delia Traverse   2 DO
Traverse, Thomas, 24 Jan. 1786, Sarah Phillips   2 DO
Traverse, Tolly, 8 March 1786, Ann Traverse   2 DO
Traverse, Wallace, 14 July 1788, Comfort Creighton   2 DO
Traviller, Thomas, 12 June 1798, Mary Brooks   4 KE-72
Travis, Charles, 1791, Mary Stewart   50 BA-391
Travis, Matthew, 28 Jan. 1796, Priscilla Harris   3 SO
Travis, Walther, 28 Jan. 1796, Priscilla Harris   1 WI-131
Trazy, Arthur, 4 July 1798, Sarah Johnson   1 WO
Treacle, Wm., 8 Aug. 1782, Annie Kirby   11 BA-5
Treadaway, Daniel, 30 July 1782, Mary Young   3 HA-6
Treakle, Christopher, 23 Dec. 1792, Mary Wilson   3 BA-259
Treakle, Stephen, 19 June 1778, Orpah Hooper   11 BA-1
Trego, Roger, 23 April 1788, Susanna Tall   2 DO
Tregoe, James, 25 Aug. 1785, Priscilla Tregoe   2 DO
Tregoe, Joseph, 7 Sept. 1796, Lilly Lane   2 DO
Tregoe, Levin, 23 April 1790, Elizabeth Christopher   2 DO
Trehearn, Cyrus, 8 May 1799, Sally Gunby   2 SO
Tremple, Samuel, 21 June 1798, Martha Schly   3 AL-5
Trent, John, 26 Nov. 1778, Eleanor Smith   4 FR
Tressler, Johannes, 15 Nov. 1791, Barbara Palmer, dau. of
          Peter   2 WA-16

```
Trevis, John, 23 May 1778, Mary Lewis                    3 MO-1
Triev, Herman, 22 July 1787, Frances West                5 BA-14
Trigal, William, 26 June 1787, Margareth Meyer          10 BA-188
Trigg, David, before 15 Sept. 1796, by Rev. Green; Charity
    Etesy                                                 4 AA
Trimble, Cornelius, 28 May 1778, Elizabeth Gates        11 BA-1
Trimble, Elisha, son of Joseph and Ann, 4th day, 4 mo.,
    1799, Anna Wilson, dau. of Benjamin and Lydia       11 SF-254
Trimble, Henry, 23 Oct. 1794, Margaret Crutchfield       2 AL-700
Trimble, James, of Joseph and Ann, 20th day, 3 mo., 1788,
    Sarah Job, of Archibald and Margaret                11 SF-215
Trimble, John, 25 May 1784, Sarah Kerby                 11 BA-7
Trimble, John, 6 Aug. 1797, Lydia Brick                  3 BA-348
Trimble, John, son of Isaac and Elizabeth, 15th day, 3 mo.,
    1798, Elizabeth Brown, dau. of David and Elizabeth
    8 SF-13
Trimble, John, 21 Oct. 1798, Julia Hugo                  6 BA
Trimble, Wm., 9 Feb. 1786, Hannah Collins               11 BA-9
Trinton, Thos., 3 April 1781, Margaret Hutchcraft        4 FR
Trip, James, 18 Dec. 1795, Jane Purnell                  1 WO
Triplet, Reuben, 11 July 1786, Rebecca Comb              2 FR-1178
    4 FR gives the bride's name as Combs.
Triplett, Thomas, 18 Oct. 1797, Elizabeth Sandes         4 FR
Tripp, Edward, 25 Feb. 1794, Eliza Barney               18 BA-6
Tripp, Henry, 5 May 1798, Jane Waters                   35 BA-6
Trippe, Daniel, 24 Feb. 1794, Henrietta Yates            2 DO
Trippe, Edward, 26 Jan. 1787, Sarah Byus                 2 DO
Trippe, Henry, 4 May 1799, Hannah Hodson                 2 DO
Trippe, James, 29 Jan. 1795, Henrietta Byus              2 DO
Trippe, John, 24 Feb. 1796, Susannah Heron               2 DO
Tritt, Peter, 3 Dec. 1799, Esther Suesz                  2 FR-1179
Tritton, John, 7 Aug. 1780, Lucy McCarty                 3 BA-180
Troth, John, son of Henry, 1st day, 1 mo., 1789, Rebecca
    Kemp, dau. of Benjamin and Ann                       4 SF-193
Troth, Samuel, son of Henry, 12th day, 10 mo., 1780, Eliza-
    beth Trew, dau. of William                           7 SF-111
Troth, Samuel, son of Henry, 2nd day, 10 mo., 1783, Ann
    Dixon, widow of Robert Dixon, and dau. of James
    Berry                                                4 SF-171
Troth, William, 11 April 1781, Amelia Dean               2 DO
Troth, William, Jr., son of William, 4th day, 5 mo., 1786,
    Elizabeth Dickenson, dau. of Daniel                  4 SF-177
Trott, James, 18 Feb. 1789, Sarah Griffith               4 AA
Trotten, George, 5 Oct. 1795, Julian Slater             29 BA-6
Trotten, John, 5 March 1793, Sarah Sollers               3 BA-264
Trout, Jacob, 9 Aug. 1780, Eliz'th Read                  4 FR
Trout, Wendle, 25 July 1794, Sarah Kephart               4 FR
Troutman, Michael, 30 Dec. 1783, Elizabeth Shrader       4 FR
Truck, Edward, 15 June 1780, Anna Ridgely Henward       11 BA-4
Truck, Esau, 17 Aug. 1785, Cath. Dewly                  11 BA-8
Trucks, John, 30 Oct. 1781, Catherine Boyle              4 FR
Trueman, Henry, 4 April 1790, Ann Bevin                  2 PG-4
Truiett, George, 20 March 1796, Nancy Rowland            6 BA
Truitt, Benj., 26 March 1798, Elener Johnson             1 WO
Truitt, Elisha, 19 Sept. 1800, Comfort Taylor            1 WO
Truitt, George, 30 Oct. 1797, Sally Bishop               1 WO
Truitt, George, 3 Aug. 1798, Elizabeth Holloway          1 WO
Truitt, James, 22 Jan. 1800, Molly Taylor                1 WO
Truitt, John K., 1 March 1796, Mary Teague               3 HA-5
Trulap, Isaac, 19 Jan. 1782, Mary Hitchcock              9 BA-142
Trump, Caspar, 21 Oct. 1798, Rachel Loor                29 BA-11
Trump, Henry, 3 Dec. 1799, Lydia Branson                 4 FR
Trundle, David, 18 Jan. 1797, Drusilla Lewis
    7 MO-29 gives the date as 19 Jan. 1797.
Trundle, Evan, 25? Jan. 1798, Anna Key                   5 mO-114
```

```
Trundle, John, 26 Feb. 1799, Mary Veatch              7 MO-29
Truson, Robert, 6 Jan. 1781, Esther Ray              2 CH-458
Truvey, Jacob, 15 Sept. 1783, Catherine Isenberger   4 FR
Tryable, John, 25 May 1784, Sarah Kirby              3 BA-187
Tryer, George, 3 March 1791, Ann Read                3 BA-234
Tubbs, James, 20 Nov. 1798, Kesiah Rain              1 WO
Tubman, James, 31 Dec. 1797, Eleanor Dement          3 PG-443
Tubman, Richard, 24 July 1794, Elizabeth Travers     2 DO
Tucker, David, 22 March 1789, Mary Ward              6 BA
Tucker, Edward, 11 April 1791, Sarah Simpson         6 BA
Tucker, Edward, 6 Nov. 1799, Sarah Riggs             4 FR
Tucker, Henry, 15 April 1790, Mary Geoghegan         2 DO
Tucker, John, 27 July 1780, Rebecca Williams         1 CA-3
Tucker, John, 10 Feb. 1782, Jane Weedon              2 CH-458
Tucker, John, 24 July 1783, Ann Tucker               3 AA-419
Tucker, John, 23 Feb. 1796, Anne Warfield            4 FR
Tucker, Jonathan, 5 Feb. 1785, Patsy Godman          4 FR
Tucker, Littleton, 2 Feb. 1786, Sarah Downing        4 FR
Tucker, Ozband, 23 Feb. 1790, Eliz. Ann Lanham       3 PG-257
Tucker, Richard, 18 Feb. 1786, Rachel Higgins        4 FR
Tucker, Richard, 24 Jan. 1794, Elizabeth Johnson     3 PG-439
Tucker, Richard, 3 Sept. 1796, by Rev. Cash; Susannah
    Cockey                                           4 AA
Tucker, William, 8 Sept. 1786, Jean Greenwood        2 DO
Tucker, William, 25 Aug. 1790, Elizabeth Jones       2 DO
Tucker, William, 10 May 1797, Betsy Dove             2 DO
Tudar, John, 29 March 1791, Ann Inloes               3 HA-3
Tudor, Joshua, 9 Oct. 1792, Susanna McCubbins        1 BA-4
Tudor, Salathiel, 20 Nov. 1791, Temperance Fugate    1 BA-3
Tudor, Wm., 14 Oct. 1783, Martha Griffith            11 BA-6
Tuedman, Allen, 8 June 1782, Sabina Fendall          2 CH-458
Tuffts, James, 8 May 1786, Mary Hurley               11 BA-9
Tuhl?, Jacob, 29 May 1794, Christina Schott          29 BA-5
Tull, Andrew, 26 Oct. 1798, Susanna Dickerson        1 WO
Tull, Henry, 5 April 1800, Jane Reed                 3 BA-384
Tull, Jesse, 12 Nov. 1790, Mary Smoot             :' 2 DO
Tull, John, 29 Nov. 1790, Nancy Madkin               2 DO
Tull, Nicholas, 10 Nov. 1796, Nelly Chaney           2 SO
    3 SO gives the date as 17 Nov. 1796.
Tull, Richard, Sept. 1796, Betsy Only                3 SO
Tull, Samuel, 2 Jan. 1798, Nancy Byrd                2 SO
Tull, Solomon, 12 Dec. 1800, Esther Only             1 WO
Tull, Stonden, 30 Nov. 1786, Lovey Whiteley          2 DO
Tully, John, 31 May 1798, Ann Rhodes                 2 SO
Tumbleson., William, 27 March 1778, Jane Hombledon   5 BA-14
Tunis, Edward, 24 Oct. 1792, Rachel Thomas           2 DO
Tunis, Elijah, 19 June 1794, Sarah Busick            2 DO
Tunis, Samuel, 18 Feb. 1800, Annaretta Powell        2 SO
Tunnells, John, 6 Oct. 1796, Mary Selby              1 WO
Turkens, Samuel, 12 Feb. 1797, Mary Warner           3 PG-443
Turnbull, Andrew, 26 Jan. 1794, Hannah Robinson      5 BA-14
Turnbull, Matthew, 28 Oct. 1800, Agnes Meekins       2 DO
Turnbull, Robert, 15 March 1790, Sarah Buchanan      1 BA-2
Turner, Abel, 6 March 1797, Mary Madden              3 HA-25
Turner, Abraham, 6 Dec. 1781, Rebecca Sadler         2 PG-3
Turner, Abraham, 11 Jan. 1798, Eleanor Brown         4 FR
Turner, Alex, 10 May 1781, Jane Johnson              3 HA-4
Turner, Andrew, 24 March 1781, Ann McDonnell         3 HA-3
Turner, Ch's, 12 Feb. 1782, Sarah Needy              11 BA-5
Turner, Edward, 8 Jan. 1784, Mary Cullember          3 AA-420
Turner, Elisha, 29 April 1797, Mary Anne Rowe        3 BA-344
Turner, Francis, 11 Nov. 1790, Ruth Bradley          6 BA
Turner, George, 19 Dec. 1799, Franky Vinson          2 DO
Turner, Jeremiah, 2 Jan. 1784, Sarah Lansdale        2 PG-5
Turner, Jno., 12 Sept. 1782, Rosanna McBride         11 BA-5
```

```
Turner, John, 6 April 1790, Martha Luton              2 FR-1178
Turner, John, 13 Sept. 1796, Anna Plummer             4 FR
Turner, Jno., 19 Oct. 1796, Mary Quinlan             29 BA-7
Turner, John, 7 Feb. 1799, by Rev. Ridgely; Sarah Beck 4 AA
Turner, Joseph, son of Isaac and Hannah, 16th day, 12 mo.,
   1789, Sarah Corse, dau. of John and Cassandra     7 SF-489
Turner, Joseph R., 31 Aug. 1798, Sarah Price          4 KE-72
Turner, Joshua, 11 Dec. 1797, Priscilla Fisher        4 FR
Turner, Lemuel, 19 Dec. 1797, Sally Parker            1 WO
Turner, Lewis, 16 Jan. 1799, Sarah Bradley            4 FR
Turner, Nathaniel, 4 Feb. 1796, Elizabeth Fitz        6 BA
Turner, Richard, 19 April 1778, Mary Ambler           3 AA-414
Turner, Richard, 4 Jan. 1784, Susanna Austin          3 AA-420
Turner, Richard, 20 Jan. 1791, Elizabeth Williams     3 PG-258
Turner, Richard, 10 Jan. 1799, Eliz. Beall            5 MO-115
Turner, Robert, 5 Jan. 1793, Eliz. Greenfield        16 BA-4
Turner, Solomon, 23 July 1786, Casander Harvy         2 FR-1178
Turner, Thomas, 12 July 1792, Eleanor Harrison        4 FR
Turner, Thomas, 24 Oct. 1797, Delia Corbin            3 HA-26
   12 BA-370 gives the date as 2 Dec. 1798.
Turner, Thomas Cockey, 21 March 1790, Polly Bossert (or
   Bessert)                                           6 FR-202
Turner, Walter, 23 April 1780, Elizabeth Blancet      2 CH-458
Turner, Wm., 25 July 1783, Martha Sheldan            11 BA-6
Turner, Wm., c.1792, by Rev. Hutchinson; Rebecca Sapping-
   ton                                                4 AA
Turner, Wm. L., 13 Nov. 1798, Sarah Harvey            2 FR-1178
Turnpaugh, John, 20 Sept. 1787, Hannah Macklascey     5 BA-14
Turpin, John, son of Nehemiah, 2 June 1791, Sarah Long,
   dau. of William                                    1 SO-174
Turpin, John, 9 Jan. 1799, Henrietta Quinton          1 WO
Turpin, Sewell, 28 April 1795, Betty Rackliffe        1 WO
Turtin, Josey Harrison, 20 Nov. 1794, Ann Jinkins     3 PG-440
Tush, Mich'l, 16 Aug. 1795, Marg. Henry              29 BA-6
   50 BA-398 gives the groom's name as Tusk.
Tutterow, Baltice, 29 Oct. 1784, Elizabeth Sleagle    4 FR
Twiford, Jonathan, 2 Dec. 1790, Elizabeth Murphey     2 SF
Twigg, Thomas, 26 Dec. 1796, Polly Anderson           2 SO
Twigg, Thomas, 13 May 1800, Sally Prior               2 SO
Twilley, George, 3 July 1795, Priscilla Taylor        1 WO
Twilley, Robert, 13 Dec. 1796, Nancy Caton            2 SO
Twine, Daniel, 19 Dec. 1797, Anne West                3 BA-353
Twomey, Daniel, 7 Nov. 1789, Sarah Sheats             4 FR
Twoshears, Geo., 19 May 1783, Barbara Hicks          11 BA-6
Tybills, James Theobald, 13 Jan. 1783, Mary Griffin   3 SM-60
Tydings, Richard, 8 Aug. 1797, Susanna Chamberlain    1 BA-8
Tyler, David, 2 Feb. 1795, Anne Foxwell               2 DO
Tyler, Isaac, March 1798, Sus. Dengler                3 WA-64
Tyler, Job, 5 June 1794, Unis Thomas                  2 DO
Tyler, John, 25 Nov. 1783, Mary Wallace               2 DO
Tyler, Dr. John, 18 April 1787, Cath. Harrison        4 FR
Tyler, John, 27 April 1797, Sally Dean                2 DO
Tyler, Robert Bradley, 2 Dec. 1779, Henrietta Beans   2 PG-7
Tyler, Samuel, 22 Jan. 1782, Verlinda Riddle          2 PG-3
Tyler, Solomon, 16 Feb. 1797, Mary Edger              2 DO
Tyler, Thomas, Nov. 1778, Ann Lewis                   1 SO-178
Tyler, William, 10 Jan. 1779, Marianne Trueman Stoddert
   2 CH-458
Tyler, William, 13 May 1798, Terran Pearson           2 DO
Tyse, John, 16 Nov. 1794, Elisab. Kinseker            3 WA-57
Tyson, Benjamin, 27 Aug. 1795, Marg. Morgan           3 WA-59
Tyson, Jacob, son of Isaac and Esther, 2nd day, 1 mo.,
   1794, Anne Perine, dau. of Peter (dec.) and Hannah
   (now Stuart                                        8 SF-1
Tyson, Jesse, son of Isaac and Esther, 4th mo., 1 day,
   1790, Marg't Hopkins, dau. of Jno. H. and Elizabeth 6 SF
```

Tyson, Nathan, 25 Jan. 1798, Sally Jackson   5 BA-14

Uhl, Bastian, 25 July 1799, Ann Cath. Bater or Pater   50 BA-405
Uhler, Philip, 20 June 1793, Mary Rodner   50 BA-393
Uhry, Christian, 25 Aug. 1796, Cath. Streip   2 FR-1180
Uhry, John, 17 April 1800, Elizabeth Hensey   2 FR-1180
Uhry, Samuel, 29 Feb. 1792, Sarah Bayer   2 FR-1180
Ulery, Aust., 8 Nov. 1796, Sarah Dolley   5 BA-14
Ulm, Daniel, 10 Nov. 1791, Catharina Wolff   2 WA-16
Ulverson, Uriah, 8 Jan. 1800, Polly Watson   3 BA-382
Umberger, Michael, 4 April 1794, Nancy Wood   4 FR
Underhill, Thomas, 30 Jan. 1799, Leah Powell   2 SO
Underwood, John, 5 May 1792, Elizabeth Davies   28 BA-2
Underwood, Nehemiah, son of Benjamin and Susanna, 30th day,
    1 mo., 1788, Mary Price, dau. of Mordecai and Mary 1 SF
Undush, Nich's, 7 Oct. 1796, Mattelene Hendricks   50 BA-400
    29 BA-7 gives the groom's name as Undust.
Unkles, Benj'n, 18 Sept. 1780, Margaret Plaister   4 FR
Updegraff, Joseph (or Josiah), son of Joseph and Mary,
    19th day, 11 mo., 1800, Hannah Farquhar, dau. of
    Allen and Phebe   3 SF
Upton, George, 8 Jan. 1778, Elizabeth Perkins   2 PG-3
Upton, George, 24 Dec. 1797, Amelia King   3 PG-443
Upton, Samuel, 4 April 1790, Mary Ann Lanham   3 PG-257
Urbush, Joseph, 21 June 1798, Polly Williams   1 WO
Urie, James, 13 June 1799, Elizabeth Long   3 BA-372
Urie, Jeremiah, 19 June 1798, Sarah Matthews   3 BA-359
Urquhart, Will'm, 18 Dec. 1783, Mary Magd'n Hall   3 AA-420
Urqurt, John, 26 Feb. 1793, Ann Low   3 PG-438
Ury, Christian, 23 Aug. 1796, Catharine Stipe   4 FR
Usher, Thomas, Jr., 18 Sept. 1783, Mary Philpot   11 BA-6
Usilton, Aquilla, 12 May 1797, Milcah Taylor   4 KE-72

Valentine, George, 22 May 1787, Mary Stull   4 FR
Valentine, Henry, 21 Sept. 1779, Elizabeth Frey   4 FR
Valentine, Jacob, 2 June 1779, Mary Free   4 FR
Valiant, George, 4 Dec. 1800, Jane Patrick   6 BA
Valiant, Levin, 19 March 1794, Peggy Vickers   2 DO
Valkman, Peter Adolph, 9 Aug. 1797, Sophia Christine
    Dorothea Amelung   4 FR
Valliant, Bennett, 19 June 1782, Martha Hurley   2 DO
Valliant, Denny, 25 Feb. 1786, Anne Vickers   2 DO
Valliant, Robert, 15 Jan. 1794, Patty Hallock   2 DO
Vanandy, Cornel, 1 Feb. 1791, Rebec. Shaghan   2 FR-1181
Vanastoste, Wm., 24 Jan. 1796, Eliz. Murray   29 BA-7
Vance, George, 3 March 1800, Patty Handy   2 SO
Vance, Samuel, 9 Oct. 1798, Mary Watters   1 BA-8
    3 HA-27 gives the date as 8 Oct. 1798.
Vance, William, 23 Feb. 1782, Martha Keeth   3 HA-6
Vandenburg, David, 23 Feb. 1790, Catharina Eperle   6 FR-202
Vanderlin, Nicholas, 10 April 1779, Mary Null   4 FR
Vane, Henry, 28 Aug. 1790, Nancy Cheshare   2 DO
Vane, Henry, 17 June 1794, Naomi Hopkins   2 DO
Vane, John, 13 Dec. 1785, Lucretia Harper   2 DO
Vanfossen, Levi, 30 Dec. 1797, Susanna Lease   4 FR
Van Horn, Benjamin, 15 Feb. 1791, Charity Sanders   1 BA-3
Vanhorn, Dennis, 31 Oct. 1782, Sarah Hutchinson   4 FR
Vanhorne, Dennis, 15 Oct. 1796, Cath. Burns   2 FR-1181
Vanoroste, Wm., 24 Jan. 1796, Eliz. Murray   50 BA-398
Vansant, Ephraim, 25 Dec. 1791, Rachel Gay   3 KE
Vansant, Joshua, 10 May 1798, Ann Davis   4 KE-72
Vansant, Peregrine, 14 Jan. 1797, Lucretia Grace   4 KE-72
Vansickle, Gilbert, 22 Sept. 1786, Leane Heather   2 DO

VanVorst, William, 19 Jan. 1799, Eleanor Hood   29 BA-10
VanZant, John, 15 July 1795, Sabina Mills   3 HA-24
  7 BA-2 gives the date as 16 July 1795.
Vaughn, Benjamin, 24 Jan. 1800, Rachel Stansbury   8 BA-1
Vaughan, Benj. Gist, (5 Oct. 1791), Rebecca Chapman   15 BA-4
Vaughan, John, 8 Aug. 1792, Sarah Tucker   2 DO
Vaughn, Ephraim, 18 June 1785, Margaret Bonwill   2 DO
Veach, Price, 11 Feb. 1786, Drusilla Layton   2 DO
Veal, William, 4 Jan. 1778, Mary Branham   4 MO-1
Veatch, Jacob, 12 Feb. 1779, Frances Masters Wilson   4 FR
Veatch, John, 16 June 1792, Nancy Weaver Davis   4 FR
Veatch, John T., 26 Feb. 1797, Mary Stone   7 MO-29
Veatch, Solomon, 3 Aug. 1793, Mary Davis   4 FR
Veazey, Robert, 21 Feb. 1798, Ann Salisbury   4 KE-72
Veazey, Thomas, March 1798, Maria Veazey   4 KE-72
Vehrly, Jno., 14 Dec. 1795, Cath. Emich   29 BA-7
Veirs, Hezekiah, (date not given; before 8 Oct. 1791)
  Ann Clarke   31 BA-1
Veist, John, 8 July 1798, Eleanor Farthing   2 FR-1181
Velum, Henry, 30 June 1791, Sarah Togood   3 PG-258
Venables, John, 22 Jan. 1800, Martha Shockley   1 WO
Venables, Richard, 26 Nov. 1796, Sarah Twilley   2 SO
Venables, Robert, 8 Oct. 1799, Sarah Ballard   2 SO
Venables, Samuel, 12 July 1787, Sarah Anderton   2 DO
Vennals, Richard, 30 Oct. 1799, Ann Miller   4 FR
Verdeick, Peter, 29 Jan. 1788, Catherine Mayauer   10 BA-190
Vermilion, Benjamin, 14 Oct. 1777, Tabatha Burch   2 CH-458
Vermilion, Caleb, 21 Dec. 1794, Mary Busey   3 PG-440
Vermilion, Giles, 26 Aug. 1790, Ann Cross   3 PG-257
Vermilion, Uriah, 16 March 1783, Susanna Barker   2 CH-458
Vermillian, Benjamin, 5 Jan. 1788, Priscilla Farr   3 PG-254
Vernon, Caleb, 6 Dec. 1790, Cloe Atchison   3 PG-257
Vessels, Elijah, 5 Jan. 1784, Ann Choram   3 SM-161
Vickars, Ezekiel, 19 June 1794, Sally Proctor   2 DO
Vickars, John, 28 Dec. 1799, Elizabeth Woolford   2 DO
Vickars, Joseph, 13 March 1797, Elizabeth LeCompte   2 DO
Vickars, Richard, 8th day, 9 mo., 1791, Celia Chilcutt   2 SF-289
Vickars, Thomas, 10 Oct. 1799, Mary Meekins   2 DO
Vickers, Clement, 4 Feb. 1793, Sarah Beckwith   2 DO
Vickers, Edward, 3 Dec. 1792, Mary Hackrage   2 DO
Vickers, Ezekiel, 25 June 1792, Mary Thomas   2 DO
Vickers, Stephen, 2 Jan. 1792, Polly Sheehawn   2 DO
Vickers, Thomas, 26 July 1782, Ann Mace   2 DO
Vickers, Thomas, 1 Oct. 1787, Nancy Cope   2 DO
Vickers, Thomas, 4 Aug. 1788, Sarah Conner   2 DO
Vickery, Nathan, 14 May 1796, Eve Crise   4 FR
Victory, Thomas, 16 March 1797, Priscilla Manning   2 SO
Vinard, Bartholomew, 24 June 1792, Susanna Roberts   3 BA-256
Vincent, George, 16 Feb. 1786, Nancy Vickers   2 DO
Vincent, Thomas, 6 Jan. 1788, Elizabeth Wilder   2 CH-458
Vincent, Thomas, 19 March 1791, Sarah Hubbert   2 DO
Vincent, Thomas, 29 Aug. 1798, Sally Taylor   2 SO
  3 SO gives the date as 30 Sept. 1798.
Vine, Patten, 28 Sept. 1778, Eleanor Walsh   11 BA-1
Vinson, Aaron, 28 Aug. 1792, Rebecca Smith   2 DO
Vinson, Eli, 11 Sept. 1797, Comfort Adams   2 SO
  3 SO gives the date as 14 Sept. 1797.
Vinson, Elijah, 11 Dec. 1800, Biddy Douglass   2 SO
Vinson, Salisbury, 9 April 1787, Eleanor Brumagem   2 DO
Vinson, Salisbury, 21 June 1792, Mary Mace   2 DO
Vinson, William, 8 Oct. 1789, Priscilla Cannon   2 DO
Vion, John, 30 March 1789, Cath. Ruff   2 FR-1181
  See also 4 FR.
Virmilion, John, 9 Jan. 1781, Janephin (Josephine?) McDaniel
  2 PG-5

Virmilion, Francis Burch, 4 Nov. 1780, Ann Wood   2 PG-3
Virmilion, William, 21 April 1778, Mary Ann Sims   2 PG-3
Vitrie, John, 4 June 1780, Mary Lockerman   3 BA-183
Vittory, John, 2 Aug. 1800, Mary Jones   2 SO
   3 SO gives the date as 4 Aug. 1800.
Vogel, Christian, 14 July 1793, Nancy Norwood   2 FR-1181
Vogel, Jos., 15 Aug. 1797, Mary Foubel   29 BA-8
Vogle, Balthasar, 3 Nov. 1789, Catherine Hertzogen   6 FR-202
Vogle, Matthis, 23 Nov. 1790, Catherine Roth   6 FR-202
Vogle, Philipp, 5 June 1791, Magdalena Spahn   6 FR-202
Volmar, John, 16 April 1795, Elizabeth Reed   3 BA-301
Von, John, 17 July 1783, Agatha Edeington   2 CH-458
Von Bremen, Daniel, 30 June 1796, Sabina Elis. Bieberin
   10 BA-198
Voss, John Eccleston, 24 Dec. 1798, Melody Wrotten   2 DO
Voss, William Cannerly, 21 Aug. 1784, Elizabeth Keene   2 DO
Vuthenrieth, Johannes, 10 July 1786, Susanna Freiburger,
   widow   10 BA-186

Wachter, George, 22 Sept. 1798, Philippina Beckebach   2 FR-1182
Waddle, George, 18 Nov. 1800, Margaret Weaver   6 BA
Waddle, William, 14 Jan. 1795, Nancy Cox   5 BA-15
Wade, Lancelot, 13 Aug. 1786, Patty Fenly   3 PG-251
Wade, Lancelot, 20 Aug. 1786, Martha Hawkins   3 PG-447
Wadigan, Christopher, 22 Jan. 1783, Catherine Thomas   4 FR
Wagers, Thomas, 12 Sept. 1794, Margaret Wooden   5 BA-15
Wages, James, 5 April 1789, Barbara Pool   2 FR-1181
Wages, Luck, 2 April 1789, Patience Phillips   10 BA-192
Waggoner, Daniel, 27 March 1800, Barb. Kline   29 BA-11
Waggoner, Geo., 24 March 1785, Juliet Cooper   11 BA-8
Waggoner, Jacob, 13 Dec. 1799, Eve Smith   4 FR
Waggoner, John, 17 March 1791, Rachael Cassell   4 FR
Wagner, Andrew, 16 Nov. 1787, Micky Moberry   29 BA-1
Wagner, Henry, 17 March 1799, Eliz'th Wolstagle   6 BA
Wagner, Jacob, 7 Aug. 1798, Rachel Raborg   29 BA-9
Wagner, John, 24 Jan. 1786, Marg. Rapp   2 FR-1181
Wagner, Mich'l, 3 Jan. 1799, Mary or Marg. Beckly   29 BA-10
Wagner, Philip, 20 May 1800, Eliz. Thiel   50 BA-407
Wagner, Valentine, 26 Dec. 1794, Phoebe Fisher   29 BA-6
Wailes, Daniel, 11 July 1799, Polly Bounds   2 SO
Wait, Thomas, 6 Dec. 1799, Rebecca Benton   3 BA-381
Waits, William Wilkinson, 4 Dec. 1792, Susanna Stansbury
   1 BA-4
Wakefield, Abel, 30 Dec. 1782, Margaret Jenkins   2 CH-458
Walcraft, Thos., 28 March 1787, Jane Beale   11 BA-10
Waldeck, Henry, 27 Oct. 1782, Rebecka Evans   4 FR
Waldrin, Peter, 15 Oct. 1780, Daley Richardson   3 HA-2
Waldron, Davis, 11 June 1782, Martha Monahan   3 HA-6
Wales, George, 23 Feb. 1798, Phoebe Button   4 KE-72
Walker, Alex'r, 18 May 1797, Edith Wane   6 BA
Walker, Rev. Archibald, 5 Feb. 1798, Mary Everitt   4 KE-72
Walker, Benjamin, 7 Jan. 1779, Margaret Pumphry   2 PG-3
Walker, Charles, 4 Sept. 1778, Sarah Ryan   2 PG-3
Walker, Charles, 2 May 1793, Mary Woodard   18 BA-5
Walker, Daniel, 21 Dec. 1799, Mary Harding   1 TA-325
   See also 1 TA-332.
Walker, David, 16 Aug. 1792, Eliza Browning   18 BA-4
Walker, George, 9 Dec. 1780, Ann Gray   2 PG-3
Walker, Henry, 10 Dec. 1780, Keziah Burgess   2 PG-5
Walker, James, 5 Sept. 1782, Mary Owens   3 AA-418
Walker, Jesse, 10 July 1787, Mary Price   6 BA
Walker, John, 25 June 1798, Selvina Crapper   1 WO
Walker, Joseph, 7 Dec. 1779, Henrietta Maria Tilghman   2 PG-1
Walker, Joseph, 11 July 1798, Mary Frasier   5 BA-15

```
Walker, Nathan, 21 July 1798, Nancy Beck                    6 MO
Walker, Nathaniel, 20 May 1785, Nellie McCallister          2 DO
Walker, Richard, 25 Aug. 1778, Mary Gilpen                  2 CH-458
Walker, Samuel, 25 Oct. 1792, Frances S. Smith              5 BA-15
Walker, Thomas, 19 March 1778, Elizabeth Brogden            2 PG-2
Walker, Thomas, 1 July 1781, Mary Littleford                2 PG-5
Walker, Thomas, 15 June 1787, Elizabeth Valliant            2 DO
Walker, Thomas, 27 Sept. 1787, Eliz'th Burnes               4 FR
Walker, Thomas, 2 June 1797, Elizabeth Miller               4 KE-72
Walkins, Christopher, 10 Dec. 1786, Sarah Grover            2 FR-1181
Wall, George, 8 March 1794, Alcey Woods                    18 BA-6
Wall, John, 23 Oct. 1790, C. Harvey                        29 BA-1
Wall, Samuel, 29 Nov. 1798, Margaret Stewart                2 DO
Wallace, Charles, 9 Jan. 1786, Sarah Wingate                2 DO
Wallace, David, 25 May 1791, Mary Langrall                  2 DO
Wallace, David, 8 July 1791, Mary Langriel                 28 BA-1
Wallace, James, 16 May 1798, Sarah Walston                  2 SO
Wallace, Jas., Sept. 1799, Sus. Stack                       3 WA-67
Wallace, John, 3 Sept. 1795, Nancy Buckingham               3 BA-311
Wallace, John, 30 Dec. 1785, by Rev. Turner; Ann Towson
    51 BA-29
Wallace, John, 13 April 1797, Mary Alexandria               5 BA-13
Wallace, John, 8 June 1798, Nicea Jones                     4 KE-72
Wallace, Joseph, 8 Jan. 1798, Amelia Ross                   2 DO
Wallace, Levin, 8 Nov. 1797, Barthula Wallace               2 DO
Wallace, Matthew, 13 Jan. 1797, Rebecca Creighton           2 DO
Wallace, Robert, 12 Dec. 1789, Rebecca Justice              6 BA
Wallace, Robert, 16 Jan. 1799, Jane Dwyre                   4 FR
Wallace, William, 22 April 1778, Drusilla Mahew             2 PG-3
Wallace, Wm., 15 June 1779, Eliz'th Hopkins                 4 FR
Wallace, William, 16 Sept. 1782, Dorothy Staplefort         2 DO
Wallace, William, 20 May 1788, Nancy McNemara               2 DO
Wallace, William, 3 Feb. 1791, Ann Burgess                 23 BA-2
Wallace, William, 12 July 1799, Nancy Tubman                2 DO
Wallace, Wm., 28 Dec. 1800, Martha Brookes                  5 MO-117
Walldeck, John, 9 Aug. 1789, Sus. Engel                     2 FR-1181
Waller, Basil, 28 June 1778, Sarah Parks                   11 BA-1
Waller, Basil, 25 Sept. 1800, Rebecka Hagerman              8 BA-2
    See also 48 BA-1.
Waller, Benjamin, 11 Dec. 1797, Mary Adams                  2 SO
    3 SO gives the date as 14 Dec. 1797.
Waller, Esme, 18 Dec. 1797, Sally Elsey                     1 WO
    3 SO gives the date as 16 Dec. 1797.
Waller, Walter, 6 June 1792, Ealy Parks                     3 BA-256
Waller, Wm., 21 May 1780, Hannah Cartright                 11 BA-4
    2 BA-11 gives the date as 25 May 1780, and the bride's
    name as Hannah Cartwright.
Waller, William, 28 Oct. 1786, Bridget Bozman, dau. of
    George and Dolly                                        3 SO
Walling, John, 29 May 1787, Susanna Reed                    4 FR
Walling, William, 27 Dec. 1796, Eliz. Delashmutt            2 FR-1182
    4 FR gives the groom's name as Wallint.
Wallingsford, John, 12 Jan. 1787, by Rev. Pigman; Ann
    Cambel                                                  4 AA
Wallingsford, Joseph, 26 Feb. 1782, Hester Lowe             2 PG-3
Wallington, Demos, 20 June 1793, Elizabeth McGee            3 BA-269
Wallis, Arthur, 12 April 1796, Mary Greber                  2 FR-1182
Wallis, Randall, 1 June 1795, Ann Worthington               3 HA-24
Wallis, Samuel, son of Samuel and Elizabeth, 11th day,
    April 1782, Sarah Sharpless, widow of Benjamin Sharp-
    less, and dau. of James and Elizabeth Rigbie            9 SF-41
Wallis, Samuel, 21 Nov. 1793, Cassandra Jolley              1 BA-6
Walls, John, 6 Sept. 1796, Elizabeth Burrier                4 FR
Walls, William, 31 March 1793, Eloner Chancy               22 BA-2
Walls, William, 18 Sept. 1799, Euphemia Johns               3 BA-377
```

Walsh, John, 12 Jan. 1797, Ann James   3 BA-341
Walsh, William, 25 Aug. 1791, Blanch Lee   1 BA-3
Walston, David, 22 Nov. 1797, Polly Moor   1 WO
Walston, George, 17 Oct. 1798, Leah Adams   2 SO
Walter, Jacob, 5 Feb. 1788, Mary Ann Wintz   4 FR
Walter, Levin, 14 Sept. 1781, Susanna Carmichael   2 DO
Walter, Thomas, 30 Jan. 1788, Polly Huffington   2 DO
Walter, Thomas, 24 July 1791, Ann Delany   1 BA-3
Walters, Charles, 29 July 1799, Elisabeth Heide   3 BA-374
Walters, Jacob, 3 April 1785, Airy Sollers   11 BA-8
Walters, Jacob, 28 Dec. 1799, Sarah Peacock   29 BA-11
Walters, James, 23 Nov. 1790, Margaret Scholls   2 FR-1182
Walters, Thomas, 1 July 1795, Nancy Angell   2 DO
Walters, William, 15 June 1797, Priscilla Walter   3 SO
Waltham, Thomas, 21 May 1795, Patty Greenfield   3 HA-24
     1 BA-7 gives the bride's name as Martha Greenfield.
Waltham, William, 16 Dec. 1780, Sarah Strong   3 HA-3
Walthen, John B., 1 June 1791, Rebecca Semmes   2 CH-458
Walton, Ezekiel, 10 Feb. 1794, Betsy Bradley   2 DO
Walton, Stephen, 28 May 1799, Rebecca Hudson   1 WO
Waltson, Zepheniah, 23 March 1799, Milley Jenkins   4 FR
Waltum, William, 13 June 1797, Priscilla Waltum   2 SO
Waltz, Frederick, 15 March 1793, Mary Linganfelder   4 FR
Waltz, John, 11 Sept. 1796, Eliz. Borger   2 FR-1182
Waltz, Reinhardt, 12 Sept. 1790, Sus. Schotter   2 FR-1182
     4 FR gives the bride's name as Shutter.
Wampler, Jacob, 21 March 1788, Mary Bare   4 FR
Wampler, John Lewis, 24 Oct. 1799, Hannah Trumbo   4 FR
Wandell, -(?)-, 25 April 1796, -(?)- Cooley   4 PG-157
Wandle, David, 26 Feb. 1792, Eleanor Mack   6 BA
Wandle, Jacob, 16 Oct. 1780, Mary Goldie   4 FR
Wann, Asa, 4 Aug. 1798, Milly Sweeney   3 HA-27
Wantrow, Blaze, 5 Aug. 1780, Modis Greene   11 BA-4
Ward, Charles, 9 Jan. 1794, Sophia Delahaye   3 BA-281
Ward, Francis, 26 Aug. 1779, Sarah Goodman   5 BA-14
Ward, Geo., 20 Dec. 1798, Ann Redman   5 MO-114
Ward, Henry, 23 Jan. 1797, Polly Becks   2 DO
Ward, James, 15 Jan. 1778, Elizabeth Harrison   3 AA-414
Ward, James, 17 July 1782, Ann Thomas   3 HA-6
Ward, James, 27 July 1785, Sarah Trigger   11 BA-8
Ward, James, 26 May 1791, Mary Poke   2 DO
Ward, John, 6 May 1794, Sarah Barber   4 FR
Ward, John, 22 Dec. 1794, Ann Cumming   2 DO
Ward, John, 24 July 1799, Euphame Marshall   1 WO
Ward, Joseph, 29 Aug. 1797, Martha Ward   2 SO
Ward, Levi, 9 Dec. 1800, Sally Scott   2 SO
Ward, Peter, 12 May 1782, Deborah Magruder   4 FR
Ward, Richard, 12 April 1780, Jane Smith   3 HA-1
Ward, Richard, 6 April 1787, Martha Bervard   1 BA-1
Ward, Southy, 30 Sept. 1790, Rachel Parks   2 DO
Ward, Thomas, 19 Feb. 1796, Sally Wheeler   2 DO
Ward, Willey, 20 Dec. 1796, Mary Harden   2 DO
Ward, William, 27 July 1777, Verlinda Harrison   2 CH-458
Ward, William, son of Robert and Elizabeth, 19th day,
     9 mo., 1799, Sarah Plummer, dau. of Yate and Artridge
     3 SF
Ward, William, c.1799, by Rev. Steuart; Barbara Phelps 4 AA
Warden, John, 3 June 1791, Ann Fisher   3 BA-234
     See also 18 BA-3.
Ware, Francis, Jr., 31 Jan. 1781, Ann Pickerell   2 CH-458
Ware, John, 19 Jan. 1778, Margaret Gosnel   11 BA-1
Ware, John, 20 March 1780, Elizabeth Kidd   3 HA-1
Warfield, Alexander, 30 Dec. 1788, by Rev. Hagerty; Eliza-
     beth Woodward   4 AA
Warfield, Beale, 28 Feb. 1797, Amelia Ridgely   5 MO-114

Warfield, Benjamin, 23 April 1796, by Rev. Ridgely; Rebeckah
   Spurrier   4 AA
Warfield, Brice, 18 April 1797, Sarah Collins   5 MO-114
Warfield, Charles, 10 July 1790, Sally Warfield   4 AA
Warfield, Edmond, 22 Dec. 1792, by Rev. Dorsey; Mary Ann
   Warfield   4 AA
Warfield, Ely, 17 Feb. 1792, by Rev. Dorsey; Frances
   Chapman   4 AA
Warfield, George F., 1 Nov. 1795, Rebecca Brown   6 BA
Warfield, Henry, 26 June 1790, by Rev. Reed; Ann Hammond
   4 AA
Warfield, James, 21 Feb. 1797, Anne Gassaway   6 BA
Warfield, John, 1790, by Rev. Forrest; Hamutal Mewshaw 4 AA
Warfield, Joseph, 6 Aug. 1778, by Rev. Magill; Elizabeth
   Dorsey   4 AA
Warfield, Richard, 7 July 1780, Anne Delashmutt   4 FR
Warfield, Samuel, 7 July 1795, by Rev. Ridgely; Susanna
   Danielson   4 AA
Warfield, Sylvanus, 31 Jan. 1778, Patience Kirby   11 BA-1
Warfield, Thomas, 13 Dec. 1778, by Rev. Magowan; Elizabeth
   Holliday   4 AA
Warfield, Thomas, 22 June 1798, by Rev. Ridgely; Elizabeth
   Marriott   4 AA
Waring, Thomas, son of Joseph and Mary, 5th day, 9 mo.,
   1798, Jane Reynolds, widow, dau. of Thomas and Ann
   King   11 SF-252
Waring?, Thomas, 22 March 1795, Margaret Berry   3 PG-441
Warlton, Charles, 30 Nov. 1793, Sarah Goslin   2 DO
Warmajorn, Jeremiah, 17 Nov. 1799, Mary Kittleman   6 BA
Warman, Benjamin, 21 March 1779, Easter Perry   2 PG-2
Warn, Jacob, 12 July 1785, Henrietta Gassaway   2 FR-1181
Warner, Aaron, son of Crosdale and Mary, 4th day, 11 mo.,
   1790, Achsah Morgan, dau. of John and Ann   9 SF-58
Warner, George, 23 May 1794, Elizabeth Waggoner   4 FR
Warner, John, 28 Aug. 1779, Biddey Henson   4 FR
Warner, Ludwick, 20 July 1797, Mary Parrott   1 TA-331
Warner, Samuel, 5 Dec. 1796, Jane Chamblin   4 FR
Warner, William, 3 Oct. 1789, by Rev. Hagerty; Alizanna
   Liger   4 AA
Warner, William, 19 Sept. 1793, Jane Hicks   6 BA
Warnick, Philip, 26 Oct. 1781, Mary Rogers   3 HA-5
Warren, Henry, 15 Sept. 1779, Elizabeth Shields   3 BA-377
Warren, John, 20 Sept. 1786, Elizabeth Shaw   2 CH-458
Warren, John Hogan, 11 Jan. 1787, Eleanor Meddise   2 DO
Warren, Matts., 5 Aug. 1799, Elizabeth Mitchell   1 WO
Warren, Thomas, 19 Nov. 1779, Marg't Fitzgerald   11 BA-3
Warren, Thomas, 8 April 1784, Mary Cohn   10 BA-180
Warren, William, 3 Aug. 1790, Lacey Addison   2 DO
Warren, William, 2 Feb. 1791, Mary McKindley   2 DO
Warren, William, 5 Feb. 1795, Bethia Howard   3 BA-299
Warrington, William, 10 Nov. 1785, Nancy Harriman   11 BA-8
Warters, James, 22 Dec. 1791, Elizabeth Bershers   3 PG-436
Warthan, Martin, 23 Dec. 1799, Hannah Ann Wilson   4 FR
Warthen, Wilfred, 6 Dec. 1799, Elizabeth Chandler   4 FR
Warwick, Wm., 25 Feb. 1799, Nelly Flemming   1 WO
Wash, William, 12 May 1783, Elizabeth Davis   3 HA-7
Washington, Nathaniel, 25 Nov. 1790, Margaret Hawkins 3 PG-257
Washington, Thornton, 26 Dec. 1779, Milly Berry   2 CH-458
Wason, Richard, 23 Jan. 1784, Sarah Lancaster   3 AA-420
Waterhouse, William, of Joshua and Elizabeth, of New Jersey,
   17th day, 5 mo., 1798, Ann Butler, dau. of Joseph and
   Mary Mitchell   8 SF-15
Waters, Aquila, 24 Dec. 1797, by Rev. Ridgely; Mary Hen-
   cock   4 AA
Waters, Basil, 19 March 1799, Ann P. Magruder   5 MO-114

Waters, Benjamin, 9 March 1797, Eliz. Becker   2 FR-1182
    4 FR gives the bride's name as Baker.
Waters, Charles, son of Jacob, 24 May 1792, Rebecca Fowler
    2 AA-114; 4 AA states the marriage was performed by
    Rev. John Long, and gives the groom's name as Charles
    S. Waters.
Waters, Clement, 27 March 1786, Sarah McNemara   2 DO
Waters, David, 30 March 1783, Mary Picket   11 BA-6
Waters, Edward, son of Samuel, 12th mo., 25 day, 1788,
    Hannah Moore Snowden, dau. of William Hopkins   6 SF
Waters, Edward, 3 Feb. 1799, by Rev. Ridgely; Rachel Jones
    4 AA
Waters, Ephraim, 22 Jan. 1797, by Rev. Ridgely; Ann Lowe 4 AA
Waters, George, 14 Dec. 1784, Sarah Austin   2 FR-1181
Waters, George, 9 July 1791, Abigail Williams; free
    blacks; see also 3 BA-253.   18 BA-3
Waters, Godfrey, 13 Nov. 1787, Martha Bradford   1 BA-1
Waters, Henry, 21 Feb. 1792, Grace Wilson   1 BA-4
Waters, Henry, 7 May 1793, Patience Bond   3 HA-22
Waters, James, 17 Sept. 1780, Draden King   1 CH-203
Waters, James, 1 Feb. 1785, Leannah Thomas   2 FR-1181
Waters, Jediah, 16 Jan. 1791, Margaret Scholls   2 FR-1182
Waters, John, 23 Aug. 1785, Christina Schoen   2 FR-1181
Waters, Jonathan, 18 Feb. 1798, Sarah Ann Mayo   1 AA-163
Waters, Josiah, 2 Feb. 1796, Ann Ballanger   4 FR
Waters, Nathaniel, 25 May 1794, by Rev. Ridgely; Mabel
    McCoy   4 AA
Waters, Philip, 9 Sept. 1789, Nelly Hincks   3 BA-221
Waters, Philipp, 4 June 1796, Sybil Gardner   6 BA
Waters, Richard, Feb. 1790, Mary Ann Mitchell   4 AA
Waters, Richard, 22 March 1791, Ann Dennis   2 DO
Waters, Richard, 4 Oct. 1795, by Rev. Ridgely; Sarah Cook
    4 AA
Waters, Richard, 20 June 1798, Mary Ann Chesney   3 SO
    2 SO gives the date as 21 June 1798, and the bride's
    name as Mary Day Chesney.
Waters, Samuel, 21st day, 2 mo., 1781, Sarah Unckles 3 SF
Waters, Spencer, 2 June 1797, Nancy Johnson   2 DO
Waters, Stanford, 23 Jan. 1790, Amy Robinson   2 DO
Waters, Stephen, 24 Feb. 1794, Sarah Dorsey   3 HA-23
Waters, Stephen, 30 March 1794, Jane Duckett   3 PG-439
Waters, Stephen, 7 July 1796, Prudence Penny   6 BA
Waters, Thomas, son of George and Betty, (date not given),
    Elizabeth Roberson   1 SO-179
Waters, Thomas, 15 Nov. 1790, Leah Kirkman   2 DO
Waters, Wm., 10 June 1782, Kitty McNeal   11 BA-5
Waters, William, 30 Oct. 1796, Anne Fallows   3 BA-329
Waters, William, 6 Feb. 1799, Sarah Boling   1 WO
Waters, William, 8 Sept. 1800, Mary Laycock   6 BA
Waters, William Gilliss, 29 May 1799, Anne Glasgow Elzey
    2 SO; 3 SO gives the date as 29 March 1799.
Waters, William Hayward, 15 July 1790, Ann Jacob, dau. of
    Robert Clark Jacob and wife Anne   1 SO-189
Waters, Wilson, 12 June 1800, Margaret Davis   1 AA-161
Waters, Zephaniah, 17 Jan. 1786, Elizabeth Morton Murphy
    1 CH-206
Waterson, James, 17 June 1800, Grace Campbell   3 BA-387
Watkin, William, 3 May 1792, Susanna Minskie   3 BA-256
Watkinduffer, Jno., 6 Nov. 1791, Lucy Branson   6 BA
Watkins, Benjamin, 16 April 1780, Elizabeth Sheckels 3 AA-416
Watkins, Charles, 15 Sept. 1780, Esther Terrel   2 PG-7
Watkins?, Ignatius, before 20 July 1793, by Rev. Blood-
    good; Eliza Gale   4 AA
Watkins, James, 17 May 1788, Rebecca Miller   3 BA-217
Watkins, Jeremiah, 23 June 1794, Deborah Purdy   4 FR

Watkins, John, 16 Aug. 1780, Elizabeth Evans   3 HA-2
Watkins, John, 14 Jan. 1783, Elizabeth Hall   3 AA-419
Watkins, John, 27 Oct. 1791, Ann Rutland   1 AA-163
Watkins, John, 8 April 1794, Sarah Fields   7 BA-1
Watkins, John, 2 June 1792, Ruth Guyton   1 BA-7
Watkins, John, son of Stephen, 5 Dec. 1797, Elizabeth
    Hall   1 AA-162
Watkins, Joseph, 26 June 1797, Polly Shaney   3 BA-346
Watkins, Nicholas, 12 Feb. 1782, Sarah Disny   3 AA-418
Watkins, Thomas, 18 Jan. 1778, Elizabeth Sprigg   2 PG-2
Watkins, Thomas, 26 Dec. 1779, Lucy Belt   2 CH-458
Watkins, Thomas, 5 Nov. 1797, by Rev. Ridgely; Sarah Disney
    4 AA
Watkins, Thomas, 20 March 1799, Elizabeth Spurrier   3 BA-369
Watkins, Wm., 17 Nov. 1791, Margaret Eccles   6 BA
Watkins, William, 13 Jan. 1799, Peggy McMillan   5 BA-15
Watson, David, 26 Feb. 1778, Elizabeth Trott   3 AA-414
Watson, David, 11 Aug. 1793, Mary Magdalen Roorbach   3 BA-271
Watson, Edward, 26 Nov. 1779, Anne Sanner   3 SM-58
Watson, George, 8 April 1781, Frances Griffen   3 AA-417
Watson, George, 14 Jan. 1800, by Rev. Ridgely; Sarah Gam-
    brill   4 AA
Watson, Jessey, 15 April 1779, Grace Bracon   1 SO-187
Watson, Joseph, 25 Sept. 1788, Fanny Moody   3 BA-218
Watson, Thomas, 7 March 1795, Anne Ogden   3 BA-301
Watson, Walter, 17 Oct. 1796, Jane Earle   4 FR
Watson, Wm., 11 Sept. 1780, Rosy Young; blacks   11 BA-4
Watters, Henry, 31 Dec. 1800, Mary Bradford   3 HA-30
Watters, Stephen, 26 Feb. 1794, by Rev. Benton Riggen;
    Sally Dorsey   4 AA
Watters, William, 1 July 1799, Elizabeth Brown   3 HA-28
Wattles, Chandler, 14 Dec. 1788, Sarah Gosling   11 BA-12
Watts, Benjamin, 13 July 1794, Susanna Griffin   3 BA-291
Watts, Edward, 9 July 1797, Elizabeth Aisquith   47 BA-1
Watts, George, 21 April 1799, by Rev. Wyatt; Mary Sark 4 AA
Watts, Henry, 22 Jan. 1799, Sarah Gwyther   4 SM-184
Watts, Isaac, 10 April 1783, Mary Smith   11 BA-6
Watts, Isaac, before 31 Aug. 1796, by Rev. Mills; Mary
    Buckingham   4 AA
Watts, Joshua, 11 Oct. 1787, Eliza Rayner   11 BA-10
Watts, Josias, 17 March 1785, Flora Perrigoe   11 BA-8
Watts, Josias, 7 June 1789, Mary Todd   6 BA
Watts, Josias, 23 Aug. 1798, Fanny Winfield   6 BA
Watts, Nathaniel, 24 Dec. 1789, Rebecca Stansbury   6 BA
Watts, Richard, 15 Dec. 1789, by Rev. Reed; Mary Packer 4 AA
Watts, Samuel, 30 March 1780, Mary Watts   11 BA-4
Watts, Thomas, 4 Sept. 1783, Lydia Bowen   11 BA-6
Watts, Thomas, 21 Nov. 1797, Elizabeth Carnons   3 BA-352
Waugh, Singleton, 3 March 1788, Elizabeth Wilworth   3 PG-254
Waugh?, William, 8 May 1784, Elizabeth Whygle   4 FR
Waughtell?, John, 19 June 1780, Elizabeth Summers   4 FR
Waver, Frederick, 2 Dec. 1797, Eliz. Maggin   3 WA-63
Wayman, Edmond, 30 July 1781, Airy Connoway   2 PG-5
Wayman, John, 17 July 1790, Margaret Elliott   4 FR
Wayman, Leonard, 16 April 1785, Eleanor Plummer   4 FR
Wayne, Ralph, 20 July 1800, Kitty Hunsman   6 BA
Weaden, John, 19 Dec. 1799, Martha Seedars   4 AA
Weale, Samuel, 25 April 1791, Kesia Cross   18 BA-3
Wear, James, 11 Sept. 1791, Charity Key   1 BA-3
Wearer, John, 6 Dec. 1794, Mary McFeel   3 BA-296
Weary, Joseph, 2 Aug. 1798, Rebecca Perrigo   3 BA-361
Weary, Peter, 11 Aug. 1785, Jemima Botts   11 BA-8
Weary, Thomas, 18 June 1795, Sarah Perigo   6 BA
Weary, William, 19 Sept. 1799, Anne Merrit   3 BA-377
Weason, Thomas, 14 March 1799, Mary Stansbury   3 BA-369

Weast, Jacob, 26 Aug. 1780, Eve Saline   4 FR
Weast, Jacob, 14 Sept. 1799, Susannah Shenkmire   4 FR
Weatherall, Henry, 2 May 1797, Charlotte E. Day   1 BA-8
     3 HA-26 gives the date as 27 April 1797.
Weatherall, William, 19 Sept. 1797, Mary Presbury   3 HA-26
     1 BA-8 gives the date as 21 Sept. 1797.
Weatherally, James, 18 Feb. 1784, Sarah Chancey   3 HA-8
Weatherby, Daniel, 23 March 1778, Sarah Woodward   11 BA-1
Weatherby, Dan'l, 8 Dec. 1785, Elizabeth Gorsuch   11 BA-9
Weatherby, William, 14 May 1795, Urith Scindall   3 BA-305
Weatherly, William, 11 Feb. 1800, Mary Leatherbury   2 SO
Weathers, Zebulon, 16 Nov. 1786, Ann Coats   11 BA-9
     See also 3 BA-191, 219.
Weaver, Casper, 12 May 1791, Ann Hatton   23 BA-2
Weaver, Dan'l, 31 May 1795, Diana Collins   29 BA-6
Weaver, George, 8 Feb. 1783, Barbara Bearinger   4 FR
Weaver, Jacob, 11 Aug. 1795, Elizabeth Nicholson   3 BA-307
Weaver, Jacob, 3 June 1798, Sarah Landerman   3 BA-359
Weaver, Jacob, 9 Oct. 1799, Elizabeth Waltz   4 FR
Weaver, Jno., 3 May 1789, Marg't Henly   11 BA-12
Weaver, Jno., 24 Sept. 1796, Sarah Currough   29 BA-7
Weaver, John, 19 Oct. 1799, Mary Govner   4 FR
Weaver, Lewis, 13 June 1794, Eliz. Lambert   29 BA-5
Weaver, Ludwick, 15 May 1797, Ruth Stevenson   4 FR
Weaver, William, 4 April 1782, Isabella Simpson   2 PG-3
Webb, Francis, 7 Jan. 1800, Rosanna Dail   2 DO
Webb, George, 8 Nov. 1798, Margaret Baughman   2 HA-350
     3 HA-27 gives the date as 5 Nov. 1798.
Webb, James, 1778, Eleanor Row; the marriage was sworn to
     on 4 May 1784, by Catherine Holland.   3 BA-186
Webb, John, 13 May 1780, Elizabeth Montgomery   3 HA-2
Webb, John, 4 Jan. 1797, Mary Hancock   1 WO
Webb, John, 10 Dec. 1799, Hetty Collins   2 SO
Webb, Peter, 9 Dec. 1782, Margaret Trippe   2 DO
Webb, Peter, 22 Feb. 1794, Sarah Trippe   2 DO
Webb, Peter, 10 May 1796, Mary Trippe   2 DO
Webb, Richard, son of John and Mary, 1st day, 12 mo.,
     1789, Mary, widow of John Malsby   1 SF
Webb, Samuel, 25 Oct. 1787, Belinda Elliott   11 BA-10
Webb, Thomas, 1 June 1799, Mary Holloway   1 WO
Webb, Wm., 11 Oct. 1785, Mary Merredith   2 FR-1181
Webe, Daniel, 15 March 1790, Sarah Tomer   50 BA-389
Weber, Henry, 31 May 1796, Elizab. Trit   2 FR-1182
Weber, Jacob, 22 Oct. 1799, Eliz. Waltz   2 FR-1182
Weber, John, 20 Oct. 1799, Mary Garner   2 FR-1182
Webster, Henry, 20 Feb. 1790, Dolly Laton   2 DO
Webster, Isaac, son of William and Ann, 4th day, 11 mo.,
     1784, Ruth Milhous, dau. of John and Margaret   11 SF-204
Webster, Isaac, 12th day, 4 mo., 1799, Elizabeth Hopkins,
     dau. of Samuel and Sarah   8 SF-19
Webster, James, 1 March 1781, Mary Brice   3 HA-3
Webster, Jesse, 7 Nov. 1797, Rebecca Traverse   2 DO
Webster, John, 27th day, 6 mo., 1778, Hannah Plummer   11 SF-189
Webster, John, son of John and Aliceanna, 15th day, 5 mo.,
     1800, Lucretia Tyson, dau. of Elisha and Mary   8 SF-31
Webster, John Skinner, 12 June 1800, Elisabeth Thornburg
     3 BA-387
Webster, John Stone, 12 Oct. 1786, Mary Lynn   3 PG-251
Webster, Joseph, 30 May 1792, Martha Chauncey   3 HA-21
Webster, Joshua, son of William and Ann, 1st day, 3 mo.,
     1798, Mary Richardson, dau. of Joseph and Dinah   11 SF-248
Webster, Philip Lewen, 20 May 1793, Elizabeth Been   3 PG-440
Webster, Richard, Jr., 14 April 1800, Rachel Mitchell   3 HA-29
Webster, Samuel, 3 Aug. 1781, Mary Baker   3 HA-4
Webster, Thomas, 21 Dec. 1785, Elizabeth Cassity   2 DO

Webster, Thomas, 23 June 1795, Rachel Beach   2 DO
Webster, William, 5 Dec. 1798, Polly Burton   1 TA-332
Weden, Nathaniel, 25 Sept. 1788, Catherine Ogden   3 PG-254
Wedge, Simon, 23 Nov. 1798, Margaret Herdich (or Hettig)
    9 BA-142
Weeden, James, 17 Jan. 1793, Sarah Wamsley   18 BA-5
Weedon, Richard, son of Richard, 15 Feb. 1800, Matilda
    Thomas, dau. of Joseph Exel Thomas   2 AA-115
Weeks, Jno., 17 March 1785, Ann Morrison   11 BA-8
Weeks, William, 3 Oct. 1797, Nancy Towson   6 BA
Weems, Col. John, 18 Dec. 1781, Mary Dorsey   3 AA-418
Weems, John, 8 April 1788, Alice Lee   2 CH-458
Weer, James, 8 March 1793, Lidia Richards   4 FR
Weihmann, Jacob, 6 Feb. 1794, Esther Penkert   10 BA-196
Weiks, Epenetus, 12 Aug. 1778, Sarah Price   11 BA-1
Weil, David, 27 May 1795, Philipine Webarn   3 WA-59
Weil, Jacob, 24 April 1795, Elis. Thomas   3 WA-58
Weiley, Robert, 24 April 1800, Mary Weiley   5 BA-15
Weinman, Heinr., 15 June 1794, Mary Irwin   50 BA-395
Weir, John, 18 July 1797, Sarah Madden   3 BA-347
Weisenthal, Barney, 21 Jan. 1792, Mary Stoner   4 FR
Weishampel, Christian, 18 Oct. 1799, Cath. Bankert   29 BA-10
Weisman, Conrad, 31 May 1790, Marg't Carne   4 FR
Weiss, Andr., 9 April 1784, An. Mar. Zeutzin   2 CL-82
Weisz, Philip, 5 Nov. 1793, Barbara Becker   2 FR-1182
Weiszman, Conrad, 31 May 1790, Marg. Kern   2 FR-1181
Welch, Edward, 11 June 1782, Dorothy Clements   2 CH-458
Welch, James, 9 Dec. 1797, Mary Ann Maynard   4 FR
Welch, Thomas, 2 June 1793, Martha Groves   1 BA-5
Welden, Ebenezer, 5 Nov. 1797, Ruthe Church   6 BA
Welfley, Christ'n, 27 Oct. 1780, Philipeana Hildebrand
    4 FR
Welfley, David, 26 Nov. 1786, Magdalena Getzendanner   4 FR
Well, John, 1790, C. Harvey   50 BA-390
Weller, Andrew, 9 March 1794, Mary Rhode   3 BA-285
Weller, Henry, 17 June 1799, Catherine Shover   4 FR
Weller, John Henry, son of John and Maria Barbara, 18
    June 1799, Catharine Schober, 2nd dau. of Peter and
    Sophia   5 FR-124
Weller, John Jacob, son of John Jacob and Anna, 14 Oct.
    1800, Margaret Weller, dau. of John Jacob and Anna
    Margaret (Harbaugh)   5 FR-125
Wellin, Amasa, 16 Jan. 1798, Linny Trundle   5 MO-114
Wells, Absolom, 28 Jan. 1798, Hellen Owings   6 BA
Wells, Bazaleel, 19 May 1795, Rebecca Risteau   4 BA-77
Wells, Charles, 4 Feb. 1783, Mary Williamson   11 BA-6
Wells, Chris., 18 Dec. 1792, Elizabeth Matts   2 AL-700
Wells, Cornelius, 13 Feb. 1783, Charlotte Craighead   3 BA-184
Wells, Cyprian, 13 Sept. 1778, Margaret White   11 BA-1
Wells, George, 9 Sept. 1778, by Rev. Wyatt; Augusta Maine?
    4 AA
Wells, James, 29 Aug. 1791, Jennett McHaffee   4 FR
Wells, John, 12 March 1782, Sarah Smith   3 HA-6
Wells, John, 1 March 1785, by Rev. West; Elizab. Welch
    51 BA-29
Wells, Jno., 12 June 1787, Sarah Hardesty   11 BA-10
Wells, Jonathan, 6 Nov. 1792, Mary Long   2 AL-700
Wells, Joseph, 16 Dec. 1781, Elizabeth Warfield   2 PG-3
Wells, Joseph, 14 March 1786, by Rev. Turner; Betsy Owings
    51 BA-29
Wells, Nathan, 15 Nov. 1798, Sophia Duley   5 MO-115
Wells, Nich's, 6 Oct. 1782, Providence Talbot   11 BA-5
Wells, Richard, 21 April 1778, Edith Coe   4 FR
Wells, Richard, 1 Nov. 1788, by Rev. Forrest; Sarah Carr 4 AA
Wells, Dr. Richard, 8 May 1793, Elizabeth Dyer   4 FR

Wells, Samuel, 13 Aug. 1778, Martha Oliver   2 CH-458
Wells, Thomas, 15 Feb. 1796, Thompsa Devall   3 BA-317
Wells, William, 12 March 1783, Cath. Smith   11 BA-6
Wells, Zenas, 4 Sept. 1799, Elizabeth Hanazan   3 HA-28
     12 BA-370 gives the date as 5 Sept. 1799, and the
     bride's name as Flanagan.
Welnor, Thomas, 26 Sept. 1799, Eleanor Henning   4 SM-184
Welsch, Philip, 11 April 1791, Elizabeth Davis   4 FR
Welsh, Aaron, 12 Nov. 1778, by Rev. Magowan; Elizabeth
     Franklin   4 AA
Welsh, Alexander, 10 Jan. 1800, Euphemia Lindsay   6 BA
Welsh, Edward, 20 Jan. 1788, Prudence Walker   6 BA
Welsh, Falise, 27 May 1782, Margaret Barns   3 HA-6
Welsh, Henry, 25 Jan. 1786, Mary Davis   4 FR
Welsh, Henry, 4 July 1791, Marg. Hamilton   29 BA-2
Welsh, Henry, 14 Aug. 1796, Barb. Shrote   29 BA-7
Welsh, James, 15 Aug. 1783, Ruth Vaughn   5 BA-14
Welsh, John, Sr., 11 July 1780, Susanna Mansfield   4 FR
Welsh, John, 15 Dec. 1785, Judith Roney   11 BA-9
Welsh, John, 19 Jan. 1794, Lucy Simpson   18 BA-6
Welsh, John, 10 May 1798, Anna Hallock   6 BA
Welsh, Mordecai, 25 Dec. 1790, by Rev. Green; Mary Watts 4 AA
Welsh, Robert, 29 Oct. 1795, by Rev. Ridgely; Sarah Merriken
     4 AA
Welsh, Tho., 3 Nov. 1785, Hannah Brooks   11 BA-8
Welsh, Thomas, 21 May 1793, Martha Groves   3 HA-22
Welsh, Walter, 8 May 1781, Eleanor Burk   5 BA-14
Welsh, William, 29 July 1794, Elizabeth Horton   3 HA-23
Welsh, William, 22 Feb. 1798, Catherine Stansbury   45 BA-2
Welty, Barnabas, 28 Feb. 1795, Mary Eichelberger   4 FR
Weltzheimer, Lewis, 8 April 1797, Margaret Meyer   4 FR
Wendlake, Lawrence, 3 Jan. 1798, Margaret Conley   3 BA-354
Wentling, John, Dec. 1798, Christina Kolern   3 WA-66
Werner, Jacob, 28 May 1787, Elizabeth Marx   1 FR-59
Werner, William, 29 Nov. 1798, Elizabeth Medcalfe   4 FR
Wertenbaker, Adam, 31 Dec. 1785, Elizabeth Rage   4 FR
Wescost, Jno., 22 Dec. 1785, Sarah Johnson   11 BA-11
Wessee, John, 19 Oct. 1786, Sarah Reeder   11 BA-9
West, David, 21st day, 1 mo., 1796, Mary Brown, dau. of
     Nicholas and Mary   7 SF-401
West, Edward, 13 Oct. 1794, Nancy Johnston   3 BA-293
West, Elijah, 3 Sept. 1789, Mary Hooper   11 BA-12
West, Enos., 18 Dec. 1800, Rebecca Hanaway   3 HA-30
West, Erasmus, 16 March 1793, Eleanor Belt   4 FR
West, Henry, 19 May 1796, Mahala Barnes   2 DO
West, Isaac, 16 June 1796, Sarah Carter   7 BA-3
West, Jacob, 8 Dec. 1794, by Rev. Benton Riggen; Mary Smith
     4 AA
West, James H., 9 Feb. 1798, Sarah W. Nicholson   2 SO
     3 SO gives the date as 11 Feb. 1798, and the groom's
     name as James U. West.
West, Joel, 19 July 1798, Juliana Francisca Repp   3 BA-360
West, John, 24 Jan. 1781, Mary Marshall   3 AA-417
West, Jonathan, 2 Nov. 1780, Jean Sturgeon   3 HA-3
West, Joseph, 9 Dec. 1784, Violetta Howard   4 BA-79
West, Joseph, 3 Nov. 1789, Anne Mollenecks   2 FR-1181
West, Luke, 27 May 1780, Sarah Bryon   3 HA-2
West, Simeon, 18 April 1797, Polly Clasby   3 BA-344
West, Stephen, 26 Nov. 1794, Ann Pue   3 BA-296
West, Thomas, 30 Dec. 1786, Sarah McGill   4 FR
West, William, 30 June 1785, Jemima Cross   6 BA
West, William, 10 Jan. 1786, Eliza Gorman   11 BA-9
Westcote, James, 9 April 1800, Mary West   3 BA-385
Westcott, John, 22 Sept. 1787, Sarah Johnson   3 BA-203
Westeberger, David, April 1800, Sus. Ox   3 WA-69

Westenhafer, Christopher, 12 Feb. 1797, Mary Downey   2 FR-1182
  4 FR gives the date as 11 Feb. 1797, and the groom's
  name as Christian Westenhaver.
Westerfield, William, 12 May 1799, Ann Cobourn   1 TA-332
Westerly, William, 19 April 1778, by Rev. Magill; Mary
  Polton   4 AA
Weston, Henry, 12 July 1796, Jenny Grover   6 BA
Weston, John, 6 Feb. 1783, Rebecca Day   11 BA-6
Weston, Joseph, 1 Jan. 1778, Rebecca Griffin   11 BA-1
Westover, Isaac, 18 Dec. 1800, Mary Berry   3 BA-396
Westwood, Jno., 3 Nov. 1796, Margaret Lowman   29 BA-8
Weyman, John, 17 July 1790, Marg. Eliot   2 FR-1182
Whalen, William, 14 June 1798, Elizabeth Kitely   6 BA
Wharton, Arthur, (27 Aug. 1785), Sarah Moore   25 BA-1
Whasky, Christian, 8 Nov. 1784, Ann Burket   11 BA-7
Wheat, Francis, 5 Nov. 1780, Sarah Upton   2 PG-3
Wheat, Jesse, 3 Dec. 1795, Sarah Soper   3 PG-441
Wheat, Zachariah, 7 Feb. 1782, Priscilla Reynolds   2 PG-3
Wheatley, Edward, 17 June 1790, Betsy Cannon   2 DO
Wheatley, Francis, 4 Feb. 1798, Prisca Edelen   3 CH-162
Wheatley, Ignatius, 25 Feb, 1796, Elizabeth Fletcher   8 MO-11
Wheatley, William, 22 March 1791, Elizabeth Harper   2 DO
Wheatly, Bent, 17 Jan. 1782, Polly Morris   2 CH-458
Wheaton, John R., 20 Nov. 1793, Elizabeth Murray   5 BA-15
Wheeler, Benedict, 23 Dec. 1779, Catherine Travers   2 CH-458
Wheeler, Benjamin, 4 Feb. 1793, Elizabeth Green   3 HA-22
Wheeler, Charles, 2 Aug. 1783, Elizabeth Thomas   2 DO
Wheeler, Charles, 20 June 1791, Sarah Woolford   2 DO
  28 BA-1 gives the date as 14 July 1791.
Wheeler, Gilbert, 14 May 1796, Drusilla Swearingen   4 FR
Wheeler, Greenbury, 11 May 1779, Susanna Welsh   5 BA-14
Wheeler, Henry, 12 Dec. 1784, Rebecca Hardy   4 FR
Wheeler, Ignatius, 19 Aug. 1783, Ann Morris   2 CH-458
Wheeler, Ignatius, 31 Jan. 1794, Rachel Newton   3 PG-439
Wheeler, John, 28 April 1785, Martha Sanders   11 BA-8
Wheeler, John, 13 Dec. 1792, Letitia Brown   3 PG-437
Wheeler, John, 30 Dec. 1799, Jenny Thomas   2 DO
Wheeler, James, 2 Feb. 1786, by Rev. Davis; Honour Cole
  51 BA-29
Wheeler, Joseph, 17 May 1786, by Rev. Turner; Rachel
  Welsh   51 BA-30
Wheeler, Joseph, 24 Aug. 1786, Sarah Smith   11 BA-9
Wheeler, Joseph, 16 Sept. 1791, Molly Slacom McNamara   2 DO
Wheeler, Joseph, 24 Nov. 1796, Sarah Waldren   7 BA-3
Wheeler, Josias, 16 June 1789, Martha Prigg   1 BA-2
Wheeler, Leonard, 7 Dec. 1797, Martha Warren   3 PG-443
Wheeler, Levin, 3 Oct. 1793, Dolly Sewers   2 DO
Wheeler, Levin, 9 Nov. 1796, Vain Cook   2 DO
Wheeler, Moses, 28 Nov. 1778, Henrietta Redman   3 SM-57
Wheeler, Nathaniel, 1787, Mary Cullen   1 SO-178
Wheeler, Nath'l, 16 Sept. 1790, Abarilla Warrell   11 BA-13
Wheeler, Philip, 19 May 1796, Mary Dines   6 BA
Wheeler, Richard, 20 Oct. 1786, by Rev. West; Rachel
  Bosley   51 BA-29
Wheeler, Richard, 22 Oct. 1797, by Rev. Ridgely; Eliza-
  beth Marriott   4 AA
Wheeler, Samuel, 29 Oct. 1780, Eleanor Wheeler   2 PG-3
Wheeler, Samuel, 7 Nov. 1783, Priscilla Williams   4 FR
Wheeler, Samuel, 13 May 1800, Mary Hendley   8 MO-24
Wheeler, Thomas, 23 June 1786, Molly Ross   2 DO
Wheeler, Thomas, 10 Feb. 1790, Eleanor Hilton   4 FR
Wheeler, Thomas, 15 June 1790, Margaret Shenton   2 DO
Wheeler, Thomas, 29 Jan. 1793, Elizabeth Martin   2 DO
Wheeler, Thomas, 18 Nov. 1794, Margaret Cottral   2 DO
Wheeler, Thomas, 26 Feb. 1795, Nancy Bowen   6 BA

Wheeler, Thomas, 28 Nov. 1799, Mary Goforth   6 BA
Wheeler, Thomas, 27 March 1800, Margaret Pickering   2 DO
Wheeler, Zadock, 28 Nov. 1796, Martha B. Dickerson   1 WO
Wheet, Joseph, 13 Dec. 1791, Rachel Bryan   3 PG-436
Whelan, Barth'w, 23 Nov. 1794, Bridget Flaherty   44 BA-1
Wheyland, William, 13 Oct. 1784, Anne Henry   2 DO
Whiffen, Joseph, 30 Oct. 1791, Susanna Knight   18 BA-3
    See also 3 BA-254.
Whip, Peter, 18 June 1788, Elizabeth Nicholls   4 FR
Whipp, Jacob, 28 Nov. 1785, Barbara Tabler   4 FR
Whipple, William, 6 Dec. 1798, Elizabeth Pate   3 BA-365
Whips, Benjamin, 23 July 1778, by Rev. Magill; Rebecca
    Pierce   4 AA
Whips, George, 11 Aug. 1778, by Rev. Magill; Elizabeth
    Pierce   4 AA
Whips, George, 3 Nov. 1792, by Rev. Dorsey; Susanna
    Shipley   4 AA
Whips, Samuel, 25 June 1792, Elizabeth Cook   4 FR
Whips, Samuel, 10 Feb. 1778, by Rev. Magill; Henrietta
    Pool; both from Baltimore Co.   4 AA
Whitacre, Hezekiah, 18 July 1784, Mary Taylor   3 HA-8
Whitacre, John, 6 Sept. 1781, Rachel Johnson   3 HA-4
Whitaker, Isaac, 9 Sept. 1796, Susannah M. Grill   3 HA-23
Whitaker, Isaac, 9 Feb. 1798, Margaret Everist   3 HA-27
    2 HA-350 gives the date as 11 Feb. 1798, and the bride's
    name as Everett.
Whitaker, Thomas, 22 Feb. 1800, Charlotte Durham   3 HA-29
Whitcraft, Edward, 25 Aug. 1792, Mary Bonham   4 FR
White, Abraham, 3 June 1797, Martha Bussey   3 HA-26
White, Archibald, 6 Feb. 1791, Mary Nash   3 PG-257
White, Archible, 22 Jan. 1793, Catherine Ekhard   2 AL-700
White, Benjamin, 5 April 1790, Susanna Carmack   2 FR-1181
White, Benjamin, 17 Dec. 1790, Rebeckah Chiswell   4 FR
White, Benoni, 16 July 1793, Elizabeth Ankerson   6 BA
White, Charles, 6 June 1778, Elizabeth Bobbs   11 BA-1
White, Davis, 2 Nov. 1799, Mary Overholtz   4 FR
White, Edw'd, 23 Jan. 1795, Mary Lush   29 BA-6
White, Gideon, 21 June 1798, by Rev. Wyatt; Anne Barber
    4 AA
White, Gowan, 25 May 1799, Biddy Hickman   2 SO
    3 SO gives the date as 20 March 1799.
White, Grafton (Grenfton?), 10 Jan. 1781, Margaret Denny
    2 CH-458; 3 HA-5 gives the date as 3 Jan. 1782.
White, Henry, 12 Jan. 1784, Elizabeth Rust   5 BA-14
White, Henry, 29 April 1784, Susanna Hendrickson   4 FR
White, Henry, 30 Jan. 1797, Sally Lister   1 WO
White, Henry, 15 Jan. 1799, Polly Jones   1 WO
White, Henry, 11 Feb. 1799, Sarah Trader   1 WO
White, Hudens, 7 July 1796, Carlenore McManners   8 MO-12
White, Jacob, 18 Dec. 1798, Polly Wilson   1 WO
White, Jacobus, 17 June 1790, Elizabeth Bonwill   2 DO
White, James, 10 Aug. 1794, Catherine Merrick   3 BA-291
White, James, 16 April 1796, Elizabeth Essang   1 AL-53
White, James, 5 June 1798, Hannah Bull   3 HA-27
    1 BA-8 gives the date as 7 June 1798.
White, John, 26 Oct. 1780, Ursula Smith   2 PG-3
White, John, 31 Dec. 1780, Mary Brown   2 PG-5
White, John, 27 June 1783, Elener Long   2 CH-458
White, John, 20 Aug. 1787, Sarah Ingram   2 DO
White, John, 1 Feb. 1791, Amelia Cohagan   3 PG-257
White, John, 9 Aug. 1792, Elizabeth Roberts   3 BA-257
White, John, 4 March 1796, Nancy Cavender   2 DO
White, John, 31 Dec. 1797, Patty Wilson   3 BA-354
White, John, 7 May 1799, Polly Selby   1 WO
White, John, 25 Dec. 1800, by Rev. Ridgely; Mary White   4 AA

White, John Cale, 1 May 1800, Harriet Lee   1 AA-162
White, Jonas, 29 Jan. 1793, by Rev. G. Ridgely; Ruth
    Marriott   4 AA
White, Joseph, 13 March 1793, Mary Fulton   2 FR-1182
White, Michael, 20 Feb. 1798, Julian Lary   3 BA-355
White, Nat, 18 Aug. 1800, Patty Gray   1 WO
White, Richard, 1 Nov. 1777, Priscilla Stewart   2 PG-2
White, Richard, c.Sept. or Oct. 1778, Dorcas Addington   3 AA-415
White, Richard, 30 April 1800, by Rev. Wyatt; Delila Pierce
    4 AA
White, Robert, 19 Sept. 1782, Keziah Wooden   11 BA-5
White, Robert, 21 Dec. 1797, by Rev. Green; Mary Ann Murphy
    4 AA
White, Sam'l, 9 Oct. 1785, Ann Parrin Hellen   11 BA-8
White, Simon, 24 July 1783, Jane Lowe   11 BA-6
White, Stephen, 1 Dec. 1794, Clementina Everett   7 BA-1
White, Thomas, 4 Nov. 1778, Sarah Gavin   4 FR
White, Thos., 21 Sept. 1780, Cath'a Devoe   11 BA-4
White, Thomas, 25 Jan. 1789, Mary Lewis   11 BA-12
White, Thomas, 26 Aug. 1795, Rebecca Gore   2 DO
White, Thomas, 20 Aug. 1796, Sarah Nairn   1 WO
White, Thomas, 16 Jan. 1798, Anne Wright   2 SO
    3 SO gives the date as 25 Jan. 1798.
White, Walter, 15 Jan. 1789, Sarah Davis   2 PG-4
White, Wm., 17 July 1782, Mary Settlemire   11 BA-5
White, William, 4 Jan. 1797, Ann Redgrave   4 KE-72
White, William, 5 Sept. 1797, Agnes Adams   3 HA-26
White, William, 24 Dec. 1798, Anne Dove   2 SO
    3 SO gives the date as 27 Dec. 1798.
White, William S., 11 April 1796, Betsey S. Waggaman   1 WO
Whiteford, Jas., 9 Oct. 1793, Marg. Butler   50 BA-393
Whiteford, Robert, 2 Feb. 1796, Nancy Kernan   3 HA-26
Whiteford, Robert, 2 Feb. 1796, Nancy McCairnan   1 BA-7
Whiteford, Samuel, 2 March 1799, Elizabeth Butler   3 HA-28
Whitehead, Edward, 5 Feb. 1793, by Rev. G. Ridgely; Anne
    Kingsbury   4 AA
Whitehead, Thomas, 7 Dec. 1780, Mary Waters   2 PG-3
Whitehill, John, 17 Aug. 1795, Mary Clemson   4 FR
Whiteley, Arthur, 23 April 1798, Rhoda Chipman   2 DO
Whiteley, David, 25 Dec. 1799, Jemima Williams   2 DO
Whiteley, Ezekiel, 2 March 1792, Peggy Harper   2 DO
Whiteley, Henry, 20 May 1796, Mary Sewers   2 DO
Whiteley, John, 2 March 1791, Nancy Hooper   2 DO
Whiteley, John, 3 Dec. 1798, Nancy Soward   2 DO
Whiteley, Nathaniel, 12 Feb. 1789, Dolly Dean   2 DO
Whiteley, Nehemiah, 31 Jan. 1781, Molly Fouks   2 DO
Whiteley, Nehemiah, 17 Aug. 1785, Rosanna Stewart   2 DO
Whiteley, Zebedee, 19 Jan. 1792, Polly Hooper   2 DO
Whitelock, John, 13 April 1800, Mary Montgomery   5 BA-15
Whitely, David, 26 Dec. 1799, Jamima Williams   1 DO-40
Whitenar, Lazarus, 25 April 1785, Wendeleana Eater   4 FR
Whitesides, Bamber, 24 Jan. 1798, Martha Weekins   3 BA-354
Whitley, Job, 28 April 1793, Sarah Willen   2 DO
Whitley, John, 7 Jan. 1792, Hannah Burns   6 BA
Whitley, Nathaniel, 10 Feb. 1784, Dolly Keene   2 DO
Whitmore, Benj., 21 July 1782, Mary Hockersmith   4 FR
Whitmore, Benjamin, 13 Feb. 1787, Eleanor Longly   3 PG-252
Whitmore, Humphery, 21 Jan. 1794, Mary Walker   3 PG-439
Whitmore, John, 1 Sept. 1778, Mary Coe   4 FR
Whitmore, Stephen, 23 Dec. 1790, Sarah Vermillion   3 PG-257
Whitney, Arthur, 25 Dec. 1791, Maria Weiss, dau. of
    George   2 WA-17
Whitney, David, 21 Jan. 1799, Rachel Evans   2 SO
    See also 3 SO.
Whitney, Gilbert, 13 May 1787, Sarah Conner   3 PG-252

Whitney, Gilbert, 25 Nov. 1794, Ann Melony   3 PG-440
Whitney, Thomas, 5 March 1795, Susanna Newel   3 BA-301
Whitterfield, William, 13 July 1798, Margaret Warfield 3 BA-360
Whittington, Benjamin, 4 Dec. 1788, by Rev. Forrest; Cassan-
   dra Smith   4 AA
Whittington, Francis, 29 Jan. 1778, Eleanor Turner   3 AA-414
Whittington, Isaac, 16 Jan. 1795, Mary Foster   2 DO
Whittington, James, 18 Dec. 1799, Sarah Coulbourn   2 SO
Whittington, John, 1 June 1780, Mary Armiger   3 AA-416
Whittington, John, 15 Oct. 1796, Rebeckah Pritchett   4 FR
Whittington, Thomas, 4 Nov. 1789, Sarah Conner   1 SO-188
Whittington, Wm., 25 Dec. 1788, by Rev. Clagett; Susanna
   Wood   4 AA
Whittington, William, 31 Dec. 1791, Nancy Ennalls   2 DO
Whittle, David, 6 Jan. 1784, Ann Wood   11 BA-7
Whittle, Joh., 12 April 1796, Charity Forrest   3 WA-60
Whittle, Rich., 7 Jan. 1784, Elizabeth Burling   10 BA-180
Whittle, Richard, 15 Dec. 1794, by Rev. Ridgely; Elisabeth
   Baldwin   4 AA
Whittle, Zachariah, 12 March 1795, by Rev. Ridgely; Eliza-
   beth Disney   4 AA
Wholey, Thomas, 21 Sept.? 1781, Priscilla Booker   3 AA-417
Whover, Christian, 6 Aug. 1796, Susy Antbebiorgez   3 WA-61
Wickery, George, 7 May 1792, Jane Prather   4 FR
Wickes, James, 18 May 1794, Easter Chance   39 BA-1
Wickham, Robert, 1 Dec. 1783, Susanna Campbell   4 FR
Wicks, Philip, 7 Sept. 1800, Margaret Higgins   6 BA
Wiesenmilder, Christ., 16 May 1785, Eliz. Schneider   2 FR-1181
Wiesenthal, Bernhardt, 22 Jan. 1792, Mary Steiner   2 FR-1182
Wiest, Jacob, 15 Sept. 1799, Sus. Schenckmayer   2 FR-1182
Wietrick, George, 7 Sept. 1799, Catherine Hargate   4 FR
Wiggard, Joh., 2 Oct. 1796, Clara Rumel   50 BA-400
Wigginton, Henry, 2 March 1778, Ann Vallandingham   2 MO-1
Wigginton, William, 7 Feb. 1778, Allison Evans   2 MO-1
Wight, John, 21 May 1797, Cary Boyd   5 MO-114
Wightt, Isle of (sic), 31 March 1783, Elizabeth Webster
   3 PG-387
Wigle, John, 23 Nov. 1784, Barbara Myer   4 FR
Wigle, Leonard, 24 Dec. 1792, Susanna Marp   4 FR
Wigley, Edward, 4 Sept. 1783, Mary Eagleston   11 BA-6
Wigley, Edward, 15 Sept. 1793, Nancy Gregory   6 BA
Wigley, George, 27 Dec. 1797, Mary Allison   4 FR
Wigley, Isaac, 6 July 1800, Sigea Johns   6 BA
Wilbone, Frederick, 10 July 1790, Catherine Weaver   4 FR
Wilcocks, James, 7 Dec. 1797, Mary or Polly McKensie 3 BA-353
Wilcox, Thomas, 24 March 1800, Nancy Littleton   2 DO
Wilcox, William, 1788, Eva Grove   50 BA-388
Wilcoxen, Jesse, 22 March 1796, Ruth Wilcoxen   5 MO-113
Wilcoxon, Levin, 16 March 1780, Mary Brashears   2 PG-3
Wilcoxon, Thomas, Jr., 24 April 1781, Mary Hardy   2 PG-5
Wilcoxon, Thos. H., 3 May 1788, Sarah Prather   5 MO-115
Wilcoxon, William, 10 Nov. 1781, Esther Taylor   3 BA-182
Wilder, John Brown, 27 May 1779, Mary Ann Smoot   2 CH-458
Wilderman, John, 25 April 1789, Margaret Wallar   6 BA
Wiles, Wm., 5 Aug. 1782, Ann Bird   4 FR
Wiley, Henry, 30 Aug. 1778, by Rev. Magowan; Mary Tanyhill
   4 AA
Wiley, Jacob, 21 Jan. 1799, Martha Block   6 BA
Wiley, Matthew, 22 May 1782, Rebecca Nelson   3 HA-6
Wilhide, Conrad, 1 Oct. 1792, Elizabeth Creager   4 FR
Wilhide, Frederick, 1800, Catharina Peitzel   5 FR-131
Wilhide, John, 1 Feb. 1785, Maria Barbara Weller, dau. of
   John Jacob and Magdalena   5 FR-133
Wilinmyer, Casp'r, 2 July 1791, Marg. Sumvalt   29 BA-2
Wiljarth, Abraham, 12 Jan. 1800, Cath. Beisser   2 FR-1182

Wilk, Peter, 24 Feb. 1800, Catherine Maguire	3 BA-383
Wilkenson, Richard, 19 Feb. 1778, Mary Askey	1 CA-1
Wilkerson, John, 28 May 1789, Elizabeth Murrey	6 BA
Wilkes, Joseph, 29 Sept. 1784, Sarah Richardson	11 BA-7
Wilkins, John, 5 June 1795, Elizabeth Christie	1 WO
Wilkinson, Joseph, 30 March 1782, Milly McCasley	2 CH-458
Wilkinson, Joseph, 16 July 1794, Mary Shock	18 BA-6
Wilkinson, Robert, 10 Dec. 1795, by Rev. Joshua Jones;	
Frances Todd Carnan	46 BA-1
Wilkinson, Wm., 18 March 1800, Eleanor Parish	29 BA-11
Wilks, Jas. or Jos., 18 June 1797, Ruth Thompson	29 BA-8
Wilks, John, 1790, Cath. South	50 BA-389
Wilks, William, 5 Aug. 1783, Eliza Morgan	11 BA-6
Willcocks, James, 29 Oct. 1789, Sarah Gray	3 BA-221
Willcox, Thomas, before 25 Nov. 1789, in Queen Annes Co.;	
Dorothy Pratt	20 BA-1
Willen, John, 9 Sept. 1799, Elizabeth Bailey	2 DO
Willet, Ninian, 1 Aug. 1778, Chloe Walker	2 PG-2
Willett, Griffith, 20 Nov. 1783, Mary Grove	4 FR
Willett, John, 15 July 1800, Deboria Butler	6 BA
Willett, Ninian, 21 July 1791, Elizabeth Sommers	3 PG-258
Willey, Absolom, 18 Dec. 1781, Clair Andrews	2 DO
Willey, Absolom, 13 June 1798, Rhoda Stinnett	1 DO-39
Willey, Archibald, 5 March 1788, Mary Robinson	2 DO
Willey, Capewell, 6 June 1791, Polly Willey	2 DO
Willey, Edward, 21 June 1791, Keziah Anderson	2 DO
Willey, Ezekiel, 3 Sept. 1797, Sarah Andrews	1 DO-39
Willey, Henry, 1 Jan. 1791, Mary Goodridge	5 BA-15
Willey, Isaac, 5 May 1796, Mary Hammond	29 BA-7
Willey, John, 15 Feb. 1796, Lurana Lewis	2 DO
Willey, John, 14 Aug. 1800, Latitia Woollen	2 DO
Willey, Joseph, 30 June 1797, Neomia Favory	29 BA-8
Willey, Littleton, 14 Jan. 1792, Hannah Wheatley	2 DO
Willey, Neddy, 6 June 1791, Amy Street	2 DO
Willey, William, 1 May 1793, Rhoda Messick	2 DO
Willey, William, 4 Oct. 1800, Perry Gadd	2 DO
Williams, Andrew, 31 March 1799, Elisabeth Duncan	5 BA-15
Williams, Benj., (20 Jan. 1789), Prudence Gorsuch	15 BA-2
Williams, Benjamin, 10 Nov. 1796, by Rev. Ridgely; Mary	
Penn	4 AA
Williams, Benjamin, 31 Oct. 1797, Elizabeth Boyer	4 KE-72
Williams, Benjamin, 6 May 1798, Elizabeth B. Harding	4 FR
Williams, Brown, 26 Feb. 1778, Ruth Cromwell	11 BA-1
Williams, Caleb, 16 Sept. 1800, Hetty Williams	1 WO
Williams, Charles, 10 Nov. 1778, Mary Rawlins	11 BA-1
Williams, Christopher, 14 June 1791, Mary Gray	29 BA-2
Williams, Edward, 3 Sept. 1790, Priscilla Beall	4 FR
Williams, Edw. O.?, 4 Dec. 1800, Eliz. Clagett	5 MO-113
Williams, Eli, 22 May 1798, Euphamy Jones	1 WO
Williams, Ennion, son of Isaac and Lydia, 9th day, 6 mo.,	
1785, Hannah Hayward, dau. of Joseph	1 SF
Williams, Enoch, son of William and Eleanor, 5th day, 11	
mo., 1778, Ann Weeks, widow of Daniel Weeks, and dau.	
of Benjamin and Rachel Lancaster	1 SF
Williams, Frederic, 13 Nov. 1794, Rachel Smith	5 BA-15
Williams, George, 1 Jan. 1784, Dorothy Meddis	2 DO
Williams, George, 30 Sept. 1795, Mary McFaron	6 BA
Williams, Hazael, 13 Sept. 1778, Mary Gore Hardy	2 MO-1
Williams, Hugh, 4 Feb. 1798, Mary Ann Dwyer	29 BA-2
Williams, Humphrey, 23 Jan. 1794, Sarah Beall	3 PG-439
Williams, Isaac, 2nd day, 10 mo., 1783, Rebecca Hayward	1 SF
Williams, Isaac, Jr., son of Isaac and Lydia, 31st day,	
12 mo., 1783, Mary Hayward, dau. of William	1 SF
See also 6 SF.	
Williams, Jacob, 22 June 1797, Polly Clower	29 BA-8

Williams, Jacob, 5 Sept. 1799, Nancy Smith   3 BA-377
Williams, James, 15 June 1797, Rachel Maid   3 BA-346
Williams, James, 11 Dec. 1800, Rebecca McCaskey   6 BA
Williams, James Pittingill, 17 Aug. 1796, Hannah Richardson
     6 BA
Williams, John, 19 Sept. 1779, Marg't Cazey   11 BA-3
Williams, John, 29 Aug. 1782, Margaret Taylor   2 PG-3
Williams, John, 5 Nov. 1782, Elizabeth Pritchard   3 HA-7
Williams, John, 10 July 1783, Alice Bond   11 BA-6
Williams, John, 4 Dec. 1783, Eliza Bowen   3 AA-420
Williams, John, 28 June 1784, Catherine Tucker   3 BA-188
Williams, John, 24 July 1784, Rosanna Ferguson   2 DO
Williams, Jno., 17 March 1785, Ann Wells   11 BA-8
     See also 3 BA-219.
Williams, John, 23 Nov. 1785, Mary Coulson   3 HA-9
Williams, Jno., 24 Dec. 1785, Eleanor Dickson   11 BA-9
Williams, John, 31 Oct. 1786, Mary Williams   2 DO
Williams, John, 8 Sept. 1788, Jane Morrison   3 BA-218
Williams, John, 5 Jan. 1789, Barbara Wrotten   2 DO
Williams, John, 8 Feb. 1790, Ruth McCollister   2 DO
Williams, John, 8 April 1790, Margaret Remmage   5 BA-15
Williams, John, 26 Jan. 1792, Rachel Vaughan   1 BA-4
Williams, John, 19 Feb. 1793, Elizabeth Hagan   4 FR
Williams, John, 7 March 1793, Elizabeth Balkett   3 PG-438
Williams, John, 28 Feb. 1796, Catherine Wood   2 FR-1182
Williams, John, 28 March 1796, Julianna Storm   2 FR-1182
Williams, John, 1 July 1797, Martha Hoggins   3 BA-347
Williams, John, 9 Nov. 1797, Lydia Robinson   5 BA-15
Williams, John, 2 Dec. 1798, Cassandra Waller   6 BA
Williams, John, 20 Feb. 1799, Martha Burns   4 FR
Williams, John, 29 Dec. 1799, Elizabeth Stone   8 MO-23
Williams, Jno., 1 Nov. 1800, Henrietta Turpin   1 WO
Williams, John, 17 Nov. 1800, Phoebe Smith   3 AL-7
Williams, Joseph, 27 April 1797, Eliz. Yeiser   29 BA-8
Williams, Lilburn, 8 Oct. 1782, Mary Thompson   2 PG-3
Williams, Luke, 20 May 1794, Dolly Webster   2 DO
Williams, Luke, 24 March 1800, Elizabeth Dean   2 DO
Williams, Mattew, 1 Sept. 1794, Nancy Brinsfield   2 DO
Williams, Nathan, 2 Aug. 1791, Sarah Parsins   29 BA-2
Williams, Otho Holland, 18 Oct. 1785, Mary Smith   5 BA-14
Williams, Philip, before 15 Sept. 1796, by Rev. Green;
     Rachel Pearce   4 AA
Williams, Purnell, 12 March 1799, Peggy Collins   1 WO
Williams, Rezin, 9 Dec. 1782, Elizabeth Fowler   4 FR
Williams, Robert, 6 Jan. 1800, Polly Griffy   6 BA
Williams, Talbot, 15 Nov. 1781, Ann Gardner   3 AA-418
Williams, Thomas, 25 Nov. 1781, Jane Jordan   11 BA-5
Williams, Thomas, 6 Aug. 1794, Elizabeth Badley   2 DO
Williams, Thomas, 27 Feb. 1797, Nancy Parker   1 WO
Williams, Thomas, 8 Nov. 1798, Sus. Steyer   2 FR-1182
Williams, Thomas, 8 Dec. 1798, Rebecca Steward   6 BA
Williams, Thomas, 7 June 1800, Eliz'th Lowell   7 BA-4
Williams, Thomas, 15 Aug. 1800, Nancy Humphries   3 BA-389
Williams, Thomas Nathaniel, 23 Feb. 1797, Nancy Parker 2 WO-54
Williams, Uriah, 18 March 1798, Sarah Roach   4 FR
Williams, Walter, 28 Jan. 1786, Ann McGill   4 FR
Williams, Walter C., 2 Aug. 1796, Christiana Heugh   5 MO-113
Williams, William, 31st day, 3 mo., 1784, Delilah Berry
     2 SF-288
Williams, Wm., 27 May 1786, Keziah Johnson   4 FR
Williams, William, 29 Sept. 1789, Rachael Conn   3 PG-255
Williams, William, 16 Dec. 1792, Milcah Fowler   1 AA-165
Williams, William, 20 Dec. 1792, Mary -(?)-   1 SO-179
Williams, William, 23 Dec. 1792, by Rev. G. Ridgely; Ruth
     Beck   4 AA

Williams, William, 22 June 1796, Anna Fowler   4 FR
Williams, William, 8 Feb. 1798, Catherine Simpson, dau.
  of James, and sister of Walter Simpson   8 MO-18a
Williams, William, 15 June 1800, Susanna Ridgeaway   8 BA-2
  See also 48 BA-1.
Williamson, Alexander, 23 Dec. 1781, Ann Kent   3 AA-418
Williamson, David, 8 June 1780, Henny Mitchell   2 PG-1
Williamson, David, free person of colour, 1 Dec. 1799,
  Lucy Williams, slave of Hercules Courtenay   3 BA-381
Williamson, Edburn, 30 Oct. 1800, Eliza Patterson   8 BA-2
  See also 48 BA-1.
Williamson, James, 1 Feb. 1780, Elizabeth Lyles   3 AA-416
Williamson, James H., 31 Oct. 1789, Nancy Raitt   4 FR
Williamson, John, 26 July 1797, Susey Lindry   4 KE-72
Williamson, Samuel, 1 June 1780, Micah Wells   5 BA-14
Williamson, Thomas, 26 Nov. 1778, Rachel Hurd   14 BA-1
Williamson, William, 5th day, 2 mo., 1789, Phebe Pasmore,
  dau. of Augustine and Hannah   11 SF-219
Williar, Andrew, son of Peter and Magdalena, 1781, Marga-
  ret Harbaugh, dau. of George and Catherine   5 FR-136
Williard, John, 11 Oct. 1799, Frances Kepler   4 FR
Williard, Peter, 1 Oct. 1792, Barbara Honeling   4 FR
Williard, Philip, 25 June 1796, Catherine Knouff   3 BA-190
Williby, William, 24 July 1785, Jane Cain   1 CA-3
Willin, Thomas, 9 Jan. 1780, Elizabeth Wood   3 PG-438
Willing, William, 31 Jan. 1793, Mary Darcey   6 BA
Willing, William, 20 Aug. 1795, Susannah Gable   3 HA-1
Willion, William, 7 Jan. 1780, Mary Scott   11 BA-6
Willis, George, 5 March 1783, Sarah Labat   11 BA-13
Willis, George, 30 Jan. 1790, Johanna Kellehan   23 BA-3
Willis, Henry, 16 March 1792, Ann Hollingsworth   2 DO
Willis, John, 20 Dec. 1783, Mary Clarkson   5 BA-15
Willis, John, 13 Dec. 1798, Nancy Hite   3 BA-213
Willis, John Winfield, 2 Nov. 1788, Ann Baker   2 DO
Willis, Joshua, 2 Sept. 1799, Elizabeth Wright   6 BA
Willis, Joshua, 22 Oct. 1799, Elizabeth Ogden   1 TA-331
Willis, Peter, 15 April 1798, Elizabeth Holmes
Willis, Philemon, 17 Dec. (year not given), Nancy Barnaby
  1 TA-331
Willis, Ricard, 27 Dec. 1796, Betsy Jones   2 DO
Williss, William, 9 Aug. 1792, Henney Chance   2 SF
Willmon, Jacob, 23 April 1797, Sarah Palmer   2 DO
Willmore, James Jones, 21 May 1783, Sarah McGaw   3 HA-8
Willmot, John, 3 Jan. 1788, Hannah Wheeler   3 BA-216
Willoughby, John, 8 Feb. 1800, Rebecca Woolford   2 DO
  1 DO-40 gives the date as 11 Feb. 1800.
Wills, Colin C., 30 July 1795, Susanna Robberds   3 BA-307
Wills, Henry, 30 Sept. 1780, Jermimah Coe   4 FR
Wills, John, 25 Dec. 1788, Margaret Fields   2 PG-4
Wills, John, 13 Aug. 1800, Polly Christopher   1 WO
Wills, Luke, 15 March 1794, Elenor Reed   3 BA-285
Willsford, George, 8 Sept. 1798, Ann Wigley   6 BA
Willson, Benjamin, 17 Nov. 1780, Hannah Morrison   3 HA-3
Willson, Francis I., 19 April 1800, Susan Daffin   2 DO
Willson, George, 6 May 1790, Eleanor Ruark   2 DO
Willson, Henry, 25 Nov. 1791, Susann Farquhar   4 FR
Willson, James, 8 Oct. 1784, Hannah Ady   3 HA-9
Willson, James, 15 Jan. 1798, Nancy Phillips   2 DO
Willson, John, 27 Aug. 1780, Letitia Kenley   3 HA-2
Willson, John, 9 Aug. 1787, Margaret Derry   3 BA-219
Willson, John, 26 April 1792, Milcah Taylor   3 BA-258
Willson, John, 2 Dec. 1795, Darcus Loon   3 BA-313
Willson, Nathaniel, 15 Oct. 1795, Elizabeth Shipway   3 BA-311
Willson, Robert, 18 April 1783, Lizzie -(?)-   3 HA-7
Willson, Robert, 28 Nov. 1791, Elizabeth Killman   2 DO

Willson, Robert, 30 Oct. 1798, Eleanor Shekells   5 MO-115
Willson, Samuel Wilmore, 7 Jan. 1792, Nancy Wheeler   2 DO
Willson, Thomas, 30 July 1782, Susanna Fogle   4 FR
Willson, Wm., 21 April 1796, Ann White   5 MO-113
Wilmen, Richard, 20 April 1795, Mary Morris   3 BA-301
Wilmer, Benjamin, 28 May 1800, Margaret Crawford   3 HA-29
   12 BA-371 gives the date as 29 May 1800.
Wilmer, William, 5 June 1797, Catherine Wetherall   3 HA-26
   12 BA-370 gives the date as 8 June 1797.
Wilsford, Geor., 29 Oct. 1791, Eleanora Hill   29 BA-2
Wilson, Alexander, 20 Aug. 1791, Frances Thomas   23 BA-2
Wilson, Amon, 11 Oct. 1787, Sarah Lowry   11 BA-10
Wilson, Aqualia, 26 Nov. 1791, Sarah Taylor   3 PG-258
Wilson, Basil, 22 Aug. 1779, Ann Scott   2 PG-3
Wilson, Benjamin, son of Benjamin and Lydia, 2nd day, 4
   mo., 1795, Anne Sidwell, dau. of Hugh and Anne   11 SF-208
Wilson, Christopher, son of John and Susanna, 10th day,
   9 mo., 1789, Margaret Coale, dau. of Skipwith and
   Sarah   1 SF
Wilson, Christopher, son of John and Aliceanna, 10th day,
   9 mo., 1789, Margaret Coale, dau. of Skipwith and
   Sarah   9 SF-54
Wilson, Clement, 6 Sept. 1778, Susannah Cecil   2 PG-3
Wilson, David, son of Samuel and Catherine, 11th day, 3 mo.,
   1784, Jane Humphrey, dau. of David and Elizabeth   1 SF
Wilson, David, 26 Aug. 1787, Hannah Wilson   6 BA
Wilson, David, 7 Dec. 1798, Mary Tatler   6 BA
Wilson, David, 3 Sept. 1799, Priscilla Covington   2 SO
Wilson, Ephraim K., 17 Dec. 1799, Sally Handy   1 WO
Wilson, Fielder, 6 Feb. 1792, Mary Suit   3 PG-436
Wilson, Francis, 10 Sept. 1780, Ruth Corbin   11 BA-4
Wilson, Gavin, 18 Nov. 1788, Delilah Roberts   6 BA
Wilson, George,27 July 1798, Hannah Wilson   35 BA-6
   See also 3 BA-361.
Wilson, Henry, 1 Dec. 1791, Sus. Forquhar   2 FR-1182
Wilson, Henry, 9 April 1795, Sarah Worthington   1 BA-7
Wilson, Hezekiah, 1 May 1784, Bethsheba Veatch   4 FR
   7 MO-29 gives the date as 9 May 1784.
Wilson, Hugh, 5 Sept. 1780, Eleanor Wilson   11 BA-4
Wilson, Hugh, 3 Feb. 1794, Hannah Hill   3 BA-281
Wilson, Jacob, 24 Jan. 1795, Rebeckah Hammet   4 FR
Wilson, James, 25 Nov. 1779, Rebecca Skinner   1 CA-3
Wilson, James, 28 Nov. 1793, Sarah Charles   2 SF
Wilson, James, 26 June 1800, Mary Davis   3 BA-387
Wilson, James, 30 Dec. 1800, Mary Shields   6 BA
Wilson, John, Jr., 2 Feb. 1779, Mary Perkins   2 KE-313
Wilson, John, 30 March 1780, Mary Scott   3 HA-1
Wilson, Jno., 1793, Ann Robinson   50 BA-393
Wilson, John, 13 May 1793, Sarah Wheeler   18 BA-5
Wilson, John, 12 Feb. 1795, Elizabeth Gordon   3 PG-440
Wilson, John, 8 June 1796, Elizabeth Chinn   4 FR
Wilson, John, 25 July 1796, Sarah Ennis   1 WO
Wilson, John, son of William, 23rd day, 11 mo., 1796,
   Anne Bowers, dau. of John   4 SF-210
Wilson, John, 12 Feb. 1797, Eleanor Ferguson   5 BA-15
Wilson, John, 18 April 1797, Norry Brady   2 HA-349
Wilson, John, 22 Nov. 1798, Margaret Smith   12 BA-370
   See also 3 HA-28.
Wilson, John, 16 Oct. 1800, Hannah Duffy   3 BA-393
Wilson, Jos., 27 Sept. 1794, Mary Reidenauer   29 BA-5
Wilson, Joseph, 20 May 1782, Hannah Pool   11 BA-5
Wilson, Joseph, 10 March 1788, by Rev. Riggin; Martha Free-
   land   4 AA
Wilson, Joshua, 2 Nov. 1786, Eliz. Grymes   11 BA-9
Wilson, Joshua, (4 Dec. 1790), Deborah Dorsey   15 BA-4

Wilson, Joshua, 28 Aug. 1793, Elizabeth Sedwick   4 FR
Wilson, Matthew, 26 Aug. 1790, Jane Conner   18 BA-2
Wilson, Nathaniel, 3 Dec. 1778, Anne Brome   1 CA-2
Wilson, Nathaniel, 17 June 1779, Martha Hanson   2 PG-3
Wilson, Nathaniel, 31 March 1782, Elizabeth Holmes   2 PG-3
Wilson, Nicholas, (12 Sept. 1789), Ruth Frizzle   15 BA-2
Wilson, Samuel, 8 Dec. 1794, Priscilla Gover   3 HA-28
Wilson, Samuel, 18 Sept. 1796, Frances Jones   2 HA-349
Wilson, Samuel, son of Benjamin and Lydia, 30th day, 5
   mo., 1799, Phebe Brown, dau. of William and Elizabeth
   11 SF-255
Wilson, Skidmore, son of William, 30th day, 5 mo., 1788,
   Sarah Dickinson, dau. of Daniel   4 SF-191
Wilson, Solomon, Sr., 13 Nov. 1788, Rachel Saffard   2 SF
Wilson, Stephen, 13 Feb. 1786, Rebecca Nelson   5 BA-14
Wilson, Thomas, 4 July 1778, Elizabeth Dunbar   11 BA-1
Wilson, Thomas, son of Peter, 7th day, 2 mo., 1788, Sarah
   Richardson, dau. of Nathan and Hannah   1 SF
   9 SF-51 states that Thomas waa a son of Peter of
   Co. Cumberland, Eng., and wife Ann.
Wilson, Thomas, 21 April 1789, Ann Hoffwider   4 FR
Wilson, Thomas, 13 Sept. 1796, Rebeckah Beale   4 FR
Wilson, Thomas, 30 Nov. 1796, Elizabeth Fisher   1 WO
Wilson, Thomas, 11 Sept. 1797, Elizabeth Hickman   3 HA-26
Wilson, Thomas, 24 Feb. 1799, Sarah Robinson   5 BA-15
Wilson, William, 7 Jan. 1779, Mary Scott   5 HA
Wilson, William, 10 Jan. 1780, Verlinda Mason   2 PG-1
Wilson, William, 6 Dec. 1782, Mary Talbott   3 HA-7
Wilson, William, 18 April 1790, Elizabeth Andrews   6 BA
Wilson, William, 13 Jan. 1795, Sarah Bivans   6 BA
Wilson, William, 17 Jan. 1796, Elenor Riddle   3 BA-317
Wilson, William, 29 Feb. 1798, Sarah Lee   3 HA-27
Wilson, William, 19 Jan. 1799, Deborah Johnson   2 SO
Wilson, William, slave, 24 March 1799, Leah Sparksman,
   free mulatto   3 BA-369
Wilson, William, 19th day, 12 mo., 1799, Uphanny Charles
   4 SF-220
Wilson, William, 14 Sept. 1800, Susanna Wolfe   3 BA-391
Wilson, William Lee, 2 March 1798, Sarah Chew Lee   1 BA-8
Wily, George, 26 Dec. 1793, Jane Smith   3 BA-279
Wilyard, Abraham, 24 Dec. 1799, Catherine Biser   4 FR
Wilyard, Jacob, 14 May 1791, Eve Grove   4 FR
Wimsatt, James, 23 March 1778, Sarah Howard   1 SM-137
Winchester, James, 21 March 1793, Sarah Owings   4 BA-75
   36 BA-1 gives the date as 11 Dec. 1793.
Winchester, Jno., 7 Jan. 1790, Eliz. Whitaker   11 BA-13
Winchester, Stephen, 17 Feb. 1792, Sarah Howard   4 FR
Winder, Dr. H., 9 May 1799, Gertrude Polk   1 WI-138
Winder, William H., 7 May 1799, Gertrude Polk   2 SO
Windle, Caleb, 27 Oct. 1796, Marha Parker   5 MO-113
Windman, Henry, 12 April 1800, Eleanora Rodes?   29 BA-11
Window, Thomas, 4 Sept. 1797, Tansey Arnett   2 DO
Windows, Charles, 22 Dec. 1787, Mary Knott   2 DO
Windsor, Luke, 24 Jan. 1797, Elizabeth Mobberly   3 PG-442
Windsar, William, 3 Oct. 1796, Kitturah Elliot   2 DO
Winebrenner, Peter, 18 March 1794, Catherine Snyder   4 FR
Winebrenner, Wm., 18 April 1799, Alice Smith   3 AL-5
Wineman, Mathias, 30 July 1799, Eliz. Martin   29 BA-10
Wingate, Ambrose, 4 Dec. 1791, Hannah Green   6 BA
Wingate, Henry, 11 Jan. 1797, Sarah Dail   2 DO
Wingate, James, 2 Jan. 1796, Elizabeth Gootee   2 DO
Wingate, James, 8 July 1798, Alice Martin   3 SO
Wingate, John, 2 Jan. 1793, Elizabeth Adams   2 DO
Wingate, Pritchett, 2 Jan. 1797, Elizabeth Pritchett   2 DO
   1 DO-39 gives the date as 4 Jan. 1797.

Wingate, Thomas, 5 Sept. 1787, Molly Ross   2 DO
Wingate, Thomas, 15 Feb. 1791, Rebecca Fallen   2 DO
Wingate, Thomas, 14 April 1793, Sarah Pottee   1 BA-5
Winhold, William, 6 Oct. 1795, Mary Mahony   4 FR
Winkfield, Christopher, 17 Jan. 1796, Sarah Ferguson   4 BA-78
Winland, Frederick, 15 June 1797, Mary Sies   29 BA-8
Winpigler, Francis, 5 Feb. 1779, Sarah Ridgely   4 FR
Winright, John, 10 Aug. 1799, Peggy McIntire   2 SO
Winright, Stephen, 20 Aug. 1779, Temperance McIntire   2 SO
Winright, Zadoc, 18 Nov. 1800, Jane Winright   2 SO
Winson, William, 8 May 1779, Eliz'th Blackmore   4 FR
Winsor, Elijah, 11 Dec. 1799, Biddy Douglas   2 SO
Winter, Abraham, 25 June 1796, Cath. Langenecker   3 WA-61
Winter, Charles Bruce, 26 June 1784, Elizabeth Mason   2 CH-458
Winter, Friedrich, 13 April 1783, Cathr. Lamperton   1 Cl÷29
Winter, John, Jan. 1790, Martha Long   2 FR-1181
Winter, John, 21 Dec. 1797, Caty Prough   4 FR
Wintkle, James, 22 Oct. 1795, Elizabeth Jenkins   3 BA-311
Wintz, Jacob, 25 Jan. 1789, Cath. Fisher   2 FR-1181
Wip, Peter, 29 June 1788, Eliz. Nickol   2 FR-1181
Wire, Peter, 25 Oct. 1783, Elizabeth Stull   4 FR
Wirkinger, Jacob, 1 Nov. 1800, Elizabeth Snyder   29 BA-12
Wirt, Henry, 30 April 1795, Jennett Ferguson   3 PG-441
Wirtenbecher, Adam, 1 Jan. 1786, Elizab. Reeb   2 FR-1181
Wirtt, Christian, 6 Sept. 1792, Mary Weaver   3 PG-437
Wirtz, Michael, 2 Feb. 1790, Catherine Delauder   4 FR
Wise, Adam, 2 Nov. 1779, Elizabeth Carter   3 SM-57
Wise, Caleb, 13 Nov. 1783, Catherine Wise   3 SM-61
Wise, Chas., 26 Nov. 1789, Elizabeth Collings   3 PG-256
Wise, John, 28 Aug. 1794, Usly Mitchell   3 PG-440
Wise, Levin, 31 May 1794, Anna Scott   5 BA-15
Wise, Thomas, 6 Dec. 1787, Mildred Robertson   3 PG-253
Wise, Thomas, 3 Dec. 1797, Mary Humpheries   3 PG-443
Wise, William, 19 Nov. 1778, Elizabeth Clocker   3 SM-57
Wise, William, 20 Nov. 1788, Elizabeth Ross   3 PG-254
Wisebach, 10 Jan. 1792, (name not given)   10 BA-194
Wisebaugh, John, 10 Dec. 1796, Mary Berry   6 BA
Wiseman, Robert, 5 Feb. 1782, Eleanor King   3 SM-60
Wiseman, Robert, 14 Jan. 1800, Eliza Phillips   2 CH-458
Wishart, James M., 29 July 1799, Sarah Carter   3 BA-374
Wisman, Jacob, 28 March 1799, Elizabeth Kephart   4 FR
Wissels, Joseph Charles, 10 Sept. 1795, Mary Ferree Yeiser
      6 BA

Wissing, Casper, 1 Jan. 1793, Cath. Altharr   50 BA-393
Wiszman, Valent., 12 Feb. 1800, Mary Gebhart   2 FR-1182
Witerich, George, 8 Sept. 1799, Cath. Herget   2 FR-1182
Withgott, James, 19 Nov. 1782, Sarah Ross   2 DO
Withgott, Joseph, 8 Aug. 1789, Sarah Thomas   2 DO
Withgott, Reuben, 27 Aug. 1798, Mary Simmons   2 DO
Withgott, Thomas, 9 Jan. 1788, Eve Sisk   2 DO
Witney, George, 17 Feb. 1799, Isabella Mulcallum   6 BA
Wittle, Richard, 1 Jan. 1784, Elizabeth Burland   10 BA-180
Wizart, John, 18 July 1784, Mary Miller   4 FR
Wobiton, 29 Jan. 1784, Cassandra Pearce   3 HA-8
Woelper, George, 13 Dec. 1798, Mary Weary   3 BA-366
Woghter, George, 19 Sept. 1798, Philipena Beckinbaugh   4 FR
Wolf, Diedrich, 2 June 1799, Gertraut Weler   50 BA-405
Wolf, Johannes, 25 Dec. 1791, Maria Hager, dau. of Michael
      2 WA-17
Wolf, Michael, 14 Nov. 1797, Mary Reiley   45 BA-2
Wolf, Samuel, 6 Feb. 1798, Healen Weamer   4 FR
Wolfe, Ludwick, 14 May 1794, Charlotte Runner   4 FR
Wolff, Adam, 7 Oct. 1787, Marg. Steinbrenner   2 FR-1181
Wolff, Henry, 25 Aug. 1793, Eliz. Haller   2 FR-1182
Wolff, Jacob, son of Paul, 28 Aug. 1769, Anna Maria Hof,
      dau. of Johan Wilhelm   6 FR-106

Wolhea, Jno., 31 Dec. 1797, Mary Myer   50 BA-402
Wolheim, John Wm., 17 March 1788, Fredericka Keplar   4 FR
Wolstenholme, Daniel, 25 Aug. 1783, Deborah Beck   3 SM-61
Woltz, Jacob, Feb. 1800, Sus. Fessler   3 WA-68
Wood, Benjamin, 13 Aug. 1778, by Rev. Magowan; Margaret
    Hutchison   4 AA
Wood, Bennett, 29 Sept. 1798, Susanna Hoy   4 FR
Wood, Charles, 26 Jan. 1793, Eleanor Eajleston   6 BA
Wood, Charles, 20 Nov. 1793, by Rev. G. Ridgely; Mary Hardy
    4 AA
Wood, Edward, 15 Sept. 1778, Rebecca Gray   1 CA-1
Wood, Henry, 23 June 1788, Sarah Mackelfresh   4 FR
Wood, Henry, 8 June 1794, Martha Griffin   3 AA-424
Wood, Icho'd, 12 Dec. 1783, Christian Woodfield   3 AA-420
Wood, Jacob, 22 March 1779, Honor Kidney   5 HA
Wood, Jacob, 22 March 1780, Honor Ridhore   3 HA-1
Wood, James, 7 May 1782, Ann Gooding   3 HA-6
Wood, James, 17 Feb. 1789, by Rev. Claggett; Minty Whit-
    tington   4 AA
Wood, James, 24 Jan. 1792, Susanna Fields   3 HA-21
Wood, Jams, 16 Aug. 1795, Cath. Flinger   3 WA-59
Wood, Jesse, 20 Jan. 1778, Hannah Wood   1 CA-1
Wood, John, 4 Dec. 1781, Martha Ogle   4 FR
Wood, John, 20 June 1783, Ann Welch   2 CH-458
Wood, John, 17 April 1785, Ann Shrier   3 BA-190
Wood, John, 1792, by Rev. Parrott; Barbara Allen   4 AA
Wood, Joshua, 26 May 1779, Mary Botts   5 HA
    3 HA-2 gives the date as 21 May 1780.
Wood, Joshua, 1 May 1797, Ann Osborn   3 HA-26
Wood, Joshua, 4 May 1797, Ann Osborne   2 HA-349
Wood, Richard, 9 Oct. 1778, Eliz'th Head   4 FR
Wood, Robert, 19 May 1783, Jane Dunn   3 BA-191
Wood, Robert, 12 Jan. 1797, by Rev. Ridgely; Ruth Leather-
    wood   4 AA
Wood, Thomas, 23 Dec. 1787, Margaret Crook   6 BA
Wood, Thomas, 2 Feb. 1797, by Rev. Ridgely; Mary Wood   4 AA
Wood, Thomas, son of Joseph and Catherine, 8th day, 11 mo.,
    1797, Elizabeth Gray, dau. of Joseph and Ann   11 SF-246
Wood, William, 10 Dec. 1780, Elizabeth Gray   2 PG-5
Wood, William, son of William and Catherine, 29th day,
    5 mo., 1781, Mary Smith, dau. of John and Elizabeth
    1 SF
Wood, Wm., 29 Oct. 1785, Martha Ridgely McCubbin   11 BA-8
Wood, William, 27 Dec. 1791, Sarah Sheppard   18 BA-4
Wood, William, 29 Jan. 1798, Ann Maria Bond   3 HA-27
Woodall, John, 30 Jan. 1798, Sarah Peacock   4 KE-72
Woodard, James, 19 Aug. 1800, Sally Asdell   2 FR-1182
Woodard, John, 31 July 1792, Rachael Johnson   3 BA-257
Woodcock, Robert, 8 Nov. 1786, by Rev. Turner; Mary Caples
    51 BA-30
Wooden, Chas., 1 Jan. 1795, Nancy Owings   29 BA-6
Wooden, John, 1 July 1790, Rachel Hooper   6 BA
Wooden, John, 11 Dec. 1796, by Rev. Ridgely; Hannah Caples
    4 AA
Wooden, Richard, 7 June 1794, Leah Bond   6 BA
Wooden, Thomas, 29 Sept. 1791, Sarah Hooper   6 BA
Wooden, William, 25 Dec. 1785, Margaret Milligan   6 BA
Woodfield, Gavin, 2 March 1796, Peggy Brawalt   1 AL-53
Woodfield, George, 3 March 1796, Peggy Bremalts   2 AL-700
Woodfield, John, 28 Feb. 1782, Elizabeth Norman   3 AA-418
Woodin, Thomas, 5 Oct. 1783, Martha Gott   3 BA-185
Wooding, Benjamin, 19 Jan. 1797, Mary Kitting   45 BA-1
Woodland, Isaac, 8 Jan. 1790, Sarah Davis   2 DO
Woodland, James, 25 Dec. 1792, Sarah Collins   1 BA-5
Woodland, John, 8 March 1799, Sarah Daffin   2 DO

Woodland, John S., 12 Dec. 1797, Charlotte Barclay   2 DO
Woodland, Levin, 3 July 1799, Nancy Booze   2 DO
Woodland, Richard, 5 Jan. 1791, Elizabeth Daffin   2 DO
Woodland, Richard, 3 June 1793, Sarah Todd   2 DO
Woodland, Solomon, 1 Jan. 1799, Betsy Gootee   2 DO
Woodland, William, 19 June 1786, Elizabeth Jones   2 DO
Woodroring, Joshua, 14 Aug. 1792, Vashta Porter   2 AL-700
Woodrough, John Williams, 29 July 1790, Elizabeth Leere   5 BA-15
Woodrow, John, 9 April 1788, Mary Roberts   4 FR
Woods, Andrew, 10 Feb. 1799, Mary Todd   3 BA-368
Woods, George, 27 July 1778, Mary Loyd   4 FR
Woods, Robert Crawford, 17 Sept. 1786, Catherine O'Brien   3 BA-191
Woods, William, 7 June 1787, Mary Hagart   16 BA-2
Woodward, Abraham B., 5 Oct. 1797, Priscilla Owens   4 FR
Woodward, Benjamin, 3 Nov. 1789, Elizabeth Pattison   2 DO
Woodward, Jacob, 12 April 1791, Jemima Phelps   4 FR
Woodward, James, 15 Aug. 1778, Tamar Bolton   11 BA-1
Woodward, Jno., 30 July 1786, Eliza Davis   11 BA-9
Woodward, Samuel, 3 April 1778, Ann Posey   2 CH-458
Woodward, Thomas, 23 May 1778, Margaret Iam   11 BA-1
Woodward, William, 22 Aug. 1799, Margaret Ingles   3 BA-376
Woodworth, Isaac, 24 Dec. 1798, Susanna Baum   29 BA-10
Woolen, Pollard, 21 May 1783, Mary Hooper   2 DO
Woolf, Henry, 19 Aug. 1793, Elizabeth Haller   4 FR
Woolf, Jacob, 20 June 1795, Ann Welch   4 FR
Woolf, Peter, 23 June 1780, Catherine Bruner   4 FR
Woolfe, George, 11 Feb. 1797, Levina Richards   4 FR
Woolfe, John, 13 April 1782, Sarah Hyatt   4 FR
Woolford, Benjamin, 28 March 1792, Anna Madkin   2 DO
Woolford, James, 6 Aug. 1783, Priscilla Hooper   2 DO
Woolford, James, 21 Dec. 1785, Mary Tully   2 DO
Woolford, James, 8 Feb. 1796, Jane Leach   2 DO
Woolford, Dr. John, 6 July 1796, Ann Irving Gillis   3 SO
Woolford, John, 27 Jan. 1799, Mary Duke   3 BA-367
Woolford, Levin, 7 Feb. 1800, Prissy Handy   2 SO
Woolford, Roger, 17 June 1798, Polly Mace   2 DO
Woolford, Roger, 17 June 1798, Polly Wall   1 DO-39
Woolford, Stevens, 25 Jan. 1783, Eleanor Jones   2 DO
Woolford, Thomas, 25 Oct. 1781, Betsy Woolford   2 DO
Woolford, Thomas, 26 July 1800, Charlotte Woolford   2 DO
Woolford, William, 25 Nov. 1796, Sarah Jones   2 DO
     1 DO-39 gives the date as 1 Dec. 1796.
Woolhead, Thomas, 25 May 1777, Caroline Hill   3 BA-173
Woollen, Benjamin, 1 July 1785, Keziah Goostree   2 DO
Woollen, John, 6 Aug- 1786, Mary Watson   2 DO
Woollen, Levin, 4 April 1799, Dolly Taylor   2 DO
Woollen, Wingate, 10 Sept. 1800, Rosanna Ruark   2 DO
Woolsey, Joseph, 28 Nov. 1785, Sarah Johnson   3 HA-10
Woolsey, William, 10 Sept. 1795, Alice Smith   3 HA-24
Wooten?, Thomas, 1 Jan. 1799, Arabella Smith   29 BA-10
Workman, Hugh, 3 June 1783, Eliza White   11 BA-6
Workman, Robert, 13 Aug. 1784, June Dunsheaf   5 BA-14
Worman, George, 26 March 1798, Susanna Towson   6 BA
Wormer, Georg, 22 Jan. 1786, Mary -(?)-   10 BA-186
Wornall, Henry, 15 April 1780, Ann Simpson   2 PG-1
Worrell, Benjamin, 23 Jan. 1797, Mary Hynson   4 KE-72
Worrell, Caleb, (26 May 1790), Rachel Gorsuch   15 BA-3
Worrell, Jesse, 6 April 1794, Agnes Morrick   6 BA
Worrell, Robert, 20 Dec. 1796, Margaret Meeks   4 KE-72
Worrell, Thomas, 12 May 1788, Mary Couden   1 BA-1
Worry, Samuel, 25 Aug. 1782, Elizabeth Underwood   2 CH-458
Wort, Herman, Oct. 1799, Sus. Miller   3 WA-68
Worthington, Abraham, 30 May 1799, Isabella Ferguson   29 BA-10

Worthington, Henry, 25 June 1778, Mary Yeisler	11 BA-1
Worthington, John, 7 Oct. 1781, Christian Magruder	2 PG-5
Worthington, Joseph, 30 May 1793, Mary Johnson	3 HA-22
Worthington, Walter, 12 Sept. 1786, Sarah Hood	29 BA-1
Worton, William, 31 Dec. 1798, Mary Saunders	4 KE-72
Wotton, Thomas, 5 June 1781, Nancy Bentley	3 SM-59
Wright, Alexander, 31 Oct. 1780, Susanna Gilbert	4 FR
Wright, Daniel, 12 March 1778, Susanna Deaver	11 BA-1
Wright, Daniel, 3rd day, 12 mo., 1785, Sarah Harriss	2 SF-288
Wright, David, 12 Nov. 1798, Susanna Thompson	4 FR
Wright, Elie, 2 Dec. 1784, Phoebe Harrison	4 FR
Wright, Elisha, 4 June 1787, Mary Medford	2 DO
Wright, George, 28 Nov. 1783, Elizabeth Johnson	4 FR
Wright, George, 1 March 1794, Sophia Wright	3 BA-285
Wright, George, 3 Jan. 1797, Bridget Simpson	2 SO
Wright, Hatfield, 16 Oct. 1790, Euphama Charles	2 SF
Wright, Hatfield, 13 Oct. 1796, Lucrecia Lowe	2 SF
Wright, Henry, 10 Jan. 1793, Dorothy Webb	2 DO
Wright, Henry, 26 Sept. 1796, Sarah Frazier	2 DO
Wright, Hezekiah, 11 July 1795, Elizabeth Riley	1 WO
Wright, Isaac, 9 March 1786, Margaret Wright	2 DO
Wright, Jacob, 5 Dec. 1789, Rhoda Harriss	2 SF
Wright, James, 6th day, 7 mo., 1778, Sarah Harriss	2 SF-288
Wright, James, 4th day, 3 mo., 1780, Sarah Wright	2 SF-288
Wright, James, son of Levin, 3 Feb. 1787, Ann Ward	2 SF
Wright, John, 13 Nov. 1778, Eleanor Coppinger	11 BA-1
Wright, John, 4 Jan. 1781, Catherine Colman	2 CH-458
Wright, John, 20 Dec. 1781, Catherine Coldham	3 HA-5
Wright, John, 6th day, 11 mo., 1784, Esther Harris	2 SF-288
Wright, John, 21 Aug. 1791, Rebecca Otherson	1 BA-3
Wright, John, 15 Oct. 1797, Nancy Hatch	5 BA-15
Wright, John Watson, 14 Jan. 1794, Ann Townshand	3 PG-439
Wright, Joseph, 26 Oct. 1789, Mary Mumford	2 FR-1181
Wright, Joshua, 19 Feb. 1781, Sarah Turpin	2 DO
Wright, Joshua, 19 June 1794, Eleanor Holmes	6 BA
Wright, Levin, son of Roger, 18th day, 6 mo., 1800,	
Lydia Dosson, dau. of John and Ann	4 SF-221
Wright, Lott, 6 Feb. 1798, Esther Evans	1 WO
Wright, Nathan, 6 Nov. 1799, Nancy Grainger	2 SO
Wright, Noble, 7 Jan. 1796, Ann? Vickers	2 DO
Wright, Perry, 9 July 1796, Mary Lord	2 DO
Wright, Reuben, 22 Nov. 1792, Elizabeth Griffiths	3 BA-257
See also 3 BA-258.	
Wright, Robert, 3 Nov. 1799, Nancy Deaver	6 BA
Wright, Samuel, 15 Feb. 1794, Sarah Dickenson	36 BA-1
Wright, Sam'l, 25 Feb. 1794, Sarah Dickenson	4 BA-76
Wright, Thomas, 16 March 1791, Ann Green	3 HA-21
1 BA-3 gives the date as 17 March 1791.	
Wright, Thomas, 31 Oct. 1795, Mary Pecker	3 BA-311
Wright, William, 19 Aug. 1794, Dorothy Morgan	4 FR
Wrightson,William, 13 Jan. 1800, Mary LeCompte	2 DO
Wrotten, John, 10 Oct. 1797, Katherine Darby	2 SO
3 SO gives the date as 19 Oct. 1797.	
Wrotten, Richard, 22 Oct. 1785, Henrietta Currier	2 DO
Wrotten, Thomas, 27 Dec. 1800, Trephena Adams	2 DO
Wroughten, William, 28 June 1799, Jemima Jarret	2 DO
Wroughton, William, 31 May 1800, Rebecca Willey	2 DO
Wullet, John, 16 May 1800, Mary Kupferschmit	2 FR-1182
Wyand, Henry, 5 April 1785, Eliz. Fein	2 FR-1181
Wyatt, Absolom, 11 Dec. 1795, Nancy Pennewell	1 WO
Wyer, William, 22 Oct. 1779, Catherine Stull	4 FR
Wyvell, Dorsey, 26 April 1790, Sarah Keene	2 DO
Xarerius, Franc., 12 Sept. 1782, Lidia True	2 CH-458

Yager, Joseph, 10 April 1800, Polly Derr   29 BA-11
Yandes, George, 31 Oct. 1798, Mary Moore   4 FR
Yardsley, John, 15 Dec. 1797, Ann Poviar   4 KE-73
Yarley, Ralph, 24 Dec. 1795, Ruth Burton   1 BA-7
Yarnal, Samuel, son of Abraham and Elizabeth, 10th day,
     1 mo., 1788, Sarah Lamb, dau. of Pierce and Rachel
     7 SF-499
Yarnall, Uriah, son of Abraham and Elizabeth, of New Castle
     Co., 4th day, 5 mo., 1786, Martha Edmondson, dau. of
     Joshua and Mary   4 SF-179
Yates, Joseph, 6 Nov. 1797, Mary Bestpitch   2 DO
Yates, Phillip, 20 March 1799, Elizabeth Hicks   2 DO
Yates, Robert Elliot, 14 Aug. 1784, Ursula Richardson   4 FR
Yates, Thomas, 7 Feb. 1799, Mary Atkinson   3 BA-368
Yearly, Nathaniel, 18 Oct. 1795, Eliza'th Robinson   7 BA-2
Yeast, Leonard, 23 Dec. 1790, Elizabeth Tompling   4 FR
Yeast, Philip, 15 June 1799, Mary Hayes   4 FR
Yeatman, Henry Lewis, 16 March 1797, Molly Evans   6 BA
Yedlis, Moses, 4 June 1778, Anne Tear   11 BA-1
Yerringto, Richard, 8 Feb. 1798, by Rev. Ridgely; Arry
     Duvall   4 AA
Yeoder, Jacob, 30 Jan. 1798, Caty Waggoner   4 FR
Yesterday, Christian, 1 April 1779, Eliz'th Huff   4 FR
Yesterday, Michael, 22 July 1784, Angel Gardner   4 FR
Yets (Yates), Jacob, 21 Oct. 1779, Ann Thompson   1 SM-137
Yoe, John, March 1781, Catherine Skinner   3 AA-417
Yokely, John, 21 Dec. 1795, Sally Hendrick   3 HA-24
Yokum, Charles, 3 Jan. 1798, Ann Evalt   3 HA-27
Yorick, Mich'l, 26 Nov. 1793, Mary Greenwell   4 FR
York, Benjamin, 30 Oct. 1800, Patty Jones   6 BA
York, Edward, 5 April 1781, Letty Doughty   2 CH-458
York, Edward, 29 Dec. 1782, Mary Hughes   3 HA-7
York, James, 3 April 1782, Nelly Daugherty   3 HA-6
York, James, 10 May 1796, Sarah Waltham   3 HA-25
     7 BA-3 gives the date as 12 May 1796.
York, John, 22 Oct. 1785, Hannah York   3 HA-10
York, Nicholas, 19 Dec. 1798, Margaret Sutton   3 HA-27
     12 BA-370 gives the date as 20 Dec. 1798.
York, Oliver, 9 Nov. 1780, Sarah Groves   3 HA-3
York, Wm., 31 July 1783, Jane Dawtridge   11 BA-6
Yost, John, 1 Aug. 1792, Juliana Young   4 FR
Yost, Ludwick, 16 Aug. 1786, Mary Everhart   4 FR
Young, Benjamin, 17 June 1799, Eleanor Cooley   4 FR
     7 MO-29 gives the date as 20 June 1799, and the bride's
     name as Eleanor Cowley.
Young, Casper, 20 Dec. 1798, Susannah Yost   4 FR
Young, Conrad, 26 March 1781, Margaret Leather   4 FR
Young, Conrad, 19 June 1790, Elizabeth Tomlinson   4 FR
Young, Cornelius, 7 March 1796, Catherine Sissler   1 AL-53
     2 AL-700 gives the date as 10 March 1796, and the
     bride's name as Siselar or Sisler.
Young, Fred., 4 Nov. 1800, Eliza Wales   2 AL-701
     3 AL-7 gives the bride's name as Wall.
Young, George, 18 March 1781, Elizabeth Husbands   3 HA-3
Young, George, 31 July 1782, Elizabeth Bull   3 HA-6
Young, George, 29 March 1798, Mary Yost   4 FR
Young, George, 4 Feb. 1799, Mary Renner   4 FR
Young, Gideon, 9 June 1790, Elizabeth Adams   6 BA
Young, Hezekiah, 6 Jan. 1789, Charity Joy Ford   3 PG-255
Young, Jacob, 16 Jan. 1781, Leah Mason   5 BA-15
Young, James, 8 July 1798, Martha Coulson   3 BA-360
Young, Jehu, 26 Aug. 1800, Margaret McKinsey   6 BA
Young, Jesse, 30 Jan. 1796, Jane McDonough   5 BA-15
Young, John, 19 June 1778, Mary Kelly   11 BA-1
Young, John, 17 Sept. 1795, Tabitha Oyster   6 BA

Young, John, 13 Dec. 1798, Martha All	3	BA-366
Young, John, 26 Nov. 1799, Sarah Johnson	8	BA-1
Young, Joseph, 11 Sept. 1794, Elizabeth Ridgly	3	BA-293
Young, Leonard, 17 April 1779, Barbara Crowl	4	FR
Young, Littleton, 11 April 1800, Jane Taylor	2	SO
Young, Nathan, 23 Jan. 1783, Eliza Todd	11	BA-6
Young, Peter, 23 Dec. 1791, Mary Powlas	4	FR
Young, Robert, 7 Feb. 1799, by Rev. Ridgely; Elizabeth Turner	4	AA
Young, Thomas, 1 May 1797, Martha Meeks	4	KE-73
Young, William, 16 Jan. 1784, Annabella Loney	3	HA-8
Young, William, 18 April 1790, Asenath Moxley	11	BA-13
Young, William, 3 Jan. 1794, Nancy Griffin	2	DO
Young, William, 14 Jan. 1796, by Rev. Ridgely; Polly Ridgely	4	AA
Young, William, 28 Jan. 1796, Mary McKinsey	2	AL-700
Young, William, 27 Nov. 1796, Ann Hoskinson	4	FR
Young, William, 19 Jan. 1797, Catherine Minsker	5	BA-15
Young, William, 20 Sept. 1797, Elizabeth Milby	4	KE-73
Young, William Price, 17 April 1785, Dinah Cox	11	BA-8
Younge, Peter, 14 Oct. 1783, Catherine Coppersmith	4	FR
Younger, Joseph, 15 April 1779, Jean Charlton	1	CA-2
Youtezell, Christ'n, 23 April 1779, Eliz'th Dickoutt	4	FR
Youtsey, John, 2 Dec. 1779, Cath. Iseminger	4	FR
Yunker, Joh., Sept. 1800, Cath. Leiser	3	WA-70
Zara, Thomas, 4 Feb. 1798, Elizabeth Dulany	2	HA-350
Zayer, Peter, 15 July 1792, Marg. Bucky	2	FR-1187
Zealer, George, 14 June 1794, Mary Frushour	4	FR
Zealer, George, 21 May 1796, Barbara Zouck	4	FR
Zeller, Andrew, 24 Feb. 1789, Cath. Gunther	2	FR-1187
Zerick, Daniel, 8 Jan. 1798, Martha Brashear	4	FR
Zerick, Jacob, 11 Sept. 1790, Marg't Plessinger	4	FR
Ziegler, George, 25 Oct. 1791, Elizabeth Pfeister, dau. of Christian	2	WA-16
Ziegler, John, Nov. 1788, Ann Kris	29	BA-1
Zierler, George, 22 May 1796, Barbara Hauck	2	FR-1187
Ziesner, Friedr., 1792, Cath. Scheveler	50	BA-392
Zimmerman, Adam, 29 July 1783, Susanna Shurte	4	FR
Zimmerman, Andrew, 27 Dec. 1796, Ruth Taylor	2	FR-1187
Zimmerman, Benj'n, 10 April 1798, Cath. Eppert	2	FR-1187
Zimmerman, Geo., 30 Oct. 1794, Rebecca Stinchcomb	29	BA-5
Zimmerman, Geo., 30 Nov. 1797, Eliz. Stinchcomb	29	BA-9
Zimmerman, Gottlieb, 17 Feb. 1798, Eva Hahn	3	WA-64
Zimmerman, Jacob, 15 July 1797, Mary Hedge	4	FR
Zimmerman, Jacob, 14 Feb. 1799, Mary Ann Snyder	4	FR
Zimmerman, John, 16 June 1798, Mary Hissey	3	BA-359
Zimmerman, Michael, 14 May 1788, Eve Cronice	4	FR
Zimmerman, Michael, 1 Nov. 1798, Barb. Taylor	2	FR-1187
Zimmerman, Nicholas, 6 June 1793, Elizabeth Troxell	4	FR
Zuilla, Wm., 30 April 1786, Clarinda Kingslane	11	BA-9
Zur, Peter, 27 Oct. 1787, Maria Herwin	10	BA-188
Zurrich, Daniel, 9 Jan. 1789, Martha Brashears	2	FR-1187
Zwisler, Jas., 7 Sept. 1795, Ann Albers	29	BA-6
Zwisler, Jas., 9 Aug. 1800, Christ. Cath. Gunderman	29	BA-11

ADDENDA

Adams, Joseph, 7 June 1789, Margaret More	8	MO-18a
Aesher, Georg Gabriel, Feb. 1795, Jacobina Hamilin	3	WA-57

Allender, Richard?, 13 June 1796, Sarah McCauley   3 WA-61
Alston, Abner, son of Israel and Sarah, 22nd day, 10 mo.,
  1794, Hannah Lamb, dau. of Pearce and Rachel   7 SF-503
Alston, Joab, 10th day, 4 mo., 1788, Hannah Lamb, dau.
  of Joshua and Susannah   7 SF-491
Amos, Benjamin, son of William, Jr., and Susanna, 22nd
  day, 5 mo., 1800, Elizabeth Cornthwait, dau. of
  Robert and Grace   8 SF-33
Amos, William, Jr., son of William and Hannah, 24th day,
  10 mo., 1799, Elizabeth Hugo, dau. of William Morgan and Ann   8 SF-23
Arnold, Henry, Sept. 1798, Mary Bowman   3 WA-65

Backer, Christian, 7 Jan. 1797, Nancy Stoul (or Stout)   3 WA-62
Baker, Maurace, 14 March 1796, Elis. McEvon   3 WA-60
Baker, Mich., 17 March 1795, Motlina Hoss   3 WA-58
Balderston, Ely, son of Isaiah and Martha, 16th day, 11
  mo., 1797, Esther Brown, dau. of William and Elizabeth
  8 SF-9
Barkdoll, Jacob, April 1800, Sus. Musselman   3 WA-69
Barkdoll, Peter, Aug. 1799, Mary Musselman   3 WA-67
Barry, Thomas, 6 Sept. 1795, Ann Adams   4 PG-157
Bateman, Henry, 4 June 1795, Mary Brown; William Bate-
  man, brother of the groom a witness   8 MO-11
Bausler, George, 28 March 1797, Motlena Metty   3 WA-62
Bayer, Jacob, 4 May 1796, Elis. Sigmond   3 WA-60
Bayer, Jacob, 2 July 1796, Barb. Anderson   3 WA-61
Bayer, Joh., 6 Feb. 1796, Elis. Krusinger   3 WA-60
Bayer, Peter, Dec. 1799, Maria Bowser   3 WA-68
Bazil and Lin, property of Jos. Boone, married 22 June
  1800   8 MO-25
Beard, Michael, 8 Aug. 1795, Hannah Hose   3 WA-59
Beckey, Joh., May 1800, Nancy Morris   3 WA-69
Benter, John, 24 July 1797, Mary Wilhelm   3 WA-63
Bergman, Jacob, 4 June 1796, Cath. Miller   3 WA-61
Bernhard, Peter, Nov. 1800, Barbara Metz   3 WA-70
Blackstone, James?, Jan. 1800, Christina Doyl (or Deyl)
  3 WA-68
Boerson, Joh., 2 May 1795, Mary Miller   3 WA-58
Bonebrake, George, 4 June 1796, Cath. Barkdoll   3 WA-61
Boram, Aaron, son of John and Ann, 3rd day, 7 mo., 1794,
  Elizabeth Johns, dau. of Nathan and Elizabeth   9 SF-67
Boughman, Andrew, 24 June 1797, Elis. Erich   3 WA-62
Bougrer, Joh., 12 April 1796, Mag. Bayer   3 WA-60
Boyer, Joh., 9 Oct. 1796, Eliz. Bauser   3 WA-61
Brandstater, John, Dec. 1798, Marg. Kifer   3 WA-66
Braun, Joh., June 1799, Nanzi Porman   3 WA-67
Brendel, George, Dec. 1799, Elis. Grave   3 WA-68
Brenner, Joh., 23 Dec. 1797, Marg. Schmidtin   3 WA-63
Brewa, Jacob, 16 Dec. 1796, Mary Angle   3 WA-62
Brinton, Joseph, son of Moses, of Leacock Twp., Lancs.
  Co., Penna.; 8th day, 10 mo., 1784, Susanna Rigbie,
  dau. of James   9 SF-45
Brooks, Isaac, son of Isaac and Hannah of Darby Twp.,
  Delaware Co., Penna.; 26th day, 12 mo., 1799, Sarah
  Hayward, dau. of Joseph and Rebecca   8 SF-27
Brown, Abner, son of Jeremiah and Anna, 11th day, 6 mo.,
  1795, Elizabeth Allen, dau. of James and Rebecca   11 SF-240
Brown, Benjamin, son of Jacob and Elizabeth, 6th day, 10
  mo., 1796, Rebeckah Sidwell, dau. of Isaac and Ann
  11 SF-242
Brown, Elihu, son of Isaac and Lydia, 29th day, 5 mo., 1782,
  Margaret Brown, dau. of Joseph and Hannah   11 SF-201
Brown, James, son of John and Mary, 18th day, 4 mo., 1799,
  Catherine Dukehart, dau. of Valerius and Margaret   8 SF-21

Brown, Uriah, son of David and Elizabeth, 10th day, 1 mo.,
   1793, Mary Brown, dau. of Jacob and Mary   11 SF-231
Burgess, John, of Fawn Twp., York Co., Penna., son of
   Joseph and Deborah of Cambel Co., Va.; 28th day,
   10 mo., 1795, Drusilla Morgan, dau. of John and Ann
   9 SF-71
Butler, Edward, free negro, 2 May 1797, Bett, slave of
   Clement Sewall   8 MO-14
Byerly, Joh., Aug. 1798, Barb. Brendle   3 WA-65

Canfair, Georg?, July 1795, Eva Nouse   3 WA-59
Carll, Andres, Feb. 1800, Nancy Brenner (or Brunner)   3 WA-68
Carter, Joel, son of Samuel and Sarah, 26th day, 7 mo.,
   1798, Margaret Reynolds, dau. of Samuel and Isabel
   11 SF-251
Carter, Joh., 5 June 1796, Rebecca Deabran   3 WA-61
Carter, John, son of John and Hannah, 14th day, 6 mo.,
   1798, Rebecca Harland, dau. of David and Alice   9 SF-77
Casenove, Antony Charles, 29 June 1797, Ann Hogan, dau.
   of Edmund   8 MO-14
Caywood, Thomas, 30 Dec. 1797, Sarah Mastaller   3 WA-63
Chamberlain, Clement, 16 July 1795, Sarah Clements   8 MO-11
Chandlee, George, son of William and Mary, 7th day, 6 mo.,
   1798, Gainer Churchman, dau. of George and Hannah 1 SF-250
Channell, John, son of John and Rachel, 12th day, 5 mo.,
   1785, Deborah Janney, dau. of Isaac and Sarah   11 SF-205
Charles, Andrew, May 1798, Margaret Vogelsang   3 WA-65
Charles, Andrew, June 1798, Marg. Vogelsang   3 WA-65
Christman, Michael, May 1799, Cath. Stick or Hick   3 WA-67
Clarck, Alex., July 1798, Sus. Swailes   3 WA-65
Clopper, Frederick, April 1798, Sarah Backer   3 WA-64
Coale, Isaac, son of William and Sarah, 7th day, 9 mo.,
   1786, Rachel Cox, dau. of William and Mary   9 SF-49
Coale, Richard, son of Philip and Ann, 6th day, 1 mo.,
   1795, Aliceanna Wilson, dau. of Thomas   9 SF-70
Coldman, Nathan, Sept. 1800, Elis. Dempster   3 WA-70
Colp, Phil., Nov. 1800, Elis. Cromer   3 WA-70
Conrad, Daniel, 27 May 1795, Ester Ruth   3 WA-59
Coock, Hennry, 13 Feb. 1798, Mary Schutz   3 WA-64
Cook, Isaac, son of Stephen and Margaret, 6th day, 11
   mo., 1788, Sarah Stubbs, dau. of Daniel and Ruth 11 SF-218
Cook, Stephen, 28 March 1796, Mary Marshall   4 PG-157
Cooper, Nicholas, son of Nicholas and Sarah, 3rd day,
   11 mo., 1791, Sarah Balderston, dau. of Isaiah and
   Martha   9 SF-60
Coppock, John, of Samuel and Ellen, 6th day, 7 mo.,
   1800, Catherine Kirk, dau. of Timothy and Lydia 11 SF-257
Corse, Thomas, son of Welthy, 18th day, 6 mo., 1778,
   Rosamond Lamb, dau. of George and Sarah   7 SF-108
Cow, Henry, 27 Oct. 1797, Mary Zimmerman   3 WA-63
Cox, Isaac, son of Isaac, 14th day, 11 mo., 1782, Rebecca
   Thomas, dau. of Henry   7 SF-115
Cresap, Thomas, 23 March 1795, Mary Briscoe   3 WA-58
Crosmock, John, 25 June 1795, Elizabeth Sleckling   4 PG-157
Cunningham, Francis, 9 Nov. 1797, Marg. Hughes   3 WA-63
Cunningham, James, May 1798, Fanny Stortzman   3 WA-65

Daugherty, James, 9 June 1795, Mary Aul   4 PG-157
Davison, Robert, 6 Feb. 1798, Sus. Burkett   3 WA-64
Dawson, Isaac, son of Benjamin and Elizabeth, 11th day,
   5 mo., 1789, Rachel Lamb, dau. of Pearce and Rachel
   7 SF-493
Dawson, William, son of Benjamin, 11th day, 3 mo., 1779,
   Sarah Lamb, dau. of George   7 SF-109

Deal, Christ., Oct. 1798, Mary Warner   3 WA-65
Delahan, Benjamin, 15 Oct. 1799, Rachel Slater, dau. of
    Thomas   8 MO-22
Deyle, Adam, 26 Feb. 1796, Cath. Updegraff   3 WA-60
Dickey, John, 18 April 1796, Mary Quirk   4 PG-157
Doyl, George, 28 Jan. 1797, Eliz. Kelhoover   3 WA-62
Draber, William, Feb. 1799, Mary Fisler   3 WA-66
Drury, Ignatius, 5 Dec. 1799, Harriet Redding 8 MO-23
Drury, Ignatius, 26 April 1800, Mary Tenny   8 MO-24
Dukehart, John, son of Valerius and Margaret, 15th day,
    12 mo., 1796, Parthenia Balderston, dau. of Isaiah
    and Martha   8 SF-5
Dusing, Adam, Aug. 1798, Cath. Buzzard   3 WA-65·
Duvall, Walter, 22 May 1798, by Rev. Ridgely; Sarah
    Duvall   4 AA

Earhart, Joh., 29 March 1795, Cath. Brundel   3 WA-58
Edmondson, John, 9th day, 2 mo., 1786, Martha Wales   7 SF-495
Edmundson, John, 3rd day, 6 mo., 1779, Margaret Johnson,
    dau. of James and Ruth   11 SF-193
Ekeberger, Walter, 3 Aug. 1794, Susanna Schneider   3 WA-57
Ellis, William, son of Benjamin and Ann of Chester Co.,
    Penna., 10th day, 2 mo., 1785, Mary Cox, dau. of
    Wm. and Mary   9 SF-47
Ely, William, son of Thomas and Sarah, 30th day, 4 mo.,
    1794, Martha Preston, dau. of Henry and Rachel   9 SF-66
England, George, son of Joseph and Elizabeth, 26th day,
    12 mo., 1799, Catherine Hooker, dau. of Thomas and
    Hannah   8 SF-25
England, John, son of Samuel and Sarah, 7th day, 8 mo.,
    1783, Elizabeth Gatchell, dau. of Jeremiah and Hannah
    11 SF-202
England, Joseph, son of Samuel and Sarah, 1st day, 9 mo.,
    1785, Hannah Pasmore, dau. of Augustine and Hannah
    11 SF-206
Ensminger, Henry, Feb. 1799, Rachel McIntire   3 WA-66
Ensminger, Lodwich, Nov. 1800, Polly Wyand   3 WA-70
Evans, Amos, of Fawn Twp., York Co., son of Griffith and
    Jane, 28th day, 9 mo., 1796, Rachel Tomkins, dau. of
    Benjamin and Mary   9 SF-73

Farmar, George, 16 Dec. 1795, Christ. Yunker   3 WA-59
Fassnecht, Barnard, April 1799, Elis. Wolf   3 WA-67
Fegly, Joh., Oct. 1799, Sus. Miller   3 WA-68
Feight, Jacob, 4 Oct. 1796, Cath. Henavel   3 WA-61
Fenick, Albin, Oct. 1799, Elis. Pryer   3 WA-68
Ferrall, John, 29 May 1795, Mary Corvy   3 WA-59
Fesler, Jacob, Feb. 1799, Cath. Grisser   3 WA-66
Fessler, Jacob, March 1799, Cath. Grisser   3 WA-66
Fiery, Jacob, April 1798, Sus. Stortzman   3 WA-64
Fiery, Joseph, 26 June 1797, Magd. Ridenauer   3 WA-62
Fisher, Price, June 1800, Mary Youngert   3 WA-69
Flager, Jacob, 10 Jan. 1797, Marg. Foltz   3 WA-62
Flenner, David, 6 Dec. 1796, Sus. Brewa   3 WA-62
Flori, Georg, March 1798, Eva Enderson   3 WA-64
Fogelsang, Christian, 23 Dec. 1797, Susana Arnold   3 WA-63
Forbes, Tom, June 1800, Cath. Selser   3 WA-69
Ford, Joseph, son of Wm. and Rosanna, 10th day, 4 mo.,
    1794, Frances Coale, dau. of Philip and Ann   9 SF-65
Foster, Samuel, son of Francis, 8th day, 12 mo., 1791,
    Elizabeth Kirk, dau. of Timothy and Lydia   11 SF-228
Frenkeberger, Conrad, July 1800, Nellie Boyd (or Beyd)   3 WA-69
Frey, Abraham, 28 Sept. 1794, Marg. Schmeistern   3 WA-57

Frey, Joh., 25 August 1795, Elis. Schlay   3 WA-59
Funch (or Fund), Jacob, 8 Aug. 1795, Sus. Ronk   3 WA-59

Gantz, Jacob, Aug. 1799, Sus. Langeneder (Langenecker) 3 WA-67
Gassman (or Hossman), Joh., Nov. 1800, Cath. Eakle   3 WA-70
George and Monica, were married 13 April 1800, with per-
    mission of their master and Mistress, Joseph Semmes
    and Mary Doyne   8 MO-23
Gerzer (or Yerzer), Michael, Nov. 1800, Marg. Scholl   3 WA-70
Gessner (or Hessner), Benjamin, 4 Jan. 1795, Barbara Menzer
    3 WA-57
Gover, Samuel, son of Philip and Mary, 3rd day, 11 mo.,
    1791, Ann Hopkins, dau. of Joseph and Mary   9 SF-61
Grau, Joh., Sept. 1798, Sus. Jaques   3 WA-65
Green, William, Aug. 1800, Elis. Henry   3 WA-69
Greist, Jacob, April 1799, Cath. Dial   3 WA-67
Griffin, Philip, 17 July 1800, Ann Jones   4 SM-184
Groffort, Joh., May 1796, Agatha Reydenauer   3 WA-61

Hadley, Richard, June 1798, Sarah Jobson   3 WA-65
Haines, Timothy, son of Job and Esther, 3rd day, 12 mo.,
    1795, Sarah Brown, dau. of Jeremiah and Hannah   11 SF-241
Hammel, Joh., Oct. 1799, Maria Curnicum   3 WA-68
Hanes, William, 3 Aug. 1797, Elis. Brunner   3 WA-63
Hanker, Jacob, 18 Dec. 1795, Cath. Butterbach   3 WA-59
Hansley (or Hausley), Levi, April 1799, Cath. Welty   3 WA-67
Harris, Samuel, son of Samuel and Margaret, 10th day, 3 mo.,
    1785, Cassandra Gover, dau. of Ephraim and Elizabeth
    9 SF-48
Hausholder, Adam, March 1798, Cath. Davis   3 WA-64
Hausholter, Fred., Oct. 1799, Cath. Lehner   3 WA-68
Hausshalter, Johannes, 5 Jan. 1797, Hanna Mehanny   3 WA-57
Hawley, Joseph, 3rd day, 4 mo., 1800, Agnes Davis   11 SF-256
Hayhurst, James, 9th day, 11 mo., 1780, Mary Warner   9 SF-40
Haynes, Jacob, 30 Dec. 1796, Mary Nisbit   3 WA-62
Heirshman, Jacob, 1 Oct. 1796, Ester Gaver   3 WA-61
Hayward, William, son of Joseph and Rebecca, 13th day,
    5 mo., 1790, Mary Husband, dau. of Joseph and Mary
    9 SF-56
Herty, Thomas, 10 Sept. 1800, Anne Ritchie   8 MO-25
Hesslich, Johann, April 1798, Magl. Alter   3 WA-64
Hetseil, Joh. Georg, 27 Oct. 1797, Cath. Hausholter   3 WA-63
Hewes, Joseph, son of Edward and Mary, 2nd day, 6 mo.,
    1800, Lydia Harrison, dau. of George and Lydia   10 SF-359
Heyberger, Conrad, 25 June 1795, Cath. Wolf   3 WA-59
Heysone, Nicholas, 6 Nov. 1797, Elis. Flenner   3 WA-63
Higdon, John Baptist, 28 Aug. 1799, Rachel Young, sis-
    ter of Robert and Elizabeth, 8 MO-22
Higgins, Joseph, 3rd day, 1 mo., 1799, Ann Bruce, dau.
    of John   9 SF-78
Hoban, James, 13 Jan. 1799, Susanna Sewell, dau. of
    Clement   8 MO-20
Hocker, Andrew, 4 Jan. 1798, Sus. Cow   3 WA-64
Hoops, Jesse, son of David and Esther, 26th day, 9 mo.,
    1794, Sarah Wilson, dau. of John and Aliceanna   9 SF-68
Hopkins, Leven Hill, son of William and Rachel, 16th day,
    5 mo., 1780, Frances Wallis, dau. of Samuel and
    Grace   9 SF-39
Hopkins, Samuel, son of William and Rachel, 2nd day, 12
    mo., 1790, Sarah Husband, dau. of Joseph and Mary   9 SF-59
Hopkins, Samuel, son of Joseph and Elizabeth, 3rd day,
    5 mo., 1798?, Rachel Worthington, dau. of John and
    Priscilla   9 SF-75

Hopkins, Thomas, son of Francis, 14th day, 10 mo., 1780,
    Sarah George, dau. of Joseph   7 SF-112
Hough, Benjamin, son of John and Elizabeth, 10th day,5
    mo., 1781, Sarah Janney, widow of Isaac   11 SF-196
Hough, Robert, son of Joseph and Mary, 15th day, 2 mo.,
    1798, Frances Martin, dau. of John and Margaret   8 SF-11
Hughes, Jesse, son of Samuel and Elizabeth, 1st day, 7 mo.,
    1780, Elizabeth Wood, dau. of William and Margaret
    11 SF-194
Husband, Joshua, son of Joseph and Mary, 27th day, 2 mo.,
    1793, Margaret Jewet?, dau. of Thadeus and Ann   9 SF-62
Hutton, Hiett, son of Thomas and Katherine, 7th day, 6 mo.,
    1792, Sarah Pugh, dau. of Joshua and Hannah   11 SF-229

Jacod, Bordet, Jan. 1799, Juliana Fasnacht   3 WA-66
Jay, Thomas, son of Stephen and Hannah, 2nd day, 3 mo.,
    1797, Sarah Wilson, dau. of Thomas and Ann   9 SF-74
Johns, Richard, son of Nathan and Elizabeth, 30th day,
    10 mo., 1794, Sarah Wilson, dau. of Benjamin and
    Elizabeth   9 SF-69
Jones, Joseph, son of Isaac and Ann, 18th day, 4 mo.,
    1787, Phebe Lukens, dau. of Benjamin and Alice   9 SF-50

King, James, son of Thomas and Ann, 3rd day, 1 mo.,
    1782, Phoebe Pyle, dau. of Moses and Mary   11 SF-199
King, Michael, son of Thomas and Ann, 9th day, 6 mo.,
    1791, Hannah Rogers, dau. of Thomas and Katherine
    11 SF-226
King, Vincent, son of Thomas and Ann, 11th day, 3 mo.,
    1789, Rachel Reynolds, dau. of Samuel and Susanna
    11 SF-221
Kinkel, Casper, Jan. 1800, Sus. Grove   3 WA-68
Kirk, Eli, son of Timothy and Ann, 19th day, 8 mo.,
    1784, Susanna Brown, dau. of Wm. and Elizabeth   11 SF-203
Kirk, Joshua, son of Timothy and Lydia, 6th day, 11 mo.,
    1794, Mary Sidwell, dau. of Abraham and Charity   11 SF-234
Kirk, William, son of Abner and Ann, 4th day, 6 mo.,
    1795, Lydia Job, dau. of Daniel and Mary   11 SF-239
Kirk, Timothy, 1st day, 3 mo., 1787, Elizabeth Wilson,
    dau. of Benjamin and Lydia   11 SF-213

Lamb, George, 20th day, 8 mo., 1783, Sarah Brisco, dau. of
    Isaac and Sarah   7 SF-119
Lukens, Charles, son of Benjamin and Alice, 4th day, 4 mo.,
    1793, Sarah Coale, dau. of Philip and Ann   9 SF-63
Lukens, Moses, son of Benjamin and Alice, 28th day, 4 mo.,
    1790, Sarah Tomkins, dau. of Benjamin and Mary   9 SF-57

McKim, John, 24th day, 9 mo., 1795, Mary Love, widow of
    William Love   8 SF-3
Mason, George, of Kennet Twp., Chester Co., son of George,
    4th day, 12 mo., 1778, Susanna Hopkins, dau. of William
    and Rachel   9 SF-38
Massey, Aquila, son of Jonathan and Cassandra, 3rd day,
    10 mo., 1793, Anna Rigbie, dau. of James and Sarah
    9 SF-64
Massey, Isaac, son of Aquila and Sarah, 10th day, 6 mo.,
    1788, Margaret Webster, dau. of Isaac and Sarah   9 SF-52
Matthews, Daniel, son of Daniel and Ann, 6th day, 4 mo.,
    1779, Mary Rowls, dau. of Hezekiah and Elizabeth 11 SF-192
Maule, John, son of Thomas and Zillah, c.1782, Susanna
    Metkiff, dau. of Curtis? and Mary   11 SF-200

Medcalfe, Abraham, son of John and Margaret, 2nd day, 3
    mo., 1786, Rebecca Morgan, dau. of William and Ann
    11 SF-209
Midcalf, Moses, son of Abraham and Mary, 11th day, 7 mo.,
    1793, Susanna Hudson, dau. of Joseph and Elizabeth
    11 SF-233
Mifflin, Daniel, of Accomac Co., Va., 6th day, 11 mo.,
    1789, Mary Husband the Elder   9 SF-55
Moore, Joseph, son of Joseph and Ann, "Autumn of 1789,"
    Mary Cutler, dau. of Benjamin and Susanna   10 SF-263
Morgan, John, son of John and Mary, 20th day, 9 mo.,
    1798, Ann Matthews, dau. of William and Ann   8 SF-17

Naylor, James, son of John and Mary, 16th day, 1 mo.,
    1800, Margaret Marsh, dau. of John and Margaret   8 SF-29
Needles, Edward, 15th day, 5 mo., 1783, Mary Lamb   7 SF-117

Offley, Michael, son of Michael and Phebe, 16th day, 5
    mo., 1781, Elizabeth Wallis, dau. of Samuel and Sary
    7 SF-113

Pennock, Moses, son of William and Alice, 18th day, 10
    mo., 1797, Elizabeth Waring, dau. of Joseph and Mary
    11 SF-245
Penock, Samuel, son of Nathaniel, 3rd day, 4 mo., 1788,
    Elizabeth Underhill, widow, dau. of Robert Johnson
    11 SF-216
Price, Israel, son of Samuel and Ann, 18th day, 5 mo., 1799,
    Hannah Brown, dau. of William and Elizabeth   8 SF-7
Pugh, Jesse, son of John and Rachel, 19th day, 3 mo., 1795,
    Elizabeth Hudson, dau. of Joseph and Elizabeth   11 SF-237
Pyle, Amos, son of Moses and Mary, 10th day, 1 mo., 1793,
    Ruth Stubbs, dau. of Daniel and Ruth   11 SF-232

Regester, David, son of John and Sarah, 11th day, 8 mo.,
    1785, Barsheba Knocks, dau. of John and Mary   7 SF-497
Reynolds, Henry, son of Jacob, 15th day, 4 mo., 1779,
    Mary Knight, dau. of William and Elizabeth   11 SF-191
Reynolds, Henry, son of Henry and Mary, 19th day, 10
    mo., 1780, Elizabeth Sidwell, dau. of Hugh and Ann
    11 SF-195
Reynolds, Jacob, son of Jacob and Rebekah, 19th day, 10
    mo., 1785, Esther Taylor, dau. of John and Mary 11 SF-207
Reynolds, Jonathan, son of Jacob, 12th day, 4 mo., 1798,
    Elizabeth Haines, dau. of Isaac   11 SF-249
Reynolds, Joseph, son of Samuel and Susannah, 6th day,
    9 mo., 1792, Mary King, dau. of Thomas and Ann   11 SF-230
Reynolds, Joshua, son of Henry and Mary, 7th day, 4 mo.,
    1791, Margaret Job, dau. of Archibald and Margaret
    11 SF-225
Reynolds, Levy, son of Samuel and -(?)-nnah, 12th day, 10
    mo., 1786, Jane King, dau. of Thomas and Ann   11 SF-212
Reynolds, Manuel, son of Henry and Mary, 8th day, 5 mo,
    1788, Sarah Sergeant, dau. of Jeremiah and Ann   11 SF-217
Reynolds, Reuben, son of Samuel and Susannah, 11th day,
    10 mo., 1781, Margaret King, dau. of Thomas and Ann
    11 SF-198
Reynolds, Richard, son of Samuel and Susannah, 8th day,
    4 mo., 1779, Rachel England, dau. of Samuel and Sarah
    11 SF-190
Reynolds, Samuel, son of Henry and Mary, 20th day, 10 mo.,
    1785, Sarah Sidwell, dau. of Richard and Ann   11 SF-208

Reynolds, Thomas, son of Jacob and Rebecca, 6th day, 12
    mo., 1786, Mary Taylor, dau. of John and Mary   11 SF-211
Richardson, Samuel, son of Joseph and Dinah, 6th day,
    11 mo., 1794, Rebecca Webster, dau. of William and
    Margaret   11 SF-235

APPENDIX

The following additions and corrections to Maryland Marriages, 1634-1777, are included here to make that volume as com-
plete and accurate as possible. I am indebted to Mr. John Dern
for the Maryland items found in the marriage register of Pastor
Stover. The source references for these marriages are given in
the List of Sources in the front of this book.

ADDITIONS

Allen, James, son of James, 8th day, 2 Mo. (April), 1742,
    Jane Brown, dau. of Messer and Jane   11 SF-51
Barrett, John, son of Arthur, 11th day, 10 mo., 1735, Mary
    Pugh, dau. of John   11 SF-23
Beeson, Richard, son of Richard, 15th day, 10 mo., 1730,
    Anne Brown, dau. of Messer   11 SF-1
Berridge, William, son of William and Elizabeth, of Gains-
    borough, Lincs., Great Britain, (born 15 April 1744),
    30 Dec. 1773, Grace Macmahan, dau. of John and Eliza-
    beth (born 29 Sept. 1751)   1 TA-308
Boothman, George, 22 Nov. 1777, by Rev. Weimer; Eve Brehem
    1 WA
Brown, Daniel, son of Daniel and Elizabeth, 27th day, 12 mo.,
    1759, Miriam Gregg, dau. of David and Lydia   11 SF-128
Brown, David, son of Messer and Dinah, 3rd day, 11 mo.,
    1757, Sarah Brown, dau. of Joshua and Hannah   11 SF-120
Brown, Eleazer, son of Thomas, 31st day, 8 mo., 1758, Mary
    Gilbert, dau. of John   11 SF-127
Brown, Eleazer, son of Thomas and Ellen, 16th day, 8 mo.,
    1769, Sarah Hewes, dau. of Joseph and Ann   11 SF-161
Brown, Elisha, son of Joshua and Hannah, 19th day, 3 mo.,
    1761, Rachel Littler, of Samuel and Mary   11 SF-132
Brown, Isaiah, son of Joshua and Hannah, 19th day, 6 mo.,
    1777, Miriam Churchman, dau. of William and Abigail
    11 SF-187
Brown, James, son of William, 4th day, 10 mo., 1734,
    Miriam Churchman, dau. of John   11 SF-36
Brown, Jeremiah, 20 July 1749, Mary Winter   11 SF-89
Brown, Joseph, son of Joseph and Mary, 27th day, 1 mo.,
    1746, Hannah Wilson, dau. of Thomas and Elizabeth
    11 SF-76
Brown, Joshua, son of Jeremiah, 15th day, 10'ber, 1736,
    Hannah Gatchell, dau. of Elisha   11 SF-31
Brown, Nathan, son of Thomas, (date not given), Margaret
    Elgar, dau. of Joseph   11 SF-63
Brown, Timothy, son of Daniel and Eliz., 26th day, 4 mo.,
    1759, Mary Jones, dau. of John and Mary   11 SF-123
Calvin, William (alias Collier), 5 Aug. 1754, Sarah Ray
    1 PG-229
Chamberlaine, Samuel, 15 Jan. 1772, Henrietta Maria Holly-
    day   1 TA-311

Clark, Henry, son of Jonathan, 5th day, 9 mo. (Nov.), 1741,
    Eliz. Underhill, dau. of John   11 SF-48
Clark, William, son of John and Hannah, 15th day, 9 mo.,
    1768, Susanna Johnson, dau. of James and Ruth   11 SF-155
Conner, James, 11 Oct. 1742, Anne Catherine Ellrodt   7 FR-383
Cook, Stephen, son of John and Eleanor, 31st day, 5 mo.,
    1759, Margaret Williams, dau. of Ennion and Frances
    11 SF-124
Cowgill, Eleazer, 29th day, 6 mo., 1739, Martha Pain, dau.
    of Josiah   11 SF-40
Cowgill, Henry, 24th day, 1 mo., 1741/2, Alice Pain, dau.
    of Josiah   11 SF-50
Cowgill, Henry, son of Henry and Mary, 19th day, 3 mo.,
    1761, Ruth Johnson, dau. of James and Ruth   11 SF-133
Cowgill, John, son of Henry and Alice, 12th day, 11 mo.,
    1772, Catherine Sheppard, dau. of William and Hannah
    11 SF-173
Day, John, 21st day, 4 mo. (June), 1733, Lydia Hoss   11 SF-30
Erhoist, Jacob, son of Paul, 28 Aug. 1769, Anna Maria
    Hoef, dau. of Johannes and Christina   6 FR-201
Fee, Tho., 6 Oct. 1733, Margaret Hook   1 PG-229
Flint, John, 26 Dec. 1721, Elizabeth -(?)-   1 PG-229
Gatchell, Elisha, son of Elisha, 3rd day, 8 mo., 1733, Mary
    Worley, dau. of Henry   11 SF-31
Gatchell, Jeremiah, son of Elisha and Mary, 3 July 1755,
    Hannah Brown, dau. of Samuel and Elizabeth   11 SF-109
Griffith, Richard, 6th day, 10 mo., 1738, Mary Sidewell,
    dau. of Jno.   11 SF-35
Grig, Aaron, son of David and Lydia, 16th day, 7 mo.,
    1767, Elizabeth Bonsall, dau. of Obadiah and Eliza-
    beth   11 SF-151
Habach, Peter, 26 Nov. 1738, Catarina Bergin   7 FR-195
Haines, Joshua, son of Jacob and Mary, 8th day, 4 mo.,
    1752, Elizabeth Harris, dau. of John and Phebe   11 SF-97
Haines, William, son of Joseph and Elizabeth, 1st day,
    11 mo., 1774, Rebekah Barnett, dau. of Thomas and
    Hannah   11 SF-182
Harbin, Joshua, 1 March 1753, Elizabeth Ray   1 PG-229
Harper, Moses, 14 Nov. 1777, by Rev. Weimer, Sarah O'Daniel
    1 WA
Harris, John, son of William, 5th day, 3 mo., 1731, Phebe
    Beeson, dau. of Richard   11 SF-5
Harris, Nathan, son of John and Phebe, 2nd day, 11 mo.,
    1774, Mary Griffe?, dau. of Richard   11 SF-181
Harris, Samuel, 25th day, 1 mo., 1753, Margaret Hopkins
    11 SF-102
Hastings, Job, son of John and Mary, 21st day, 9 mo., 1751,
    Mary Reese, dau. of Morris and Sarah   11 SF-94
Hopkinton, Thomas, 25 March 1740, Ann -(?)-   1 PG-229
Hutzel, Georg, 17 June 1739, Eliesabetha Schweinhardtin
    7 FR-238
Jacob, Benjamin, 6th day, 5 mo., 1756, Prudence Butterfill,
    dau. of John   11 SF-115
Jacob, John, son of Thomas and Mary, 8th day, 3 mo., 1744,
    Elizabeth Kirk, dau. of Roger and Elizabeth 11 SF-67
James, Mordecai, son of George and Ann, 26th day, 3 mo.,
    1727, Gayner Lloyd, dau. of Robert and Lowry   10 SF-103
James, Mordecai, son of George and Ann, 4th day, 9 mo.,
    1736, Dinah Churchman (als. Brown), dau. of John
    and Hannah   10 SF-104
James, Mordecai, 3rd day, 12 mo., 1767, Susanna Pasmore,
    widow of Samuel   11 SF-152
Job, Archibald, son of Thomas and Elizabeth, 30 July
    1752, Margaret Rees, dau. of Morris and Sarah   11 SF-100
Job, Daniel, son of Thomas and Elizabeth, 26th day, 10
    mo., 1758, Mary Brown, dau. of Samuel and Eliz.   11 SF-121

Job, Enoch, son of Andrew, 6th day, 3 mo. (May), 1731,
    Abigail Gatchell, dau. of Elisha   11 SF-6
Job, Joshua, son of Andrew, 11 March 1731, Margaret M'Koy,
    dau. of Robert   11 SF-3
Johns, Aquila, son of Richard, 16th day, 9 mo., 1704,
    Mary H -(?)-, dau. of Henry   5 SF
Ogden, Nehemiah, 21 Nov. 1733, Mary Cooper   1 PG-229
Owen, Robert, 25 Feb. 1731, Rachel Hook   1 PG-229
Patterson, William, 13 Nov. 1777, by Rev. Weimer; Phebe
    O'Daniel   1 WA
Pool, John, 30th day, 10 mo., 1768, Aney Wallis   2 SF-289
Pouits, John, 27 Aug. 1777, by Rev. Young; Jean Slover 1 WA
Rigbie, Nathan, Jr., 20 Oct. 1747, Sarah Giles   11 SF-82
Schaffer, Peter, 21 May 1740, Anna Schaubin   7 FR-284
Schaiteler, Joh. Georg, 20 Dec. 1739, Margaretha Neffin
    7 FR-272
Schmidt, Joh. Peter, 11 Oct. 1742, Eva Rosina Fauthin 7 FR-383
Sidewell, Hugh, son of John, 28th day, 8 mo., 1741, Hannah
    Berry, dau. of Samuel   11 SF-46
Sidewell, Richard, son of Hugh, 23rd day, 11 mo., 1739,
    Margaret King, dau. of Thomas   11 SF-41
Slicer, Thomas, son of Robert, of Tewkesbury, Glouces-
    tershire, Eng., 16th day, 4 mo. (June), 1737, Mary
    Harris, dau. of William   11 SF-33
Traut, Joh. Heinrich, 24 Nov. 1738, Anna Maria Baumin 7 FR-194

CORRECTIONS

p. 9 - Marriage date of Henry Barns and Elizabeth Green should
       be 27 Oct. 1754.
p. 24 - Marriage date of Redman Buck and Eleanor Buck should be
        27 July 1777.
p. 57 - Reference for marriage of Jonathan Edwards and Rachel
        Huff should be 11 SF-142.
p. 67 - Garrett Garrettson married Elizabeth Freeborne on 15 Dec.
        1702.
p. 81 - Delete marriage of Charles Harryman to Millicent Haile.
p. 85 - Marriage date of Edward Hewes and Mary Stubbs should be
        11th day, 10 mo., 1760.
p. 95 - Marriage date of Henry Jackson and Mary Bond should be
        3 April 1766.
p. 113- Capt. George McCliston should be Capt. George McClister.
p. 131- John Huill Nutter should be John Huitt Nutter.
p. 143 Marriage date of John Price and Alce (?) should be 6 Sept.
       1690.
p. 155- Marriage date of William Rogers and Elizabeth Harris
        Brown should be 6th day, 3 mo., 1760.

INDEX

ADDENDA